Lecture Notes in Computer Science 7690

Commenced Publication in 1973
Founding and Former Series Editors:
Gerhard Goos, Juris Hartmanis, and Jan van Leeuwen

T0223913

Dong Hoon Lee   Moti Yung (Eds.)

Information Security Applications

13th International Workshop, WISA 2012
Jeju Island, Korea, August 16-18, 2012
Revised Selected Papers

 Springer

Volume Editors

Dong Hoon Lee
Korea University, Center for Information Security Technologies
Anam-dong 5(o)-ga, Seoul 136-713, Korea
E-mail: donghlee@korea.ac.kr

Moti Yung
Columbia University, Computer Science Department
Amsterdam Avenue 1214, New York, NY 10027, USA
E-mail: moti@cs.columbia.edu

ISSN 0302-9743   e-ISSN 1611-3349
ISBN 978-3-642-35415-1   e-ISBN 978-3-642-35416-8
DOI 10.1007/978-3-642-35416-8
Springer Heidelberg Dordrecht London New York

Library of Congress Control Number: 2012953045

CR Subject Classification (1998): C.2, K.6.5, E.3, D.4.6, H.4, J.1

LNCS Sublibrary: SL 4 – Security and Cryptology

Typesetting: Camera-ready by author, data conversion by Scientific Publishing Services, Chennai, India

Printed on acid-free paper

Springer is part of Springer Science+Business Media (www.springer.com)

Preface

WISA 2012, the 13th International Workshop on Information Security Applications, was held during August 16–18 in the Ocean Suites Jeju Hotel, Jeju Island, Republic of Korea. The conference was hosted by the Korea Institute of Information Security and Cryptology (KIISC) and sponsored by the Ministry of Public Administration and Security (MoPAS). It was also co-sponsored by the National Security Research Institute (NSRI), the Korea Internet Security Agency (KISA), and the Electronics and Telecommunications Research Institute (ETRI).

We received 100 valid submissions from 16 countries, of which 26 were accepted for full-paper track and 14 for short abstract track. These proceedings contain the revised versions of 26 full papers and 8 short papers. Every paper received at least three independent reviews, and papers with Program Committee (PC) contributions got five or more. To fill a final odd ten slots, partitioning the DI papers into topical categories helped.

For the Best Paper Award, the PC selected "N-Victims: An Approach to Determine N-Victims for APT Investigations" by Shun-Te Liu, Yi-Ming Chen, and Hui-ching Huang, "AIGG Threshold-Based HTTP GET Flooding Attack Detection" by Yang-seo Choi, Ik-Kyun Kim, Jin-Tae Oh, and Jong-Soo Jang and "Three Phase Dynamic Current Mode Logic: A More Secure DyCML to Achieve a More Balanced Power Consumption" by Hyunmin Kim, Vladimir Rozic, and Ingrid Verbauwhede. There were two invited talks, Suraj C. Kothari delivered "Preventing Catastrophe from Sophisticated Software Sabotage" on August 16 and Gil-young Song spoke on "Social Media Mining Technology and Applications" on August 17.

We would like to thank the authors of all submissions regardless of whether their papers were accepted or not. Their work made this conference possible. We are extremely grateful to the PC members for their enormous investment of time and effort in the difficult and delicate process of review and selection. We would like to thank Jin Kwak, who was the Organizing Chair in charge of the local organization and finances. Special thanks go to Shai Halevi for providing and setting up the splendid review software. We are most grateful to Hwaseong Lee, who provided support for the entire WISA 2012 process. We are also grateful to Souhwan Jung, the WISA 2011 Program Chair, for his timely information and replies to the host of questions we posed during the process.

August 2012

Dong Hoon Lee
Moti Yung

Organization

General Chair

Chang-Seop Park   Dankook University, Korea

Advisory Committee

Bongsik Ko	FSA, Korea
Hyunsook Cho	ETRI, Korea
Kiwook Sohn	NSRI, Korea
Sungtaek Chi	NSRI, Korea
Youjae Won	KISA, Korea

Steering Committee

Bart Preneel	Katholieke University Leuven, Belgium
Dong Ho Won	Sungkyunkwan University, Korea
Dae Ho Kim	Joongbu University, Korea
Heung-YoulYoum	Soonchunhyang University, Korea
Hideki Imai	Chuo University, Japan
Hong Sub Lee	Konkuk University, Korea
Joo Seok Song	Yonsei University, Korea
Kil Hyun Nam	Korea National Defense University, Korea
Kwan Jo Kim	KAIST, Korea
Man Young Rhee	Kyung Hee University, Korea
Min Sub Rhee	Dankook University, Korea
Pil Joong Lee	POSTEC, Korea
Sang Jae Moon	Kyungpook National University, Korea
Se Hun Kim	KAIST, Korea

Program Committee

Co-chairs

Dong Hoon Lee	Korea University, Korea
Moti Yung	Columbia University, USA

Committee Members

Gail-Joon Ahn	Arizona State University, USA
Frederik Armknecht	University of Mannheim, Germany
Kefei Chen	Shanghai Jiaotang University, China
Ed Dawson	Queensland University of Technology, Australia
Rafael Dowsley	University of California at San Diego, USA
Pierre-Alain Fouque	Ecole normale superieure, France

Shaojing Fu	National University of Defense Technology, China
David Galindo	University of Luxembourg, Luxembourg
Pierrick Gaudry	University of Lorraine, France
Dieter Gollmann	Hamburg University of Technology, Germany
JaeCheol Ha	Hoseo University Korea
Swee-Huay Heng	Multimedia University, Malaysia
Jiankun Hu	University of New South Wales, Australia
Hiroaki Kikuchi	Tokai University, Japan
Taekyoung Kwon	Sejong University, Korea
Mun-Kyu Lee	Inha University, Korea
Benoit Libert	Universite catholique de Louvain, Belgium
Dongdai Lin	Chinese Academy of Sciences, China
Atsuko Miyaji	JAIST, Japan
Yutaka Miyake	KDDI R&D Laboratories, Japan
Tae (Tom) Oh	Rochester Institute of Technology, USA
Rolf Oppliger	eSECURITY Technologies, Switzerland
Carles Padro	Nanyang Technological University, Singapore
Dan Page	University of Bristol, UK
Susan Pancho-Festin	University of the Philippines, Philippines
C. Pandu Rangan	IIT, India
Christian Rechberger	DTU, Denmark
Kouichi Sakurai	Kyushu University, Japan
Nitesh Saxena	University of Alabama at Birmingham, USA
Willy Susilo	University of Wollongong, Australia
Tzong-Chen Wu	National Taiwan University of Science and Technology, Taiwan
Wenling Wu	Chinese Academy of Sciences, China
Yongjin Yeom	NSRI, Korea
Jeong Hyun Yi	Soongsil University, Korea
Kazuki Yoneyama	NTT, Japan
Dae Hyun Yum	POSTECH, Korea
Rui Zhang	Chinese Academy of Sciences, China

Organizing Committee

Chair

Jin Kwak	Soonchunhyang University, Korea

Committee Members

Hyo Beom Ahn	Kongju National University, Korea
Im-Yeong Lee	Soonchunhyang University, Korea
Jungtaek Seo	NSRI, Korea
KijungAhn	Jeju National University, Korea
Kyungho Lee	Korea University, Korea
Namje Park	Jeju National University, Korea
Soomi Lee	FSA, Korea

Table of Contents

Symmetric Cipher

Secure Hardware/Public Key Crypto Application

Cryptographic Protocols/ Digital Forensics

Network Security

Trust Management/Database Security

Security on LBlock
against Biclique Cryptanalysis

Yanfeng Wang, Wenling Wu, Xiaoli Yu, and Lei Zhang

Institute of Software, Chinese Academy of Sciences, Beijing 100190, P.R. China
{wangyanfeng,wwl}@is.iscas.ac.cn

Abstract. LBlock is a lightweight block cipher, with a 64-bit block size and an 80-bit key length, which was proposed at ACNS 2011. It can be implemented efficiently not only in hardware environment but also in software platforms. Because biclique cryptanalysis was proposed recently, the security of LBlock against this method has not been evaluated. This paper presents an optimized brute force attack on full LBlock by using the biclique cryptanalysis with partial matching and match with precomputation techniques. Moreover, the low diffusion of key schedule algorithm is the major contributor to the success of this attack. Therefore, a new key schedule algorithm is proposed with sufficient diffusion, considering both the implementations on 8-bit Micro-controller and the security under related-key attack.

Keywords: Lightweight block cipher, LBlock, Meet-in-the-middle, Biclique cryptanalysis, Complexity.

1 Introduction

With the large development of communication and electronic applications, the low resource devices such as RFID tags and sensor nodes have been used in many aspects of our life such as access control, parking management, eHealth and so on. This kind of new cryptography environment is ubiquitous but constrained. Traditional block cipher is not suitable for this extremely constrained environment. Therefore, research on designing and analyzing lightweight block ciphers has become a hot topic. Recently, a number of lightweight block ciphers have been proposed, like PRESENT[1], MIBS[2], KATAN & KTANTAN[3], TWIS[4], PRINT[5], KLEIN[6], LED[7], Piccolo[8] etc.

LBlock[9] is a 64-bit lightweight block cipher with 80-bit key length. It was designed to be suitable for low-cost devices. Up to now, the security of LBlock against various attacks has been evaluated. For the related-key attack, we present a 13-round distinguisher, which exploits a 13-round related-key characteristic. For the differential analysis, we find that the probability of 15-round characteristic can be lower than 2^{-64}. Recently, a key recovery attack on 21-round LBlock is presented in ISPEC 2012, which takes advantage of a 14-round impossible differential[10]. For the integral attack, we presented a key recovery attack on 20-round LBlock by using a 15-round integral distinguisher. And Yanjun Li

D.H. Lee and M. Yung (Eds.): WISA 2012, LNCS 7690, pp. 1–14, 2012.
© Springer-Verlag Berlin Heidelberg 2012

improved the key recovery attack to 22-round by exploiting the same round distinguisher[11].

MITM attack, introduced by Diffie and Hellman[12], is a typical method in the cryptanalysis of block cipher, whose outstanding property is the extremely low data complexity. The method has been improved with many techniques to carry out the preimage attack on hash functions[13]. These techniques include spice-and-cut framework, initial structure, partial matching etc. Variants have also been developed, for example three-subset MITM[14]. Recently, Andrey Bogdanov *et al.* gave the first attack on full AES-128/-192/-256 with the biclique technique[15]. Using the characteristic of key expansion in cipher algorithm, adversary can construct an initial structure named biclique and filter out wrong keys based on the result of partial matching, which is the main idea of the method. As a matter of fact, biclique cryptanalysis is an optimized brute force attack by using meet-in-the-middle attack with biclique, following the strategy of initial structure and partial matching.

In this paper, we study the security of LBlock from the aspect of biclique cryptanalysis. Bicliques can be built under two independent key differential trails and the choice of key differences will largely influence the results of key recovery attack. Then we perform a computer-based algorithm to evaluate the computational and data complexity of different attacks with different choice of original key difference. Based on the chosen key differential trails, we successfully construct 8-round bicliques of dimension 4 for LBlock. Exploiting these bicliques and additional techniques, e.g., the partial matching and the match with precomputation, a key recovery attack of full-round LBlock is developed. The key recovery attack is with data complexity of 2^{52} chosen plaintexts and with time complexity of $2^{78.40}$ encryptions. Furthermore, we find that the success of biclique analysis is largely due to the low diffusion of key schedule algorithm. Therefore, a new key schedule algorithm is proposed to improve the diffusion of whole cipher, considering both the software implementations on 8-bit platform and the security against related-key attack.

This paper is organized as follows. Section 2 provides a brief description of LBlock and the notations used throughout this paper. Section 3 presents the general structure of the biclique cryptanalysis. The key recovery attacks on full-round LBlock is shown in Section 4. Section 5 summarizes this paper and describes the new key schedule algorithm.

2   A Brief Description of LBlock

We first introduce some notations used throughout this paper and then give a simple description of the lightweight block cipher LBlock.

2.1   Notations

K: the master key.
K_r: r-th[1] round subkey.

---

[1] All counts involved in the text always start from 0.

$K_{\{a,b\}}$: a-th and b-th bits of master key K.

X_r: 64-bit input of the r-th round function.

$X_r^{c,d}$: c-th and d-th nibble[2] of X_r.

2.2   Description of LBlock

Encryption Algorithm. The general structure of LBlock is a variant of Feistel Network, which is depicted in Figure 1. The number of iterative rounds is 32. The round function of LBlock includes three basic functions: AddRoundKey AK, confusion function S and diffusion function P. The confusion function S consists of eight 4×4 S-boxes in parallel. The diffusion function P is defined as a permutation of eight 4-bit words.

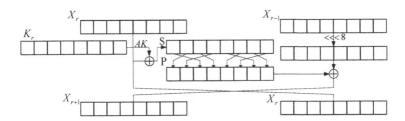

Fig. 1. The encryption of block cipher LBlock

Key Schedule Algorithm. To reduce the cost of hardware and to decrease key set-up time, the key schedule of LBlock is rather simple. The 80-bit master key K is stored in a key register and represented as $K = k_{79}k_{78}...k_0$. At round i, the leftmost 32 bits of current contents of register K are output as the round key K_i, i.e., $K_i = k_{79}k_{78}...k_{48}$. After extracting the round subkey K_i, the key register is updated as follows:

1. $[k_{79}k_{78}k_{77}...k_1k_0] = [k_{50}k_{49}k_{48}...k_1k_0k_{79}k_{78}k_{77}...k_{52}k_{51}]$
2. $[k_{79}k_{78}k_{77}k_{76}] = s_9[k_{79}k_{78}k_{77}k_{76}]$
   $[k_{75}k_{74}k_{73}k_{72}] = s_8[k_{75}k_{74}k_{73}k_{72}]$
3. $[k_{50}k_{49}k_{48}k_{47}k_{46}] = [k_{50}k_{49}k_{48}k_{47}k_{46}] \oplus [i]_2$

3   Biclique Cryptanalysis of LBlock

Here we first introduce the notion of biclique [15] and present the general structure of biclique cryptanalysis of LBlock.

---

[2] A nibble is composed of 4-bit words.

3.1 Definition of Biclique

Let f be a subcipher that connects 2^d plaintexts $\{P_i\}$ to 2^d states $\{S_j\}$ with 2^{2d} keys $\{K[i,j]\}$:

$$\{K[i,j]\} = \left\{ \begin{array}{l} K[0,0] \qquad K[0,1] \quad \ldots \quad K[0, 2^d-1] \\ \ldots \qquad\qquad \ldots \\ K[2^d-1,0] \ K[2^d-1,1] \ldots K[2^d-1, 2^d-1] \end{array} \right\}$$

If $S_j = f_{K[i,j]}(P_i)$ for all $i,j \in \{0, \ldots, 2^d-1\}$, the 3-tuple $[\{P_i\}, \{S_j\}, \{K[i,j]\}]$ is called a d-dimensional biclique. Figure 2 shows the relationships between 3-tuple. Moreover, the vertexes of the graph stand for states while the edges stand for keys. Besides dimension, the length, which is defined as the number of rounds that f covered, is also a significant characteristic of a biclique.

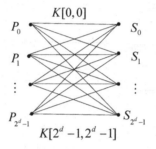

Fig. 2. d-dimensional biclique

According to the definition of biclique, a d-dimensional biclique needs to establish 2^{2d} relationships simultaneously. Bogdanov et al. have proposed an approach to find a d-dimensional biclique from related-key differentials [15]. And we find it is difficult to construct a long biclique for cipher algorithms with well diffusion. Moreover, the efficiency of biclique cryptanalysis depends on the diffusion property of both encryption algorithm and key schedule algorithm. We evaluate the security of LBlock against biclique cryptanalysis because of the fact that key schedule and encryption of LBlock are both with unsufficient diffusion.

3.2 Pattern of Biclique Cryptanalysis of LBlock

In fact, the biclique cryptanalysis of LBlock is a meet-in-the-middle attack with biclique, following the strategy of initial structure and partial matching. The general structure of biclique cryptanalysis of LBlock is described in Figure 3.

The single encryption oracle illustrates that the attack described in our paper is in the single-key model. And the procedure of our attacks can be described as follows:

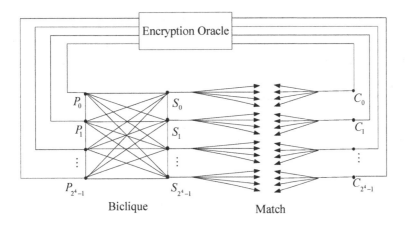

Fig. 3. Structure of Biclique Cryptanalysis against LBlock

Step 1 *Divide Key Space.* Divide the full key space into disjoint groups. To guarantee the success rate to be 1, the following steps are exhaustively applied to every group.

Step 2 *Build Bicliques.* Construct a biclique of appropriate dimension for every key group. In our attack, the dimension of biclique is 4, so the number of $\{P_i\}$ and $\{S_j\}$ are both 2^4.

Step 3 *Filter Out Keys.* For every biclique:

1. Choose a position as the matching internal variable, denoted by v.
2. Ask for the encryptions of plaintexts P_i obtained during Step 2, and get the corresponding ciphertexts denoted by C_i.
3. Let $S_j \to v$ be forward direction computation and $v \leftarrow C_i$ be backward direction computation. As a matter of fact, if one of the tested keys $K[i,j]$ is the correct key, it will map state S_j to the ciphertext C_i. So delete the keys that don't match in the internal matching variable.

Step 4 *Search Candidates.* Exhaustively test the remaining key candidates until the correct key is found.

Since the number of produced plaintexts is proportional to the number of bicliques and the length of keys are larger than plaintexts, we have to avoid covering the full codebook. The attack that we propose is to keep only those bicliques whose plaintexts belong to a particular set of cardinality smaller than 2^{64}. In order to get the best results of key recovery, an algorithm is executed to optimize the choice of related-key differential trails. Taking advantage of these chosen related-key differentials, we can construct 8-round bicliques of dimension 4 for LBlock.

Considering the low diffusion property of encryption algorithm, the technique of partial matching can largely reduce the time complexity of key recovery attack and may cause a better attack. When the dimension of bicliques are fixed to 4, three options of internal matching variable are equivalent to provide the key recovery attack on full round LBlock with the least computational complexity.

4   Key Recovery for Full-Round LBlock

In this section, we show the process of key recovery attack on full round LBlock in detail. The parameters of the key recovery attack are summarized in Table 1.

Table 1. Parameters of key recovery for LBlock

Cipher	Rounds	BLength	BDimension	Matching v	Forward Rounds	Backward Rounds
LBlock	32	8(0-7)	4	$X_{19}^{2,7}$	8-19	20-31

† v :matching variable.
† BLength: Length of Biclique;
† BDimension: Dimension of Biclique.

For all the variants of Feistel structure, bicliques can not be built under inter-leaving differential trails. The iterative structure of LBlock is one of the variants of Feistel structure. Therefore, we need to find two independent related-key differential trails to successfully build bicliques. Considering the time complexity of whole attack, one searching algorithm illustrates that choosing bits $K_{\{75,76,77,78\}}$ and $K_{\{14,15,16,17\}}$ as original positions of key difference is optimal for LBlock.

4.1   Key Partitioning

For more clarity, we define the key groups with respect to the master key and enumerate the groups by 2^{72} base keys. We divide the LBlock key space into 2^{72} groups of 2^8 keys each. The base keys of these groups are all possible 80-bit values with the $\{75, 76, 77, 78, 14, 15, 16, 17\}$-th bits fixed to 0 and the remaining 72 bits running over all values. The following steps are exhaustively applied to every key group. Next, we take one group as an example to explain the process of filtering out wrong keys.

As mentioned before, there are 2^8 keys in one group and they share common 72 bits except the $\{75, 76, 77, 78\}$-th and $\{14, 15, 16, 17\}$-th bits. We denote them by $K[i,j]$ $(i,j \in \{0,1\}^4)$ and the different values are distinguished as follows:

$$K[i,j]_{\{75,76,77,78\}} = i \quad K[i,j]_{\{14,15,16,17\}} = j$$

Obviously, for a fixed i, the keys $\{K[i,j], j \in \{0,1\}^4\}$ share common 76 bits and are only different in the $\{14, 15, 16, 17\}$-th bits. Similarly, the keys $\{K[i,j], i \in \{0,1\}^4\}$ are only different in the $\{75, 76, 77, 78\}$-th bits. In the sequel, the difference will be called active. Taking the master key set $\{K[i,j], j \in \{0,1\}^4\}$ as an example, round subkeys and S-boxes computed during the key schedule shall the common values in parts without color, which is shown in the bottom part of Table 2. Meanwhile, S-boxes and subkeys noted with red color are influenced active. Similarly, influence of the active $\{75, 76, 77, 78\}$-th bits are described in the top part of Table 2.

Having known the relationships of keys in one group, let's see the process of building a biclique covering these 2^8 keys.

Table 2. Key schedule of LBlock influenced by key difference

Active Bits: 78-77-76-75

Round	0				1				2				3				4				5				6				7			
0	79	78	77	76	75	74	73	72	71	70	69	68	67	66	65	64	63	62	61	60	59	58	57	56	55	54	53	52	51	50	49	48
1	50	49	48	47	46	45	44	43	42	41	40	39	38	37	36	35	34	33	32	31	30	29	28	27	26	25	24	23	22	21	20	19
2	21	20	19	18	17	16	15	14	13	12	11	10	9	8	7	6	5	4	3	2	1	0	79	78	77	76	75	74	73	72	71	70
3	72	71	70	69	68	67	66	65	64	63	62	61	60	59	58	57	56	55	54	53	52	51	50	49	48	47	46	45	44	43	42	41
4	43	42	41	40	39	38	37	36	35	34	33	32	31	30	29	28	27	26	25	24	23	22	21	20	19	18	17	16	15	14	13	12
5	14	13	12	11	10	9	8	7	6	5	4	3	2	1	0	79	78	77	76	75	74	73	72	71	70	69	68	67	66	65	64	63
6	65	64	63	62	61	60	59	58	57	56	55	54	53	52	51	50	49	48	47	46	45	44	43	42	41	40	39	38	37	36	35	34
7	36	35	34	33	32	31	30	29	28	27	26	25	24	23	22	21	20	19	18	17	16	15	14	13	12	11	10	9	8	7	6	5
8	7	6	5	4	3	2	1	0	79	78	77	76	75	74	73	72	71	70	69	68	67	66	65	64	63	62	61	60	59	58	57	56
9	58	57	56	55	54	53	52	51	50	49	48	47	46	45	44	43	42	41	40	39	38	37	36	35	34	33	32	31	30	29	28	27
10	29	28	27	26	25	24	23	22	21	20	19	18	17	16	15	14	13	12	11	10	9	8	7	6	5	4	3	2	1	0	79	78
11	0	79	78	77	76	75	74	73	72	71	70	69	68	67	66	65	64	63	62	61	60	59	58	57	56	55	54	53	52	51	50	49
12	51	50	49	48	47	46	45	44	43	42	41	40	39	38	37	36	35	34	33	32	31	30	29	28	27	26	25	24	23	22	21	20
13	22	21	20	19	18	17	16	15	14	13	12	11	10	9	8	7	6	5	4	3	2	1	0	79	78	77	76	75	74	73	72	71
14	73	72	71	70	69	68	67	66	65	64	63	62	61	60	59	58	57	56	55	54	53	52	51	50	49	48	47	46	45	44	43	42
15	44	43	42	41	40	39	38	37	36	35	34	33	32	31	30	29	28	27	26	25	24	23	22	21	20	19	18	17	16	15	14	13
16	15	14	13	12	11	10	9	8	7	6	5	4	3	2	1	0	79	78	77	76	75	74	73	72	71	70	69	68	67	66	65	64
17	66	65	64	63	62	61	60	59	58	57	56	55	54	53	52	51	50	49	48	47	46	45	44	43	42	41	40	39	38	37	36	35
18	37	36	35	34	33	32	31	30	29	28	27	26	25	24	23	22	21	20	19	18	17	16	15	14	13	12	11	10	9	8	7	6
19	8	7	6	5	4	3	2	1	0	79	78	77	76	75	74	73	72	71	70	69	68	67	66	65	64	63	62	61	60	59	58	57
20	59	58	57	56	55	54	53	52	51	50	49	48	47	46	45	44	43	42	41	40	39	38	37	36	35	34	33	32	31	30	29	28
21	30	29	28	27	26	25	24	23	22	21	20	19	18	17	16	15	14	13	12	11	10	9	8	7	6	5	4	3	2	1	0	79
22	1	0	79	78	77	76	75	74	73	72	71	70	69	68	67	66	65	64	63	62	61	60	59	58	57	56	55	54	53	52	51	50
23	52	51	50	49	48	47	46	45	44	43	42	41	40	39	38	37	36	35	34	33	32	31	30	29	28	27	26	25	24	23	22	21
24	23	22	21	20	19	18	17	16	15	14	13	12	11	10	9	8	7	6	5	4	3	2	1	0	79	78	77	76	75	74	73	72
25	74	73	72	71	70	69	68	67	66	65	64	63	62	61	60	59	58	57	56	55	54	53	52	51	50	49	48	47	46	45	44	43
26	45	44	43	42	41	40	39	38	37	36	35	34	33	32	31	30	29	28	27	26	25	24	23	22	21	20	19	18	17	16	15	14
27	16	15	14	13	12	11	10	9	8	7	6	5	4	3	2	1	0	79	78	77	76	75	74	73	72	71	70	69	68	67	66	65
28	67	66	65	64	63	62	61	60	59	58	57	56	55	54	53	52	51	50	49	48	47	46	45	44	43	42	41	40	39	38	37	36
29	38	37	36	35	34	33	32	31	30	29	28	27	26	25	24	23	22	21	20	19	18	17	16	15	14	13	12	11	10	9	8	7
30	9	8	7	6	5	4	3	2	1	0	79	78	77	76	75	74	73	72	71	70	69	68	67	66	65	64	63	62	61	60	59	58
31	60	59	58	57	56	55	54	53	52	51	50	49	48	47	46	45	44	43	42	41	40	39	38	37	36	35	34	33	32	31	30	29

Active Bits: 17-16-15-14

Round	0				1				2				3				4				5				6				7			
0	79	78	77	76	75	74	73	72	71	70	69	68	67	66	65	64	63	62	61	60	59	58	57	56	55	54	53	52	51	50	49	48
1	50	49	48	47	46	45	44	43	42	41	40	39	38	37	36	35	34	33	32	31	30	29	28	27	26	25	24	23	22	21	20	19
2	21	20	19	18	17	16	15	14	13	12	11	10	9	8	7	6	5	4	3	2	1	0	79	78	77	76	75	74	73	72	71	70
3	72	71	70	69	68	67	66	65	64	63	62	61	60	59	58	57	56	55	54	53	52	51	50	49	48	47	46	45	44	43	42	41
4	43	42	41	40	39	38	37	36	35	34	33	32	31	30	29	28	27	26	25	24	23	22	21	20	19	18	17	16	15	14	13	12
5	14	13	12	11	10	9	8	7	6	5	4	3	2	1	0	79	78	77	76	75	74	73	72	71	70	69	68	67	66	65	64	63
6	65	64	63	62	61	60	59	58	57	56	55	54	53	52	51	50	49	48	47	46	45	44	43	42	41	40	39	38	37	36	35	34
7	36	35	34	33	32	31	30	29	28	27	26	25	24	23	22	21	20	19	18	17	16	15	14	13	12	11	10	9	8	7	6	5
8	7	6	5	4	3	2	1	0	79	78	77	76	75	74	73	72	71	70	69	68	67	66	65	64	63	62	61	60	59	58	57	56
9	58	57	56	55	54	53	52	51	50	49	48	47	46	45	44	43	42	41	40	39	38	37	36	35	34	33	32	31	30	29	28	27
10	29	28	27	26	25	24	23	22	21	20	19	18	17	16	15	14	13	12	11	10	9	8	7	6	5	4	3	2	1	0	79	78
11	0	79	78	77	76	75	74	73	72	71	70	69	68	67	66	65	64	63	62	61	60	59	58	57	56	55	54	53	52	51	50	49
12	51	50	49	48	47	46	45	44	43	42	41	40	39	38	37	36	35	34	33	32	31	30	29	28	27	26	25	24	23	22	21	20
13	22	21	20	19	18	17	16	15	14	13	12	11	10	9	8	7	6	5	4	3	2	1	0	79	78	77	76	75	74	73	72	71
14	73	72	71	70	69	68	67	66	65	64	63	62	61	60	59	58	57	56	55	54	53	52	51	50	49	48	47	46	45	44	43	42
15	44	43	42	41	40	39	38	37	36	35	34	33	32	31	30	29	28	27	26	25	24	23	22	21	20	19	18	17	16	15	14	13
16	15	14	13	12	11	10	9	8	7	6	5	4	3	2	1	0	79	78	77	76	75	74	73	72	71	70	69	68	67	66	65	64
17	66	65	64	63	62	61	60	59	58	57	56	55	54	53	52	51	50	49	48	47	46	45	44	43	42	41	40	39	38	37	36	35
18	37	36	35	34	33	32	31	30	29	28	27	26	25	24	23	22	21	20	19	18	17	16	15	14	13	12	11	10	9	8	7	6
19	8	7	6	5	4	3	2	1	0	79	78	77	76	75	74	73	72	71	70	69	68	67	66	65	64	63	62	61	60	59	58	57
20	59	58	57	56	55	54	53	52	51	50	49	48	47	46	45	44	43	42	41	40	39	38	37	36	35	34	33	32	31	30	29	28
21	30	29	28	27	26	25	24	23	22	21	20	19	18	17	16	15	14	13	12	11	10	9	8	7	6	5	4	3	2	1	0	79
22	1	0	79	78	77	76	75	74	73	72	71	70	69	68	67	66	65	64	63	62	61	60	59	58	57	56	55	54	53	52	51	50
23	52	51	50	49	48	47	46	45	44	43	42	41	40	39	38	37	36	35	34	33	32	31	30	29	28	27	26	25	24	23	22	21
24	23	22	21	20	19	18	17	16	15	14	13	12	11	10	9	8	7	6	5	4	3	2	1	0	79	78	77	76	75	74	73	72
25	74	73	72	71	70	69	68	67	66	65	64	63	62	61	60	59	58	57	56	55	54	53	52	51	50	49	48	47	46	45	44	43
26	45	44	43	42	41	40	39	38	37	36	35	34	33	32	31	30	29	28	27	26	25	24	23	22	21	20	19	18	17	16	15	14
27	16	15	14	13	12	11	10	9	8	7	6	5	4	3	2	1	0	79	78	77	76	75	74	73	72	71	70	69	68	67	66	65
28	67	66	65	64	63	62	61	60	59	58	57	56	55	54	53	52	51	50	49	48	47	46	45	44	43	42	41	40	39	38	37	36
29	38	37	36	35	34	33	32	31	30	29	28	27	26	25	24	23	22	21	20	19	18	17	16	15	14	13	12	11	10	9	8	7
30	9	8	7	6	5	4	3	2	1	0	79	78	77	76	75	74	73	72	71	70	69	68	67	66	65	64	63	62	61	60	59	58
31	60	59	58	57	56	55	54	53	52	51	50	49	48	47	46	45	44	43	42	41	40	39	38	37	36	35	34	33	32	31	30	29

† yellow color: positions of S-boxes during the key schedule(exclude the 0-th round);
† blue color and red color: active positions of corresponding round subkeys caused by key difference.

4.2   8-Round Biclique of Dimension 4

We construct an 8-round (f: 0-th round to 7-th round) biclique of dimension 4 for every key group. Known the keys covered by the biclique, we need to determine 2^4 plaintexts and 2^4 states that satisfy the definition of the biclique.

P is plaintext of the encryption algorithm and the state S is defined as X_8 and X_7, which is the output of the 7-th round encryption. The procedure of computing the plaintexts and states is depicted in Figure 4 and can be described as follows:

Step 1. Fix $P_0 = 0_{(64)}$ and derive $S_0 = f_{K[0,0]}(P_0)$. The process is stored and called as basic computation.

Step 2. Encrypt P_0 under different keys $K[0,j]$ ($0 < j < 2^4$) and the corresponding states are denoted by S_j (Figure 4, Left). Because of the same starting point with basic computation, the time complexity of this process is determined by the influence of difference between $K[0,j]$ and $K[0,0]$. As the

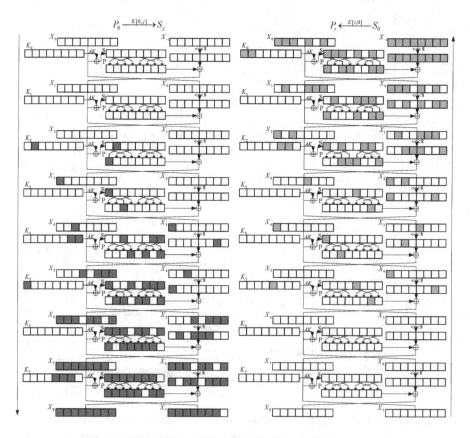

Fig. 4. Construction of 8-round biclique with 4 dimension

definition, keys $\{K[0,j], j \in \{0,1\}^4\}$ are only different in the $\{14, 15, 16, 17\}$-th bits and the round subkeys are different in parts filled with red color(Table 2, Bottom). So the process share common values with basic computation in white parts and difference parts are marked with red color. As a result, the red parts need to be computed 2^4 times because the number of keys in $\{K[0,j]~(0 < j < 2^4)\}$ is 2^4.

Step 3. Decrypt S_0 under different keys $K[i,0]~(0 < i < 2^4)$ and let P_i be the corresponding plaintexts (Figure 4, Right). This process shares common ending point with basic computation. Similarly, keys $\{K[i,0]~(0 < i < 2^4)\}$ are only different in the $\{75, 76, 77, 78\}$-th bits and the influence of the key difference is marked with blue color.

Now, we have established the relationships of $P_0 \xrightarrow{K[0,j]} S_j~(j \in \{0,1\}^4)$ and $P_i \xrightarrow{K[i,0]} S_0~(i \in \{0,1\}^4)$. Because of the low diffusion of the key schedule and encryption algorithm, two differential trails share no active S-boxes during first 8-round as demonstrated in Figure 4. It is easy to prove that $P_i \xrightarrow{K[i,j]} S_j~(i, j \in \{0,1\}^4)$ is always true. Until now, we obtain a corresponding 4-dimensional biclique for every key group as discussed above.

4.3   Matching over 24 Rounds

Taking the computational complexity into account, we choose $v = X_{2,7}^{19}$, which is a 8-bit output of round 19, as the internal matching variable. Another two choices is equivalent to this position, that is $X_{2,7}^{20}$ and $X_{2,7}^{21}$. Next, compute the values of matching variable in both directions and delete keys that don't match.

S-boxes are the major contributor to the computational complexity of the attack. Therefore, in order to evaluate the complexity simply, we firstly count the number of S-boxes that to be computed and then compare it to that in 32-round LBlock.

Forward computation: We aim to get the values of corresponding internal matching variable. Let S_j be fixed and use keys $K[i,j]~(i \in \{0,1\}^4)$ to partly encrypt S_j to derive the values of $X_{2,7}^{19}$, which is corresponding denoted by $v_{i,j}$. We first compute and store the process of $S_j \xrightarrow{K[0,j]} V_{0,j}$. When encrypting the same S_j under keys $K[i,j]~(i \in \{0,1\}^4 and~i \neq 0)$, we only compute the different parts compared to that process under $K[0,j]$. Because of the same starting point, the computational complexity is determined by the influence of differences between $K[i,j]~(i \neq 0)$ and $K[0,j]$. We know the keys are only different in the $\{75, 76, 77, 78\}$-th bits and the round subkeys are different in parts filled with blue color(Table 2, Top). As demonstrated in the left of Figure 5, it makes no difference between the S-boxes marked with yellow color, while the blue parts represent active parts. Besides, we can skip the parts without color because they do not affect the values of matching variable. As a result, for a single S_j, the matching values can be obtained after computing 43 S-boxes 2^4 times and 21 S-boxes once.

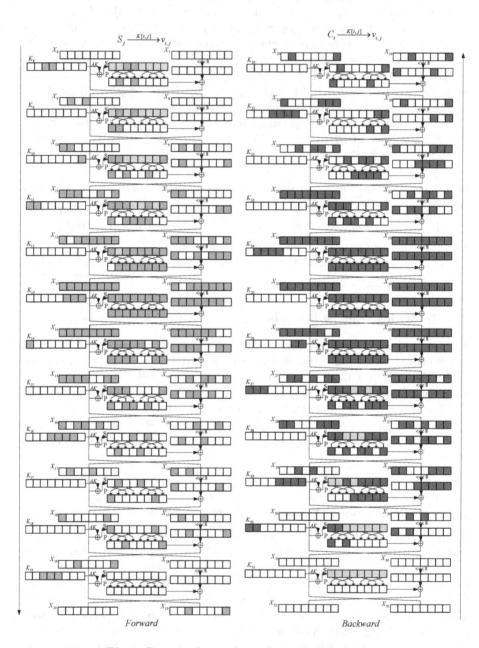

Fig. 5. Process of partial matching over 24 rounds

Backward computation: Now we evaluate the amount of computation in backward direction. First of all, ask for the encryptions of plaintexts P_i ($i \in \{0,1\}^4$) and get 2^4 ciphertexts C_i. Then decrypt the ciphertexts C_i with the keys $K[i,j]$ ($j \in \{0,1\}^4$) to $X_{2,7}^{19}$. We know the keys are only different in the $\{14,15,16,17\}$-th bits and the round subkeys are different in parts filled with red color(Table 2, Bottom). Taking a fixed C_i for example, the process of backward matching can be described as right parts of Figure 5. There is no difference between the S-boxes marked by yellow color for all the decryptions and we can skip the computation of the states without color obtaining the matching variables. As a result, for a single C_i, the matching values can be obtained after computing 54 S-boxes 2^4 times and 22 S-boxes once.

4.4   Search Candidates

Exhaustively test the remaining key candidates in each key group until the correct key is found. Because we test 2^8 keys to see whether 8 bit values match or not, the number of remaining key candidates in each key group is $2^{8-8} = 1$ on the average.

4.5   Complexity

Now we evaluate the complexity of the key recovery for full round LBlock. The construction of biclique and the process of matching are applied to 2^{72} key groups exhaustively and each key group only includes 2^8 keys. So the memory complexity is not exceed 2^8 full-round LBlock states. Thus, the memory complexity can be ignored compared to the computational complexity.

Data Complexity. The data complexity is determined by the number of plaintexts that to be encrypted. We fix $P_0 = 0_{(64)}$ for every biclique and all the plaintexts P_i ($i \in \{0,1\}^4$) share the same values in the $\{3,5,7\}$-th nibble of X_0(Figure 4), so the data complexity does not exceed 2^{52} chosen plaintexts.

Computational Complexity. First, let us see the complexity of constructing a single biclique with $P_0 = 0_{(64)}$. As before, we first count the S-boxes that need to be computed. The basic computation costs 8 S-boxes for each round, 64 S-boxes in total. In order to get P_i ($0 < i < 2^4$), we need to compute 16 S-box for 2^4 times. Similarly, computing S_j ($0 < j < 2^4$) involves 23 S-boxes 2^4 times. Thus, a biclique is constructed with complexity of 688 S-boxes.

In the matching part, we compute eight bits in two directions as discussed before. It spends $2^4(21+2^4 \times 43)$ S-boxes in forward direction and $2^4(22+2^4 \times 54)$ S-boxes in backward direction. In total, it costs 25520 S-boxes per biclique.

The number of S-boxes cost in 32-round LBlock is $32 \times 8 + 31 \times 2 = 318$ S-boxes as we have to take the key schedule nonlinearity into account. Obviously, the complexity of the key schedule in every biclique should also be taken into consideration. There are 2^8 master keys in every group. As shown in

Table 2, positions of active S-boxes under these two active model are independent. Moreover, those S-boxes marked with red or blue color need to be computed for 2^4 times because the keys are only different with base key in only four bits. So, the complexity of the key schedule per biclique is $2^4 \times 19 + 43 = 347$ S-boxes.

Altogether, we build 2^{72} bicliques. The whole computational complexity is estimated as:

$$C = 2^{72}(\frac{688 + 25520 + 347}{318} + 1) \approx 2^{78.40}$$

Since the groups has fully covered the key space, the success probability is 1.

Table 3. Summary of attacks on LBlock

Single-Key Model				
Round	Method	Data(CP)	Time(Enc)	Reference
20	Integral Attack	$2^{63.7}$	$2^{63.7}$	[9]
21	Impossible DC	$2^{62.5}$	$2^{73.7}$	[10]
22	Integral Attack	$2^{61.6}$	$2^{71.2}$	[11]
32	Biclique Cryptanalysis	2^{52}	$2^{78.40}$	**This paper**

† DC : Differential Cryptanalysis.
† CP: Chosen Plaintexts; † Enc: Encryptions.

5   Conclusion

Table 3 summarized the previous results on LBlock under the single key model. Moreover, we find that the two key differentials used in this paper share no active subkey bits over full 32 rounds. Besides, the subkeys of the last round are not influenced by every bit of master key. Thus, we can draw the conclusion that the diffusion of key schedule algorithm of LBlock is poor.

In order to improve the security of LBlock, we try to modify the key schedule algorithm to get sufficient diffusion. There are two kinds of evaluation criteria can be referred to. Each round subkey is affected by any bit of master key and every bit of subkey is affected by every bit of master key. Furthermore, three main aspects are considered to give the improvement. Firstly, the bit-wise key schedule is revised to nibble-wise algorithm to get a faster implement on 8-bit platform. Secondly, some operations of XOR are added to improve the diffusion. Finally, we analyzed the security of the new algorithm against biclique cryptanalysis and related-key attack. And the new key schedule algorithm can be described as follows:

The 80-bit master key K is stored in a key register and denoted as $K = k_{79}k_{78}...k_0$. Output the leftmost 32 bits of register K as subkey K_0. For $i = 0, 1, ..., 30$, update the key register K as follows:

1. $K \lll 24$
2. $[k_{55}k_{54}k_{53}k_{52}] = s[k_{79}k_{78}k_{77}k_{76}] \oplus [k_{55}k_{54}k_{53}k_{52}]$
   $[k_{31}k_{30}k_{29}k_{28}] = s[k_{75}k_{74}k_{73}k_{72}] \oplus [k_{31}k_{30}k_{29}k_{28}]$
   $[k_{67}k_{66}k_{65}k_{64}] = [k_{71}k_{70}k_{69}k_{68}] \oplus [k_{67}k_{66}k_{65}k_{64}]$
   $[k_{51}k_{50}k_{49}k_{48}] = [k_{11}k_{10}k_{9}k_{8}] \oplus [k_{51}k_{50}k_{49}k_{48}]$
3. $[k_{54}k_{53}k_{52}k_{51}k_{50}] = [k_{54}k_{53}k_{52}k_{51}k_{50}] \oplus [i]_2$
4. Output the leftmost 32 bits of current content of register K as round subkey K_{i+1}.

Acknowledgments. We would like to thank anonymous referees for their helpful comments and suggestions. The research presented in this paper is supported by the National Natural Science Foundation of China (No. 61272476 and No. 61202420) and National Program on Key Basic Research Project (973 Program).

References

1. Bogdanov, A., Knudsen, L.R., Leander, G., Paar, C., Poschmann, A., Robshaw, M.J.B., Seurin, Y., Vikkelsoe, C.: PRESENT: An Ultra-Lightweight Block Cipher. In: Paillier, P., Verbauwhede, I. (eds.) CHES 2007. LNCS, vol. 4727, pp. 450–466. Springer, Heidelberg (2007)
2. Izadi, M., Sadeghiyan, B., Sadeghian, S., Khanooki, H.: MIBS: A New Lightweight Block Cipher. In: Garay, J.A., Miyaji, A., Otsuka, A. (eds.) CANS 2009. LNCS, vol. 5888, pp. 334–348. Springer, Heidelberg (2009)
3. De Cannière, C., Dunkelman, O., Knežević, M.: KATAN and KTANTAN — A Family of Small and Efficient Hardware-Oriented Block Ciphers. In: Clavier, C., Gaj, K. (eds.) CHES 2009. LNCS, vol. 5747, pp. 272–288. Springer, Heidelberg (2009)
4. Ojha, S.K., Kumar, N., Jain, K., Sangeeta: TWIS – A Lightweight Block Cipher. In: Prakash, A., Sen Gupta, I. (eds.) ICISS 2009. LNCS, vol. 5905, pp. 280–291. Springer, Heidelberg (2009)
5. Knudsen, L., Leander, G., Poschmann, A., Robshaw, M.J.B.: PRINT CIPHER: A Block Cipher for IC-Printing. In: Mangard, S., Standaert, F.-X. (eds.) CHES 2010. LNCS, vol. 6225, pp. 16–32. Springer, Heidelberg (2010)
6. Gong, Z., Nikova, S., Law, Y.W.: KLEIN: A New Family of Lightweight Block Ciphers. In: Juels, A., Paar, C. (eds.) RFIDSec 2011. LNCS, vol. 7055, pp. 1–18. Springer, Heidelberg (2012)
7. Guo, J., Peyrin, T., Poschmann, A., Robshaw, M.: The LED Block Cipher. In: Preneel, B., Takagi, T. (eds.) CHES 2011. LNCS, vol. 6917, pp. 326–341. Springer, Heidelberg (2011)
8. Shibutani, K., Isobe, T., Hiwatari, H., Mitsuda, A., Akishita, T., Shirai, T.: *Piccolo*: An Ultra-Lightweight Blockcipher. In: Preneel, B., Takagi, T. (eds.) CHES 2011. LNCS, vol. 6917, pp. 342–357. Springer, Heidelberg (2011)
9. Wu, W., Zhang, L.: LBlock: A Lightweight Block Cipher. In: Lopez, J., Tsudik, G. (eds.) ACNS 2011. LNCS, vol. 6715, pp. 327–344. Springer, Heidelberg (2011)
10. Liu, Y., Gu, D., Liu, Z., Li, W.: Impossible Differential Attacks on Reduced-Round LBlock. In: Ryan, M.D., Smyth, B., Wang, G. (eds.) ISPEC 2012. LNCS, vol. 7232, pp. 97–108. Springer, Heidelberg (2012)

11. Li, Y.: Integral Cryptanalysis on Block Ciphers. Institute of Software, Chinese Academy of Sciences, Beijing (2012)
12. Diffie, W., Hellman, M.E.: Special feature exhaustive cryptanalysis of the NBS data encryption standard. Computer 10(6), 74–84 (1977)
13. Sasaki, Y.: Meet-in-the-Middle Preimage Attacks on AES Hashing Modes and an Application to Whirlpool. In: Joux, A. (ed.) FSE 2011. LNCS, vol. 6733, pp. 378–396. Springer, Heidelberg (2011)
14. Bogdanov, A., Rechberger, C.: A 3-Subset Meet-in-the-Middle Attack: Cryptanalysis of the Lightweight Block Cipher KTANTAN. In: Biryukov, A., Gong, G., Stinson, D.R. (eds.) SAC 2010. LNCS, vol. 6544, pp. 229–240. Springer, Heidelberg (2011)
15. Bogdanov, A., Khovratovich, D., Rechberger, C.: Biclique Cryptanalysis of the Full AES. In: Lee, D.H., Wang, X. (eds.) ASIACRYPT 2011. LNCS, vol. 7073, pp. 344–371. Springer, Heidelberg (2011)

Improved Impossible Differential Attacks
on Reduced-Round MISTY1

Keting Jia[1] and Leibo Li[2,*]

[1] Institute for Advanced Study, Tsinghua University, China
ktjia@mail.tsinghua.edu.cn
[2] Key Laboratory of Cryptologic Technology and Information Security, Ministry of Education,
Shandong University, China
lileibo@mail.sdu.edu.cn

Abstract. MISTY1 is a Feistel block cipher with a 64-bit block and a 128-bit key. It is one of the final NESSIE portfolio of block ciphers, and has been recommended for Japanese e-Government ciphers by the CRYPTREC project. In this paper, we improve the impossible differential attack on 6-round MISTY1 with 4 FL layers introduced by Dunkelman et al. with a factor of 2^{11} for the time complexity. Furthermore, combing with the FL function properties and the key schedule algorithm, we propose an impossible differential attack on 7-round MISTY1 with 3 FL layers, which needs 2^{58} known plaintexts and $2^{124.4}$ 7-round encryptions. It is the first attack on 7-round MISTY1 in the known plaintext model to the best of our knowledge. Besides, we show an improved impossible differential attack on 7-round MISTY1 without FL layers with $2^{92.2}$ 7-round encryptions and 2^{55} chosen plaintexts, which has lower time complexity than previous attacks.

Keywords: MISTY1, Impossible Differential, Cryptanalysis, Block Cipher.

1 Introduction

MISTY1 is a 64-bit block cipher with 128-bit key, proposed by Matsui in FSE 1997 [14]. Now MISTY1 has been recommended in many cryptographic standards and applications, such as the CRYPTREC e-government recommended ciphers, one of the final NESSIE portfolio of block ciphers, as well as an ISO standard. Moreover, it is widely used in the world.

MISTY1 has an 8-round Feistel structure with an FL layer every 2 rounds, which has not been broken, but there are many results on the reduced versions. Since the FL layer makes the cryptanalysis of MISTY1 more difficult, most results are only related to the reduced versions without FL layer. For example, Kühn [8] gave the first 6-round impossible differential cryptanalysis [1, 6], which was improved by Lu et al. with low data complexity and time complexity [12]. For the reduced versions with FL layers, a slicing attack on 4 rounds was shown by Kühn [9]. Later, Dunkelman et al. combined the generic impossible differential attack against 5-round Feistel constructions and the slicing attack to give a 6-round cryptanalytic result for MISTY1 with FL

---

* Corresponding author.

D.H. Lee and M. Yung (Eds.): WISA 2012, LNCS 7690, pp. 15–27, 2012.
© Springer-Verlag Berlin Heidelberg 2012

layers and a 7-round cryptanalytic result without FL layers [4]. Higher order differential [10] is another method which was usually used to analyze MISTY1, for the low order degree of the S-boxes used in the block cipher. Babbage gave the first higher order differential cryptanalysis of 5-round MISTY1 without FL layers [2]. Tsunoo et al. introduced the higher order differential cryptanalysis of 7-round MISTY1 with FL layers [17] with $2^{54.1}$ chosen plaintexts and $2^{120.7}$ 7-round encryptions, which is a chosen plaintext attack. Under certain weak key assumptions, the related-key differential or amplified boomerang cryptanalysis of MISTY1 were given [3, 11, 13]. However, the related-key setting assumes that the attacker knows the relationship between one or more pairs of unknown keys, which renders the resulting attack inapplicable in most real-world usage scenarios.

In this paper, we improve the impossible differential attack on 6 rounds of MISTY1 applying an observation of FL functions to filter the wrong keys more efficiently, which costs $2^{112.4}$ 6-round encryptions with $2^{52.5}$ chosen plaintexts. Moreover, an impossible differential attack on 7-round MISTY1 with 3 FL layers is proposed, which is the first attack on 7-round MISTY1 in known plaintext model. For the attack, we consider the generical 5-round impossible differential and the key schedule algorithm to select special differential characteristic for the extended rounds to filter wrong keys as early as possible. In this process some FL function properties are used to reduce the time complexity. For the 7-round MISTY1, the data complexity is 2^{58} known plaintexts, and the time complexity is $2^{124.4}$ 7-round encryptions. For the 7-round MISTY1 without FL layers, our attack needs $2^{92.2}$ 7-round encryptions with 2^{55} chosen plaintexts. Table 1 summaries our and previously published main cryptanalytic results on MISTY1 without related keys, where CP and KP refer respectively to the numbers of chosen plaintexts and known plaintexts, Enc. refers to the required number of encryption operations of the relevant version of MISTY1.

The paper is organized as follows. We give a brief description of the block cipher MISTY1 in Sect. 2. Section 3 presents impossible differential attacks on 6-round and 7-round MISTY1 versions. We summarize the paper in Sect. 4.

Table 1. Some cryptanalytic results on MISTY1

Rounds	Attack Type	FL layer	Data	Time
5	Higher-Order Differential [2]	None	$2^{10.5}$ CP	2^{17} Enc
6	Impossible Differential [8]	None	2^{54} CP	2^{61} Enc
7	Impossible Differential [4]	None	$2^{50.2}$ KP	$2^{114.1}$ Enc
7	Higher-Order Differential [16]	None	$2^{11.9}$ CP	$2^{125.1}$ Enc
7	Higher-Order Differential [5]	None	$2^{36.5}$ CP	$2^{112.0}$ Enc
7	Impossible Differential (Sect. 3.4)	None	2^{55} CP	$2^{92.2}$ Enc
4	Collision Search [8]	3	2^{28} CP	2^{76} Enc
4	Slicing Attack [9]	3	$2^{27.2}$ CP	$2^{81.6}$ Enc
5	Integral Attack [7]	3	$2^{10.5}$ CP	$2^{22.11}$ Enc
6	Integral Attack [15]	4	2^{32} CP	$2^{126.09}$ Enc
6	Impossible Differential [4]	4	2^{51} CP	$2^{123.4}$ Enc
6	Impossible Differential (Sect. 3.2)	4	$2^{52.5}$ CP	$2^{112.4}$ Enc
7	Impossible Differential (Sect. 3.3)	3	2^{58} KP	$2^{124.4}$ Enc

2 Description of MISTY1

MISTY1 works on a 64-bit block and a 128-bit key. We give a brief description of MISTY1 in the following. MISTY1 has eight rounds with a Feistel structure, which contains FL and FO functions. The FO function provides the non-linear property in each round, which is another three-round Feistel structure consisting of three FI functions and key mixing stages. The MISTY1 encryption function, FO, FI and FL functions are shown in Fig.1. For convenience, some notations used in this paper are listed firstly.

Notations

FL_i	: the i-th FL function of MISTY1 with subkey KL_i.
FO_i	: the i-th FO function of MISTY1 with subkey (KO_i, KI_i).
FI_{ij}	: the j-th FI function of FO_i with subkey KI_{ij}.
$\wedge$	: bitwise AND.
$\vee$	: bitwise OR.
$\oplus$	: bitwise XOR.
$X\|Y$	: the concatenation of X and Y.
$z[i]$	: the i-th bit of z, and '0' is the least significant bit.
$z[i_1 - i_2]$	: the $(i_2 - i_1 + 1)$ bits from the i_1-th bit to i_2-th bit of z.
$f \circ g$	: the composite function of f and g.
f^{-1}	: the inverse function of f.

The FL function is a simple key-dependent boolean function. Let the input of the FL_i be $XL_i = XL_{i,l}\|XL_{i,r}$, the output be $YL_i = YL_{i,l}\|YL_{i,r}$, where $XL_{i,l}, XL_{i,r}, YL_{i,l}$ and $YL_{i,r}$ are 16-bit integers. The FL function is defined as follows.

$$YL_{i,r} = (XL_{i,l} \wedge KL_{i1}) \oplus XL_{i,r}, \tag{1}$$

$$YL_{i,l} = (YL_{i,r} \vee KL_{i2}) \oplus XL_{i,l}. \tag{2}$$

The FO function provides the non-linear property in each round, which is another three-round Feistel structure consisting of three FI functions and key mixing stages. The FO function is depicted in Fig.1 (b). There is a 112-bit subkey[1] in FO function of each round (48 subkey bits used in the FI functions and 64 subkey bits in the key mixing stages). Let $XO_i = XO_{i,l}\|XO_{i,r}$, $YO_i = YO_{i,l}\|YO_{i,r}$ be the input and output of the FO_i function, where $XO_{i,l}, XO_{i,r}, YO_{i,l}, YO_{i,r}$ and $\overline{XI}_{i3}$ are 16-bit integers. Then the FO function has the form

$$\overline{XI}_{i,3} = FI((XO_{i,l} \oplus KO_{i1}), KI_{i1}) \oplus XO_{i,r},$$
$$YO_{i,l} = FI((XO_{i,r} \oplus KO_{i2}), KI_{i2}) \oplus \overline{XI}_{i,3} \oplus KO_{i4},$$
$$YO_{i,r} = FI((\overline{XI}_{i3} \oplus KO_{i3}), KI_{i3}) \oplus YO_{i,l} \oplus KO_{i4}.$$

The FI function uses two S-boxes S_7 and S_9 which are permutations of 7-bit to 7-bit and 9-bit to 9-bit respectively. Suppose the input of the FI_{ij} function is XI_{ij}, and the output is YI_{ij}, where XI_{ij} and YI_{ij} are 16-bit integers. Let $KI_{ij1} = KI_{ij}[9 - 15]$, $KI_{ij2} = KI_{ij}[0 - 8]$, $\overline{YI}_{ij2}, YI_{ij2}$ be 9-bit variable, and $\overline{YI}_{ij1}, YI_{ij1}$ be 7-bit variable. The structure of FI is depicted in Fig.1 (d). The FI function is definition as

---

[1] In [8] it was observed that the round function has an equivalent description that accepts 105 equivalent subkey bits.

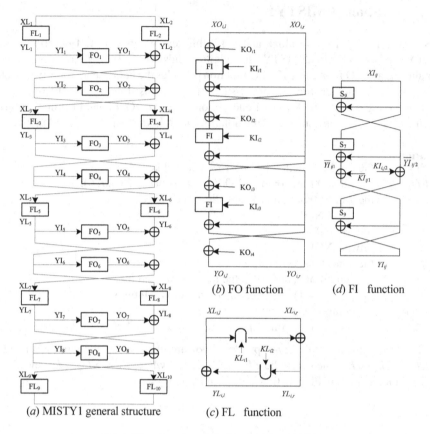

(a) MISTY1 general structure

(b) FO function

(d) FI function

(c) FL function

Fig. 1. The structure of the block cipher MISTY1

$$\overline{YI}_{ij2} = S_9(XI_{ij}[7 - 15]) \oplus XI_{ij}[0 - 6],$$
$$\overline{YI}_{ij1} = S_7(XI_{ij}[0 - 6]) \oplus \overline{YI}_{ij2}[0 - 6],$$
$$YI_{ij1} = \overline{YI}_{ij1} \oplus KI_{ij1},$$
$$YI_{ij2} = S_9(\overline{YI}_{ij2} \oplus KI_{ij2}) \oplus YI_{ij1}.$$
$$YI_{ij} = YI_{ij1} \| YI_{ij2}.$$

The key schedule of MISTY1 takes the 128-bit key, and treats it as eight 16-bit words $K_1, K_2, \ldots, K_8$. From this set of subkeys, another eight 16-bit words are generated according to $K_i' = FI_{K_{i+1}}(K_i)$. The subkeys $KL_i = (KL_{i1}, KL_{i2})$, $KO_i = (KO_{i1}, KO_{i2}, KO_{i3}, KO_{i4})$, $KI_i = (KI_{i1}, KI_{i2}, KI_{i3})$ are listed in Tab. 2.

3   Impossible Differential Attacks on MISTY1

In this section, we give improved impossible differential attacks on the block cipher MISTY1 in exploitation of some new observations of the FL functions to eliminate the wrong keys as early as possible.

Table 2. The subkeys generated with K_i and K'_i for each round

KO_{i1}	KO_{i2}	KO_{i3}	KO_{i4}	KI_{i1}	KI_{i2}	KI_{i3}	KL_{i1}		KL_{i2}	
K_i	K_{i+2}	K_{i+7}	K_{i+4}	K'_{i+5}	K'_{i+1}	K'_{i+3}	$K_{\frac{i+1}{2}}$ (odd i)		$K'_{\frac{i+1}{2}+6}$ (odd i)	
							$K'_{\frac{i}{2}+2}$ (even i)		$K_{\frac{i}{2}+4}$ (even i)	

3.1 Some Observations of MISTY1

Observation 1. *[9] Let X, X' be l-bit variable, and $\Delta X = X \oplus X'$. Then there are two difference properties of AND and OR operations, such that*

$$(X \wedge K) \oplus (X' \wedge K) = \Delta X \wedge K,$$
$$(X \vee K) \oplus (X' \vee K) = \Delta X \oplus (\Delta X \wedge K).$$

We define FL'_i as the function on the input and output differences of FL_i, which is deduced by the definition of FL function and Observation 1. Let $\Delta X = \Delta X_l \| \Delta X_r$, $\Delta Y = \Delta Y_l \| \Delta Y_r$ be the input and output differences of FL_i respectively, and $\Delta Y = FL'_i(\Delta X)$ has the form

$$\Delta Y_r = (\Delta X_l \wedge KL_{i1}) \oplus \Delta X_r,$$
$$\Delta Y_l = (\Delta Y_r \wedge KL_{i2}) \oplus \Delta Y_r \oplus \Delta X_l. \tag{3}$$

By equation (3), we know FL'_i is linear and invertible, which can be represented as 16 parallelized bit equations. Let $\Delta x_j = (\Delta X_l[j], \Delta X_r[j])$, $\Delta y_j = (\Delta Y_l[j], \Delta Y_r[j])$, each bit equation is denoted as $f_j : \Delta x_j \rightarrow \Delta y_j$,

$$\Delta Y_r[j] = (\Delta X_l[j] \wedge KL_{i1}[j]) \oplus \Delta X_r[j], \qquad j = 0, 1, \ldots, 15.$$
$$\Delta Y_l[j] = (\Delta Y_r[j] \wedge KL_{i2}[j]) \oplus \Delta Y_r[j] \oplus \Delta X_l[j],$$

There are 9 possible values of $(\Delta x_j, \Delta y_j)$, which are listed in Tab. 3.

When $(\Delta x_j, \Delta y_j)$ are chosen from the uniform set $\{0, 1\}^4$, there are 3 cases holding with probability 1, 6 cases holding with probability $1/2$ for given $KL_{i2}[j]$. Thus f_j holds with probability $\frac{3}{16} \times 1 + \frac{6}{16} \times \frac{1}{2} = \frac{3}{8}$. Moreover equation (3) holds with probability $(3/8)^{16} = 2^{-22.6}$ for given KL_{i2} on average.

Observation 2. *Let $\delta \| \delta$, $b_0 \| b_1$ be the input and output differences of the FL_i function respectively. Then $\delta = b_0 \vee b_1$, and there are 2^{16} KL_i such that $(b_0 \| b_1) = FL'_i(\delta \| \delta)$. Some bits of KL_i are computed as follows:*

$$KL_{i1}[j] = b_1[j] \oplus 1 \text{ when } b_0[j] \vee b_1[j] = 1, \qquad j = 0, 1, \ldots, 15. \quad (4)$$
$$KL_{i2}[j] = b_0[j] \text{ when } b_1[j] = 1,$$

Proof. By equation (3), the following equations are deduced

$$b_1 = (\delta \wedge KL_{i1}) \oplus \delta,$$
$$b_0 = (b_1 \wedge KL_{i2}) \oplus b_1 \oplus \delta.$$

Table 3. The input and output differences and the corresponding subkeys for bit equation f_j of the FL function

Δx_j	Δy_j	$KL_{i1}[j]$	$KL_{i2}[j]$
(0,0)	(0,0)	0 or 1	0 or 1
(0,1)	(0,1)	0 or 1	1
(0,1)	(1,1)	0 or 1	0
(1,0)	(1,0)	0	0 or 1
(1,0)	(0,1)	1	0
(1,0)	(1,1)	1	1
(1,1)	(1,0)	1	0 or 1
(1,1)	(0,1)	0	0
(1,1)	(1,1)	0	1

Each FL'_i function can be represented as a parallel application of 16 equations for $j = 0, \ldots, 15$.

$$b_1[j] = (\delta[j] \wedge KL_{i1}[j]) \oplus \delta[j],$$
$$b_0[j] = = (\delta[j] \wedge KL_{i1}[j]) \oplus (\delta[j] \wedge KL_{i2}[j]) \oplus (\delta[j] \wedge KL_{i1}[j] \wedge KL_{i2}[j]). \tag{5}$$

There are four cases for each equation (5), which are corresponding to the values in Tab. 3 when $\Delta x = (0,0)$ or $(1,1)$. Then we get $\delta[j] = b_0[j] \vee b_1[j]$. Moreover, $\delta = b_0 \vee b_1$. It is obvious that there are four subkeys when $(b_0[j], b_1[j]) = (0,0)$, there are two subkeys when $(b_0[j], b_1[j]) = (1,0)$, and there are only one subkey for the other cases respectively. Suppose $(b_0 \| b_1)$ are chosen from the uniform set $\{0, 1\}^{32}$. The expected number of subkeys such that $(b_0 \| b_1) = FL'_i(\delta \| \delta)$ is

$$\sum_{i=0}^{16} \binom{16}{i} \left(\sum_{j=0}^{16-i} \binom{16-i}{j} \times (1/2)^j \times (2/4)^{(16-i-j)} \right) = 2^{16}. \qquad \square$$

We also conclude that given input difference $b_0 \| b_1$ of the FL_i function, the output difference is of the form $\delta \| \delta$. Then $\delta = b_0 \vee b_1$.

It is obvious that given the output differences of FL_i, the 16-bit value δ is independent of the 32 subkey bits (KL_{i1}, KL_{i2}) when input difference of FL_i is of the form (δ, δ). With this observation, we divided the key recovery into two independent parts for the impossible differential attack on 6-round MISTY1.

Observation 3. *Let $(0, \alpha)$ be the input difference of round 2, $(\beta, 0)$ be the output difference of round 6, and then $(0, \alpha) \xrightarrow{5R} (\beta, 0)$ is an impossible differential for rounds 2 to 6 when $FL'_3(\alpha) = FL'^{-1}_5 \circ FL'^{-1}_7(\beta)$.*

The input difference of round 2 is $(0, \alpha)$, and the output difference of round 6 is $(\beta, 0)$, so we deduce that the input difference of FO_4 is nonzero, and the output difference of FO_4 is $FL'^{-1}_5 \circ FL'^{-1}_7(\beta) \oplus FL'_3(\alpha) = 0$. See Fig. 2. Hence $(0, \alpha) \xrightarrow{5R} (\beta, 0)$. The similar impossible differential was used for the first 5 rounds in reference [4].

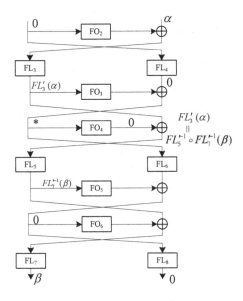

Fig. 2. Five round impossible differential of MISTY1

Observation 4. *Let* $\phi = FL_7' \circ FL_5' \circ FL_3'$, $X = X_l \| X_r$, $Y = Y_l \| Y_r$, *such that* $Y = \phi(X)$. *Then* X, Y *necessarily satisfy*

$$(X_l \wedge X_r) \oplus X_l \oplus X_r \oplus (Y_l \wedge Y_r) \oplus Y_l \oplus Y_r = 0x0000. \tag{6}$$

And the equation (6) holds with probability $2^{-10.85}$, *when* X, Y *both are chosen from the uniform set* $\{0, 1\}^{16}$.

Proof. As FL_i' is linear and invertible, $\phi = FL_7' \circ FL_5' \circ FL_3'$ is also linear and invertible. ϕ can be represented as 16 parallelized bit equations g_j, $(Y_l[j], Y_r[j]) = g_j(X_l[j], X_r[j])$ is one-to-one mapping, and $(Y_l[j], Y_r[j]) = (0, 0)$, if and only if $(X_l[j], X_r[j]) = (0, 0)$. Hence $(X_l[j] \wedge X_r[j]) \oplus X_l[j] \oplus X_r[j] \oplus (Y_l[j] \wedge Y_r[j]) \oplus Y_l[j] \oplus Y_r[j] = 0$. There are 10 values which are possible of all 16 values $(X_l[j], X_r[j], Y_l[j], Y_r[j])$, so the equation (6) holds with probability $(10/16)^{16} = 2^{-10.85}$. $\qquad\square$

Observation 5. *[8] For* FO_i *function, let the input difference be* (β_l, β_r), *the output difference be* (δ, δ), *where* β_l, β_r *and* δ *are 16-bit variable. Then the input and output differences of* FI_{i3} *are 0, the input and output differences of* FI_{i1} *are* β_l, β_r, *and the input and output differences of* FI_{i2} *are* β_r, δ. *The difference of* FO_i *function depends only on the 50 subkey bits* KO_{i1}, KO_{i2}, KI_{i12} *and* KI_{i22}.

Observation 6. *For* FO_i *function, let the input difference be* $(\alpha_l, 0)$, *the output difference be* (β_l, β_r), *where* α_l, β_l *and* β_r *are 16-bit variable. Then the input and output differences of* FI_{i2} *are 0, the input and output differences of* FI_{i1} *are* α_l, β_l, *and the input and output differences of* FI_{i3} *are* $\beta_l, \beta_l \oplus \beta_r$. *The difference of* FO_i *function depends only on the 50 subkey bits* KO_{i1}, KO_{i3}, KI_{i12} *and* KI_{i32}.

Observations 2 and 5 are used to eliminate the wrong keys for greater efficiency to improve the impossible differential attack on 6-round MISTY1.

3.2 An Improved Impossible Differential Attack on 6-Round MISTY1

In this section, an improved impossible differential attack on 6 rounds of MISTY1 with 8 FL functions is presented. The impossible differential is the same as reference [4], and extend a round at the end. Special differentials are used to deduce the time complexity in the key recovery process. Let the output difference ΔYO_6 of the 6-th round is of the form (δ, δ). By Observation 2, δ is independent of the subkey KL_7. Consequently, we guess or compute the subkey bits in FO_6 and FL_8 which bring about the input and output values of the impossible differential, and then match the subkey KL_7 which make the input difference of FL_7 be of the form (δ, δ). The impossible differential with the extended round is depicted in Fig. 3. And we demonstrate our improved impossible differential attack on 6-round MISTY1 in the following process.

1. Ask for encrypting m structures of 2^{32} plaintexts $(A, *)$, such that in each structure, the left half of all the plaintexts is equal to some random value A, while the right half obtains all possible values. As a result, the differences between two plaintexts in the same structure are of the form $(0, \alpha)$. For each structure, find the pairs whose output differences are of the form $(*, \beta)$, such that $\alpha \to \beta$ is possible though $FL'_8 \circ FL'_6 \circ FL'_4 \circ FL'_2$. There are $m \times 2^{63-10.85} = m \times 2^{52.15}$ pairs kept on average.

2. For every pair, since the output difference ΔYO_6 is of the form $(\delta\|\delta)$, then $\delta = \Delta C_{l,l} \vee \Delta C_{l,r}$ by Observation 2. We get $\Delta YI_{6,2} = \delta$, and $\Delta YI_{6,1} = \Delta XO_{6,r}$. Guess $KL_8(K_8, K'_6)$ to compute the FO_6's input $XO_6 = XL_8$ with FL_8. Then ΔYI_{621} is obtained by FI_{62}. If ΔYI_{621} is not equal to $\delta[9-15]$, then start a new guess. Otherwise compute the key $KI_{622}(K'_7[0-8])$ by the input and output differences of S_9 S-box[2].

3. Guess 7-bit $K'_7[9-15]$, and compute the K_7 and K_6 by key schedule. Then ΔYI_{611} is obtained by FI_{61}. If ΔYI_{611} is not equal to $\Delta XI_{62}[9-15]$, then start a new guess. Otherwise compute $KI_{612}(K'_3[0-8])$ by the input and output differences of S_9 S-boxes.

4. Guess K_5 to compute the subkey K'_5. Then get K'_4 and $K'_3[9-15]$ by function $\beta = FL'_8 \circ FL'_6 \circ FL'_4 \circ FL'_2(\alpha)$. Then compute $K_4(KL_{71})$ by key schedule, and $KL_{72}(K'_2)$ are deduced from FL_7, for we know the input and output differences and KL_{71}. Finally, we compute K_2 by key schedule. Thus the key words $(K_2, K_3, K_4, K_5, K_6, K_7, K_8)$ produce the impossible differential, discard it from the list of the 2^{112} possible values and start a new guess. Hence, the number of pairs remaining for each subkey $(K_2, K_3, K_4, K_5, K_6, K_7, K_8)$ guess is about $m \times 2^{52.15-32-21.15-16} = m \times 2^{-17}$ [3].

5. There are about $2^{112} \times e^{-m \times 2^{-17}}$ key words $(K_2, K_3, K_4, K_5, K_6, K_7, K_8)$ kept after the $m \times 2^{52.15}$ pairs filter. Exhaustively search for the 16-bit key word K_1, and get the right key. Otherwise go to Step 2, and repeat the above process.

---

[2] This can be done easily by examining the difference distribution table of S_9.

[3] In [4], let $G = FL'_8 \circ FL'_6 \circ FL'_4 \circ FL'_2$, which is linear and invertible. There are 6^{16} possible G functions in total. And the expected number of G functions is $\sum_{j=0}^{16} \binom{16}{j} \times (9/10)^j \times 2^j \times (1/10)^{(16-j)} \times 6^{16-j} = (12/5)^{16}$ for given α and β. Therefore a function $\beta = G(\alpha)$ holds with probability $(2/5)^{16} = 2^{-21.5}$ for given α and β.

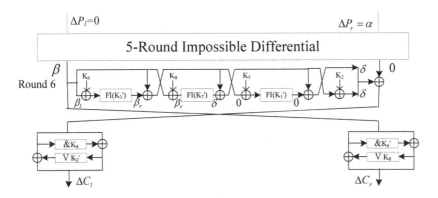

Fig. 3. An impossible differential attack on 6-round MISTY1

Complexity Evaluation. There are $m \times 2^{32}$ 6-round encryptions and $m \times 2^{63}$ computations of equation (6) in Step 1. Step 2 needs $2^{32} \times m \times 2^{52.15} = m \times 2^{84.15}$ FL computations. There are about $m \times 2^{84.15} \times 3$ FI computations in Step 3. Step 4 costs about $m \times 2^{84.15-7+16} = m \times 2^{93.15}$ FI computations and $m \times 2^{93.15} \times 4$ FL functions. We spend $2^{128} \times e^{-m \times 2^{-17}}$ encryptions in Step 5. The two most time consuming steps of the attack are Steps 4 and 5. We take the moderate assumption that an FI function computation is equivalent to 3 FL function computation, so the the time complexity of 4 FL functions and an FI function evaluations is not greater than 1/6 of the time required for a 6-round encryption. By balance the time complexity of Steps 4 and 5, i.e. $2^{128} \times e^{-m \times 2^{-17}} = m \times 2^{93.15} \times 1/6$. Then we get $m = 2^{20.5}$, the time complexity is about $2^{112.4}$ 6-round encryptions and the data complexity is $2^{52.5}$ chosen plaintexts.

3.3 The Impossible Differential Attack on 7-Round MISTY1

In this section, we propose the first impossible differential attack on 7 rounds of MISTY1 with 6 FL functions. We apply the impossible differential $(0, \alpha) \overset{5R}{\nrightarrow} (0, \beta)$ with $\beta = \phi(\alpha)$, and extend one round backward and forward respectively(seen Fig. 4), where $\phi = FL'_7 \circ FL'_5 \circ FL'_3$ is the same definition as Observation 4.

Precomputation. We take FI as a key dependent S-box. As KI_{ij1} has no impact on the output difference of FI, we construct a key dependent difference distribution table of FI. For all 2^{31} possible input pairs (XI, XI') of the FI function, and 2^9 possible subkeys KI_{ij2}, compute the corresponding output difference pairs ΔYI. Store the value XI in a hash table T_1 indexed by 41-bit value $(KI_{ij2}\|\Delta XI\|\Delta YI)$, and then each XI corresponds to an index on average. We take an access to this table as a computation of FI function.

Data Collection. Collect 2^m plaintexts $P = (P_l\|P_r)$ and their corresponding ciphertexts $C = (C_l\|C_r)$, and store the (P, C) pairs in a hash table with index $C_{l,l} \oplus C_{l,r}$. There are about 2^{2m-17} pairs kept with $\Delta C_{l,l} = \Delta C_{l,r}$. We extend one round at the beginning and end of the impossible differential respectively, and then $\alpha = \Delta P_l, \beta = \Delta C_r$. Hence the input difference ΔP_l and output difference ΔC_r should satisfy $\Delta C_r = \phi(\Delta P_l)$ by

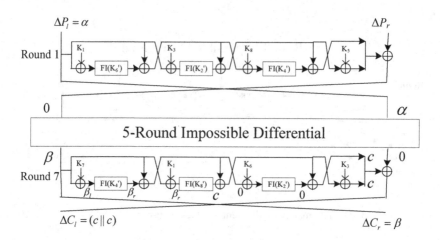

Fig. 4. Impossible differential attack on 7 rounds of MISTY1

Observation 3. We apply Observation 4 to filter some pairs which can not bring about the impossible differential. At last there are $2^{2m-17-10.85} = 2^{2m-27.85}$ pairs kept.

Key Recovery

1. For every pair, we get $\Delta XI_{7,2} = \Delta C_{r,r}, \Delta YI_{7,2} = \Delta C_{l,l}$. Guess 9-bit $KI_{722}(K_8'[0-8])$, $XI_{7,1}$ is obtained by looking up the hash table T_1. Then $K_1 = XI_{72} \oplus C_{r,r}$, or $K_1 = XI_{72} \oplus C_{r,r}'$.

2. Guess 9-bit $KI_{112}(K_6'[0-8])$, and compute the output difference ΔYI_{11} by the function FI_{11}. Then the output difference of FI_{12} is $\Delta YI_{12} = \Delta YI_{11} \oplus \Delta P_{r,l}$, and input difference is $\Delta XI_{12} = \Delta P_{l,r}$.

3. Guess 9-bit $KI_{122}(K_2'[0-8])$, access the hash table T_1 to get the FI_{12}'s input XI_{12}, and $K_3 = XI_{12} \oplus P_{l,r}$ or $K_3 = XI_{12} \oplus P_{l,r}'$.

4. Detect the subkeys KL_3, KL_5, KL_7, which make $\Delta C_r = \phi(\Delta P_l)$ hold or not. As the subkeys $K_1, K_3, K_2'[0-8]$ have been obtained in the above steps, guess 7-bit $K_2'[9-15]$, and then K_2, K_1' are deduced by key schedule algorithm. As ϕ can be represented as 16 parallel bit equations, check $\Delta C_r = \phi(\Delta P_l)$ bit by bit. Since the subkeys $KL_{31}, KL_{32}[0-8], KL_{51}, KL_{52}$ are known, then we get $\Delta XL_{7,l}[0-8], \Delta XL_{7,r}[0-8]$ by FL_3' and FL_5' functions. Detect $(\Delta C_{r,l}[j], \Delta C_{r,r}[j]) = f_j(\Delta XL_{7,l}[j], \Delta XL_{7,r}[j])$ for $j = 0, 1, \ldots, 8$, with KL_{72}, which hold with probability $(3/8 \times 16/10)^9 = 2^{-6.63}$. [4] If the equation does not hold, start a new guess.

5. As $\Delta XI_{7,1} = \Delta C_{r,l}, \Delta YI_{7,1} = \Delta C_{r,r}$, guess 9-bit $KI_{712}(K_4'[0-8])$, $XI_{7,1}$ is obtained by accessing the hash table T_1. Then $K_7 = XI_{7,1} \oplus C_{r,l}$, or $K_7 = XI_{7,1} \oplus C_{r,l}'$. The input difference of FI_{13} is $\Delta XI_{13} = \Delta YI_{11} \oplus \Delta P_{l,r}$, the output difference is $\Delta YI_{1,3} = \Delta P_{r,l} \oplus \Delta P_{r,r}$, and $KI_{132} = K_4'[0-8]$. Then XI_{13} is obtained by accessing

---

[4] Since the pairs for which the differential $(0, \Delta P_l) \xrightarrow{5R} (\Delta C_r, 0)$ is impossible were already discarded in data collocation process

the hash table T_1. The equivalent subkey $K_8 \oplus (K'_6[9-15] \| 00 \| K'_6[9-15])$ is deduced by XI_{13} and the function FI_{11}.

6. For $j = 9, \ldots, 15$, guess $K'_8[j]$, and compute $\Delta XL_{7,l}[j]$, $\Delta XL_{7,r}[j]$. Then we detect $(\Delta C_{r,l}[j], \Delta C_{r,r}[j]) = f_j(\Delta XL_{7,l}[j], \Delta XL_{7,r}[j])$, which holds with probability $3/8 \times 16/10 = 0.6$. If the equation does not hold, start a new guess. Otherwise deduce K_8 by key schedule, and get K'_6 by the equivalent key $K_8 \oplus (K'_6[9-15] \| 00 \| K'_6[9-15])$.

7. By $\Delta C_r = FL'_7(\Delta XL_7)$, deduce the key word $K_4 = KL_{71}$, there are $(3/9 \times 2 + 6/9)^{16} = (4/3)^{16}$. Then we deduce K_8, K_6 by key schedule. Thus the key words $(K_1, K_2, K_3, K_4, K'_4[0-8], K_6, K_7, K_8)$ produce the impossible differential, discard it from the list of the 2^{121} possible values and start a new guess. For each pair there are about $2^{41} \times (0.6)^{16} \times (4/3)^{16} = 2^{35.85}$ key $(K_1, K_2, K_3, K_4, K'_4[0-8], K_6, K_7, K_8)$.

8. There are about $2^{121} \times e^{-2^{2m-113}}$ key words $(K_1, K_2, K_3, K_4, K'_4[0-8], K_6, K_7, K_8)$ kept after the $2^{2m-27.85}$ pairs filter. Exhaustively search for the 9-bit key word $K'_4[9-15]$, and get the right key. Otherwise go to Step 1, and repeat the above process.

Complexity Evaluation. Step 1 needs $2^9 \times 2^{2m-27.85} = 2^{2m-18.85}$ FI computations. There are about $2^{18} \times 2^{2m-27.85} = 2^{2m-9.85}$ FI computations in Step 2. Step 3 costs about $2^{27} \times 2^{2m-27.85} = 2^{2m-0.85}$ FI computations. We speed $2^{34} \times 2^{2m-27.85} = 2^{2m+6.15} \times 2$ FI computations in Step 4. There are $2^{43-6.63} \times 2^{2m-27.85} = 2^{2m+8.52} \times 2$ FI computations in Step 5. Step 6 costs $2^{43-6.63} \times (2 + 2^2 \times 0.6 + \cdots + 2^7 \times (0.6)^6) \times 2^{2m-27.85} \times 2 = 2^{2m+14.21}$ FL computations. We spend $2^{41} \times (0.6)^{16} \times 2^{2m-27.85} = 2^{2m+1.36}$ FL computations in Step 7. There are about $2^{128} \times e^{-2^{2m-113}}$ 7-round encryptions in Step 8. We know the time complexity is about $2^{2m+8.38}$ 7-rounds encryption in the first 7 steps. Let $2^{2m+8.38} = 2^{128} \times e^{-2^{2m-113}}$ to achieve the least overall time complexity. Then $m = 58$, the total time complexity is about $2^{124.4}$ 7-round encryptions.

3.4 An Impossible Differential Attack on 7-Round MISTY1 without FL

For MISITY1 without FL layers, the general impossible differential was utilized to analyze 7-round MISTY1 in [4]. The underlying impossible differential characteristic is: $(0, a) \overset{5R}{\nrightarrow} (0, a)$, where a is a 32-bit non-zero value. In this section, we specify the 5-round impossible differential as:

$$(0, a_l \| 0) \overset{5R}{\nrightarrow} (0, a_l \| 0),$$

where a_l is 16-bit non-zero value. The choice of difference $a_l \| 0$ can minimize the key words guessing when the differential is extended to 7-round. Combined with the key words distribution, we mount the 5-round impossible differential from round 2 to round 6, and extend one round forward and backward respectively.

The impossible differential attack on the 7-round variant of MISTY1 is described in the following.

1. Choose the 2^n structures of plaintexts, and each structure contain 2^{48} plaintexts $(P_l, P_r) = (* \| x, * \| *)$, where x is a fixed 16-bit value, '$*$' take all the possible 16-bit values. Query their corresponding ciphertexts (C_l, C_r) and store (P_l, P_r, C_l, C_r) in a hash table H indexed by 32-bit values $P_{1,l} \oplus C_{r,l}$ and $C_{r,r}$. Sieve the plaintext and ciphertext pair, which satisfy $\Delta P_{l,l} = \Delta C_{r,l}$ and $\Delta C_{r,r} = 0$. There are $2^{n+95-32} = 2^{n+63}$ pairs remain on average.

2. For each plaintext-ciphertext pair, we know the input and output differences of FI_{71}, where $\Delta XI_{71} = \Delta C_{r,l}, \Delta YI_{71} = \Delta C_{l,l}$. Guess 9-bit subkey $KI_{711}(K'_4[0-8])$, XI_{71} is obtained by looking up the hash table T_1. Then $K_1 = XI_{72} \oplus C_{r,r}$, or $K_1 = XI_{72} \oplus C'_{r,r}$. As $\Delta XI_{13} = \Delta P_{r,l}, \Delta YI_{13} = \Delta P_{r,l} \oplus \Delta P_{r,r}$, and $KI_{131} = K'_4[0-8]$, then XI_{13} is obtained by accessing the hash table T_1.

3. As $\Delta XI_{73} = \Delta C_{l,l}, \Delta YI_{73} = \Delta C_{r,l} \oplus \Delta C_{r,r}$, guess 9-bit subkey $KI_{731}(K'_2[0-8])$, and XI_{71} is obtained by looking up the hash table T_1. Then we get the equivalent key $K_6 \oplus (K'_4[9-15]\|00\|K'_4[9-15])$.

4. Guess 7-bit $K'_4[9-15]$, and deduce K_6 from the above equivalent key. Then compute K'_6 by the key schedule algorithm. Since $\Delta XI_{11} = \Delta P_{l,l}, \Delta YI_{11} = \Delta P_{r,l}$, we get XI_{11} by accessing the hash table T_1. Then $K_1 = XI_{11} \oplus P_{l,l}$, or $K_1 = XI_{11} \oplus P'_{l,l}$, and YI_{11} is obtained by FI_{11}. Hence, we get K_8 from YI_{11} and XI_{13}.

5. For each guess of $(K'_4, K'_2[0-8])$, there are about several 64-bit subkeys (K_1, K_6, K_7, K_8) left after 2^{63+n}-pair filters. Search for the remaining subkey K_2, K_3, K_4 to obtain the right key. Otherwise, return to Step 2, and repeat the above process.

Complexity. In Step 1, we need about 2^{n+48} encryptions to get the corresponding ciphertexts. Step 2 costs $2^{n+63+9} = 2^{n+72} \times 2$ FI computations. We need $2^{n+72+9} = 2^{n+81}$ FI computations in Step 3. Step 4 are $2^{n+88} \times 3$ FI computations. In step 5, there are about $\epsilon = 2^{128}(1 - \frac{1}{2^{64}})^{2^{63+n}}$ 7-round encryptions to find the right key. By balance the complexity of step 4 and 5, we get $n = 7$. The time complexity is about $2^{92.2}$ encryptions and the data complexity is 2^{55} chosen plaintexts.

4   Conclusion

In this paper, we show new observations on FL functions of MISTY1. Taking advantage of these observations and early abort technique, we improve a previous impossible differential attack on 6-round MISTY1 with FL functions, which costs $2^{112.2}$ 6-round encryptions with $2^{52.5}$ chosen plaintexts. Furthermore, selecting special differential characteristic in the extended rounds, we present impossible differential cryptanalysis on 7-round MISTY1 with 6 FL functions, which is the first known plaintexts attack on the 7-round MISTY1. The impossible differential attack on 7-round MISTY1 needs $2^{124.4}$ encryptions with 2^{58} known plaintexts. Besides, an improved impossible differential attack on 7-round MISTY1 without FL functions is presented, which needs $2^{92.2}$ 7-round encryptions with 2^{55} chosen plaintexts.

For the impossible differential cryptanalysis, the special differential characteristic in the extended rounds with less key words is helpful to filter the wrong keys more efficiently. For the block ciphers, there are available key relations in exploitation of the linear key schedule algorithm to recovery key. The observations of FL functions can also be used to the differential cryptanalysis of MISTY1 to detect the secret key.

Acknowledgments. We would like to thank anonymous reviewers for their very helpful comments on the paper. This work is supported by the National Natural Science Foundation of China (Grant No. 61133013 and 60931160442), China Postdoctoral Science Foundation(20110490442) and the Tsinghua University Initiative Scientific Research Program (No.20111080970).

References

1. Biham, E., Biryukov, A., Shamir, A.: Cryptanalysis of Skipjack Reduced to 31 Rounds Using Impossible Differentials. In: Stern, J. (ed.) EUROCRYPT 1999. LNCS, vol. 1592, pp. 12–23. Springer, Heidelberg (1999)
2. Babbage, S., Frisch, L.: On MISTY1 Higher Order Differential Cryptanalysis. In: Won, D. (ed.) ICISC 2000. LNCS, vol. 2015, pp. 22–36. Springer, Heidelberg (2001)
3. Dai, Y., Chen, S.: Weak key class of MISTY1 for related-key differential attack. In: Moti, Y., Wu, C.K. (eds.) INSCRYPT 2011 (2011) (to appear)
4. Dunkelman, O., Keller, N.: An Improved Impossible Differential Attack on MISTY1. In: Pieprzyk, J. (ed.) ASIACRYPT 2008. LNCS, vol. 5350, pp. 441–454. Springer, Heidelberg (2008)
5. Igarashi, Y., Kaneko, T.: The 32nd-order Differential Attack on MISTY1 without FL Functions. In: 2008 International Symposium on Information Theory and its Applications, WTI-4-4 (2008)
6. Knudsen, L.R.: DEAL -a 128-bit block cipher. Technical report, Department of Informatics, University of Bergen, Norway (1998)
7. Knudsen, L.R., Wagner, D.: Integral Cryptanalysis. In: Daemen, J., Rijmen, V. (eds.) FSE 2002. LNCS, vol. 2365, pp. 112–127. Springer, Heidelberg (2002)
8. Kühn, U.: Cryptanalysis of Reduced-Round MISTY. In: Pfitzmann, B. (ed.) EUROCRYPT 2001. LNCS, vol. 2045, pp. 325–339. Springer, Heidelberg (2001)
9. Kühn, U.: Improved Cryptanalysis of MISTY1. In: Daemen, J., Rijmen, V. (eds.) FSE 2002. LNCS, vol. 2365, pp. 61–75. Springer, Heidelberg (2002)
10. Lai, X.: Higher Order Derivatives and Differential Cryptanalysis. Communications and Cryptography: Two Sides of One Tapestry, pp. 227–233 (1994)
11. Lee, S., Kim, J., Hong, D., Lee, C., Sung, J., Hong, S., Lim, J.: Weak Key Classes of 7-round MISTY 1 and 2 for Related-key Amplied Boomerang Attacks. IEICE Transactions on Fundamentals of Electronics, Communications and Computer Sciences 91-A(2), 642–649 (2008)
12. Lu, J., Kim, J.-S., Keller, N., Dunkelman, O.: Improving the Efficiency of Impossible Differential Cryptanalysis of Reduced Camellia and MISTY1. In: Malkin, T. (ed.) CT-RSA 2008. LNCS, vol. 4964, pp. 370–386. Springer, Heidelberg (2008)
13. Lu, J., Yap, W., Wei, Y.: Weak Keys of the Full MISTY1 Block Cipher for Related-Key Cryptanalysis, IACR Cryptology ePrint Archive 2012: 66 (2012)
14. Matsui, M.: New Block Encryption Algorithm MISTY. In: Biham, E. (ed.) FSE 1997. LNCS, vol. 1267, pp. 54–68. Springer, Heidelberg (1997)
15. Sun, X., Lai, X.: Improved Integral Attacks on MISTY1. In: Jacobson Jr., M.J., Rijmen, V., Safavi-Naini, R. (eds.) SAC 2009. LNCS, vol. 5867, pp. 266–280. Springer, Heidelberg (2009)
16. Tanaka, H., Hatano, Y., Sugio, N., Kaneko, T.: Security Analysis of MISTY1. In: Kim, S., Yung, M., Lee, H.-W. (eds.) WISA 2007. LNCS, vol. 4867, pp. 215–226. Springer, Heidelberg (2008)
17. Tsunoo, Y., Saito, T., Shigeri, M., Kawabata, T.: Higher Order Differential Attacks on Reduced-Round MISTY1. In: Lee, P.J., Cheon, J.H. (eds.) ICISC 2008. LNCS, vol. 5461, pp. 415–431. Springer, Heidelberg (2009)

Efficient Parallel Evaluation
of Multivariate Quadratic Polynomials on GPUs

Satoshi Tanaka[1], Tung Chou[2], Bo-Yin Yang[2], Chen-Mou Cheng[3],
and Kouichi Sakurai[1]

[1] Kyushu University, Fukuoka, Japan
{tanasato@itslab.inf,sakurai@csce}.kyushu-u.ac.jp
[2] Academia Sinica, Taipei, Taiwan
{blueprint,by}@crypto.tw
[3] National Taiwan University, Taipei, Taiwan
ccheng@cc.ee.ntu.edu.tw

Abstract. QUAD is a provably secure stream cipher, whose security is based on the hardness assumption of solving multivariate quadratic polynomial systems over a finite field, which is known to be NP-complete. However, such provable security comes at a price, and QUAD is slower than most other stream ciphers that do not have security proofs.

In this paper, we discuss two efficient parallelization techniques for evaluating multivariate quadratic polynomial systems on GPU, which can effectively accelerate the QUAD stream cipher. The first approach focuses on formula of summations in quadratics, while the second approach uses parallel reduction to summations. Our approaches can be easily generalized and applied to other multivariate cryptosystems.

Keywords: Stream cipher, efficient implementation, multivariate cryptography, GPGPU.

1 Introduction

1.1 Background

Multivariate cryptography uses multivariate polynomial systems as public keys. The security of multivariate cryptography is based on the hardness of solving non-linear multivariate polynomial systems over a finite field [1]. Multivariate cryptography is considered to be a promising tool for fast digital signature because it often involves arithmetic operations in smaller algebraic structures compared with traditional public-key cryptosystems like RSA.

Non-linear multivariate polynomials can also be used to construct symmetric-key cryptosystems, e.g., the QUAD stream cipher [3]. The security of QUAD depends on the hardness of the multivariate quadratic (MQ) problem. QUAD has a provable security, but it is slow compared with other symmetric ciphers. It would be nice if we could accelerate QUAD while having a security proof, combining the strengths from the two worlds.

D.H. Lee and M. Yung (Eds.): WISA 2012, LNCS 7690, pp. 28–42, 2012.
© Springer-Verlag Berlin Heidelberg 2012

1.2   Related Works

Berbain et al. proposed several efficient implementation techniques for multivariate cryptography [2]. GPU implementation result of the QUAD stream cipher [5]. In this paper, we reconsider GPU implementations of the QUAD stream cipher. We note that a preliminary version of this paper, "Fast Implementation and Experimentation of Multivariate Cryptography," was presented at the 6th Joint Workshop on Information Security, 2011. This version includes the results of further investigation after the preliminary version was presented at the workshop.

1.3   Contributions

Our main contribution is to accelerate the evaluation of quadratic polynomials in the QUAD stream cipher. The bottleneck computation in QUAD's encryption is to evaluate multivariate quadratic polynomial systems. In particular, we accelerate the computation of the summation in evaluating quadratic polynomials.

We investigated two parallelization strategies to evaluate summations in multivariate quadratic polynomials. The first approach focuses on formula of summations in quadratics, while the second uses parallel reduction to summations. Our techniques apply to multivariate public-key cryptography as well.

Finally, even if QUAD cannot be accelerated a lot by the proposed techniques, having a GPU implementation is still useful because we will be able to offload the computation from CPU to GPU on busy servers.

2   Multivariate Cryptography

Multivariate cryptography is a candidate of post-quantum cryptography. In multivariate cryptography, we can encrypt plaintext to ciphertext by evaluating appropriate multivariate polynomial systems over $\mathbb{GF}_q$. Or we can use it to generate keystream bits as in QUAD. In the rest of this section, we will give an overview of the multivariate stream cipher QUAD and the problems it faces.

2.1   Multivariate Polynomial Systems

Multivariate Polynomials. A term is a primitive unit which can be denoted only by using multiplications. A term consists of one constant and some unknowns. A monomial consists of a single term, and a polynomial consists a finite sum of terms, as shown in Equation 1, where x_i variables, and $\alpha, \beta_i, \gamma_{i,j}$, constants.

$$\alpha + \sum_{i=1}^{n} \beta_i x_i + \sum_{i=1}^{n} \sum_{j=1}^{n} \gamma_{i,j} x_i x_j + \dots \tag{1}$$

Equation 2 gives a general description of a multivariate quadratic polynomial in n unknowns.

$$\sum_{1 \leq i \leq j \leq n} \alpha_{i,j} x_i x_j + \sum_{1 \leq i \leq n} \beta_i x_i + \gamma \tag{2}$$

Multivariate Polynomials Systems and MP Problem. A multivariate polynomial system which is constructed with n unknowns and m polynomials is given in Equation 3.

$$MP(x_1, \ldots, x_n) = \{f_1(x_1, \ldots, x_n), \ldots, f_m(x_1, \ldots, x_n)\} \qquad (3)$$

Solving such a system is called the MP problem. It is known as a NP-hard problem over a finite field [10] even for quadratics.

2.2 QUAD Stream Cipher

QUAD is a stream cipher proposed by Berbain et al. [3] and its security is based on the MQ assumption.

Keystream Generation. QUAD uses a random multivariate quadratic system as a pseudorandom number generator. We can construct QUAD using n unknowns and a system S consisting of m multivariate quadratic equations over $\mathbb{GF}(q)$. We denote such an instance as $\mathrm{QUAD}(q, n, r)$, where $r = m - n$ is the number of output keystream bits. The sketch illustrating the keystream generation algorithm is shown in Figure 1. The generator can then output an essentially endless stream of bits by repeating the above steps.

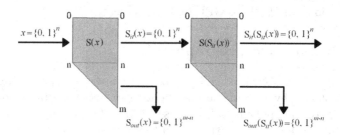

Fig. 1. Generating keystream

Computational Cost of QUAD. The computational cost of multivariate quadratics depends heavily on computing quadratic terms. The summation of quadratic terms requires $n(n + 1)/2$ multiplications and additions. Therefore, the computational costs of evaluating one multivariate quadratic is $O(n^2)$. $\mathrm{QUAD}(q, n, r)$ requires to compute m multivariate quadratics. Since $m = kn$, the computational cost of generating key stream is $O(n^3)$.

Security Level of QUAD. The security level of QUAD is based on the MQ assumption. Berbain et al. [3] proofs that solving QUAD can be reduced to solving MQ problem. However, according to the analysis of QUAD using the XL-Wiedemann algorithm proposed by Yang et al. [11], $\mathrm{QUAD}(256, 20, 20)$ has 45-bit security, $\mathrm{QUAD}(16, 40, 40)$ has 71-bit security, and $\mathrm{QUAD}(2, 160, 160)$ has less than 140-bit security.

Actually, secure QUAD requires larger constructions such as QUAD(2, 256, 256) or QUAD(2, 320, 320).

3   CUDA Computing

3.1   GPGPU

Originally, Graphics Processing Units (GPUs) are processing units for accelerating computer graphics. Recently, some online network games and simulators require very high amount of computer graphics computation. The GPU performance is growing to satisfy such requirements. As a result, GPU has a large amount of power for computation.

GPGPU is a technique for performing general-purpose computation using GPUs. In cryptography, it has been used to accelerate the encryption and decryption processes of various cryptosystems. For example, Manavski proposed an implementation of AES on GPU, which is 15 times faster than on CPU in 2007 [7]. Moreover, Osvik et al. presented a result of an over 30 Gbps GPU implementation of AES in 2010 [9]. On the other hand, GPGPU techniques have also been used for cryptanalysis. Bonenberger et al. used a GPU to accelerate polynomial generations in the General Number Field Sieve [4].

GPUs have a SIMD architecture, so it is better to handle several simple tasks simultaneously. On the other hand, the performance of a GPU core is not higher than CPU. Therefore, if we use GPU for sequential processing, it is not effective. In the GPGPU techniques, how to parallelize algorithms is an important issue.

3.2   CUDA

CUDA is NVIDIA's development environment for GPU based on C language. Various tools for using GPU existed before CUDA, but they often require hacking OpenGL or DirectX and hence are not easy to users. CUDA allows more efficient development of GPGPU by allowing the developers to work in the familiar C language.

In CUDA's terminology, "hosts" correspond to computers, while "devices" correspond to GPUs. In CUDA, the host controls the device. A kernel represents a unit of computation that a host asks a device to perform. In order to fully exploit the computational power of a GPU, a program needs to parallelize its computation in a kernel. A kernel handles some blocks in parallel. A block also handles many threads in parallel. Therefore, a kernel can handle many threads simultaneous.

NVIDIA GeForce GTX 580. In this paper, we use NVIDIA GeForce GTX 580 graphics card to perform our experiments. It is a high-end GPU in the GeForce 500 series, which was released in November, 2010. GTX 580 belongs to the Fermi architecture family, which is the successor to Tesla, the first-generation

CUDA-capable architecture. GTX 580 has 16 streaming multiprocessors (SMs), each of which consists of 32 CUDA cores, as opposed to 8 CUDA cores in Tesla.

4   Parallelization Strategies

4.1   Previous Works by Berbain et al.

Berbain et al. proposed several efficient implementation techniques of computing multivariate polynomial systems for multivariate cryptography [2]. In this paper, we use the following strategies from their work.

- Variables are treated as vectors. For example, C language defines int as a 32-bit integer variable. Therefore, we can use int as a 32-vector of boolean variables. This technique is often referred to as "bitslicing" in the literature.
- We precompute each quadratic term. Because in multivariate quadratic systems, we must compute the same $x_i x_j$ for every polynomial, so precomputing helps to save some computations.
- We compute only non-zero terms in $\mathbb{GF}(2)$. The probability of $x_i = 0$ is $1/2$, and the probability of $x_i x_j = 0$ is $3/4$. Therefore, we can reduce computational cost to about $1/4$.

4.2   Parallelizing on the GPU

In GPGPU, the most important point is the parallelization of algorithms. Because the performance of a single GPU core is worse than that of CPU, serial implementations with GPU are expected to be slower than CPU implementations.

Since the polynomials of a multivariate quadratic system are independent of each other, parallelization of a system is straightforward. Moreover, we parallelize the evaluation of each polynomial in a multivariate quadratic system. We propose two parallelization techniques, as shown in Figure 4.

The Basic Strategy of Parallelization. Let $t_{i,j} = \alpha_{i,j} x_i x_j$. Summation of quadratic terms can be considered as summation of every element of a triangular matrix, as shown on the left side of Figure 2. We assume that other elements from the matrix are zero. Therefore, we can compute summation of quadratic terms as summation of a rectangular matrix, as shown on the right side of Figure 2. Then, we can compute the summation as $\sum_{i=1}^{n} \sum_{j=1}^{n} \alpha_{i,j} x_i x_j = \sum_{i=1}^{n} \sum_{j=1}^{n} t_{i,j}$ as follows.

1. We compute $S_k(x) = \sum_{i=1}^{n} t_{k,i}$ for all k in parallel.
2. We compute $\sum_{k=1}^{n} S_k(x)$.

However, such a strategy introduces some overhead caused by the extra unnecessary computations.

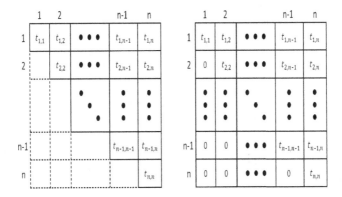

Fig. 2. Left: Evaluating quadratics on a triangular matrix. Right: Evaluating quadratics on a padded rectangle matrix.

Parallelization Method 1. Next we introduce the first strategy to reduce unnecessary computations. We reshape a triangular matrix to a rectangular matrix as shown in Figure 3, in which method of matrix reshaping is depicted. By this reshaping, we can efficiently reduce about 25% of the cost for evaluating a multivariate quadratic polynomial system.

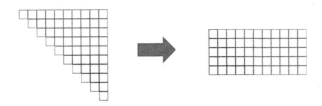

Fig. 3. Reshaping triangular to rectangular matrix

Parallelization Method 2. In the second strategy, we treat a polynomial as a vector as opposed to a matrix. Assuming that n_c is the number of GPU cores, we separate a vector into n_c-subvectors.

Moreover, we use the parallel reduction technique to compute all subvectors in parallel. The parallel reduction technique works as follows.

1. We substitute the length of subvectors for n_c.
2. We add $n_c/2 + i$-th elements to i-th elements.
3. We compute $n_c = n_c/2$.
4. While n_c is larger than 1, we iterate step 2 and 3.

The entire parallel reduction technique consists of $\log n_c$ iterations of the above steps. Therefore, we can evaluate polynomials efficiently.

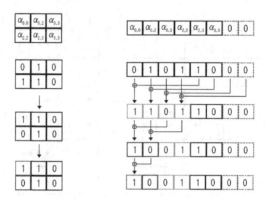

Fig. 4. Pallalelization strategies. Left: Strategy 1; right: Strategy 2

4.3 Optimization on GPU Architectures

On GPU implementations, we must consider its characteristics. Together, the cores on a GPU provide a tremendous amount of computing power, but each single GPU core is much slower than a CPU core. Therefore, we need to minimize the number of inactive GPU cores.

Optimization of Matrix Calculation. An NVIDIA GeForce GTX 580 GPU has 16 SMs, each of which has 32 CUDA cores. Since each SM handles 32 threads at a time, the number of threads should be an integral multiple of 32. In the same way, we should make sure that the algorithm can be handled by 16 SMs in parallel. Together, the total number of threads should be an integral multiple of $32 \times 16 = 512$.

In parallelization method 1, we can compute an summation in a polynomial as multiple co-summations of rows of a matrix. An n-unknown quadratic polynomial has $n(n+1)/2$ monomials. Then the long side of a rectangular matrix that is reshaped from an n-dimensional triangular matrix has n or $n+1$ elements. Although a number of a long side's elements can be counted in a process, counting incurs extra cost in the computation. Therefore, we assume that $n = 31k$, where k is a natural number. By handling a summation in a polynomial as a triangular matrix which elements are k-dimensional square submatrices, we can handle a summation as a 16×31 rectangle matrix, as shown in Figure 5. Thus we can parallelize the calculation of a matrix for 16 SMs with 32 CUDA cores per SM.

In parallelization method 2, we can parallelize a summation by the number of cores that can efficiently share data. In CUDA, we can share data in a block. Then we can parallelize a summation by 32 monomials on NVIDIA GeForce GTX 580. Therefore, we assume that $n = 32k$, where k is a natural number. Iterating time of parallelize reduction in a summation is $k(32k+1)/2$.

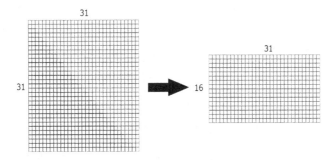

Fig. 5. Handling as a 16×31 matrix

Further Optimizations. In order to improve the efficiency, we need to break down the computation into small chunks of similar computations for parallel processing. Moreover, GPUs can't handle conditional branches efficiently, so we need to handle conditional branches differently than we do on CPU. In this case, we use a different kernel for each different number of non-zero terms. However, using a kernel for each possible number of non-zero terms would incur an extremely large amount of overhead. Therefore, we make kernels just every number of k. For example, for $QUAD(2, 512, 512)$, the maximum k is 17, so we need only 17 kernels.

4.4   Analysis of Potential Speedup

Parallelization Speedup. Originally, each polynomial in $QUAD(q, n, n)$ requires $(n+1) \times (n+2)/2$ additions and multiplications. Moreover, $QUAD(q, n, n)$ requires evaluation of $2n$ polynomials. Using the strategies proposed by Berbain et al. [3], we can compute each polynomial in $QUAD(q, n, n)$ with $(n+1) \times (n+2)/8$ additions and multiplications. Therefore, we can compute $QUAD(q, n, n)$ with $n/16$ times the cost of evaluating a single polynomial using 32-bit vectors.

Such techniques can be used by CPU implementation as well as GPU implementation. By parallelization on GPU, we can compute $QUAD(q, n, n)$ in parallel. We can compute multiplications of a polynomial before additions. We can compute $\alpha_{i,j} x_i x_j$ in n multiplications time by we parallelize multiplications in each i and compute by every j. When we use a multivariate polynomial system over $\mathbb{GF}(2)$, we can compute multiplications by reducing monomials with a strategy of Berbain et al.

Parallelization method 1 with optimizations computes a summation in a polynomial by as a rectangle matrix, which elements are k-dimensional square submatrices. Since NVIDIA GeForce GTX 580 has 16×32 cores, each submatrices can be computed on each CUDA cores in parallel. Then, computational time of summations k-dimensional matrices is k^2 additions. Moreover, we should compute submatrices of every polynomials, then it takes mk^2; m is the number of polynomials divided by 32. After that, we compute row co-summations in matrices. So we can compute row co-summations at one time, computational cost of row co-summations is 31 additions. When $m \leq 32$ (the number of polynomials ≤ 1024), we can compute row co-summations of all polynomials in once time. Finally, we compute a summation of row co-summations' result in 15 additions. Then, the computational costs of summations of a multivariate quadratic polynomial system can be denoted by $mk^2 + 46$ additions.

In parallelization method 2, we compute summations by parallel reductions. Parallel reductions can be computed co-summations of 32 elements on NVIDIA GeForce GTX 580 at once. Then, co-summations can be computed in 5 additions. Assuming $n = 32k$, we can compute co-summations of a polynomial by $k(32k + 1)/2$ times. Since we can compute 16 co-summations at once, actually, we can compute co- summations by $\lceil k(32k+1)/32 \rceil$ times. When $n \leq 512 = 32 \times 16$, we can compute co-summations at most $n/2$ times. Finally, we compute summations of co-summations' result of a polynomial as parallelization method 1. Then, the computational costs of summations of a multivariate quadratic polynomial system can be denoted by $(5m + 1)n/2$ additions.

5   Experiments

In this section, we present and discuss experiment results. We used NVIDIA GeForce GTX 580 GPU, as well as Intel Core $i7$ $875K$ CPU with 8 GB of memory.

5.1   Experiment Setup

We implement the evaluation of systems of $2n$-polynomials in n-unknowns for $n = 32, 64, 96, \ldots, 512$ on CPU and GPU. Finally, we compare the results of GPU and CPU implementations.

CPU Implementation. We implement evaluation of multivariate quadratic polynomial systems on the CPU by C language. We apply strategies of Berbain et al. [2] to CPU implementations.

GPU Implementation. We also apply them to GPU implementations. Moreover, we implement evaluation of multivariate quadratic polynomial systems with the parallelization strategies 1 and 2 as mentioned previously.

5.2   Experiment Results

We present the results of evaluation time of multivariate quadratic systems in Table 1. Evaluation time with the parallelization strategy 1 increase in the number of unknowns n rapidly. On the other hand, the parallelization strategy 2 increase in n slowly. Therefore, the strategy 2 is more efficient than the strategy 1.

Table 1. Evaluation time for multivariate quadratic polynomial systems

Unknowns	Polynomials	Evaluation time (μs)		
n	$2n$	CPU	Strategy 1	Strategy 2
32	64	2.7	21.758	15.927
64	128	16.9	23.483	15.849
96	192	52.7	24.110	16.071
128	256	118.8	24.325	16.537
160	320	236.2	25.058	17.166
192	384	417.8	29.845	17.184
224	448	656.5	34.549	18.125
256	512	992.5	41.864	18.651
288	576	1505.4	52.442	19.408
320	640	2322.2	71.663	19.841
352	704	3409.2	90.264	20.236
384	768	4906.2	111.951	20.710
416	832	6666.4	146.331	21.420
448	896	8453.5	193.567	21.892
480	960	10545.1	256.538	22.259
512	1024	12902.0	336.299	22.785

Table 2. Encryption thoroughput of QUAD

		Throughput[Mbps]	
		QUAD$(2, 160, 160)$	QUAD$(2, 320, 320)$
CPU		0.646	0.131
GPU	Strategy 1	5.086	3.768
	Strategy 2	11.693	14.567
Berbain et al. [2]		8.45	—
Chen et al. [5]	CPU	—	6.1
	GPU	—	2.6

Futhermore, we compare result of QUAD implementations with Berbain et al. [2] and Chen et al. [5] on QUAD$(2, 160, 160)$ and QUAD$(2, 320, 320)$ in Table2. Unfortunately, QUAD$(2, 160, 160)$ with the parallelization strategy 2 is not so fast, compared with the results of Berbain et al. [2] However, QUAD$(2, 320, 320)$ with the parallelization strategy 2 is 2.3 times faster than Chen et al. [5] Moreover, it is faster than QUAD$(2, 160, 160)$. Therefore, we think that strategy 2 is suited to QUAD$(2, n, n)$, which n is a large number.

6 Conclusions

We presented two parallelization strategies for accelerating the evaluation of multivariate quadratic polynomial systems. A GPU implementation with parallelization strategy 2 is the fastest implementation compared with previous works. Moreover, it might be suited to large finite fields. The security of QUAD depends on the scale of multivariate quadratic polynomial systems. We expect QUADs with the strategy 2 will become efficient and secure stream ciphers. Our approaches can be applied not only to the QUAD stream cipher but potentially also to other multivariate cryptosystems.

Acknowledgment. This work is partially supported by Japan Science and Technology agency (JST), Strategic Japanese-Indian Cooperative Programme on Multidisciplinary Research Field, which combines Information and Communications Technology with Other Fields, entitled "Analysis of Cryptographic Algorithms and Evaluation on Enhancing Network Security Based on Mathematical Science." The authors are grateful to Takashi Nishide for his valuable comments on our proposal.

References

1. Bard, G.V.: Algebraic Cryptranalysis. Springer (2009)
2. Berbain, C., Billet, O., Gilbert, H.: Efficient Implementations of Multivariate Quadratic Systems. In: Biham, E., Youssef, A.M. (eds.) SAC 2006. LNCS, vol. 4356, pp. 174–187. Springer, Heidelberg (2007)
3. Berbain, C., Gilbert, H., Patarin, J.: QUAD: A Practical Stream Cipher with Provable Security. In: Vaudenay, S. (ed.) EUROCRYPT 2006. LNCS, vol. 4004, pp. 109–128. Springer, Heidelberg (2006)
4. Bonenberger, D., Krone, M.: Factorization of RSA-170,
   http://public.rz.fh-wolfenbuettel.de/~kronema/pdf/rsa170.pdf
5. Chen, M.-S., Chen, T.-R., Cheng, C.-M., Hsiao, C.-H., Niederhagen, R., Yang, B.-Y.: What price a provably secure stream cipher? In: Fast Software Encryption, 2010, Rump session (2010)
6. Liu, F.-H., Lu, C.-J., Yang, B.-Y.: Secure PRNGs from Specialized Polynomial Maps over Any $\mathbb{F}_q$. In: Buchmann, J., Ding, J. (eds.) PQCrypto 2008. LNCS, vol. 5299, pp. 181–202. Springer, Heidelberg (2008)
7. Manavski, S.: CUDA compatible GPU as an efficient hardware accelerator for AES cryptography. In: 2007 IEEE International Conference on Signal Processing and Communications, pp. 65–68 (2007)
8. NVIDIA CUDA, http://developer.NVIDIA.com/object/CUDA.html
9. Osvik, D.A., Bos, J.W., Stefan, D., Canright, D.: Fast Software AES Encryption. In: Hong, S., Iwata, T. (eds.) FSE 2010. LNCS, vol. 6147, pp. 75–93. Springer, Heidelberg (2010)
10. Patarin, J., Goubin, L.: Asymmetric cryptography with s-boxes. In: First International Conference on Information and Communication Security, pp. 369–380 (1997)
11. Yang, B.-Y., Chen, O.C.-H., Bernstein, D.J., Chen, J.-M.: Analysis of QUAD. In: Biryukov, A. (ed.) FSE 2007. LNCS, vol. 4593, pp. 290–308. Springer, Heidelberg (2007)

A   Program Sources of Evaluating a 320-Unknowns 640-Polynomials System

A.1   CPU Implementaions

```c
#include <stdio.h>
#include <stdlib.h>

/* Extract non-zero unknowns */
int checkXX(int *x, int *x1) {
    int i, k;
    for (i = 0; i < 321; i++)   if (x[i]) { x1[k] = i; k++; }
    if (k & 0x01) { x1[k] = 321; k++; }
    return k;
}

/* Evaluate a system. */
int evaluateSystem(int *x1, int *S, int ***A, int k) {
    int i, j, l, tx1, tx2, tx3;
    for (i = 0; i < k / 2; i++) {
        tx1 = x1[i]; tx2 = x1[k-i-1];
        for (j = 0; j < k; j++) {
            tx3 = xx[j];
            for (l = 0; l < 20; l++) S[l] = S[l] ^ (A[l][tx1][tx3] | A[l][tx2][tx3]);
        }
    }
    return k;
}

int main(void) {
    int ***A, *x;      /* A: coefficients: 20x321x321, x: unknowns */
    int *x1, Nx1;      /* x1: non-zero unknowns. Nx1: the number of x1s */
    Nx1 = checkXX(x, x1);      /* Extract non-zero variables */
    (void)evaluateSystem(x1, KS, A, Nx1);      /* Evaluate a system */
    return 0;
}
```

A.2   GPU Implementations

Overview
```c
#include <stdio.h>
#include <stdlib.h>
#include <cutil.h>
#include <cuda_runtime.h>

int main(int argc, char** argv) {
```

```
int *x, *x1, *Gx1, Nx1, *S, *T1, *T2, *T3, *A;
Nx1 = checkXX(x, x1);    /* Extract non-zero variables */
    (*) Evaluating a multivariate quadratic polynomial system
return 0;
}
```

Evaluating a System with Parallelization Strategy 1

```
/* bx: blockIdx.x, by: blockIdx.y, tx: threadIdx.x, ty: threadIdx.y */
/* Reshape from a triangular matrixt to a rectangle matrix */
__global__ void SetArray6(int *xx, int *Axx) {
    __shared__ int Pxx1[192];
    int i, j, k;
    i = (by << 4) + bx;   j = (ty << 5) + tx;   k = i * 192 + j;
    Pxx1[j] = xx[j]; __syncthreads();
    if (i < j) {
        Axx[k] = (Pxx1[i] * 322) + Pxx1[j-1];
    } else {
        Axx[k] = (Pxx1[191-i] * 322) + Pxx1[191-j];
    }
}
```

```
/* Compute a row summation of a submatrix n=161-192 */
__global__ void ComputeSRow6(int *Axx, int *T, int *A) {
    int i, j, k, t1, t2, t3, t4, t5, t6, *p1, *p2;
    i = ((ty << 4) + bx) << 5) + tx;   j = 3072 * by;   k = i + j;
    p1 = Axx + (6 * i);   p2 = A + (103684 * by);
    t1 = *p1++; t2 = *p1++; t3 = *p1++; t4 = *p1++; t5 = *p1++; t6 = *p1;
    T[k] = *(p2+t1) ^ *(p2+t2) ^ *(p2+t3) ^ *(p2+t4) ^ *(p2+t5) ^ *(p2+t6));
}
```

```
/* Compute a culumn summation of a submatrix n=161-192 */
__global__ void ComputeSCul6(int *S, int *T) {
    int i, t1, t2, t3, t4, t5, t6, *p;
    i = (ty << 9) + (bx << 5) + tx;   p = S + (6 * i);
    t1 = *p++; t2 = *p++; t3 = *p++; t4 = *p++; t5 = *p++; t6 = *p;
    T[i] = t1 ^ t2 ^ t3 ^ t4 ^ t5 ^ t6;
}
```

```
/* Compute a row summation of a 32x16 matrix */
__global__ void ComputeRow(int *S, int *T) {
    int i, k1, k2, k3, k4, t1, t2, t3, t4, t5, t6, t7, t8, *p;
    i = (tx << 4) + bx;   p = S + (i << 5);
    t1 = *p++; t2 = *p++; t3 = *p++; t4 = *p++;
    t5 = *p++; t6 = *p++; t7 = *p++; t8 = *p++;
    k1 = t1 ^ t2 ^ t3 ^ t4 ^ t5 ^ t6 ^ t7 ^ t8;
```

```
      t1 = *p++; t2 = *p++; t3 = *p++; t4 = *p++;
      t5 = *p++; t6 = *p++; t7 = *p++; t8 = *p++;
    k2 = t1 ^ t2 ^ t3 ^ t4 ^ t5 ^ t6 ^ t7 ^ t8;
      t1 = *p++; t2 = *p++; t3 = *p++; t4 = *p++;
      t5 = *p++; t6 = *p++; t7 = *p++; t8 = *p++;
    k3 = t1 ^ t2 ^ t3 ^ t4 ^ t5 ^ t6 ^ t7 ^ t8;
      t1 = *p++; t2 = *p++; t3 = *p++; t4 = *p++;
      t5 = *p++; t6 = *p++; t7 = *p++; t8 = *p++;
    k4 = t1 ^ t2 ^ t3 ^ t4 ^ t5 ^ t6 ^ t7 ^ t8;
    T[i] = k1 ^ k2 ^ k3 ^ k4;
}

/* Compute a culumn summation of a 32x16 matrix */
_global_ void ComputeSCul(int *S, int *T) {
    int k1, k2, t1, t2, t3, t4, t5, t6, t7, t8, *p;
    p = S + (tx << 4);
      t1 = *p++; t2 = *p++; t3 = *p++; t4 = *p++;
      t5 = *p++; t6 = *p++; t7 = *p++; t8 = *p++;
    k1 = t1 ^ t2 ^ t3 ^ t4 ^ t5 ^ t6 ^ t7 ^ t8;
      t1 = *p++; t2 = *p++; t3 = *p++; t4 = *p++;
      t5 = *p++; t6 = *p++; t7 = *p++; t8 = *p++;
    k2 = t1 ^ t2 ^ t3 ^ t4 ^ t5 ^ t6 ^ t7 ^ t8;
    T[threadIdx.x] = k1 ^ k2;
}
```

(*) Evaluating a multivariate quadratic polynomial system in main function
```
    cudaMemcpy(Gx1, x1, 352 * sizeof(int), cudaMemcpyHostToDevice);
    switch (Nx1) {
        case 6: /* Nx1 = 161-192 */
            /* Bl[i]: dim3(16, i, 1), Th[i]: dim3(32, i, 1) */
            SetArray6<<<Bl[6], Th[6]>>>(Gx1, GAxx);
            ComputeSRow6<<<Bl[20], Th[6]>>>(GAxx, T1, A);
            ComputeSCul6<<<Bl[1], Th[20]>>>(T1, T2);
            break;
        case 5: /* Nx1 = 129-160 */
            ...
    }
    ComputeRow<<<16, 20>>>(T2, T3);
    ComputeCul<<<1, 20>>>(T3, S);
```

Evaluating a System with Parallelization Strategy 2
```
/* bx: blockIdx.x, by: blockIdx.y, tx: threadIdx.x */
/* Divide a quadratic polynomial as sub-vector */
_global_ void setArray20(int *x1, int *Axx, int *A) {
```

```
  __shared__ int X[320];
  int NH, x0, i, j, Ai;
  X[tx] = x1[tx+1]; __syncthreads();
  x0 = x1[0];   Ai = ((X[bx] * (321-X[bx])) >> 1) + X[tx] - X[bx] - 1;
  i = (bx * xx0) - (((bx-1) * bx) >> 1) + tx -bx - 1;   NH = ((x0-1)*x0) >> 1;
  if (tx < bx)
     for (j = 0; j < 20; j++) { Axx[i] = A[Ai]; i += NH; Ai += 103684; }
  }
}


/* Compute summations of sub-vectors */
__global__ void compLog(int *Axx, int *T) {
  __shared__ int sm[512];
  int i = (by*gridDim.x + bx) << 9;
  smem[tx]=Axx[i+tx]; __syncthreads();
  if (tx < 256) sm[tx] ^= sm[tx+256]; __syncthreads();
  if (tx < 128) sm[tx] ^= sm[tx+128]; __syncthreads();
  if (tx < 64) sm[tx] ^= sm[tx+64]; __syncthreads();
  if (tx < 32) {
     sm[tx] ^= sm[tx+32]; sm[tx] ^= sm[tx+16]; sm[tx] ^= sm[tx+8];
     sm[tx] ^= sm[tx+4]; sm[tx] ^= sm[tx+2]; sm[tx] ^= sm[tx+1];
  }
  if (tx == 0) T[i+bx] = sm[0];
}


/* Compute summations of a system */
__global__ void compLastLog(int *T1, int *S) {
  __shared__ int sm[256];
  int i = bx << 8;
  sm[tx] = T1[threadIdx.x+i];   __syncthreads();
  if (tx < 128) sm[tx] ^= sm[tx+128]; __syncthreads();
  if (tx < 64) sm[tx] ^= sm[tx+64]; __syncthreads();
  if (tx < 32) {
     sm[tx] ^= sm[tx+32]; sm[tx] ^= sm[tx+16]; sm[tx] ^= sm[tx+8];
     sm[tx] ^= sm[tx+4]; sm[tx] ^= sm[tx+2]; sm[tx] ^= sm[tx+1];
  }
  if (tx == 0) S[bx]=sm[0];
}


(*) Evaluating a multivariate quadratic polynomial system in main function
     cudaMemcpy(Gx1, x1, (x1[0]+1) * sizeof(int), cudaMemcpyHostToDevice);
     setArray20<<<x1[0], x1[0]>>>(Gx1, GAxx, A);
     compLog<<<Bl[Nx1], 512>>>(GAx1, T1); /* Bl[i]: dim3(i,20,1) */
     compLastLog<<<20, 256>>>(T1, S);
```

Enumeration of Even-Variable Boolean Functions with Maximum Algebraic Immunity

Wentao Zhao[1], Xin Hai[2], Shaojing Fu[1,3,4], Chao Li[2], and Yanfeng Wang[3]

[1] College of Computer, National University of Defense Technology,
Changsha, China
[2] Dept of Mathematics and System Science, College of Science, National University
of Defense Technology, Changsha, China
[3] State Key Laboratory of Information Security, Institute of Information
Engineering, Chinese Academy of Sciences, Beijing, China
[4] Shanghai Key Laboratory of Integrate Administration Technologies for Information
Security, Shanghai, China

Abstract. Enumerating the Boolean functions satisfying one or several cryptographic criteria is useful. However, for a given number of variables, the number of Boolean functions with maximum AI is not known, either the previous known bound on the number is not good. In this paper, we investigate the enumeration of Boolean functions with maximum AI. First, we improve the lower bound on the number of even-variable Boolean functions with maximum AI, our new lower bound is better than the previous lower bounds. Then, for the first time, a significant lower bound on the number of 1-resilient Boolean functions with maximum AI is provided.

Keywords: Stream cipher, Boolean Function, Algebraic Attacks, Algebraic Immunity, Resiliency.

1 Introduction

In recent years algebraic attack [5] has become an important tool in cryptanalysis of symmetric cipher systems. A new cryptographic property for designing Boolean functions to resist this kind of attack, called algebraic immunity(AI), has been introduced [15]. It has been showed that, for any n-variable Boolean function, its AI is bounded by $\lceil n/2 \rceil$. If the bound is achieved, we say the Boolean function has maximum AI. And several classes of Boolean functions with maximum AI have been investigated and constructed in order to against the algebraic attack[1-4,7-10,12-23].

There are two reasons for counting the Boolean functions satisfying one or several cryptographic criteria. Firstly, it indicates for which values of the parameters there is a chance of finding good cryptographic functions by random search. Secondly, a large number of functions is necessary if we want to impose extra constraints on the functions or if we want to use the function as part of the secret key.

D.H. Lee and M. Yung (Eds.): WISA 2012, LNCS 7690, pp. 43–54, 2012.

It is Li et al. [13] who first studied the enumeration of Boolean functions with maximum AI. They found a relation between the special matrices and Boolean function with maximum AI. As a result, a lower bound on the number of Boolean functions with maximum AI was obtained. Then in [12], the lower bound was improved when the number of variables is even. In this paper, we improve the lower bound on the number of Boolean functions with maximum AI. Our new lower bound is better than the previous results. Then, for the first time, we provide a significant lower bound on the number of 1-resilient Boolean functions with maximum AI.

2   Preliminaries

Let $\mathbb{F}_2$ be the binary finite field, the vector space of dimension n over $\mathbb{F}_2$ is denoted by $\mathbb{F}_2^n$. For vector $X = (x_1, x_2, \cdots, x_n) \in \mathbb{F}_2^n$, the support of X is denoted by $supp(X) = \{i | x_i \neq 0\}$, and the weight of X is the cardinality of $supp(X)$, and is denoted by $wt(X)$. A Boolean function on n-variable may be viewed as a mapping from $\mathbb{F}_2^n$ into $\mathbb{F}_2$. We denoted by B_n the set of all n-variable Boolean function.

Any $f \in B_n$ can be interpreted as a multivariate polynomial over $\mathbb{F}_2$, that is,

$$f(x_1, x_2, \cdots, x_n) = \sum_{I \subseteq \{1,2,\cdots,n\}} a_I \prod_{i \in I} x_i = \sum_{I \subseteq \{1,2,\cdots,n\}} a_I x^I$$

where the coefficients a_I are in $\mathbb{F}_2$. This representation of f is called the algebraic normal form (ANF) of f. The maximum cardinality of $I(\#I)$ with $a_I \neq 0$ is called the algebraic degree, or simply the degree of f and denoted by $\deg(f)$. The support of f is the set $\{X | f(X) = 1\}$ and is denoted by $supp(f)$, and the weight of f is the cardinality of $supp(f)$. We say an n-variable Boolean function f is balanced iff $wt(f) = 2^{n-1}$. The walsh transform of f is a real-valued function defined as

$$W_f(u) = \sum_{X \in \mathbb{F}_2^n} (-1)^{f(X)+X \cdot u},$$

where the dot product of vectors X and u is defined as $X \cdot u = x_1 u_1 + x_2 u_2 + \cdots + x_n u_n$.

An n-variable Boolean function f is called t-resilient if and only if its Walsh transform satisfies

$$W_f(u) = 0, \quad for \ 0 \leq wt(u) \leq t. \tag{1}$$

A nonzero n-variable Boolean function g is called an annihilator of f if $f * g = 0$. We denote the set of all annihilators of f by $AN(f)$.

Definition 1. *The algebraic immunity(AI) of f is the minimum degree of nonzero functions $g \in B_n$ such that $g * f = 0$ or $g * (f + 1) = 0$. Namely,*

$$AI(f) = \min\{\deg(g) | 0 \neq g \in AN(f) \cup AN(1 + f)\}$$

Let $g = \sum_{I \subseteq \{1,2,\cdots,n\}} b_I x^I \in AN(f)$ with $deg(g) < d$. Then we have $g(x) = 0$ for $x \in supp(f)$. So

$$\sum_{I \subseteq \{1,2,\cdots,n\}, \#I < d} b_I x^I = 0, \quad \text{for } x \in supp(f).$$

The above equations on b_I are homogeneous linear. Denote the coefficient matrix of the equations by $V(f,d)$, which is a $wt(f) \times \sum_{i=0}^{d-1} \binom{n}{i}$ matrix. Then f has no annihilator of degree $< d$ if and only if the rank of the matrix $V(f,d)$ has a column full rank. Given a set Ω, denoted $V(\Omega,d)$ by the set $V(f,d)$ such that $supp(f) = \Omega$.

Lemma 1. *[13] Let $f \in B_n$, then f does not have a nonzero annihilator of degree $\leq d$ if and only if $V(f,d)$ has full column rank.*

Lemma 2. *[6]The Majority Boolean function $F_n(X)$:*

$$F_n(X) = \begin{cases} 1, wt(X) < \lceil \frac{n}{2} \rceil, \\ 0, wt(X) \geq \lceil \frac{n}{2} \rceil. \end{cases}$$

satisfy $AI(F_n) = \lceil \frac{n}{2} \rceil$.

3   Enumeration of Boolean Functions with Maximum AI

In this section, we study the number of Boolean function with maximum AI. We first use a binary string of length 2^n to represent an n-variable Boolean function. We denote by "$||$" the concatenation of binary strings. For the denotation "$||$", given two Boolean function $f, g \in B_n$, then $f||g = (1 + x_{n+1})f + x_{n+1}g$.

We start with the following proposition.

Proposition 1. *[1] Let f, g be two n-variable Boolean functions with $AI(f) = d_1$ and $AI(g) = d_2$. Let $h = f||g$.*
(1). If $d_1 \neq d_2$, then $AI(h) = \min\{d_1, d_2\} + 1$.
(2). If $d_1 = d_2 = d$, then $d \leq AI(h) \leq d + 1$, and $AI(h) = d$ if and only if there exists f_1, g_1 of algebraic degree d such that $\{f * f_1 = 0, g * g_1 = 0\}$ or $\{(1 + f) * f_1 = 0, (1 + g) * g_1 = 0\}$ and $\deg(f_1 + g_1) \leq d - 1$.

The following Lemma was proved in [13].(There is a small error in [13]. In fact $\{\alpha_1, \alpha_2, \ldots, \alpha_m\} \cup \{\beta_{j_1}, \ldots, \beta_{j_k}\} \setminus \{\alpha_{i_1}, \ldots, \alpha_{i_k}\}$ should change to $\{\alpha_1, \alpha_2, \ldots, \alpha_m\} \setminus \{\alpha_{i_1}, \ldots, \alpha_{i_k}\} \cup \{\beta_{j_1}, \ldots, \beta_{j_k}\}$. So the following is the modified Lemma of [13].)

Lemma 3. *Let U be an m-dimension vector space, $\{\alpha_1, \alpha_2, \ldots, \alpha_m\}$ and $\{\beta_1, \beta_2, \ldots, \beta_m\}$ be two bases of U, then for any integer $1 \leq k \leq m$, and k integers $1 \leq i_1 < i_2 < \ldots < i_k \leq m$, there exist $1 \leq j_1 < j_2 < \ldots < j_k \leq m$, such that*

$$\{\alpha_1, \alpha_2, \ldots, \alpha_m\} \setminus \{\alpha_{i_1}, \ldots, \alpha_{i_k}\} \cup \{\beta_{j_1}, \ldots, \beta_{j_k}\}$$

and

$$\{\beta_1, \beta_2, \ldots, \beta_m\} \setminus \{\beta_{j_1}, \ldots, \beta_{j_k}\} \cup \{\alpha_{i_1}, \ldots, \alpha_{i_k}\}$$

are two bases of U.

In the rest of this paper, we assume that $n = 2m$, and we have some notation: $M = \sum_{i=0}^{m-2} \binom{2m-1}{i}$, $M^* = \binom{2m-1}{m}$, $W^{\geq k} = \{x \in \mathbb{F}_2^n | wt(x) \geq k\}$, $W^{=k} = \{x \in \mathbb{F}_2^n | wt(x) = k\}$, $W^{\leq k} = \{x \in \mathbb{F}_2^n | wt(x) \leq k\}$. The following is the counting results on $2m - 1$-variable Boolean functions(The counting results in Ref. [21] are improved here).

Lemma 4. *The number of $2m - 1$-variable Boolean functions with maximum AI is not less than*
$$Num_1 \triangleq 2^{2^{2m-2}} + \sum_{k=0}^{m-2} \binom{2m-1}{k}\binom{2m-1-k}{m-k} + \binom{2m-1}{m} \times 2^m - 2^{2m-2} +$$
$$2^{n-m+1} \prod_{d=2}^{m} 2^{(d-1)\binom{n-d}{m-2}} - 2^{1+\sum_{d=2}^{m}\binom{n-d}{m-2}}$$

Proof. Note that the Majority Boolean function F_{2m-1} has maximum AI, then by Lemma 1, $V(F_{2m-1}, m-1)$ and $V(F_{2m-1}+1, m-1)$ has full column rank.

If we choose a vector $Y_1 \in supp(F_{2m-1}) \setminus W^{=m-1}$, then we can choose $Y_2 \in W^{=m}$ to obtain a new Boolean function F^* with

$$supp(F^*) = supp(F_{2m-1}) \cup \{Y_2\} \setminus \{Y_1\}.$$

If $supp(Y_1) \subseteq supp(Y_2)$, then F^* has maximum AI. Note that for a given Y_1, we can select at least $\binom{2m-1-wt(Y_1)}{m-wt(Y_1)}$ different Y_2, so the number is $\sum_{k=0}^{m-2}\binom{2m-1}{k}\binom{2m-1-k}{m-k}$. Similarly, if we choose a vector $Y_1 \in W^{=m-1}$, then we can choose $Y_2 \in W^{\geq m}$ to obtain a new Boolean function with maximum AI, and the number is $\binom{2m-1}{m} \times 2^m$.

On the other hand, note that $|supp(F_{2m-1})| = |supp(F_{2m-1}+1)| = 2^{2m-2}$, the rows of $V(supp(F_{2m-1}), m-1)$ and the rows of $V(F_{2m-1}+1, m-1)$ are two bases of 2^{2m-2}-dimension vector space.

Then by Lemma 3, for any $k(2 \leq k \leq 2^{2m-2})$ vectors $X_1, X_2, \ldots, X_k$ in $supp(F_{2m-1})$, we can always obtain a new Boolean function with maximum AI by finding another k vectors $Y_1, Y_2, \ldots, Y_k$ in $supp(F_{2m-1}+1)$, such that both

$$V(supp(F_{2m-1}) \cup \{Y_1, \ldots, Y_k\} \setminus \{X_1, \ldots, X_k\}, m-1)$$

and

$$V(supp(F_{2m-1}+1) \cup \{X_1, \ldots, X_k\} \setminus \{Y_1, \ldots, Y_k\}, m-1)$$

have full column rank. Since the new Boolean functions are different as the selected k vectors are different, so the number is $\binom{2^{2m-2}}{2} + \binom{2^{2m-2}}{3} + \cdots + \binom{2^{2m-2}}{2^{2m-2}}$.

Denoted by Ω the set $\{X | wt(X) = m-1, wt(X+e_1) \geq m\}$ (Here $e_1 = (1, 0, \cdots, 0)$), then $|\Omega| = \sum_{d=2}^{m}\binom{n-d}{m-2}$, and for any $X \in \Omega$, we construct 2^{d-1} different Boolean functions with maximum AI where d is the minimum integer such that $x_d \neq 0$. So, we have $2^{n-m+1}\prod_{d=2}^{m}2^{(d-1)\binom{n-d}{m-2}}$ different Boolean functions with maximum AI. By removing the duplicate functions, we get the number is

$$2^{n-m+1}\prod_{d=2}^{m}2^{(d-1)\binom{n-d}{m-2}} - 2^{1+\sum_{d=2}^{m}\binom{n-d}{m-2}}.$$

This completes the proof. $\qquad\square$

Lemma 5. *Let Ψ_1 be the set of $2m - 1$-variable Boolean functions such that* $\Psi_1 = \{f \in B_{2m-1} | AI(f) \geq m - 1\}$, *then*

$$|\Psi_1| \geq \frac{373}{256} \times 2^{2M^*+M} \triangleq Num_2$$

Proof. Consider $f_1(X) \in B_{2m-1}$ with $supp(f_1)$ satisfies,

$$supp(f_1) = D \cup W^{\leq m-2}$$

where D is a subset of $\{X | wt(X) = m-1, m\}$. Note that both $V(W^{\leq m-2}, m-2)$ and $V(W^{\geq m+1}, m-2)$ have full column rank, then $f_1 \in \Psi_1$. The number of different f_1 is equal to the number of different D, that is 2^{2M^*}, and

$$|supp(f_1) \cap (W^{\leq m-2} \cup W^{\geq m+1})| = M \tag{2}$$

Given f_1, by Lemma 1 and Lemma 3, for any $k(0 \leq k \leq M)$ vectors in $W^{\leq m-2}$, we can always obtain a new Boolean function with maximum AI by finding another $k(0 \leq k \leq M)$ vectors in $W^{\geq m+1}$, and the new Boolean function also satisfies Relation (2). Since the new functions obtained are different as the selected k vectors are different, so the number is 2^M.

Thus, we can construct $2^M \times 2^{2M^*}$ different Boolean functions by using 2^{2M^*} different f_1.

Now, consider another Boolean function $f_2(X) \in B_{2m-1}$ with $supp(f_2)$ as follow,

$$supp(f_2) = D \cup \{(\underbrace{1,\cdots,1}_{m-1},\underbrace{0,\cdots,0}_{m})\} \cup W^{\leq m-2} \setminus \{(0,\cdots,0)\}$$

where D is a subset of $\{X | wt(X) = m-1, m\} \setminus \{(\underbrace{1,\cdots,1}_{m-1},\underbrace{0,\cdots,0}_{m})\}$. It is clear that $AI(f_2) \geq m - 1$. So the number of different f_2 is 2^{2M^*-1}, and

$$|supp(f_2) \cap (W^{\leq m-2} \cup W^{\geq m+1})| = M - 1 \tag{3}$$

For given f_2, by Lemma 1 and Lemma 3, for any $k(0 \leq k \leq M - 1)$ vectors in $W^{\leq m-2} \setminus \{(0,\cdots,0)\}$, we can always obtain a new function with maximum AI by finding other $k(0 \leq k \leq M - 1)$ vectors in $W^{\leq m+1}$. Since the new functions obtained are different as the sets of k vectors are different, so the number is 2^{M-1}.

For $f_2^*(X) \in B_{2m-1}$ with $supp(f_2^*)$ as follow,

$$supp(f_2^*) = D \cup \{(\underbrace{1,\cdots,1}_{m-1},\underbrace{0,\cdots,0}_{m})\} \cup W^{\leq m-2} \setminus \{(1,0,\cdots,0)\}$$

where D is a subset of $\{X|wt(X) = m-1, m\} \setminus \{(\underbrace{1,\cdots,1}_{m-1}, \underbrace{0,\cdots,0}_{m})\}$. It is clear that $AI(f_2^*) \geq m-1$, the number of different f_2^* is 2^{2M^*-1}, and

$$|supp(f_2^*) \cap (W^{\leq m-2} \cup W^{\geq m+1})| = M-1 \qquad (4)$$

For given f_2^*, by Lemma 1 and Lemma 3, for any $k(0 \leq k \leq M-1)$ vectors in $W^{\leq m-2} \setminus (\{(0,\cdots,0),(1,0,\cdots,0)\})$, we can always obtain a new function with maximum AI by finding other $k(0 \leq k \leq M-2)$ vectors in $W^{\geq m+1}$. Since the new functions obtained are different as the sets of k vectors are different, so the number is 2^{M-2}.

Thus, we have construct $3 \times 2^{M-2} \times 2^{2M^*-1}$ different Boolean functions by using 2^{2M^*-1} different f_2.

Let $B = \{(0,\cdots,0),(0,\cdots,0,1)\}$, $A = \{(\underbrace{1,\cdots,1}_{m-1}, \underbrace{0,\cdots,0}_{m}), (\underbrace{1,\cdots,1}_{m-2}, \underbrace{0,\cdots,0}_{m},$
$1)\}$, and D is a subset of $\{X|m-1 \leq wt(X) \leq m\} \setminus A$. Then, by using f_3 as follows,

$$supp(f_3) = W^{\leq m-2} \cup D \cup A \setminus B$$

we can construct $2^{M-2} \times 2^{2M^*-4}$ different Boolean functions with maximum AI, and $|supp(f_3) \cap (W^{\leq m-2} \cup W^{\geq m+1})| = M-2$.

Similarly, we can find $f_i(i \geq 4)$ with

$$|supp(f_i) \cap (W^{\leq m-2} \cup W^{\geq m+1})| = M - i + 1$$

to construct different Boolean functions. However, when i become big, the number decreases dramatically, so here we stop at $i = 5$.

Thus, we complete the proof.   □

Lemma 6. *Let Ψ_2 be the set of $2m-1$-variable Boolean functions such that $\Psi_2 = \{f \in B_{2m-1}|AI(f) = m-1\}$. Then*

$$|\Psi_2| \geq Num2 - \sum_{i=0}^{5} 2^{M-i} \times \binom{2M^*-i}{M^*-i} \triangleq Num3.$$

Proof. Note that a $2m-1$-variable Boolean function has maximum AI if the function is balanced. Consider $f_1(X) \in B_{2m-1}$ with $supp(f_1)$ satisfies,

$$supp(f_1) = D \cup W^{\leq m-2}$$

where D is a subset of $\{X|wt(X) = m-1, m\}$ such that $|D| \neq M^*$. Note that both $V(W^{\leq m-2}, m-2)$ and $V(W^{\geq m+1}, m-2)$ have full column rank, and then f_1 is not balanced, so $f_1 \in \Psi_2$. The number of different f_1 is equal to the number of different D, that is $2^{2M^*} - 2^M \times \binom{2M^*}{M^*}$, and

$$|supp(f_1) \cap (W^{\leq m-2} \cup W^{\geq m+1})| = M \qquad (5)$$

Similarly, we can find unbalanced $f_i (i \geq 2)$ with

$$|supp(f_i) \cap (W^{\leq m-2} \cup W^{\geq m+1})| = M - i + 1 \tag{6}$$

to construct different Boolean functions which have algebraic immunity $m - 1$.

Consider all the Boolean functions constructed by unbalanced $f_i (i \geq 1)$, we have $|\Psi_2| \geq Num2 - \sum_{i=0}^{5} 2^{M-i} \times \binom{2M^*-i}{M^*-i} \triangleq Num3$. □

Lemma 7. *Let Λ_1, Λ_2 be the set of $2m - 1$-variable Boolean functions such that*
$\Lambda_1 = \{f \in B_{2m-1}|AI(f) = m - 1, \min\{\deg(g)|g \in AN(f)\} \geq m\};$
$\Lambda_2 = \{f \in B_{2m-1}|AI(f) = m - 1, \min\{\deg(g)|g \in AN(f+1)\} \geq m\}.$
Then $|\Lambda_1|=|\Lambda_2| \geq (2^{2m-2} + 1)(2^{M^*} - 2) + 1.$

Proof. Consider $l(X) \in B_{2m-1}$ with $supp(l)$ satisfies,

$$supp(l) = D \cup W^{\leq m-2}$$

where D is a strict subset of $W^{=m-1}$. Then $l \in \Lambda_2$, and the number of different l is $2^{M^*} - 1$.

For any $\alpha \in W^{\geq m}$ we can find $\beta \in W^{=m-1}$ such that $supp(\beta) \subseteq supp(\alpha)$, then $V(W^{\geq m} \cup \{\beta\} \setminus \{\alpha\}, m - 1)$ has full column rank. Let $l^* \in B_{2m-1}$ with support as follows,

$$supp(l^*) = D^* \cup \{\alpha\} \cup W^{\leq m-2}$$

where D^* is a strict subset of $W^{=m-1} \setminus \{\beta\}$, then $l^* \in \Lambda_2$, and the number of different $2^{2m-2}(2^{M^*} - 2)$.

So $|\Lambda_2| \geq (2^{2m-2} + 1)(2^{M^*} - 2) + 1$. It is clear that $|\Lambda_1| = |\Lambda_2|$, this completes the proof. □

The accurate number of $2m$-variable Boolean functions with maximum AI is hard to calculate. However, by Lemma 4, Lemma 5, Lemma 6, and Lemma 7, we can obtain a low bound.

Theorem 1. *The number of $2m$-variable Boolean functions with maximum AI is not less than $Num1 \times (Num2 + Num3) + 2 \times (2^{2m-2} + 1)^2 (2^{M^*} - 1)^2 + \sum_{k=0}^{M^*-2} \binom{2^{n-2}-1}{k} \sum_{i=0}^{M^*-2-k} \binom{M^*-1}{i}.$*

Proof. For a $2m$-variable Boolean functions $h = f||g$, let N_1 be the number of h with $AI(f) \geq m-1$ and $AI(g) = m$; N_2 be the number of h with $AI(f) = m$ and $AI(g) = m - 1$; N_3 be the number of h with $AI(f) = m - 1$ and $AI(g) = m - 1$. Then $N_1 \geq Num1 \times Num2$ and $N_2 \geq Num1 \times Num3$.

Now we give a lower bound of N_3. Note that if $(f, g) \in (\Lambda_1, \Lambda_2)$ or $(f, g) \in (\Lambda_2, \Lambda_1)$, then by Proposition 1 we have $h = (1 + x_{2m})f + x_{2m}g$ such that $AI(f) = m - 1$ and $AI(g) = m - 1$, and the number is not less than $2 \times [(2^{2m-2} + 1)(2^{M^*} - 2) + 1]^2$.

On the other hand, note that $h_1 \in B_{2m}$ with

$$supp(h_1) = W^{\leq m-1} \cup \{(0, 1, \ldots 0, 1)\} \setminus \{(0, \ldots 0)\}$$

has $AI(h_1) = m$. Suppose that $h_1(x_1, \cdots, x_{2m}) = (1 + x_{2m})f(x_1, \cdots, x_{2m-1}) + x_{2m}g(x_1, \cdots, x_{2m-1})$, then if $x_{2m} = 1$, $h_1 = g$; $x_{2m} = 0$, $h_1 = f$. So $supp(f) = \{X|X \in supp(h), x_{2m} = 0\}$, which indicates that $wt(f) = 2^{2m-2} - 1$. Then $wt(g) = \sum_{i=0}^{m-1}\binom{2m}{m-1} - 2^{2m-2} + 1 = 2^{2m-2} - M^* + 1$. Then f and g are not balanced, so $AI(f) = AI(g) = m-1$. By Lemma 1 and Lemma 3, for given $k(0 \leq k \leq M^*-2)$ vectors in $supp(f)\backslash\{(0,1,0,1,\cdots,0,1)\}$, we can always obtain a new Boolean function h^* with maximum AI by finding another k vectors in $W^{\geq m+1}$, and it is clear that $wt(h^*) = \sum_{i=0}^{m-1}\binom{2m}{m-1}$, the number of choice is $\binom{2^{2m-2}-1}{k}$. Let $h^*(x_1, \cdots, x_{2m}) = (1 + x_{2m})f^*(x_1, \cdots, x_{2m-1}) + x_{2m}g^*(x_1, \cdots, x_{2m-1})$, then

$$2^{2m-2} - k - 1 \leq wt(f^*) \leq 2^{2m-2} - 1$$

and

$$2^{2m-2} - M^* + 1 \leq wt(g^*) \leq 2^{2m-2} - M^* + 1 + k.$$

So, f^* and g^* are not balanced, thus $AI(f^*) = AI(g^*) = m - 1$. Note that for any given h^* obtained by changing $k(0 \leq k \leq M^* - 2)$ vectors, if we select $M^* - 2 - k$ vectors from $\{X|wt(X) = m, x_{2m} = 1\}$ to change the output from 0 to 1, then we can have other new Boolean functions with maximum AI such that $AI(f) = m - 1$ and $AI(g) = m - 1$. And the number is $\sum_{i=0}^{M^*-2-k}\binom{M^*-1}{i}$. Thus, the total number of functions obtained by h_1 is

$$\sum_{k=0}^{M^*-2}\binom{2^{n-2}-1}{k}\sum_{i=0}^{M^*-2-k}\binom{M^*-1}{i}$$

Thus, the total number of $2m$-variable Boolean functions with maximum AI is not less than $Num1 \times (Num2 + Num3) + 2 \times (2^{2m-2} + 1)^2(2^{M^*} - 1)^2 + \sum_{k=0}^{M^*-2}\binom{2^{n-2}-1}{k}\sum_{i=0}^{M^*-2-k}\binom{M^*-1}{i}$.　□

We compare our lower bound with the previous lower bounds in Table 1. Table 1 clearly shows the superiority of lower bound.

Table 1. The lower bound on the number of n-variable Boolean functions with maximum AI

n	[13]	[12]	[21]	Theorem 1
6	4.39×10^{12}	8.02×10^{12}	1.09×10^{13}	1.20×10^{13}
8	1.16×10^{49}	2.22×10^{49}	3.03×10^{49}	3.29×10^{49}
10	1.14×10^{192}	2.22×10^{192}	2.98×10^{192}	3.27×10^{192}

Let $h \in B_{2m}$ is balanced and $h = f||g$. If $AI(h) = m$, then h can be classified into three types,

Type A: $AI(f) \geq m - 1$, $AI(g) = m$, and $wt(f) = wt(g) = 2^{2m-2}$.
Type B: $AI(f) = m$, $AI(g) = m - 1$, and $wt(f) = wt(g) = 2^{2m-2}$.
Type C: $AI(f) = m - 1$, $AI(g) = m - 1$, and $wt(f) + wt(g) = 2^{2m-1}$.

By Lemma 4, Lemma 5, Lemma 6, and Lemma 7, and Theorem 1, we can improve the lowed bound on $2m$-variable balanced Boolean functions with maximum AI as follows.

Theorem 2. *The number of $2m$-variable balanced Boolean functions with maximum AI is not less than $Num1 \times \{\sum_{i=0}^{2m-1} 2^{M-i}\binom{2M^*-i}{M^*} + 2^{M-2}\binom{2M^*-1}{M^*} + \sum_{k=1}^{m-1}\binom{2m-1}{k}[2^{2m-2} - \sum_{i=m-k}^{2m-1-k}\binom{2m-1-k}{i}]\} + 2\sum_{k=0}^{M^*-1}[\binom{M^*}{k} + 2^{2m-2}\binom{M^*-1}{k-1}]^2$.*

In the end of this section, we compare this new lower bound on balanced Boolean functions with the previous lower bounds.

Table 2. Lower bound on the number of balanced Boolean functions with MAI

n	[13]	[11]	Theorem 2
6	7.75×10^{11}	1.06×10^{12}	1.14×10^{12}
8	1.11×10^{48}	1.51×10^{48}	1.63×10^{48}
10	5.73×10^{190}	7.73×10^{190}	8.29×10^{190}

4   The Number of 1-Resilient Boolean Functions with Maximum AI

In this section, we study the number of 1-resilient Boolean function with maximum AI. Let $h \in B_{2m}$ is balanced and $h(x_1, \cdots, x_{2m}) = (1 + x_{2m})f(x_1, \cdots, x_{2m-1}) + x_{2m}g(x_1, \cdots, x_{2m-1})$. Then for $u = (u_1, \cdots, u_{2m}) \in \mathbb{F}_2^{2m}$,

$$W_h(u) = \sum_{(x_1, \cdots, x_{2m}) \in \mathbb{F}_2^{2m}} (-1)^{\sum_{i=1}^{2m} x_i u_i + h(x_1, \cdots, x_{2m})}$$

$$= \sum_{(x_1, \cdots, x_{2m-1}) \in \mathbb{F}_2^{2m-1}} (-1)^{\sum_{i=1}^{2m-1} x_i u_i + f} + \sum_{(x_1, \cdots, x_{2m-1}) \in \mathbb{F}_2^{2m-1}} (-1)^{\sum_{i=1}^{2m-1} x_i u_i + g + u_{2m}}$$

$$= W_f(u_1, \cdots, u_{2m-1}) + (-1)^{u_{2m}} W_g(u_1, \cdots, u_{2m-1})$$

Now we have the following proposition.

Proposition 2. *If $h = f\|g$ is 1-resilient, then $wt(f) = wt(g) = 2^{2m-2}$, and $W_f(u_1, \cdots, u_{2m-1}) = -W_g(u_1, \cdots, u_{2m-1})$ for $wt(u_1, \cdots, u_{2m-1}) = 1$.*

Proof. If h is 1-resilient Boolean function, then

$$W_f(u_1, \cdots, u_{2m-1}) + (-1)^{u_{2m}} W_g(u_1, \cdots, u_{2m-1}) = 0$$

for any $wt(u_1, \cdots, u_{2m}) \le 1$.

Since we have $W_f(0, \cdots, 0) + W_g(0, \cdots, 0) = 0$ and $W_f(0, \cdots, 0) - W_g(0, \cdots, 0) = 0$, then $wt(f) = wt(g) = 2^{2m-2}$. For $wt(u_1, \cdots, u_{2m-1}) = 1$, then $W_h(u_1, \cdots, u_{2m-1}, 0) = 0$, so $W_f(u_1, \cdots, u_{2m-1}) = -W_g(u_1, \cdots, u_{2m-1})$.

Let Λ be the set of $2m - 1$-variable Boolean functions such that $\Lambda = \{f \in B_{2m-1} | wt(f) = 2^{2m-2}, AI(f) = m - 1, \min\{\deg(g)|g \in AN(f)\} \geq m\}$.

Theorem 3. *The number of 1-resilient $2m$-variable Boolean functions with maximum AI is not less than $Num1 + \#\Lambda$.*

Proof. Let $h \in B_{2m}$ is balanced and $h(x_1, \cdots, x_{2m}) = (1 + x_{2m})f(x_1, \cdots, x_{2m-1}) + x_{2m}g(x_1, \cdots, x_{2m-1})$.

If f is a $2m - 1$-variable Boolean functions with maximum AI, let $g = f + 1$, then h is a 1-resilient Boolean functions with maximum AI, and the number is $Num1$.

If f is a $2m - 1$-variable Boolean functions such that $f \in \Lambda$, let $g = f + 1$, then h is a 1-resilient Boolean functions with maximum AI, and the number is $\#\Lambda$.

This completes the proof. □

However, we can not estimate $\#\Lambda$, the following table are the number of 1-resilient Boolean functions with maximum AI obtained by Theorem 3(We take $\#\Lambda = 0$ here). It shows that the number of 1-resilient Boolean functions with maximum AI is very small, compared to the number of balanced Boolean functions with maximum AI.

Table 3. The number of 1-resilient Boolean functions with maximum AI

n	Theorem 3
6	≥ 65536
8	$\geq 1.85 \times 10^{19}$
10	$\geq 1.16 \times 10^{77}$

5   Conclusion

Algebraic immunity has been considered as one of significant properties for Boolean functions, and having maximum AI is a necessary criteria for Boolean functions used in stream ciphers against algebraic attacks. In this paper, we present a lower bound on the number of Boolean functions, in any even number of variables, with maximum AI, and our new low bound is better than the previous lower bounds. Furthermore, we also provide a lower bound on the number of 1-resilient even-variable Boolean functions with maximum AI.

However, the bounds we have obtained are not so good. For instance, in the case of Boolean functions in six variables. The lower bound on the number of 6-variable Boolean functions in Table-1 is 1.18×10^{13}, which is very small compare to the number of 6-variable Boolean functions. So, how to improve these low bounds will be our future study.

Acknowledgments. This work are supported by the National Natural Science Foundation of China (No:61103191,61272484,61070215), the opening project of Shanghai Key Laboratory of Integrate Administration Technologies for Information Security (No:AGK 2012001), and the open research fund of State key Laboratory of Information Security.

References

1. Carlet, C., Dalai, D.K., Gupta, K.C., Maitra, S.: Algebraic Immunity for Cryptographically Significant Boolean Functions: Analysis and Construction. IEEE Transactions on Information Theory 52, 3105–3121 (2006)
2. Carlet, C., Feng, K.: An Infinite Class of Balanced Functions with Optimal Algebraic Immunity, Good Immunity to Fast Algebraic Attacks and Good Nonlinearity. In: Pieprzyk, J. (ed.) ASIACRYPT 2008. LNCS, vol. 5350, pp. 425–440. Springer, Heidelberg (2008)
3. Carlet, C., Zeng, X.Y., Li, C.L., Hu, L.: Further properties of several classes of Boolean functions with optimum algebraic immunity. Design, Codes and Cryptography 52, 303–338 (2009)
4. Chen, Y.D., Lu, P.Z.: Two classes of symmetric Boolean functions with optimum algebraic immunity: construction and analysis. IEEE Transactions on Information Theory 57, 2522–2538 (2011)
5. Courtois, N., Meier, W.: Algebraic Attacks on Stream Ciphers with Linear Feedback. In: Biham, E. (ed.) EUROCRYPT 2003. LNCS, vol. 2656, pp. 345–359. Springer, Heidelberg (2003)
6. Dalai, D.K., Maitra, S., Sarkar, S.: Basic theory in construction of Boolean functions with maximum possible annihilator immunity. Design, Codes and Cryptography 40, 41–58 (2006)
7. Du, Y.S., Pei, D.Y.: Construction of Boolean functions with maximum algebraic immunity and count of their annihilators at lowest degree. SCIENCE CHINA Information Sciences 53(4), 780–787 (2010)
8. Fu, S.J., Qu, L.J., Li, C., Sun, B.: Balanced Rotation Symmetric Boolean Functions with Maximum Algebraic Immunity. IET Information Security 5(2), 93–99 (2011)
9. Fu, S.J., Li, C., Matsuura, K., Qu, L.J.: Construction of Even-variable Rotation Symmetric Boolean Functions with Maximum Algebraic Immunity. SCIENCE CHINA Information Sciences (2012), doi:10.1007/s11432-011- 4350
10. Fu, S.J., Qu, L.J., Li, C., Sun, B.: Blanced 2p-variable Rotation Symmetric Boolean Functions with Maximum Algebraic Immunity. Applied mathematical Letters 24, 2093–2096 (2011)
11. Hai, X., Fu, S.J., Li, C.: On the Number of Balanced Even-Variable Boolean Function with Maximum Algebraic Immunity. In: 2011 International Conference on Information Technology for Manufacturing Systems (ITMS 2011), pp. 227–232 (2011)
12. Li, Y., Yang, M., Kan, H.B.: Constructing and counting Boolean functions on even variables with maximum algebraic immunity. IEICE Transactions on Fundamentals E93-A(3), 640–643 (2010)
13. Li, N., et al.: On the construction of Boolean functions with optimal algebraic immunity. IEEE Transactions on Information Theory 54(3), 1330–1334 (2008)
14. Liu, M.C., Du, Y.S., Pei, D.Y., Lin, D.D.: On designated-weight Boolean functions with highest algebraic immunity. Sci. China Math. 53(11), 2847–2854 (2010)

15. Meier, W., Pasalic, E., Carlet, C.: Algebraic Attacks and Decomposition of Boolean Functions. In: Cachin, C., Camenisch, J.L. (eds.) EUROCRYPT 2004. LNCS, vol. 3027, pp. 474–491. Springer, Heidelberg (2004)
16. Pan, S.S., Fu, X.T., Zhang, W.G.: Construction of 1-Resilient Boolean Functions with Optimal Algebraic Immunity and Good Nonlinearity. Journal of computer science and technology 26(2), 269–275 (2011)
17. Qu, L.J., Li, C.: On the 2^m-variable symmetric Boolean functions with maximum algebraic immunity. SCIENCE CHINA Information Sciences 51(2), 120–127 (2008)
18. Qu, L.J., Feng, K.Q., Liu, F., Wang, L.: Constructing Symmetric Boolean Functions With Maximum Algebraic Immunity. IEEE Transactions on Information Theory 55, 2406–2412 (2009)
19. Tu, Z.R., Deng, Y.P.: A Conjecture on Binary String and Its Applications on Constructing Boolean Functions of Optimal Algebraic Immunity. Designs, Codes and Cryptography 60(1), 1–14 (2011)
20. Wang, Q., Peng, J., Kan, H., Xue, X.: Constructions of cryptographically significant Boolean functions using primitive polynomials. IEEE Transactions on Information Theory 56(6), 3048–3053 (2010)
21. Xiong, X., Fu, S.J., Qu, L.J.: The Number of Even-Variable Boolean Function with Maximum Algebraic Immunity. In: Chinacrypt 2010, Beijing (October 2010)
22. Zeng, X.Y., Carlet, C., Shan, J.Y., Hu, L.: More Balanced Boolean Functions with optimum Algebraic Immunity and good Nonlinearity and Resistance to Fast Algebraic Attacks. IEEE Transactions on Information Theory 57(9), 6310–6320 (2011)
23. Zhang, F.L., Hu, Y.P., Xie, M., Wei, Y.Z.: Constructions of 1-resilient Boolean functions on odd number of variables with a high nonlinearity. Security and Communication Networks (2011), doi:10.1002/sec.356

Multi-precision Multiplication for Public-Key Cryptography on Embedded Microprocessors*

Hwajeong Seo and Howon Kim**

Computer engineering, Pusan National University, Pusan Republic of Korea
{hwajeong,howonkim}@pusan.ac.kr
http://infosec.pusan.ac.kr

Abstract. In this paper, we revisit the "operand caching" method for multi-precision multiplication, which reduces the number of required *load* instructions by caching the operands [6]. With the previous method, we can achieve high performance in terms of multiplication speed with modern micro-processors. However, this method does not provide full operand caching when changing the row of partial products. To overcome this problem, we propose a novel method, i.e., "consecutive operand caching". We divide partial products and reconstruct them yielding common operands between previous and new partial products. Finally, we reduce the number of *load* instructions and boost the speed of multi-precision multiplication by 3.85%, as compared to previous best known results.

Keywords: Multi-precision Multiplication, Public-Key Cryptography, Consecutive Operand-Caching Method, Embedded Microprocessors.

1 Introduction

Public key cryptography methods such as RSA [1], ECC [2], and pairing [3] involve computation-intensive arithmetic operations; in particular, multiplication accounts for most of the execution time of microprocessors. Several technologies have been proposed to reduce the execution time and computation cost by decreasing the number of memory accesses, i.e., the number of clock cycles.

A row-wise method called "operand scanning" is used for short looped programs. This method loads all operands in a row. The alternative Comba method is a common schoolbook method that is also known as the "product scanning method." This method computes all partial products in a column [4]. The hybrid method combines the useful features of operand scanning and product scanning. By adjusting row and column width, the number of operand accesses and result updates are reduced. This method has an advantage over a microprocessor equipped with many general purpose registers [5]. Recently, the "operand caching

---

* This work was supported by the National Research Foundation of Korea(NRF) grant funded by the Korea government(MEST) (No.2010-0026621).
** Corresponding author.

D.H. Lee and M. Yung (Eds.): WISA 2012, LNCS 7690, pp. 55–67, 2012.
© Springer-Verlag Berlin Heidelberg 2012

method" was proposed [6]. This method significantly reduces the number of *load* operations, which are regarded as expensive operations, via caching of operands.

In this paper, we propose a novel multiplication method that highly optimizes the number of *load* instructions required for operand loading. From initial partial products to the final partial products, the required operands are cached and not *loaded* repeatedly. For this reason, the number of required *load* instructions is reduced. The remainder of this paper is organized as follows. In Section 2, we describe different multi-precision multiplication techniques and in Section 3, we compare them with our method. In Section 4, we describe the performance evaluation in terms of memory accesses and clock cycles. Finally, Section 5 concludes the paper.

2   Multi-precision Multiplication Techniques

In this section, we introduce various multi-precision multiplication techniques, including "operand scanning", "product scanning", "hybrid scanning" and "operand caching". Each method has unique features for reducing the number of *load* and *store* instructions. In particular, "operand caching" reduces the number of memory accesses by caching operands to the registers. However, after partial row products, no common operands exist. Therefore, operands should be reloaded for the next row computation. To overcome this problem, we present an advanced operand caching method that ensures operand caching throughout the processes. As a result, the number of required *load* instructions is reduced.

To describe the multi-precision multiplication method, we use the following notations. Let A and B be two m-bit operands that are multiple-word arrays. Each operand is written as follows: $A = (A[n-1], ..., A[2], A[1], A[0])$ and $B = (B[n-1], ..., B[2], B[1], B[0])$. The division of operand-size(m) by word-size(w) represents the number of elements(n) in the operand array. The result of multiplication is twice as large as operand $C = (C[2n-1], ..., C[2], C[1], C[0])$.

For clarity, we describe the method using a multiplication structure and rhombus form, as shown in Figure. 1. Each point represents a multiplication $A[i] \times B[j]$. The rightmost corner of the rhombus represents the lowest indices $(i, j = 0)$, whereas the leftmost represents corner the highest indices $(i, j = n-1)$. The lowermost side represents result indices $C[k]$, which ranges from the rightmost corner $(k = 0)$ to the leftmost corner $(k = 2n - 1)$.

2.1   Operand-Scanning Method

This method consists of two parts, i.e., inner and outer loops. In the inner loop, operand $A[i]$ holds a value and computes the partial product with all multiple values of the multiplicand $B[j]$ $(j = 0...n - 1)$. In the outer loop, the index of operand $A[i]$ increases by a word-size and then the inner loop is executed.

Figure. 1. (a) shows the "operand scanning" method. The arrows indicate the order of computation and computations are performed from the rightmost corner to the leftmost corner. In each row, $2n$ *load* and n *store* instructions

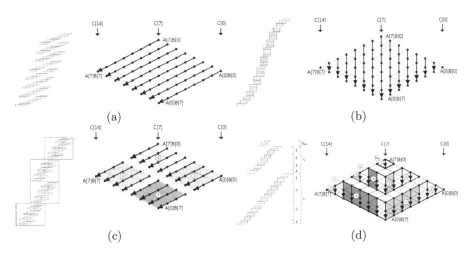

Fig. 1. Multi-precision Multiplication Techniques. (a)Operand-Scanning. (b)Product-Scanning. (c)Hybrid-Scanning. (d)Operand-Caching [6].

are executed for loading the multiplicand result and storing the result of the partial product. The number of memory accesses is $n^2 + 3n$ to $3n^2 + 2n$, which is determined by the number of available general purpose registers for caching intermediate results.

2.2   Product-Scanning Method

This method computes all partial products in the same column by multiplication and addition [4]. Because each partial product in the column is computed and then accumulated, registers are not needed for intermediate results. The results are stored once, and the stored results are not reloaded because all computations have already been completed. To perform multiplication, three registers for accumulation and two registers for the multiplicand, i.e., a total of five registers are required. As the number of registers increases, the remaining registers can be used for caching operands.

Figure. 1. (b) shows the "product scanning" method. The arrows are directed from the top of the rhombus to the bottom, which means that the partial products are computed in the same column. The partial products are computed from right to left. For computation, $2n^2$ *load* instructions are executed for loading the operands $A[i]$ and $B[j]$ $(0 \leq i, j \leq n-1)$ and $2n$ *store* instructions are executed for storing the results $C[k]$ $(0 \leq k \leq 2n - 1)$. Therefore, $2n^2 + 2n$ memory accesses are required.

2.3   Hybrid-Scanning Method

This method combines the useful features of "operand scanning" and "product scanning" [5]. multiplication is performed on a block scale using "product scanning". The number of rows within the block is defined as d, and inner block partial products follow the "operand scanning" rule. Therefore, the method reduces the number of *load* instructions by sharing the operands within the block. As the number of available registers increases, the number of rows also increases. Therefore, the number of memory accesses can be reduced by maximizing the shared operands.

Figure. 1. (c) shows the "hybrid" method in the case of $(d = 4)$. The computation order is from block 1 to 4. After computing block 2, the next computation is block 3. In the transition, there are no common operands between block 2 and block 3. For this reason, all operands should be reloaded from memory. The total cost of memory access is $2\lceil n^2/d \rceil + 2n$, which is determined by the number of rows in block (d).

2.4   Operand-Caching Method

This method follows the "product scanning" method, but it divides the calculation into several row sections [6]. By reordering the sequence of inner and outer row sections, previously loaded operands in working registers are reused for the next partial products. A few *store* instructions are added, but the number of required *load* instructions is reduced. The number of row section is given by $r = \lfloor n/e \rfloor$, and e denotes the number of words used to cache digit in the operand.

Figure. 1. (d) shows the "operand caching" method in the case of $(e = 3)$. Given $n = 8$, the number of row section is $r = \lfloor 8/3 \rfloor = 2$. The remaining section, b_{init}, is first computed, and the main algorithm parts, r_0 and r_1 are subsequently computed. In a row, at part 2, 3, 4, and 5, operands are cached and reused. For example, between part 2 and part 3 in r_0, operands $A[i]$ are used for both parts $(i = 3, 4, 5)$. The subsequent have the parts have the same features. Therefore, the number of required operand *load* instructions is reduced. However, between part 4 of r_0 and part 1 of r_1, there is no common operand. The operand *load* should be executed for the next partial products. The required number of memory accesses for the *load* and store instructions is $2n^2/e$ and $n^2/e + n$, respectively.

3   Consecutive Operand-Caching Method

In this section, we first introduce a novel multi-precision multiplication, i.e., "consecutive operand-caching". Because this method is based on "operand-caching", it can perform multiplication with a reduced number of memory accesses for operand *load* instructions by using caching operands. However, previous method has to reload operands whenever a row is changed, which generates unnecessary overheads.

To overcome these shortcomings, we divided the rows and re-scheduled the multiplication sequences. Thus, we found a contact point among rows that share the same operands for partial products. Therefore, we can cache the operands by sharing the operands by sharing them, even when a row is changed. A detailed example is shown in Figure. 2.

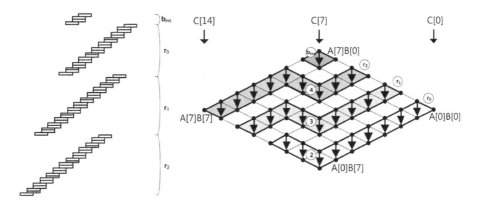

Fig. 2. Consecutive Operand-Caching Method

The size of the caching operand e and the number of elements n are set to 2 and 8, respectively. The value e is determined by the number of working registers in the platform. The number of rows is $r = 4$, following the notation $r = \lfloor n/e \rfloor$. Given the number of working registers w, the value is $w = 3 + 2e$. Three working registers are used for accumulating the intermediate results obtained from the partial products. The algorithm is divided into three parts. The initialization block b_{top} is the top of the rhombus and the remaining rows are divided into two parts, b_{bottom} and b_{middle}. The b_{bottom} part is located in the bottom of the rhombus. The remaining rows, b_{middle}, are divided into two parts based on the following condition. If $\lfloor n/e \rfloor = n/e$ is true, b_{middle} is not divided; otherwise, b_{middle} is divided into b_{middle} and b_{last} parts. The b_{last} part is the last sequence of the rows which has a different operand size compared to the other rows because the size of operands A in the last part, $n - re$, is smaller than e. An example of b_{last} is shown in Figure. 5. (b, e, f ,g, h). All the partial products are computed from right to left, and the detailed process is described as follows.

Top of the Rhombus b_{top}. The block located at the top of the rhombus executes "product scanning" using operands of size $n - re$. In Figure. 2, the operands $A[6, 7]$ and $B[0, 1]$ are used for the b_{top} process. While computing the partial products, the number of caching operands is smaller than the number of required operands e. Therefore, the operand reload process does not occur. If $\lfloor n/e \rfloor = n/e$ is true, the b_{top} process is skipped.

Processing the Row. The row parts compute the overlapping *store* and *load* instructions between the bottom and upper rows. In Figure. 2. r_1 is located over r_0; hence memory addresses storing the intermediate results $C[k]$ $(2 \leq k \leq 11)$ are accessed twice to update previous results. Throughout the computations, operands are consecutively cached. When operands $B[j]$ are loaded for partial products in the rows, the operands $A[i]$ are maintained and vice versa. Whenever the row is changed, the operand $A[i]$ is still maintained for the next partial product of the row. For this reason, the number of *load* instructions is significantly reduced.

Bottom of the Row b_{bottom}. The block located in the bottom of the rhombus can reuse caching operands $B[0]$ and $B[1]$ from b_{top}. First, operands $A[i], (i = 0, 1)$ are loaded as caching operands, and then, partial products are computed with operands $B[j], (j = 0, ..., 7)$. When partial products with caching operands $A[i]$ are completed, the next sequence of operands $A[i], (i = 2, 3)$ is loaded and the partial products are computed by e, the size of the caching operand.

Middle of the Row b_{middle}. The block located between b_{top} and b_{bottom} can use caching operands $A[i]$ from the previous row block. The partial products are computed with operands $B[j]$. The range of j increases for the remaining partial products in a row. In the second row(r_1), the range of j is $0 \le j \le 5$. After the operands $B[4]$ and $B[5]$ are cached, the next sequence of operands $A[i], (i = 4, 5)$ is loaded and the partial products are computed by e. Finally the remaining partial products, with operands $A[i]$ on the left side of the rhombus, are computed.

End of the Row b_{last}. The b_{last} part occurs when the condition is $\lfloor n/e \rfloor \ne n/e$. Most processes are equal to b_{middle}, but in the last part, computing partial products using operands $A[i], (re \le i < n)$ with $B[j], (n - re \le j < n)$ is different. Because the remaining operands $A[i]$ are smaller than the size of the caching operand e, the partial products are computed with a narrow width of operands than b_{middle}.

4   Results

In this section, we evaluate the proposed method by comparing its results with the previous best results. Table 1. lists the number of total *load* and *store* instructions. Operand load indicates the overhead for saving the operand to registers, and result load indicates the reloading of intermediate results. The result store is used for storing the complete results. In the following subsection, we provide the detailed computation costs.

4.1   Operand-Caching Method

The best known result of the "operand caching" method is evaluated by calculating the total costs of the *load* and *store* instructions. Equation 1. expresses the complexity of *load* instructions, which consist of operand load and intermediate result reload. Equation 2. expresses the costs for *store* instructions. The notation p denotes the index of the row for the partial product.

$$2(n - re) + \sum_{p=0}^{r-1}(4n - 4pe - 2e) = 2n + 4rn - 2er^2 - 2er \tag{1}$$

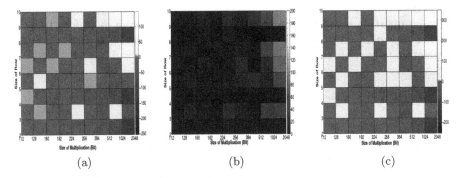

(a)   (b)   (c)

Fig. 3. Differences in number of memory accesses of proposed and operand-caching method (#(proposed method)-#(operand-caching)) period, (a),(b),(c) represent *load*, *store* and *total(load + store)* respectively, The x and y axes represent the size of multiplication and size of caching operands, respectively

$$2(n - re) + \sum_{p=0}^{r-1}(2n - 2pe) = 2n + 2rn - er^2 - er \qquad (2)$$

4.2   Consecutive Operand-Caching Method

The "consecutive operand caching" method is evaluated under two different conditions, depending on the size of caching operands e. The case $\lfloor n/e \rfloor = n/e$ represents case a. The other case $\lfloor n/e \rfloor \neq n/e$ represents case b. The difference in the size of caching operands e makes results in a difference in computation costs. The *load* and *store* instruction costs are listed in Table 2. The detailed information is described in the following subsection. Equations 3 and 4 express the costs of *load* instructions for case a and b, and Equations 5 and 6 express the costs for *store* instructions for case a and b, respectively.

$$7n - 4re + 3e + (r - 2)(2n + 2e) = 3n - 2re - e + 2rn \qquad (3)$$

$$2e + n + 3e + (r - 2)(2n + 2e) = e - 3n + 2rn + 2er \qquad (4)$$

$$4n - 3re + e + (r - 1)(n + 2e) = 3n - re + rn - e \qquad (5)$$

$$2e + (r - 1)(n + 2e) = rn - n + 2er \qquad (6)$$

Figure. 3. shows the efficiency of memory accesses. The *load* instruction is significantly reduced because operands are fully cached throughout the process.

However, additional *store* instructions are needed because b_{last} has an inefficient computation structure. The total efficiency ranges from -6.88% to 14.28%, which is dependent on the set parameters. Therefore, we should consider the parameters to execute multiplication more efficiently.

Table 1. Comparison of number of *load* and *store* instructions

Method	Operand Load	Result Load	Result Store
Operand Caching	$2n + 2rn - er^2 - er$	$2rn - er^2 - er$	$2n + 2rn - er^2 - er$
Consecutive[a]	$2n - re + rn$	$n - re + rn - e$	$3n - re + rn - e$
Consecutive[b]	$rn + er - n + e$	$rn - 2n + er$	$rn - n + 2er$

Table 2. Memory-access complexity of $b_{top}, b_{bottom}, b_{middle}$ and b_{last}, The case $\lfloor n/e \rfloor = n/e$ represents case a. The other case $\lfloor n/e \rfloor \neq n/e$ represents case b.

Component	Load Instr[a]	Load Instr[b]	Store Instr[a]	Store Instr[b]	Total[a]	Total[b]
b_{top}	$2(n - re)$	$2e$	$2(n - re)$	$2e$	$4(n - re)$	$4e$
b_{bottom}	$2n - re + 2e$	$n + 3e$	$n + 2e$	$n + 2e$	$3n - re + 4e$	$2n + 5e$
b_{middle}	$2(n + e)$	$2(n + e)$	$n + 2e$	$n + 2e$	$3n + 4e$	$3n + 4e$
b_{last}	$3n + e - re$	$-$	$2n + e - re$	$-$	$5n - 2re + 2e$	$-$

Evaluation Result with Embedded Microprocessors. We evaluated the performance of the proposed method by using MICAz mote, which is equipped with an ATmega128 8-bit processor clocked at 7.3728 MHz. It has a 128 kB EEPROM chip and 4 kB RAM chip [7]. The ATmega128 processor has a RISC architecture with 32 registers. Among them, 6 registers (r26-r31) serve as the special pointers for indirect addressing. The remaining 26 registers are available for arithmetic operations. One arithmetic instruction incurs one clock cycle, and memory instructions or memory addressing or 8-bit multiplication incurs two processing cycles [8]. We used 6 registers for the operand and result pointer, 2 for the result of multiplication, 4 for accumulating the intermediate result, and the remaining registers for caching operands.

Table 3 lists the clock cycles for computation in the case of 160-bit multiplication. The addition instructions are computed to accumulate the results of the partial product and the intermediate results. The *clear* operation is executed when changing the column to clear the accumulated registers. The number of additions is $3n^2 + n - re + nr - e$ and $3n^2 + nr - 2n + re$ for case a and b, respectively. The number of clear operations is $3n - re - e + nr - 2$ and $nr + 2re - 2r - n$ for case a and b, respectively. Table 4 shows a comparison of the total clock cycles in case of 160-bit multiplication. The proposed method shows the highest performance among all methods. Table 5 shows the total clock cycles for multi-precision multiplication depending on the size of multiplication

Table 3. Computation costs of clock cycles for instructions in 160-bit multiplication using consecutive operand-caching method

r	e	load	store	mul	add	clear	Total
10	2	764	440	800	1,560	200	3,764
6	3	522	318	800	1,438	145	3,223
5	4	368	240	800	1,360	110	2,878
4	5	290	200	800	1,320	92	2,702
3	6	276	192	800	1,312	88	2,668
2	7	210	158	800	1,278	73	2,519
2	8	200	152	800	1,272	70	2,494
2	9	190	146	800	1,266	67	2,469
2	10	140	120	800	1,240	56	2,356

Table 4. Instruction counts for a 160-bit multiplication on the ATmega128

Method	load	store	mul	add	others	Total
Operand Scanning	820	440	400	1,600	466	5,427
Product Scanning	800	40	400	1,200	161	3,957
Hybrid (d=4)	200	40	400	1,250	311	2,904
Operand Caching (e=10)	80	60	400	1,240	70	2,395
Consecutive Operand Caching (e=10)	70	60	400	1,240	56	2,356

Table 5. Multi-precision multiplication result using proposed method with different parameters

e	Size of multiplication									
	112	128	160	192	224	256	384	512	1024	2048
2	1,838	2,404	3,764	5,428	7,396	9,668	21,796	38,788	155,396	622,084
3	1,583	2,104	3,223	4,574	6,380	8,231	18,358	33,032	131,239	525,384
4	1,452	1,840	2,878	4,148	5,650	7,384	16,640	29,608	118,600	474,760
5	1,339	1,806	2,702	3,927	5,384	7,073	15,764	27,879	111,684	447,102
6	1,314	1,684	2,668	3,724	5,136	6,780	14,924	26,742	107,068	426,404
7	1,228	1,659	2,519	3,690	4,906	6,505	14,487	26,116	103,611	412,585
8	1,212	1,564	2,494	3,514	4,872	6,248	14,068	25,024	100,208	401,104
9	1,196	1,548	2,469	3,489	4,838	6,214	14,016	24,954	98,997	394,155
10	1,180	1,532	2,356	3,464	4,644	6,180	13,624	24,400	96,744	387,260

and caching operands. Figure. 4 shows the differences in the clock cycles required for operand caching and the proposed method. The proposed method for multi-precision multiplication performs from -0.93% to 3.85%.

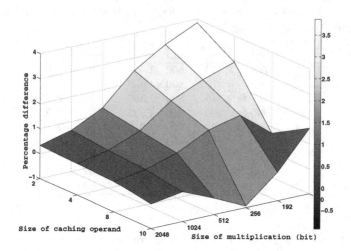

Fig. 4. Differences of total clock cycle between operand-caching and proposed method

5   Conclusion

The previous best known method reduced the number of *load* instructions by using caching operands. However, there is little room to improve the performance by reducing the number of *load* instructions.

In the paper, we present a novel method, i.e., "consecutive operand caching", for multi-precision multiplication. The method fully caches the operands by re-sequencing the partial products. Evaluation results show an improvement of method by analyzing the total number of *load* and *store* instructions. For more practical results, we implement the method using a microprocessor, and we evaluate the clock cycles for the operation.

References

1. Rivest, R.L., Shamir, A., Adleman, L.: A method for obtaining digital signatures and public-key cryptosystems. Comm. ACM 21(2), 120–126 (1977)
2. Hankerson, D., Menezes, A., Vanstone, S.: Guide to Elliptic Curve Cryptography. Springer (2004)
3. Devegili, A.J., Scott, M., Dahab, R.: Implementing Cryptographic Pairings over Barreto-Naehrig Curves. In: Takagi, T., Okamoto, T., Okamoto, E., Okamoto, T. (eds.) Pairing 2007. LNCS, vol. 4575, pp. 197–207. Springer, Heidelberg (2007)
4. Comba, P.: Exponentiation cryptosystems on the IBM PC. IBM Systems Journal 29(4), 526–538 (1990)
5. Gura, N., Patel, A., Wander, A., Eberle, H., Shantz, S.C.: Comparing Elliptic Curve Cryptography and RSA on 8-bit CPUs. In: Joye, M., Quisquater, J.-J. (eds.) CHES 2004. LNCS, vol. 3156, pp. 119–132. Springer, Heidelberg (2004)

6. Hutter, M., Wenger, E.: Fast Multi-precision Multiplication for Public-Key Cryptography on Embedded Microprocessors. In: Preneel, B., Takagi, T. (eds.) CHES 2011. LNCS, vol. 6917, pp. 459–474. Springer, Heidelberg (2011)
7. Hill, J.L., Culler, D.E.: Mica: A wireless platform for deeply embedded networks. IEEE Micro 22, 12–24 (2002)
8. Atmel, 8 bit AVR Microcontroller ATmega128(L) Manual (2004)

Appendix. A. Algorithm for Consecutive Operand-Caching Method

Input: word size n, parameter e, where $n \geq e$, Integers $a, b \in [0, n), c \in [0, 2n)$.

Output: $c = ab$.

$r = \lfloor n/e \rfloor$.

if $(r == n/e)$

$\quad r = r - 1$.

$R_A[e - 1, ..., 0] \leftarrow M_A[n - 1, ..., re]$.

$R_B[e - 1, ..., 0] \leftarrow M_B[n - re - 1, ..., 0]$.

$ACC \leftarrow 0$.

for $i = 0$ to $n - re - 1$ do

$\quad$ for $j = 0$ to i do

$\quad\quad ACC \leftarrow ACC + R\_A[j] \times R\_B[i - j]$.

$\quad$ end for

$\quad M_c[re + i] \leftarrow ACC_0$.

$\quad (ACC_1, ACC_0) \leftarrow (ACC_2, ACC_1)$.

$\quad ACC_2 \leftarrow 0$.

end for

for $i = 0$ to $n - re - 2$ do

$\quad$ for $j = i + 1$ to $n - re - 1$ do

$\quad\quad ACC \leftarrow ACC + R\_A[j] \times R\_B[n - re - j + i]$.

$\quad$ end for

$\quad M_c[n + i] \leftarrow ACC_0$.

$\quad (ACC_1, ACC_0) \leftarrow (ACC_2, ACC_1)$.

$\quad ACC_2 \leftarrow 0$.

end for

$M_C[2n - re - 1] \leftarrow ACC_0$.

$ACC_0 \leftarrow 0$.

for $p = 0$ to $r - 1$ do

$\quad R_A[e - 1, ..., 0] \leftarrow M_A[(p + 1)e - 1, ..., pe]$.

$\quad R_B[e - 1, ..., 0] \leftarrow M_B[e - 1, ..., 0]$.

$\quad$ for $i = 0$ to $e - 1$ do

$\quad\quad$ for $j = 0$ to i do

$\quad\quad\quad ACC \leftarrow ACC + R_A[j] \times R_B[i - j]$.

$\quad\quad$ end for

$\quad\quad M_C[pe + i] \leftarrow ACC_0$.

$\quad\quad (ACC_1, ACC_0) \leftarrow (ACC_2, ACC_1)$.

$$ACC_2 \leftarrow 0.$$
end for
for $i = 0$ **to** $n - (p+1)e - 1$ **do**
  $R_B[e-1, ..., 0] \leftarrow M_B[e+i], R_B[e-2, ..., 1].$
  for $j = 0$ **to** $e - 1$ **do**
    $ACC \leftarrow ACC + R_A[j] \times R_B[e-1-j].$
  end for
  $ACC \leftarrow ACC + M_C[(p+1)e + i].$
  $M_C[(p+1)e + i] \leftarrow ACC_0.$
  $(ACC_1, ACC_0) \leftarrow (ACC_2, ACC_1).$
  $ACC_2 \leftarrow 0.$
end for
if $p == r - 1$
  $k = n - re - 1$
else
  $k = e - 1$
for $i = 0$ **to** k **do**
  $R_A[e-1, ..., 0] \leftarrow M_A[(p+1)e + i], R_A[e-2, ..., 1].$
  for $j = 0$ **to** $e - 1$ **do**
    $ACC \leftarrow ACC + R_A[j] \times R_B[e-1-j].$
  end for
  $ACC \leftarrow ACC + M_C[n+i].$
  $M_C[n+i] \leftarrow ACC_0.$
  $(ACC_1, ACC_0) \leftarrow (ACC_2, ACC_1).$
  $ACC_2 \leftarrow 0.$
end for
for $i = k$ **to** $k + e - 2$ **do**
  for $j = i + 1$ **to** $k + e - 1$ **do**
    $ACC \leftarrow ACC + R_A[j] \times R_B[e-j+i].$
  end for
  $ACC \leftarrow ACC + M_C[n+i+pe].$
  $M_C[n+i+pe] \leftarrow ACC_0.$
  $(ACC_1, ACC_0) \leftarrow (ACC_2, ACC_1).$
  $ACC_2 \leftarrow 0.$
end for
for $i = 0$ **to** $pe - 1$ **do**
  $R_B[e-1], ..., 0] \leftarrow M_B[(r-p+1)e + i], R_B[e-2, ..., 1].$
  for $j = 0$ **to** $e - 1$ **do**
    $ACC \leftarrow ACC + R_A[j] \times R_B[e-1-j].$
  end for
  $ACC \leftarrow ACC + M_C[(p+1)e + i].$
  $M_C[n + (p+1)e + i] \leftarrow ACC_0.$
  $(ACC_1, ACC_0) \leftarrow (ACC_2, ACC_1).$
  $ACC_2 \leftarrow 0.$
end for

$$M_C[2n - 1 - pe] \leftarrow ACC_0.$$
$$ACC_0 \leftarrow 0.$$
end for
Return c.

Appendix. B. Examlple: 160-Bit Consecutive Operand-Caching Method

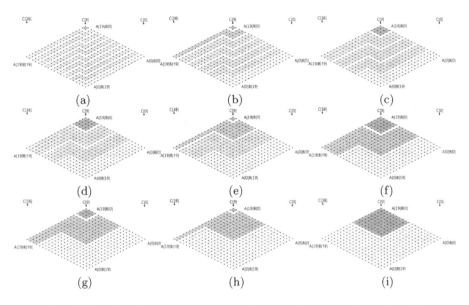

Fig. 5. Rhombus form of proposed method, (a~i) represents (e=2 ~ 10)

Three Phase Dynamic Current Mode Logic:
A More Secure DyCML
to Achieve a More Balanced Power Consumption

Hyunmin Kim, Vladimir Rozic, and Ingrid Verbauwhede

Katholieke Universiteit Leuven, ESAT-SCD-COSIC
Kasteelpark Arenberg 10, B-3001, Leuven-Heverlee, Belgium
{Hyunmin.kim,Vladimir.Rozic,Ingrid.Verbauwhede}@esat.kuleuven.be

Abstract. In order to protect cryptographic devices against power analysis attacks, circuit level countermeasures can be used. Using dynamic current mode logic(DyCML) is an efficient countermeasure providing that the routing of dual-rail signals is balanced. In this paper, we have developed a new logic style based on DyCML, which provides side-channel security without the balanced routing requirement. Simulations of 1-bit full adder were performed to compare the proposed logic style with SABL and DyCML in terms of side-channel security. Post layout simulation results show improvement of normalized energy deviation(NED) of 50% and normalized standard deviation(NSD) of 63% compared with DyCML. Finally, for the AES Sbox simulation, our proposed logic style improves by 31% in NED and by 40% in NSD compared to other secure logics.

Keywords: DyCML, side channel attack, hardware countermeasure, secure logic style.

1 Introduction

Side channel attacks are used to reveal secret data from cryptographic devices by exploiting physical information such as computation time, power consumption or electromagnetic radiation. Differential power analysis is known to be very powerful since the power consumption is closely correlated to the values of intermediate results [1]. Different countermeasures at the algorithm and architecture level have been proposed to prevent power analysis attacks. However, unexpected side-channel vulnerabilities can appear in the hardware implementations due to data dependent power consumption of logic gates. For this reason, a number of logic styles have been proposed to remove these vulnerabilities at the transistor level. In these logic styles the power consumption of each gate is not dependent on the input and output values.

Logic styles with data-independent power consumption can be classified into two categories: Dual-Rail Pre-Charge (DRP) logic styles and Current Mode Logic (CML) styles.

D.H. Lee and M. Yung (Eds.): WISA 2012, LNCS 7690, pp. 68–81, 2012.

- **DRP style logic.** In these logic styles a pre-charge phase and complementary signaling on dual outputs are used. Power consumption doesn't depend on the operated data providing that dual outputs have the same capacitive loads. Sense Amplifier Based Logic(SABL) [2], Three-Phase Dual-Rail precharge Logic(TDPL) [3] and Wave Dynamic Differential Logic(WDDL) [4] are in this category.
- **CML style logic.** These logic styles operate using a small voltage swing at the output and have constant current at the internal nodes. These logic styles are suitable for low power implementations since energy consumption is 50% lower than DRP logic styles [5]. MOS Current Mode Logic(MCML) [6–9] can be used as a countermeasure against power analysis attack. However, high static power consumption is the main drawback of this logic style. For this reason, dynamic logic styles such as Dynamic Current Mode Logic(DyCML) [5, 10–12] have been proposed as an alternative.

However, previous DRP and CML logic styles have an unbalanced capacitance resulting from implementation environment and process conditions. This unbalanced load capacitance becomes a weakness against power analysis attack. Therefore, it is necessary to make up for the unbalanced load capacitance. Although symmetrical rail dividing method using back annotation or fat wire layout [13] is introduced, it doesn't have a completely balanced capacitive load due to process variation and coupling capacitance [14]. To solve the unbalanced load capacitance problem the Three-Phase Dual-Rail Precharge Logic(TDPL) based on DRP style logic has been proposed [3]. The TDPL adds an additional discharge operation and this additional function makes power consumption constant in every clock cycle. However, this logic style consumes two times more power than other DRP style logics. This increased power limits the use of TDPL at the cryptographic device.

In this paper, we apply the three phase design method, which was introduced in [3], to DyCML and propose a new logic style, which we will refer to as Three Phase Dynamic Current Mode Logic(TPDyCML). This logic style is robust against the unbalance of capacitive loads, so it can be used in an automated design environment without additional routing restrictions.

To verify the side-channel security of the proposed logic style, we observed the power consumption of basic gates implemented in SABL, DyCML and TPDyCML. Unbalanced capacitive loads are used at the output nodes, since we assume unbalanced load capacitance after automatic logic synthesis. Also, we simulated a 1-bit full adder implemented in SABL, DyCML and TPDyCML for all possible 64 input transitions. For a more precise evaluation of the effect of the unbalanced capacitance in a real implementation environment, the post layout simulation of a 1bit full adder was evaluated to compare balanced power consumption characteristics for DyCML and TPDyCML.

To investigate the performance of a crypto device, we implemented an AES Sbox [15] using SABL, TDPL, DyCML, TPDyCML. The presented simulation results show that the Normalized Standard Deviation(NSD) of TPDyCML gates is improved by at least with 40% compared to the other four secure logic styles. We confirm the security advantage of our TPDyCML through this simulation.

This paper is organized as follows; The next section introduces the previous representative secure DRP and CML logic styles. Section 3 gives description of the proposed TPDyCML logic family. In section 4 simulation results are presented. Section 5 highlights the contribution and concludes the paper.

2   Background and Related Work

A lot of secure logic styles have been proposed until now. Most commonly used logic styles are developed based on some basic secure logic such as SABL and DyCML. So, in this section, we briefly review these basic forms of secure logic styles that provide outstanding efficiency compared to most commonly used logic solution, such as CMOS logic style.

2.1   Sense Amplifier Based Logic Style(SABL)

SABL is a Dynamic and Differential Logic(DDL) and operates using exactly one transition in every clock cycle. During this switching, all capacitances of internal nodes are charged (dynamic mode) and discharged (differential mode). This makes the total power consumption constant in every clock cycle. Therefore, it is independent on input transitions. Figure 1 shows the general structure of SABL.

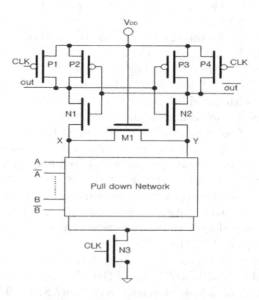

Fig. 1. SABL general structure

SABL operates using two phases: precharge and discharge. In a precharge phase (dynamic mode), two output nodes are charged during a low level phase of a clock cycle, whereas evaluation phase (differential mode), activates during a high level phase. In this phase, according to input transitions of in(A,B) or $\overline{in}(\overline{A},\overline{B})$ charge is stored on output node capacitance and current flows down one impedance path of the pull down network. Also, all internal nodes are connected to output nodes so that all consumed power are the same in every clock cycle.

However, since SABL was developed, a lot of secure logic style which are proposed until now are more improved than SABL in secure characteristic, such as DyCML and TDPL. Furthermore, as automatic design flow has been used more frequently, SABL like other dual rail logic styles has also increased the unbalanced load capacitance after logic synthesis.

2.2   Dynamic Current Mode Logic Style(DyCML)

DyCML is a dynamic current mode logic family, designed to reduce static power consumption of CML logic styles.

DyCML gate consists of four parts: a logic block for function evaluation(i.e. inverter/buffer, nand/and, xor/nxor), precharge circuit (P1,P4), dynamic current source(Q1,Q2,C1) and a latch(P2,P3). The latch transistors speed up the evaluation and preserve the logic value. The dynamic current source operates as a virtual ground and as an active element resistance to reduce static power consumption. Additionally, it consumes less power because of small swing operation. Therefore, this logic style is suitable for reducing power consumption and chip area, which makes it easy to apply to a digital system and to a small portable device. Figure 2 shows the basic structure of DyCML.

The dynamic operation of the DyCML is as follows. During the low clock phase, the transistor Q2 is switched ON to discharge capacitor C1 to GND.

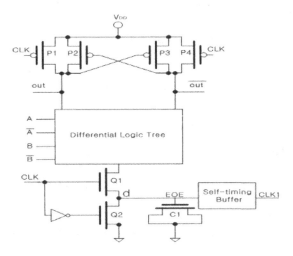

Fig. 2. DyCML general structure

Simultaneously, transistor Q1 is OFF, eliminating the DC current flow paths from V_{DD} to GND. Then, during the high clock phase, the precharge transistor Q2, P1 and P4 switch OFF, while transistor Q1 switches ON, creating a current path from the two precharged output nodes to the capacitor C1. The capacitor C1 acts as a virtual ground. If the DyCML gate connects with the other DyCML gate, a buffer is required to connect with the following clock input because of clock delay. Figure 3 presents a self timing buffer which is one of the most commonly used buffers for DyCML.

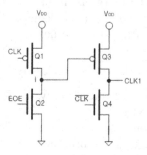

Fig. 3. The structure of self timing buffer

Dual-rail configuration of logic block of DyCML has two rail paths from V_{DD} to GND. These two paths have a different impedance, depending on the logic function and inputs. This difference is much larger if the automatic design flow is used for placement and routing. Therefore, the security of DyCML has to be evaluated under the unbalanced capacitive load condition.

3   Three Phase Dynamic Current Mode Logic

This paper proposes a TPDyCML family. The need for balancing wire capacitance of dual signals is eliminated by using a three phase configuration: charge, evaluation and discharge phase. In addition, the total power consumption is reduced compare to DRP logic style because of the small swing operation.

3.1   Structure of the Proposed Logic

Figure 4 shows the basic architecture of the TPDyCML. TPDyCML gate consists of the following: A differential logic tree, precharge circuits(P1,P4), virtual ground circuit(C1,C2), a p-type latch to preserve the logic value after evaluation(P2,P3), dynamic operation part of TPDyCML(Q1,Q2), three phase part(additional discharge) and one additional self timing buffer compared to DyCML. The self timing buffer for discharge phase is used to enable discharge clk delay, which makes TPDyCML operation more robust.

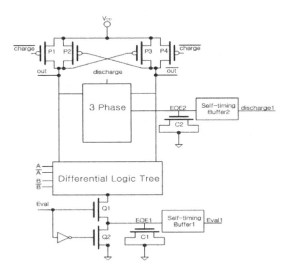

Fig. 4. TPDyCML general structure

Discharge phase control transistors are added to enable TPDyCML operation in a three phase mode, same as TDPL. The additional discharge phase makes the consumed energy balanced. Thus, the following operation occurs. First, during the evaluation phase, the proper line is discharged to GND according to the processed data. Second, the discharge control transistors are switched ON just before the end of the clock cycle. Finally, unbalanced charge at output nodes discharge simultaneously. Thus, energy consumed over one clock cycle becomes constant. Figure 5 presents TPDyCML NAND/AND and XOR/XNOR gates.

3.2 Operation of the Proposed Logic

Precharge Phase: At the beginning of every clock cycle, output node capacitances are charged to the high logic value. The upper PMOS transistors(P1,P4) of the circuit, switch ON when $\overline{charge}$ signal has a low level and power source charges output node capacitances. In addition, transistor Q2 switches ON and charge stored in the virtual ground flows to the GND because Eval signal is also set to low level.

Evaluation Phase: At this phase, PMOS transistors(P1,P4) switch OFF. Charge stored in the output node flows in the source of transistor Q1 through the path in the logic block that depends on input values. Since Eval signal is high, transistor Q1 switches ON and a discharge current flows to the virtual ground.

Discharge Phase: In this phase, the residual charge stored in the output node, is removed through transistors Q3 and Q4 in the three phase block. Even if TPDyCML style gates have an unbalanced load capacitance, this

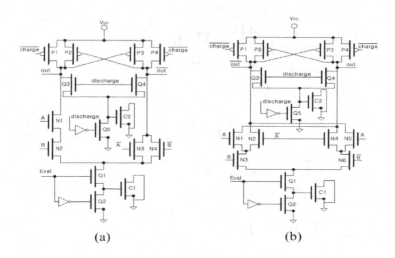

(a)   (b)

Fig. 5. TPDyCML NAND/AND and XOR/XNOR gate

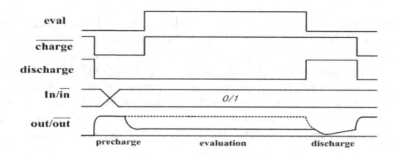

Fig. 6. TPDyCML timing diagram

operation balances power consumption. Figure 6 shows a timing diagram of TPDyCML.

When TPDyCML gates are cascaded, one more self timing buffer is connected to the output of the discharge signal compared to DyCML. In figure 7, more details on how TPDyCML is connected using two self timing buffer are described.

4   Case Study

To check the performance of TPDyCML, we simulate basic gates and 1bit full adder with unbalanced capacitance loads and AES Sbox. At basic gates and a 1bit full adder simulation, we connect unbalanced load capacitances at output nodes of each NAND/AND or XOR/NXOR gates to verify the security characteristic when unexpected unbalanced node capacitances are present due to

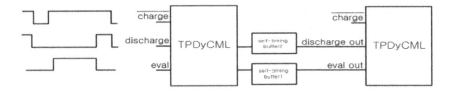

Fig. 7. Cascaded circuit of TPDyCML

automatic design flow or operation environment. Through the post layout simulation of DyCML and TPDyCML, we confirm improvement of TPDyCML and verify the influence of parasitic capacitance after layout design.

In addition, we compare different logic styles with respect to the NED and NSD using AES Sbox implementation. NED is defined as $(\max(E)\text{-}\min(E))$ / $\max(E)$ and NSD formulated as $\sigma_E/\bar{E}$, where σ and $\bar{E}$ are standard deviation and mean calculated per a complete clock cycle [2]. Energy consumption is given by the formula $E = V_{DD} \cdot \int_0^T I_{DD}(t)dt$.

For these simulations, the BSIM3v3 model of UMC 0.13um technology at core voltage Vdd=1.5v and 200MHz operating frequency at basic gate and 1bit full adder simulation is used. For the AES S-box simulation, we use a 100KHz operating frequency because it is normally used for RFID [16]. The simulations are performed using HSPICE.

4.1   Unbalanced Capacitance Load Test

This configuration is used to evaluate the performance of secure logic gates at unbalanced capacitance condition. Table 1 and figure 8 show the results of an unbalanced capacitance load test.

Basic Gate Simulation. The DUT testbench simulation connects to unbalanced load capacitance similar to [3]. Figure 9 shows a DUT testbench circuit.

We test all 16 transition of NAND/AND gate and XOR/NXOR gate. The results of this simulation show that TPDyCML has improved NED and NSD compared to SABL and DyCML. The improvement of NED 47%, 51% and 25%, 23% are compared to SABL and DyCML respectively. The improvement of NSD are 33%, 45% and 27%, 30%.

1bit Full Adder Simulation. A 1bit full adder is designed as shown in figure 10. Between two cascaded gates, a static inverter is inserted in SABL. This is because a static inverter blocks the race condition following domino rule at DRP logic style. The static inverters don't have effect on unbalanced power consumption because every inverters flip the same number of times [3]. However, in CML logic styles, a self timing buffer is a substitute for the static inverter because

Table 1. Normalized Standards Deviation(NSD) and Normalized Energy Deviation(NED) of basic gates and 1 bit full adder

	Normalized Standard Deviation(NSD,%)			
logic style	basic gate		1 bit full adder	
	NAND/AND	XOR/NXOR	pre-layout	post-layout
SABL	24	29	9	—
DyCML	22	23	8	0.95
TPDyCML	16	16	4	0.35
	Normalized Energy Deviation(NED,%)			
logic style	basic gate		1 bit full adder	
	NAND/AND	XOR/NXOR	pre-layout	post-layout
SABL	57	64	33	—
DyCML	40	40	25	4
TPDyCML	30	31	12	2

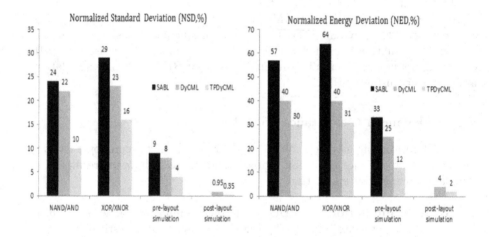

Fig. 8. Simulation result graph of basic gates and 1bit full adder

the CML logic styles have a clock delay problem rather than a race condition. Furthermore, the same unbalanced capacitance values with basic gate simulation are used and those are connected to output nodes of every NAND/AND and XOR/NXOR gates of figure 10.

In this simulation, all 64 transitions are used to evalute NED and NSD. The 1bit full adder simulation shows that TPDyCML improves NED by 33% compared to SABL and by 52% compared to DyCML. At NSD, TPDyCML are 56% better than SABL and 50% better than DyCML.

We also look into the effect of parasitic capacitance after layout design. We evaluate the post layout simulation of a 1bit full adder using DyCML and

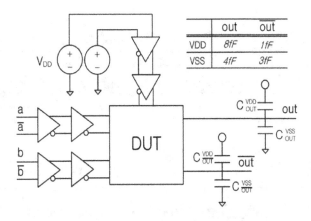

	out	$\overline{out}$
VDD	8fF	1fF
VSS	4fF	3fF

Fig. 9. DUT testbench

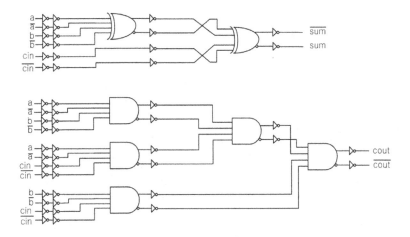

Fig. 10. 1 bit full adder configuration

TPDyCML. The results show that TPDyCML improves by 50% in NED and by 63% in NSD compared to DyCML. Therefore, even if there are some unbalanced capacitance after layout design, TPDyCML will have constant power consumption. Figure 11 shows the layout design and figure 12 presents the post layout simulation current waveform obtained by the transient analysis of DyCML and TPDyCML for all 64 input transitions. It can be seen from figure 12 that variations of power are indeed smaller for TPDyCML compared to DyCML.

4.2 AES S-Box Simulation

Figure 13 shows the structure of an AES Sbox. We implemented the compact AES Sbox presented in [15] using SABL, TDPL, DyCML, TPDyCML. Inside all

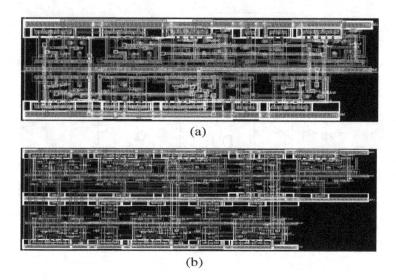

Fig. 11. Layout design of DyCML(a) and TPDyCML(b)

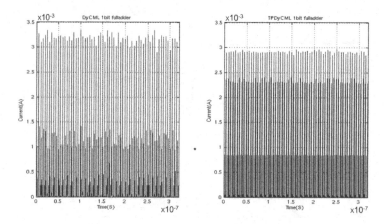

Fig. 12. 1-bit full adder current waveforms

function of the AES Sbox the static inverter is also inserted in SABL and TDPL and the self timed buffer in DyCML and TPDyCML. The circuit implementation of four logic styles has logic depth 25. All 256 input transitions are simulated to check NED and NSD. Table 2 shows the obtained NED and NSD values of AES Sbox and figure 14 presents the result graph.

Presented simulation results confirm that the proposed TPDyCML is more secure compared to SABL, TDPL, DyCML. An improvement of more than 40% for NSD and 31% of NED has been observed.

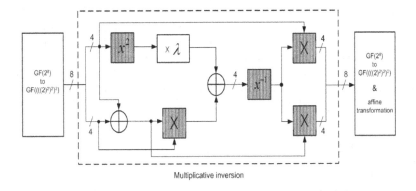

Multiplicative inversion

Fig. 13. Structure of the AES S-box implementation

Table 2. Normalized Standards Deviation(NSD) and Normalized Energy Deviation(NED) of AES S-box simulation

logic style	AES S-box	
	NSD(%)	NED(%)
SABL	33	87
TDPL	11	54
DyCML	5	26
TPDyCML	3	18

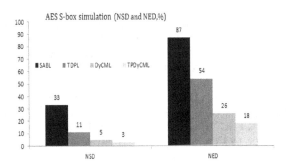

Fig. 14. Simulation result graph of AES S-box

5   Conclusion

In this paper, TPDyCML is introduced. This logic style uses a three phase and dynamic current mode logic. Unbalanced capacitive loads caused by automatic design flow present a weakness against power analysis attack. An additional final discharge phase reduces this effect. In addition, AES SBox simulation confirms the suitability of the proposed logic style for secure applications. In the case study we simulate basic gate and 1bit full adder for an unbalanced capacitance load test and AES SBox for a test of security device. TPDyCML shows an improvement of NED and NSD by 50% and 63% in 1bit full adder after layout design and more than 31% and 40% in the AES SBox simulation. As a result, it proves that the proposed TPDyCML enhances side channel security.

Further Work

Although NED and NSD values indicate higher resistance against power analysis, real attack simulation needs to be done. Our work is planned to configure real attack model, such as correlation power analysis or mutual information analysis. In addition, our AES Sbox is to be optimized using binary decision(BDD) model to reduce logic depth and reduce delay.

After that, we will develop with current mode based TPDyCML sequential elements(Flip-flops, latches) that utilize three phase operation.

Acknowledgment. This research was supported by Basic Science Research Program through the National Research Foundation of Korea(NRF) funded by the Ministry of Education, Science and Technology(2011-0026354).

References

1. Kocher, P.C., Jaffe, J., Jun, B.: Differential Power Analysis. In: Wiener, M. (ed.) CRYPTO 1999. LNCS, vol. 1666, pp. 388–397. Springer, Heidelberg (1999)
2. Tiri, K., Akmal, M., Verbauwhede, I.: A Dynamic and Differential CMOS Logic with Signal Independent Power Consumption to Withstand Differential Power Analysis on Smart Cards. In: ESSCIRC 2002, pp. 403–406 (2002)
3. Bucci, M., Giancane, L., Luzzi, R., Trifiletti, A.: Three-Phase Dual-Rail Pre-charge Logic. In: Goubin, L., Matsui, M. (eds.) CHES 2006. LNCS, vol. 4249, pp. 232–241. Springer, Heidelberg (2006)
4. Tiri, K., Verbauwhede, I.: A Logic Level Design Methodology for a Secure DPA Resistanct ASIC of FPGA Implementation. In: DATE 2004, pp. 246–251 (2004)
5. Mace, F., Standaert, F.X., Hassoune, I., Legat, J.D., Quisquater, J.J.: A Dynamic Current Mode Logic to Counteract Power Analysis Attacks. In: DCIS 2004, pp. 186–191 (2004)
6. Yamashina, M., Yamada, H.: Mos current mode logic MCML circuit for low-power GHz processors. NEC Research Development 36(1), 54–63 (1995)
7. Regazzoni, F., Eisenbarth, T., Poschmann, A., Großschädl, J., Gurkaynak, F., Macchetti, M., Toprak, Z., Pozzi, L., Paar, C., Leblebici, Y., Ienne, P.: Evaluating Resistance of MCML Technology to Power Analysis Attacks Using a Simulation-Based Methodology. In: Gavrilova, M.L., Tan, C.J.K., Moreno, E.D. (eds.) Trans. on Comput. Sci. IV. LNCS, vol. 5430, pp. 230–243. Springer, Heidelberg (2009)
8. Badel, S., Guleyupoglu, E., Inac, O., Martinez, A.P., Vietti, P., Gurkaynak, F., Leblebici, Y.: A generic standard cell design methodology for differential circuit styles. In: DATE 2008, pp. 843–848 (2008)

9. Hassan, H., Anis, M., Elmasry, M.: Design and optimization of MOS current mode logic for parameter variations. VLSI Journal 38, 417–437 (2005)
10. Allam, M.W., Elmasry, M.: Dynamic Current Mode Logic(DyCML): A New Low-Power High-Performance Logic Style. IEEE Journal of Solid-State Circuits 36(3), 550–558 (2001)
11. Ren, F., Markovic, D.: True energy-performance analysis of the MTJ-Based logic-in-memory architecture(1-bit full adder). IEEE Transactions on Electron Devices 57(5), 1023–1028 (2010)
12. Sundstrom, J., Alvandpour, A.: A comparative analysis of logic styles for secure IC's against DPA attacks. In: NORCHIP 2005, pp. 297–300 (2005)
13. Tiri, K., Verbauwhede, I.: Place and Route for Secure Standard Cell Design. In: CARDIS 2004, pp. 143–158 (2004)
14. Lin, L., Burleson, W.: Analysis and Mitigation of Process Variation impacts on Power-Analysis Tolerance. In: DAC 2009, pp. 238–243 (2009)
15. Mentens, N., Batina, L., Preneel, B., Verbauwhede, I.: A Systematic Evaluation of Compact Hardware Implementations for the Rijndael S-Box. In: Menezes, A. (ed.) CT-RSA 2005. LNCS, vol. 3376, pp. 323–333. Springer, Heidelberg (2005)
16. Feldhofer, M., Dominikus, S., Wolkerstorfer, J.: Strong Authentication for RFID Systems Using the AES Algorithm. In: Joye, M., Quisquater, J.-J. (eds.) CHES 2004. LNCS, vol. 3156, pp. 357–370. Springer, Heidelberg (2004)

Improved Differential Fault Analysis
on Block Cipher ARIA

JeaHoon Park[1] and JaeCheol Ha[2],[*]

[1] The Attached Institute of ETRI, Korea
jenoon65@ensec.re.kr
[2] Dept. of Information Security, Hoseo Univ., 336-795, Korea
jcha@hoseo.edu

Abstract. Differential Fault Analysis (DFA) is a kind of fault injection attack on block ciphers. To retrieve the master secret key embedded in hardware device, an attacker should obtain some faulty outputs that occur after a fault injection during the operation of a cryptographic algorithm. This paper proposes an improved DFA on the block cipher ARIA. To retrieve the 128-bit full secret key of ARIA, 33 faulty ciphertexts are sufficient for the proposed DFA. Our proposal is more efficient than the previous DFA introduced by W. Li *et al.*, which requires about 45 faulty ciphertexts. And, the experimental results on the commercial microcontroller ATmega128 give the validity and effectiveness for our DFA.

1 Introduction

Fault injection attacks have already broken many kinds of implementation of cryptographic algorithms. Fault injection attacks analyze the faulty outputs that occur as a result of a fault injection during the operation of a cryptographic device. We usually call a fault injection attack on block cipher a Differential Fault Analysis (DFA). The focus of a DFA attack is to retrieve the secret key by analyzing the differences between the pairs of correct and faulty outputs.

DFA was first proposed in 1997 by E. Biham and A. Shamir as an attack on DES [5]. Similar attacks have been proposed on AES [9,2,11,3,1,7], Triple-DES [10], RC4 [6] and CLEFIA [8,12], etc. Recently, a DFA attack on the ARIA algorithm, which is the Korean standard block cipher, was proposed by W. Li *et al.* [13]. They showed that the 128-bit full secret key of ARIA can be retrieved with about 45 faulty ciphertexts that are caused by a single byte random fault on the intermediate value during the encryption process. To the best of our knowledge, their method is currently the most efficient fault attack on ARIA.

This paper proposes a more efficient DFA on the ARIA algorithm. Unlike W. Li *et al.*'s method, in which they try to find the intermediate ciphertext value, our DFA directly exploits the round keys of ARIA. In order to retrieve the full master secret key, we should recover at least four round keys. Thus, we first find the final round key and then recover the remaining three round keys in

---

[*] Corresponding author.

D.H. Lee and M. Yung (Eds.): WISA 2012, LNCS 7690, pp. 82–95, 2012.
© Springer-Verlag Berlin Heidelberg 2012

reverse order. After getting the final round key, we are faced with the problem of retrieving the three remaining round keys because these remaining three rounds have a diffusion layer. To solve this problem, we introduce some analytical tricks in which we interchange the order of the round functions: the round key addition and the diffusion layer. Having applied this trick to our DFA for retrieving the three remaining round keys, we can easily guess the target round key. As a result, our method needs roughly 33 faulty ciphertexts to retrieve the full master secret key of ARIA. Additionally, our DFA can be applied when a fault is injected during the key expansion process as well as when one is injected during the encryption process.

This paper is organized as follows. In section 2, we briefly introduce the ARIA algorithm and the previous DFA as described by W. Li *et al.*. We propose our improved DFA on the ARIA in section 3. In section 4, we present the experimental results of our DFA using a commercial microcontroller. Finally, we conclude our paper in section 5.

2   Related Works

2.1   ARIA Block Cipher

The ARIA block cipher was introduced by D. Kwon *et al.* in 2003 and has been used as the Korean standard block cipher since 2004 [4].

ARIA Key Expansion Algorithm. The key expansion process of ARIA consists of two parts, which are initialization and round key generation, as follows.

- Initialization: In the initialization part, four 128-bit values W_0, W_1, W_2, W_3 are generated from the master secret key by using a 3-round 256-bit Feistel cipher, which is described in [4].

- Round key generation: In the generation part, the four values W_i are combined to obtain an encryption round key ek_i as follows.

$$ek_1 = W_0 \oplus W_1^{>>>19}, \ ek_2 = W_1 \oplus W_2^{>>>19},$$
$$\ldots, \ ek_{12} = W_0^{>>>67} \oplus W_3, \ ek_{13} = W_0 \oplus W_1^{>>>97}. \tag{1}$$

For the ARIA decryption process, we derive the decryption round keys dk_i from the encryption round keys as follows.

$$dk_1 = ek_{n+1}, \ dk_2 = DL(ek_n),$$
$$dk_3 = DL(ek_{n-1}), \cdots, \ dk_n = DL(ek_2), \ dk_{n+1} = ek_1 \tag{2}$$

, where $DL(\ )$ denotes diffusion layer of the ARIA encryption algorithm.

ARIA En/Decryption Algorithm. ARIA algorithm uses a 128-bit input message and 128, 192, 256-bit variable size secret keys, for which the number of rounds are 12, 14, and 16, respectively. And, ARIA is an involution SPN block cipher for which the encryption procedure is the same as the decryption

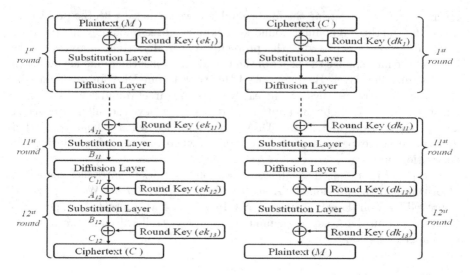

Fig. 1. Round functions of ARIA block cipher

procedure. In Fig. 1, $A_i, B_i,$ and C_i denote the intermediate values of the i-th round of the ARIA encryption process and ek_i, dk_i represents the i-th round key.

Each round of the ARIA encryption consists of three layers: a substitution layer (SL), a diffusion layer (DL), and a round key addition (RKA) as shown in Fig. 1. In the substitution layer, the intermediate data is substituted by the substitution table called the S-Box. ARIA has two kinds of S-Boxes, type 1 and 2. In the diffusion layer, a simple 16×16 binary matrix (equation (3)) is multiplied with the intermediate data in such a way that a single byte of input affects the seven bytes of output.

$$
\begin{pmatrix} o_0 \\ o_1 \\ o_2 \\ o_3 \\ o_4 \\ o_5 \\ o_6 \\ o_7 \\ o_8 \\ o_9 \\ o_{10} \\ o_{11} \\ o_{12} \\ o_{13} \\ o_{14} \\ o_{15} \end{pmatrix} = \begin{pmatrix} 0\,0\,0\,1\,1\,0\,1\,0\,1\,1\,0\,0\,0\,1\,1\,0 \\ 0\,0\,1\,0\,0\,1\,0\,1\,1\,1\,0\,0\,1\,0\,0\,1 \\ 0\,1\,0\,0\,1\,0\,1\,0\,0\,0\,1\,1\,1\,0\,0\,1 \\ 1\,0\,0\,0\,0\,1\,0\,1\,0\,0\,1\,1\,0\,1\,1\,0 \\ 1\,0\,1\,0\,0\,1\,0\,0\,1\,0\,0\,1\,0\,0\,1\,1 \\ 0\,1\,0\,1\,1\,0\,0\,0\,0\,1\,1\,0\,0\,0\,1\,1 \\ 1\,0\,1\,0\,0\,0\,0\,1\,0\,1\,1\,0\,1\,1\,0\,0 \\ 0\,1\,0\,1\,0\,0\,1\,0\,1\,0\,0\,1\,1\,1\,0\,0 \\ 1\,1\,0\,0\,1\,0\,0\,1\,0\,0\,1\,0\,0\,1\,0\,1 \\ 1\,1\,0\,0\,0\,1\,1\,0\,0\,0\,0\,1\,1\,0\,1\,0 \\ 0\,0\,1\,1\,0\,1\,1\,0\,1\,0\,0\,0\,0\,1\,0\,1 \\ 0\,0\,1\,1\,1\,0\,0\,1\,0\,1\,0\,0\,1\,0\,1\,0 \\ 0\,1\,1\,0\,0\,0\,1\,1\,0\,1\,0\,1\,1\,0\,0\,0 \\ 1\,0\,0\,1\,0\,0\,1\,1\,1\,0\,1\,0\,0\,1\,0\,0 \\ 1\,0\,0\,1\,1\,1\,0\,0\,0\,1\,0\,1\,0\,0\,1\,0 \\ 0\,1\,1\,0\,1\,1\,0\,0\,1\,0\,1\,0\,0\,0\,0\,1 \end{pmatrix} \cdot \begin{pmatrix} i_0 \\ i_1 \\ i_2 \\ i_3 \\ i_4 \\ i_5 \\ i_6 \\ i_7 \\ i_8 \\ i_9 \\ i_{10} \\ i_{11} \\ i_{12} \\ i_{13} \\ i_{14} \\ i_{15} \end{pmatrix} \qquad (3)
$$

In the round key addition, the intermediate data of each round is XORed with the round key which is generated from the master secret key (MK) using the round key generation process. In the final round, the diffusion layer is replaced by the additional round key addition.

2.2 The Previous DFA for ARIA

In 2008, W. Li *et al.* introduced a DFA for ARIA that was the first DFA attack on ARIA [13]. They assumed that an attacker can change only one byte of the intermediate data before the diffusion layer to a random value by a fault injection. To recover the final round key, an attacker computes the difference of the intermediate data, and then deduces the input of the 12-th round S-Box A_{12} based on a brute force search for the S-Box input difference ΔA_{12} using equation (4). The output difference of the j-th ($0 \le j \le 15$) S-Box in the 12-th round can be represented by $\Delta b_{j,12} = (\Delta B_{12})_j = (\Delta C)_j$. The j-th ($0 \le j \le 15$) byte of A_{12} satisfies:

$$a_{j,12} \in IN(\Delta a_{j,12}, \Delta b_{j,12}), \qquad (4)$$

where $IN(\Delta a_{j,i}, \Delta b_{j,i}) = \{a_{j,i} | a_{j,i} \in \{0,1\}^8, S(a_{j,i}) \oplus S(a_{j,i} \oplus \Delta a_{j,i}) = \Delta b_{j,i}\}$.

Thus, the attacker can compute the final round key $ek_{13}(= C \oplus B_{12} = C \oplus SL(A_{12}))$. To retrieve the 128-bit full master secret key of ARIA, an attacker needs about 45 faulty ciphertexts on average. Please refer [13] for detailed method and process.

3 Proposed Differential Fault Analysis for ARIA

In our proposal, we assume that an attacker can induce a random single byte error in the intermediate value before the diffusion layer of each round during the encryption process, and get the faulty ciphertexts. This is the same assumption as made in W. Li *et al.*'s research of DFA on ARIA. However, unlike the previous DFA, in which an attacker tries to guess and compute the intermediate value of the encryption round and then deduce the round key, we directly guess the round keys and remove the candidate keys.

Our DFA attack is based on the fact that a single byte error injected as an input of the diffusion layer is propagated to the seven bytes of output. Since the diffusion layer is a linear function, the difference between the correct and faulty input bytes to the diffusion layer is the same as the differences between the seven correct and faulty output bytes from the diffusion layer.

In order to complete our DFA, we divide the process into two phases. One is the basic phase for recovering the final round key and another extended phase for the remaining three round keys: 12-th to the 10-th. To recover the remaining three round keys after finding out the final round key, we use additional tricks, which will be explained in section 3.2.

3.1   Basic DFA for Recovering the Last Round Key

In this subsection, we describe a basic DFA on ARIA to recover the final round key. First, we try to recover the seven bytes of the final round key using two ciphertexts: correct and faulty ciphertexts. The faulty ciphertext is the output after injecting a byte fault to the intermediate value before the diffusion layer in the 11-th round. As an example we can look at Fig. 2, in which a fault is injected at the most significant byte (MSB) of the intermediate value before the 11-th round diffusion layer.

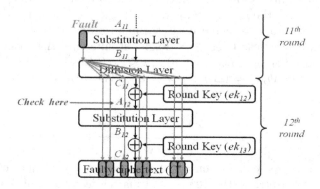

Fig. 2. Fault injection to recover the last round key

The faulty ciphertext (C^*) has the seven byte errors at the 3, 4, 6, 8, 9, 13 and 14-th bytes. To recover the seven bytes of ek_{13}, we introduce equation (5). The equation is based on the property of diffusion layer (eq. 3). It is fact that the differences of the seven output bytes are the same since they result from a single faulty input byte to the diffusion layer.

$$\Delta_3 = SL^{-1}(C_3 \oplus ek_{3,13}) \oplus SL^{-1}(C_3^* \oplus ek_{3,13}),$$
$$\Delta_4 = SL^{-1}(C_4 \oplus ek_{4,13}) \oplus SL^{-1}(C_4^* \oplus ek_{4,13}),$$
$$\vdots$$
$$\Delta_{14} = SL^{-1}(C_{14} \oplus ek_{14,13}) \oplus SL^{-1}(C_{14}^* \oplus ek_{14,13}),$$
$$\Delta_3 = \Delta_4 = \ldots = \Delta_{13} = \Delta_{14}. \tag{5}$$

Here, Δ_i means the difference for the i-th byte as reckoned from the MSB and C_i is the i-th byte from the MSB of the ciphertext ($0 \le i \le 15$). $ek_{j,i}$ means the j-th byte from the MSB of the i-th round key ($0 \le j \le 15$, $1 \le i \le 13$). $SL^{-1}()$ denotes the inversion of the S-Box.

In our method, we first guess the two bytes among bytes 3, 4, 6, 7, 8, 13, 14 of the round key. We test the two round key byte candidates using equation (5). As there are many candidates that satisfy equation (5), we try to recover the correct two bytes of the round key using two correct ciphertexts (C, D) and the two faulty ciphertexts (C^*, D^*) using arbitrary plaintext inputs $X1$ and $X2$, where C and C^* use the same plaintext $X1$, D and D^* use $X2$ respectively. We repeat the same guessing method to recover other secret byte keys, which are in the same byte position as the seven bytes fault position of the faulty ciphertext. The detailed procedure of our DFA attack is as follows. Our DFA also does not restrict the position of the injected faulty bytes. We just choose two faulty ciphertexts which are caused by a byte fault of the same position. For the simplicity, we will describe the case when the MSB of the intermediate value before the diffusion layer in the 11-th round is modified by a fault injection.

Step 1. Obtain two ciphertexts (C, D) by encrypting arbitrary plaintexts $X1$ and $X2$ with a master secret key. And, obtain two faulty ciphertexts (C^*, D^*) which are caused by a random byte error before the diffusion layer in the 11-th round during the ARIA encryption process with plaintexts $X1$ and $X2$, respectively.

Step 2. To confirm the position of the fault injected bytes and select proper faulty ciphertexts, compute the difference between the correct and faulty ciphertexts $(\Delta = C \oplus C^*, \Delta' = D \oplus D^*)$. First, to recover the 3-rd and 4-th bytes of the round key $(ek_{3,13}, ek_{4,13})$, we check equation (6) using the 2^{16} possible values of the two bytes. Through this checking process we obtain several candidates for the two secret bytes.

$$\Delta_3 = SL^{-1}(C_3 \oplus ek_{3,13}) \oplus SL^{-1}(C_3^* \oplus ek_{3,13}),$$
$$\Delta_4 = SL^{-1}(C_4 \oplus ek_{4,13}) \oplus SL^{-1}(C_4^* \oplus ek_{4,13}),$$
$$\Delta_3' = SL^{-1}(D_3 \oplus ek_{3,13}) \oplus SL^{-1}(D_3^* \oplus ek_{3,13}),$$
$$\Delta_4' = SL^{-1}(D_4 \oplus ek_{4,13}) \oplus SL^{-1}(D_4^* \oplus ek_{4,13}),$$
$$\text{Check } (\Delta_3 = \Delta_4 \ \& \ \Delta_3' = \Delta_4') \ \text{ or } \ \text{not.} \tag{6}$$

Then we add to the round key candidate list L, those $ek_{3,13}$ and $ek_{4,13}$ values which values pass the checking equation (6).

Step 3. Recover the next byte of the round key (6-th) using one of the two candidates $(ek_{3,13}, ek_{4,13})$ from the list $L = \{L_3, L_4\}$. In this case, we use the 4-th byte candidates in the L_4 to recover one more round key byte. In a similar way to Step 2, we compute equation (7) using the 2^8 possible values for the byte $ek_{6,13}$ and the candidate list L_4.

$$\Delta_4 = SL^{-1}(C_4 \oplus L_4) \oplus SL^{-1}(C_4^* \oplus L_4),$$
$$\Delta_6 = SL^{-1}(C_6 \oplus ek_{6,13}) \oplus SL^{-1}(C_6^* \oplus ek_{6,13}),$$
$$\Delta_4' = SL^{-1}(D_4 \oplus L_4) \oplus SL^{-1}(D_4^* \oplus L_4),$$
$$\Delta_6' = SL^{-1}(D_6 \oplus ek_{6,13}) \oplus SL^{-1}(D_6^* \oplus ek_{6,13}),$$
$$\text{Check } (\Delta_4 = \Delta_6 \ \& \ \Delta_4' = \Delta_6') \ \text{ or } \ \text{not.} \tag{7}$$

The list L is updated by $L = \{L_3, L_4, L_6\}$, in which the L_6 is the candidates for $ek_{6,13}$.

Step 4. Repeat Step 3 while extending the key byte. When there are only seven byte values in the list L, these seven values become seven bytes of the final round key.

Step 5. Repeat Steps 1 to 4 three more times, changing randomly the position of the fault injection at the intermediate value before the diffusion layer in the 11-th round to obtain the ultimate list $L = \{ek_{0,13}, ..., ek_{15,13}\}$, the correct 128-bit final round key ek_{13}.

3.2   Extended DFA for Recovering the Three Remaining Round Keys

After finding out the final round key, we try to recover the three remaining round keys: from 12 to 10. In this extended DFA for recovering the three remaining round keys, the attack scenarios are almost the same as the basic DFA for recovering the last round key. In order to recover the 12-th round key ek_{12}, we should inject a fault to the intermediate value before the diffusion layer of the 10-th round. And we should trace back to the input of the diffusion layer of the 11-th round. This means that we should compute the differences of the correct and faulty intermediate values, which are outputs from the substitution layer in the 11-th round. However, as can be seen in Fig. 3, these differences cannot easily compute because we should totally guess the 128-bit 12-th round key ek_{12}.

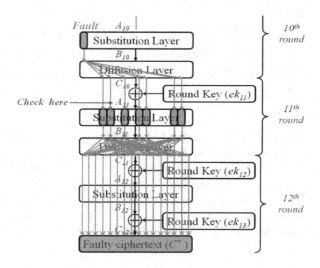

Fig. 3. Fault injection to recover the 12-th round key

Although we cannot compute the input of diffusion layer, we want to guess the input of substitution layer for applying our extended DFA. Thus, we utilized some analytic tricks. It is necessary to keep in mind that the (inverse) diffusion layer and the round key addition are both composed solely of XOR operations and so are linear functions. Thus, we can change the computation order of the (inverse) diffusion layer and the round key addition as follows:

$$\text{Output} = DL(\text{Input}) \oplus key, \tag{8}$$

$$\text{Input} = DL^{-1}(\text{Output} \oplus key) = DL^{-1}(\text{Output}) \oplus DL^{-1}(key). \tag{9}$$

Since we know ek_{13} by the basic DFA attack, we can trace back from an original ciphertext as follows.

$$B_{11} = DL^{-1}((SL^{-1}(C \oplus ek_{13})) \oplus ek_{12}). \tag{10}$$

As a result of interchanging, the equation (10) can be rewritten as follows.

$$B_{11} = DL^{-1}(SL^{-1}(C \oplus ek_{13})) \oplus DL^{-1}(ek_{12}). \tag{11}$$

Due to this property of ARIA, our DFA can be applied to recovering the intermediate round keys. Without loss of generality, we can assume that a fault is injected at the MSB of the intermediate value before the 10-th round diffusion layer. Then the output of the 10-th round diffusion layer has seven byte errors at the 3, 4, 6, 8, 9, 13 and 14-th bytes. The extended DFA attack procedure is as follows.

Step 1. Obtain two ciphertexts (C, D) by encrypting arbitrary plaintexts $X1$ and $X2$ with a master secret key. And, obtain the two faulty ciphertexts (C^*, D^*) that result from a random byte fault before the diffusion layer in the 10-th round during the ARIA encryption process with plaintexts $X1$ and $X2$, respectively.

Step 2. Recover the inputs of S-Box $(A_{12}^C, A_{12}^{C^*}, A_{12}^D, A_{12}^{D^*})$ in the 12-th round using the recovered final round key ek_{13} as follows:

$$A_{12}^C = SL^{-1}(C \oplus ek_{13}), \ \ A_{12}^{C^*} = SL^{-1}(C^* \oplus ek_{13}),$$
$$A_{12}^D = SL^{-1}(D \oplus ek_{13}), \ \ A_{12}^{D^*} = SL^{-1}(D^* \oplus ek_{13}). \tag{12}$$

And then, interchange the inverse computational order of the diffusion layer and the round key addition of ek_{12}. Thus, the inversion of the diffusion layer is computed as follows:

$$\hat{B}_{11}^C = DL^{-1}(A_{12}^C), \ \ \hat{B}_{11}^{C^*} = DL^{-1}(A_{12}^{C^*}),$$
$$\hat{B}_{11}^D = DL^{-1}(A_{12}^D), \ \ \hat{B}_{11}^{D^*} = DL^{-1}(A_{12}^{D^*}). \tag{13}$$

$\hat{B}_{11}^C$ is different from the original input of the diffusion layer (B_{11}^C) because we changed the order with the round key addition. To confirm the fault injected byte and select proper faulty ciphertexts, we compute the difference between the correct and faulty ciphertexts as follows:

$$\Delta = \hat{B}_{11}^C \oplus \hat{B}_{11}^{C^*}, \ \ \Delta' = \hat{B}_{11}^D \oplus \hat{B}_{11}^{D^*}. \tag{14}$$

First, to recover the 3-rd and 4-th bytes of the temporary round keys $(\hat{ek}_{3,12}, \hat{ek}_{4,12})$, we check equation (15) using 2^{16} possible values of two bytes. The temporary round key is different from the real round key $(ek_{3,12}, ek_{4,12})$, but we can deduce the real round key using the relationship $\hat{ek}_{12} = DL^{-1}(ek_{12})$. By checking the following equation (15), we can get candidates for the two secret bytes.

$$\Delta_3 = SL^{-1}((\hat{B}^C_{11})_3 \oplus \hat{ek}_{3,12}) \oplus SL^{-1}((\hat{B}^{C^*}_{11})_3 \oplus \hat{ek}_{3,12}),$$
$$\Delta_4 = SL^{-1}((\hat{B}^C_{11})_4 \oplus \hat{ek}_{4,12}) \oplus SL^{-1}((\hat{B}^{C^*}_{11})_4 \oplus \hat{ek}_{4,12}),$$
$$\Delta'_3 = SL^{-1}((\hat{B}^D_{11})_3 \oplus \hat{ek}_{3,12}) \oplus SL^{-1}((\hat{B}^{D^*}_{11})_3 \oplus \hat{ek}_{3,12}),$$
$$\Delta'_4 = SL^{-1}((\hat{B}^D_{11})_4 \oplus \hat{ek}_{4,12}) \oplus SL^{-1}((\hat{B}^{D^*}_{11})_4 \oplus \hat{ek}_{4,12}),$$
$$\text{Check } (\Delta_3 = \Delta_4 \ \& \ \Delta'_3 = \Delta'_4) \ \text{ or } \ \text{not.} \tag{15}$$

Here, $(\hat{B}^C_{11})_i$ means the i-th byte from the MSB of the 11-th round diffusion layer's input in the 11-th round. Then we add $\hat{ek}_{3,12}$ and $\hat{ek}_{4,12}$ values to the temporary round key candidate list L of values which have passed the checking equation (15).

Step 3. Recover the next 6-th byte of the temporary round key with one of two candidates $(\hat{ek}_{3,12}, \hat{ek}_{4,12})$ in the list $L = \{L_3, L_4\}$. In this case, we use the 4-th byte round key candidates in the list L_4. In a similar way to that described in Step 2., we compute equation (16) using the 2^8 possible values for the byte $ek_{6,12}$ and the candidate list L_4.

$$\Delta_4 = SL^{-1}((\hat{B}^C_{11})_4 \oplus L_4) \oplus SL^{-1}((\hat{B}^{C^*}_{11})_4 \oplus L_4),$$
$$\Delta_6 = SL^{-1}((\hat{B}^C_{11})_6 \oplus \hat{ek}_{6,12}) \oplus SL^{-1}((\hat{B}^{C^*}_{11})_6 \oplus \hat{ek}_{6,12}),$$
$$\Delta'_4 = SL^{-1}((\hat{B}^D_{11})_4 \oplus L_4) \oplus SL^{-1}((\hat{B}^{D^*}_{11})_4 \oplus L_4),$$
$$\Delta'_6 = SL^{-1}((\hat{B}^D_{11})_6 \oplus \hat{ek}_{6,12}) \oplus SL^{-1}((\hat{B}^{D^*}_{11})_6 \oplus \hat{ek}_{6,12}),$$
$$\text{Check } (\Delta_4 = \Delta_6 \ \& \ \Delta'_4 = \Delta'_6) \ \text{ or } \ \text{not.} \tag{16}$$

The list L is updated by $L = \{L_3, L_4, L_6\}$, in which the L_6 indicates candidates of $\hat{ek}_{6,12}$.

Step 4. Repeat Step 3 while extending the key byte. If there are only seven byte values in the list L, these seven values become seven bytes of the 12-th temporary round key.

Step 5. Repeat Steps 1 to 4 three more times, changing randomly the position of the fault injection at the intermediate value before the diffusion layer in the 10-th round to obtain the ultimate list $L = (\hat{ek}_{0,12}, ... \hat{ek}_{15,12})$, is the correct temporary round key $\hat{ek}_{12}$. Since we can find the 128-bit temporary round key $(\hat{ek}_{12})$ by interchanging the order of the two round functions, we can actually recover the real 12-th round key (ek_{12}) from this process by using the diffusion function, i.e. $ek_{12} = DL^{-1}(\hat{ek}_{12})$.

Step 6. Recover the round key ek_{11} by repeating from Step 1 to Step 5 with faults injected before the diffusion layer in the 9-th round.

Step 7. Recover the round key ek_{10} by repeating from Step 1 to Step 5 with faults injected before the diffusion layer in the 8-th round.

Step 8. The master secret key of ARIA can be calculated from the recovered four round keys.

4   Application and DFA Experiment

4.1   Application to Key Expansion Algorithm

When there is a single byte error of the intermediate value in the key expansion algorithm, can our DFA be applied? This was mentioned as a future work in W. Li *et al.*'s paper. But, our DFA and W. Li *et al.*'s also can be applied when a fault is injected to the intermediate value of the key expansion procedure of ARIA. In the key expansion case, since each round key is only concerned with the four 128-bit initial values (W_0, W_1, W_2, W_3), there is no relationship between each round key generation algorithm as shown in equation (1). This means that an error in a one round key generation algorithm does not affect the other round key generation algorithm. Therefore, a byte fault injected to the intermediate value of the key expansion algorithm can cause one byte fault of the intermediate value before the diffusion layer in the encryption algorithm. An example is given in Fig. 4 where we inject a single byte fault to the intermediate value in the key expansion procedure of ek_{11}. These faulty effects are the same as the basic attack's effects on the recovery of the ek_{13}.

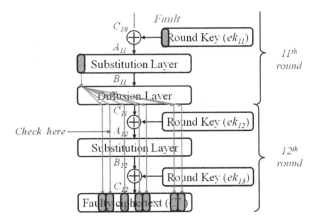

Fig. 4. Fault injection to retrieve the last round key in the key expansion algorithm

4.2   DFA Attack Experiment on the ARIA

First, we simulate our DFA on a PC with a 2.83GHz Core2 Quad with 2GB memory using Visual C++ software. In our simulation, we intensively modify the one byte of the intermediate value with a random value to realize a fault injection effect. Table 1 shows that the required number of faulty ciphertexts necessary to recover each round key with the proposed DFA or W. Li *et al.*'s DFA. To recover the round key, our DFA needs eight faulty ciphertexts in most of the simulation results. Thus, roughly 33 faulty ciphertexts are sufficient to retrieve the 128-bit master secret key.

Table 1. Simulation result : the required number of faulty ciphertexts

No.	Proposed DFA					W. Li *et al.*'s DFA				
	$\sharp FC_{13}$	$\sharp FC_{12}$	$\sharp FC_{11}$	$\sharp FC_{10}$	$\sharp FC_{MK}$	$\sharp FC_{13}$	$\sharp FC_{12}$	$\sharp FC_{11}$	$\sharp FC_{10}$	$\sharp FC_{MK}$
1	8	8	8	8	32	13	12	13	8	46
2	8	8	8	9	33	14	17	18	8	57
3	8	8	8	8	32	13	10	8	11	42
4	8	9	8	8	33	10	10	10	11	41
5	8	8	8	8	32	10	10	10	9	39
6	8	8	8	8	32	7	12	12	15	46
7	8	8	8	9	33	9	8	10	11	38
8	8	8	9	8	32	12	11	9	10	42
9	8	8	8	8	32	9	11	13	12	45
10	8	8	8	8	32	12	12	12	11	47

* $\sharp FC_i$ and * $\sharp FC_{MK}$: the number of faulty ciphertexts to recover ek_i and MK.

When we make 1000 simulations, Table 2 shows that most trials need just eight faulty ciphertexts to recover each round key. For example, among 1000 simulations to recover the final round key, 929 simulations require eight faulty ciphertexts, 34 simulations require nine and the seven simulations require ten. As you can see from Table 2, about 8.1 faulty ciphertexts are sufficient to recover each round key and about 32.38 faulty ciphertexts are enough to recover the 128-bit master secret key. These results surpass those of the previous research, W. Li *et al.*'s DFA on ARIA. In the simulation of the faulty model in the key expansion procedure, we can also recover each round key, which shows the same result as that of the encryption case.

Table 2. Simulation result : proportion of the required faulty ciphertexts

	8 faulty ciphertext	9 faulty ciphertext	10 faulty ciphertext	11 faulty ciphertext
Last Round (ek_{13})	929	34	7	-
12-th Round (ek_{12})	910	85	5	-
11-th Round (ek_{11})	906	87	6	1
10-th Round (ek_{10})	901	92	7	-

For the practical DFA experiment, we used ATmega128 microcontroller [14] on which a software ARIA algorithm was implemented. In order to inject a fault using a laser, an EzLaze 3 laser system [15] was used. For the simple injection of a fault, a target ATmega128 chip was decapsulated in advance. Fig. 5 shows the experimental setting for DFA on ARIA.

The combination of the laser and an optical microscope enable to inject a laser beam to desired locations, such as RAM, CPU, EEPROM, and BUS. The EzLaze 3 system can inject a laser beam with a several *ns* laser pulse, and we can control the time of a laser beam injection in steps of 10 *ns* using a function

Fig. 5. Experimental setting for DFA

generator. And, the microcontroller is controlled by a computer which can send some commands and inputs through serial line. Fig. 6 shows the power trace for the encryption processing of the ARIA and several I/O signals.

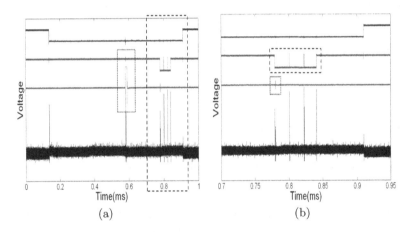

Fig. 6. Signals captured by oscilloscope: (a)Original signal, (b)Zoomed signal

Fig. 6(a) shows the power trace of the whole ARIA encryption process (low state of the first top signal, 0.13ms ∼ 0.91ms). The dotted square indicates the trigger signal for the laser injection. The EzLaze 3 laser injection tool shoots a laser beam at the target chip after about 200μs delay. Fig. 6(b) shows a close up of the dashed square of the Fig. 6(a). In Fig. 6(b), the dashed square includes the I/O signal for the distinction of the 11-th round ARIA round functions: the round key addition (0.78ms ∼ 0.80ms), the substitution layer (0.80ms ∼ 0.82ms), and the diffusion layer (0.82ms ∼ 0.84ms). And, the dotted square in Fig. 6(b) indicates the real laser injection point, which is located in the round key addition.

As a result of the laser injection, we can get the faulty ciphertexts as shown in Fig. 7. The underlined outputs are faulty ciphertexts. As can be seen from Fig. 7, only seven bytes (3, 4, 6, 8, 9, 13 and 14-th) are different from the correct ciphertext, which results means that the laser fault only injected MSB one byte of the intermediate data before the 11-th round diffusion layer. As explained earlier, our DFA can get the seven bytes round key of the final round using the outputs in the Fig. 7. Finally, we could retrieve all 128-bit master keys with four applications of the experimental DFA on ARIA, changing the position of the fault injection. In the experiment, controlling the time of a laser beam injection, we could change the position of the faulty injection randomly.

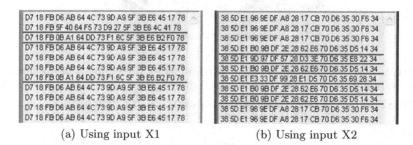

(a) Using input X1   (b) Using input X2

Fig. 7. Outputs of the target chip with the fault injection using laser system (master key : 000102030405060708090A0B0C0D0E0F, X1 : 00112233445566778899AA-BBCCDDEEFF, X2 : FFEEDDCCBBAA99887766554433221100)

5   Conclusion

This paper proposed a more efficient DFA for the block cipher ARIA algorithm. Unlike W. Li *et al.*'s method, in which they compute the intermediate values of each round, our DFA directly tries to recover the round keys. The proposed DFA to recover the final round key is based on the fact that the seven output byte differences of two outputs in the diffusion layer, resulting from a single byte input error, are the same. In order to recover three more round keys after finding out the final round key, we introduced some tricks. To simplify guessing of the round keys, we interchange the inverse computational order of the two round functions, the round key addition and the diffusion layer. Thus, we can directly retrieve the master secret key with only 33 faulty ciphertexts, according to simulation results. Also, our experimental results on a commercial microcontroller demonstrate that the DFA based on random byte error really threatens software implementation of cryptographic algorithms. Furthermore, our DFA model can be extended to the key expansion algorithm of ARIA and get the same result with the fault attack on the encryption process. In future work, DFA experiments on hardware implemented ARIA and other fault injection techniques should be considered.

References

1. Moradi, A., Shalmani, M.T.M., Salmasizadeh, M.: A Generalized Method of Differential Fault Attack Against AES Cryptosystem. In: Goubin, L., Matsui, M. (eds.) CHES 2006. LNCS, vol. 4249, pp. 91–100. Springer, Heidelberg (2006)
2. Chen, C., Yen, S.: Differential Fault Analysis on AES Key Schedule and Some Countermeasures. In: Safavi-Naini, R., Seberry, J. (eds.) ACISP 2003. LNCS, vol. 2727, pp. 118–129. Springer, Heidelberg (2003)
3. Giraud, C.: DFA on AES. In: Dobbertin, H., Rijmen, V., Sowa, A. (eds.) AES 2005. LNCS, vol. 3373, pp. 27–41. Springer, Heidelberg (2005)
4. Kwon, D., Kim, J., Park, S., Sung, S., Sohn, Y., Song, J., Yeom, Y., Yoon, E., Lee, S., Lee, J., Chee, S., Han, D., Hong, J.: New Block Cipher: ARIA. In: Lim, J.-I., Lee, D.-H. (eds.) ICISC 2003. LNCS, vol. 2971, pp. 432–445. Springer, Heidelberg (2004)
5. Biham, E., Shamir, A.: Differential Fault Analysis of Secret Key Cryptosystems. In: Kaliski Jr., B.S. (ed.) CRYPTO 1997. LNCS, vol. 1294, pp. 513–525. Springer, Heidelberg (1997)
6. Biham, E., Granboulan, L., Nguyên, P.: Impossible Fault Analysis of RC4 and Differential Fault Analysis of RC4. In: Gilbert, H., Handschuh, H. (eds.) FSE 2005. LNCS, vol. 3557, pp. 359–367. Springer, Heidelberg (2005)
7. Piret, G., Quisquater, J.-J.: A Differential Fault Attack Technique against SPN Structures, with Application to the AES and KHAZAD. In: Walter, C.D., Koç, Ç.K., Paar, C. (eds.) CHES 2003. LNCS, vol. 2779, pp. 77–88. Springer, Heidelberg (2003)
8. Chen, H., Wu, W., Feng, D.: Differential Fault Analysis on CLEFIA. In: Qing, S., Imai, H., Wang, G. (eds.) ICICS 2007. LNCS, vol. 4861, pp. 284–295. Springer, Heidelberg (2007)
9. Blömer, J., Seifert, J.-P.: Fault Based Cryptanalysis of the Advanced Encryption Standard (AES). In: Wright, R.N. (ed.) FC 2003. LNCS, vol. 2742, pp. 162–181. Springer, Heidelberg (2003)
10. Hemme, L.: A Differential Fault Attack Against Early Rounds of (Triple-)DES. In: Joye, M., Quisquater, J.-J. (eds.) CHES 2004. LNCS, vol. 3156, pp. 254–267. Springer, Heidelberg (2004)
11. Dusart, P., Letourneux, G., Vivolo, O.: Differential Fault Analysis on A.E.S. In: Zhou, J., Yung, M., Han, Y. (eds.) ACNS 2003. LNCS, vol. 2846, pp. 293–306. Springer, Heidelberg (2003)
12. Shirai, T., Shibutani, K., Akishita, T., Moriai, S., Iwata, T.: The 128-Bit Block-cipher CLEFIA (Extended Abstract). In: Biryukov, A. (ed.) FSE 2007. LNCS, vol. 4593, pp. 181–195. Springer, Heidelberg (2007)
13. Li, W., Gu, D., Li, J.: Differential fault analysis on the ARIA algorithm. Information Sciences 178, 3727–3737 (2008)
14. Atmel Corp. webpage, http://www.atmel.com/dyn/resources/prod_documents/doc2467.pdf
15. New Wave Research webpage, http://www.new-wave.com/1nwrProduct-s/EZLaze3.html

Multi-Level Controlled Signature

Pairat Thorncharoensri[1,2], Willy Susilo[1,*], and Yi Mu[1]

[1] School of Computer Science & Software Engineering, University of Wollongong,
Australia
pt78@uowmail.edu.au, {wsusilo,ymu}@uow.edu.au
[2] Department of Information Systems, Faculty of Business,
City University of Hong Kong, Hong Kong
pthornch@cityu.edu.hk

Abstract. In this work, we present and establish a new primitive called *Multi-level Controlled Signature*. This primitive allows a signer to specify a security level to limit the verifiability of the signature. This primitive works as follows. Without losing generality, we assume the security levels of a group of users are defined in ascending order, where "A" represents the lowest security level and "Z" represents the highest security level, respectively. When a signer signs a message by specifying a security level "C", all users who have a security level greater than "C" will be able to verify while other users whose security levels are "A", "B" or "C" cannot verify the authenticity of this message. This primitive resembles some similarities with other existing primitives, such as Hierarchical Identity-based Encryption/Signatures, policy-based cryptography, but we stress that this primitive is unique in the sense that other primitives cannot satisfy all requirements as stated above efficiently. In this paper, we develop a security model for such a primitive. We present two concrete constructions that are proven secure in our model. The first scheme has a constant signature size, while the second scheme is more efficient in terms of verifier's private information. We provide a comparison between our schemes and illustrate where each scheme is applicable in the real world scenario.

1 Introduction

Multi-level marketing (MLM) is a marketing strategy that is aimed at compensating promoters of selling companies not only for product sales they personally generate, but also for the sales of others they introduced to the company. Consider a scenario where Alice, who is a representative at the MLM company, would like to inform the amount of sale to her "upline" distributors (meaning that all distributors who are higher than her level). In this situation, Alice would like to convince only people in the "upline" connection, rather than everyone who has a level below her. In this situation, Alice's signature on the message must be "designated" to everyone whose level is higher than her.

---

[*] This work is supported by the ARC Future Fellowship (FT0991397).

D.H. Lee and M. Yung (Eds.): WISA 2012, LNCS 7690, pp. 96–110, 2012.
© Springer-Verlag Berlin Heidelberg 2012

Note that at the first glance, the notion of designated verifier signature, as introduced in [10], might be used to solve this situation by allowing Alice to sign her message multiple times designated to *all* members who have higher level than her. Nevertheless, in this situation, Alice may not know who are the other members whose level are higher than her (other than the one who is directed above her level, i.e. the person who introduced her to the company). Hence, the notion of designated verifier signature cannot really solve this problem.

According to the best of our knowledge, there exists no cryptographic primitives that can be used to solve the above problem efficiently. Therefore, in this work, we introduce the notion of *multi-level controlled signatures* to solve the aforementioned problem. We present the security model to capture this notion, together with two concrete schemes. Our first scheme benefits from its constant signature size, and this scheme is suitable for an organization where there are many security levels involved. The second scheme benefits from the short credential involved and therefore, it is suitable for an organization where the security levels involved are not widely spread.

1.1   Related Work

In this section, we will review some work in the literature that are closely related to our proposed notion.

The notion of policy-based cryptography was put forth by Bagga and Molva in [1]. This notion includes policy-based encryption schemes and policy-based signature schemes. In the policy-based signature schemes, a signer can only sign a message if he/she satisfies the required policy. Policy-based signatures ensure the security of the scheme from the signer's point of view, namely message integrity, authenticity and non-repudiability. In policy-based signatures, any verifier can verify the authenticity of the message, but nobody can forge the authenticity of the signatures that have been signed by a signer that satisfies a stated policy. This is in contrast to multi-level controlled signatures. In multi-level controlled signatures, the policy will guard the verifiers, and hence, only verifiers who satisfy some policies will be able to verify the authenticity of the message.

The other related notion is the notion of Hierarchical Identity-based Encryption/Signature. The Hierarchical Identity-based Encryption (HIBE) system [8,9,3,5] is a unified concept between a hierarchy system and Identity-based Encryption (IBE) system [11,4] where an identity at level k of the hierarchical system can issue a private key for its descendant identity, but it cannot decrypt a message on behalf of other identity except its descendants. At the first sight, it seems quite straightforward to construct multi-level controlled signatures from HIBE and a standard signature scheme. This is done as follows. First, a public key generator (PKG) in HIBE assumes the role of a trusted authority (TA) in the scheme. PKG generates HIBE private keys as credentials for verifiers. Second, a signer S generates the signature by signing on a concatenation of the actual message M and some uniformly random dummy message M_R in the plaintext space of the HIBE scheme. Next, by using ID as the security level, S uses HIBE to encrypt M_R with ID as his/her public key. Finally, the multi-level controlled signature consists of the signature on $M||M_R$ and the HIBE ciphertext of M_R. Without having the credentials allowing to decrypt the HIBE ciphertext and to obtain M_R, the signature cannot be verified. The above generic construction seems to be correct, but unfortunately there is a big drawback to the scheme. If a verifier who holds the valid credentials (and hence, allowing him/her to decrypt the HIBE ciphertext) exposes M_R with the above signature, then everyone can verify this signature without the need of having the credentials to decrypt the HIBE ciphertext. This contradicts with the security model of the multi-level controlled signature, which will be presented in the Section 3. Essentially, this is the basic security requirement of the multi-level controlled signature to avoid someone from exposing some information that will be affecting the security of the scheme. Hence, it is clear that the above generic construction scheme is indeed insecure in the required security model.

The Hierarchical Identity-based Signature (HIBS) scheme [8,6,9] is a natural conversion from the HIBE scheme. Similar to the HIBE, the ancestor identity of the hierarchical system can issue a private key for its descendant identity. However, it cannot sign on a message on behalf of other identities except its descendants. The purpose of HIBE systems is to reduce the bottleneck in a large network, where the PKG of the IBE system is applied, and to limit the scope of key escrow. For the HIBS, it is, however, similar to policy-based signature schemes where it only provides for the signer in the message integrity, and the authenticity and non-repudiation but not the authorization for the verifier.

The other work related to this notion is the designated verifier signature proofs, as mentioned earlier. It was introduced by Jakobsson, Sako and Impagliazzo in [10]. A proof does not provide only authentication of a message but it also provides the deniability property that allows the signer to deny the signature (since the verifier can also generate such a proof). Hence, only the designated verifier can verify the proof on the message.

1.2   Our Contributions

In this paper, we introduce the notion of multi-level controlled signature (MLCS) schemes and present two concrete constructions of MLCS schemes. The notion of MLCS scheme allows only receivers, who hold a credential for a certain security level specified by the sender (or signer), to verify the authenticity of the signed message. Furthermore, we define and formalize the notion of MLCS scheme and its security model. Our concrete constructions are proven secure in our model.

Organization of The Paper

The paper is organized as follows. In the next section, we review some preliminaries that will be used throughout this paper. In the Section 3, we introduce the definition of MLCS and its security notions. Next, the first concrete scheme together with its security proof will be provided in Section 4. Then, in the Section 5, we will provide the second concrete scheme and its security proof. Finally, the comparison of two concrete schemes and conclusion of the paper will be presented in the last section.

2   Preliminaries

2.1   Notation

Throughout this paper, the following notations will be used. When we say that a function $f : \mathbb{N} \to \mathbb{R}$ is *negligible*, it means that, for all constant $c > 0$ and for all sufficiently large n, $f(n) < \frac{1}{n^c}$. Let $poly(.)$ be a deterministic polynomial function. For all polynomials $poly(k)$ and for all sufficiently large k, we say that q is polynomial-time in k if $q \le poly(1^k)$. Let $l \xleftarrow{\$} L$ denote the operation of picking l at random from a (finite) set L.

2.2   Bilinear Pairing

We denote by $\mathbb{G}_1$ and $\mathbb{G}_2$ cyclic multiplicative groups. Their generators are g_1 and g_2, respectively. Let p be a prime and the order of both generators. Let $\mathbb{G}_T$ be another cyclic multiplicative group with the same order p. We denote by $\hat{e} : \mathbb{G}_1 \times \mathbb{G}_2 \to \mathbb{G}_T$ a bilinear mapping with the following properties:

1. *Bilinearity:* $\hat{e}(g_1^a, g_2^b) = \hat{e}(g_1, g_2)^{ab}$ for all $g_1 \in \mathbb{G}_1, g_2 \in \mathbb{G}_2$, $a, b \in \mathbb{Z}_p$.
2. *Non-degeneracy:* There exists $g_1 \in \mathbb{G}_1$ *and* $g_2 \in \mathbb{G}_2$ such that $\hat{e}(g_1, g_2) \neq 1$.
3. *Computability:* There exists an efficient algorithm to compute $\hat{e}(g_1, g_2)$ for all $g_1 \in \mathbb{G}_1$, $g_2 \in \mathbb{G}_2$.

Note that there exists $\varphi(.)$ function which maps $\mathbb{G}_1$ to $\mathbb{G}_2$ or vice versa in one time unit.

2.3   Complexity Assumptions

Definition 1 (Computation Diffie-Hellman (CDH) Problem). *Given a 3-tuple* $(g, g^x, g^y \in \mathbb{G}_1)$ *as input, output* $g^{x \cdot y}$. *An algorithm $\mathcal{A}$ has advantage ϵ' in solving the CDH problem if*

$$\Pr[\mathcal{A}(g, g^x, g^y) = g^{x \cdot y}] \ge \epsilon'$$

where the probability is over the random choice of $x, y \in \mathbb{Z}_q^*$ and the random bits consumed by $\mathcal{A}$.

Assumption 1. Computation Diffie-Hellman Assumption [7,2]   We say that the (t, ϵ')-CDH assumption holds if no PPT algorithm with time complexity $t(.)$ has advantage at least ϵ' in solving the CDH problem.

Definition 2 (Decision Bilinear Diffie-Hellman (DBDH) Problem). *Given a random 4-tuple* $(g, g^x, g^y, g^z) \in \mathbb{G}_1$ *and a random integer $Z \in \mathbb{G}_T$ as input, decide whether or not $Z = \hat{e}(g, g)^{xyz}$. An algorithm $\mathcal{A}$ is said to (t, ϵ) solves the DBDH problem in $\mathbb{G}_1, \mathbb{G}_T$, if $\mathcal{A}$ runs in time t, and*

$$\left| \Pr[\mathcal{A}(g, g^x, g^y, g^z, Z = \hat{e}(g, g)^{xyz}) = 1] - \Pr\left[\mathcal{A}\left(g, g^x, g^y, g^z, Z = \hat{e}(g, g)^d\right) = 1\right] \right| \ge \epsilon,$$

where the probability is taken over the random choices of $x, y, z, d \in \mathbb{Z}_p$, $g \in \mathbb{G}_1$, and the random bits consumed by $\mathcal{A}$.

Assumption 2. Decision Bilinear Diffie-Hellman Assumption   We say that the (t, ϵ')-DBDH assumption in $\mathbb{G}_1, \mathbb{G}_T$ holds if there is no PPT algorithm with time complexity $t(.)$ has advantage at least ϵ' in solving the DBDH problem.

3   Multi-Level Controlled Signature Schemes (MLCS)

Model

Let TA be a trusted authority who issues credentials associated with a security level in the multi-level security system. In multi-level controlled signature schemes, there are three main players called a signer, a verifier and a trusted authority TA. A signer S generates a signature, which can be verified *only* by a verifier V who holds a credential satisfying the multi-level security policy. TA is responsible to issue a credential for V. Let A_V denote a security level in the multi-level security policy. We define MP to be a multi-level security policy which contains a policy that indicates a level of security clearance of the verifier. Without losing generality, we assume that the order of the security levels is increasing, for example, the higher number is the higher security level[1]. Let $MP = $ "$A_V > n$" where n is the number indicated the security level. Generally, we can use other type of index or symbol to indicate the security level. In the following, we provide a definition of multi-level controlled signature scheme as follows.

Definition 3. *A multi-level controlled signature scheme Σ is an 6-tuple (Setup, TKeyGen, SKeyGen, CreGen, Sign, Verify) such that*

Signature Scheme Setup
  - *System Parameters Generation (Setup):*
    On input a security parameter $\mathcal{K}$, a PPT algorithm named Setup outputs the system parameters param. That is, param $\leftarrow$ Setup($1^{\mathcal{K}}$).
  - *TA Key Generator (TKeyGen) :*
    On input the system parameters param, a PPT algorithm named TKeyGen outputs strings (sk_{TA}, pk_{TA}) where they denote a secret key and a public key of trusted authority, respectively. That is, $\{pk_{TA}, sk_{TA}\} \leftarrow TKeyGen(\text{param})$.
  - *Signer Key Generator (SKeyGen) :*
    On input the system parameters param, a PPT algorithm named SKeyGen outputs strings (sk_S, pk_S) where they denote a secret key and a public key of a signer, respectively. That is, $\{pk_S, sk_S\} \leftarrow SKeyGen(\text{param})$.
  - *Verifier Credential Generator (CreGen) :*
    On input the system parameters param, the TA's public key, and an assertion A_V indicated a security level of verifier, a PPT algorithm named CreGen outputs a credential for verifier VCR. That is, $VCR \leftarrow CreGen(\text{param}, pk_{TA}, sk_{TA}, A_V)$.

---

[1] We note that for a decreasing order security levels, our scheme can be modified trivially.

Multi-level Controlled Signature Signing ($Sign$):
> $Sign$ is a PPT algorithm that, on input the system parameters **param**, the trusted authority's public key pk_{TA}, the signer's secret key sk_S, the signer's public key pk_S, a message M and the multi-level security policy MP, it outputs signer's signature σ. That is, $\sigma \leftarrow Sign(\text{param}, M, sk_S, pk_S, pk_{TA}, MP)$.

Multi-level Controlled Signature Verification ($Verify$):
> $Verify$ is an algorithm that, on input the system parameters **param**, the trusted authority's public key pk_{TA}, the signer's public key pk_S, the multi-level security policy MP, a credential VCR, a message M and a signature σ, it outputs a verification decision $d \in \{Accept, Reject\}$. That is, $d \leftarrow Verify(\text{param}, M, \sigma, pk_{TA}, pk_S, MP, VCR)$.

3.1   Security Model

Before modelling the ability of the adversaries in breaking the security of MLCS schemes, we first describe the oracles used in the security model as follows:

$\mathcal{SSO}$ **oracle:** An adversary $\mathcal{A}$ can make at most q_S query to $\mathcal{SSO}$ for signatures σ on its choice of a message M. $\mathcal{SSO}$ outputs a response by running the $Sign$ algorithm to generate a signature σ on a message M corresponding with pk_{TA}, pk_S and MP. Then, $\mathcal{SSO}$ returns σ to $\mathcal{A}$.

$\mathcal{VCO}$ **oracle:** $\mathcal{A}$ can make at most q_C query to $\mathcal{SSO}$ for credentials VCR corresponding to a security level A_V. $\mathcal{VCO}$ responds $\mathcal{A}$ with a corresponding credential VCR.

$\mathcal{VSO}$ **oracle:** By giving σ, M to $\mathcal{VSO}$ as inputs, $\mathcal{A}$ can make at most q_V query for the verification of a signature σ. $\mathcal{VSO}$ returns with `Accept` or `Reject` depending on the validation of signature σ and the message M.

Unforgeability. The unforgeability property of MLCS schemes is to prevent an attacker, who has an access to the credential oracle, to generate a new multi-level controlled signature σ_* on a message M^*. Formally, the unforgeability in this model provides an assurance that one, with an access to $\mathcal{SSO}$ oracle, $\mathcal{VCO}$ oracle, the signer's public parameters pk_S and the trusted authority's public key, should be unable to produce a new multi-level controlled signature on a message M^* even with arbitrarily chosen multi-level security policy MP, a message M and the entire credentials as inputs.

Let $CM\text{-}A$ denote the adaptive chosen message and credential exposure attack and let $EUF\text{-}MLCS$ denote the existential unforgeability of MLCS scheme. The following experiment between the adversary $\mathcal{A}^{CM\text{-}A}_{EUF\text{-}MLCS}$ and a simulator $\mathcal{F}$ models a security against existential unforgeability under the adaptive chosen message and credential exposure attack.

With an adaptive strategy, $\mathcal{A}$ arbitrarily makes queries to $\mathcal{SSO}$ and $\mathcal{VCO}$ oracle on its choice of a message M. Let $\overline{VCR}$ be the credentials for the entire security level. After the queries process, assume that $\mathcal{A}$ outputs a forged signature σ_* on a message M^* with respect to the public key pk_S and multi-level security policy MP^*. $\mathcal{A}$ wins the experiment if:

1. $Accept \leftarrow Verify(M^*, \sigma_*, pk_S, MP^*, \overline{VCR})$.
2. σ_* is not the output of that $\mathcal{A}$ previously made a request to SSO oracle.

Let $Succ^{CM\text{-}A}_{EUF\text{-}MLCS}(.)$ be the success probability function of that $\mathcal{A}^{CM\text{-}A}_{EUF\text{-}MLCS}$ wins the above experiment.

Definition 4. *A MLCS scheme is (t,q_H,q_S,q_C,ϵ)-secure existentially unforgeable under a chosen message and credential exposure attack if there are no PPT adversary $\mathcal{A}^{CM\text{-}A}_{EUF\text{-}MLCS}$ such that the success probability $Succ^{CM\text{-}A}_{EUF\text{-}MLCS}(k) = \epsilon$ is negligible in k, where $\mathcal{A}^{CM\text{-}A}_{EUF\text{-}MLCS}$ runs in time at most t, makes at most q_H hash queries, q_S signing queries, and q_C verification queries.*

Coalition-Resistance. In this section, we will describe the coalition-resistant property of MLCS schemes. This property is to prevent an attacker, as a group of corrupted credential holders (verifiers), to verify a multi-level controlled signature σ_* on a message M^* with a multi-level security policy MP, in which the attacker does not have a credential satisfied the security level indicated in MP.

Let $CR\text{-}MLCS$ denote the existential coalition-resistance of MLCS scheme. Let $\mathcal{A}^{CMP\text{-}A}_{CRI\text{-}PCS}$ be the adaptively chosen message and chosen multi-level security policy distinguisher and let $\mathcal{F}$ be a simulator. The following game between $\mathcal{F}$ and $\mathcal{A}$ describes the existential coalition-resistance of MLCS scheme under a chosen message and chosen multi-level security policy attack. We divide the game into two phases and run them as follows:

1. **Phase 1:** With any adaptive strategies, $\mathcal{A}$ arbitrarily issues a request of queries to SSO and VCO oracles. The oracles response as per their design.
2. **Challenge:** After the first phase, $\mathcal{A}$ outputs M^* and $MP^* = \text{``}A_V \geq l\text{''}$ such that:
   a. On input MP^* and M^*, $\mathcal{A}$ never issued a request for a multi-level controlled signature to SSO queries.
   b. With $MP^* = \text{``}A_V \geq l\text{''}$, $\mathcal{A}$ can issue a request of credential to VCO queries for a security level $A_V < l$.

   If the above condition is satisfied, $\mathcal{F}$ chooses a random bit $b \overset{\$}{\leftarrow} \{0,1\}$. If $b = 1$ then, on input a multi-level security policy MP^* and a message M^*, $\mathcal{F}$ issues a request for a multi-level controlled signature to SSO queries. Then $\mathcal{F}$ responds $\mathcal{A}$ with σ^* as an output from SSO queries. Otherwise, on input a multi-level security policy MP^*, a message M^*, a valid policy-controlled signature σ on message M^* with policy MP^* and a credentials VCR, $\mathcal{F}$ computes a (simulated) invalid multi-level controlled signature σ^*. Then $\mathcal{F}$ responds $\mathcal{A}$ with σ^*.
3. **Phase 2:** In this phase, $\mathcal{A}$ can arbitrarily return to *Phase 1* or *Challenge*. With one condition, at least one set of challenges M^*, MP^*, σ^* must be valid and satisfy the condition in the challenge phase.
4. **Guessing:** $\mathcal{A}$ finally outputs a guess b' based on a challenge M^*, MP^*, σ^*. The distinguisher wins the game if $b = b'$.

We denote by $Succ^{CMP\text{-}A}_{CR\text{-}MLCS}(.)$ the success probability function of that $\mathcal{A}^{CMP\text{-}A}_{CR\text{-}MLCS}$ wins the above experiment.

Definition 5. *A MLCS scheme is* $(\mathsf{t},q_H,q_S,q_C,\epsilon)$*-secure existentially coalition-resistance under a chosen message and chosen multi-level security policy attack if there are no PPT distinguisher* $\mathcal{A}_{CR\text{-}MLCS}^{CMP\text{-}A}$ *such that the success probability* $Succ_{CR\text{-}MLCS}^{CMP\text{-}A}(k)=|\Pr[b=b']-\Pr[b\neq b']|=\epsilon$ *is negligible in* k, *where* $\mathcal{A}_{CR\text{-}MLCS}^{CMP\text{-}A}$ *runs in time at most* t, *make at most* q_H *hash queries,* q_S *signing queries, and* q_C *verification queries.*

4   The First MLCS Scheme

In this section, we present our first concrete construction of MLCS schemes. Let $H:\{0,1\}^*\to\mathbb{G}_1$ be a collision-resistant hash function. Let $h:\{0,1\}^*\to\mathbb{Z}_p^*$ be a collision-resistant hash function. Let $\mathbb{G}_1$ and $\mathbb{G}_T$ denote two groups of prime order p. Let $\hat{e}$ be the bilinear mapping function, which maps $\mathbb{G}_1$ to $\mathbb{G}_T$. The above mapping function is defined as $\hat{e}:\mathbb{G}_1\times\mathbb{G}_1\to\mathbb{G}_T$. The scheme is described as follows.

Setup: On input a security parameter $\mathcal{K}$, a trusted third party randomly chooses a prime $p\approx poly(1^{\mathcal{K}})$. Choose a random generator $g\in\mathbb{G}_1$ and a bilinear mapping function $\hat{e}$. Select two hash functions $H(.)$ and $h(.)$ Let us denote by param $=(p,\hat{e},g,H,h)$ the system parameters. Then, *Setup* returns param.

TKeyGen: Let n be a number of security levels. On input a system parameters param, a trusted authority TA randomly generates a private key sk_{TA} and a public key pk_{TA} for each security level as follows: select random integers $\mu_1,...,\mu_n,\gamma_1,...,\gamma_n,a,b,c_1,...,c_n\in\mathbb{Z}_p$. Let $pk_{TA}=(U_1=g^{\mu_1},...,U_n=g^{\mu_n},W_1=g^{\gamma_1},...,W_n=g^{\gamma_n},\mathbb{A}=g^a,\mathbb{B}=g^b)$ denote a public key. Then, $TKeyGen$ returns $sk_{TA}=(\mu_1,...,\mu_n,\gamma_1,...,\gamma_n,a,b,c_1,...,c_n)$ as a private key of the trusted authority and $pk_{TA}=(U_1,...,U_n,W_1,...,W_n,\mathbb{A},\mathbb{B})$ as a public key of the trusted authority.

SKeyGen: On input a system parameters param, a signer S randomly generates a private key sk_S and a public key pk_S as follows. First, choose a random integer $x\in\mathbb{Z}_p$. Let $\mathbb{X}=g^x;\mathbb{W}=\mathbb{A}^x;\mathbb{U}=\mathbb{B}^x$ denote a public key. Then, $SKeyGen$ set $sk_S=x$ as a private key of the signer and $pk_S=(\mathbb{X},\mathbb{W},\mathbb{U})$ as a public key of the signer. Finally, $SKeyGen$ returns sk_S,pk_S.

CreGen: Let A_V indicate a security level of verifier, for example, $A_V=$"D". On input a system parameters param, the trusted authority's public key pk_{TA}, the trusted authority's private key sk_{TA} and a security level of verifier $A_V=l$ that verifier is satisfied to obtain, a trusted authority TA randomly generates a set of credential strings $VCR=(CV_1,...,CV_l,CR_1,...,CR_l)$, where i is an index of security level, as follows: TA randomly selects $\nu_1,...,\nu_l\in\mathbb{Z}_p^*$ and computes each credential $CV_i=g^{c_i\cdot\nu_i}$; $CR_i=g^{(\mu_i\cdot\gamma_i-\mu_{i-1}\cdot\gamma_{i-1}-a\cdot c_i\cdot\nu_i)/(b)}$ and then returns $VCR=(CV_1,...,CV_l,CR_1,...,CR_l)$ to the verifier as a credential for a security level assertion $A_V=l$. The verifier checks the validity of each CV_i and CR_i as follows:

$$\hat{e}(U_i,W_i)\stackrel{?}{=}\hat{e}(\mathbb{A},CV_i)\hat{e}(\mathbb{B},CR_i)\hat{e}(U_{i-1},W_{i-1}).$$

Sign: Given param, pk_{TA}, sk_S, pk_S, $MP = $ "$A_V \geq l$" and a message M, S computes a multi-level controlled signature σ on a message M as follows:

$$r, k \xleftarrow{\$} \mathbb{Z}_p, \ \sigma_1 = g^r, \ \sigma_2 = \mathbb{X}^r, \ \sigma_3 = \mathbb{W}^r, \ \sigma_4 = \mathbb{U}^r,$$
$$\Gamma = \sigma_1 ||\sigma_2||\sigma_3||\sigma_4||pk_S||pk_{TA}||MP, \ \sigma_5 = g^k, \ \sigma_6 = H(\Gamma)^x,$$
$$\sigma_7 = h(\hat{e}(U_l, W_l)^{x \cdot r}) + h(M||\Gamma||\sigma_5), \ \sigma_8 = k + \sigma_7 \cdot x.$$

The multi-level controlled signature on a message M is $\sigma = (\sigma_1, \sigma_2, \sigma_3, \sigma_4, \sigma_5, \sigma_6, \sigma_7, \sigma_8)$. S publishes M, σ, MP.

Verify: Let $VCR = CV_1, ..., CV_l, CR_1, ..., CR_l$, be a set of credentials that verifier possessed. Parse $\Gamma = \sigma_1||\sigma_2||\sigma_3||\sigma_4||pk_S||pk_{TA}||MP$. Given pk_S, pk_{TA}, pk_V, VCR, $MP = $ "$A_V \geq l$", σ and a message M, a verifier V checks whether

$$\hat{e}(\sigma_1, \mathbb{X}) \overset{?}{=} \hat{e}(\sigma_2, g), \ \hat{e}(\sigma_3, g) \overset{?}{=} \hat{e}(\sigma_2, \mathbb{A}), \ \hat{e}(\sigma_4, g) \overset{?}{=} \hat{e}(\sigma_2, \mathbb{B}),$$
$$\hat{e}(\sigma_6, g) \overset{?}{=} \hat{e}(H(\Gamma), \mathbb{X}), \ g^{\sigma_8} \overset{?}{=} \sigma_5 \cdot \mathbb{X}^{\sigma_7}$$
$$\sigma_7 \overset{?}{=} h(M||\Gamma||\sigma_5) + h(\hat{e}(\sigma_3, \prod_{i=1}^{l} CV_i)\hat{e}(\sigma_4, \prod_{i=1}^{l} CR_i)),$$

hold. If it does not hold, then V outputs `reject`. Otherwise, it outputs `accept`.

4.1 Security Analysis

Unforgeability

Theorem 1. *The above multi-level controlled signature scheme is existentially unforgeable under an adaptive chosen message and credential exposure attack if the CDH assumption holds in the random oracle model.*

Proof. Assume that there exists a forger algorithm $\mathcal{A}$ running the existentially unforgeable game defined in Section 3.1. Then we will show that, by using $\mathcal{A}$, an adversary $\mathcal{F}$ solves the CDH problem.

We now begin with the the construction of oracles. To begin with, $\mathcal{F}$ runs *Setup* and *TKeyGen* to obtain a system parameter param, a secret key sk_{TA} and a public key of TA. Next, on input g, g^x and g^y as an instance of the CDH problem, $\mathcal{F}$ sets $\mathbb{X} = g^x; \mathbb{W} = \mathbb{X}^a; \mathbb{U} = \mathbb{X}^b$ as the signer public key pk_S. $\mathcal{F}$ sets g^y as one of the answers for the hash query to the random oracle. Then, $\mathcal{F}$ construct oracles as follows:

$\mathcal{HO}$ **oracle:** On input a string Γ, if it is a request for a hash value of $H(\Gamma)$, $\mathcal{HO}$ oracle randomly choose $d \xleftarrow{\$} \{0, 1\}$ such that the probability of $d = 1$ is $\frac{1}{q_H}$. If $d = 1$, set $H(\Gamma) = g^y$ and return $H(\Gamma)$. Otherwise, $l \xleftarrow{\$} \mathbb{Z}_p$; $H(\Gamma) = g^l$ and return $H(\Gamma)$. In case of $h(\Gamma)$, $\mathcal{HO}$ chooses $\iota \xleftarrow{\$} \mathbb{Z}_p$ and then returns $h(\Gamma) = \iota$. Then $\mathcal{HO}$ keeps l and ι in the list and this list can be accessed only by $\mathcal{F}$.

$\mathcal{VCO}$ **queries:** On input a secret key sk_{TA}, $\mathcal{VCO}$ runs $CreGen$ to generate the credential VCR for the security level assertion $A_V = l$ and then returns VCR.

$\mathcal{SSO}$ **queries:** On input $MP =$ "$A_V \geq l$" and a message M, $\mathcal{SSO}$ computes a multi-level controlled signature as follows:

$$r, k \overset{\$}{\leftarrow} \mathbb{Z}_p, \ \sigma_1 = g^r, \ \sigma_2 = \mathbb{X}^r, \ \sigma_3 = \mathbb{W}^r, \ \sigma_4 = \mathbb{U}^r,$$
$$\Gamma = \sigma_1||\sigma_2||\sigma_3||\sigma_4||pk_S||pk_{TA}||MP.$$

Before processing the next step, on access to the list of l and ι, $\mathcal{F}$ checks whether $H(\Gamma) \overset{?}{=} g^y$. If it holds, output $\perp$. Otherwise, $\mathcal{F}$ gives l to $\mathcal{SSO}$. Next, $\mathcal{F}$ randomly selects $\iota' \overset{\$}{\leftarrow} \mathbb{Z}_p$; $K \overset{\$}{\leftarrow} \mathbb{G}_1$ and $\mathcal{F}$ adds $\iota', h(M||\Gamma||K)$ to the list. Then, $\mathcal{F}$ returns K to $\mathcal{SSO}$. As a result, $\mathcal{SSO}$ computes the rest of signature as follows:

$$z \overset{\$}{\leftarrow} \mathbb{Z}_p, \ \sigma_8 = z, \ \sigma_6 = \mathbb{X}^l, \ \sigma_7 = h(\hat{e}(\mathbb{X}, W_l)^{\mu_l \cdot r}) + h(M||\Gamma||K), \ \sigma_5 = g^{\sigma_8} \mathbb{X}^{-\sigma_7}.$$

At the end of the process, on input σ_5 from $\mathcal{SSO}$, $\mathcal{F}$ updates $\iota', h(M||\Gamma||\sigma_5)$ to the list. Hence, a multi-level controlled signature on message M is $\sigma = (\sigma_1, \sigma_2, \sigma_3, \sigma_4, \sigma_5, \sigma_6, \sigma_7, \sigma_8)$. $\mathcal{SSO}$ then responds with M, σ, MP.

Now, we begin the game by giving an access to the above oracles to $\mathcal{A}$. Assume that $\mathcal{A}$ always makes a query for a string or a message to $\mathcal{HO}$ oracle before it outputs a potential forgery, denoted by M^*, σ^*, MP^*. After executing an adaptive strategy with the above oracles, $\mathcal{A}$ outputs a forgery σ^* on a message M^* with respect to MP^*. $\mathcal{A}$ wins the game if a multi-level controlled signature σ^* on message M^* with respect to MP^* is valid and is not an output from the $\mathcal{SSO}$ queries.

We denote by ϵ the success probability $Succ_{EUF\text{-}MLCS}^{CM\text{-}A}(.)$ that $\mathcal{A}$ wins the game. Let e be the base of the natural logarithm. As we mentioned early, a query for a hash of a string or message to $\mathcal{HO}$ is always issued before $\mathcal{A}$ issues a query for a signature to $\mathcal{SSO}$ queries, hence, $q_H \geq q_S$. Now, we can analyze the success probability that $\mathcal{A}$ outputs a signature σ^* on message M^* with respect to MP^*, where $\sigma_6^* = H(\Gamma)^x = (g^y)^x$, and wins the above game as follows:

- E_1: *$\mathcal{F}$ does not abort during the issuing of queries to the $\mathcal{SSO}$.* The probability of this event $\Pr[E_1]$ is $(1 - \frac{1}{q_H})^{q_S}$. It is because $\mathcal{A}$ needs to have at least one query for $H(\Gamma)$ to output σ_6^* which is a part of forgery. Since $q_H \geq q_S$, the upper bound for $\mathcal{SSO}$ queries is then $q_H - 1$ and $\Pr[E_1] \geq (1 - \frac{1}{q_H})^{q_H - 1} \approx \frac{q_H}{e \cdot (q_H - 1)}$.
- E_2: *$\mathcal{F}$ does not abort after $\mathcal{A}$ output σ^*.* $\mathcal{F}$ aborts the experiment after $\mathcal{A}$ output σ^* when only $H(\Gamma) \neq g^y$. Therefore, the probability of this event is greater than $(1 - \frac{1}{q_H})^{q_H - 1} \approx \frac{q_H}{e \cdot (q_H - 1)}$.

To summarize the probability, $\mathcal{A}$ wins the above game and outputs a signature σ^* on a message M^*, where $H(\Gamma) = g^y$ and $\sigma_6^* = H(\Gamma)^x$, with a probability equal to

$\Pr[Succ^{CM-A}_{EUF-MLCS}] \cdot \Pr[Succ^{CM-A}_{EUF-MLCS}|E_1|E_2] \geq \epsilon(\frac{q_H}{e \cdot (q_H-1)})^2$. From the above results, $\mathcal{F}$ outputs $\sigma_6^* = H(\Gamma)^x = g^{xy}$ as an answer to CDH problem and the above success probability shows that our multi-level controlled signature scheme secures against existentially unforgeable under an adaptive chosen message and credential exposure attack if the success probability of solving CDH problem is negligible.

Coalition-Resistance

Theorem 2. *The above multi-level controlled signature scheme is existentially coalition-resistance against the adaptively chosen message and chosen multi-level security policy distinguisher $\mathcal{A}^{CMP-A}_{CR-MLCS}$ if the DBDH assumption is hold in the random oracle model.*

Due to the page limitation, please find the proof for Theorem 2 in the full version of this paper [12].

5   The Second MLCS Scheme

In this section, we present the second construction of MLCS schemes. The scheme is described as follows.

Setup: On input a security parameter $\mathcal{K}$, a trusted third party randomly selects a prime $p \approx poly(1^{\mathcal{K}})$. Choose a random generator $g \in \mathbb{G}_1$ and a bilinear mapping function $\hat{e}$. Select two hash functions $H(.)$ and $h(.)$ Let param $= (p, \hat{e}, g, H, h)$ denote the system parameters. Then, *Setup* returns param.

TKeyGen: Let n be a number of security levels. On input a system parameters param, a trusted authority TA randomly generates a private key sk_{TA} and a public key pk_{TA} for each security level as follows: select random integers $\mu, a, b, w_1, ..., w_n \in \mathbb{Z}_p$. Let $pk_{TA} = (U = g^\mu, \mathbb{A} = g^a, \mathbb{B} = g^b, W_1 = g^{w_1}, ..., W_n = g^{w_n}$ denote a public key. Then, *TKeyGen* returns $sk_{TA} = (\mu, a, b, w_1, ..., w_n)$ as a private key of the trusted authority and $pk_{TA} = (\mathbb{A}, \mathbb{B}, U, W_1, ..., W_n,)$ as a public key of the trusted authority.

SKeyGen: On input a system parameters param, a signer S randomly generates a private key sk_S and a public key pk_S as follows. Choose a random integer $x \in \mathbb{Z}_p$. Let set $pk_S = (\mathbb{X} = g^x, \mathbb{U} = U^x, \mathbb{W}_1 = W_1^x, ..., \mathbb{W}_n = W_n^x)$ to a public key. Then, *SKeyGen* returns $sk_S = x$ as a private key of the signer and $pk_S = (\mathbb{X}, \mathbb{U}, \mathbb{W}_1, ..., \mathbb{W}_n)$ as a public key of the signer.

CreGen: Let A_V indicates a security level of verifier. On input a system parameters param, the trusted authority's public key pk_{TA}, the trusted authority's private key sk_{TA} and a security level of verifier $A_V = l$ that verifier is satisfied to obtain, a trusted authority TA randomly generates a credential strings $VCR = (CV, CR)$ as follows: TA randomly selects $s \in \mathbb{Z}_p^*$ and computes each credential $CV = g^s$; $CR = g^{((a \cdot b - s \cdot \mu)/w_l)}$ and then returns $VCR = (CV, CR)$ to the verifier as a credential for a security level assertion $A_V = l$. Verifier checks the validity of CV, CR as follows:

$$\hat{e}(\mathbb{A}, \mathbb{B}) \stackrel{?}{=} \hat{e}(U, CV)\hat{e}(W_l, CR).$$

Sign: Given param, pk_{TA}, sk_S, pk_S, $MP = $ "$A_V \geq l$" and a message M, S computes a multi-level controlled signature σ on a message M as follows:

$$r, k \xleftarrow{\$} \mathbb{Z}_p, \; \sigma_1 = g^r, \; \sigma_2 = \mathbb{X}^r, \; \sigma_3 = (\mathbb{W}_l^r, ..., \mathbb{W}_n^r)\sigma_4 = \mathbb{U}^r,$$
$$\Gamma = \sigma_1||\sigma_2||\sigma_3||\sigma_4||pk_S||pk_{TA}||MP,$$
$$\sigma_5 = g^k, \; \sigma_6 = H(\Gamma)^x, \; \sigma_7 = h(\hat{e}(\mathbb{A}, \mathbb{B})^{x \cdot r}) + h(M||\Gamma||\sigma_5), \; \sigma_8 = k + \sigma_7 \cdot x.$$

The multi-level controlled signature on a message M is $\sigma = (\sigma_1, \sigma_2, \sigma_3, \sigma_4, \sigma_5, \sigma_6, \sigma_7, \sigma_8)$. S publishes M, σ, MP.

Verify: Let $VCR = (CV, CR)$ be a credential that verifier possessed for a security level "$A_V = t$", where $l \leq t \leq n$. Let prase $\Gamma = \sigma_1||\sigma_2||\sigma_3||\sigma_4||pk_S||pk_{TA}||MP$ Given pk_S, pk_{TA}, pk_V, VCR, $MP = $ "$A_V \geq l$", σ and a message M, a verifier V checks whether, for $i = l$ to n, $\hat{e}(\sigma_{3,i}, g) \stackrel{?}{=} \hat{e}(\sigma_2, W_i)$ and, then, check whether

$$\hat{e}(\sigma_1, \mathbb{X}) \stackrel{?}{=} \hat{e}(\sigma_2, g), \; \hat{e}(\sigma_4, g) \stackrel{?}{=} \hat{e}(\sigma_2, U), \; \hat{e}(\sigma_6, g) \stackrel{?}{=} \hat{e}(H(\Gamma), \mathbb{X}),$$
$$\sigma_7 \stackrel{?}{=} h(M||\Gamma||\sigma_5) + h(\hat{e}(\sigma_4, CV)\hat{e}(\sigma_{3,t}, CR)), \; g^{\sigma_8} \stackrel{?}{=} \sigma_5 \cdot \mathbb{X}^{\sigma_7}$$

hold. If it does not hold, then V outputs `reject`. Otherwise, it outputs `accept`.

5.1   Security Analysis

Unforgeability

Theorem 3. *Our second multi-level controlled signature scheme is existentially unforgeable under an adaptive chosen message and credential exposure attack if the CDH assumption holds in the random oracle model.*

Proof. Assume that there exists a forger algorithm $\mathcal{A}$ running the existentially unforgeability game defined in Section 3.1. Then we will show that, by using $\mathcal{A}$, an adversary $\mathcal{F}$ solves the CDH problem.

We now begin with the the construction of oracles. To begin with, $\mathcal{F}$ runs *Setup* and *TKeyGen* to obtain a system parameter param, a secret key sk_{TA} and a public key of TA. Next, on input g, g^x and g^y as an instance of the CDH problem, $\mathcal{F}$ sets $\mathbb{X} = g^x; \mathbb{U} = \mathbb{X}^\mu; \mathbb{W}_1 = \mathbb{X}^{w_1}; ...; \mathbb{W}_n = \mathbb{X}^{w_n}$ as the signer public key pk_S. $\mathcal{F}$ sets g^y as one of the answers for the hash query to the random oracle. Then, $\mathcal{F}$ constructs oracles as follows:

$\mathcal{HO}$ **oracle:** On input a string Γ, if it is a request for a hash value of $H(\Gamma)$, $\mathcal{HO}$ oracle randomly choose $d \xleftarrow{\$} \{0, 1\}$ such that the probability of $d = 1$ is $\frac{1}{q_H}$. If $d = 1$, set $H(\Gamma) = g^y$ and return $H(\Gamma)$. Otherwise, $l \xleftarrow{\$} \mathbb{Z}_p; H(\Gamma) = g^l$ and return $H(\Gamma)$. In case of $h(\Gamma)$, $\mathcal{HO}$ chooses $\iota \xleftarrow{\$} \mathbb{Z}_p$ and then returns $h(\Gamma) = \iota$. Then $\mathcal{HO}$ keeps l and ι in the list and this list can be accessed only by $\mathcal{F}$.

$\mathcal{VCO}$ **queries:** On input a secret key sk_{TA}, $\mathcal{VCO}$ runs $CreGen$ to generate the credential VCR for the security level assertion $A_V = l$ and then returns VCR.

$\mathcal{SSO}$ **queries:** On input $MP = $ "$A_V \geq l$" and a message M, $\mathcal{SSO}$ computes a multi-level controlled signature as follows:

$$r, k \xleftarrow{\$} \mathbb{Z}_p, \ \sigma_1 = g^r, \ \sigma_2 = \mathbb{X}^r, \ \sigma_3 = (\mathbb{W}_l^r, ..., \mathbb{W}_n^r), \ \sigma_4 = \mathbb{U}^r,$$
$$\Gamma = \sigma_1 || \sigma_2 || \sigma_3 || \sigma_4 || pk_S || pk_{TA} || MP.$$

Before processing the next step, on access to the list of l and ι, $\mathcal{F}$ checks whether $H(\Gamma) \stackrel{?}{=} g^y$. If hold, output $\perp$. Otherwise, $\mathcal{F}$ gives l to $\mathcal{SSO}$. Next, $\mathcal{F}$ randomly selects $\iota' \xleftarrow{\$} \mathbb{Z}_p$; $K \xleftarrow{\$} \mathbb{G}_1$ and $\mathcal{F}$ adds $\iota', h(M||\Gamma||K)$ to the list. Then, $\mathcal{F}$ returns K to $\mathcal{SSO}$. As a result, $\mathcal{SSO}$ computes the rest of signature as follows:

$$z \xleftarrow{\$} \mathbb{Z}_p, \ \sigma_8 = z, \ \sigma_6 = \mathbb{X}^l, \ \sigma_7 = h(\hat{e}(\mathbb{X}, \mathbb{A})^{b \cdot r}) + h(M||\Gamma||K), \ \sigma_5 = g^{\sigma_8} \mathbb{X}^{-\sigma_7}.$$

In the end of the process, on input σ_5 from $\mathcal{SSO}$, $\mathcal{F}$ updates $\iota', h(M||\Gamma||\sigma_5)$ to the list. Hence, a multi-level controlled signature on message M is $\sigma = (\sigma_1, \sigma_2, \sigma_3, \sigma_4, \sigma_5, \sigma_6, \sigma_7, \sigma_8)$. $\mathcal{SSO}$ then responds with M, σ, MP.

Now, we begin the game by giving an access to the above oracles to $\mathcal{A}$. Assume that $\mathcal{A}$ always make a query for a string or a message to $\mathcal{HO}$ oracle before it outputs a potential forgery, denoted by M^*, σ^*, MP^*. After executing an adaptive strategy with the above oracles, $\mathcal{A}$ outputs a forgery σ^* on a message M^* with respect to MP^*. $\mathcal{A}$ wins the game if a multi-level controlled signature σ^* on message M^* with respect to MP^* is valid and is not an output from the $\mathcal{SSO}$ queries.

We denote by ϵ the success probability $Succ_{EUF\text{-}MLCS}^{CM\text{-}A}(.)$ that $\mathcal{A}$ wins the game. Let e be the base of the natural logarithm. As we mentioned early, a query for a hash of a string or message to $\mathcal{HO}$ is always issued before $\mathcal{A}$ issues a query for a signature to $\mathcal{SSO}$ queries, hence, $q_H \geq q_S$. Now, we can analyze the success probability that $\mathcal{A}$ outputs a signature σ^* on message M^* with respect to MP^*, where $\sigma_6^* = H(\Gamma)^x = (g^y)^x$, and wins the above game as follows:

- E_1: $\mathcal{F}$ *does not abort during the issuing of queries to the $\mathcal{SSO}$*. The probability of this event $\Pr[E_1]$ is $(1 - \frac{1}{q_H})^{q_S}$. It is because $\mathcal{A}$ needs to have at least one query for $H(\Gamma)$ to output σ_6^* which is a part of forgery. Since $q_H \geq q_S$, the upper bound for $\mathcal{SSO}$ queries is then $q_H - 1$ and $\Pr[E_1] \geq (1 - \frac{1}{q_H})^{q_H - 1} \approx \frac{q_H}{e \cdot (q_H - 1)}$.

- E_2: $\mathcal{F}$ *does not abort after $\mathcal{A}$ output σ^**. $\mathcal{F}$ aborts the experiment after $\mathcal{A}$ output σ^* when only $H(\Gamma) \neq g^y$. Therefore, the probability of this event is greater than $(1 - \frac{1}{q_H})^{q_H - 1} \approx \frac{q_H}{e \cdot (q_H - 1)}$.

To summarize the probability, $\mathcal{A}$ wins the above game and outputs a signature σ^* on a message M^*, where $H(\Gamma) = g^y$ and $\sigma_6^* = H(\Gamma)^x$, with a probability equal to

$\Pr[Succ^{CM-A}_{EUF-MLCS}] \cdot \Pr[Succ^{CM-A}_{EUF-MLCS}|E_1|E_2] \geq \epsilon(\frac{q_H}{e \cdot (q_H - 1)})^2$. From the above results, $\mathcal{F}$ outputs $\sigma_6^* = H(\Gamma)^x = g^{xy}$ as an answer to CDH problem and the above success probability shows that our multi-level controlled signature scheme secures against existentially unforgeable under an adaptive chosen message and credential exposure attack if the success probability of solving CDH problem is negligible.

Coalition-Resistance

Theorem 4. *Our second multi-level controlled signature scheme is existentially coalition-resistance against the adaptively chosen message and chosen multi-level security policy distinguisher $\mathcal{A}^{CMP-A}_{CR-MLCS}$ if the DBDH assumption is hold in the random oracle model.*

Due to the page limitation, please find the proof for Theorem 4 in the full version of this paper [12].

Version / Size of	First Scheme	Second Scheme
PK_{TA}	$(2n+2)|\mathbb{G}_1|$	$(n+3)|\mathbb{G}_1|$
SK_{TA}	$(3n+2)|p|$	$(n+3)|p|$
PK_S	$3|\mathbb{G}_1|$	$(n+1)|\mathbb{G}_1|$
SK_S	$|p|$	$|p|$
VCR_V	$(2l)|\mathbb{G}_1|$	$2|\mathbb{G}_1|$
Signature	$6|\mathbb{G}_1| + 2|p|$	$(5+n-l)|\mathbb{G}_1| + 2|p|$
Signing Computation	$7E + M + P$	$(6+n-l)E + M + P$
Verification Computation	$E + 2lM + 10P$	$E + (2(n-l)+8)P$

Fig. 1. The comparison of two concrete schemes

6   Conclusion

We presented a security model for MLCS schemes to capture the message integrity and authenticity, together with authorization of the verifiers. Two concrete schemes and their proof of security have been presented. A signature of the first scheme has a constant size. A private information (credentials) of verifier is shorter in the second scheme. Our schemes are shown to be secure in our model. The comparison between the two schemes is provided in Fig 1. It is interesting to study how to provide a constant size signature while the size of verifier's credential is also constant. Moreover, it is also interesting to study how to construct MLCS schemes in the standard model. We discussed the insecure generic construction from HIBE, however, it is also interesting to study how to construct a generic construction scheme that will be secure in our model such that the verification can be done only by an appropriate verifier. Note that, in Fig 1, l is a security level in the multi-level security policy where $MP = $ "$A_V \geq l$". n is the number of security level. Let E denote a computation of exponential in $\mathbb{G}_1$ or $\mathbb{G}_T$. Let M be a computation of multiplication in $\mathbb{G}_1$. Let P be a computation of bilinear pairing function $\hat{e}$.

References

1. Bagga, W., Molva, R.: Policy-Based Cryptography and Applications. In: S. Patrick, A., Yung, M. (eds.) FC 2005. LNCS, vol. 3570, pp. 72–87. Springer, Heidelberg (2005)
2. Boneh, D.: The Decision Diffie-Hellman Problem. In: Buhler, J.P. (ed.) ANTS 1998. LNCS, vol. 1423, pp. 48–63. Springer, Heidelberg (1998)
3. Boneh, D., Boyen, X., Goh, E.-J.: Hierarchical Identity Based Encryption with Constant Size Ciphertext. In: Cramer, R. (ed.) EUROCRYPT 2005. LNCS, vol. 3494, pp. 440–456. Springer, Heidelberg (2005)
4. Boneh, D., Franklin, M.: Identity-Based Encryption from the Weil Pairing. In: Kilian, J. (ed.) CRYPTO 2001. LNCS, vol. 2139, pp. 213–229. Springer, Heidelberg (2001)
5. Boyen, X., Waters, B.: Anonymous Hierarchical Identity-Based Encryption (Without Random Oracles). In: Dwork, C. (ed.) CRYPTO 2006. LNCS, vol. 4117, pp. 290–307. Springer, Heidelberg (2006)
6. Chow, S.S.M., Hui, L.C.K., Yiu, S.-M., Chow, K.P.: Secure Hierarchical Identity Based Signature and Its Application. In: López, J., Qing, S., Okamoto, E. (eds.) ICICS 2004. LNCS, vol. 3269, pp. 480–494. Springer, Heidelberg (2004)
7. Diffie, W., Hellman, M.E.: New directions in cryptography. IEEE Transactions on Information Theory IT-22(6), 644–654 (1976)
8. Gentry, C., Silverberg, A.: Hierarchical ID-Based Cryptography. In: Zheng, Y. (ed.) ASIACRYPT 2002. LNCS, vol. 2501, pp. 548–566. Springer, Heidelberg (2002)
9. Horwitz, J., Lynn, B.: Toward Hierarchical Identity-Based Encryption. In: Knudsen, L.R. (ed.) EUROCRYPT 2002. LNCS, vol. 2332, pp. 466–481. Springer, Heidelberg (2002)
10. Jakobsson, M., Sako, K., Impagliazzo, R.: Designated Verifier Proofs and Their Applications. In: Maurer, U.M. (ed.) EUROCRYPT 1996. LNCS, vol. 1070, pp. 143–154. Springer, Heidelberg (1996)
11. Shamir, A.: Identity-Based Cryptosystems and Signature Schemes. In: Blakely, G.R., Chaum, D. (eds.) CRYPTO 1984. LNCS, vol. 196, pp. 47–53. Springer, Heidelberg (1985)
12. Thorncharoensri, P., Susilo, W., Mu, Y.: Multi-level controlled signature (full version). can be obtained from the first author (2012)

Tate Pairing Computation
on Generalized Hessian Curves*

Liangze Li and Fan Zhang

LMAM, School of Mathematical Sciences, Peking University, Beijing 100871, China
liliangze2005@163.com, viczf@pku.edu.cn

Abstract. In this paper, we present explicit formulae for Miller's algorithm to compute the Tate pairing on generalized Hessian curves using
projective coordinates. Firstly, we propose the geometric interpretation
of the group law and construct Miller function on generalized Hessian
curves. The computation of Tate pairing using these functions in Miller's
algorithm costs $10\mathbf{m}$ in addition steps and $5\mathbf{m}+6\mathbf{s}$ in doubling steps. Finally, we present the parallel algorithm for computing Tate pairing on
generalized Hessian curves.

Keywords: Elliptic curves, Hessian curves, Tate pairing, Miller algorithm, Cryptography.

1 Introduction

Pairings on elliptic curves have, in recent years, been discussed on various elliptic
curve models. A well known elliptic curve model is Weierstrass model, and many
efficient formulae for pairing computation for this model can be found in [5] and
[1]. Recently, other models, for example, Edwards curves [8] and twisted Edwards
curves [3] are widely used. Pairing computation on twisted Edward curves was
first considered by Das and Sarkar [7], and then by Ionic and Joux[11]. In 2009,
Arène, Lange et al. [1] developed more efficient formulae of pairing computation
on twisted Edwards curves.

The use of Hessian curves in cryptology was explained in [6], [12] and [15].
Joye and Quisquater [12] suggested that the unified addition formulas on Hessian
curves could be used to prevent side-channel attack. Subsequently pairing computation on Hessian curves was first proposed by Gu, Gu and Xie[10] in 2010.
They pointed out that their algorithm for computing Tate pairing was faster
than all algorithms of Tate pairing computation on Edwards and Weierstrass
curves except for some special cases.

In 2010, R.Farashahi and Joye [9] defined the generalized Hessian curves
which cover more isomorphism classes of elliptic curves than Hessian curves.
In this paper, we consider the computation of Tate pairing on generalized Hessian curves. Firstly, we give the Miller function on generalized Hessian curves,

---

* Supported in part by the National Natural Science Foundation of China No.
11101002.

D.H. Lee and M. Yung (Eds.): WISA 2012, LNCS 7690, pp. 111–123, 2012.

then propose explicit formulas for the doubling and addition steps in Miller's algorithm. To gain speed up, we use the denominator elimination technique. More precisely, if one chooses the subgroups as $\mathbb{G}_1 = \mathbf{H}_{c,d}[r] \bigcap Ker(\pi_q - [1])$ and $\mathbb{G}_2 = \mathbf{H}_{c,d}[r] \bigcap Ker(\pi_q - [q])$, then the denominator of Miller's function can be eliminated by the final exponent. If $\mathbf{m}$ and $\mathbf{s}$ denote the costs of multiplication and squaring in the base field $\mathbb{F}_q$; $\mathbf{M}$ and $\mathbf{S}$ denote the costs of multiplication and squaring in the extension field $\mathbb{F}_{q^k}$; $\mathbf{m_C}$ denotes the cost of multiply by a constant in the base field. By using the denominator elimination technique, the addition steps in Miller's algorithm can be done in $\mathbf{12m+km+M}$; if one uses mixed addition the cost of addition steps can be reduced to $\mathbf{10m+km+M}$. And the doubling steps can be done in $\mathbf{5m+6s+km+S+M}$.

The remainder of this paper is organized as follows: In section 2 we introduce the bilinear pairings, Miller's algorithm and background on generalized Hessian curves briefly. In section 3, we give the Miller function on generalized Hessian curves. In section 4, firstly we discuss the denominator elimination technique; then we give explicit formulas of the doubling and addition steps in Miller's algorithm to compute the Tate pairing; finally we present the parallel algorithm of computing the Tate pairing. In section 5, we conclude our paper.

2   Preliminaries

2.1   Tate Pairing

This section briefly recalls the definition of the Tate pairing. An excellent survey of Tate pairing can be found in [4] or [14].

Let p be a prime, $p > 3$, $\mathbb{F}_q$ a finite field with $q = p^n$ elements, E an elliptic curve defined over $\mathbb{F}_q$. Let r be a prime such that $r \mid \sharp E(\mathbb{F}_q)$, k the smallest positive integer such that r divides $q^k - 1$, such integer is called the embedding degree of E. For technical reasons we assume that r^2 does not divide $q^k - 1$. With the above choice of r and k, one has $E[r] \subset E(\mathbb{F}_{q^k})$.

Let $P \in E[r]$, $D_P \in Div^0(E)$ such that $D_P = (P) - (O)$, then there exists a rational function $f_P \in \mathbb{F}_q(E)$ such that $(f_P) = rD_P$. Let $Q \in E(\mathbb{F}_{q^k})$, $D_Q = (Q + R) - (R)$ with R a random point in $E(\mathbb{F}_{q^k})$. Suppose that D_P and D_Q have disjoint supports, then the Tate pairing is well-defined as follows:

$$E[r] \times E(\mathbb{F}_{q^k})/rE(\mathbb{F}_{q^k}) \to \mathbb{F}_{q^k}^*/(\mathbb{F}_{q^k}^*)^r$$

$$t_r(P, Q) \mapsto f_P(D_Q) \tag{1}$$

From the above definition, one can prove that Tate pairing is bilinear and non-degenerate.

The output of this pairing is only defined up to a coset of $(\mathbb{F}_{q^k}^*)^r$, however, for protocols we will require a unique element of $\mathbb{F}_{q^k}^*$, hence to obtain a unique representative, one defines the reduced Tate pairing as:

$$t_r(P, Q) = f_P(D_Q)^{(q^k - 1)/r} \tag{2}$$

Although the Tate pairing as defined in (1) allows arguments $P \in E[r]$ and $Q \in E(\mathbb{F}_q^k)$, in practice one often works with specific subgroups to speed-up the pairing computation. Let π_q be the Frobenius endomorphism, i.e. $\pi_q : E \to E : (x, y) \mapsto (x^q, y^q)$, then we choose the following two subgroups: $\mathbb{G}_1 = E[r] \cap Ker(\pi_q - [1])$ and $\mathbb{G}_2 = E[r] \cap Ker(\pi_q - [q])$.

2.2 Miller's Algorithm

From the formula (1) in section 2.1, to calculate the Tate pairing, we need to compute $f_P(D_Q)$. It is not difficult to show that, if $k > 1$ one can ignore working with the divisor D_Q, and simply work with the point Q (see [2]). So we only need to calculate $f_P(Q)$. In his unpublished manuscript, Miller gave an elegant and efficient algorithm for this calculation. The main ideal of Miller's algorithm is to inductively build up such a function f_P by constructing the function $f_{n,P}$. The function $f_{n,P}$ is defined by $(f_{n,P}) = n(P) - ([n]P) - (n-1)(O)$, n is an integer smaller than r.

Let E is an elliptic curve given by a Weierstrass equation, $P, T \in E$. Let $\ell_{P,T}$ be the normalized linear function, such that $\ell_{P,T} = 0$ is the equation of the line passing through P and T, v_{P+T} the vertical line through $P + T$. Obviously $(\ell_{P,T}) = (P) + (T) + (-P-T) - 3(O)$ and $(v_{P+T}) = (P+T) + (-P-T) - 2(O)$, then the Miller function $g_{P,T}$ is defined as follows:

$$g_{P,T} := \frac{\ell_{P,T}}{v_{P+T}} \tag{3}$$

From the definition of addition and the divisor of a rational function, we have

$$(g_{P,T}) = (P) + (T) - (P+T) - (O)$$

Since all lines are chosen to be normalized, $g_{P,T}$ is also normalized. In fact, any functions defined over $\mathbb{F}_q$ with the divisor $(g_{P,T})$, will multiply $g_{P,T}$ by a factor in $\mathbb{F}_q^*$. And (2) shows that when we compute the reduced Tate pairing the factor will be eliminated by the final exponent. So the problem whether the lines are normalized or not can be ignored in this paper.

If $P \in E$, define $f_{0,P} = f_{1,P} = 1$. Inductively, for $n > 0$, define $f_{n+1,P} := f_{n,P} g_{P,nP}$, then we have

$$f_{m+n,P} = f_{m,P} f_{n,P} g_{mP,nP}$$

that is:

$$f_{m+n,P} = f_{m,P} f_{n,P} \frac{\ell_{nP,mP}}{v_{(n+m)P}} \tag{4}$$

Let the binary representation of r be $r = \sum_{i=0}^{t} r_i 2^i$, where $r_i \in \{0, 1\}$. Using the double-and-add method, Miller's algorithm to calculate the value of a function f_P is described in algorithm 1.

Algorithm 1. Miller's algorithm(P, Q, r)

Input: $r = \sum_{i=0}^{t-1} r_i 2^i$, where $r_i \in \{0, 1\}$, $r_t \neq 0$. $P, Q \in E$.
Output: $f_{r,P}(Q)$

1: $f \leftarrow 1, T \leftarrow P$
2: **for** $i = t - 1$ down to 0 **do**
3:     $f \leftarrow f^2 \cdot \frac{l_{T,T}(Q)}{v_{2T}(Q)},\; T \leftarrow 2T$
4:     **if** $r_i = 1$ **then**
5:        $f \leftarrow f \cdot \frac{l_{T,P}(Q)}{v_{T+P}(Q)},\; T \leftarrow T + P$
6:     **end if**
7: **end for**
8: **return** f

2.3   Background on General Hessian Curves

A Hessian curves over a field $\mathbb{F}_q$ is given by the cubic equation

$$H_d : x^3 + y^3 + 1 = dxy$$

for some $d \in \mathbb{F}_q$ with $d^3 \neq 27$ [13]. In 2010, R.Farashahi and Joye [9] defined the family of generalized Hessian curves which cover more isomorphism classes of elliptic curves than Hessian curves:

Definition 1. *Let c, d be elements of $\mathbb{F}_q$ such that $c \neq 0$ and $d^3 \neq 27c$. The generalized Hessian curves $H_{c,d}$ over $\mathbb{F}_q$ is defined by the equation:*

$$H_{c,d} : x^3 + y^3 + c = dxy$$

Clearly, a generalized Hessian curve $H_{c,d}$ with $c = 1$ is a Hessian curve H_d. The projective closure of the curve $H_{c,d}$ is:

$$\mathbf{H}_{c,d} : X^3 + Y^3 + cZ^3 = dXYZ$$

The neutral element (1: -1: 0) of $\mathbf{H}_{c,d}$ is denoted by O. For the points $P = (X_1 : Y_1 : Z_1)$ on $\mathbf{H}_{c,d}$, we have $-P = (Y_1 : X_1 : Z_1)$. The formulae of point addition and doubling are as follows:

Point Addition. Let the sum of the points $(X_1 : Y_1 : Z_1)$, $(X_2 : Y_2 : Z_2)$ on $\mathbf{H}_{c,d}$ be the point $(X_3 : Y_3 : Z_3)$, then:

$$X_3 = X_2 Z_2 Y_1{}^2 - X_1 Z_1 Y_2{}^2$$

$$Y_3 = Y_2 Z_2 X_1{}^2 - Y_1 Z_1 X_2{}^2$$

$$Z_3 = X_2 Y_2 Z_1{}^2 - X_1 Y_1 Z_2{}^2$$

Point Doubling. Let the doubling of the point $(X_1 : Y_1 : Z_1)$ on $\mathbf{H}_{c,d}$ be the point $(X_3 : Y_3 : Z_3)$, then:

$$X_3 = Y_1(cZ_1{}^3 - X_1{}^3)$$
$$Y_3 = X_1(Y_1{}^3 - cZ_1{}^3)$$
$$Z_3 = Z_1(X_1{}^3 - Y_1{}^3)$$

3 Miller Function on Generalized Hessian Curves

In this section, firstly we give the construction of Miller function on generalized Hessian curves, then we give the explicit equations of projective lines which appear in Miller function.

3.1 The Construction of Miller Function

Here, instead of using the linear affine function ℓ in formula (3) in section 2.2, we consider projective lines which are given by homogeneous projective equations $L = 0$. In this paper, we still use the symbol L to denote projective lines. Any projective line has exactly three intersections with $\mathbf{H}_{c,d}$, counted by multiplicity. Although these linear equations are not functions on $\mathbf{H}_{c,d}$, their divisors can be well defined as:

$$(L) = \sum_{P \in L \cap \mathbf{H}_{c,d}} n_P(P) \tag{5}$$

where n_P is the intersection multiplicity of L and $\mathbf{H}_{c,d}$ at P. However, the quotient of two homogeneous projective equations is a rational function of $\mathbf{H}_{c,d}$ which gives a principal divisor.

Let P and T are two different points on $\mathbf{H}_{c,d}$, $L_{P,T}$ denotes the projective line passing through P and T. And $-P - T$ is the third intersection, by (5) we can get:

$$(L_{P,T}) = (P) + (T) + (-P - T)$$

Similarly, $L_{P+T,-P-T}$ intersects with $\mathbf{H}_{c,d}$ at $P + T$, $-P - T$ and O, then:

$$(L_{P+T,-P-T}) = (-P - T) + (P + T) + (O)$$

Thus,

$$\left(\frac{L_{P,T}}{L_{P+T,-P-T}}\right) = (P) + (T) - (P + T) - (O)$$

The Miller function $g_{P,T}$ over $\mathbf{H}_{c,d}$ is defined as:

$$g_{P,T} = \frac{L_{P,T}}{L_{P+T,-P-T}} \tag{6}$$

Particularly, if $T = P$, Miller function $g_{T,T}$ over $\mathbf{H}_{c,d}$ is defined as:

$$g_{T,T} = \frac{L_{T,T}}{L_{2T,-2T}} \tag{7}$$

Notice that Miller's Algorithm 1 in section 2.2 uses the double-and-add method, so we only need to display explicit formulas for the addition and doubling steps.

3.2   Addition Steps

By Algorithm 1 and (6), we know that the value of f in addition step is computed as follows:

$$f \leftarrow f \cdot \frac{L_{P,T}(Q)}{L_{P+T,-P-T}(Q)} \tag{8}$$

So in this section we give the equation of $L_{P+T,-P-T}$ and $L_{P,T}$.

Equation of $L_{P+T,-P-T}$. Let $P = (X_p : Y_P : Z_P), T = (X_T : Y_T : Z_T)$, and $L_{P+T,-P-T} : C_X X + C_Y Y + C_Z Z = 0$ is the projective line passing through $P + T = (X_{P+T} : Y_{P+T} : Y_{P+T})$ and $O = (1 : -1 : 0)$, then:

$$C_X X_{P+T} + C_Y Y_{P+T} + C_Z Z_{P+T} = 0, C_X = C_Y$$

Thus, we can get the (projective) solutions:

$$C_X = C_Y = Z_{P+T}, C_Z = X_{P+T} + Y_{P+T} \tag{9}$$

So that, $L_{P+T,-P-T}$ has the following equation:

$$L_{P+T,-P-T} : Z_{P+T}(X + Y) - (X_{P+T} + Y_{P+T})Z = 0 \tag{10}$$

Equation of $L_{P,T}$. Let $L_{P,T} : C_X X + C_Y Y + C_Z Z = 0$ be the projective line passing through two different points P and T, then:

$$C_X X_P + C_Y Y_P + C_Z Z_P = 0$$

$$C_X X_T + C_Y Y_T + C_Z Z_T = 0$$

Thus, we can get the (projective) solutions:

$$C_X = Y_P Z_T - Y_T Z_P, C_Y = Z_P X_T - Z_T X_P, C_Z = X_P Y_T - X_T Y_P \tag{11}$$

So that, $L_{P,T}$ has the following equation:

$$L_{P,T} : (Y_P Z_T - Y_T Z_P)X + (Z_P X_T - Z_T X_P)Y + (X_P Y_T - X_T Y_P)Z = 0 \tag{12}$$

3.3   Doubling Steps

By Algorithm 1 and (7), we know that the value of f in doubling step is computed as follows:

$$f \leftarrow f^2 \cdot \frac{L_{T,T}(Q)}{L_{2T,-2T}(Q)} \tag{13}$$

So in this section we give the equation of $L_{2T,-2T}$ and $L_{T,T}$.

Equation of $L_{2T,-2T}$. $L_{2T,-2T} : C_X X + C_Y Y + C_Z Z = 0$ is the projective line passing through $2T = (X_{2T} : Y_{2T} : Z_{2T})$ and $O = (1 : -1 : 0)$, then by the similar method of $L_{P+T,-P-T}$, we can get:

$$L_{2T,-2T} : Z_{2T}(X + Y) - (X_{2T} + Y_{2T})Z = 0 \tag{14}$$

Equation of $L_{T,T}$. Let $L_{T,T}$ be the tangent to $\mathbf{H}_{c,d}$ at T, then

$$L_{T,T} : \frac{\partial \mathbf{H}_{c,d}}{\partial X}(T)X + \frac{\partial \mathbf{H}_{c,d}}{\partial Y}(T)Y + \frac{\partial \mathbf{H}_{c,d}}{\partial Z}(T)Z = 0$$

So we can get the equation of $L_{T,T}$ as follows:

$$(3X_T{}^2 - dY_T Z_T)X + (3Y_T{}^2 - dX_T Z_T)Y + (3cZ_T{}^2 - dX_T Y_T)Z = 0 \qquad (15)$$

4 Computation of Tate Pairing on Generalized Hessian Curves

In this section, firstly we discuss the denominator elimination technique; then we give explicit formulas of the doubling and addition steps in Miller's algorithm to compute the Tate pairing; finally we present the parallel algorithm of computing the Tate pairing.

4.1 Denominator Elimination

To compute the Tate pairing on generalized Hessian curves, this section mainly discusses how to use the technique of *denominator elimination* to improve the implementation.

Let p be a prime, $p > 3$, $\mathbb{F}_q$ a finite field with $q = p^n$ elements, $\mathbf{H}_{c,d}$ an generalized Hessian curve defined over $\mathbb{F}_q$. Let r be a prime, $r > 3$, such that $r \mid \sharp \mathbf{H}_{c,d}(\mathbb{F}_q)$. In this section, we assume that the embedding degree k is even and r^2 does not divide $q^k - 1$. With the above choice of r and k, one has $\mathbf{H}_{c,d}[r] \subset \mathbf{H}_{c,d}(\mathbb{F}_{q^k})$.

Let $\mathbb{G}_1 = \mathbf{H}_{c,d}[r] \bigcap Ker(\pi_q - [1])$, $\mathbb{G}_2 = \mathbf{H}_{c,d}[r] \bigcap Ker(\pi_q - [q])$, $P \in \mathbb{G}_1$, $Q \in \mathbb{G}_2$. From formula (6) in section 3.1, the Miller function's value at point Q in addition step is:

$$g_{T,P}(Q) = \frac{L_{P,T}(Q)}{L_{P+T,-P-T}(Q)}$$

From formula (7) in section 3.1, the Miller function's value at point Q in doubling step is:

$$g_{T,T}(Q) = \frac{L_{T,T}(Q)}{L_{2T,-2T}(Q)}$$

Here the point T is nP for some integer n, so $T \in \mathbb{G}_1$. The *denominator elimination* technique is based on the following theorem:

Theorem 1. *Suppose $\mathbf{H}_{c,d}$ is defined over F_q, r is a prime, $r \mid \sharp \mathbf{H}_{c,d}(F_q)$, the embedding degree k is even, $Q \in \mathbb{G}_2$, $f \in \mathbb{F}_{q^{k/2}}(H_{c,d})$ is regular at Q, $F_{q^k} = F_{q^{k/2}}(\alpha)$ with $\alpha^2 \in F_{q^{k/2}}$. Then $f(Q) \in \mathbb{F}_{q^{k/2}}$ when f is even function; $\frac{f(Q)}{\alpha} \in \mathbb{F}_{q^{k/2}}$ when f is odd function.*

Proof. Since $Q \in \mathbb{G}_2 = \mathbf{H}_{c,d}[r] \cap Ker(\pi_q - [q])$, then $\pi_q(Q) = qQ$. We know that $r \mid q^k - 1 = (q^{k/2} + 1)(q^{k/2} - 1)$, while r does not divide $q^{k/2} - 1$, so $r \mid q^{k/2} + 1$ hence $(q^{k/2} + 1)Q = 0$. That is to say $\pi_{q^{k/2}}(Q) = q^{k/2}Q = -Q$. Let σ be the non-trivial element of $Gal(F_{q^k}/F_{q^{k/2}})$, then $Q^\sigma = \pi_{q^{k/2}}(Q)$. If f is even function we have:

$$(f(Q))^\sigma = f(Q^\sigma) = f(-Q) = f(Q)$$

In another word, $f(Q) \in \mathbb{F}_{q^{k/2}}$.

$\mathbb{F}_{q^k} = \mathbb{F}_{q^{k/2}}(\alpha)$, with $\alpha^2 \in \mathbb{F}_{q^{k/2}}$, then $(\alpha^2)^\sigma = \alpha^2$, we can get $\alpha^\sigma = -\alpha$. If f is odd function we have:

$$\left(\frac{f(Q)}{\alpha}\right)^\sigma = \frac{(f(Q))^\sigma}{\alpha^\sigma} = \frac{f(Q^\sigma)}{\alpha^\sigma} = \frac{f(-Q)}{-\alpha} = \frac{f(Q)}{\alpha}$$

In another word, $\frac{f(Q)}{\alpha} \in \mathbb{F}_{q^{k/2}}$. $\qquad\square$

Corollary 1. *Using the notation of theorem 1, suppose $r > 3$ and $Q \neq O$. Then there exist $a, b \in \mathbb{F}_{q^{k/2}}$ such that $Q = (X_Q : Y_Q : Z_Q)$ where $X_Q = a + b\alpha$, $Y_Q = a - b\alpha$, $Z_Q = 1$.*

Proof. Because $r > 3$, Q cannot be a 3-torsion point, that is to say Q is not on the line $Z = 0$. Thus we can consider the affine coordinate functions $x = \frac{X}{Z}$ and $y = \frac{Y}{Z}$ at Q. Since $-Q = (Y_Q : X_Q : Z_Q)$, we know that $(x+y)(Q) = (x+y)(-Q)$, i.e. $x+y$ is even. So we can get $(x+y)(Q) \in \mathbb{F}_{q^{k/2}}$ by theorem 1. Similarly $x-y$ is odd, and again theorem 1 shows $\frac{(x-y)(Q)}{\alpha} \in \mathbb{F}_{q^{k/2}}$. So there are $a, b \in \mathbb{F}_{q^{k/2}}$ such that: $(x + y)(Q) = 2a$ and $\frac{(x-y)(Q)}{\alpha} = 2b$. Thus $X_Q = a + b\alpha$, $Y_Q = a - b\alpha$ when choosing $Z_Q = 1$. $\qquad\square$

For a projective line L, we define $L(Q)$ to be the value of $\frac{L}{Z}(Q)$, which is actually the value of L when substituting the coordinates of Q with $Z_Q = 1$. The equations of $L_{P+T,-P-T}$ and $L_{2P,-2P}$ are given in section 3.2 and section 3.3. And from the inverse formula of generalized Hessian curves, we know $\frac{L_{P+T,-P-T}}{Z}$ and $\frac{L_{2P,-2P}}{Z}$ are exactly even. Then theorem 1 tells us that $L_{P+T,-P-T}(Q)$ and $L_{2P,-2P}(Q)$ are in $\mathbb{F}_{q^{k/2}}$. Thus,

$$L_{P+T,-P-T}(Q)^{\frac{q^k-1}{r}} = (L_{P+T,-P-T}(Q)^{q^{\frac{k}{2}}-1})^{\frac{q^{\frac{k}{2}}+1}{r}} = 1$$

$$L_{2T,-2T}(Q)^{\frac{q^k-1}{r}} = (L_{2T,-2T}(Q)^{q^{\frac{k}{2}}-1})^{\frac{q^{\frac{k}{2}}+1}{r}} = 1$$

which means that $L_{P+T,-P-T}(Q)$ and $L_{2P,-2P}(Q)$ can be eliminated in Miller's algorithm of computing reduced Tate pairing. That is to say, if we choose the subgroups as $\mathbb{G}_1 = \mathbf{H}_{c,d}[r] \cap Ker(\pi_q - [1])$ and $\mathbb{G}_2 = \mathbf{H}_{c,d}[r] \cap Ker(\pi_q - [q])$, then the *denominator elimination* technique can be used to improve the implementation.

4.2   Formulas for Pairing

Let $T = (X_T : Y_T : Z_T)$, $P = (X_P : Y_P : Z_P)$ and $Q = (X_Q : Y_Q : Z_Q)$, where $X_Q = a + b\alpha$, $Y_Q = a - b\alpha$, $Z_Q = 1$. In this section, we denote $\mathbf{m}$ and $\mathbf{s}$ the costs of multiplication and squaring in the base field $\mathbb{F}_q$, $\mathbf{M}$ and $\mathbf{S}$ the costs of multiplication and squaring in the extension field $\mathbb{F}_{q^k}$, $\mathbf{m_C}$ the cost of multiplying by a constant in the base field.

Formulas for Addition Steps. By applying denominator elimination, the value of f in addition steps can be simply computed as follows:

$$f \leftarrow f \cdot L_{P,T}(Q) \tag{16}$$

From this formula, in the addition steps we need to compute the coordinates of $P + T$, the coefficients of $L_{P,T}$ and its value at $Q = (a + b\alpha : a - b\alpha : 1)$ i.e. $L_{P,T}(Q)$. Then the explicit formulae of addition steps are given as follows:

$$A = Y_P Z_T, B = Y_T Z_P, C = Z_P X_T, D = Z_T X_P, E = X_P Y_T, F = X_T Y_P$$

$$C_X = A - B, C_Y = C - D, C_Z = E - F$$

$$X_{P+T} = AF - EB, Y_{P+T} = ED - FC, Z_{P+T} = CB - DA$$

$$L_{P,T}(Q) = (C_X + C_Y)a + (C_X - C_Y)b\alpha + C_Z$$

Thus,the total computation in addition steps of Miller's algorithm can be done in $\mathbf{12m + km + M}$. In fact, one can use the mixed addition, which means $Z_P = 1$, then the above cost can be reduced to $\mathbf{10m + km + M}$.

Formulas for Doubling Steps. Similarly, by applying denominator elimination $L_{2T,-2T}(Q)$ can be eliminated, so the value of f in doubling steps can be simply computed as follows:

$$f \leftarrow f^2 \cdot L_{T,T}(Q) \tag{17}$$

To benefit our computation, we multiply the coordinates of $2T$ by 6 and compute $2T = (6X_{2T} : 6Y_{2T} : 6Z_{2T})$; we multiply the equation (15) by 2:

$$L_{T,T} : (6X_T^2 - 2dY_T Z_T)X + (6Y_T^2 - 2dX_T Z_T)Y + (6cZ_T^2 - 2dX_T Y_T)Z = 0$$

From (17), in the doubling steps we need to compute the coordinates of $2T$, the coefficients of $L_{T,T}$ and its value at $Q = (a + b\alpha : a - b\alpha : 1)$ i.e. $L_{T,T}(Q)$. The explicit formulae of doubling steps are given as follows:

$$A = X_T^2, B = Y_T^2, C = Z_T^2$$

$$D = (Y_T + Z_T)^2 - C - B, E = (X_T + Z_T)^2 - A - C, F = (X_T + Y_T)^2 - A - B$$

$$C_X = 6A - dD, C_Y = 6B - dE, C_Z = 6cC - dF$$

$$G = X_T C_X, H = Y_T C_Y$$

$$6X_{2T} = -Y_T(2G + H), 6Y_{2T} = X_T(G + 2H), 6Z_{2T} = Z_T(G - H)$$

$$L_{T,T}(Q) = (C_X + C_Y)a + (C_X - C_Y)b\alpha + C_Z$$

Thus, the total computation in doubling steps of Miller's algorithm can be done in $\mathbf{5m + 6s + km + 4m_C + S + M}$. If $c = 1$, the computation in doubling steps can be done in $\mathbf{3m + 6s + km + 3m_C + S + M}$ by the method of Gu, Gu and Xie[10].

Formulas for the Special Case $d = 0$. Particularly, if $d = 0$, then the generalized Hessian curves has equation:

$$\mathbf{H}_{c,0} : X^3 + Y^3 + cZ^3 = 0$$

which is isomorphic to the elliptic curve:

$$E : Y'^2 Z' = X'^3 + a_6 Z'^3$$

where, $a_6 = \frac{c^2}{3^6 2^2}$. Let $\varepsilon \in \mathbb{F}_q$ such that $\varepsilon^2 + \varepsilon + 1 = 0$, there is an $F_q(\varepsilon)$-isomorphism:

$$E \to H_{c,0}$$
$$(X' : Y' : Z') \mapsto (X : Y : Z)$$

which is given by:

$$X = (\varepsilon - 1)Y' - \frac{c}{18}(\varepsilon + 1)Z', Y = -(\varepsilon + 2)Y' + \frac{c}{18}\varepsilon Z', Z = X'$$

The inverse isomorphism:

$$H_{c,0} \to E$$
$$(X : Y : Z) \mapsto (X' : Y' : Z')$$

is given by:

$$X' = Z, Y' = -\frac{(\varepsilon + 1)}{2(1 + 2\varepsilon)}Y - \frac{\varepsilon}{2(1 + 2\varepsilon)}X, Z' = -\frac{3^2(\varepsilon - 1)}{c(1 + 2\varepsilon)}Y - \frac{3^2(\varepsilon + 2)}{c(1 + 2\varepsilon)}X$$

Then the total computation in addition steps of Miller's algorithm can be done in **10m+km+M** by mixed addition. While the cost of doubling steps of Miller's algorithm can be reduced to **5m+3s+km+m$_C$+S+M** as follows:

$$A = X_T{}^2, B = Y_T{}^2, C = Z_T{}^2$$

$$C_X = 6A, C_Y = 6B, C_Z = 6cC$$

$$D = AX_T, E = BY_T, F = -D - E$$

$$X_{2T} = Y_T(F - D), Y_{2T} = X_T(E - F), Z_{2T} = Z_T(D - E)$$

$$L_{T,T}(Q) = (C_X + C_Y)a + (C_X - C_Y)b\alpha + C_Z$$

4.3   Comparison

In 2009, Arène, Lange et al.[1] proposed new pairing formulae for Edwards curves. And they pointed out that, their new formulae beat all previous formulae on Edwards curves. While, our pairing formulae for generalized Hessian curves are faster than their formulae on Edwards curves. In their paper,

Arène, Lange et al.[1] also proposed some improvements to pairing formulae for two special Weierstrass curves. One special case is Weierstrass curves with $a_3 = -3$, and the other special case is Weierstrass curves with $a_4 = 0$. And our pairing formulae for generalized Hessian curves with $d = 0$ are faster than their formulae for the above two special Weierstrass curves.

In 2010, Gu, Gu and Xie et.al [10] gave pairing formulae for Hessian curves. Their formulae for addition steps are as fast as our formulae for generalized Hessian curves. While their formulae for doubling steps are faster than our formulae, that is because when $c = 1$ a special technique (see [10]) can be used to reduce the cost. Generalized Hessian curves discussed here doesn't limit c to 1, which cover more isomorphism classes of elliptic curves than Hessian curves discussed by Gu, Gu and Xie et. al.

The following table shows the concrete comparison. Any mixed addition step (mADD) or addition step (ADD) needs **1M+km** for evaluation at Q and the update of f; each doubling step (DBL) needs **1M+km+S** for the evaluation at Q and the update of f. So we do not comment on these expenses in the following table. We denote Edwards coordinates by $\mathcal{E}$ and Jacobian coordinates by $\mathcal{J}$.

	DBL	mADD	ADD
$\mathcal{J}$,$a_4 = -3$ [1]	$6m + 5s$	$6m + 6s$	$9m + 6s$
$\mathcal{J}$,$a_4 = 0$ [1]	$3m + 8s$	$6m + 6s$	$9m + 6s$
$\mathcal{E}$ [1]	$6m + 5s$	$12m$	$14m$
$H_{1,d}$ [10]	$3m + 6s$	$10m$	$12m$
$H_{c,d}$, this paper	$5m + 6s$	$10m$	$12m$
$H_{c,0}$, this paper	$5m + 3s$	$10m$	$12m$

4.4 Parallelizing the Tate Pairing

In [15], it is observed that the addition and doubling steps of Miller's algorithm on Hessian curves can be performed independently. In this subsection we show how the computation of Tate pairing on generalized Hessian curves can be performed independently. We propose 3-Processor Tate pairing algorithm, the more processors cases can be derived with similar approaches.

Cost	Step	Processor 1	Processor 2	Processor 3
1m	1	$A_1 = Y_P Z_T$	$B_1 = Y_T Z_P$	$C_1 = Z_P X_T$
1m	2	$A_2 = Z_T X_P$	$B_2 = X_P Y_T$	$C_2 = X_T Y_P$
$-$	3	$A_3 = A_1 - B_1$	$B_3 = C_1 - A_2$	$C_3 = B_2 - C_2$
2m	4	$A_4 = A_1 C_2 - B_1 B_2$	$B_4 = A_2 B_2 - C_1 C_2$	$C_4 = B_1 C_1 - A_1 A_2$
$\frac{k}{2}$m	5	$A_5 = a(A_3 + B_3)$	$B_5 = b(A_3 - B_3)\alpha$	$-$

From the above table, we know that when compute $f \leftarrow f \cdot L_{P,T}(Q) = f \cdot (A_5 + B_5 + C_3)$ in Miller's algorithm, the cost of addition steps by 3-Processor Tate pairing algorithm is **4m+$\frac{k}{2}$m+M**.

Cost	Step	Processor 1	Processor 2	Processor 3
1s	1	$A_1 = X_T^2$	$B_1 = Y_T^2$	$C_1 = Z_T^2$
1s	2	$A_2 = (Y_T + Z_T)^2 - B_1 - C_1$	$B_2 = (X_T + Z_T)^2 - A_1 - C_1$	$C_2 = (X_T + Y_T)^2 - A_1 - B_1$
–	3	$A_3 = 6A_1 - dA_2$	$B_3 = 6B_1 - dB_2$	$C_3 = 6cC_1 - dC_2$
1m	4	$A_4 = X_T A_3$	$B_4 = Y_T B_3$	–
1m	5	$A_5 = -Y_T(2A_4 + B_4)$	$B_5 = X_T(A_4 + 2B_4)$	$C_5 = Z_T(A_4 - B_4)$
$\frac{k}{2}m$	6	$A_6 = a(A_3 + B_3)$	$B_6 = b(A_3 - B_3)\alpha$	–

Finally, when compute $f \leftarrow f^2 \cdot L_{T,T}(Q) = f^2 \cdot (A_6 + B_6 + C_3)$ in Miller's algorithm, the cost of doubling steps by 3-Processor Tate pairing algorithm is **2s+2m+$\frac{k}{2}$m+M+S**.

5　Conclusion

In this paper, we firstly give the Miller function on generalized Hessian curves. Furthermore we propose explicit formulas for the doubling and addition steps in Miller's algorithm to compute the Tate pairing on generalized Hessian curves. After applying denominator elimination, the addition steps in Miller's algorithm can be done in **12m+km+M**, and **10m+km+M** under mixed addition; the doubling steps in Miller's algorithm can be done in **5m+6s+km+S+M**. Finally, we present the parallel algorithm of computing the Tate pairing on generalized Hessian curves.

References

1. Arène, C., Lange, T., Naehrig, M., Ritzenthaler, C.: Faster computation of the Tate pairing, Arxiv preprint, arXiv:0904.0854 (2009)
2. Barreto, P.S.L.M., Kim, H.Y., Lynn, B., Scott, M.: Efficient Algorithms for Pairing-Based Cryptosystems. In: Yung, M. (ed.) CRYPTO 2002. LNCS, vol. 2442, pp. 354–369. Springer, Heidelberg (2002)
3. Bernstein, D.J., Birkner, P., Joye, M., Lange, T., Peters, C.: Twisted Edwards Curves. In: Vaudenay, S. (ed.) AFRICACRYPT 2008. LNCS, vol. 5023, pp. 389–405. Springer, Heidelberg (2008)
4. Blake, I.F., Seroussi, G., Smart, N.P.: Advances in elliptic curve cryptography. Cambridge Univ. Pr. (2005)
5. Chatterjee, S., Sarkar, P., Barua, R.: Efficient Computation of Tate Pairing in Projective Coordinate over General Characteristic Fields. In: Park, C.-S., Chee, S. (eds.) ICISC 2004. LNCS, vol. 3506, pp. 168–181. Springer, Heidelberg (2005)
6. Chudnovsky, D.V., Chudnovsky, G.V.: Sequences of numbers generated by addition in formal groups and new primality and factorization tests. Advances in Applied Mathematics 7(4), 385–434 (1986)
7. Das, M.P.L., Sarkar, P.: Pairing Computation on Twisted Edwards Form Elliptic Curves. In: Galbraith, S.D., Paterson, K.G. (eds.) Pairing 2008. LNCS, vol. 5209, pp. 192–210. Springer, Heidelberg (2008)
8. Edwards, H.M.: A normal form for elliptic curves. Bulletin of the American Mathematical Society 44(3), 393–422 (2007)

9. Farashahi, R.R., Joye, M.: Efficient Arithmetic on Hessian Curves. In: Nguyen, P.Q., Pointcheval, D. (eds.) PKC 2010. LNCS, vol. 6056, pp. 243–260. Springer, Heidelberg (2010)

10. Gu, H., Gu, D., Xie, W.: Efficient Pairing Computation on Elliptic Curves in Hessian Form. In: Rhee, K.-H., Nyang, D. (eds.) ICISC 2010. LNCS, vol. 6829, pp. 169–176. Springer, Heidelberg (2011)

11. Ionica, S., Joux, A.: Another Approach to Pairing Computation in Edwards Coordinates. In: Chowdhury, D.R., Rijmen, V., Das, A. (eds.) INDOCRYPT 2008. LNCS, vol. 5365, pp. 400–413. Springer, Heidelberg (2008)

12. Joye, M., Quisquater, J.-J.: Hessian Elliptic Curves and Side-Channel Attacks. In: Koç, Ç.K., Naccache, D., Paar, C. (eds.) CHES 2001. LNCS, vol. 2162, pp. 402–410. Springer, Heidelberg (2001)

13. Ostrowski, A.: Über dirichletsche reihen und algebraische differentialgleichungen. Mathematische Zeitschrift 8(3), 241–298 (1920)

14. Silverman, J.H.: The arithmetic of elliptic curves, vol. 106. Springer (2009)

15. Smart, N.P.: The Hessian Form of an Elliptic Curve. In: Koç, Ç.K., Naccache, D., Paar, C. (eds.) CHES 2001. LNCS, vol. 2162, pp. 118–125. Springer, Heidelberg (2001)

Reduction-Centric Non-programmable Security Proof for the Full Domain Hash in the Random Oracle Model⋆

Mario Larangeira and Keisuke Tanaka

Department of Mathematical and Computing Sciences,
Tokyo Institute of Technology,
2-12-1 Oookayama, Meguro-ku, Tokyo, Japan
{larangeira.m.aa@m,keisuke@is}.titech.ac.jp

Abstract. The security proofs which do not rely on the programmability of the Random Oracle Model (ROM) have the advantage that the reduction of the proof can be actually constructed. This feature contrasts with reductions that rely on the programmability, because hash functions with programmability capacities are not known to exist in the level required in actual proofs of security for important cryptographic schemes. Recent work in Asiacrypt 2010 by Fischlin et al. [7] has shown that proofs without programmability are not likely to exist for the Full Domain Hash (FDH) signature scheme. We propose the strengthening of the one-wayness of the trapdoor permutation underlying the FDH. More formally, we assume one-way trapdoor permutations that cannot be inverted in a number of points of the domain, even when the adversary has access to the inverter oracle for a restricted number of queries, say ℓ. This approach resembles the one-more RSA problem studied by Bellare et al. [1], a generalization of the regular one-wayness assumption. We show that even in the naive case, where the sign and hash queries are less than ℓ, a non-programmable security reduction is possible in Fischlin's model. We also study the more general case where the number of sign and hash queries is greater than ℓ.

Keywords: Random Oracle Model, RSA, FDH, Programmability.

1 Introduction

In the ROM methodology one considers a function $h : X \to Y$, for finite sets X and Y, as an ideal hash function. Moreover, it is common to choose arbitrary (but convenient for some security game) values for the outputs of the function h in security proofs of cryptographic schemes. This ability is denoted as the *programmability* of the random oracle.

⋆ This research was supported in part by NTT Information Sharing Platform Laboratories and JSPS Global COE program "Computationism as Foundation for the Sciences".

D.H. Lee and M. Yung (Eds.): WISA 2012, LNCS 7690, pp. 124–143, 2012.

Very often proofs in the random oracle model use this ability. As an example, consider the notion of *existential unforgeability under the adaptive chosen message attack* (EUF-CMA) [9] by Goldwasser, Micali and Rivest. Briefly, in this notion the adversary is expected to compute a forged signature given a public key, and the access to both the random and the signing oracles. Once the adversary outputs a valid forgery of the form $\sigma = h(m)^d \mod N$, i.e., the RSA-FDH signature scheme by Bellare and Rogaway [3], it is known that the value $h(m)$ must have been delivered to the adversary by the random oracle. In other words, the adversary cannot sample it by itself, since, in such a case, σ would be a *valid* forgery (the verification procedure returns 1) only with negligible probability due to the model. Similar ideas were used to construct security proofs in [4, 5, 13], i.e., the reduction algorithm embeds the challenge of the security proof into the outputs of the random oracle, therefore using the programmability.

These observations received special attention after the work of Nielsen [12]. His result showed that there is a gap between the models with and without programmability.

1.1   Motivation and Related Work

In a simulation-based security proof as in [12] recall that the simulator $\mathcal{S}$ always programs the random oracle, both in the non-programmable and the programmable settings. It may seem contradictory, however the difference is that in the former, the *only good simulation* is when $\mathcal{S}$ repeats the value received from $\mathcal{O}$. Otherwise, the distinguisher easily distinguishes the executions by asking itself the same query directly to $\mathcal{O}$. Obviously, this argument does not work in the programmable setting.

For almost seven years, since [12] the programmability of ROM remained as a understudied topic until recent work carried by Wee [15] and Fischlin et al. [7]. The latters were the first to introduce a framework to address the programmability on reductions, i.e., reduction-centric, instead of the simulation-based approach of the original model of Nielsen. They point out that this approach is indeed relevant, since even in the simulation-based proof one needs to construct a reduction from an instance problem to the distinguisher and this may require the programmability. Their framework is the best model in the literature to formally study proofs with and without programmability.

Their framework introduced a new model named *weakly programmable random oracle model* (WPROM). Briefly, their model prevents programmability by relying on the one-wayness of the one-way function ρ, by giving the adversary access to two interfaces. In one it receives the image $\rho(r)$, while in the other it receives the preimage r, both as the output of the random oracle. A reduction which tries to program the random oracle, can choose $\rho(r)$ but does not know r due to the one-wayness of ρ, therefore the model is non-programmable.

The authors of [7] remark that their model allows what they named *randomly programming*, that is, a reduction can still choose values for r. In comparison, their model addresses a restrictive sort of non-programmability, i.e., all reductions which program the oracle is expected to fail, due to the one-wayness of ρ, if they set directly the values of $\rho(r)$. One of the observations of their study is that this very specific restriction on the programmability in WPROM is enough to show that no reduction exists to prove FDH secure. In particular no algorithm reduces efficiently from the one-wayness of the trapdoor permutation to an adversary breaking the FDH in their model.

In the *standard model*, i.e., the hash function is not the random oracle, Dodis, Oliveira and Pietrzak [6] previously studied the FDH scheme and found that, essentially, no property of the trapdoor permutation allows a security proof. Moreover it is not known whether any number-theoretic assumption would allow a proof of security.

The interest for the study of programmability, in particular for proofs that do not rely on programmability, is explained since no concrete hash function known so far has features which allow them to be programmed as it is often required in security proofs[1]. The consequence is that a security reduction may not be constructed in practice as observed in [7].

The results in the standard model [6] and in the non-programmable ROM [7] combined leave the security of FDH in state of uncertainty regarding the real construction of the reduction presented by the current security proofs [2, 4]. The practical implications of such real constructions are of prime importance since widely used cryptographic standards [11] for digital signatures rely on them.

Our work takes a different approach. Although the security of the RSA-FDH scheme perfectly holds in the ROM, the previous proofs do not provide a construction for the reduction because they are built in the programmable ROM. Since it is hopeless to look for a property of the trapdoor permutation in the standard model, an alternative is to look for it in the non-programmable ROM. This work provides the first non-programmable security proof for the RSA-FDH, which means that at least in the Fischlin's model the non-programmable security is possible. We see our work as an effort to put the security of the RSA-FDH on more firm grounds.

1.2 Our Contribution

The main finding of our work is that a non-programmable security reduction for RSA-FDH in the Fischlin's WPROM is possible. It may sound to the reader that it is a contradiction to the previous work, therefore we remark that for the security proof we also propose a strengthening of the one-way assumption for the trapdoor permutation. We adapted the one-more RSA assumption introduced by Bellare et al. in [1] to the WPROM.

Although this notion is not as weak as the standard notion often used for signature schemes, it is a natural and reasonable generalization for the classical one-wayness. Furthermore, we show that combined with the randomly programming of Fischlin's WPROM, it brings the advantage to permit the construction of a non-programmable security proof based on the random oracle model.

---

[1] Programmable hash functions were introduced by Hofheinz and Kiltz[10], but unfortunately their hash functions still lack the level of programmability required in the regular proofs of security.

Table 1. Security reduction for the FDH in the programmable and non-programmable ROM, and the standard model

Trapdoor permutations			
∀ property (essencially)	One-way		One-more One-way
Standard model	non-prog. ROM	prog. ROM	non-prog. ROM
∄ security reduction [6]	∄security reduction [7]	∃ security reduction (theoretical reduction) [2, 4]	∃ security reduction (**Fischlin's Model**) [This work]

In a theoretical point of view, our result is relevant since we show a middle ground between the general result of [6] and the one in the Fischlin's model. Moreover, our result still relies on crucial properties of the random oracle described earlier, i.e., when the adversary outputs a valid forgery, it can be assumed that the hash of the message was delivered by the random oracle. Thus, a conclusion is that in random oracle based proofs, this property may play a more crucial role in comparison to the programmability of the ROM for proving the security of RSA-FDH scheme.

1.3   Overview of Our Approach

We base our work on the described property. We prove two theorems about the security of RSA-FDH regarding the number of hash and sign queries, respectively, q_h and q_s, and ℓ, where ℓ is the parameter for the one-more one-wayness assumption. In particular we present the following

- Naive approach: q_h and q_s, are less than ℓ (Theorem 1, Lemmas 1 and 2).
- Tighter version: $q_h + q_s \geq \ell$, (Theorem 2 and Lemma 3) in Section 6, and the security analysis regarding q_s, ℓ and the security parameter k in Section 7. That is, whenever $q_s < \ell - k \cdot \ln(2)$ the RSA-FDH is secure.

The proofs are based in two disjoint cases: when a forgery would be generated by (1) the (unlikely) collision found by the adversary using the (weakly programmable) random oracle, and (2) a collision have not happened and the adversary inverted the trapdoor permutation. We focus our analysis in (2) (Lemma 2 and Lemma 3).

Recall that in the standard one-wayness of the trapdoor permutation f_{pk}, an algorithm, say, $\mathcal{I}$, receives a random value from the domain and the public key pk, and is required to output $z = f_{sk}^{-1}(y)$. The approach using this property is not suitable for the non-programmable setting since in the classical EUF-CMA the adversary receives several points sampled by the random oracle.

Our approach is to consider a definition more similar to the model of attack (i.e., EUF-CMA) and more general, since in [7] only the particular case of *none* signature queries was considered. That is the adversary and the reduction receive arbitrary points in the domain of the trapdoor but choose one to compute the inverted value for the trapdoor on that point (i.e., construct the forgery as in (2) in our analysis) after received at most $q - 1$ inverted values (i.e., signature queries). This translates into a property similar to the one-more RSA assumption [1], that is the inverter algorithm $\mathcal{I}$ to query the inverter oracle f_{sk}^{-1} at most $\ell - 1$ times. The challenge starts by $\mathcal{I}$ receiving the pk and ℓ values r_i. It is expected to output ℓ inverted values $z_1, \ldots, z_\ell$, such that $f_{pk}(z_i) = y_i$ with at most $\ell - 1$ queries to the inverter oracle f_{sk}^{-1}, for uniformly random y_i chosen by the random oracle $\mathcal{O}$. Adapting it to WPROM, this means that y_i are $\rho(r_i)$, where ρ is defined by the model.

Note that, $\mathcal{I}$ is not expected to invert a single value as in the classical one-wayness notion. Instead, it chooses among the received *arbitrary* values y_i sampled randomly from the domain. Needless to say that $\mathcal{I}$ cannot choose the points y_i, which are chosen by the random oracle $\mathcal{O}$.

2   Basic Definitions

In this work, PPT stands for *probabilistic polynomial-time*. When a pair (y, x) is said to be defined, it means that the value x has already been queried to the random oracle and y was returned. It is said that a function f is negligible in k, i.e., negl(k), if for any $c, d \in \mathbb{N}$ there exists $k_0 \in \mathbb{N}$ such that for all $k > k_0$ and for all $x \in \{0, 1\}^{k^d}$, it holds that $f(x, k) < k^{-c}$. Finally, assume that $\mathcal{M} = \{0, 1\}^l$ is the message space for the scheme and k is the security parameter in the rest of the paper.

We start by reviewing a few basic definitions.

2.1   The One-Way Trapdoor Permutations

Definition 1 (Collection of one-way trapdoor permutations [8]). *The tuple $(\mathcal{K}, \mathcal{F}, \mathcal{G}, \mathcal{R})$ is a collection of one-way trapdoor permutations with security parameter k, if $\mathcal{K}$ is an infinite index set, $\mathcal{F} = \{f(pk, \cdot) = f_{pk}(\cdot) : D_{pk} \to D_{pk}\}_{pk \in \mathcal{K}}$ is a set of permutations for a domain D_{pk}, the key/trapdoor-generator $\mathcal{G}$ and the domain-generator $\mathcal{R}$ are PPT algorithms, and the following holds:*

Easy to compute (generator algorithm): *$\mathcal{G}(1^k) \to (pk, sk)$ generates pairs of keys and trapdoors, where $pk \in \mathcal{K} \cap \{0, 1\}^{p(k)}$ for some fixed polynomial $p(k)$. Nonetheless $f_{pk}(\cdot)$ is PPT for $r \in D_{pk}$ and computes $f_{pk}(r)$.*
Easy to sample (domain set algorithm): *$\mathcal{R}(pk) \to r$, and r is uniformly random in D_{pk}.*
Hard to invert: *For any PPT algorithm $\mathcal{A}$ the probability over the randomnesses of the algorithms $\mathcal{G}$ and $\mathcal{R}$ that $\mathcal{A}(pk, f_{pk}(r)) = r$ is negligible in k.*
Easy to invert with the trapdoor: *There   is   a   PPT   algorithm $f^{-1}(sk, f_{pk}(r)) := f_{sk}^{-1}(f_{pk}(r)) = r$, for all $\mathcal{G} \to (pk, sk)$ and $r \in D_{pk}$.*

2.2   The RSA Cryptosystem

One of the most popular candidates for collection of trapdoor (one-way) permutations is presented in the next definition.

Definition 2 (RSA collection [8]). *Let the tuple* $(\mathsf{RSA}, \mathsf{D}_{RSA}, \mathsf{F}_{RSA})$ *be called RSA collection with security parameter* $k \in \mathbb{N}$, *if the key/trapdoor-generation algorithm* RSA *and the domain-generator* D_{RSA} *are PPT algorithms in* k, *and the following holds.*

- RSA, *on input* 1^k, *outputs except with negligible probability a modulo* N *and two integers* e *and* d, *such that* $e \cdot d = 1 \mod (p-1) \cdot (q-1)$, *for two* $k-bit$ *long prime numbers* p *and* q *whose product is* N.
- $\mathsf{D}_{RSA}(N, e)$ *samples an element from* $\{1, \ldots, N\}$.
- $\mathsf{F}_{RSA} = \{f((N, e), \cdot) : \mathsf{D}_{RSA}(N, e) \to \mathsf{D}_{RSA}(N, e)\}$, *with* $f((N, e), x) = x^e \mod N$.

2.3   The Digital Signature Schemes

A digital signature is a string dependent of a message m and a secret value sk only known to the signer. Anyone can verify the signature given the public key pk, the message m and the signature.

Definition 3 (Signature scheme). *The tuple* (gen, sig, ver) *is a digital signature scheme with respect to a message space* $\mathcal{M}$ *if the three above mentioned algorithms are as follows.*

- *The key generation algorithm* $gen(1^k)$ *outputs the secret/public key pair* $(\mathsf{pk}, \mathsf{sk})$ *given the security parameter* k. *That is* $gen(1^k) \to (\mathsf{sk}, \mathsf{pk})$.
- *The sign algorithm* $sig_{\mathsf{sk}} := sig(\mathsf{sk}, \cdot)$ *output the signature* σ *when given the message* $m \in \mathcal{M}$. *That is* $sig_{\mathsf{sk}}(m) \to \sigma$.
- *The verification algorithm* $ver_{\mathsf{pk}} := ver(\mathsf{pk}, \cdot, \cdot)$ *outputs a bit* b *such that* $b = 1$ *if the signature* σ *is accepted with respect to* m *and* pk, *otherwise* b *equals to* 0. *That is* $ver_{\mathsf{pk}}(m, \sigma) \to b$.

2.4   The Full Domain Hash Signature Scheme (FDH)

The FDH is the signature scheme $(gen, sig_{\mathsf{sk}}, ver_{\mathsf{pk}})$ where the algorithms sig_{sk} and ver_{pk} have oracle access to a hash function $h : \{0,1\}^l \to \{0,1\}^k$ and $gen(1^k) \to (\mathsf{pk}, \mathsf{sk})$.

$sig_{\mathsf{sk}}(m)$	$ver_{\mathsf{pk}}(m, \sigma)$
$h(m) \to y$	$f_{\mathsf{pk}}(\sigma) \to y'$
$f_{\mathsf{sk}}^{-1}(y) \to \sigma$	if $h(m) = y'$
return σ	return 1
	else
	return 0

Next, we review the classical security game for digital signature schemes.

2.5   The EUF-CMA Security Game

This is the standard security game for digital signature schemes.

Definition 4 (EUF-CMA security game [9]). *Given a signature scheme S, the existential forgery under adaptive chosen message attack game is defined by the following.*

$\mathbf{Game}^{h}_{EUF-CMA}(k)$

1. *The generation algorithm* $gen(1^k)$ *is run to obtain the keys* (sk, pk).
2. *Adversary* $\mathcal{A}$ *is given* pk.
3. *The adversary submits hash queries by sending* x_i, *and receives the values* $h(x_i)$.
4. *The adversary submits sign queries by sending* m_j, *and receives the values* q_j.
5. *Eventually,* $\mathcal{A}$ *outputs a forged signature* σ^* *for* m^*.
6. *If* $\forall j$, $m^* \neq m_j$ *and* $ver_{pk}(m^*, \sigma^*) = 1$, $\mathcal{A}$ *wins the game and therefore output* 1. *Otherwise* $\mathcal{A}$ *loses, consequently output* 0.

Definition 5. *For an adversary* $\mathcal{A}$ *and a signature scheme S, we define the advantage of* $\mathcal{A}$ *in the above game, written* $Adv_{S^h}^{EUF-CMA}(\mathcal{A})$, *as follows*

$$Adv_{S^h}^{EUF-CMA}(\mathcal{A}) = \Pr[Game^{h}_{EUF-CMA}(k) \rightarrow 1]$$

where the probability is taken over the randomness of the game.

2.6   The RSA-FDH

Now we are ready to properly review the RSA-FDH signature scheme[2] which is given by the table below.

$gen(1^k)$	$sig_{sk}(m)$	$ver_{pk}(m, \sigma)$
$RSA(1^k) \rightarrow (N, e, d)$	$h(m) \rightarrow y$	$\sigma^e \rightarrow y'$
$(N, e) \rightarrow$ pk	$y^d \rightarrow \sigma$	if $h(m) = y'$
$(N, d) \rightarrow$ sk	return σ	return 1
return (pk, sk)		else
		return 0

The security of the RSA-FDH is based on the assumption that the RSA Cryptosystem, as in Definition 2, is a collection of one-way trapdoor permutations, as in Definition 1, in the (programmable) ROM.

Next, we review the WPROM, in particular the ρ-WPROM, therefore it is possible to choose a proper function ρ which gives the non-programmable ROM.

---

[2] Consider $h : \{0, 1\}^l \rightarrow \{0, 1\}^k$ and exponentiations are done modulo N.

3   The Weakly Programmable Random Oracle Model

Here we review the WPROM. In particular we review the definitions for ρ-WPRO and the fully-black-box (BB) WPROM reduction from [7].

3.1   The WPROM and ROM

For comparison, we start the section by recalling the standard definition for the random oracle $\mathcal{O}$.

Definition 6 (Random oracle $\mathcal{O}$). *The parties (and the adversary) are allowed to evaluate values $x \in \{0,1\}^l$ and receive the value $z \in \{0,1\}^k$ chosen uniformly at random independent of previous evaluations, except for the evaluation on the same value x, in which $\mathcal{O}$ returns z again.*

In order to move to the WPROM, first we need to review the definition for GOOD function ρ.

Definition 7 (GOOD function ρ [7]). *Given two sets COINS and RNG, a function $\rho :$ COINS $\to$ RNG is named GOOD for RNG, if and only if*

1. *COINS is a finite set*
2. *|RNG| divides |COINS|*
3. *ρ is regular, that is $\forall y \in$ RNG*

$$|\{r \in \text{COINS} : \rho(r) = y\}| = \frac{|\text{COINS}|}{|\text{RNG}|}.$$

From now we consider RNG $= \{0,1\}^k$ and COINS $= \{0,1\}^c$ for a fixed integer c and the security parameter k as given by the RSA-FDH scheme from Section 2.6.

Now we need to review the weakly programmable random oracle (WPRO).

Definition 8 (ρ-WPRO [7]). *Given a GOOD function ρ, and two pairwise tables T and R, the weakly programmable random oracle $\mathcal{O}^\rho$, or ρ-WPRO, is composed by the honest and the adversary interfaces, that is $\mathcal{O}^\rho = (\mathcal{O}^\rho_{hon}, \mathcal{O}^\rho_{adv})$, where the two interfaces are defined as follows*

$\mathcal{O}^\rho_{hon}(x):$	$\mathcal{O}^\rho_{adv}(x):$
if $\exists$ a pair $(z,x) \in$ T	if $\exists$ a pair $(z,x) \in$ T
return z	return z and r
	(such that $(r,x) \in$ R)
else	else
sample $r \leftarrow$ COINS	sample $r \leftarrow$ COINS
set $z \leftarrow \rho(r)$	set $z \leftarrow \rho(r)$
add (z,x) in T	add (z,x) in T
add (r,x) in R	add (r,x) in R
return z	return z and r

Remark 1. As an example, if the adversary $\mathcal{A}$ submits a hash query on x, it would receive two values, namely r and $\rho(r)$, through the adversarial interface $\mathcal{O}^\rho_{adv}$.

Remark 2. As discussed in [7], depending on the properties of ρ, the WPROM may vary from non-programmable to fully-programmable ROM. In particular,

- If ρ is the identity function, then WPROM is equivalent to the programmable ROM.
- If ρ is one-way function, then WPROM is non-programmable ROM.

It is easy to see that when ρ is one-way function it becomes difficult for any reduction to program the random oracle. In particular, any PPT reduction, given a value z' for the output of the random oracle, will find difficult to compute $\rho^{-1}(z')$ in order to find a suitable r'. Since we are interested in the non-programmable ROM, it is convenient to give an extra definition.

Definition 9 (GOOD$_{OW}$ function ρ). *A function ρ : COINS $\to$ RNG is said to be GOOD$_{OW}$ if it is GOOD for RNG and it is also one-way function.*

Remark 3. From now, assume for the rest of the work that ρ is GOOD$_{OW}$ function.

It is also known from [7, Theorem 4.6], that ROM and WPROM are equivalent models. In addition that being a weakly programmable random oracle is in fact a *weaker requirement* than being a full-fledged random oracle, in the sense that it is possible to construct a random oracle out of a WPRO.

From now, we can properly give the formal definition for the fully-black box (BB) security reduction in WPROM, i.e., WPROM reduction for short.

3.2 Black-Box Reduction in WPROM

Given a cryptographic scheme S with access to $\mathcal{O}^{\rho}_{hon}$, and which uses a primitive f, written $S^{\mathcal{O}^{\rho}_{hon}}[f]$, a reduction $\mathcal{B}$ that breaks the property π' of the primitive f, using an adversary $\mathcal{A}$, which, respectively, attacks the property π of the scheme S is formalized in the following definition.

Definition 10 (WPROM reduction [7]). *For $q_{\mathcal{A}}$ instances of the adversary $\mathcal{A}$, q_ρ queries to ρ, q_f queries to f and running time t, the $(\pi' \leftarrow \pi, \delta, t, q_\rho, q_f, q_{\mathcal{A}})$-fully-BB WPROM security reduction for S is an oracle machine $B^{(\cdot,\cdot,\cdot)}$ with the property that for all π-adversaries $\mathcal{A}^{(\cdot)}$, all GOOD functions ρ for RNG, and all π'-candidates f, if*

$$Adv^{\pi}_{S^{\mathcal{O}^{\rho}_{hon}}[f]}(\mathcal{A}^{\mathcal{O}^{\rho}_{adv}}) > \varepsilon$$

for ρ-WPRO $\mathcal{O}^{\rho} = (\mathcal{O}^{\rho}_{hon}, \mathcal{O}^{\rho}_{adv})$

$$Adv^{\pi'}_{f}(B^{(\rho,f,\mathcal{A}^{(\cdot)})}) > \delta(\varepsilon, q_{\mathcal{A}}, q_\rho, q_f, t).$$

The intuition is that given an adversary $\mathcal{A}$ with minimal success probability ε in breaking π, then the reduction B with oracle access to ρ, f and $\mathcal{A}$ in WPROM has minimal success probability δ in breaking π'.

As pointed in Remark 2, if ρ is GOOD$_{OW}$ the reduction B will find very difficult to simulate the *adversarial interface* $\mathcal{O}^{\rho}_{adv}$, i.e., the pair (z', r'), for an arbitrary z' and $r' = \rho^{-1}(z')$. In fact, for such simulation, the success probability of B can be showed negligible in the non-programmable setting.

Next, we describe our approach to give a stronger property for the collection of one-way trapdoor permutation of Definition 1.

4   Strengthening the One-Way Trapdoor Permutation

In this section we give the strengthening of the regular one-way trapdoor permutation assumption adapted to the WPROM.

4.1   The One-More Variant

Here we give the strengthening of Definition 1.

Our notion for the one-wayness resembles the one considered in [1] and [14] based on the one-more RSA problem, i.e. ℓ-OM-RSA, which suggests that the RSA collection of trapdoor (one-way) permutations satisfies this extra requirement.

For comparison, we briefly recall the one-more problem for a collection of trapdoor $(\mathcal{K}, \mathcal{F}, \mathcal{G}, \mathcal{R})$ from Definition 1.

Definition 11 (One-more trapdoor permutation problem)
Given the generation algorithm $\mathcal{G}$, the trapdoor permutation $f_{\mathsf{pk}} \in \mathcal{F}$ and $\ell = \ell(k)$, for all PPT inverter algorithm $\mathcal{I}$ which does at most $\ell - 1 > 0$ queries to the inverter oracle f_{sk}^{-1}, we have that the probability

$$\Pr \left[\begin{array}{l} \mathcal{G}(1^k) \to (\mathsf{sk}, \mathsf{pk}); \\ \mathcal{R} \to (r_1, \ldots, r_\ell); \\ \mathcal{I}^{f_{\mathsf{sk}}^{-1}}(r_1, \ldots, r_\ell, \mathsf{pk}) \end{array} : \mathcal{I}^{f_{\mathsf{sk}}^{-1}} \to \begin{array}{l} (f_{\mathsf{sk}}^{-1}(r_1), \\ \ldots, f_{\mathsf{sk}}^{-1}(r_\ell)) \end{array} \right] \leq \varepsilon_{OM}$$

where the probability is taken over the randomnesses of the algorithms $\mathcal{G}$, $\mathcal{R}$ and $\mathcal{I}^{f_{\mathsf{sk}}^{-1}}$.

4.2   The One-More Variant in WPROM

We now formally state our definition for the one-more problem variant in the ρ-WPROM, i.e., WP-OM.

Definition 12 $((\ell, \varepsilon_{WP\text{-}OM})$-WP-OM). *Let k be the security parameter and ρ be a GOOD$_{OW}$ function. Given the generation algorithm $\mathcal{G}$, the trapdoor permutation $f_{\mathsf{pk}} \in \mathcal{F}$ and $\ell = \ell(k)$, for all PPT inverter algorithm $\mathcal{I}$ which does at most $\ell - 1 > 0$ queries to the inverter oracle f_{sk}^{-1}, we have that the probability*

$$\Pr \left[\begin{array}{l} \mathcal{G}(1^k) \to (\mathsf{sk}, \mathsf{pk}); \\ \mathcal{R} \to (r_1, \ldots, r_\ell); \\ \text{GOOD}_{OW} \to \rho; \\ \mathcal{I}^{f_{\mathsf{sk}}^{-1}, \rho}(r_1, \ldots, r_\ell, \mathsf{pk}) \end{array} : \mathcal{I}^{f_{\mathsf{sk}}^{-1}, \rho} \to \begin{array}{l} (f_{\mathsf{sk}}^{-1}(\rho(r_1)), \\ \ldots, f_{\mathsf{sk}}^{-1}(\rho(r_\ell))) \end{array} \right] \leq \varepsilon_{WP\text{-}OM}$$

where the probability is taken over the randomnesses of the algorithms $\mathcal{G}$, $\mathcal{R}$ and $\mathcal{I}^{f_{sk}^{-1},\rho}$.

The difference is that the inverter algorithm $\mathcal{I}^{f_{sk}^{-1},\rho}$ receives the public key pk and $\ell(k)$ points in the domain, moreover it can query f_{sk}^{-1} and the GOOD_{OW} function ρ in a restricted number of times.

Intuitively, this definition is stronger than the standard one-wayness (when ℓ is fixed and equals to 1) of the trapdoor permutation. Consider, for example, that the algorithm $\mathcal{I}^{f_{sk}^{-1},\rho}$ can choose which value it will try to invert among the ones it received from $\mathcal{R}$. This does not apply to the Definition 1, since, in there, $\mathcal{I}^{f_{sk}^{-1},\rho}$ receives the single value it is expected to invert.

They were chosen by the arbitrary sampler algorithm $\mathcal{R}$, which samples them uniformly at random, and ρ.

Remark 4. As observed in [1] and [14], for $\ell_2 \geq \ell_1$, ℓ_2-OM-RSA reduces to ℓ_1-OM-RSA. The 1-OM-RSA is identical to the problem induced by Definition 1, i.e., the problem of inverting the one-way trapdoor permutation.

Remark 5. Note the number of points is $\ell := \ell(k)$, that is it depends on the security parameter k.

5   The RSA-FDH in the WPROM

Here we give our security analysis of the RSA-FDH in WPROM.

For the next theorem, let $S = (gen, sig_{sk}, ver_{pk})$ be the RSA-FDH given by Section 2.6 and $\ell = \ell(k)$, where k is the security parameter.

Theorem 1. *Assume that the RSA cryptosystem, from Definition 2, is a collection of $(\ell, \varepsilon_{WP-OM})$-WP-OM one-way trapdoor permutation as in Definition 12. Then, for all adversary $\mathcal{A}$ performing the EUF-CMA with at most q_s signature queries and q_h hash queries, such that $q_s + q_h \leq \ell - 1$, we have*

$$Adv_{S^{O\rho}}^{EUF-CMA}(\mathcal{A}) \leq \frac{q_s \cdot (q_s + q_h)}{2^k} + \varepsilon_{WP-OM},$$

where the probabilities are taken over the randomnesses of the adversary, the generation algorithm gen and WPRO.

Proof.   Consider a challenger C which simulates to the adversary $\mathcal{A}$ the $\textbf{Game}_{\textbf{EUF-CMA}}^{O\rho}$ as in Definition 4 with fresh randomness and security parameter k.

The challenger C simulates both the honest and the adversary interfaces as outlined in Definition 8. In other words, C keeps tables T and R, and samples uniformly random values r from the COINS set.

Assume for the sake of contradiction that $\mathcal{A}$ produces a valid forgery σ^* for some message m^* with non-negligible probability and denote by WIN the event that $\mathcal{A}$ outputs a valid forgery. The Definition 5 gives that

$$Adv_{S^{O\rho}}^{EUF-CMA}(\mathcal{A}) = \Pr[\text{WIN}]$$

with probabilities taken over the randomness of the challenger C.

Let also QUERY be the event that $\mathcal{A}$ has queried m^* to the random oracle $\mathcal{O}^\rho$ and received z^* and r^*, while C defined $z^* = \rho(r^*)$ for a uniformly random value r^* as in Definition 8.

It is straightforward that

$$\Pr[\mathsf{WIN}] = \Pr[\mathsf{WIN} \wedge \overline{\mathsf{QUERY}}] + \Pr[\mathsf{WIN} \wedge \mathsf{QUERY}]$$
$$\leq \Pr[\mathsf{WIN}|\overline{\mathsf{QUERY}}] + \Pr[\mathsf{QUERY}]$$

where the probabilities are taken from the randomnesses of challenger C and the generation algorithm gen.

We estimate the two probabilities $\Pr[\mathsf{WIN}|\overline{\mathsf{QUERY}}]$ and $\Pr[\mathsf{QUERY}]$ separately in the following two lemmas. The theorem follows.

Lemma 1. *Given a* GOOD$_{OW}$ *function* ρ*, if the hash function* h *is modeled as the* ρ*-WPRO, then*

$$\Pr[\mathsf{WIN}|\overline{\mathsf{QUERY}}] \leq \frac{q_s \cdot (q_s + q_h)}{2^k}.$$

Proof. The event $\overline{\mathsf{QUERY}}$ means that the adversary did not submit a hash query on m^*. That is, the value $z^* = \rho(r^*)$ and r^* must have been defined in a signature query during the simulation of $\mathbf{Game}^{\mathcal{O}^\rho}_{\mathbf{EUF-CMA}}$ given by C.

In order to understand why it must have been defined in a signature query, assume that the adversary $\mathcal{A}$ outputs (m^*, σ^*) without submitting m^* for a sign query nor a hash query. We show, next, that the probability that $ver(\mathsf{pk}, m^*, \sigma^*) \to 1$ for such adversary is negligible. Therefore this adversary is often not considered in security proofs based on the random oracle model.

Let SIGN be the event that m^* is submitted for a sign query in the simulation provided by C. Formally, we need to show that $\Pr[ver(\mathsf{pk}, m^*, \sigma^*) \to 1|\overline{\mathsf{SIGN}} \wedge \overline{\mathsf{QUERY}}]$ is negligible in k. First, observe that this probability is equal to

$$\Pr[\mathsf{COINS} \to r' : y^* = \rho(r')]$$

where $y^* = (\sigma^*)^e$ is fixed by $\mathcal{A}$ by the time it outputs (m^*, σ^*), and r' is uniformly chosen at random because $\overline{\mathsf{SIGN}}$ and $\overline{\mathsf{QUERY}}$, i.e., $(r', m^*) \notin \mathsf{R}$, for R being the table for the WPRO simulation provided by the challenger C as in Definition 8. Since $(r', m^*) \notin \mathsf{R}$, we are confident to state that by the time C checks the validity of σ^*, some r' is chosen when C runs $ver(\mathsf{pk}, m^*, \sigma^*)$.

Recall that ρ is GOOD$_{OW}$, in particular, it is *regular*, therefore the size of the set of such values for r' is $\frac{|\mathsf{COINS}|}{|\mathsf{RNG}|}$. Moreover ρ is a $\{0,1\}^c \to \{0,1\}^k$ function, where k is the security parameter as defined by the RSA-FDH scheme. Hence the probability that the verification procedure picks the correct r' is upper bounded by

$$\Pr[\mathsf{COINS} \to r' : y^* = \rho(r')] = \frac{1}{|\mathsf{COINS}| \cdot \frac{1}{\frac{|\mathsf{COINS}|}{|\mathsf{RNG}|}}} = \frac{1}{2^k},$$

where r' is chosen uniformly at random. Therefore,

$$\Pr[ver(\mathsf{pk}, m^*, \sigma^*) \to 1|\overline{\mathsf{SIGN}} \wedge \overline{\mathsf{QUERY}}] \leq \frac{1}{2^k}.$$

The conclusion is that if the adversary outputs a *valid* forgery for m^* for the RSA-FDH, i.e., the verification algorithm returns 1, then we can assume that m^* was necessarily asked in a hash or a signature query.

Since by assumption QUERY does not happen during the simulation in the previous reasoning, we feel confident enough to assume that $z^* = \rho(r^*)$ and r^* must have been defined in a signature query. Then the challenger must have chosen, for some $m_i \neq m^*$ (otherwise it would not be a valid forgery), r_i such that $z^* = \rho(r^*) = \rho(r_i) = z_i$. This means

$$\Pr[\mathsf{WIN}|\overline{\mathsf{QUERY}}] = \sum_{i=1}^{q_s} \Pr[\mathsf{COINS} \to r^* : \rho(r_i) = \rho(r^*)|\mathsf{COINS} \to r_i].$$

Since by Definition 8, the values of r_i are chosen uniformly at random, the terms in the summation in the previous equation are upper bounded by all possible hashed values queried in q_s signatures and q_h hash queries,

$$\Pr[\mathsf{COINS} \to r^* : \rho(r_i) = \rho(r^*)|\mathsf{COINS} \to r_i] \leq \frac{q_s + q_h}{2^k}$$

for a fixed sign query i. Therefore, we have that

$$\Pr[\mathsf{WIN}|\overline{\mathsf{QUERY}}] \leq \frac{q_s \cdot (q_s + q_h)}{2^k}$$

for $0 < i \leq q_s$.   □

Lemma 2. *Given a* GOOD$_{OW}$ *function* ρ *and* $q_s + q_h \leq \ell - 1$, *if the hash function* h *is modeled as the* ρ-*WPRO and the RSA Cryptosystem has the property described in Definition 12, then*

$$\Pr[\mathsf{QUERY}] \leq \varepsilon_{WP\text{-}OM}.$$

Proof. The adversary submitted a hash query on m^*, where m^* is the message which the signature was forged. Thus the value $z^* = \rho(r^*)$ and r^* must have been defined by the challenger C, i.e., there is a pair (r^*, m^*) in table R and a pair (z^*, m^*) in table T that C keeps during the simulation of $\mathbf{Game}^{\mathcal{O}^\rho}_{\mathbf{EUF\text{-}CMA}}$.

In order to bound the probability of the event QUERY to happen, assume that a direct hash query on m^* did happen, then we construct the inverter algorithm $\mathcal{I}^{f_{sk}^{-1},\rho}$ as outlined in Definition 12. The inverter $\mathcal{I}^{f_{sk}^{-1},\rho}$ is a black-box WPROM reduction as described in Definition 10.

The Construction of $\mathcal{I}^{f_{sk}^{-1},\rho}$. Let $\{r_1, \ldots, r_\ell\}$ be the input sampled by the sampling algorithm $\mathcal{R}$ which was received by the inverter algorithm $\mathcal{I}^{f_{sk}^{-1},\rho}$ with pk. The inverter delivers pk to $\mathcal{A}$ and simulates the WPRO by keeping the tables T and R, as in Definition 8, and two lists, named USED and INVERTED, both initially empty.

The algorithm $\mathcal{I}^{f_{sk}^{-1},\rho}$ answers the hash and sign queries by using its ρ and f_{sk}^{-1} oracles, respectively, and through manipulation of INVERTED and USED, as follows:

- Hash query on x_i: choose a value r uniformly at random from $\{r_1, \ldots, r_\ell\} \setminus$ USED and add it to USED.
  1. forward r to the ρ oracle, and receive $\rho(r)$;
  2. add the pairs $(\rho(r), x_i)$ and (r, x_i), respectively, to the tables T and R;
  3. return r and $\rho(r)$ to the adversary;
- Sign query on m_i: If there is no x, such that $x = m_i$, for the pairs $(r, x) \in R$ and $(\rho(r), x) \in T$, then use the hash query procedure described earlier for m_i and run again the sign procedure. Otherwise, there is a pair $(\rho(r), m_i) \in T$, then
  1. forward $\rho(r)$ to the oracle f_{sk}^{-1}, and receive $f_{sk}^{-1}(\rho(r))$, then;
  2. deliver $f_{sk}^{-1}(\rho(r))$ to the adversary as the signature σ_i for m_i;
  3. add $f_{sk}^{-1}(\rho(r))$ to INVERTED.

By assumption QUERY occurs. Note that, by definition, whenever the event QUERY happens the adversary $\mathcal{A}$ outputs a valid forgery σ^* for the message m^*. Then, it is known that $\sigma^* = f_{sk}^{-1}(\rho(r^*))$ for a pair $(\rho(r^*), m^*) \in T$. Therefore, $\mathcal{I}^{f_{sk}^{-1},\rho}$ adds $f_{sk}^{-1}(\rho(r^*))$ to INVERTED.

For all remained value $r \in \{r_1, \ldots, r_\ell\} \setminus$ USED, submit it to the oracle ρ and then to f_{sk}^{-1} and add the received value $f_{sk}^{-1}(\rho(r))$ to INVERTED. Whereas, for all the values in USED which there is no inverted value in INVERTED, submit to the f_{sk}^{-1} oracle. Thus, $\mathcal{I}^{f_{sk}^{-1},\rho}$ outputs INVERTED.

Analysis of $\mathcal{I}^{f_{sk}^{-1},\rho}$. Clearly, the running time of $\mathcal{I}^{f_{sk}^{-1},\rho}$ is polynomial-time in k . The key observation is that since h is modeled as a (non-programmable) random oracle, there are pairs $(r^*, m^*) \in R$ and $(\rho(r^*), m^*) \in T$. In order to see this, recall that it is very unlikely that the adversary can choose by itself a value $\rho(r^*)$ for a valid forgery when h is the random oracle. In other words, we may assume that the adversary received the correct (for a valid forgery) value $\rho(r^*)$ from the simulation.

In addition, since, by construction, all the values delivered in the hash queries are inputs of $\mathcal{I}^{f_{sk}^{-1},\rho}$ and $q_s + q_h \le \ell - 1$, our inverter algorithm does at most $\ell - 1$ queries to its f_{sk}^{-1} oracle.

Hence, if the direct hash query on m^* happens and the adversary computes a forgery with non-negligible probability, that means

$$\Pr[\text{QUERY}] = \Pr[\mathcal{I}^{f_{sk}^{-1},\rho} \to (f_{sk}^{-1}(\rho(r_1)), \cdots, f_{sk}^{-1}(\rho(r_\ell)))].$$

On the other hand, we assumed, from Definition 12, that for all PPT inverter algorithm $\mathcal{I}^{f_{sk}^{-1},\rho}$,

$$\Pr[\mathcal{I}^{f_{sk}^{-1},\rho} \to (f_{sk}^{-1}(\rho(r_1)), \cdots, f_{sk}^{-1}(\rho(r_\ell)))] \le \varepsilon_{WP-OM},$$

therefore we have

$$\Pr[\mathsf{QUERY}] \leq \varepsilon_{WP-OM}$$

thereby giving the proof of the lemma.   □

6   A Tighter Security Reduction

For the next lemma, we consider the case when $q_s + q_h > \ell$. Let again ρ an GOOD_{OW} function, and now consider an arbitrary probability p. Our next construction for the inverter algorithm spreads the values from the one-more challenge within the hash values, in the hope that when the adversary output a forgery, it comes from $\{r_1, \ldots, r_\ell\}$ since the adversary has no way to distinguish them.

The proof is more technical than the early one, therefore for reading convenience, let INPUT be the set $\{r_1, \ldots, r_\ell\}$.

Lemma 3. *If the hash function h is modeled as the ρ-WPRO and the RSA Cryptosystem has the property described in Definition 12, and $q_s + q_h > \ell$ for $q_s \leq \ell - 1$, then*

$$\Pr[\mathsf{QUERY}] \leq (1-p)^{q_h} + \frac{\varepsilon_{WP-OM}}{1 - q_s \cdot (q_h - (\ell - q_s)) \cdot (1-p)} \cdot \frac{1}{1 - q_s \cdot (1 - (1-p)^{q_h}) \cdot \frac{1-p}{p}}.$$

Proof. A direct hash query on m^* did happen, therefore the value $z^* = \rho(r^*)$ and r^* must have been defined by the challenger C, i.e., there is a pair (r^*, m^*) in table R and a pair (z^*, m^*) in table T that C keeps during the simulation of $\mathsf{Game}_{\mathsf{EUF-CMA}}^{\mathcal{O}^\rho}$.

If QUERY happens it means that the adversary could find the inverted value $f_{\mathsf{sk}}^{-1}(\rho(r^*))$. Similarly, consider the next inverter algorithm $\mathcal{I}^{f_{\mathsf{sk}}^{-1}, \rho}$ as outlined in Definition 12.

The Construction of $\mathcal{I}^{f_{\mathsf{sk}}^{-1}, \rho}$. The construction is similar to the one in the proof of Lemma 2, the differences are in the definitions of the simulations for the sign and the hash queries.

The inverter $\mathcal{I}^{f_{\mathsf{sk}}^{-1}, \rho}$ answers the hash and sign queries by using its ρ and f_{sk}^{-1} oracles, respectively, and through manipulation of $\mathsf{INPUT} \setminus \mathsf{USED}$, as follows:

-   Hash query on x_i: If $\mathsf{INPUT} \setminus \mathsf{USED}$ is not empty, with arbitrary probability p, choose a value r uniformly at random from $\mathsf{INPUT} \setminus \mathsf{USED}$ and add it to USED. Otherwise, with probability $p - 1$ or $\mathsf{INPUT} \setminus \mathsf{USED}$ is empty, choose a uniformly random value r. Then,
    1. If r is in R, i.e., $(r, x_i) \in \mathsf{R}$, then return r and $\rho(r)$, such that $(\rho(r), x_i) \in \mathsf{T}$, to the adversary.
    2. Otherwise, i.e., if $r \notin \mathsf{R}$, forward r to the ρ oracle, and receive $\rho(r)$.
    3. Add the pairs $(\rho(r), x_i)$ and (r, x_i), respectively, to the tables T and R;
    4. Return r and $\rho(r)$ to the adversary;

– Sign query on m_i:

If there is any $x = m_i$, such that $(r, x) \in \mathsf{R}$ and $(\rho(r), x) \in \mathsf{T}$. Then,

1. If $r \in \mathsf{INPUT}$, then
   (a) Forward $\rho(r)$ to the oracle f_{sk}^{-1}, and receive $f_{\mathsf{sk}}^{-1}(\rho(r))$;
   (b) Deliver $f_{\mathsf{sk}}^{-1}(\rho(r))$ to the adversary as the signature σ_i for m_i.
   else
   (a) Abort and let this event denote Input-Abort.

Else (if there is no x such that $x = m_i$)

1. If $\mathsf{INPUT} \backslash \mathsf{USED}$ is not empty
   (a) Forward $\rho(r)$ to the oracle f_{sk}^{-1}, and receive $f_{\mathsf{sk}}^{-1}(\rho(r))$;
   (b) Deliver $f_{\mathsf{sk}}^{-1}(\rho(r))$ to the adversary as the signature σ_i for m_i.
   (c) add $f_{\mathsf{sk}}^{-1}(\rho(r))$ to $\mathsf{INVERTED}$.
   else
   (a) Abort and let this event denote Empty-Abort.

By assumption, QUERY happens. As in the proof of Lemma 2 the adversary $\mathcal{A}$ outputted a valid forgery σ^*, and $\mathcal{I}^{f_{\mathsf{sk}}^{-1}, \rho}$ behaves in the same way as in the construction of the proof of Lemma 2.

Analysis of $\mathcal{I}^{f_{\mathsf{sk}}^{-1}, \rho}$. Clearly, the running time of $\mathcal{I}^{f_{\mathsf{sk}}^{-1}, \rho}$ is polynomial-time in k. The inverter algorithm succeeds if the following conditions are fulfilled:

– The value $r^* \in \mathsf{INPUT}$ (therefore the event QUERY occurs); and
– $\mathcal{I}^{f_{\mathsf{sk}}^{-1}, \rho}$ does not abort.

This means

$$\Pr[\mathcal{I}^{f_{\mathsf{sk}}^{-1}, \rho} \text{ succeeds}] = \Pr[\mathsf{QUERY} | r^* \in \mathsf{INPUT}] \cdot \Pr[r^* \in \mathsf{INPUT}] \cdot \Pr[\mathcal{I}^{f_{\mathsf{sk}}^{-1}, \rho} \text{ does not abort}]. \quad (1)$$

On the other hand, it is straightforward to see that

$$\Pr[\mathsf{QUERY}] \leq \Pr[r^* \notin \mathsf{INPUT}] + \Pr[\mathsf{QUERY} | r^* \in \mathsf{INPUT}] \cdot \Pr[r^* \in \mathsf{INPUT}]. \quad (2)$$

From both equations 1 and 2, we have

$$\Pr[\mathcal{I}^{f_{\mathsf{sk}}^{-1}, \rho} \text{ succeeds}] \geq (\Pr[\mathsf{QUERY}] - \Pr[r^* \notin \mathsf{INPUT}]) \cdot \Pr[\mathcal{I}^{f_{\mathsf{sk}}^{-1}, \rho} \text{ does not abort}]. \quad (3)$$

The Definition 12 states that for all PPT inverter algorithm $\mathcal{I}^{f_{\mathsf{sk}}^{-1}, \rho}$,

$$\Pr[\mathcal{I}^{f_{\mathsf{sk}}^{-1}, \rho} \text{ succeeds}] \leq \varepsilon_{WP-OM}.$$

Therefore, Equation 3 gives

$$\Pr[\mathsf{QUERY}] \leq \frac{\varepsilon_{WP-OM}}{\Pr[\mathcal{I}^{f_{\mathsf{sk}}^{-1}, \rho} \text{ does not abort}]} + \Pr[r^* \notin \mathsf{INPUT}]. \quad (4)$$

At this point, we need to estimate the probabilities $\Pr[\mathcal{I}^{f_{sk}^{-1},\rho} \text{ does not abort}]$ and $\Pr[r^* \notin \mathsf{INPUT}]$.

Estimation of $\Pr[\mathcal{I}^{f_{sk}^{-1},\rho} \text{ does not abort}]$. By our construction for $\mathcal{I}^{f_{sk}^{-1},\rho}$, note that

$$\Pr[\mathcal{I}^{f_{sk}^{-1},\rho} \text{ does not abort}] = \Pr[\overline{\mathsf{Input\text{-}Abort}}] \cdot \Pr[\overline{\mathsf{Empty\text{-}Abort}}].$$

We bound the probabilities separately. However, in both cases, consider without loss of generality that by the time of the j-th sign query there has been i hash queries already.

We start by $\Pr[\overline{\mathsf{Empty\text{-}Abort}}]$.

First recall that the inverter algorithm may have used at most j values through sign queries from its input values r, letting at least $\ell - j$ values left. Then the probability can be conditioned as follows

$$\Pr[\mathsf{Empty\text{-}Abort}] = \Pr[\mathsf{Empty\text{-}Abort}|\ell - j > i] \cdot \Pr[\ell - j > i]$$
$$+ \Pr[\mathsf{Empty\text{-}Abort}|\ell - j \le i] \cdot \Pr[\ell - j \le i].$$

The set $\mathsf{INPUT} \backslash \mathsf{USED}$ is not empty when $\ell - j > i$, therefore

$$\Pr[\mathsf{Empty\text{-}Abort}|\ell - j > i] = 0.$$

Since

$$\Pr[\overline{\mathsf{Empty\text{-}Abort}}] = 1 - \Pr[\mathsf{Empty\text{-}Abort}]$$

then we know

$$\Pr[\overline{\mathsf{Empty\text{-}Abort}}] > 1 - \Pr[\mathsf{Empty\text{-}Abort}|\ell - j \le i].$$

In other words, the probability $\Pr[\mathsf{Empty\text{-}Abort}|\ell - j \le i]$ is the same probability that, among the i hash queries, the inverter has sampled, from the set $\{r_1, \ldots, r_\ell\} \backslash \mathsf{USED}$, $\ell - j$ times (instead of picking a random value). The algorithm, by construction, chooses between values from the abovementioned set with arbitrary probability p and uniformly random values with probability $1 - p$, therefore

$$\Pr[\mathsf{Empty\text{-}Abort}|\ell - j \le i] = (1 - p).$$

Consequently, if $\ell - j \le i \le q_h$, then

$$\Pr[\mathsf{Empty\text{-}Abort}|\ell - j \le q_h] = \sum_{i=\ell-j}^{q_h} (1 - p) = (q_h - (\ell - j)) \cdot (1 - p)$$

for a fixed j signature queries.

The probability that the event Empty-Abort in any of the q_s signature queries is

$$\Pr[\text{Empty-Abort}] = \sum_{j=1}^{q_s}(q_h - (\ell - j)) \cdot (1 - p) = q_s \cdot (q_h - (\ell - q_s)) \cdot (1 - p),$$

and therefore

$$\Pr[\overline{\text{Empty - Abort}}] = 1 - q_s \cdot (q_h - (\ell - q_s)) \cdot (1 - p).$$

It remains to bound $\Pr[\overline{\text{Input-Abort}}]$.

Note that on the j-th signature query, the event Input-Abort happens with highest probability when, among all the i hash queries, the inverter $\mathcal{I}^{f_{\text{sk}}^{-1},\rho}$ has not chosen any value from the set INPUT\USED. This event happens with probability $(1 - p)^i$ for a fixed number of hash queries i. Thus, we know that for $i \leq q_h$

$$\Pr[\text{Input-Abort}|\text{on the } j\text{-th sign query}] \leq \sum_{i=1}^{q_h}(1 - p)^i. \tag{5}$$

When $1 \leq j \leq q_s$,

$$\Pr[\text{Input-Abort}] \leq \sum_{j=1}^{q_s}\sum_{i=1}^{q_h}(1 - p)^i \leq q_s \sum_{i=1}^{q_h}(1 - p)^i,$$

$$\leq q_s \cdot (1 - (1 - p)^{q_h}) \cdot \frac{1 - p}{p}.$$

Consequently,

$$\Pr[\overline{\text{Input-Abort}}] \geq 1 - q_s \cdot (1 - (1 - p)^{q_h}) \cdot \frac{1 - p}{p}. \tag{6}$$

Estimation of $\Pr[r^* \notin \text{INPUT}]$. Similarly to the Equation 5, the worst case is when there was no query which $\mathcal{I}^{f_{\text{sk}}^{-1},\rho}$ used values from its inputs, i.e., the set INPUT\USED, among the q_h hash queries. Therefore we have the following upper-bound

$$\Pr[r^* \notin \text{INPUT}] \leq (1 - p)^{q_h}. \tag{7}$$

The Equations 5, 6 and 7 plugged in the Equation 4 give that

$$\Pr[\text{QUERY}] \leq (1 - p)^{q_h} + \frac{\varepsilon_{WP-OM}}{1 - q_s \cdot (q_h - (\ell - q_s)) \cdot (1 - p)} \cdot \frac{1}{1 - q_s \cdot (1 - (1 - p)^{q_h}) \cdot \frac{1-p}{p}}.$$

Therefore we have the lemma.   □

Note that in the case of $p = 1$, we have the upper bound of the Lemma 2.

The Lemma 3 and the early mentioned Lemma 2 allow us to state a more general version of the Theorem 1.

Theorem 2. *Given an arbitrary probability $p < 1$, assume that the RSA cryptosystem, from Definition 2, is a collection of $(\ell, \varepsilon_{WP\text{-}OM})$-WP-OM one-way trapdoor permutation as in Definition 12. Then, for all adversary $\mathcal{A}$ performing the EUF-CMA with at most $q_s < \ell - 1$ signature queries and $q_s + q_h > \ell$ hash queries, we have*

$$Adv_{SOP}^{EUF-CMA}(\mathcal{A}) \le \frac{q_s \cdot (q_s + q_h)}{2^k} + (1-p)^{q_h} + \frac{\varepsilon_{WP-OM}}{1 - q_s \cdot (q_h - (\ell - q_s)) \cdot (1-p)}$$
$$\cdot \frac{1}{1 - q_s \cdot (1 - (1-p)^{q_h}) \cdot \frac{1-p}{p}},$$

where the probabilities are taken over the randomnesses of the adversary, the generation algorithm gen and WPRO.

Proof. The proof follows from Lemma 1 and Lemma 3.   □

Note that upper bound given by Theorem 2 does not give a proof of security since the term $(1-p)^{q_h}$ is not negligible in general. However this can be set arbitrarily negligible by limiting the maximum number of signatures the signer party can issue. In other words, given the value ℓ, it is possible to derive the maximum number of signatures for which RSA-FDH remains EUF-CMA secure for a certain security parameter k.

We conclude by discussing the security regarding ℓ, k and q_s in the next section.

7   Conclusion

Our more general result, the Theorem 2, means that if one assumes that the one-more RSA assumption holds for a fixed and concrete value ℓ, it is possible to derive a maximum number of signatures to be generated in order to remain the advantage negligible. As pointed by Coron in [4][Section 4], arbitrarily limiting the number of signatures is practical. We quote: *"This is practical significance since in the real-world applications, the number of hash calls is only limited by the computational power of the forger, whereas the number of signature queries can be deliberately limited."*

In other words, by setting $p = \frac{\ell - q_s}{q_h}$ and considering natural constraints, such as a high number of hash queries q_h and arbitrarily large value for $\ell - q_s$, the term $(1-p)^{q_h}$ is not greater than $e^{-(\ell - q_s)}$, thus

$$Adv_{SOP}^{EUF-CMA}(\mathcal{A}) \le \frac{q_s \cdot (q_s + q_h)}{2^k} + e^{-(\ell - q_s)} + \frac{\varepsilon_{WP-OM}}{1 + q_s},$$

thereby giving us a proof of security even in the non-programmable random oracle model, whenever $q_s < \ell - k \cdot \ln(2)$ signatures, where ln is the natural logarithm.

Note that in all cases, our results rely on the key (but not new) observation that the message from the forgery can be assumed to be computed by the hash oracle. Our result also shows that this property of the weaker variants of ROM seems to be even more crucial than the programmability of ROM.

References

[1] Bellare, Namprempre, Pointcheval, Semanko: The one-more-RSA-inversion problems and the security of Chaum's blind signature scheme. Journal of Cryptology 16, 185–215 (2008)

[2] Bellare, M., Rogaway, P.: Random oracles are practical: A paradigm for designing efficient protocols, pp. 62–73. ACM Press (1993)

[3] Bellare, M., Rogaway, P.: The Exact Security of Digital Signatures - How to Sign with RSA and Rabin. In: Maurer, U.M. (ed.) EUROCRYPT 1996. LNCS, vol. 1070, pp. 399–416. Springer, Heidelberg (1996)

[4] Coron, J.-S.: On the Exact Security of Full Domain Hash. In: Bellare, M. (ed.) CRYPTO 2000. LNCS, vol. 1880, pp. 229–235. Springer, Heidelberg (2000)

[5] Coron, J.-S.: Optimal Security Proofs for PSS and Other Signature Schemes. In: Knudsen, L.R. (ed.) EUROCRYPT 2002. LNCS, vol. 2332, pp. 272–287. Springer, Heidelberg (2002)

[6] Dodis, Y., Oliveira, R., Pietrzak, K.: On the Generic Insecurity of the Full Domain Hash. In: Shoup, V. (ed.) CRYPTO 2005. LNCS, vol. 3621, pp. 449–466. Springer, Heidelberg (2005)

[7] Fischlin, M., Lehmann, A., Ristenpart, T., Shrimpton, T., Stam, M., Tessaro, S.: Random Oracles with(out) Programmability. In: Abe, M. (ed.) ASIACRYPT 2010. LNCS, vol. 6477, pp. 303–320. Springer, Heidelberg (2010)

[8] Goldreich, O.: Foundations of Cryptography Vol. I - Basic Tools. Cambridge University Press (2006)

[9] Goldwasser, S., Micali, S., Rivest, R.L.: A digital signature scheme secure against adaptive chosen-message attacks. SIAM J. Comput. 17(2), 281–308 (1988)

[10] Hofheinz, D., Kiltz, E.: Programmable Hash Functions and Their Applications. In: Wagner, D. (ed.) CRYPTO 2008. LNCS, vol. 5157, pp. 21–38. Springer, Heidelberg (2008)

[11] The Internet Engineering Task Force (IETF). Public-key cryptography standards (pkcs) #1: RSA cryptography specifications version 2.1 (2003)

[12] Nielsen, J.B.: Separating Random Oracle Proofs from Complexity Theoretic Proofs: The Non-committing Encryption Case. In: Yung, M. (ed.) CRYPTO 2002. LNCS, vol. 2442, pp. 111–126. Springer, Heidelberg (2002)

[13] Numayama, A., Isshiki, T., Tanaka, K.: Security of Digital Signature Schemes in Weakened Random Oracle Models. In: Cramer, R. (ed.) PKC 2008. LNCS, vol. 4939, pp. 268–287. Springer, Heidelberg (2008)

[14] Paillier, P.: Impossibility Proofs for RSA Signatures in the Standard Model. In: Abe, M. (ed.) CT-RSA 2007. LNCS, vol. 4377, pp. 31–48. Springer, Heidelberg (2006)

[15] Wee, H.: Zero Knowledge in the Random Oracle Model, Revisited. In: Matsui, M. (ed.) ASIACRYPT 2009. LNCS, vol. 5912, pp. 417–434. Springer, Heidelberg (2009)

An Authentication and Key Management Scheme for the Proxy Mobile IPv6[*]

Hyun-Sun Kang[1] and Chang-Seop Park[2]

[1] Department of General Education, Namseoul University,
Cheonan, Choongnam, Republic of Korea
sshskang@nsu.ac.kr
[2] Department of Computer Science, Dankook University,
Chonan, Choongnam, Republic of Korea
csp0@dankook.ac.kr

Abstract. Proxy Mobile IPv6 (*PMIPv6*) is a protocol for network-based mobility management. Without a proper protection mechanism of the signaling messages to be used for mobility support in *PMIPv6*, *PMIPv6* is vulnerable to several security attacks such as *Redirection*, *MITM* (Man-In-The-Middle), and *DoS* (Denial of Service) attacks. In this paper, we point out some security problems of previous authentication scheme associated with *PMIPv6*, and also propose a new authentication scheme and key management scheme applicable to *PMIPv6*. In addition, it is also shown that the proposed one is more efficient and secure than the previous ones.

Keywords: Proxy Mobile Ipv6, Authentication, Key Management.

1   Introduction

Mobile IPv6 (*MIPv6*) [1] provides a mobile node (MN) with IP mobility when it performs a handover from one access router to another. *MIPv6* requires client functionality in the IPv6 stack of the MN and the exchange of the signaling messages between the MN and Home Agent (HA) to support IP mobility. However, this process poses a huge burden for a resource-constrained MN, so *MIPv6* is not utilized in actual commercial services. *Proxy MIPv6* (*PMIPv6*) [2] provides IP mobility to MN that does not support *MIPv6* functionality. A proxy agent in the network performs the mobility management signaling on behalf of MN. The core functional entities defined in *PMIPv6* are *Local Mobility Anchor* (LMA) and *Mobile Access Gateway* (MAG). LMA is the modified *MIPv6* HA and is the entity that manages the address binding state of MN. MAG manages the mobility-related signaling of MN that is attached to its access link. It is responsible for detecting the MN's movements to and from the access link and for initiating binding registrations to the MN's LMA. Fig. 1 shows the

---

[*] This research was supported by Basic Science Research Program through the National Research Foundation of Korea (NRF) funded by the Ministry of Education, Science and Technology (2011-0002734).

D.H. Lee and M. Yung (Eds.): WISA 2012, LNCS 7690, pp. 144–160, 2012.

signaling call flow when MN initially accesses a new *PMIPv6* network [2]. A *RtrSol* (*Router Solicitation*) message from MN may arrive at any time after the MN's attachment. For updating the current location of the MN, the MAG_A sends a *PBU* (*Proxy Binding Update*) message to LMA. Upon accepting it, LMA responds with a *PBA* (*Proxy Binding Acknowledgement*) message including the MN's HNP (Home Network Prefix). It also creates the BCE (Binding Cache Entry) and sets up its endpoint of the tunnel to MAG_A. BCE contains MN's identifier, HNP, timestamp and other information related with MN. MAG_A on receiving the *PBA* message also sets up its endpoint of the tunnel to LMA for the purpose of forwarding the MN's traffic. MAG_A sends a *RtrAdv* (*Router Advertisement*) message containing the MN's HNP to MN. MN upon receiving the *RtrAdv* message configures its interface based on HNP. LMA being the topological anchor point for the MN's HNP receives any packets that are sent to MN by any node in or outside the *PMIPv6* domain. LMA forwards these received packets to MAG_A through the established tunnel. MAG_A forwards the packet to MN on the access link.

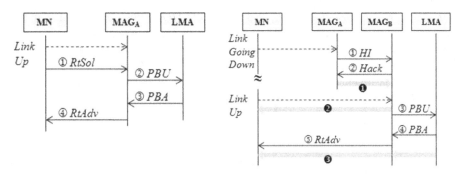

Fig. 1. Initial Network Access in PMIPv6   **Fig. 2.** Fast Handover for PMIPv6

Fast Handover for MIPv6 (*FH-MIPv6*) [3] has been proposed to reduce the handover latency in *MIPv6* by allowing a MN to send packets as soon as it detects a new subnet link, and by delivering packets to MN as soon as its attachment is detected by the new access router. *Fast Handover for PMIPv6* (*FH-PMIPv6*) [4] has also been proposed for the same reason. Fig. 2 shows the signaling call flow when MN handovers from MAG_A to MAG_B in the *FH-PMIPv6*. MN detects that a handover is imminent and reports to MAG_A the identifier of itself and MAG_B to which MN is most likely to move. By exchanging both *HI* (*Handover Initiate*) and *Hack* (*Handover Acknowledge*) messages, a tunnel is established between MAG_A and MAG_B, and the packets destined for MN are forwarded from MAG_A to MAG_B over this tunnel (❶ and ❷). Subsequently, LMA and MAG_B exchange a *PBU* and *PBA* messages. From this time on, the packets to/from MN go through MAG_B instead of MAG_A (❸).

Without a proper protection scheme for the signaling messages in *PMIPv6*, *PMIPv6* is also vulnerable to several security attacks such as *Redirection* attack, *MITM* (Man-In-The-Middle) attack, and *DoS* (Denial of Service) attack just as in *MIPv6* [6-8]. Recently, authentication schemes to protect the signaling messages in

PMIPv6 have been studied [11-15]. However, they are still vulnerable to several security attacks. In this paper, we point out some security problems of previous authentication schemes, and we then propose a new authentication scheme and key management scheme applicable to *PMIPv6*. Unlike the previously proposed ones, our proposed authentication scheme does not interact with the AAA (Authentication, Authorization, and Accounting) server during a handover. Therefore, the handover delay due to the authentication can be minimized. The rest of this paper is organized as follows. Section 2 specifies security threats to the *PMIPv6* and Section 3 points out some security problems of previous authentication schemes. Section 4 explains the proposed authentication scheme, and Section 5 describes the security and performance analysis. Finally, in Section 6, the concluding remarks are given.

2   Security Threats to PMIPv6

If no proper protection scheme is provided for the signaling messages in *PMIPv6*, *PMIPv6* remains vulnerable to several security attacks [9]. Security threats to the *PMIPv6* such as *Redirection* attack, *DoS* attack, and *MITM* attack are described in this section. *Redirection* attack is a threat that an attacker redirects MN's traffic to a different address. *DoS* attack against a LMA is a threat that LMA cannot support legitimate binding update requests. On the other hand, *MITM* attack is a threat that an attacker that manages to interject itself between entities can act as a man-in-the-middle. It can forge, modify, or drop the signaling messages.

2.1   Redirection Attack

Suppose an attacker sends a forged *PBU* message including MAGID' (forged MAGID) instead of legitimate MAGID (MAG IDentifier) in order to redirect MN's traffic. Since the signaling messages between LMA and MAG are not protected at all, LMA updates BCE according to the *PBU* message without verification. Eventually, the MN's traffic is redirected due to the forged MAGID' so that MN loses its traffic. *Redirection* attack is also possible by an attacker who resides on a different MAG, MAG'. Suppose an attacker who can forge MN's identity sends a forged *RtrSol* message to the MAG'. Upon receiving the *RtrSol* message, MAG' sends a *PBU* message to LMA to update BCE without verification. Eventually, the MN's traffic is redirected to the forged MAGID'.

2.2   DoS Attack

DoS attack can be mounted against LMA by an attacker who can impersonate a legitimate MAG. Suppose an attacker sends a storm of forged *PBU* messages for non-existing MNs to a targeted LMA. Since the signaling messages between LMA and MAG are not protected at all, LMA will establish BCE for each of the non-existing

MNs without verification. The unexpected growth of BCE may eventually cause LMA to reject legitimate binding updates.

2.3   MITM Attack

A MAG sends a *PBU* message to the LMA in order to update the current location of an MN. Suppose an attacker eavesdrops on the *PBU* message, and then sends a *PBA* message including HNP′ (forged HNP) to MAG. Since the signaling messages between LMA and MAG are not protected at all, MAG will send a *RtrAdv* message to MN without verification. MN will configure the address with HNP′ and MN loses its traffic. *MITM* attack is also possible by an attacker who can impersonate a legitimate MAG. After being attached to a new MAG, MN sends a *RtrSol* message to MAG in order to handover and MAG sends *PBU* message to LMA. Upon receiving *PBU* message, LMA sends a *PBA* message including HNP to MAG. Suppose that an attacker sends a forged *RtrAdv* message including HNP′ to the MN. MN will configure the address with forged HNP′ without verification and MN loses its traffic.

3   Previous Works

Recently, authentication schemes have been studied in order to protect the signaling messages in *PMIPv6* and *FH-PMIPv6* [11-15]. In Section 3.1, a previous authentication scheme [11] is investigated and its security problems are pointed out. Other authentication schemes [12-15] are also analyzed in Section 3.2.

3.1   Zhou-Zhang-Yajuan's Authentication Scheme

Zhou, et. al. [11] have proposed an authentication scheme based on the AAA server in order to protect the signaling messages for both the initial network access in *PMIPv6* and *FH-PMIPv6*. It is assumed that there are pre-established long-term keys, K_{MN}, $K_{AAA\text{-}MAGA}$, and $K_{AAA\text{-}LMA}$, shared between MN and AAA server, AAA and MAG_A, AAA and LMA, respectively. The AAA server in each *PMIPv6* domain has a profile of a MN and it also shares a long-term key with MN. It is also assumed that the long-term key between MAGs is shared. In Fig. 3, the signaling messages in the dotted box are proposed in [11] for authenticating MN and establishing a new security association between LMA and MAG_A.

When MN initially accesses a new *PMIPv6* network, MN receives a challenge value from the MAG_A (❶). MN computes a response to the challenge using the pre-established long-term key K_{MN} shared with AAA server. Both the challenge and response values are sent to MAG_A through the *RtrSol* message. Upon receiving it, MAG relays it to the AAA server (❷) since MAG_A cannot verify the response. The AAA server checks if the received response from MN is valid using K_{MN}. If MN is successfully authenticated, the AAA server generates a session key $K_{LMA\text{-}MAGA}$ shared between LMA and MAG_A, and sends it to both LMA and MAG_A (❷, ❸, and ❹).

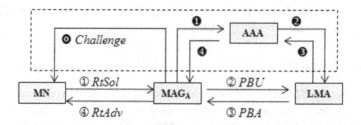

Fig. 3. Authentication Scheme for Initial Network Access [11]

When distributing the session key, two shared long-term keys, $K_{AAA\text{-}MAGA}$ and $K_{AAA\text{-}LMA}$, between AAA and MAG$_A$, AAA and LMA are used. The *PBU* and the *PBA* messages are now protected by the newly shared session key $K_{LMA\text{-}MAGA}$. However, since there is no security association between MN and MAG$_A$, the *RtrSol* message and the *RtrAdv* message are not protected. So, it is vulnerable to several security attacks such those as introduced in Section 2.

When MN changes its point of attachment in the *PMIPv6* domain, MN performs a *FH-PMIPv6* operation. Fig. 4 shows an authentication scheme for *FH-PMIPv6*. Same as in Fig. 3, the signaling messages in the dotted box in Fig. 4 have been supplemented in [11] for authenticating MN and establishing a new security association between LMA and MAG$_B$.

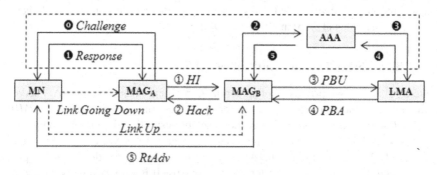

Fig. 4. Authentication Scheme for *FH-PMIPv6* [11]

When MN changes its point of attachment in the *PMIPv6* domain, MN computes a response to the challenge using the pre-established long-term key K_{MN} shared with AAA (❶ and ❷). Both the challenge and response values are sent to AAA via MAG$_A$ and MAG$_B$ (① and ❷). After that, the purpose of exchanging the messages (❸, ❹, and❺) in Fig. 4 is the same as that of exchanging (❷, ❸, and ❹) in Fig. 3. Namely, upon successfully authenticating MN, another session key is distributed to both LMA and MAG$_B$, which can be used to protect the *PBU* and *PBA* messages. However, the authentication scheme in [11] has some problems in terms of security and efficiency. First, the MN should interact with the AAA server whenever a handover occurs, which induces a long handover delay. Second, there is no security association between MN and MAG. Therefore, the signaling message between MN and MAG is not protected, so it is vulnerable to the *Redirection* and *DoS* attacks introduced in Section 2. Third, it is also exposed to the *Replay* attack. Even though a timestamp has been used, the timestamp is not protected at all.

3.2   Other Authentication Schemes

A scheme [12] to authenticate MN based on the AAA server has been proposed, while reducing packet loss during handover. When MAG_A becomes aware of the MN's detachment, it sends the *PBU* message on behalf of MAG_B to establish a tunnel between LMA and MAG_B as soon as possible. However, MN has to interact with the AAA server whenever a handover occurs, which is another source of packet loss. An authentication scheme [13] based on a concept of ticket introduced in Kerberos [5] has been proposed. A ticket includes an encrypted authentication key between MN and MAG as well as an expiration time. This ticket can be used continuously whenever MN handovers until reaching the expiration time. In this case, if the authentication key is exposed, then perfect backward and forward securities are not guaranteed. Also, it has a fundamental problem in that it needs to interact with the AAA server again when the lifetime of the ticket is expired. A MNID (MN IDentifier) has been used as one-time key to authenticate MN [14]. When MN attaches to a new MAG, MN generates one-time key based on the device ID and current time, and sends it to LMA via MAG to authenticate MN. However, it is not easy to synchronize when the MNID is generated. An authentication scheme has been proposed in [15], which is to authorize a MN according to security levels. And, authentication traffic in terms of cost has been also analyzed. However, the authentication scheme has not been described in detail so that it is not suitable for comparative analysis with our proposed authentication scheme.

4   Proposed Authentication Scheme

4.1   Assumptions and Design Principles

First, there are no security associations between MN and MAG in most previous schemes including [11]. So, the signaling messages between MN and MAG are not protected and vulnerable to several security attacks. On the other hand, in the proposed scheme, a security association (shared secret key) can be established between them, and the signaling messages are protected by MAC (Message Authentication Code) computed using the shared secret key. **Second**, while the pre-established long-term key is used in [11] to authenticate the signaling messages, the proposed scheme generates and uses a new session key whenever a handover occurs. The session key is generated based on both the long-term key and timestamp. Thus, the accidental exposure of one of them does not expose the other one. Namely, the Domino effect is suppressed by the proposed scheme. **Third**, in [11], interaction with the AAA server is required every handover in order to authenticate MN and to distribute a secret key shared between network entities. However, in the proposed scheme, interaction with AAA server occurs only once during the initial network access procedure. In our scheme, LMA acts as a kind of *local key distribution center*, so it performs fast and secure handovers. **Fourth**, the proposed scheme uses a timestamp in order to prevent *Replay* attacks. Since it is used more like a sequence number, strict time synchronization is not required between network entities. When an entity receives a signaling message with a timestamp, the timestamp in the message is compared with the stored one. In the proposed scheme, it is assumed that the AAA server shares a pre-established secret key K_{MN} with MN, and also shares the public keys with LMA, MAG_A, and MAG_B. The notations used in the proposed scheme are shown in Table 1.

Table 1. Notations

Notation	Description
PK_X, SK_X	public key and private key of X
$prf(.)$	pseudo-random function
$MAC(K)$	MAC computed over all preceding message fields using K
$[m]PK_X$	encryption of m with the public key, PK_X.
$Sig(SK_X)$	digital signature based on SK_X covering all preceding fields
T_0, T_1	initial timestamp and handover timestamp
MN, MAG_A, MAG_B, LMA	unique identifier of MN, MAG_A, MAG_B and LMA, respectively
SA (X, Y)	security association between X and Y
K_{MN}	a long-term symmetric key shared between MN and AAA server

4.2   Authentication Scheme for Initial Network Access

Suppose MN enters a new *PMIPv6* domain as in Fig. 5. Two signaling messages, *Auth_Req* and *Auth_Rsp*, in the dotted box are supplemented to authenticate MN as well as to establish SA (MN, MAG_A) and SA (LMA, MAG_A). Each original signaling message (①, ②, ③, and ④ in Fig. 5) of *PMIPv6* has several inherent fields. However, since most of them are not related with the security, they are excluded for the simplicity of explanation. Instead, only the security-related fields are shown in each message.

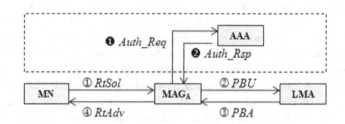

Fig. 5. Proposed Authentication Scheme for Initial Network Access

① $RtrSol$ {$MN, T_0, MAC(K^*)$}
❶ $Auth\_Req$ {$MN, T_0, MAC(K^*), Sig(SK_{MAGA})$}
❷ $Auth\_Rsp$ {$LMA, T_0, [K_{MN\text{-}MAGA}, K_{LMA\text{-}MAGA}]PK_{MAGA}, [MN, K^*]PK_{LMA}, Sig(SK_{AAA})$}
② PBU {$T_0, [MN, K^*]PK_{LMA}, MAC(K_{LMA\text{-}MAGA})$}
③ PBA {$T_0, MAC(K_{LMA\text{-}MAGA})$}
④ $RtrAdv$ {$T_0, MAC(K_{MN\text{-}MAGA})$}

$K^* = prf(K_{MN}, T_0)$ $K_{MN\text{-}MAGA} = prf(K^*, MAG_A)$ $K_{LMA\text{-}MAGA} = prf(K^*, MAG_A, LMA)$

MN generates an initial timestamp T_0 and a master session key $K^* = prf(K_{MN}, T_0)$ using the shared secret K_{MN} with the AAA server. MN sends the $RtrSol$ message (①) protected with the MAC computed using K^* to MAG_A. The verification of the MAC value is delayed until MAG_A receives the $Auth\_Rsp$ message from the AAA server. MAG_A signs the received message using its private key and sends the $Auth\_Req$ message (❶) to the AAA server. When receiving the $Auth\_Req$ message, the AAA server verifies the MAC and the digital signature. If the verification fails, the protocol stops. However, upon successful verification, the AAA server generates session keys $K_{MN\text{-}MAGA}$ and $K_{LMA\text{-}MAGA}$ to be shared between MN and MAG_A, LMA and MAG_A, respectively. The AAA server encrypts them using MAG_A's public key and encrypts K^* using LMA's public key, and then sends the $Auth\_Rsp$ message (❷) to MAG_A. When receiving the $Auth\_Rsp$ message, MAG_A obtains {$K_{MN\text{-}MAGA}, K_{LMA\text{-}MAGA}$} after decryption with its private key. The subsequent signaling messages (②, ③, and ④) are protected with the secret keys distributed by the AAA server. Especially, when receiving the PBU message containing [$MN, K^*]PK_{LMA}$, LMA can compute $K_{LMA\text{-}MAGA}$ $= prf(K^*, MAG_A, LMA)$.

4.3   Authentication Scheme for FH-PMIPv6

When MN changes its point of attachment in the $PMIPv6$ domain, MN performs FH-$PMIPv6$ operation. The signaling messages (❶, ❷, and ❸) in the dotted box in Fig. 6 are supplemented for security purpose, and the security-related fields are also padded into each original signaling message (①, ②, ③, ④, and ⑤) of FH-$PMIPv6$. A main role of the proposed authentication scheme for FH-$PMIPv6$ is to establish both SA (MN, MAG_B) and SA (LMA, MAG_B).

When MN detects a handover from the MAG_A to MAG_B, MN sends a $Start\_Auth$ message (❶) to notify MAG_A that it intends to handover to MAG_B. By exchanging $Auth\_Req$ (❷), $Auth\_Rsp$ (❸), and HI (①) messages, two session keys {$K_{MN\text{-}MAGB}$, $K_{LMA\text{-}MAGB}$} are generated and distributed to MAG_B. The one is a session key to be shared between MN and MAG$_B$, and the other is a session key to be shared between LMA and MAG$_B$. The two session keys are used to protect the signaling messages (③, ④, and ⑤). LMA plays a role of local *key distribution center* for MAGs in the *PMIPv6* domain.

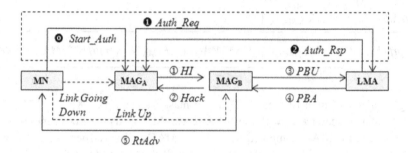

Fig. 6. Proposed Authentication Scheme for *FH-PMIPv6*

---

❶ *Start_Auth* {MN, MAG$_B$, T_1, MAC($K_{MN-MAGA}$)}
❶ *Auth_Req* {MN, MAG$_B$, T_1, PK_{MAGB}, MAC($K_{LMA-MAGA}$)}
❷ *Auth_Rsp* {LMA, T_1, [$K_{MN-MAGB}$, $K_{LMA-MAGB}$] PK_{MAGB}, MAC($K_{LMA-MAGA}$)}
① *HI* {MN, LMA, T_1, [$K_{MN-MAGB}$, $K_{LMA-MAGB}$] PK_{MAGB}, $Sig(SK_{MAGA})$}
② *Hack* {T_1, $Sig(SK_{MAGB})$}
③ *PBU* {T_1, MAC($K_{LMA-MAGB}$)}
④ *PBA* {T_1, MAC($K_{LMA-MAGB}$)}
⑤ *RtrAdv* {T_1, MAC($K_{MN-MAGB}$)}

$K_{MN-MAGB} = prf(K^*, T_1, MAG_B)$ $K_{LMA-MAGB} = prf(K^*, T_1, MAG_B, LMA)$

A key hierarchy of the proposed authentication scheme consists of three levels as shown in Fig. 7. A network entity on a specific level of the key hierarchy can access the secret keys on the same level as well as lower levels. Namely, MN and AAA can access all secret keys in the key hierarchy, while MAG can access only the secret keys shared with MN or LMA. From the long-term symmetric key K_{MN} shared between MN and the AAA server, a master session key K^* is generated. The master session key is valid until MN terminates its session in the *PMIPv6* domain.

When MN is attached to MAG$_A$ for the first time, two session keys $K_{MN-MAGA}$ and $K_{LMA-MAGA}$ are generated by the AAA server, which will be used to protect the signaling messages. Upon handover from MAG$_A$ to MAG$_B$, two more session keys $K_{MN-MAGB}$ and $K_{LMA-MAGB}$ are generated for the same purpose. However, in this case, they are generated by LMA which is a local *key distribution center*.

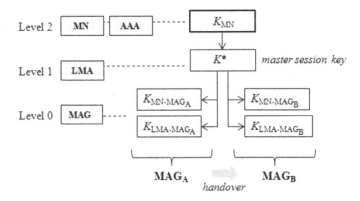

Fig. 7. Key Hierarchy of the proposed scheme

5   Discussions and Analysis

5.1   Establishing Security Associations

In Fig. 8, the solid lines between network entities represent pre-established security associations (SAs), and the dotted lines between them represent the new security associations derived from other existing security associations. SAs (❶, ❷, ❸, and ❹) are pre-established in both our proposed scheme (Fig. 8-(a)) and [11] (Fig. 8-(b)).

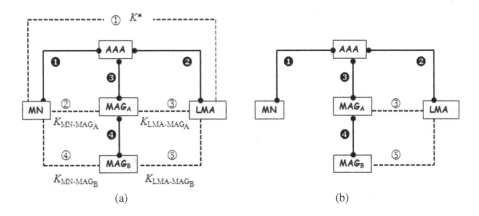

Fig. 8. Security Associations of the proposed scheme and [11]

In Fig. 8-(b), new SAs ③ and ⑤ are derived transitively from ❷ and ❸, ❷, ❸ and ❹, respectively, which will be denoted as (❷, ❸) ⇒ ③ and (❷,❸,❹) ⇒ ⑤. The authentication scheme proposed in [11] does not derive any more SAs from the existing SAs. Especially, no SAs exist between MN and MAG, which induces several security attacks. On the other hand, there exists SA between any two network entities in our proposed authentication scheme, as is shown in Fig. 8-(a). Based on the following pre-established SAs, new SAs can be derived. When MN enters the *PMIPv6* network for the first time, three new SAs ①, ②, and ③ are derived owing to our proposed authentication scheme. Subsequently, as MN handovers from MAG_A to MAG_B, two new SAs ④ and ⑤ are also derived. As seen in Fig. 8, the number of pre-established SAs in our proposed scheme is the same as that of [11].

SA ❶ : long-term symmetric key K_{MN}	SA ❷ : LMA's public key PK_{LMA}
SA ❸ : MAG_A's public key PK_{MAGA}	SA ❹ : Each other's public key

$(❶,❷) \Rightarrow ①$ $(❶,❸) \Rightarrow ②$ $(❷, ❸) \Rightarrow ③$ $(②,❹) \Rightarrow ④$ $(③,❹) \Rightarrow ⑤$

However, the total number of SAs derived from the pre-established SAs can differ depending on what kind of security-related fields are inserted into each signaling message, namely how to design the authentication scheme.

5.2   Timestamp and Replay Attack

In our proposed scheme, a single timestamp is used to guarantee the freshness of each of signaling messages, namely T_0 in Fig. 5 and T_1 in Fig. 6. It is shown here that why a single timestamp is enough for such purpose. Suppose A and B perform the following 2-way handshake protocol exchanging two messages, *2WH1* and *2WH2*, where *T* is a timestamp generated by A and two messages are protected by *MAC(K)*.

[Protocol 1]

- A $\Rightarrow$ B : *2WH1* { ..., *T*, *MAC(K)* }
- A $\Leftarrow$ B : *2WH2* { ..., *T*, *MAC(K)* }

Since T is generated by A and it is contained in the *2WH2* message, it is a kind of challenge-response protocol so that the freshness of the *2WH2* message is guaranteed. Suppose B maintains a *timestamp cache* to store the timestamp received previously from A. Then, when receiving the *2WH1* message, B compares *T* in the message with *stored_T* in the *timestamp cache*. If *T* > *stored_T*, then the *2WH1* message is proven to be fresh and *stored_T* is replaced by *T*. Therefore, a single timestamp generated by one side can be used to guarantee the freshness of two messages. On the other hand, if the *timestamp cache* for A is not yet created at B, then it means that the *2WH1* message is received by B for the first time so that it can be considered as fresh. Subsequently, B creates the *timestamp cache* for A and stores *T* in it. Fig. 9 shows how the timestamp is handled in our proposed authentication scheme for *FH-PMIPv6*. From now on, only the timestamp is verified if it is new, and the MAC verification is assumed to be done. It is assumed that MAG_A and LMA maintain the *timestamp caches* for MN, where T_0 has already been stored as a result of the initial network access in *PMIPv6* in Fig. 5. Since MAG_B is a new MAG to which MN tries to attach during handover, the *timestamp cache* of MN has not yet been created at MAG_B.

When receiving T_1 in ❶, MAG_A compares T_1 in ❶ with T_0 in the *timestamp cache*. If $T_1 > T_0$, then it is considered as fresh, and the *FH-MIPv6* protocol continues. Otherwise, it just silently drops the message and the protocol stops. The following pairs of messages are used for a kind of 2-way handshake protocol: (❶, ❷), (①, ②), and (③, ④). The freshness of each pair can be proven according to [Protocol 1]. In case of (❶, ❷), when receiving ❶, LMA can verify it by comparing T_1 with T_0 in its *timestamp cache*.

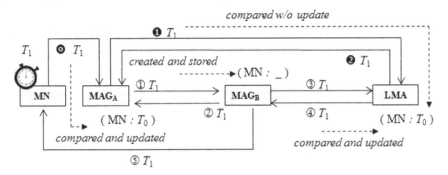

Fig. 9. Timestamp Handling in Fig. 6

If the verification is successful, then ❶ is proven to be fresh. In this case, the *timestamp cache* of LMA is not yet updated unlike [Protocol 1], it will be updated later. The meaning of the MAG_A's receiving T_1 in ❷ is that the freshness of ❷ is verified. Now, the *timestamp cache* in MAG_A is updated with T_1. (①, ②) and (③, ④) can also be processed in the same way as (❶, ❷). Especially, in case of (③, ④), LMA updates its *timestamp cache* with T_1. Finally, when receiving ⑤, MN checks if T_1 in ⑤ is the same as T_1 in ❶. If they are identical, then ⑤ is considered as fresh.

5.3   Security Analysis

In our proposed scheme, the signaling messages between MAG and LMA, MM and MAG are protected thanks to security associations established between them. In this section, we analyze the security of the proposed scheme against the threats of *PMIPv6* introduced in Section 2. First, in our proposed scheme, a *Redirection* attack is not feasible. An attacker has to be able to forge the *RtrSol* message or *PBU* message to succeed in a *Redirection* attack. However, in our scheme, the secret keys, K_{MN-MAG} and $K_{LMA-MAG}$, are shared between MN and MAG, LMA and MAG, respectively, which can be used to protect the signaling messages. Therefore, an attacker who does not know the secret key cannot compute a correct MAC value of the forged message. Second, in the proposed scheme, a *DoS* attack is not possible either. An attacker impersonating a legitimate MAG must be able to forge the *PBU* message for non-existing MNs or replay eavesdropped *PBU* message in order to mount the *DoS* attack mentioned in Section 2. However, the attacker does not know the secret key to compute a correct MAC value for the forged message. Third, in the proposed scheme, a *MITM* attack is impossible. An attacker must be able to forge the *PBA* message after eavesdropping the *PBU* message, or must be able to forge the *RtrAdv* message after eavesdropping *RtrSol* message. However, since the attacker does not know the shared secret key between MAG and LMA, the corresponding messages cannot be forged.

Table 2 shows the security comparisons between the previous schemes and ours. In [11] and [14], the signaling messages between MAG and MN are not protected at all, since there is no security association established between them. In [13], a security association exists between MAG and MN. However, it is vulnerable to *Redirection* and *DoS* attacks, since there is no security association between MAG and LMA. In [12] and [15], there are no security associations between MAG and MN, MAG and LMA, so they are also vulnerable to *Redirection*, *DoS*, and *MITM* attack.

Table 2. Security Comparison

secure against	*Redirection attack*	*DoS attack*	*MITM attack*
[11]	O	X	X
[12]	X	X	X
[13]	X	X	O
[14]	O	X	X
[15]	X	X	X
[proposed]	O	O	O

5.4   Performance Analysis

Our proposed authentication scheme is compared with [11]. First, we describe the system model for performance evaluation. Then, we analyze and compare handover costs and numerical results.

System Model. For performance evaluation, we adapt the hexagonal network model and Fluid Flow (FF) model as the network model and mobility model [15-16], respectively. It is assumed that each subnet has a hexagonal shape and they have the same size. The inmost subnet is labeled '0', called the center cell, and surrounded by its neighboring subnets which are labeled by '1'. Let r ($r \geq 1$) be the label of ring. The number of cells in the r-th ring is $6r$. It is also assumed that a hexagonal network model is a *PMIPv6* domain and a cell is a subnet. Let k be the number of rings and R the radius for subnet. We can calculate the number of subnets $N(k)$, perimeter $L(k)$ and coverage area $S(k)$ of the given *PMIPv6* domain as follows.

$$N(k) = \sum_{(r = 1 \text{ to } k)} (6r + 1) \tag{1}$$

$$L(k) = (12k + 6) \cdot R \tag{2}$$

$$S(k) = (2.6 \cdot R^2) \cdot (3k \cdot (k + 1) + 1) \tag{3}$$

$$\lambda_i = v \cdot L(k) / \pi \cdot S(k) \tag{4}$$

The authentication procedure is performed as MN handovers between MAGs. Hence, the handover rate is closely related with the MN's mobility pattern. In the FF model, the average cell crossing rate in the given *PMIPv6* domain, λ_i, is equal to the average handover rate, and the direction of an MN's movement is uniformly distributed in the range of $(0, 2\pi)$ [15-16]. v is the average velocity of MN and i is an indicator of user group. The user group is divided into two groups, pedestrian user (pu) and vehicular user (vu) [15].

Handover Cost Analysis. The handover costs of our proposed scheme and [11], namely Fig. 4 and Fig. 6, are analyzed and compared. In this section, the handover cost is defined as the sum of signaling cost and processing cost to implement *FH-PMIPv6* supplemented with the authentication scheme. Let j be the authentication method index ([11] or [proposed]). Let $C_{j,s}$ and $C_{j,p}$ be the signaling cost and processing cost when an authentication method j is applied. Let AC_j be the average handover cost of an authentication method j in a unit time. λ_i represents the average handover rate in a unit time.

$$AC_j = \lambda_i \cdot C_j, \text{ where } C_j = (C_{j,s} + C_{j,p}) \tag{5}$$

We define that C_{wired}, C_{wireless}, $H_{\text{MN-MAG}}$, $H_{\text{MAG-LMA}}$, $H_{\text{MAG-MAG}}$, $H_{\text{AAA-LMA}}$ and $H_{\text{MAG-AAA}}$ are the transmission cost on wired link, transmission cost on wireless link, number of hops between MN and MAG, number of hops between MAG and LMA, number of hops between MAG and MAG, number of hops between AAA and LMA, and the number of hops between MAG and AAA. It is also defined that P_{MN}, P_{MAGA}, P_{MAGB}, P_{LMA} and P_{AAA} are the processing costs on MN, MAG$_A$, MAG$_B$, LMA and AAA, respectively. Then, the handover cost C_j and average handover cost in time unit AC_j are calculated based on the parameters in Table 3 as follows.

Table 3. Comparison of Authentication Costs

$C_{[11]} = 3H_{\text{MN-MAG}}C_{\text{wireless}} + 2H_{\text{MAG-MAG}}C_{\text{wired}} + 2H_{\text{MAG-AAA}}C_{\text{wired}} + 2H_{\text{AAA-LMA}}C_{\text{wired}} +$ $2H_{\text{MAG-LMA}}C_{\text{wired}} + P_{\text{MN}} + P_{\text{MAGA}} + P_{\text{MAGB}} + P_{\text{AAA}} + P_{\text{LMA}}$	
$P_{\text{MN}} = C_{\text{enc}}$	$P_{\text{AAA}} = 2C_{\text{enc}} + C_{\text{dec}} + C_{\text{key}}$
$P_{\text{MAGA}} = C_{\text{hash}} + C_{\text{veri}}$	$P_{\text{LMA}} = C_{\text{hash}} + C_{\text{veri}} + C_{\text{dec}} + C_{\text{key}}$
$P_{\text{MAGB}} = 2C_{\text{hash}} + 2C_{\text{veri}}$	
$AC_{[11]} = \lambda_i \cdot C_{[11]}$	
$C_{[\text{proposed}]} = 2H_{\text{MN-MAG}}C_{\text{wireless}} + 2H_{\text{MAG-MAG}}C_{\text{wired}} + 4H_{\text{MAG-LMA}}C_{\text{wired}} + P_{\text{MN}} +$ $P_{\text{MAGA}} + P_{\text{MAGB}} + P_{\text{LMA}}$	
$P_{\text{MN}} = C_{\text{hash}} + C_{\text{veri}} + C_{\text{key}}$	$P_{\text{MAGB}} = 2C_{\text{hash}} + C_{\text{veri}} + C_{\text{enc}} + 2C_{\text{dec}}$
$P_{\text{MAGA}} = C_{\text{hash}} + 2C_{\text{veri}} + C_{\text{enc}} + C_{\text{dec}}$	$P_{\text{LMA}} = 2C_{\text{hash}} + 2C_{\text{veri}} + C_{\text{enc}} + 2C_{\text{key}}$
$AC_{[\text{proposed}]} = \lambda_i \cdot C_{[\text{proposed}]}$	

Numerical Results. In this section, we present the numerical results. The parameter values are presented in Table 4. Note that the values are defined relatively [13, 15], so that the cost does not mean the actual authentication cost for the scheme.

Table 4. Parameters for Evaluation

Symbol	Description	Value
C_{wired}	Transmission cost on a wired link	10
$C_{wireless}$	Transmission cost on a wireless link	20
C_{hash}	MAC generation cost	1
C_{veri}	MAC validation cost	1
C_{enc}	Encryption/Signature cost	1
C_{dec}	Decryption/Validation cost	1
C_{key}	Key generation cost	1
$H_{MN\text{-}MAG}$	Number of hops between MN and MAG	1
$H_{MAG\text{-}LMA}$	Number of hops between MAG and LMA	2
$H_{MAG\text{-}MAG}$	Number of hops between MAG_A and MAG_B	1
$H_{AAA\text{-}LMA}$	Number of hops between LMA and AAA	2
$H_{MAG\text{-}AAA}$	Number of hops between MAG and AAA	4

Fig. 10 shows the numerical results of the average handover cost in time unit AC_j. R and k are fixed as 0.05 km and 10, respectively. The solid line in Fig. 10 shows the average handover cost of the proposed scheme, $AC_{[proposed]}$ and the dotted line shows the average handover cost of [11], $AC_{[11]}$. As seen in the figures, the proposed scheme performs at a lower handover cost than [11].

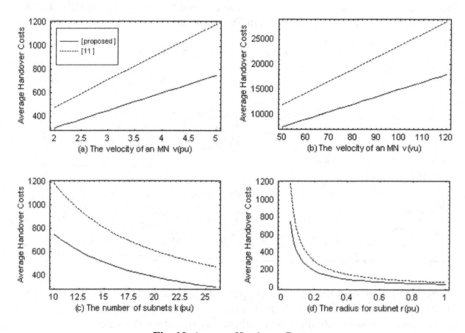

Fig. 10. Average Handover Costs

Fig. 10-(a) and (b) show the average handover cost in time unit of the pedestrian user and vehicular user. The velocity of pu is varied from 2km/h to 5km/h, and the velocity of vu is also varied from 50km/h to 120km/h. As we can see, the average handover cost in a unit time increases as the velocity increases. Fig. 10-(c) and (d) reveal the effect of the number of subnet and the subnet size on the handover cost in a time unit. As we can see, as the number of subnet increases, the average handover cost in a time unit decreases and as the subnet size increases, the average handoff cost in a time unit rapidly decreases. Therefore, the number of subnet and the subnet size are important for achieving an efficient handover.

6   Conclusion

Without a proper protection scheme for the signaling messages in *PMIPv6*, it is vulnerable to several security attacks such as *Redirection* attack, *MITM* attack and *DoS* attack. In this paper, we pointed out the security problems of the previous authentication scheme proposed for *PMIPv6*, and also proposed a new authentication scheme and key management scheme applicable to *PMIPv6*. In the proposed scheme, the secret keys between MN and MAG and between MAG and LMA are used for achieving authentication of signaling message. It is based on *FH-PMIPv6* and minimizes the handover delay by interacting only once with the AAA server. As shown in Section 5, our proposed scheme is more secure and efficient than the previous authentication schemes.

References

1. Johnson, D., Perkins, C., Arkko, J.: Mobility Support in IPv6. RFC3775 (June 2004)
2. Gundavelli, S., Leung, K., Devarapalli, V., Chowdhury, K., Patil, B.: Proxy Mobile IPv6. RFC5213 (August 2008)
3. Koodli, R.: Fast Handovers for Mobile IPv6. RFC4068 (July 2005)
4. Yokota, H., Chowdhury, K., Koodli, R., Patil, B., Xia, F.: Fast Handovers for Proxy mobile IPv6. RFC 5949 (2010)
5. Web page of Krb Working Group,
   http://www.ietf.org/html.charters/krb-wg-charter.html
6. Aura, T., Roe, M., Arkko, J.: Security of Internet Location Management. In: Proc. of 18th Annual Computer Security Applications Conference, Las Vegas (December 2002)
7. Nikander, P., Arkko, J., Aura, T., Montenegro, G., Nordmark, E.: Mobile IP version 6 Route Optimization Security Design Background. RFC4225 (December 2005)
8. Nikander, P., Arkko, J., Aura, T., Montenegro, G., Nordmark, E.: Mobile IP version 6 Route Optimization Security Design Background. RFC4225 (December 2005)
9. Vogt, C.: Security Threats to Network-Based Localized Mobility Management (NETLMM). RFC 4832 (2007)
10. Laganier, J., Narayanan, S., McCann, P.: Interface between a Proxy MIPv6 Mobility Access Gateway and a Mobile Node. Internet Draft, draft-ietf-netlmm-mn-ar-if-03 (2008)
11. Zhou, H., Zhang, H., Qin, Y.: An Authentication Method for Proxy Mobile IPv6 and Performance Analysis. Security and Communication Networks 2, 445–454 (2009)

12. Ryu, S., Kim, G., Kim, B., Mun, Y.: A Scheme to Reduce Packet Loss during PMIPv6 Handover considering Authentication. In: Proc. of International Conference on Computational Sciences and Its Applications, ICCSA, pp. 47–51 (2008)

13. Lee, J., Lee, J., Chung, T.: Ticket-based Authentication Mechanism for Proxy Mobile IPv6 Environment. In: Proc. of Third International Conference on Systems and Networks Communications 2008, pp. 304–309 (October 2008)

14. Song, J., Ha, S.: One-time Key Authentication Protocol for PMIPv6. In: Proc. of Third 2008 International Conference on Convergence and Hybrid Information Technology, pp. 1150–1153 (November 2008)

15. Lee, J., Chung, T.: A Traffic Analysis of Authentication Methods for Proxy Mobile IPv6. In: Proc. of 2008 International Conference on Information Security and Assurance, pp. 512–517 (2008)

16. Wang, W., Akyildiz, I.F.: Intersystem Location Update and Paging Schemes for Multitier Wireless Networks. In: Proc. of International Conference on Mobile Computing and Networking (MobiCom 2000), pp. 99–109 (August 2000)

17. Baek, S., Pack, S., Kwon, T., Choi, Y.: Localized Authentication, Authorization, and Accounting (AAA) Protocol for Mobile Hotspots. In: Proc. of IEEE/IFIP Annual Conference on Wireless on demand Network Systems and Services (WONS 2006), Les Menuires, France (January 2006)

18. Krawczyk, H., Bellare, M., Canetti, R.: HMAC:Keyed-Hashing for Message Authentication. RFC 2104 (Feburuary 1997)

Payment Approval for PayWord

László Aszalós and Andrea Huszti

Faculty of Informatics
University of Debrecen
Debrecen, Hungary
{aszalos.laszlo,huszti.andrea}@inf.unideb.hu

Abstract. In case of micropayment schemes, all costs that appear during functioning should be minimized. This includes cost of disputes and charge backs that result in penalties for the vendor. We extend the PayWord micropayment scheme with payment approval to minimize disputes, charge backs or to avoid attacks that ruin the reputation of the vendor. Payment approval is achieved by employing a MAC function per a purchase, that does not increase time complexity significantly. A formal evaluation in applied π and a proof that our scheme fulfills secure payment authorization, payment approval and secrecy of payment information are also given.

1 Introduction

The more people use Internet in their everyday life, the larger variety of payment solutions are required. Typical payment technologies that were invented as a consequence of Internet applications are the micropayment schemes. In particular, there are content and service providers that charge very small amount (e.g. less than a dollar). The usual online purchasing method - payment by credit cards - requires minimal transaction fee and other extra costs, hence it is not applicable for charging small amounts. Special payment systems, so-called micropayment schemes, are required. One can read an overview of micropayment schemes in [14]. One of the most well known micropayment scheme is the PayWord scheme [12].

In case of micropayment schemes all costs that appear during functioning should be minimized. This includes the cost of disputes and charge backs that result in penalty for the vendor. Our goal is to minimize risks that cause disputes or ruin reputation of the vendor by applying cryptographic techniques. We decrease the trust level of the user, so the user should not only give precise information about what he would like to buy and what price he tends to pay for it, but should provide a proof of this information. Therefore the system avoids misunderstandings between the user and the vendor. We decrease the trust level of the vendor also, we assume there might be an adversary who tries to masquerade him. We extend PayWord to prevent this attack that causes disputes or ruins the reputation of the vendor.

Cryptographic schemes employing strong cryptographic tools, but weakly designed allow frauds. Thus substantial evaluation should be provided in order to

D.H. Lee and M. Yung (Eds.): WISA 2012, LNCS 7690, pp. 161–176, 2012.
© Springer-Verlag Berlin Heidelberg 2012

prevent flaws. Many researchers use general purpose model checkers [9], [11], others use theorem provers [4], [10] and strand spaces [13] for verifying security properties of cryptographic protocols. We used applied π calculus with an automatic protocol verifier called Proverif [6], [7], [8] for verifying security properties. According to our best knowledge PayWord is formalized in spi-calculus in [2], but detailed formal security analysis is not made before.

2   Security Requirements of Micropayment Schemes

In case of macropayment systems the amount of money transfer for each transaction is large enough for unrestricted utilization of cryptographic techniques and on-line activities to detect possible attacks. Micropayment systems should keep all their financial and computational costs per a transaction low, meaning on-line processing time and cost of database handling and use of public key cryptography should be minimized. At the same time loosing the sum of money that consumer usually pays per a transaction is not a big loss neither for the consumer, nor for the vendor.

In order to be efficient and keep the transaction cost low design of micropayment schemes demands special care. Besides the cost of a successful transaction, the cost of disputes and charge backs also should be considered. There are several security requirements that micropayment systems should achieve [5]. Usually necessity of payment authorization, unreusability and secrecy of payment information are considered. Additionally we detail importance of payment approval, too.

Payment Authorization

It is essential for the vendor to have a proof, that there are funds on the consumer's account to cover the payment. In case of credit card based payment systems the vendor verifies validity of the credit card and whether the amount of the payment is available *for each transaction*. Since this solution is costly, it is not applicable for micropayment schemes. We should also pay attention to the large computational overhead of employing public key signatures. Secure payment authorization also includes the protection against unauthorized overspending, meaning a consumer proceeds more payments than the funds available in his account.

Payment Approval

Mainly for credit card purchasing, but to some extent to any on-line purchasing, there are laws protecting consumers' right to dispute when transactions were not approved by the consumer, and often when they were not properly fulfilled[14]. *Payment approval* process addresses that a consumer agrees to pay a certain amount of money for a particular product, to accomplish *secure payment approval*, a proof of the acceptance of a payment for a third party is also necessary, *i.e.* to achieve non-repudiation. An obvious solution for secure payment approval would be applying digital signatures, but it is too costly for micropayment schemes. One of the most challenging duty is to provide secure payment approval for micropayments.

Unreusability

Unreusability or also called double-spending detection means protection against dishonest participants proceeding the same payment more than once. Unreusability for the PayWord scheme that is typically a one-vendor scheme, means concentrating only on the situation when an attacker tries to spend the same payment at *the same* vendor more than once.

Secrecy of Payment Information

For electronic payment systems it is essential that confidential data - credit card information - should be kept secret. The only participant, besides the owner, who should be aware of payment information is the broker or the bank.

3   PayWord

Let us review the micropayment scheme called PayWord according to [12]. There are three participants: consumer or user (U), vendor (V) and broker (B). A user asks for the broker's authorization to make micropayments to the vendor, hence we have a user-broker and a user-vendor relationship. Vendors initiate a pay-off procedure with the broker, so we also have a broker-vendor relationship. Among the three relationships the user-vendor one is short-term, the other two are long-term. User-vendor relationship occurs ad-hoc and should be kept alive for short time, usually just few hours, hence an on-line payment and delivery last only for seconds, but could be repeated several times. On the other hand, broker-vendor and user-broker relationships might be off-line, and these kind of transactions happen rarely, maximum once a day, hence the computational cost is not so important.

Let us describe PayWord micropayment scheme in details. We employ digital signatures, where public and secret keys of the users and brokers are denoted by K_U^+, K_B^+ and K_U^-, K_B^-, respectively. We denote by $\{M\}_{K_i^-}$ the application of the secret key on message M, where $i \in \{U, B\}$.

User-Broker Relationship

User U initiates a relationship with broker B by requesting an authorized PayWord Certificate. U transports his credit-card number, the requested amount and his public key K_U^+ to B on an authenticated encrypted channel.

$$1.\ U \to B : U, K_U^+$$

B generates U's certificate by signing digitally B, U, K_U^+ and E with key K_B^-. It means that broker B issues this certificate to user U, whose public key is K_U^+

and the certificate's expiration date is E. This certificate ensures any vendor that valid amounts will be paid-off before date E.

$$2.\ B \to U : \{B, U, K_U^+, E\}_{K_B^-}$$

User-Vendor Relationship

For the first purchase U generates a *payword chain* $w_0, w_1, \ldots w_n$ in the following way. First U generates a random number w_n, then calculates

$$w_i = H(w_{i+1}),$$

where $i \in \{n-1, n-2, \ldots, 0\}$. We call $w_1, \ldots w_n$ paywords, w_0 is the root of the chain. U chooses the number n arbitrarily beyond the requested amount and generates a certificate containing the vendor's identification information V, his PayWord Certificate, w_0 as a commitment and the actual date D. This certificate is signed by the user's secret key K_U^-. The user should keep track of commitments he sent.

$$3.\ U \to V : \{V, \{B, U, K_U^+, E\}_{K_B^-}, w_0, D\}_{K_U^-}$$

The vendor verifies U's signature by public key K_U^+, and B's signature by K_B^+, checks whether D is before E and stores w_0 with the user information.

After sending the certificate, U makes his payment. A payment is a pair of a payword and the corresponding index (w_i, i), where $i \in \{1, 2, \ldots, n\}$. It is important that the user sends his paywords starting from w_1, the w_2 and so on.

$$4.1\ U \to V : (w_1, 1)$$

$$4.2\ U \to V : (w_2, 2)$$

$$\vdots$$

$$4.n\ U \to V : (w_n, n)$$

Vendor V verifies the received payword w_i by applying i times the hash function on it, *i.e.* checks $H^i(w_i) = w_0$ in case of the first shopping. If U requests products from V not for the first time, then V will verify w_i with the stored payword w_j, where $j < i$, *i.e.* checks $H^{i-j}(w_i) = w_j$. By storing the payword with the highest index, V prevents double spending.

Vendor-Broker Relationship

Vendor V sends all necessary information to B for pay-off. V transmits the certificate generated by U, the last payword received from U and the corresponding index.

$$5.\ V \to B : \{V, \{B, U, K_U^+, E\}_{K_B^-}, w_0, D\}_{K_U^-}, w_l, l$$

B verifies the signature of user's certificate with K_U^+, checks whether identity information of the vendor received matches with V, the expiring date and validity of the payword, *i. e.* $H^l(w_l) = w_0$. If all verifications hold, then B pays the proper amount to V.

4   Payment Approval for PayWord

Purchases made electronically call forth more disputes and charge backs than face-to-face ones. Frequent disputes result in penalty payments for vendors, hence vendors are concerned about minimizing the possibility of disputes. Payment approval might prevent a large number of conflicts. We have extended PayWord in order to achieve payment approval, *i.e.* for each payment the user generates a proof of order information for the vendor, the fact that he agrees to pay the requested amount of money for that product. After completing the payment phase the vendor is able to verify this proof. The obvious way would be to achieve payment approval to employ digital signatures, but this solution is computationally intensive for micropayments. Number of public key operations should be minimized, we applied message authentication codes (MAC) instead. Payment approval prevents misunderstandings between the user and the vendor that decrease number of disputes and charge backs.

For achieving payment approval besides having a proof of order and price information, authentication of the user and the vendor is also necessary. In the PayWord system each payword is selfauthenticating, only the user is capable of disclosing the next element of the payword chain. On the other hand the vendor is not authenticated, hence an attacker can masquerade the vendor and may receive all the paywords the user generated. An attacker is able to send these valid paywords to the vendor and able to gain products without paying. If the adversary does not send any product back to the user, then he or she ruins the good reputation of the vendor. The algorithm works out repeatedly if the attacker provides products for the user that are acceptable. Let us give an example. A user would like to buy short stories on-line, chooses several stories and pays for them. After each successful payment the adversary provides the story with the proper text at the beginning only that is available for free, and some junk text at the end. Since PayWord does not possess payment approval the adversary is able to order any kind of products he needs, even different from the ones ordered by the user. Although the lack of vendor authenticity is already mentioned in [3], it does not change the buying phase itself.

We have extended the user-vendor relationship with the authentication of the vendor by applying a public key encryption that should be run only once, when the user starts the communication with the vendor. So it does not increase the complexity significantly. We have extended the user-vendor relationship with the following messages, where (K_V^+, K_V^-) denote public and secret keys of the vendor for encrypting messages:

$$3'\ U \to V : \{V, \{B, U, K_U^+, E\}_{K_B^-}, w_0, D, \{K\}_{K_V^+}\}_{K_U^-}$$

$$4.1'\ U \to V : OrderInf_1, Mac((OrderInf_1, w_1), K)$$

$$V \to U : Product_1$$

$$U \to V : (w_1, 1)$$

$$4.2'\ U \to V : OrderInf_2, Mac((OrderInf_2, w_2), K)$$

$$V \to U : Product_2$$

$$U \to V : (w_2, 2)$$

$$\vdots$$

$$4.n' \; U \to V : OrderInf_n, Mac((OrderInf_n, w_n), K)$$

$$V \to U : Product_n$$

$$U \to V : (w_n, n)$$

Before the first payment the user generates a symmetric MAC key (K) and sends it to the vendor encrypted. For each payment we add order information and a proof for the vendor, a MAC of order information and the payword the consumer tends to pay. Please note that the vendor sends the requested product without verifying the payword, since hash and MAC verification happen after the user receives the product. In case of micropayments loosing the amount of one payment is not a large loss, if either the hash or the MAC verification is unsuccessful, then the vendor might decide to refuse other purchases. We also employ PayWord as a post-paid system, hence the user first receives the product and pays for it afterwards. The cost of payment approval is only an application of MAC for each payment, that does not increase the total complexity significantly. The only data that should be stored besides the last payword is the MAC key. Authentication of the vendor happens with public key decryption, hence we prevented the aforementioned attack.

We should also remark, that we do not achieve non-repudiation, since after completing a payment phase the vendor is able to forge the MAC value. Our goal was to provide assurance for the vendor of what the consumer is ready to buy and the price he would pay for it, preventing misunderstandings between the user and the vendor. If MAC verifications are successful repetitively, the vendor is affirmed about the consumer's satisfaction. Please notice, that the user might decide not to pay for a product, if he is unsatisfied, then the vendor might refuse next orders till completing the payment. Our solution protects against honest users who misunderstood the payment process or made an error by accident, but does not protect against malicious attacker, who misleads the vendor during the payment phase and initiates a dispute.

5   Applied π Calculus

In this section we briefly review the applied π calculus that is based on the π calculus. Detailed description of this topic can be found in [1]. A signature $\sum$ is a set of function symbols, each with an arity. A function symbol f with arity 0 is a constant symbol. The set of terms is built from names, variables, and function symbols. Let us denote channel names by a, b, c, and names of any sort by m, n.

Also, let x, y, z range over variables.

$$L, M, N, T, U, V ::= \qquad\qquad\qquad\qquad \textbf{terms}$$
$$a, b, c, \ldots, k, \ldots, m, n, \ldots, s \qquad\qquad\qquad \text{name}$$
$$x, y, z \qquad\qquad\qquad\qquad\qquad \text{variable}$$
$$f(M_1, ..., M_l) \qquad\qquad \text{function application}$$

The grammar for processes is the following:

$$P, Q, R ::= \qquad\qquad\qquad\qquad\qquad \textbf{processes}$$
$$\mathbf{0} \qquad\qquad\qquad\qquad\qquad \text{null process}$$
$$P | Q \qquad\qquad\qquad \text{parallel composition}$$
$$!P \qquad\qquad\qquad\qquad \text{replication}$$
$$\nu n.P \qquad\qquad \text{name restriction (new)}$$
$$if \; M = N \; then \; P \; else \; Q \qquad\qquad \text{conditional}$$
$$u(x).P \qquad\qquad\qquad \text{message input}$$
$$\overline{u}\langle N \rangle.P \qquad\qquad\qquad \text{message output}$$

Replication of process P means infinite number of copies of P running in parallel. Name restriction process $\nu n.P$ creates a new, private name and behaves as P. Finally, process $u(x).P$ is ready to input from channel u, then to run P with the message replaced for the formal parameter x, and process $\overline{u}\langle N \rangle.P$ is ready to output N on channel u, then to run P. We extend processes with active substitution. We denote the substitution that replaces the variable x with the term M by $\{M/x\}$.

Operational Semantics

Given a signature $\sum$ we equip it with an equational theory, *i.e.* an equivalence relation on terms that is closed under substitution of terms for variables. We write $E \vdash M = N$ for equality and $E \nvdash M = N$ for inequality in the theory associated with $\sum$. Operational semantics of the applied-pi calculus is defined in terms of structural equivalence ($\equiv$) and internal reduction ($\rightarrow$). Structural equivalence captures rearrangements of parallel compositions and restrictions, and the equational rewriting of the terms in a process. Internal reduction defines the semantics of process synchronizations and conditionals. Observational equivalence ($\approx$) captures the equivalence of processes with respect to their dynamic behavior.

5.1   ProVerif

For cryptographic verification of our modified PayWord micropayment system we employed a software package called ProVerif that is an automatic cryptographic protocol verifier. We refer to [7] for a detailed description of the system. ProVerif handles input files encoded in applied π. We can formalize cryptographic primitives such as symmetric, asymmetric encryptions, digital signatures etc., and ProVerif is capable of proving reachability properties, correspondence assertions and observational equivalences that help analyzing security properties of secrecy, authentication etc..

For modeling PayWord scheme, we use syntax of ProVerif, that is similar to the one in applied π. There are some differences, though, we write *new n; P* for name restriction and we add a restriction to active substitution as follows: $\nu x.(\{M/x\}|P)$ that corresponds to *let x = M in P*. We use $in(c,m)$ and $out(c,m)$ denoting input and output of message m on channel c, respectively.

We give formalization for cryptographic primitives as follows:

Hash Function, Message Authentication Code. We represent a oneway hash function as a unary function symbol H with no equations. The absence of an inverse for H models the onewayness of H. Similarly we denote a oneway MAC function as a binary function symbol Mac, where the second argument corresponds to the secret key of MAC.

fun H/1.
fun Mac/2.

Symmetric Encryption. We take binary function symbols *senc* and *sdec* for encryption and decryption, respectively, with the equation: $sdec(senc(x,y),y) = x$. Here x represents the plaintext and y the secret key.

fun senc/2.
reduc sdec(senc(x,y),y) = x.

Asymmetric Encryption. In case of asymmetric encryption we have to generate a keypair, a public and a secret key. We have an unary function symbol *pk* for generating the public key, where the secret key is the argument. Similarly to symmetric encryption we represent asymmetric encryption and decryption with binary function symbols *penc* and *pdec* with the equation of $pdec(penc(x,pk(y)),y) = x$, where x denotes the plaintext and y is the secret key.

fun pk/1.
fun penc/2.
reduc pdec(penc(x,pk(y)),y) = x.

Digital Signatures. In order to formalize digital signatures that also employ secret and public keys we use function symbol *pk* for generating public keys, and binary function symbols *sign, checksign*. We interpret digital signatures with message recovery, meaning we have equation $checksign(sign(m,k),pk(k)) = m$, where m is the message and k is the secret key.

fun pk/1.
fun sign/2.
reduc checksign(sign(m,k),pk(k)) = m.

Security Properties

ProVerif is capable of analyzing properties reachability, correspondence assertions and observational equivalences. We mention that ProVerif is sound, but not complete. If ProVerif results that a property is satisfied, then the model guarantees the property, but ProVerif may not be able to prove a property that holds.

For security evaluations ProVerif uses queries that might be a fact or a correspondence. In case of **reachability** the query is a fact, we test whether the fact holds. Especially, we query whether a term m is secret for the attacker: $query\ attacker : m.$

A **correspondence** is a form of $F \Longrightarrow H$, that means if F holds then H also holds. We define events in the model as important stages and we test whether if an event a has been executed, then event b has been previously executed before. The $query\ ev :\ a(x,y) \Longrightarrow ev :\ b(y,z).$ means that, for all x,y, for each occurrence of $a(x,y)$, there is a previous occurrence of $b(y,z)$ for some z. For proving one-to-one relationship we apply injective correspondences. The $query\ evinj :\ a(x,y) \Longrightarrow evinj :\ b(y,z).$ means for each occurrence of the event $a(x,y)$, there is a *distinct* earlier occurrence of the event $b(y,z)$ for some z.

The notion of indistinguishability is called **observational equivalence** in the formal model, denoted by $P \approx Q$. Two processes are observationally equivalent if an active adversary cannot distinguish them. Further information can be found in [7].

6   Formal Security Evaluation

In order to prove security properties, such as secure payment authorization, payment approval and secrecy of payment information we employ applied π calculus with the help of ProVerif. As a first step we model the extended PayWord, then we evaluate it with ProVerif queries.

6.1   Modeling Extended PayWord

In this section we give a detailed formal security evaluation of our extended PayWord scheme. We extended the basic PayWord scheme with use of nonces that are freshly generated random numbers that are used only once. We use nonces as challenges for entity authentication processes and also to verify freshness of messages. We should mention here that handling database - inserting, searching data - in applied π calculus is cumbersome.

We model our scheme in a way that users apply for the PayWord certificate on-line. We establish a secure authenticated channel between the user and the broker by employing asymmetric, symmetric encryptions and digital signatures. Payment information is sent through this channel.

We implemented the hash chain with only three elements, where one of them is the commitment, hence there are two purchases in the user process. In case the length of the hash chain is longer, proofs will work out similarly. Two payments serve for us in order to prove our requirements.

We leave the vendor-broker relationship open, which means we do not specify whether it is on-line or off-line. In case we consider it to be on-line, then the channel used for communication should be an authenticated channel.

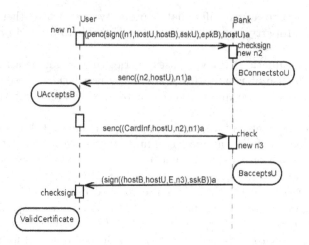

Fig. 1. User-Broker relationship

There are four processes: a main process, that makes calls for processes of the user, the vendor and the broker. We have infinite number of copies of the processes of the participants.

In order to follow interactions between the participants please check Figures 1, 2 and 3.

The Main Process. In the main process secret and public keys are generated and an identification number for each participant. Secret and public keys are generated for signature schemes for the broker and the user, also keypairs are generated for encrypting and decrypting messages for the vendor and the broker. For the formal description we refer to Figure 4.

The User Process. User first generates a symmetric encryption key $(n1)$ that is sent to the broker encrypted by broker's public key. This symmetric key is used for transmitting payment information encrypted. Authentication of the broker is proceeded by challenge-response, where the user challenges the broker whether he is able to decrypt. We inserted event *UacceptsB* that happens if user makes sure of communicating with the broker. Authentication of the user is achieved by a digital signature. User finishes user-broker relationship with event *ValidCertificate* that happens after verifying PayWord certificate after sending correct payment information.

User starts user-vendor relationship with generating the first element of the hash chain (wn) and the MAC key (K). Event *UReadytoPurchase* happens at the beginning of buying phase, $n4$ is a nonce for verifying freshness of signature generated by the user and also behaves as a challange for user authentication. Events *UStartsFirstPayment* and *UStartsSecondPayment* show the beginning of the first and the second purchase. For the formal description we refer to Figure 5.

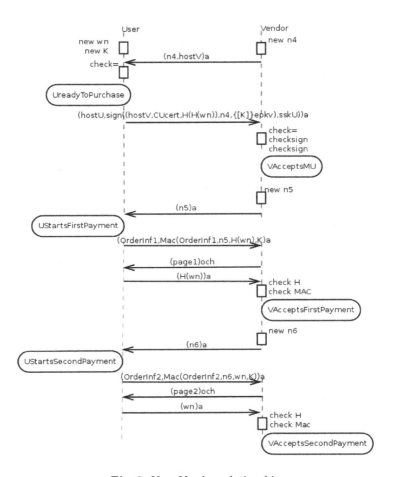

Fig. 2. User-Vendor relationship

The Broker Process. Event *BconnectstoU* happens after decrypting the message received from the user, shows that the broker initializes connection with the user. Event *BacceptsU* happens after the broker authenticates the user by his credit card information. Broker sends the PayWord certificate afterwards.

The second part of the process is already part of the pay off, broker verifies the signatures and the hash value before paying to the vendor. For the formal description we refer to Figure 6.

The Vendor Process. Event *VAcceptsMU* happens after authenticating the user by challenge-response, verifying PayWord certificate, user's signature and decrypting the symmetric MAC key. After each successful purchase an event happens, namely *VAcceptsFirstPayment* and *VAcceptsSecondPayment* that shows that MAC and hash values are correct. Finally the pay off procedure starts with the event *VPaymentReq*. For the formal description we refer to Figure 7.

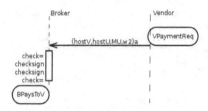

Fig. 3. Vendor-Broker relationship

```
process
     new sskU;  (*User's secret sign. key*)
     new sskB;  (*Broker's secret sign. key*)
     new eskV;  (*Vendor's secret dec. key*)
     new eskB;  (*Broker's secret dec. key*)
     let epkB=pk(eskB) in    (*Broker's public enc. key*)
     let epkV=pk(eskV) in    (*Vendor's public enc. key*)
     let spkU=pk(sskU) in    (*User's public sign. ver. key*)
     let spkB=pk(sskB) in    (*Broker's public sign. ver. key*)
     let hostV=host(epkV) in (*Vendor id*)
     let hostU=host(spkU) in (*User id*)
     let hostB=host(spkB) in (*Broker id*)
     out(b,(hostB,epkB));out(b,hostU);out(b,hostV);(*ids made public*)
     ( (!processU) | (!processB) | (!processV) )
```

Fig. 4. Main process

6.2   Security Analysis

We prove that our proposed scheme accomplish secure payment authorization, payment approval and secrecy of payment information. We first give precise definitions of these security requirements, then we give a formal proof using ProVerif.

Payment Authorization. Payment authorization guarantees a proof for the vendor, that there is sufficient fund on the user's account. This proof or certificate is created by the broker.

Definition 1. *We state that a payment scheme fulfills payment authorization if the following conditions hold:*

1. *Broker authentication: The consumer successfully authenticates the broker, it is indisputable that the certificate is authorized by the broker.*
2. *Consumer authentication: The broker successfully authenticates the consumer, it is indisputable that the consumer's account is questioned.*
3. *Certificate: There is a proof for the vendor, that the sufficient fund is available.*

Secure *payment authorization is achieved, if the certificate is undeniable.*

Payment Approval. Payment approval process generates a proof for the vendor that a consumer agrees to pay a certain amount of money for a particular product. We would like to emphasize requisiteness of vendor authentication, since if the consumer sends the proof to an adversary, then the adversary might be able to masquerade the consumer.

```
let processU =
  new n1;
  out(a,(penc(sign((n1,hostU,hostB),sskU),epkB),hostU));
  in(a,mes);
  let (n2B,=hostU)=sdec(mes,n1) in
   event UacceptsB(hostU,hostB,n1,n2B);
  out(a,senc((CardInf,hostU,n2B),n1));
   in(a, CUcert);
    let (=hostB,=hostU,EB,n3B)=checksign(CUcert,spkB) in
     event ValidCertificate(hostU,hostB,n1,n2B);
     new wn; new K;
     in(a,(n4V,hostY));
     if hostY=hostV then
      event UReadytoPurchase(hostU,hostV,H(H(wn)),K,n4V);
      out(a,(hostU,sign((hostV,CUcert,H(H(wn)),n4V,penc(K,epkV)),sskU)));
      in(a,n5V);
      event UStartsFirstPayment(hostU,hostV,H(wn),K,n5V);
      out(a,(OrderInf1,Mac((OrderInf1,n5V,H(wn)),K)));
      in(och,page1); out(a,H(wn));
      in(a,n6V);
      event UStartsSecondPayment(hostU,hostV,wn,K,n6V);
      out(a,(OrderInf2,Mac((OrderInf2,n6V,wn),K)));
      in(och,page2); out(a,wn).
```

Fig. 5. User process

```
let processB =
        in(a,(s,hostX));
        if hostX=hostU then
         let sig=pdec(s,eskB) in
         let (n1U,=hostU,=hostB)=checksign(sig,spkU) in
         new n2;
         event BconnectstoU(hostU,hostB,n1U,n2);
         out(a,senc((n2,hostU),n1U));
         in(a,mes);
          let inf=sdec(mes,n1U) in
        let (Cinf,=hostU,=n2)=sdec(mes,n1U) in
         event BacceptsU(hostU,hostB,n1U,n2);
         new n3;
         out(a,sign((hostB,hostU,E,n3),sskB));
         in(a,(hostY,hostZ,MUpayment,w2V));
         if hostZ=hostU then
          let (=hostY,CUcert,w0,n4B,ciphB)=checksign(MUpayment,spkU) in
          let (=hostB,=hostU,E,=n3)=checksign(CUcert,spkB) in
           if H(H(w2V))=w0 then
            event BPaysToV(hostB,hostY,w2V).
```

Fig. 6. Broker process

Definition 2. *We state that a payment scheme fulfills payment approval if the following conditions hold:*

1. *Consumer authentication: The vendor successfully authenticates the consumer, it is indisputable that the proof originates from the consumer.*
2. *Vendor authentication: The consumer successfully authenticates the vendor, it is indisputable that the certificate is sent to the vendor.*
3. *Order information: The proof contains precise description of the product.*
4. *Price information: The proof contains the amount of money the consumer tends to pay.*

Secure *payment approval is achieved, if the proof is undeniable.*

```
let processV =
      new n4;
      out(a,(n4,hostV));
      in(a,(hostX,signMU));
      if hostX=hostU then
       let (=hostV,CUcertV,w0,=n4,ciph)=checksign(signMU,spkU) in
        let (=hostB,=hostU,EB,n3)=checksign(CUcertV,spkB) in
         let KU=pdec(ciph,eskV) in
          event VAcceptsMU(hostU,hostV,w0,KU,n4);
          new n5; out(a,n5);
          in(a,(OrderInfV1,pw1st)); out(och,page1);
          in(a,w1);
          if H(w1)=w0 then
           if pw1st=Mac((OrderInfV1,n5,w1),KU) then
            event VAcceptsFirstPayment(hostU,hostV,w1,KU,n5);
            new n6; out(a,n6);
            in(a,(OrderInfV2,pw2nd)); out(och,page2);
            in(a,w2);
            if H(w2)=w1 then
             if pw2nd=Mac((OrderInfV2,n6,w2),KU) then
              event VAcceptsSecondPayment(hostU,hostV,w2,KU,n6);
              event VPaymentReq(hostB,hostV,w2);
              out(a,(hostV,hostU,signMU,w2)).
```

Fig. 7. Vendor process

Secrecy of Payment Information. In case of payment schemes it is crucial that payment information such as credit card information should be kept secret.

Definition 3. *We state that a payment scheme possesses secrecy of payment information, if confidential payment information is not revealed for adversaries.*

Theorem 1. *Our proposed extended PayWord scheme accomplish secure payment authorization, payment approval and secrecy of payment information.*

Proof. Our scheme fulfills *secure payment authorization*, since it provides an undeniable certificate, namely a PayWord certificate: $sign((hostB, hostU, spkU, E, n3), sskB)$. Broker and consumer authentication are achieved, because the following queries return logical value true:

query evinj : $BacceptsU(x, y, z, t) \implies (evinj : UacceptsB(x, y, z, t) \implies evinj : BconnectstoU(x, y, z, t))$.

query evinj : $ValidCertificate(x, y, z, t) \implies evinj : BconnectstoU(x, y, z, t)$.

Our scheme fulfills *payment approval*, since it provides a proof of order and price information: $Mac((OrderInf, n5, H(wn)), K)$ and fulfills consumer and vendor authentication, since the following queries return true:

query evinj : $VAcceptsMU(x, y, z, t, s) \implies evinj : UReadytoPurchase(x, y, z, t, s)$.

query evinj : $VAcceptsFirstPayment(x, y, z, s, t) \implies (evinj : UStartsFirstPayment(x, y, z, s, t) \implies evinj : VAcceptsMU(x, y, H(z), s, l))$.

query evinj : $VAcceptsSecondPayment(x, y, z, s, t) \implies evinj : UStartsSecondPayment(x, y, z, s, t)$.

query evinj : $UStartsSecondPayment(x, y, z, s, t) \implies evinj : VAcceptsMU(x, y, H(H(z)), s, k)$.

Our scheme possesses *secrecy of payment information*, since the following query returns true:

query attacker : $CardInf$.

7   Conclusion

By extending the basic PayWord scheme with payment approval we avoid misunderstandings between the consumer and the vendor that would cause penalty for the vendor or ruin its reputation. We achieved payment approval with employing a MAC function per a purchase, that do not increase time complexity significantly. We have also proved that our scheme fulfills secure payment authorization and secrecy of payment information. Our future plan to make formal examination of unreusability.

Acknowledgment. The work is supported by TÁMOP 4.2.1/B-09/1/KONV-2010-0007 and TÁMOP 4.2.2/C-11/1/KONV-2012-0001 projects. The projects are implemented through the New Hungary Development Plan co-financed by the European Social Fund, and the European Regional Development Fund. The second author is supported by the Hungarian National Foundation for Scientific Research Grant No. K75566 and NK 104208.

References

1. Abadi, M., Fournet, C.: Mobile Values, New Names, and Secure Communication. In: 28th ACM Symposium on Principles of Programming Languages (POPL 2001), pp. 104–115 (2001)
2. Aszalós, L., Huszti, A.: Applying Spi-calculus for Payword. In: Proceedings of ICAI 2010 8th International Conference on Applied Informatics, pp. 295–302 (2010)
3. Azbel, I.: PayWord Micro-Payment Scheme. Strengths, Weaknesses and Proposed Improvements, http://citeseerx.ist.psu.edu/
4. Bella, G., Massacci, F., Paulson, L.C.: Verifying the set purchase protocols. J. Autom. Reasoning 36(1-2), 5–37 (2006)
5. Bellare, M., Garay, J., Hauser, R., Herzberg, A., Krawczyk, H., Steiner, M., Van Herrenweghen, E., Waidner, M.: Design, Implementation and Deployment of the iKP Secure Electronic Payment System. IEEE Journal of Selected Areas in Communications 18(4), 611–627 (2000)
6. Blanchet, B.: Automatic verification of correspondences for security protocols. Journal of Computer Security
7. Blanchet, B., Smyth, B.: ProVerif 1.85:Automatic Cryptographic Protocol Verifier, User Manual and Tutorial (2011), http://www.proverif.ens.fr/manual.pdf
8. Kusters, R., Truderung, T.: Using proverif to analyze protocols with diffie-hellman exponentiation. In: Computer Security Foundations Symposium, pp. 157–171. IEEE (2009)
9. Lowe, G.: Casper: A compiler for the analysis of security protocols. In: CSFW, pp. 18–30. IEEE Computer Society (1997)
10. Meadows, C.: Language generation and verification in the nrl protocol analyzer. In: CSFW, pp. 48–61. IEEE Computer Society (1996)

11. Mitchell, J.C., Mitchell, M., Stern, U.: Automated analysis of cryptographic protocols using mur-phi. In: IEEE Symposium on Security and Privacy, pp. 141–151. IEEE Computer Society (1997)

12. Rivest, R., Shamir, A.: PayWord and MicroMint: Two simple Micropayment Schemes. In: Lomas, M. (ed.) Security Protocols 1996. LNCS, vol. 1189, pp. 69–87. Springer, Heidelberg (1997)

13. Javier Thayer, F., Herzog, J.C., Guttman, J.D.: Strand spaces: Why is a security protocol correct? In: IEEE Symposium on Security and Privacy, pp. 160–171. IEEE Computer Society (1998)

14. Kou, W.: Payment Technologies for E-Commerce. Springer (1998)

Anonymity-Based Authenticated Key Agreement with Full Binding Property[*]

Jung Yeon Hwang[1], Sungwook Eom[2], Ku-Young Chang[1], Pil Joong Lee[2], and DaeHun Nyang[3,**]

[1] ETRI, Daejeon, Republic of Korea
{videmot,jang1090}@etri.re.kr
[2] POSTECH, Pohang, Republic of Korea
sweom@oberon.postech.ac.kr, pjl@postech.ac.kr
[3] Inha University, Incheon, Republic of Korea
nyang@inha.ac.kr

Abstract. In this paper we propose anonymity-based authentication and key agreement protocols where no participant's identity is revealed. The proposed protocols guarantee stronger notion of security which is called *full binding* property for communication messages. Under the notion of full binding, a verifier can confirm that an anonymous participant has not turned over a session to another anonymous participant while connecting to the verifier and also a session hijacking does not happen. Our approach is to use an anonymous signature scheme with a signer-controlled yet partially enforced linkability. We formally prove that the constructed protocols are secure.

Keywords: Anonymity, Authentication, Key Agreement, Full Binding Property, Session Turn-over, Session Hijacking.

1 Introduction

Demands on privacy enhancing technologies are increasing, and anonymous cryptographic primitives such as group signature and direct anonymous authentication (DAA) are playing important role in the anonymous service structure. Considering that today's web-oriented service structures require sessions to facilitate the communication, however, relying only on those primitives is not enough because they are just signing algorithms for a single message not for entire protocol messages or a session. So, it is necessary to have an anonymous session establishing protocol using those primitives.

An effective way to achieve a secure session establishment is to use a key agreement (KA) protocol with an identity. A protocol achieving key agreement and authentication is called an authenticated key agreement (AKA) protocol.

---

[*] This work was supported by the IT Research and Development program of MKE, Korea (Development of Privacy Enhancing Cryptography on Ubiquitous Computing Environment).

[**] Corresponding author.

D.H. Lee and M. Yung (Eds.): WISA 2012, LNCS 7690, pp. 177–191, 2012.

It can be used to establish a secure session [32]. In practice, Kerberos [29], SSL (Secure Socket Layer) [22] and X.509 an authentication framework [27] have been used for the user identification and key agreement. An agreed key via AKA is used not only for confidentiality and message integrity, but also for *binding* a communicating peer with the identity.

Recently, Walker et al. have proposed an anonymous authenticated key exchange protocol with DAA [34], called DAA-SIGMA. They showed formal security proof in Canetti-Krawcyzk model. The protocol can be used as a way to establish an anonymous session. Also, by applying a group signature instead of a normal signature to an AKA protocol, one can easily obtain an anonymous AKA protocol. In those protocols, one can manage an anonymous session using the agreed session key. Though DAA-SIGMA and group signature based AKA protocols are enough when a verifier does not mind each individual user's behavior but it is interested only in the group behavior, it is also desirable if the verifier is able to be sure that a user who has been authenticated is the same user who has just sent a message during the established session. In that sense, DAA-SIGMA and group signature based AKA protocols are not strong enough.

Assume that an anonymous authentication protocol is dependent upon a session key established during the authentication for binding each message with a user as AKA is. Then a user may transfer its session key to another user, but the verifier cannot recognize it. Consequently, a user is able to turn over its session to another user while the verifier is not aware. This happens in DAA-SIGMA and in group signature based AKA. This unrecognized turn-over or misbinding may cause unwanted effects in some scenarios.

While a user wants to remain anonymous after authentication, he might also want the verifier to maintain his rewarding points. However, the misbinding might disturb the verifier's record of rewarding points. Or, a verifier might want to record an individual user's misbehavior while not knowing who he is so that a verifier should block the misbehaving user later. Thus, the misbinding might cause some confusion in the verifier's record of misbehaviors. The rewarding/penalty system needs to singulate an anonymous user while not being aware of the user's identity.

The session turn-over may not be critical in AKA unlike anonymous AKA. In an AKA using a normal signature scheme, an individual user is clearly known to a verifier, so he does not have much motivation to turn over the session by transferring the session key, whereas in an anonymous AKA protocol, anonymous users cannot be singulated among group members, so an anonymous user is likely to abuse the misbinding when it is possible.

Singulating a user correctly is important not only to prevent *the session turn-over* but also *a session hijacking* caused from a stolen session key. Assume that a user was watching a video content from a server anonymously, and changed his device to continue to watch the video at home in a large screen. While changing the devices, his session key was stolen. Then, neither a server nor a user could recognize this session hijacking. This type of hijacking from a stolen session key is always possible considering that a session key resides in RAM that is not secure at all, while a long-term key is stored in a secured area like Tamper-Proof-Module.

In this paper, we introduce a new notion of *full binding* in anonymous authentication protocol and give a formal definition of it. Intuitively, for example, the full binding guarantees that a protocol participant has only one-partnered party of a session for two-party anonymous authentication. In addition, we present a formal security model for an anonymity-based AKA (AAKA) protocol with the full binding notion. We also propose AAKA protocols with the full binding property and formally prove that the proposed AAKA protocols are secure in the presented security model. Our protocols mainly make use of DAA for anonymous authentication. In particular, in order to achieve the full binding property, our protocols rely on the signer-controlled but partially enforced linking feature of the underlying DAA scheme. By eliminating the dependency on a session key, our protocols can resolve the session turn-over and the session hijacking effectively. As long as a user's long-term key is stored securely in TPM, a user and a server can expect correct anonymous singulation. Though still it is possible to turn over a session by transferring his DAA private key to another user, transferring the permanent private key is much more critical and sensitive than transferring the temporary session key, which would discourage a user to turn over a session.

Finally, we present AAKA protocols with a relaxed binding property. Here not all of the outgoing messages but only the messages that might be necessary for singulation of the anonymous user later are anonymously signed with DAA. In terms of computational overhead, these protocols gain advantages because some messages can be authenticated by MAC which may be more efficiently computed than DAA. Our protocols can be modified to achieve additional properties such as revocable anonymity or unilateral anonymity.

Related Works. In order to deal with anonymity-based authentication, various anonymous digital signature schemes such as group signatures, DAA, anonymous credentials have been proposed. These schemes mainly focus on how to control two properties, unlinkability on signatures and anonymity on signer identity.

A group signature was first introduced in [15]. It allows a member of a group to anonymously sign a message. Boneh et al. proposed a novel short group signature scheme based on Strong Diffie-Hellman assumption in a bilinear map [6]. Previous group signatures were based on Strong RSA assumption [1,12]. The group signature scheme provided approximately the same security and signature length as standard RSA signature scheme [6]. Formal definitions and security properties for a group signature are well presented for static and dynamic groups at [2,4]. There were many researches related to revocation [33,31]. Recently, Hwang et al. proposed a short group signature scheme for dynamic membership with controllable linkability. The controllable linkability enables an entity that possesses a special linking key to check whether two signatures are from the same signer or not [25].

Direct anonymous attestation (DAA) was first introduced by Brickell et al. using the RSA cryptosystem [7]. It is a cryptographic protocol which enables the remote anonymous authentication of a trusted platform module (TPM). Many improvement schemes were proposed in the aspect of privacy and performance using RSA cryptography [10,23,21]. Recently several groups of researchers have constructed pairing-based DAA schemes to achieve better efficiency. The first pairing-based DAA scheme was proposed by Brickell et al.[8,9]. Chen et al. improved the [8,9] schemes to increase the security and flexibility with the asymmetric pairing [18,19]. These schemes are all built on LRSW assumption [13]. Brickell et al. proposed an extension of DAA scheme based q-SDH assumption [5,20]. In 2010 Chen reduced the size of the private signing key [16] and Brickell et al. reduced a computational cost [11].

Leung et al. introduced an anonymous authenticated KA protocol using DAA [30]. Cesena et al. proposed an anonymous authenticated KA protocol to protect sharing credential [14] and Chen et al. proposed a protocol for mobile embedded device [17]. Walker et al. proposed the security model for key exchange with anonymous authentication and anonymous authenticated KA protocol which provides a binding property [34].

Organization. The rest of this paper is organized as follows. In Section 2 we briefly review some preliminaries for our construction. In Section 3 we present a security model for an AAKA protocol and a binding property on transmission messages. In Section 4 we propose various AAKA protocols with the full binding property and proves their security. Finally, we conclude in Section 5.

2   Preliminaries

In this section we review some preliminaries for our construction.

2.1   Computational Assumptions

Let $\mathbb{G}$ be a cyclic group of order q and g a random generator of $\mathbb{G}$ where q is a large prime number.

Decisional Diffie-Hellman (DDH) Problem. A DDH algorithm $\mathcal{A}$ for $\mathbb{G}$ is a PPT algorithm satisfying, for some fixed $\alpha > 0$ and sufficiently large n: $\left| \Pr \left[\mathcal{A}(p, g, g^a, g^b, g^{ab}) = 1 \right] - \left[\mathcal{A}(p, g, g^a, g^b, g^c) = 1 \right] \right| > 1/n^\alpha$, where a, b, and c are selected from $\mathbb{Z}_q^*$ uniformly at random. We say that $\mathbb{G}$ satisfies the DDH assumption if there is no DDH algorithm for $\mathbb{G}$.

2.2   Cryptographic Primitives

Message Authentication Code (MAC). An MAC consists of two algorithms MAC-Gen and MAC-Vrfy. The algorithms are associated to key space $\mathcal{K}$ that is typically defined by $\{0, 1\}^\kappa$. MAC-Gen takes as input a message m and a key

$s \in \mathcal{K}$ to generate a MAC-tag $\mathtt{tag}$. MAC-Vrfy takes as input a message m, a MAC-tag $\mathtt{tag}$ and a key s, and verifies the MAC-tag. We say that a MAC scheme is (t, ϵ)-secure if, for any PPT adversary $\mathcal{A}$ running in time at most t, we have $\Pr\left[s \leftarrow \mathcal{K}; \langle M, \mathtt{tag}\rangle \leftarrow \mathcal{A}^{MAC_s(\cdot)} : \mathsf{MAC\text{-}Vrfy}_s(M, \mathtt{tag}) = 1, M \notin \mathcal{M}\right] \leq \epsilon$, where $\mathcal{M}$ is the set of messages that $\mathcal{A}$ submitted to its oracle $MAC_s(\cdot)$.

Pseudorandom Function. Let $F : \{0,1\}^* \times \{0,1\}^* \to \{0,1\}^*$ be an efficient, length-preserving, keyed function. We say that F is a pseudorandom function if for all PPT distinguishers D, there exists fixed $\alpha > 0$ for sufficiently large n such that: $\left|\Pr\left[D^{F_k(\cdot)}(1^n) = 1\right] - \Pr\left[D^{f(\cdot)}(1^n) = 1\right]\right| \leq 1/n^\alpha$, where $k \in \{0,1\}^n$ is chosen uniformly at random and f is chosen uniformly at random from the set of functions mapping n-bit strings to n-bit strings.

2.3   A Review of DAA

In this section we review a DAA scheme that is used as the main building block for constructing our AAKA protocols with the full binding property.

In general, a DAA scheme has three types of players, i.e., an issuer $\mathcal{I}$, a signer $\mathcal{S}_i{}^1$, and a verifier $\mathcal{V}_j$. A DAA scheme consists of the following polynomial-time algorithms or an interactive protocol, Setup, Join, Sign, Vrfy, and Link:

- Setup: It takes as input a security parameter 1^λ and then outputs a pair $(\mathtt{gpk}, \mathtt{mik})$ where $\mathtt{mik}$ is the master issuing key secretly managed by the Issuer $\mathcal{I}$ and $\mathtt{gpk}$ is the group public key including the global public parameters. We assume that anyone can access $\mathtt{gpk}$.
- Join: It is an interactive protocol run by a signer $\mathcal{S}_i$ and the issuer $\mathcal{I}$. To perform the joining process, $\mathcal{S}_i$ generates its own secret key $\mathtt{usk}_i$. After the completion of the protocol, $\mathcal{S}_i$ obtains a full DAA signing key, $\mathtt{sk}_i{=}(\mathtt{usk}_i, \mathtt{cre}_i)$ where $\mathtt{cre}_i$ is a membership credential issued by $\mathcal{I}$. The value of $\mathtt{sk}_i$ is unknown to the issuer.
- Sign: It takes as input, $\mathtt{gpk}$, $\mathtt{sk}_i = (\mathtt{usk}_i, \mathtt{cre}_i)$, a basename $\mathtt{bsn}_j$, and a message m, and then outputs a signature σ on m. The basename $\mathtt{bsn}_j$ can be either an arbitrary string such as the name of a verifier or a special symbol $\perp$ that represents a randomly selected string. It can be used for controlling the linkability.
- Vrfy: It takes as input, $\mathtt{gpk}$, $\mathtt{bsn}_j$, message m, signature σ, and then outputs 0 or 1. Here '0' and '1' mean 'invalid' and 'valid', respectively.
- Link: It takes as input, two valid signatures σ_0 and σ_1, and then outputs 0 or 1. Here '0' and '1' mean 'unlinked' and 'linked', respectively.

We say that a DAA scheme is secure if the following properties hold: For the concrete formal definition of the security of DAA, refer to [7,9,34].

---

[1] Actually a DAA signer should be defined by the combination of TPM $\mathcal{M}_i$ and a host $\mathcal{H}_i$ because $\mathcal{M}_i$ and $\mathcal{H}_i$ form a platform in the trusted computing environment and share the role of a DAA signer $\mathcal{S}_i$. For simplicity, the DAA signer is treated as a single entity in the paper.

- Correctness. A signature generated with a valid signing key should be verified correctly.
- Anonymity. It must be hard for an adversary to learn the identity of a signer of signatures.
- Unforgeability. It must be hard for an adversary to forge a signature if he does not hold a valid (or non-revoked) signing key.
- User-controlled Linkability. Signatures created by the same set of $\mathsf{sk} = (\mathsf{usk}, \mathsf{cre})$, bsn can be linked. However, signatures cannot be linked if they are created using different basenames (or if $\mathsf{bsn} = \perp$).

If a signature σ was created using $\mathsf{bsn} = \perp$, then σ is called a random based signature; otherwise, σ is called a name based signature.

As mentioned in the introduction, DAA signature schemes have been constructed using various mathematical assumptions.

3   Security Model

In this section we present a formal security model for a two-party AAKA protocol by modifying the security model of [3,28,34]. In particular, this model captures the notion of a *binding property* to guarantee that a participant has only one anonymous partner in a run of a two-party AAKA protocol.

3.1   Security Model for a Two-Party AAKA Protocol

Participants and Initialization. Let α be a polynomial on a security parameter and $\mathcal{U} = \{U_1, ..., U_\alpha\}$ denote a set of α users for a AAKA protocol. A pair of users in $\mathcal{U}$ is allowed to invoke the AAKA protocol in order to share a session key and run the protocol concurrently. During some initialization phase a key generation process is executed to generate a group public key, gpk which is known to all users and also an adversary. The group public key is not bound to a specific user. In addition, each user U_i generates a long-term secret key, sk_{U_i}, possibly with the help of a trusted entity. We assume that all long-term keys are honestly generated.

Session IDs, Partner IDs, and Related Notions. A user $U \in \mathcal{U}$ is allowed to run the protocol multiple times with different participants; these multiple executions of user U is modeled via the use of instances such that instance i of user U is denoted by Π_U^i and the index i sequentially increases according to the number of executions of U [3,28].

A session ID of instance Π_U^i (denoted by sid_U^i) is defined as the set of the common transcripts of two anonymous players executing the protocol. As we consider anonymity-based authentication, the identity of a user will not be revealed during an execution of the protocol. Accordingly, a partner ID is not defined explicitly when a user U (or instance Π_U^i) first initiates the protocol. Instead, the partner ID for instance Π_U^i can be defined with temporal *pseudo-identities* of anonymous players (including U itself) who take part in a run of the protocol to establish a session key. We simply view the partner ID as the session ID. However, to clarify the description of the model, we define pid_U^i as the set of the identities of the real players taking part in the protocol.

We say an instance Π_U^i accepts when it computes a session key sk_U^i. If an instance computes a session key sk_U^i, we assume that it outputs $(\text{sid}_U^i, \text{sk}_U^i)$. Finally, we say that a pair of instances Π_U^i and Π_V^j (with $U \neq V$) are (anonymously) *partnered* if and only if (1) $\text{sid}_U^i = \text{sid}_V^j$ and (2) they have both accepted.

Adversarial Model. Behaviors of an adversary are modeled through the following oracle queries and the corresponding responses:

- $\text{Execute}(U, i, V, j)$. The oracle executes the protocol between instances Π_U^i and Π_V^j, and outputs the transcripts generated from the execution.
- $\text{Send}(U, i, M)$. The oracle sends message M to instance Π_U^i and outputs the response generated by this instance.
- $\text{Corrupt}(U)$. The oracle outputs the long-term secret key sk_U of user U.
- $\text{Reveal}(U, i)$. The oracle outputs session key sk_U^i for a terminated instance Π_U^i. This query models the leakage of a session key via break-ins and side-channel attacks, etc.
- $\text{Test}(U, i)$. This query is allowed only when Π_U^i has accepted. The oracle picks a random bit $b \in \{0, 1\}$. If $b = 0$, it outputs a random session key, and otherwise, i.e., if $b = 1$, it outputs the session key sk_U^i computed by Π_U^i. The adversary is allowed to access this oracle only once.

AKA Security. We say a player U is *corrupted* if the adversary makes a query with $\text{Corrupt}(U)$. A session sid is corrupted if there exists an anonymous player U who is corrupted while there is an instance $\Pi_{U'}^i$ associated with this session (possibly with $U' = U$) who has not yet terminated. We say an instance Π_U^i associated with session sid is *fresh* if (1) the adversary has never queried $\text{Reveal}(U', j)$ for any instance $\Pi_{U'}^j$ associated with sid, and (2) the session sid is not corrupted. The adversary succeeds if it queries the Test oracle regarding a fresh instance, and correctly guesses the value of the bit b used by the Test oracle. Let denote this event by Succ and define the advantage of adversary $\mathcal{A}$ attacking protocol π to be $\text{Adv}_{\mathcal{A},\pi}^{\text{AKE}} = | \Pr[\text{Succ}] - \frac{1}{2} |$. We say that KA protocol π is *AKA-secure* if, for any PPT adversary $\mathcal{A}$, the advantage $\text{Adv}_{\mathcal{A},\pi}^{\text{AKE}}$ is negligible.

Anonymity. We consider the following (unilateral) anonymity game between a challenger $\mathcal{C}$ and an adversary $\mathcal{A}$. First $\mathcal{A}$ issues Send, Corrupt, and Reveal queries. Then $\mathcal{A}$ chooses users $\hat{U}_0$, $\hat{U}_1$, and V from $\mathcal{U}$. $\mathcal{A}$ must not have made any corrupt query on either $\hat{U}_0$ or $\hat{U}_1$. $\mathcal{C}$ chooses a bit b uniformly at random, and then runs a KA protocol π using $(\hat{U}_b, V)$. $\mathcal{A}$ issues Send, Corrupt, and Reveal queries adaptively. $\mathcal{A}$ must not have made any corrupt query on either $\hat{U}_0$ or $\hat{U}_1$. Finally, $\mathcal{A}$ returns a guess bit b'. We say that the adversary wins the game if $b = b'$. We denote by CGus the event that the adversary correctly guesses the bit. The advantage of adversary $\mathcal{A}$ attacking protocol π is defined by $\text{Adv}_{\mathcal{A},\pi}^{\text{Anon-L}} = | \Pr[\text{CGus}] - \frac{1}{2} |$. We say that KA protocol π is *unilaterally* *anonymous* if, for any PPT adversary $\mathcal{A}$, $\mathsf{Adv}_{\mathcal{A},\pi}^{\mathsf{Anon\text{-}L}}$ is negligible. For full (or bilateral) anonymity, i.e., anonymity on both players, $\mathcal{A}$ performs a similar test in the above game with $(V, \hat{U}_b)$. In this case, the advantage of $\mathcal{A}$ attacking protocol π is defined by $\mathsf{Adv}_{\mathcal{A},\pi}^{\mathsf{Anon\text{-}R}} =\mid \Pr[\mathrm{CGus}] - \frac{1}{2} \mid$. We say that KA protocol π is anonymous if, for any PPT adversary $\mathcal{A}$, both advantages, i.e., $\mathsf{Adv}_{\mathcal{A},\pi}^{\mathsf{Anon\text{-}L}}$ and $\mathsf{Adv}_{\mathcal{A},\pi}^{\mathsf{Anon\text{-}R}}$ are negligible.

We say that KA protocol π is a secure AAKA protocol if π is AKA-secure and anonymous.

Binding Property. Assume that a pair of instances Π_U^i and Π_V^j (with $U \neq V$) are (anonymously) *partnered* for a session. Let $\mathcal{T}_U^i$ be a collection of all session transcripts that are generated by the instance Π_U^i for the session sid_U^i. If it is guaranteed that $\mathsf{sid}_U^i \setminus \mathcal{T}_U^i$, i.e., all the remaining session transcripts except $\mathcal{T}_U^i$ are generated only by Π_V^j then we say that a unilateral full binding property[2] holds for Π_U^i. Similarly, if it is guaranteed that $\mathsf{sid}_U^i \setminus \mathcal{T}_U^i$ is generated only by Π_U^i then we say that a unilateral full binding property holds for Π_V^j. If the binding properties hold for both instances then we say that a KA protocol achieves the (bilateral) full binding property. Intuitively, the full binding property guarantees that a party must have only one partnered party of a session.

The above notion can be relaxed to capture a partial binding property to guarantee that some partial session transcripts are generated by a party.

4   Our AAKA Protocols

In this section, we propose two-party AAKA protocols with the full binding property. The main idea to achieve our goal is to use a DAA scheme. Basically anonymous authentication can be provided under the anonymity of the underlying DAA scheme. Furthermore, because of the user-controlled linkability, we can build a proper structure to achieve the full binding property while preserving anonymity for participants.

Assume that a DAA scheme, $\mathrm{DAA} = (\mathsf{Setup}, \mathsf{Join}, \mathsf{Sign}, \mathsf{Vrfy}, \mathsf{Link})$ is given. Before running the proposed protocols, Setup is performed to generate a group public key, gpk and a secret master issuing key, mik. Each user ID obtains a signing key, $\mathsf{sk}_{ID} = (\mathsf{usk}_{ID}, \mathsf{cre}_{ID})$ by performing Join with the Issuer who can access mik. Here cre_{ID} is a membership credential and usk_{ID} is a secret key that is generated by user ID and is unrevealed to the Issuer. Assume that usk_{ID} is generated to be a value of which randomness is contributed by both a user and the Issuer. This can be easily done by using known secure multiparty computation methods. This feature is necessary to achieve the full binding property in our protocols.

The proposed protocols make use of a message authentication code MAC and a pseudorandom function PRF, and a cryptographic hash function $H : \{0,1\}^* \to$

---

[2] Our full binding property is different from the notion of a binding property considered in [34] mainly to prevent so-called misbinding attacks.

$\{0,1\}^\ell$. Let $\mathbb{G}$ be a cyclic group of order q and g a random generator of $\mathbb{G}$ where q is a large prime number.

4.1   Three Pass AAKA Protocol I

The basic structure of this protocol is similar to that of the KA protocol [24] that runs in three rounds. However our protocol performs a mutual anonymity-based authentication process. For explicit key confirmation, our protocol uses a DAA signature. See Fig. 1.

Theorem 1. *The above proposed protocol is a secure AAKA protocol that achieves the full binding property if the underlying DAA signature scheme is secure.*

Proof. We can directly prove the theorem by using Lemma 1 and Lemma 2. □

Lemma 1. *The above proposed protocol is a secure AAKA protocol if the DDH assumption in $\mathbb{G}$ holds and the underlying DAA signature scheme is secure.*

Proof. First, we show that the proposed protocol is AKA-secure. Let $\mathcal{A}$ be an adversary attacking the proposed AAKA protocol. We assume that the adversary makes q_{ex} and q_s calls to the Execute and the Send oracles. We define two

$U(\mathbf{sk}_U)$		$V(\mathbf{sk}_V)$
$x \leftarrow_R \mathbb{Z}_q; X \leftarrow g^x$		
$\mathbf{bsn}_U \leftarrow H(X)$		
$Sign_U \leftarrow \mathsf{Sign}_{\mathbf{sk}_U}(\mathbf{gpk}, \mathbf{bsn}_U, X)$	$\xrightarrow{\;[X, Sign_U]\;}$	$\mathbf{bsn}_U \leftarrow H(X)$
		If $1 \neq \mathsf{Vrfy}(\mathbf{gpk}, \mathbf{bsn}_U, X, Sign_U)$,
		abort. Otherwise
		$y \leftarrow_R \mathbb{Z}_q; Y \leftarrow g^y$
		$K \leftarrow X^y = g^{xy}$
		$k_0 \leftarrow \mathrm{PRF}_K(0), k_1 \leftarrow \mathrm{PRF}_K(1)$
		$\mathbf{bsn}_V \leftarrow H(Y); h_v = H(Y, X, k_0)$
$K \leftarrow Y^x = g^{xy}$	$\xleftarrow{\;[Y, Sign_V]\;}$	$Sign_V \leftarrow \mathsf{Sign}_{\mathbf{sk}_V}(\mathbf{gpk}, \mathbf{bsn}_V, h_v)$
$k_0 \leftarrow \mathrm{PRF}_K(0), k_1 \leftarrow \mathrm{PRF}_K(1)$		
$h_v = H(Y, X, k_0)$		
If $1 \neq \mathsf{Vrfy}(\mathbf{gpk}, \mathbf{bsn}_V, h_v, Sign_V)$,		
abort. Otherwise		
$h_u = H(X, Y, k_0)$		
$Sign'_U \leftarrow \mathsf{Sign}_{\mathbf{sk}_U}(\mathbf{gpk}, \mathbf{bsn}_U, h_u)$	$\xrightarrow{\;[Sign'_U]\;}$	$h_u = H(X, Y, k_0)$
		If $1 \neq \mathsf{Vrfy}(\mathbf{gpk}, \mathbf{bsn}_U, h_u, Sign'_U)$,
		abort.
		If $1 \neq \mathsf{Link}(Sign_U, Sign'_U)$, abort.
Session Key: k_1		Session Key: k_1

Fig. 1. Three pass AAKA protocol

independent events, Forge and Repeat. Forge is the event that $\mathcal{A}$ outputs a forged DAA signature on a new message before issuing a Corrupt(U) query. Obviously, Pr[Forge] is negligible because the underlying DAA signature scheme is assumed to be unforgeable and $\mathcal{A}$ can use at most $|\mathcal{U}|$ DAA signatures in parallel where $|\mathcal{U}|$ is the number of all users, which is polynomially bounded in a security parameter. Repeat is the event that an honest user generates an ephemeral DH public key g^r twice. Let λ be the bit-length of the order of the (mathematical) group $\mathbb{G}$. We can show Pr[Repeat] $\leq \frac{q_s \cdot (q_s + q_{ex})}{2^\lambda}$ via birthday paradox because a user selects a random element at most $q_s + q_{ex}$ times. Pr[Repeat] is negligible because λ is assumed to be sufficiently large.

Now, (unless Forge and Repeat occur,) we can show that an efficient algorithm $\mathcal{D}$ solving the DDH problem in $\mathbb{G}$ can be constructed using $\mathcal{A}$ who attacks the proposed protocol. Note that $\mathcal{A}$'s Test query can be asked to an instance which was initialized via an Execute query or a Send query. We denote by $\mathsf{Test_E}$ the event that $\mathcal{A}$ asks its Test query to an instance which was initialized via Execute query. Here we only give an analysis for $\mathsf{Test_E}$. For the case of an Send query, we can similarly analyze it because an Execute query can be simulated via multiple calls to the Send oracle. For more details, refer to the full version of this paper.

$\mathcal{D}$ generates all private DAA signing keys and a group public key by running Setup and Join algorithms of the underlying DAA scheme. Assume that $\mathcal{D}$ is given a random DDH instance $(g, A = g^a, B = g^b, Z = g^c)$. The goal of $\mathcal{D}$ is to determine whether $Z = g^{ab}$ or not. $\mathcal{D}$ guesses $\alpha \in \{1, ..., q_{ex}\}$ uniformly at random such that $\mathcal{A}$ makes its Test query to an instance which was initialized via the αth Execute query. On the αth Execute query, denoted by Execute(U, i, V, j), $\mathcal{D}$ defines the response by $\mathsf{sid}_U^i = \mathsf{sid}_V^j = \{(X = g^a, Sign_U), (Y = g^b, Sign_V), (Sign'_U)\}$ where $\{Sign_U, Sign'_U\}$ and $Sign_V$ are generated with DAA signing keys of U and V, respectively. Note that a session ID is the same to a set of all transcripts generated from an honest execution of the protocol and thus $\mathsf{sid}_U^i = \mathsf{sid}_V^j$ can be the response to Execute(U, i, V, j). $\mathcal{D}$ can generate the signatures easily using DAA signing keys that he generated. Then $\mathcal{D}$ defines the resulting session key sk by Z. Except the αth Execute query, responses to other oracle queries can be made in an obvious way because $\mathcal{D}$ is aware of the long-term private DAA keys of all users. When $\mathcal{A}$ issues Test(U, t) for a terminated instance, $\mathcal{D}$ finds related session ID, sid_U^t for the instance, and the corresponding session key that are associated with the instance. If sid_U^t is not the session ID for the αth Execute query, then $\mathcal{D}$ aborts and outputs a random bit. Otherwise, $\mathcal{D}$ returns sk $= g^c$ to $\mathcal{A}$. $\mathcal{D}$ outputs the bit that $\mathcal{A}$ outputs. When $\mathsf{Test_E}$ occurs, $\mathcal{D}$ does not abort with probability $1/q_{ex}$. In addition, unless $\mathcal{D}$ aborts, there exist two possible cases in the above simulation as follows: If $Z = g^{ab}$, i.e., (g, g^a, g^b, Z) is a valid DDH tuple then the simulation is a correct execution of the proposed protocol, that is, sk is a real session key. Otherwise, i.e., $Z = g^c$ for random $c \in \mathbb{Z}_q^*$, sk is a random key obviously. Hence $\mathcal{D}$ can solve the given DDH instance using the same advantage of the adversary $\mathcal{A}$. In other words, the proposed protocol is AKA-secure if the DDH assumption in $\mathbb{G}$ holds.

Next we show that the proposed AAKA protocol is anonymous. The AAKA protocol combines the ephemeral Diffie-Hellman KA protocol and a DAA signature scheme. Each message is transmitted together with a DAA signature generated for the message. By assumption, a DAA signature scheme provides anonymity on a signer [34]. Basically, a verifier cannot learn the identity of the signer from a given signature due to the anonymity of the DAA signature. Since the anonymity of the DAA signature is independent of the position of protocol participants, the proposed protocol achieves the bilateral anonymity, i.e., it is anonymous. □

Lemma 2. *The above proposed protocol achieves the full binding property if the underlying DAA signature scheme is secure.*

Proof. Assume that a pair of instances Π_U^i and Π_V^j for two different users U and V are anonymously *partnered* for a session after an execution of the protocol. We denote a session ID generated from the execution by $\mathsf{sid}_U^i = \mathsf{sid}_V^j = \{(X = g^x, Sign_U), (Y = g^y, Sign_V), (Sign_U')\}$ where $Sign_U$, $Sign_U'$, and $Sign_V$ are valid DAA signatures. Let $\mathcal{T}_U^i = \{(X = g^x, Sign_U), (Sign_U')\}$ and $\mathcal{T}_V^j = \{(Y = g^y, Sign_V)\}$. Since $Sign_U$ is a valid DAA signature associated with the message X, both of X and $Sign_U$ consisting of the first transcript of $\mathcal{T}_U^i$ should be generated and sent only by an anonymous user. The third transcript of $\mathcal{T}_U^i$ consisting of a valid single signature is trivially generated only by an anonymous user. By construction of the protocol, we must have $1 = \mathsf{Link}(Sign_U, Sign_U')$, that is, $Sign_U$ and $Sign_U'$ should be linked. Note that the two DAA signatures are generated with the same basename $\mathsf{bsn}_U = H(X)$. In other words, this means that the two DAA signatures were generated by a single signer. Hence $\mathcal{T}_U^i$ was generated only by the anonymous user, i.e. the unilateral full binding property holds for Π_V^j. It is easy to see that the unilateral full binding property holds for Π_U^i, because $Sign_V$ is a valid DAA signature associated with Y and thus both of the messages, Y and $Sign_V$ consisting of the first transcript of $\mathcal{T}_V^i$ should be generated and sent only by a user. Hence the proposed protocol achieves the bilateral full binding property. □

4.2   Two Pass Parallel AAKA Protocol

In this section we present a two pass AAKA protocol. Consider the delay tolerant network where the communication delay overwhelms the computation time. For example, the computation time is in mili-second order, but the communication delay is in hours or even in days. The delay tolerant network also known as the pocket switching network or opportunistic network has very high delay due to its inherent nature of very limited connectivity. Because of this high latency, reducing the number of passes in a protocol significantly improves the session establishing time and also in the consequent communication time.

The basic structure of our protocol is similar to the KA protocol of [26]. The protocol runs in two rounds. However our protocol performs a mutual anonymous authentication process. For explicit key confirmation this protocol uses a DAA signature. See Fig. 2.

U	V
$x \leftarrow_R \mathbb{Z}_q; X \leftarrow g^x$	$y \leftarrow_R \mathbb{Z}_q; Y \leftarrow g^y$
$\mathsf{bsn}_U \leftarrow H(X)$	$\mathsf{bsn}_V \leftarrow H(Y)$
$Sign_U \leftarrow \mathsf{Sign}_{sk_U}(\mathbf{gpk}, \mathsf{bsn}_U, X)$	$Sign_V \leftarrow \mathsf{Sign}_{sk_V}(\mathbf{gpk}, \mathsf{bsn}_V, Y)$
If $1 \neq \mathsf{Vrfy}(\mathbf{gpk}, \mathsf{bsn}_V, Y, Sign_V)$,	If $1 \neq \mathsf{Vrfy}(\mathbf{gpk}, \mathsf{bsn}_U, X, Sign_U)$,
abort. Otherwise	abort. Otherwise
$K \leftarrow Y^x = g^{xy}$	$K \leftarrow X^y = g^{xy}$
$k_0 \leftarrow \mathrm{PRF}_K(0), k_1 \leftarrow \mathrm{PRF}_K(1)$	$k_0 \leftarrow \mathrm{PRF}_K(0), k_1 \leftarrow \mathrm{PRF}_K(1)$
$h_u = H(X, Y, k_0)$	$h_v = H(Y, X, k_0)$
$Sign'_U \leftarrow \mathsf{Sign}_{sk_U}(\mathbf{gpk}, \mathsf{bsn}_U, h_u)$	$Sign'_V \leftarrow \mathsf{Sign}_{sk_V}(\mathbf{gpk}, \mathsf{bsn}_V, h_v)$
$h_v = H(Y, X, k_0)$	$h_u = H(X, Y, k_0)$
If $1 \neq \mathsf{Vrfy}(\mathbf{gpk}, \mathsf{bsn}_V, h_v, Sign'_V)$,	If $1 \neq \mathsf{Vrfy}(\mathbf{gpk}, \mathsf{bsn}_U, h_u, Sign'_U)$,
abort.	abort.
If $1 \neq \mathsf{Link}(Sign_V, Sign'_V)$, abort.	If $1 \neq \mathsf{Link}(Sign_U, Sign'_U)$, abort.
Session Key: k_1	Session Key: k_1

Messages exchanged: $\xrightarrow{[X, Sign_U]}$, $\xleftarrow{[Y, Sign_V]}$, $\xrightarrow{[Sign'_U]}$, $\xleftarrow{[Sign'_V]}$

Fig. 2. Two pass parallel AAKA protocol

Theorem 2. *The above protocol is a secure AAKA protocol with the full binding property if the DDH assumption in $\mathbb{G}$ holds and the underlying DAA signature scheme is secure.*

Proof. The theorem can be proved using a similar proof idea of Theorem 1. We omit concrete proof details. Refer to the full version of this paper for more details. □

4.3 MAC-Based AAKA Protocols

We can convert the previous AAKA protocols into AAKA protocols using a MAC-tag for explicit key confirmation. As MAC can be efficiently executed compared to an anonymous signature such as a DAA signature, the MAC-based protocols can gain advantages in the computational cost. However, the protocols provide a weakened binding property that is the same to the property presented in [34], instead of the full binding property.

We briefly depict these MAC-based protocols in Fig. 3 and Fig. 4. For more details, refer to the full version. Our MAC-based protocols are similar to the DAA-SIGMA of [34]. We can prove the security of the above protocols using a similar proof idea of [34] under the hardness of the DDH problem.

4.4 Variants

The proposed AAKA protocols are constructed in a modular manner by independently combining cryptographic primitives such as the DH key exchange method, the DAA signature scheme, and MAC. Naturally, we can modify the

Round 1.	$U \to V$:	$X = g^x, Sign_U$
Round 2.	$U \leftarrow V$:	$Y = g^y, Sign_V, MAC_V$
Round 3.	$U \to V$:	MAC_U
Session Key	U, V:	$k_1 = \text{PRF}_{g^{xy}}(1)$

Fig. 3. Three pass MAC-based AAKA protocol

Round 1.	$U \to V$:	$X = g^x, Sign_U$
	$U \leftarrow V$:	$Y = g^y, Sign_V$
Round 2.	$U \to V$:	MAC_U
	$U \leftarrow V$:	MAC_V
Session Key	U, V:	$k_1 = \text{PRF}_{g^{xy}}(1)$

Fig. 4. Two pass MAC-based Parallel AAKA protocol

AAKA protocols to achieve various properties by replacing components properly. For example, the proposed protocols can provide revocable anonymity to identify signers by replacing the DAA signature scheme (that supports only linking capability) with the group signature scheme that supports opening and linking capability in [25]. For another example, our AAKA protocols can be modified to provide only unilateral anonymous authentication by replacing an anonymous signature with a standard signature for one party.

5   Conclusions

We have presented AAKA protocols that provides the full binding property on communications, which is a new security notion for anonymous authentication protocol. This notion is useful when we consider more refined anonymous services such as rewarding/penalty systems. The binding property should be crucially achieved for anonymous authentication. Our approach is based on the use of an anonymous signature scheme with a signer-controlled but partially enforced linkability. It would be an open issue to design other efficient methods to achieve the full binding property.

References

1. Ateniese, G., Camenisch, J.L., Joye, M., Tsudik, G.: A Practical and Provably Secure Coalition-Resistant Group Signature Scheme. In: Bellare, M. (ed.) CRYPTO 2000. LNCS, vol. 1880, pp. 255–270. Springer, Heidelberg (2000)
2. Bellare, M., Micciancio, D., Warinschi, B.: Foundations of Group Signatures: Formal Definitions, Simplified Requirements, and a Construction Based on General Assumptions. In: Biham, E. (ed.) EUROCRYPT 2003. LNCS, vol. 2656, pp. 614–629. Springer, Heidelberg (2003)
3. Bellare, M., Rogaway, P.: Entity Authentication and Key Distribution. In: Stinson, D.R. (ed.) CRYPTO 1993. LNCS, vol. 773, pp. 232–249. Springer, Heidelberg (1994)

4. Bellare, M., Shi, H., Zhang, C.: Foundations of Group Signatures: The Case of Dynamic Groups. In: Menezes, A. (ed.) CT-RSA 2005. LNCS, vol. 3376, pp. 136–153. Springer, Heidelberg (2005)

5. Boneh, D., Boyen, X.: Short Signatures Without Random Oracles. In: Cachin, C., Camenisch, J.L. (eds.) EUROCRYPT 2004. LNCS, vol. 3027, pp. 56–73. Springer, Heidelberg (2004)

6. Boneh, D., Boyen, X., Shacham, H.: Short Group Signatures. In: Franklin, M. (ed.) CRYPTO 2004. LNCS, vol. 3152, pp. 41–55. Springer, Heidelberg (2004)

7. Brickell, E.F., Camenisch, J., Chen, L.: Direct anonymous attestation. In: ACM Conference on Computer and Communications Security, pp. 132–145 (2004)

8. Brickell, E., Chen, L., Li, J.: A New Direct Anonymous Attestation Scheme from Bilinear Maps. In: Lipp, P., Sadeghi, A.-R., Koch, K.-M. (eds.) Trust 2008. LNCS, vol. 4968, pp. 166–178. Springer, Heidelberg (2008)

9. Brickell, E., Chen, L., Li, J.: Simplified security notions of direct anonymous attestation and a concrete scheme from pairings. Int. J. Inf. Sec. 8(5), 315–330 (2009)

10. Brickell, E., Li, J.: Enhanced privacy id: a direct anonymous attestation scheme with enhanced revocation capabilities. In: WPES, pp. 21–30 (2007)

11. Brickell, E., Li, J.: A Pairing-Based DAA Scheme Further Reducing TPM Resources. In: Acquisti, A., Smith, S.W., Sadeghi, A.-R. (eds.) TRUST 2010. LNCS, vol. 6101, pp. 181–195. Springer, Heidelberg (2010)

12. Camenisch, J.L., Lysyanskaya, A.: Dynamic Accumulators and Application to Efficient Revocation of Anonymous Credentials. In: Yung, M. (ed.) CRYPTO 2002. LNCS, vol. 2442, pp. 61–76. Springer, Heidelberg (2002)

13. Camenisch, J.L., Lysyanskaya, A.: Signature Schemes and Anonymous Credentials from Bilinear Maps. In: Franklin, M. (ed.) CRYPTO 2004. LNCS, vol. 3152, pp. 56–72. Springer, Heidelberg (2004)

14. Cesena, E., Löhr, H., Ramunno, G., Sadeghi, A.-R., Vernizzi, D.: Anonymous Authentication with TLS and DAA. In: Acquisti, A., Smith, S.W., Sadeghi, A.-R. (eds.) TRUST 2010. LNCS, vol. 6101, pp. 47–62. Springer, Heidelberg (2010)

15. Chaum, D., van Heyst, E.: Group Signatures. In: Davies, D.W. (ed.) EUROCRYPT 1991. LNCS, vol. 547, pp. 257–265. Springer, Heidelberg (1991)

16. Chen, L.: A daa scheme requiring less tpm resources. IACR Cryptology ePrint Archive 2010, 8 (2010)

17. Chen, L., Dietrich, K., Löhr, H., Sadeghi, A.R., Wachsmann, C., Winter, J.: Lightweight anonymous authentication with tls and daa for embedded mobile devices. IACR Cryptology ePrint Archive 2011, 101 (2011)

18. Chen, L., Morrissey, P., Smart, N.P.: Pairings in Trusted Computing. In: Galbraith, S.D., Paterson, K.G. (eds.) Pairing 2008. LNCS, vol. 5209, pp. 1–17. Springer, Heidelberg (2008)

19. Chen, L., Morrissey, P., Smart, N.P.: Daa: Fixing the pairing based protocols. IACR Cryptology ePrint Archive 2009, 198 (2009)

20. Park, C.-M., Lee, H.-S.: Pairing-friendly curves with minimal security loss by cheon's algorithm. ETRI Journal 33(4), 656–659 (2011)

21. Feng, D.G., Xu, J., Chen, X.F.: A forward secure direct anonymous attestation scheme. In: Proceedings of the 11th WSEAS International Conference on Mathematical Methods and Computational Techniques in Electrical Engineering, MMACTEE 2009, pp. 182–188. World Scientific and Engineering Academy and Society, Stevens Point (2009)

22. Freier, A.O., Karlton, P., Kocher, P.C.: The ssl protocol — version 3.0. Internet Draft, Transport Layer Security Working Group (November 1996)

23. Ge, H., Tate, S.R.: A Direct Anonymous Attestation Scheme for Embedded Devices. In: Okamoto, T., Wang, X. (eds.) PKC 2007. LNCS, vol. 4450, pp. 16–30. Springer, Heidelberg (2007)

24. Harkins, D., Carrel, D.: The Internet Key Exchange (IKE). RFC 2409 (Proposed Standard), obsoleted by RFC 4306, updated by RFC 4109 (November 1998), http://www.ietf.org/rfc/rfc2409.txt

25. Hwang, J.Y., Lee, S., Chung, B.H., Cho, H.S., Nyang, D.: Short group signatures with controllable linkability. In: Workshop on Lightweight Security and Privacy: Devices, Protocols, and Applications, pp. 44–52 (2011)

26. ISO/IEC 9798-3 Information Technology - Security techniques - Entity Authentication Mechanisms - Part 3: Mechanisms using digital signature techniques, 2nd ed. (1998)

27. ITU-T recommendation X.509: information technology - open systems interconnection - the directory: authentication framework, ITU-T (1997)

28. Katz, J., Yung, M.: Scalable Protocols for Authenticated Group Key Exchange. In: Boneh, D. (ed.) CRYPTO 2003. LNCS, vol. 2729, pp. 110–125. Springer, Heidelberg (2003)

29. Kohl, J., Neuman, C.: The kerberos network authentication service (v5). Tech. rep., RFC 1510 (September 1993)

30. Leung, A., Mitchell, C.J.: Ninja: Non Identity Based, Privacy Preserving Authentication for Ubiquitous Environments. In: Krumm, J., Abowd, G.D., Seneviratne, A., Strang, T. (eds.) UbiComp 2007. LNCS, vol. 4717, pp. 73–90. Springer, Heidelberg (2007)

31. Libert, B., Peters, T., Yung, M.: Scalable Group Signatures with Revocation. In: Pointcheval, D., Johansson, T. (eds.) EUROCRYPT 2012. LNCS, vol. 7237, pp. 609–627. Springer, Heidelberg (2012)

32. Menezes, A., van Oorschot, P.C., Vanstone, S.A.: Handbook of Applied Cryptography. CRC Press (1996)

33. Nakanishi, T., Fujii, H., Hira, Y., Funabiki, N.: Revocable Group Signature Schemes with Constant Costs for Signing and Verifying. In: Jarecki, S., Tsudik, G. (eds.) PKC 2009. LNCS, vol. 5443, pp. 463–480. Springer, Heidelberg (2009)

34. Walker, J., Li, J.: Key Exchange with Anonymous Authentication Using DAA-SIGMA Protocol. In: Chen, L., Yung, M. (eds.) INTRUST 2010. LNCS, vol. 6802, pp. 108–127. Springer, Heidelberg (2011)

A Study for Classification of Web Browser Log and Timeline Visualization*

Junghoon Oh[1], Namheun Son[2], Sangjin Lee[2], and Kyungho Lee[2,**]

[1] A-FIRST
AhnLab, Sungnam, Korea
jh.oh@ahnlab.com
[2] Center for Information Security Technologies,
Korea University, Seoul, Korea
{pida2,sangjin,kevinlee}@korea.ac.kr

Abstract. Types of logs, such as cache, history, cookie and downloads list, are created by a web browser. Digital forensic investigators analyze these logs and obtain useful information related to cases. In fact, most of the existing tools simply parse log files. As a result, investigators have to classify and analyze log data at firsthand in the process of digital forensic investigation. In particular, in the case of massive data, they should spend enormous time analyzing the data. Therefore, in this paper, with parsed information on cache, history, cookie and download list, we propose data classification and timeline visualization method to improve analysis in efficient way for reducing investigation time and work. Also, "WEFA", a developed tool based on the research work, is to be introduced.

Keywords: Web Browser Log, Data Classification, Timeline Visualization.

1 Introduction

A web browser is one of the most used application programs in the current society. Most people gather information and handle their business work with a web browser. The information collected through the web browsing is saved into log files, such as cache, history, cookie and downloads list.

For this reason, when log files created by a web browser are analyzed in the process of digital forensic investigation, a lot of information on suspects can be acquired. For example, a suspect is likely to use a web browser to get information on a crime or find a way to conceal a crime.

These days, there are many studies and tools assist analysing web browsers' log files, but most existing researches focus on the structure of log files, and the current tools simply remain in the down level to parse log files. Therefore, inspectors

---

* This work was supported by the IT R&D program of MKE/KEIT 10035157, Development of Digital Forensic Technologies for Real-Time Analysis.
** Corresponding author.

D.H. Lee and M. Yung (Eds.): WISA 2012, LNCS 7690, pp. 192–207, 2012.

should classify and analyze the parsed data at firsthand in the process of digital forensic investigation. In particular, in the case of massive data, they should spend enormous time to analyze the data. Therefore, in this paper, with parsed information on cache, history, cookie, and downloads list, we propose data classification and timeline visualization method to improve the way of analyzing those data.

This paper is comprised of as follows: In section 2, the existing web browser forensic studies and tools are introduced, and then their limits are described; in section 3, data classification of basic web browser logs-cache, history, cookie and downloads list-is described; in section 4, "WEFA", a tool to support data classification and visualization, is introduced; in section 5, WEFA is compared with the existing tools in terms of functions; and in section 6, conclusions are drawn, and future research direction is described.

2   Related Research

2.1   Existing Research

General research on Web browser forensics has been targeted to structural analysis of particular log files.

Jones [1] explained the structure of the index.dat file and how to extract deleted activity records from Internet Explorer. He also introduced the Pasco tool to analyze the index.dat file. Also he described forensics in Firefox 2 using a cache file. The cache file in Firefox 2 is not saved in the same way as in IE, so he suggested an analysis method using the cache file structure.

Pereira [2] explained in detail the changes in the history system that occurred when Firefox 2 was updated to Firefox 3 and proposed a new method of searching deleted history information using unallocated fields. The author suggests a method of extracting history information from Firefox 3 by examining the SQLite database structure.

2.2   Existing Tools

Web browser forensic tools currently released focus on parsing log files created by a web browser. Most of them do not support a function to classify parsed data. As a result, as investigators perform an analysis with these tools, they should classify and analyze the data at firsthand. As shown in Table 1, most tools simply provide a function to parse log files, yet do not offer a function to classify parsed data.

3   A Classification of Web Browser Log Data

As investigators analyze log data with existing tools, they cant identify directly what the parsed data mean. Particularly, in the case of massive data, this analysis requires a myriad of time. In the respect, to shorten the analysis time, it is necessary to perform data classification prior to an analysis.

Table 1. Representative Forensic Tools for Web Browsers

Tools	Targeted Data	Data Classification
Pasco	Index.dat	No
Web Historian 1.3	History	No
Index.dat Analyzer 2.5	Index.dat	No
Firefox Forensic 2.3	History, Cookie, Download List, Bookmarks	No
Chrome Analysis 1.0	History, Cookie, Download List, Bookmarks	No
NetAnalysis 1.53	Cache, History	No
CacheBack 3.1.7	Cache, History, Cookie	Only Facebook Cache
Encase 6.18	History, Cookie, Download List, Bookmarks	No
FTK 3.2	Cache, History, Cookie	No

In this section, data classification method of basic web browser logs, such as cache, history, cookie, and downloads list , is explained. The web browser and OS used for research are Internet Explorer 8 and Windows XP SP3.

3.1   A Classification of Cache Data

A cache in a web browser is data that are automatically downloaded from a web server. The downloaded data help a user access the same web site quickly, because the data are not downloaded again and consequently shorten web page loading time. General types of cache data include HTML, text, image, XML, Java Script, and Shock Wave Flash Object files.

In this sub-section, we explain the classification method of cache data. The factors used to classification are filename, extension and URL.

Filename Classification. Every cache data has a filename, and some specific web application generates unique filename. At the time users pc downloads cache data, all browsers except Internet Explorer save cache data with it's original filename which is unchanged. In case of Internet Explorer, the cache data has square brackets at the end of it's filename, and a number is located between each bracket. (e.g. filename[N]) The reason Internet Explorer uses this way is to avoid same filenames located in same folder. So, if filename of some cache data is already located in the folder, the number between each bracket is increased. In conclusion, the unique filename generated by web application can be used to classify the cache data.

The following Table 2 is an outcome of research about data classification with cache filename.

Extension Classification. The classification of cache data with extension can be divided into two parts.

First part is simple classification about file type. With this classification, the investigator can easily find the cache data like html file which contain site content or document file viewed by user through web browser.

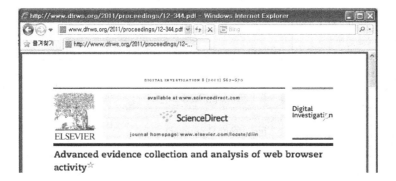

Fig. 1. Viewing Document on a Web Browser

Second part is detecting suspicious file to cyber attack. Generally, Most malicious programs frequently download another dangerous program into a user's computer with "URLDownloadToFile" API. These files downloaded in the way above are saved into Content.IE5, a temporary internet files folder of Internet Explorer. In addition, PDF or SWF(Shock Wave Flash) file can be downloaded by malicious server to attack vulnerability of Adobe Reader or Adobe Flash Player.

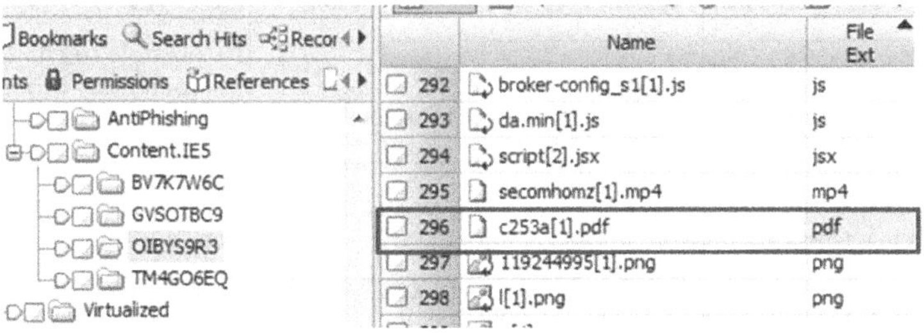

Fig. 2. Suspicious PDF File in Cache Data

So, if the extension of some cache file is included in PE(exe, dll, sys) , pdf, swf, the investigator should suspect that file for attack.

URL Classification. In the classification with URL, the specific keyword in URL is important factor. With this specific keyword, the useful information can be extracted from cache URL.

Table 2. Classification of Cache Data with Filename

Data Type	Filename	Detail
Gmail - Mail List	mail.htm (deleted after application closing)	Data signature is "\003cspan class"
Yahoo Mail - Mail List	launch.htm (deleted after application closing)	Data signature is ""subject":"
Hot Mail - Mail List	mail.htm (deleted after application closing)	Data signature is <div class="SbB"> <ahref=#>
Gmail - Mail List	mail.htm (deleted after application closing)	Data signature is "\003cspan class"
Outlook Express - Mail Body (IE Only)	wbk###.tmp (# : hexadecimal number) (deleted after application closing)	Its possible to confirm the content by browser
Windows Live Mail - Mail Body (IE Only)	wbk####.tmp	Its possible to confirm the content by browser
Facebook - Main Page	facebook_com.htm (deleted after application closing)	Its possible to confirm the content by browser
Google Docs - View Document List	docs_google_com.htm (deleted after application closing)	Its possible to confirm the content by browser
Google Docs - Edit Document	edit.htm (deleted after application closing)	The content is located after "s":
Google Docs - Edit Presentation	edit.htm (deleted after application closing)	The content is located after "title":
Google Docs - Edit Spreadsheet	ccc.htm (deleted after application closing)	Its possible to confirm the content by browser. The content is stored until 100 rows
Google Docs - View Content	viewer.txt	Text data extracted from document
	viewer.png, CA .png (XP) viewerCA .png(Win 7)	Each page or Slide screenshot
Google - Search	search.htm	Its possible to confirm the content by browser
	s	Data signature is first d:
Yahoo - Search	search;_ylt=[Random].htm	Its possible to confirm the content by browser
Baidu - Search	s.htm	Its possible to confirm the content by browser
Bing - Search	search_nsuggest	Data signature is "rq :"

The typical example of URL classification is search word extraction. This search word extraction can be applied to history URL. So, if the search words are extracted from history URL, it is not necessary to extract search word from cache URL.

But, there are some exception. When a user uses a Google search engine with Internet Explorer, URLs related to searching are not left in history log by Google's instant search function. But, as soon as the instant search function is executed, search.htm file is saved into cache data, and consequently URLs relevant to searching are left in Cache log. Therefore, the search information not extracted from history log can be found in cache log. The way to extract search words from cache URL is identical to the one to extract them from history URL. More details about it are explained in the next section which mainly describes about history data classification.

3.2   A Classification of History Data

Web browser history refers to data recorded into a log file as a user visits the web site. The history log includes visited URLs, site titles, sequence time of visit to a website, and other information.

In the actual investigation process, investigators should visit relevant websites to figure out the characteristics of the sites and the behavior and intention of a user. This process, however, requires a lot of time as massive log files are needed to be analyzed.

Therefore, in this section, history data classification to improve analysis is explained. In fact, unlike cache data, In fact, unlike cache data, every information is in the URL. There is no file included in history data. So, the investigator should extract useful information just in URL. As a result of research, we find two category of classification: search word extraction and classification of user behavior.

Search Words Extraction. As mentioned earlier in the cache data classification section, in the digital forensic investigation process, search words are the most intuitive data to understand a user's intention.

Generally, the search words, which are entered in search engine, are recorded in URL in the way of GET as shown in the following.

http://www.google.com/search?hl=en&source=hp&q=forensic&aq=f&oq= &aqi=g10

In the URL above, a search word is "forensic", a value of variable 'q'. So, if information related to the search words is able to be extracted from URL, it is possible to easily figure out a suspect's plan and intention.

Additionally, if search words are not English, the search word is encoded with UTF-8 or Unicode or Code Page based URL encoding, depending on a search engine. As a result, For understanding non-English search word, relevant

Table 3. Host, Path, Search Word Location for Different Search Engines

Search Engine	Host	Path	Search Word Location
Google	google.com	#sclient	After variable q
Yahoo	search.yahoo.com	/search	After variable p
Baidu	baidu.com	/s	After variable wd
Bing	bing.com	/search	After variable q
Ask	ask.com	/web	After variable q
AOL	search.aol.com	/search/	After variable q
Excite	msxml.excite.com	/results/	After path /Web/
Lycos	Search.lycos.com		After variable query
Alta vista	altavista.com	/search	After variable p

decoding process is required[7]. Table 3 shows the typical host, path, and search word locations in the URL of each search engine.

Therefore, if the URL includes search words, the investigator can classify the relevant URL as a search behavior.

A Classification of User Behavior. A history log can be classified by user behavior. The user behavior on web browser is generally classified with information acquisition, download, purchase, work, relationship and entertainment as shown in Table 4.

Table 4. Classification of User Behavior

User Behavior	Detailed classification
Information Acquisition	Search, Wikipedia, Viewing the Document, Education, Blog, Map, News, Weather
Download	Nothing
Purchase	Shopping, Reservation
Work	Mail, Calendar, Cloud, Banking
Relationship	SNS, Community, Chatting
Entertainment	Game, Movie, Music, Cartoon, Sports, Radio, Adult

The best classification method for user's behavior from a history log is saving any specific behavior and specific signature collected from URL to database and then classify signatures.

For example, if there is signature facebook.com in a URL, a user's behavior is classified as SNS. This method, however, contains limitation which is impossible to extract signatures from all of the web sites in the world. With this respect, more generalized method is need.

Like URL structure in Fig.3, URL consists of protocol, domain, path, page file and variable-value pairs[5].

URLs usually include special keyword presenting the work and contents of relevant web pages, because URL information is created by humans.

Protocol://	Domain	/	Path(/../../)	Page File	?	Variable & Value	...

Fig. 3. Viewing Document on a Web Browser

Table 5. General Keywords used by Classification

User Behavoir		General Keyword & Classification Method
Information Acquisition	search	If search word is extracted in URL, the behavior is "Search"
	Wikipedia	wikipedia
	Viewing Document	.doc(x), .ppt(x), .xls(x), .pdf, .txt
	Blog	blog
	Education	lecture, study, learn
	Map	map
	News	news
	Weather	weather
	Dictionary	dic, dictionary
Download		ftp://, download
Purchase	Shopping	shop, store
	Reservation	reservation, ticket
Relationship	SNS	Nothing, Using DB Signature (facebook.com, twitter.com ...)
	Community	forum, cafe, club, group, community
	Chatting	chat
Work	Mail	mail, email, e-mail
	Calendar	calendar
Cloud	SNS	Nothing, Using DB Signature (docs.google.com, zoho, aws.amazon)
	Banking	bank
	Application	apply, application
	Registration	register
Entertainment		game, movie, music, cartoon, sport, radio, adult, porn, sex

So, if web sites are classified with generally used keyword, a user's behavior can be classified on the basis of the keyword.

However, a simple searching method for URL by targeting keyword is most likely giving a wrong result. For instance, Researching on the sites which have URL including mail keyword returns only about 40 percent of the sites providing real mail service. Therefore, the more accurate classification method on user behavior is required.

The classification method suggested in this paper is presented as follows.

Step 1. URL is an input. If a search word can be extracted from URL, the user behaviors on URL is classified as "Search". If any search words are not extracted, go to Step 2.

Step 2. Specific signatures saved into DB are searched for in URL. If any specific signature is found in URL, relevant behaviors are returned and the process is finished. Otherwise, go to Step 3.

Step 3. Download keyword is searched for the whole URL. If the keyword is found in URL, the behaviors on relevant URL is classified as "Download". Otherwise, go to Step 4. The reason for this process is that all URL including download keyword can be classified into Download behavior exceptionally.

Step 4. Executing URL is divided into protocol, domain, path, page file and variable-value pairs area. If ftp://keyword is found in protocol area, the behaviors on relevant URL is classified as "Download". Otherwise, go to Step 5.

Step 5. If the extender of document such as, .doc, .ppt, or .txt is founded in page file area, the behaviors on relevant URL is classified as " Viewing the document. Otherwise, go to Step 6.

Step 6. General keywords are searched in domain area. If specific keyword is founded in domain area, make sure there are characters such as /,.,-on both side of the keyword. If the keyword is distinguished by above characters, relevant behaviors are returned. Otherwise, go to Step 7. The reason for this process is that sometimes the domain including keyword which is not distinguished by above character do not mean relevant behavior. For instance, www.emailquestions.com doesnt mean Mail behavior, but mail.google.com means Mail behavior.

Step7. General keywords are searched in path area. The depth of path performed by searching process varies for each keyword. For instance, mail keyword is searched until 1 depth, but shop keyword is searched until 2 depth. In case of particular keyword, the search depth is increasingly down as the probability of misclassification is increasing. This mean that /mail/../../has high probability of classification into Mail behavior, but ../../mail has low probability of that. If the classification is success with above process, relevant behaviors are returned and the process is finished. Otherwise, go to Step 8.

Step 8. Since behaviors related to relevant information are not able to be classified more, NULL value is returned.The general keyword used by classification process can be confirmed in Table 5. The result of applying this classification process is that about 80 percent of the sites classified Mail behavior provide real mail service. Therefore, with the above process, investigators can classify history data on the basis of a user's behavior then the classified data make possible the shortening of the analysis time and the efficient web browser forensic analysis.

3.3   A Classification of Cookie Data

In a web browser, cookie data refer to small sized text data saved into a user's computer by a web site. When a user accesses the same web site, cookie data are uploaded to site for discerning a user or providing individual services. So, the cookie data vary from site to siter, and it is impossible to figure out exactly what the cookie data means in each site. As a result of research, however, we find some standards for classification of cookie data : User Identifier and Google Analytics.

User Identifier. When a user turns on the 'Stay signed in' function, most sites provide an automatic log-on function through cookie data such like user identifier. Generally, user identifier is unique numbers or mail address. In the

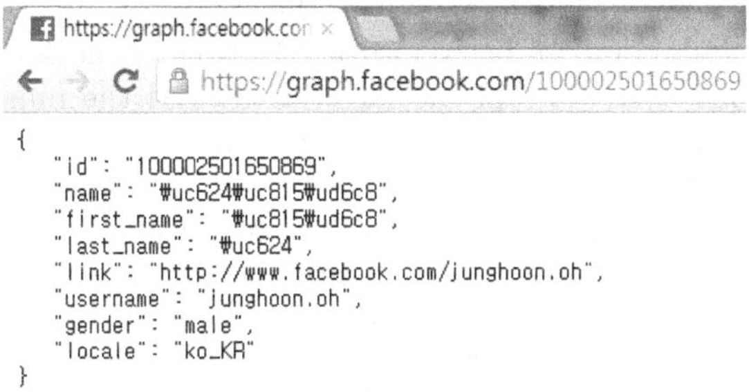

```
{
    "id": "100002501650869",
    "name": "₩uc624₩uc815₩ud6c8",
    "first_name": "₩uc815₩ud6c8",
    "last_name": "₩uc624",
    "link": "http://www.facebook.com/junghoon.oh",
    "username": "junghoon.oh",
    "gender": "male",
    "locale": "ko_KR"
}
```

Fig. 4. Facebook Graph API

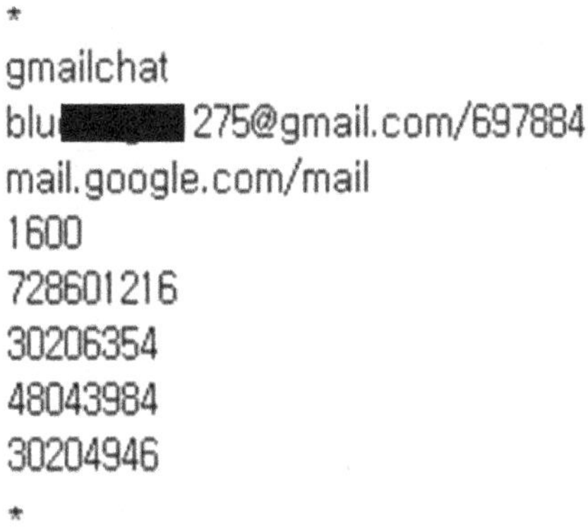

Fig. 5. Google ID in cookie

case of Facebook as an example, unique user numbers can be acquired from cookie data, and with Graph API basically offered by Facebook, a user's basic information as shown in Fig.4 can be acquired.

Another example is Google ID. The Google ID is saved into cookie as shown in Fig.5. So, if the investigator have some signatures like host, path, and variable name, he can extract user identifier from cookie data. In addition, This ID can be utilized as a signature to search for a password left in a memory.

Google Analytics. Google Analytics generates details statistics about visitors to a website. When a user accesses a website using the service, Google Analytics cookie data is left in the user's computer, and the website gets statistical information by utilizing the data saved into the cookie. As a result, all websites using Google Analytics service have Google Analytics cookie left in users' computers, and consequently the information can be useful for investigators.

Variable types of Google Analytics Cookie include __utma, __utmb, __utmc, and __utmz. Each variable's value is consist of sub values divided by .. All time information saved in the cookie is based on UNIX Time [6].

Each variable is described as follows. Variable __utma is used to identify visitors. The value includes domain hash, visitor IDs, time of the first visit to a site, time of the previous visit, time of the latest visit, and the number of current sessions. Variable __utmb and __utmc are used to discern sessions.

Variable __utmb includes domain hash, the number of pages loaded into a domain, and time of loading the last page, where as variable __utmc only includes domain hash. In the case of __utmc, once a visitor accesses a website, and a session is activated, the variable is saved into a memory.

Variable __utmz includes the most meaningful data from the perspective of digital forensic investigation. The variable value consists of domain hash, the latest updated time, the number of sessions of the current site, the number of resources used in the current site and sub variables.

Table 6. Google Analytics Cookie

Cookie	Detail
__utma	\<domain hash\>.\<visitor ID\>.\<first visit time\>.\<previous visit time\>.\<last visit time\>
__utmb	\<domain hash\>. \<pages count viewed\>.10.\<last visit time\>
__utmc	\<domain hash\>
__utmz	\<domain hash\>.\<last visit time\>.\<session count\>.\<source count\>.\<sub variables\>

The sub variables are discerned with —, and their types are utmcsr, utmccn, utmcmd, and utmctr/utmcct. The utmcsr includes the route information as to how the current site is accessed. The utmcmd includes the information on access type that is divided into Organic, Referral, and Direct.

Organic type is set as a website is accessed through a search engine like Google. Referral type is set as a website is accessed through other sites' web link. Direct type is set as a user enters a website address on the URL bar or as a website is accessed through bookmarks or through a web link in documents and emails.

The utmccn includes campaign information used for Google Adwords, but is mostly identical to utmcmd. In the case of the utmctr, as the access type is set to Organic, it includes search words entered into a search engine to look for the accessed site. The utmcct includes the path of a page in which the link for the access to a website is found, as the access type is set to Referral.

3.4   A Classification of Download List

Downloads list data is a log of file downloaded directly by a user with the use of a web browser. From a classification viewpoint, a classification of download list is as same as a classification of cache data with extension. So, it is possible to apply same methodology used in cache classification to classification of download list.

Actually, Most of the entrance path of malicious programs is downloading attached file of mail or malicious PE file disguised normal PE file. Therefore, if the investigator can find these kind of files quickly, it is very helpful to find sources of files related to cases or of malicious program.

Table 7. Sub Variables of __utmz

Sub Variable	Detail
utmcsr	Last Source/Site
utmccn	Campaign Information, Usually the same as utmcmd
utmcmd	Last type of access Organic : referred by search engine Referral : referred by other sites Direct : typing the URL directly
utmctr	Keywords used in search engine(Organic)
utmcct	The path to the page on the site of referring link(Referral)

4   Tool Development and Timeline Visualization

In this section, "WEFA", a developed tool based on the research work, is introduced. Available tool environments include Windows 2000, XP, Vista, and 7, and the targeted Web browsers for analysis are Internet Explorer, Firefox, Chrome, Safari, and Opera. WEFA basically supports functions for integrated analysis, search word extraction, URL decoding, cache data preview and recovery for deleted log data. The basic details of WEFA can be acquired from Advanced Evidence Collection and Analysis of Web Browser Activity[7]. The following is additional functions to WEFA based on this paper

4.1   Data Classification

WEFA executes data classification process with collected information on cache, history, cookie, downloads list. Based on the research work, the work of data classification is performed and signatures for data classification are written as regular expression. These signatures are saved into SQLite database and can be added and deleted. So, investigators can improve the accuracy of the data classification function by adding or deleting signatures suitable for each country and region. The results after the execution of data classification process by each information are presented as follows.

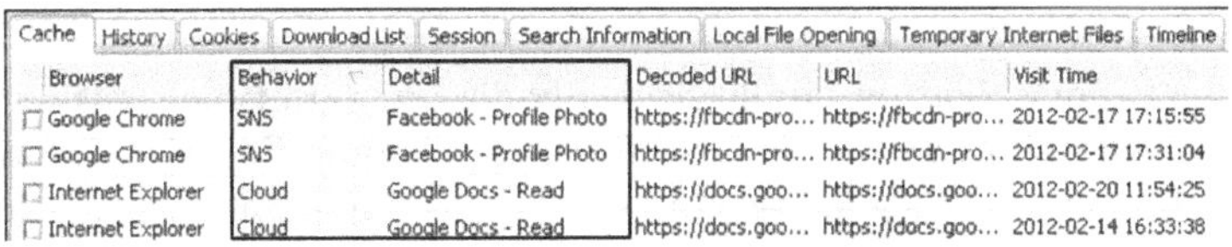

Fig. 6. Cache Classification

Cache	History	Cookies	Download List	Session	Search Information	Local File Opening	Temporary Internet Files	Timeline

Browser	Behavior	Search Information	Decoded URL	URL	Visit Time
☐ Internet Explorer	Dictionary		http://endic.nav...	http://endic.nav...	2012-02-20 14:29:54
☐ Internet Explorer	Search	return that	http://dic.daum...	http://dic.daum...	2012-02-20 14:30:13
☐ Internet Explorer	Cloud		https://docs.goo...	https://docs.goo...	2012-02-21 11:54:25
☐ Internet Explorer	Search	2 depth	http://endic.nav...	http://endic.nav...	2012-02-20 15:13:03

Fig. 7. History Classification

Cache	History	Cookies	Download List	Session	Search Information	Local File Opening	Temporary Internet Files	Timeline

Browser	Host	Path	Last Access Time	Name	Value	Detail
☐ Opera	fomos.kr		2012-02-16 14:43:32	__utmb	33252009....	Google Analytics
☐ Opera	fomos.kr		2012-02-16 14:43:32	__utmz	33252009....	Google Analytics
☐ Internet Explorer	accounts.google....		2012-02-20 15:17:57	GAUSR	mail:bluean...	Google Account ID : mail:bl██████275@gmail.com
☐ Google Chrome	accounts.google....		2012-02-17 16:02:00	GAUSR	mail:bluean...	Google Account ID : mail:bl██████275@gmail.com

Fig. 8. Cookie Classification

Cache	History	Cookies	Download List	Session	Search Information	Local File Opening	Temporary Internet Files	Timeline

Browser	File Name	Extension	URL	Download Path	Download Time
☐ Google Chrome	[2012.05.01]Decoding Prefetch Files for F...	pdf	http://forensic.k...	C:\Users\blue...	2012-07-06 17:59:36
☐ Google Chrome	Evernote_4.5.7.7146.exe	exe	http://evernote....	C:\Users\blue...	2012-07-10 14:50:16
☐ Google Chrome	Evernote_4.5.7.7146 (1).exe	exe	http://evernote....	C:\Users\blue...	2012-07-10 14:51:32
☐ Google Chrome	Evernote_4.5.7.7146 (2).exe	exe	http://evernote....	C:\Users\blue...	2012-07-10 15:01:33

Fig. 9. Download List Classification

Such results will help investigators shorten the time to find proper data, and consequently will help reduce their analysis time.

4.2   Timeline Visualization

Based on the data classification function described earlier, WEFA supports timeline visualization for the information on cache, history, cookie, downloads list, local file opening, and temporary internet files. As shown in the Fig. 10, the vertical graph represents one day, and each log data are displayed on the vertical graph as a horizontal line. Data classification is presented with the colors of horizontal lines displayed on the timeline (e.g : Search=red, Mail =orange...).

Accordingly, investigators can intuitively discern data type right away, and that can be helpful for them to shorten their analysis time. The time information of data can be displayed as a mouse pointer is put over relevant data. The interval of the timeline can be set to 3 months, 1 month, or 1 week, and the basis day of the timeline is also changeable.

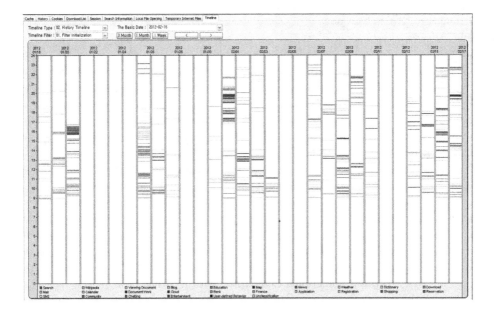

Fig. 10. Timeline Visualization

Timeline	Browser	URL Parameter		
Visit Date ▽		Browser	URL	Behavior
2012-02-06 23:01:16		Internet Explorer	https://ahnban...	Mail
2012-02-06 23:01:07		Internet Explorer	https://ahnban...	Mail
2012-02-06 22:56:47		Internet Explorer	http://www.fo...	Community
2012-02-06 22:56:31		Internet Explorer	http://www.fo...	Community
2012-02-06 22:56:10		Internet Explorer	http://www.fac...	SNS

2012
02/07
2012-02-06 23:27:00
2012-02-06 21:33:00

Fig. 11. Instant Period Search

Instant Period Search. WEFA offers a function to search a certain period in the timeline. While analyzing the timeline, investigators can get details about the data related to a certain period by mouse drag. That is, investigators click on the left button of a mouse from the starting point of the period, and then drag the mouse through the end point of the period, and release the left button.

Timeline Filtering. When massive data are analyzed in timeline, it is difficult to make them classified due to the large size of visualized data. For the reason, WEFA offers a filtering function to make the data investigators want displayed in the timeline. For instance, if the "Search" filtering is applied in the history timeline as shown in the Fig 12., only the data classified as "Search" behavior are left on the timeline. The function is also helpful to shorten the analysis time.

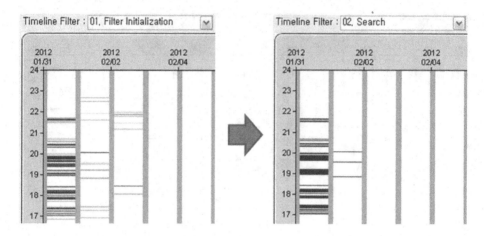

Fig. 12. Timeline Filtering

Table 8. Functional Comparison with Existing Tools

Function	WEFA	CacheBack 3.17	Encase 6.18	FTK 3.2	NetAnalysis 1.52
Cache Classification	O	△	X	X	X
Search Word Extraction	O	X	X	X	X
History Classification	O	X	X	X	X
Cookie Classification	O	X	X	X	X
Download Classification	O	O	O	O	O
Timeline Visualization Based on Classification of Log Data	O	X	X	X	X
Instant Period Search	O	X	X	X	X
Timeline Filtering	O	X	X	X	X

5   Functional Comparison with Existing Tools

The authors performed a comparison between WEFA and existing tools that investigator use in the forensic field today. Results are shown in Table.

Most tools except for CacheBack do not support a function to classify parsed data. Therefore, as investigators perform an analysis with the tools, they should directly identify all data on a web browser. Even CacheBack supports a function only limited to Facebook cache data. Also these tools do not support a timeline visualization based on classification of log data.

WEFA, however, supports a function to classify the data of all logs, such as cache, history, cookie, downloads list, session, local time list, temporary internet files. And, since it supports visualization, instant period search, and timeline filtering on the basis of the classified data, investigators can considerably shorten the analysis time.

6   Conclusion

In the web browser forensic investigation process, classification of log data and timeline visualization process are required to shorten the analysis time. In this paper, a study on data classification for fundamental web browser logs-cache, history, cookie, and downloads list-is performed. And, based on the research work, WEFA, a tool to support data classification function and timeline visualization, was introduced.

In the case of WEFA's data classification function, all signatures used in the tool are saved into SQLite database. As a result, investigators can freely add and delete signatures.

In the case of the timeline visualization, the tool supports intuitive data classification with colors, instant period search through a mouse drag, and timeline filtering function with which the data investigators want are displayed on the timeline.

Therefore, WEFA help investigators improve the analysis efficiency for reducing time and work load of forensic investigation process. Future research will involve researching method to find the usage traces of web browsers in other locations except web browser logs.

References

1. Jones, K.J.: Forensic Analysis of Internet Explorer Activity Files. Foundstone (2003), http://www.foundstone.com/us/pdf/wp_index_dat.pdf
2. Pereira, M.T.: Forensic analysis of the Firefox3 Internet history and recovery of deleted SQLite records. Digital Investigation 5, 93–103 (2009)
3. Browser Forensics, Forensic Analysis of Microsoft Internet Explorer Disk Cache, http://www.browserforensics.com/?p=32
4. Facebook Graph API, https://developers.facebook.com/docs/reference/api/
5. Berners-Lee, T., Masinter, L.: RFC 1738: Uniform Resource Locator, http://tools.ietf.org/html/rfc1738
6. Nelson, J.S.: Google Analytics Cookies and the Forensic Implications, http://www.dfinews.com/article/google-analytics-cookies-and-forensic-implications?page=0,6
7. Oh, J.: Advanced Evidence Collection and Analysis of Web Browser Activity. In: DFRWS (2011), http://www.dfrws.org/2011/proceedings/12-344.pdf

Intellectual Property Protection for Integrated Systems Using Soft Physical Hash Functions

François Durvaux, Benoît Gérard, Stéphanie Kerckhof,
François Koeune, and François-Xavier Standaert

Université catholique de Louvain, UCL Crypto Group,
B-1348 Louvain-la-Neuve, Belgium

Abstract. Intellectual property right violations are an important problem for integrated system designers. We propose a new solution for mitigating such violations, denoted as soft physical hash functions. It combines previously introduced ideas of soft hash functions (in the field of image processing) and side-channel leakage (in the field of cryptographic hardware). For this purpose, we first introduce and formalize the components of an intellectual property detection infrastructure using soft physical hash functions. Next, we discuss its advantages over previous proposals aiming at similar goals. The most important point here is that the proposed technique can be applied to already deployed products. Finally, we validate our approach with a first experimental study.

1 Introduction

While technology shrinking has been the enabling factor for producing increasingly powerful micro- and nano-electronic devices, it has also made the manufacturing process of these devices an increasingly difficult and expensive task. Besides, the high complexity of present hardware/software co-designs leads most system developers to assemble various pieces of hardware and software produced by different companies. This has motivated the development of new businesses, relying on the selling of Intellectual Property (IP) cores. A recent study from Semico Research estimated that the IP core market reached 4 billion US$ in 2009, i.e. a growth of 23,2% compared to the 2005 figures [28]. The advantages of re-using IP cores are enormous in terms of cost and development time reductions. But they also raise important risks regarding IP theft. Namely, the high-valued nature of hardware/software systems naturally creates a strong incentive for piracy, cloning of products and copyright infringement. In addition, the selling of IP cores implementing certain functionalities, that have to be integrated in larger developments, raise compatibility constraints that make the situation even more challenging. This is in part due to the versatility of these IP, that can be distributed under different shapes. For example, IP can be found in high-level format (i.e. described with a high-level language) or in low-level format (i.e. as completely laid out functional blocks restricted to a given technology). As a result, various solutions have been proposed to decrease the risk of unlicensed IP usage.

D.H. Lee and M. Yung (Eds.): WISA 2012, LNCS 7690, pp. 208–225, 2012.

Looking at low-level IP, two main general approaches are usually suggested in the literature. A first line of research can be denoted as "permission-based". The idea is that before running, any functional system performs some test in order to make sure that it has the right permissions. The use of passwords is a typical example of such an approach. More robust ideas have also been introduced in two main directions. On the one hand, the test could check the presence of a cryptographically-enhanced security chip (rather than a simple password), as typically suggested in [3,22]. On the other hand, one can also take advantage of Physically Unclonable Functions, in order to make sure that the system is running on the correct (unique) piece of hardware, e.g. as suggested in [16,29].

A second active line of research is to exploit watermarking techniques. In general, a watermark is a piece of information that is embedded in a digital signal, in order to verify its authenticity or the identity of its owners. Its main evaluation criteria are *robustness* (i.e. the watermark should be detectable even if the digital signal is slightly modified by some processing, e.g. filtering), *imperceptibility* (i.e. the original signal and the masked signal should be perceptually close) and *capacity* (i.e. the embedded mark should be large). By contrast to the permission-based approach, watermarking is useful a posteriori, in order to detect illegal copies at lower cost than reverse engineering. While first investigated in the context of image processing, watermarking has also been applied for software IP protection [7,25]. More recently, it has attracted attention for hardware IP protection, e.g. [1,18,19].

Two types of limitations can be highlighted for these approaches. The first one mainly applies to the performance and security of permission-based protections. That is, in order to include such mechanisms in a circuit, one needs to modify its original layout. This means that some logic gates are lost (and consume power) for this purpose. Besides, as permission checks imply the addition of some circuitry in the chips, an adversary who has access to the source code (by reverse engineering or any other means) can remove this part of the designs, hence producing illegal copies without any protection. The second limitation is more general and relates to the flexibility of the solutions. Namely, for both types of IP protections, the decision to protect an implementation has to be part of the design process (and must sometimes be made early in this process). Hence, it cannot help for already deployed products.

In parallel, security enhancements that are specific to high-level IP and take advantage of software facilities have also been proposed. One typical example is source code or bitstream encryption that is used, e.g. in FPGA [9]. While this solution is useless in the case of hardwired IP, as there is no code to encrypt/decrypt, it can be a useful complement in some IP protection systems, where a part of the value to preserve is software. Note that the encryption/decryption of the source code or bitstream then has to be secure against other types of physical attacks, e.g. using side-channels [24]. It is also necessary that the encryption/decryption keys are stored in a sufficiently secure memory (a problem for which the tamper resistant property of PUF could help [31]).

In this paper, we propose a new IP protection scheme that applies both to high-level and low-level IP. It mitigates some of the limitations, and can be efficiently combined with, previously introduced solutions for this purpose. More precisely, we take advantage of two main ingredients. First, we build on the idea of soft (aka robust, aka perceptual) hash functions, that are yet another tool used to protect the copyright of digital data (e.g. images) [13,21,23,32]. Second, we exploit the physical representation of the IP, e.g. through its power consumption, as proposed with side-channel watermarks [4,35]. In addition, we use the formalism introduced in the context of Physically Unclonable Functions [2], in order to specify the components of our IP detection infrastructure. Combining these elements, we introduce soft physical hash functions as a powerful yet flexible way to deal with the IP of microelectronic circuits and systems. We then define the main properties of such functions, namely their *content sensitivity* and *perceptual robustness*. Finally, we instantiate a first soft physical hash function with simple signal processing tools and analyze its properties based on an experimental case study. Namely, and based on the implementation of 10 different block ciphers in an Atmel microcontroller that have been made public through the ECRYPT project [11], we show experimentally that a soft physical hash function can efficiently discriminate these different implementations, while being robust to some elementary code transformations that should not modify the IP (perceptually).

2   IP in Hardware and Software Design Flows

This section briefly introduces the hardware and software design flows, and discusses where the IP lies in such systems. We conclude by describing two general attacks against IP in integrated systems. The hardware design flow is illustrated in the left part of Figure 1. It is essentially made of five successive steps for which a succint description is given next.

1. *Description.* This step consists in specifying the implementation of an algorithm with a Hardware Description Language (HDL), e.g. VHDL and Verilog. Such languages determine the number and type of operations that have to be implemented on chip, as well as their scheduling. The result of this step is called the hardware source code.
2. *Synthesis.* This step consists in converting the hardware source code into an idealized electronic circuit. The synthesis tools automatically translate a high-level description into a lower-level one (e.g. gate-level). It is functionally equivalent to the hardware source code and corresponds to the target platform (e.g. ASIC or FPGA). The result of this step is called a netlist. Netlists are idealized in the sense that they do not correspond to a physical description of the chip. Yet, the result of synthesis is highly dependent on the tool options (e.g. space- or time-oriented optimizations).
3. *Place and route.* At this point of the design flow, the automated tools build a physical model for all the logic and memory elements of the netlist. They

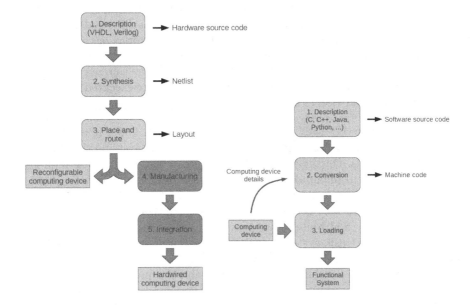

Fig. 1. Hardware (left) and software (right) design flows.

also simulate their mapping on the circuit surface, taking the position of each cell, the width and length of connections, ... into account. The result of this step is called the layout. It is again dependent on the tool options.

Note that for reconfigurable devices such as FPGA, the design flow essentially stops here (i.e. moves to final Step 5). Namely the layout can be directly loaded into the device that will next act as a dedicated circuit with the same functionality. By contrast for ASIC, an additional Step 4 has to be carried out:

4. *Manufacturing.* Once the design of the chip is finished, its layout is sent to a manufacturer in order to be physically built. Manufacturing usually includes a packaging step that consists in protecting the chip with a plastic coating.
5. *Integration.* Eventually, and optionally, the chip can be integrated into a larger system, combining different electronic pieces together.

In general, most systems used in current applications combine (hardwired or reconfigurable) computing devices with software programming. Software is used either to control the dedicated hardware, or to perform some general purpose computations for which standard computing platforms (microcontrollers, microprocessors) provide sufficient performance. The software design flow is illustrated in the right part of Figure 1. It is essentially made of three steps that we describe next.

1. *Description.* As for the hardware flow, a high-level description language is used (e.g. C, C++, Java, ...). It specifies a sequence of (sometimes data-dependent) operations to execute on some fixed hardware in order to perform an algorithmic task. The result of this step is called the software source code.

2. *Conversion.* This step consists in converting the high-level software source code into a lower-level description, denoted as the machine code. As for the hardware flow, it exploits automated tools (i.e. interpreters or compilers) the options of which may significantly affect the final performances.
3. *Loading.* This last step consists in writing the machine source code into the computing device memory, from which instructions are executed. As a result, a fully functional system is obtained and ready to use in actual applications.

Where Does the IP Lie? From the previous design flows, it appears that different types of IP are manipulated by the functional systems that are used in final applications. On the one hand, the source codes contain the high-level IP. They are easy to manipulate and provide the most readable description of algorithmic tricks used to obtain efficient implementations. In addition, they are extremely *malleable*, as it is easy to slightly modify them, or to run again the synthesis and place and route (resp. conversion) steps, in order to produce two computing devices (resp. systems) with the same functionality and slightly different layouts (resp. machine codes). On the other hand, the layout and machine codes contain the low-level IP that is less malleable but possibly includes further optimization efforts performed during the synthesis and place and route (resp. conversion) steps. The netlist in a hardware design flow falls between these two extremes.

Attacks against the IP. Leaving technical details aside, two main types of attacks can be mounted to violate IP. First, "recovery and clone" attacks imply that the adversary just re-uses the stolen IP as such. They typically target the layouts or machine codes. Second, "recovery and modify" attacks imply that the adversary modifies the IP before re-using it in an illegal system. They typically target source codes. Clearly, the second attacks are much more powerful and, in general, harder to prevent. As mentioned in the introduction, permission-based IP protections are useless against such attacks, as the adversary can remove them in his modified design. But in cases where a watermark is somewhat "additive" (e.g. [4,35]), the risk that an adversary identifies the watermark insertion and removes it also increases. In practice, there exist many ways in which attacks against the IP can be implemented. Reverse engineering generally comes in the first place for ASIC. A rather complete survey is given in [30]. One can also mention approaches taking advantage of side-channel analysis [8,12,17,27]. But threats caused by dishonest manufacturers, producing more chips than licenced, or industrial IP theft, are other examples. There finally exist many attacks that are specific to one technology. For example, bitstream security is a serious issue for SRAM-based FPGA [34]. In order to remain generic, most of our discussions in the following section are independent of the technical solutions used to perform IP theft.

3   A New Approach Based on Soft Hash Functions

Looking at previous works, the protection of IP in integrated circuits and systems appears to easily take advantage of general solutions for the protection of digital data. As a result, and besides the watermarking and permission-based techniques, it is natural to investigate other tools that have been proposed to prevent the piracy of digital images. Following, we propose to exploit robust hash functions [13,32], also known as soft hash functions [21] or perceptual hash functions [23], for this purpose. We will use the term "soft hash functions" in the rest of the paper. By contrast to cryptographic hash functions, for which the output string is highly sensitive to small perturbations of the input, soft hash functions are such that similar objects should return highly correlated digests (i.e. be *perceptually robust*), while different objects should produce uncorrelated ones (i.e. be *content-sensitive*). Soft hash functions exist in keyed and un-keyed version. We will only consider the second category and leave the design of a keyed version as a scope for further research.

In practice, the soft hash functions we will consider are generally made of two main ingredients. First, a *feature vector evaluation* phase outputs an intermediate response that is expected to represent the object to characterize in the most accurate manner. In other words, this intermediate string should be very content-sensitive. Second, an *extraction phase* should apply signal processing and summarize the feature vector into a smaller output hash value that best trades content sensitivity for perceptual robustness. In addition, soft hash function infrastructures use a *detection tool* in order to compare different hashes and determine whether they correspond to the same object. The main idea that we propose in this paper is to extract a physical feature from the objects to protect. We denote the resulting tool as a *Soft Physical Hash function* (SPH) that will be the main component of our *IP detection infrastructure*. Interestingly, SPH can be viewed as a particular type of physical function systems, as formally defined in [2]. But whereas this previous work focuses on the robustness, unclonability and unpredictability of physical functions, we rather care about the previously mentioned perceptual robustness and content sensitivity. Relations with the formal definitions from [2] will be given in the next section. Intuitively, an IP detection infrastructure can be specified as follows:

1. *Object to protect.* This could be any type of IP, namely a source code, a netlist, a layout, or a machine code, as defined in Section 2.
2. *Physical feature vector evaluation.* This could be any physical emanation of the device running the IP. For example, side-channels such as the power consumption [20] or the electromagnetic radiation [14] are natural candidates.
3. *Extraction.* This could be any signal processing outputting a hash value that best represents the IP. For example, one could compress by selecting the "points of interest" in a side-channel measurement trace.
4. *Detection.* This could be any statistical tool that allows determining the level of similarity between two hash values. Again, techiques from the side-channel attack community could help, e.g. correlation [5] or template attacks [6].

In addition, one generally has to consider the context in which the IP protection mechanism will be applied. Namely, we could consider:

1. *Known or unknown inputs.* That is, can the IP claimer select the data that is manipulated by the target device during the physical feature evaluation (in which case the soft hash can characterize both operation and data dependencies)? Or is he limited to executions on random, and possibly unknown, inputs (in which case the soft hash only characterizes operation dependencies)?

2. *Known or unknown source code.* That is, does the IP claimer know the full source code he is trying to detect or does he only have access to its soft physical hash value (e.g. if the IP claimer is a third party)?

3. *Same or different technologies.* That is, are the soft hash values to be compared extracted from devices in the same technology or not?

4. *Same or different setups.* That is, are the soft hash values to be compared extracted with the same measurement apparatus or not?

Obviously, certain scenarios are more challenging than others and the perceptual robustness and content sensitivity of a SPH can significantly vary accordingly. Before entering into more details and instantiation issues, we would like to point out a few advantages of the proposed approach. In the first place, and contrary to the permission-based and watermarking approaches, using SPH does not require to modify the designs a priori. This allows improved flexibility, as one can decide even after implementation to exploit this idea for IP theft detection. It also means that implementing the protection mechanism implies no performance overhead at all. Second, SPH theoretically allow preventing some recovery and modify attacks. This is due to the fact that there is nothing to remove from a protected design, but the IP itself (i.e. the protection is fully intrinsic). Of course, the detection phase will be significantly more challenging when modifications are substantial (because content sensitivity is inherently limited once modified designs become too different), but it can at least tolerate some malleability in the objects to protect. Third, the proposed solution remains cheaper than reverse engineering, as it only requires to measure a physical feature.

4   Definitions

4.1   The IP Detection Infrastructure

The main goal of this section is to provide some formalism to define and study the aforementioned IP detection procedure, based on the idea of SPH. This procedure naturally fits in the generic framework for physical functions presented in [2], that is depicted in Figure 2. Indeed, SPH perfectly correspond to the definition of *physical function systems*. Hence, we reuse and lighten the formalism provided in [2] and apply it to our IP detection using SPH. The generic framework we propose for IP detection is illustrated in Figure 3, where a *soft physical hash function* is a *probabilistic procedure* $\mathrm{SPH}(\mathrm{IP}, \mathrm{X})$ that returns a *hash value* h.

$$\mathrm{SPH} : (\mathrm{IP}, X) \mapsto h.$$

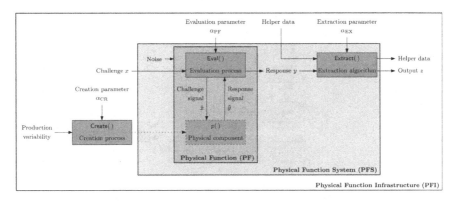

Fig. 2. Generic framework for physical functions [2]

Such outputs are obtained in two steps. First, a *physical feature vector* is obtained (with the Eval(·) procedure), corresponding to the measurement of some physical quantity observed during the processing of data X (that may contain more than one input) by a device running the given IP. The probabilistic nature of a SPH comes from this procedure and is due to many different reasons, such as the variability that can be observed between different devices running the same IP, or the noise in the measurements. This part of the system is the one bringing the *content sensitivity* property but, as just stated, there is a non-negligible variability that should be removed for reaching *perceptual robustness*. This is precisely the role of the Extract(·) procedure. During this second step, the physical feature vector is processed to extract the robust information it contains, returning a hash value that should characterize the IP running on the device.

Next, an *IP detection infrastructure* is composed of two *soft physical hash functions* $\mathrm{SPH(IP_{ref}, \cdot)}$ and $\mathrm{SPH(IP_{sus}, \cdot)}$, corresponding to the reference and the suspicious devices. Each SPH outputs a hash value that should identify the IP running on the device under test. Additionally to these two SPH, a detection tool Detect(·, ·) is used to compare the hash values h_{ref} and h_{sus} returned by the SPH. This procedure outputs a *similarity score* that should be close to 1 for similar IP, and close to 0 for different ones:

$$\mathrm{Detect} : (h_{\mathrm{ref}}, h_{\mathrm{sus}}) \mapsto s \in [0, 1].$$

Performance metrics are required to evaluate SPH. In the following section, we define *perceptual robustness* and *content sensitivity*, so that we will be able to quantify these properties and to determine relevant tools for extracting hash values.

4.2   Performance Metrics

The IP detection infrastructure aims at confirming/invalidating the presence of an IP running on a suspicious device. As mentioned earlier in the paper, this

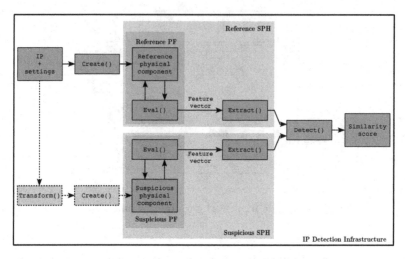

Fig. 3. Generic framework for IP detection

IP can be of different nature, such as a layout or source code for instance. The main difficulty for formally defining our problem comes from the fact that some modifications of the source code should not be considered as defining a new IP. For example, trivial modifications (e.g. changing variable names, switching registers, adding dummy operations, changing compiler options) can clearly be regarded as preserving the IP, but other modifications such as code optimizations can also be considered as improving, yet relying on, the initial IP. Defining the boundary between IP reuse and new IP definition is outside the scope of this paper[1]. Here we assume the existence of such a definition and concentrate on providing a tool allowing us to decide whether a given device is based on a given IP or not, in the sense of this definition. More formally, we consider a set $\mathcal{F}_{pre}$ of *IP-preserving transformations*. The detection tool should consider as "close" an IP and its transform if the transformation function belongs to $\mathcal{F}_{pre}$, and as "distant" if the transformation belongs to $\bar{\mathcal{F}}_{pre}$.

Remark. The use of sets $\mathcal{F}_{pre}$ and $\bar{\mathcal{F}}_{pre}$ is a purely formal way of dealing with the perceptual notion of closeness involved in this problem. These sets should be complementary but obviously, in practice, we will only consider some transformations in both sets. Notice that $\bar{\mathcal{F}}_{pre}$ may contain modifications of an IP, but also transformations that simply consist in changing the IP. For instance, let IP_1 be the IP corresponding to the source code of a social network and IP_2 be the one corresponding to a plane autopilot. Then, formally, there exists $\bar{F} \in \bar{\mathcal{F}}_{pre}$ such that $IP_1 = \bar{F}(IP_2)$. Nevertheless, and as will be clear in the next section, such a definition is useful to capture practical transforms that can be considered as IP-preserving, while providing the flexibility to evaluate a wide range of scenarios.

---

[1] In Section 5 we will run experiments on typical examples, where, on the one hand, IPs are modified and reused, and, on the other hand, different IPs are considered.

As a result, the robustness and sensitivity of a SPH are related to the set of transformations considered to be IP-preserving, to the detection tool that is used, to the threshold τ that has been fixed to make the decision, and to the data complexity N corresponding to the number of IP runs that will be measured. We denote by $\mathcal{X}_N$ the set of N-input requests that can be sent to the devices and define our evaluation metrics as follows.

Definition 1. *(τ-perceptual robustness): Let $\tau \in [0,1]$, the τ-perceptual robustness of a SPH relatively to a detection tool Det, a set of transformations $\mathcal{F}_{\mathrm{pre}}$ and a data complexity N, is the probability that the similarity score of a reference IP and its transformation by $F \in \mathcal{F}_{\mathrm{pre}}$ is larger than τ:*

$$\mathrm{PeRo}_\tau^N(\mathrm{Det}, \mathcal{F}_{\mathrm{pre}}) \triangleq \mathrm{Pr}_{\mathrm{IP}, X \in \mathcal{X}_N, F \in \mathcal{F}_{\mathrm{pre}}} \left[\mathrm{Det}\left(\mathrm{SPH(IP},X), \mathrm{SPH}(F(\mathrm{IP}), X) \right) \geq \tau \right].$$

Definition 2. *(τ-content sensitivity): Let $\tau \in [0,1]$, the τ-content sensitivity of a SPH relatively to a detection tool Det, a set of transformations $\bar{\mathcal{F}}_{\mathrm{pre}}$ and a data complexity N, is the probability that the similarity score of a reference IP and its transformation by $\bar{F} \in \bar{\mathcal{F}}_{\mathrm{pre}}$ is smaller than τ:*

$$\mathrm{CoSe}_\tau^N(\mathrm{Det}, \bar{\mathcal{F}}_{\mathrm{pre}}) \triangleq \mathrm{Pr}_{\mathrm{IP}, X \in \mathcal{X}_N, \bar{F} \in \bar{\mathcal{F}}_{\mathrm{pre}}} \left[\mathrm{Det}\left(\mathrm{SPH(IP},X), \mathrm{SPH}(\bar{F}(\mathrm{IP}), X) \right) \leq \tau \right].$$

An IP detection infrastructure aims at combining an SPH to a relevant detection tool in order to ensure good performances regarding both perceptual robustness and content sensitivity. This context is the one of binary hypothesis testing where τ corresponds to a threshold, $1 - \mathrm{PeRo}$ is non-detection error probability and $1 - \mathrm{CoSe}$ is the false-alarm error probability.

5   First Experimental Results

This section demonstrates the use of SPH based on power consumption traces to perform IP detection. First, we propose a simple instance of IP detection infrastructure, that uses classical tools in signal processing and side-channel attacks. Then, we provide experimental results that confirm the content sensitivity and perceptual robustness of this instance. These results are obtained for a particular set of IP and some representative code transformations that we considered as IP-preserving.

5.1   An Exemplary Instance

We first present our instance by specifying the four elements that define an IP detection infrastructure enumerated in Section 3. Then, we detail the context we consider for detecting IP. Finally, we provide information about our measurement setup.

Object to protect. As a first case study, we investigated the relevance of our IP detection based on SPH in the context of software implementations. In particular, we took advantage of the cryptographic algorithms made available as open source codes in [11]. We considered the assembly codes of these lightweight ciphers as IP to protect, in order to analyze situations ranging from very similar algorithms to totally different ones.

Physical feature evaluation. Inspired by side-channel attacks, we characterize an IP by measuring the power consumption of a device running this IP. As the literature on power analysis attacks suggests, such a physical feature vector is expected to be highly content sensitive.

Extraction. We somehow need to compress the feature vector, removing part of the variability due to the "noise"[2], while keeping the content sensitive information. The Fourier transform is a natural candidate for such compressing and filtering purposes. The technique we propose is to apply a Fast Fourier Transform (FFT) to the traces obtained, to take its modulus, and to only extract the values corresponding to frequencies below the clock frequency. Information in higher frequencies does not refer to logic gates but to the device itself. We provide below (Figure 5) results that emphasize the positive effect of this preprocessing.

Detection. As a detection tool, we propose to use the widespread Pearson correlation coefficient that has shown its interest in many previous works in the domain of power-based cryptanalysis [5]. Let us recall that the Pearson correlation coefficient between two vectors x and y of length n having mean values $\bar{x}$ and $\bar{y}$ is defined as:

$$\rho(x, y) \triangleq \frac{\sum_{i=1}^{n}(x_i - \bar{x}) \cdot (y_i - \bar{y})}{\sqrt{\sum_{i=1}^{n}(x_i - \bar{x})^2}\sqrt{\sum_{i=1}^{n}(y_i - \bar{y})^2}}.$$

Context. As mentioned in Section 3, the IP detection infrastructure can be used in different contexts. We specify the settings of our experimental work as follows. First, inputs to the device are unknown to the detection infrastructure and a single trace is used to perform the detection. Second, the source code is also unknown to the IP detection infrastructure. Third, the same technology, i.e. an Atmel 644P, has been used to perform all the measurements. Finally, the same measurement setup has been used for all these measurements.

Measurement setup. We obtained power consumption traces by measuring the voltage variations around an inductance at the input of the power supply of the microcontroller. The clock frequency of the controller was fixed to 20 MHz, and the sampling frequency to 50 MHz. For each IP, a reference trace corresponding to a single encryption was stored. Next, the suspicious traces were cut or padded

---

[2] We stress that the term noise is generic. It can refer to measurement noise, but also to noise due to minor transformations of the code or the use of different inputs for the evaluation phase.

(by re-encrypting the ciphertext), in order to deal realistically with the (frequent) situation were IP have different cycles counts[3].

5.2   Testing Content Sensitivity

Using Different Ciphers. As a first step, we applied our instance of SPH on different ciphers. We chose to focus on the 10 block ciphers in Table 1. This first experiment aims at confirming that the proposed IP detection infrastructure indeed provides content sensitivity and perceptual robustness in a simple case, where the set of IP-preserving transformations $\mathcal{F}_{pre}$ is reduced to identity, and the set $\bar{\mathcal{F}}_{pre}$ consists in choosing another cipher in the list.

Table 1. Table of ciphers used as IP

AES	DESXL	HIGHT	KASUMI
KATAN	MCRYPTON	NOEKEON	PRESENT
	SEA	TEA	

For each of the 100 possible couples of IP (reference, suspicious) we measured 20 traces (corresponding to different inputs) for both IP, and applied the IP detection tool for each of the 400 possible pairs of traces. The similarity scores obtained are plotted in Figure 4.

Black dots are the scores obtained when IP are compared to $F(\text{IP})$ with $F \in \mathcal{F}_{pre}$ and gray dots are the one obtained when the transformation belongs to $\bar{\mathcal{F}}_{pre}$. This picture is encouraging : both content sensitivity and perceptual robustness are reached in experiments using a single trace. Indeed, for any τ value between 0.86 and 0.27, the detection rule makes no mistake for this particular set of IP and these particular sets $\mathcal{F}_{pre}$ and $\bar{\mathcal{F}}_{pre}$.

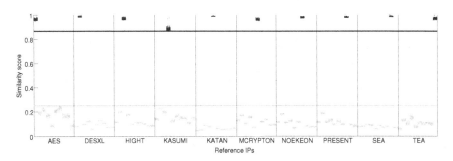

Fig. 4. Similarity scores for different IP

---

[3] We first ran tests with a single execution of the IP but then it was too easy to detect IPs. Since a cipher is generally used to encrypt more than one block we chose to perform tests on looping IPs.

Remark on KASUMI. The reader may have noticed that almost all reference ciphers lead to scores higher than 0.95, except for KASUMI. The explanation is quite simple. Indeed, the execution path of KASUMI depends on the data being processed. To avoid timing attacks, cryptographers usually add nop operations to make the implementation time-constant. While this prevents the execution time from being data-dependent, this is not the case of instructions performed: traces obtained by processing different outputs will correspond to different instruction sequences. This explains why we observe these smaller scores for KASUMI. Note also that a few scores are larger than 0.9 in Figure 4: they correspond to the comparison of two traces obtained with the same input.

Using Different Implementations of a Same Cipher. As the setting of Figure 4 is quite favorable (since we are comparing totally different IP), we now move to a more challenging context and consider a single block cipher, namely the standard AES, and four of its implementations. Three of them are the *Fast, Furious* and *Fantastic* implementations that can be found in [26]. The fourth one is proposed in [11] and named *Francesco* in reference to the first-name of its programmer. Again, for each of the 16 possible couples of reference/suspicious IP, we performed 2500 experiments (corresponding to 50 traces for both IP). To highlight the positive effect of using an FFT, we plotted the results obtained with/without such extraction, in the right/left parts of Figure 5.

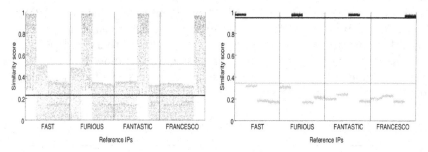

Fig. 5. Similarity scores for different AES implementations using the FFT (right) or not (left)

As can easily be seen, and as expected, using the FFT in the extraction step drastically decreases the variance observed in the similarity scores in the case where traces are directly compared (left part), while keeping the content sensitivity property. Indeed, each implementation should be considered as a different IP since they are really different one from the other. This emphasizes the need of an extraction tool that compresses the feature vector to ensure robustness: using FFT there is a wide range of thresholds (namely 0.37 to 0.95) for which both perceptual robustness and content sensitivity are equal[4] to 1 (that is, a 100%

---

[4] Obviously these values are only estimates since one cannot consider all possible IPs and all possible code modifications.

success rate) while without this tool, any value of the threshold will induce a non-zero error probability.

Yet, it remains that the content sensitivity could come from the simple fact that each implementation requires a different number of cycles to perform an encryption. In order to rule out this possibility, we additionally tuned the *Fast* and the *Furious* implementations in such a way that they have the same number of clock cycles and their only differences consist in actual round variations. For this purpose, the key expansion, first key addition, and final rounds remained the same and the inner rounds of the *Fast* implementation has been padded with `nop` operations. As can be observed in Figure 6, and even in this case, both implementations are detected as different IP with, again, a large range of thresholds leading to perceptual robustness and content sensitivity of 1.

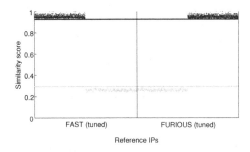

Fig. 6. Similarity scores for tuned versions of *Fast* and *Furious* AES implementations

5.3 Testing Perceptual Robustness

The previous experiments exhibit the good behavior of our SPH instance regarding content sensitivity. We now focus on its perceptual robustness. That is, can we still detect an IP when minor modifications have been applied to the original code? As previously mentioned, testing perceptual robustness requires to agree on a set of *IP-preserving* transformations. We identified two types of transformations, depending on whether they alter the performances or not:

- `addr`: i.e. changing registers or SRAM **addr**esses (non-altering);
- `swap`: i.e. **swap**ping instructions if possible (non-altering);
- `dumo`: i.e. adding **dum**my operations **o**ut of the rounds (altering);
- `dumi`: i.e. adding **dum**my operations **i**n the rounds (altering).

We chose to apply these modifications to the *Furious* implementation of AES. Our results are given in Figure 7. Dots correspond to scores obtained when comparing the reference implementation (`ref`) to its modification by one or more of the listed transformations. The number of added dummy-operations is the same for both `dumo` and `dumi` (57 additional cycles). As can be seen, the proposed instance is directly robust regarding all non altering transformations. Concerning the addition of dummy operations, we can observe that increasing

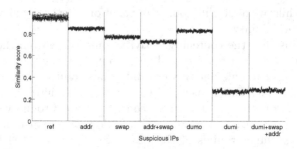

Fig. 7. Similarity scores for transforms of the *Furious* implementation

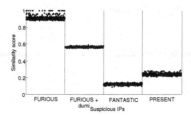

Fig. 8. Improved similarity scores for the *Furious* implementation, its `dumi` transform and other IP

the encryption time does not always critically decrease the robustness (cf. `dumo`) but, that adding dummy operations inside a repetitive part of the cipher is more damaging. This observation naturally relates more to the simple nature of our extraction and detection procedures than to the very idea of SPH. Interestingly, simple tweaks allow to deal with such more challenging contexts, as illustrated in Figure 8.

In this final figure, we slightly modified our SPH in order to first identify the block cipher rounds (using cross-correlation). Next, we applied the FFT separately on the different rounds, and used the average correlation over these rounds as detection procedure. While this approach remains clearly heuristic, the experimental results in Figure 8 show that it allows discriminating the addition of dummy operations within the rounds from the move towards another implementation of the AES.

To conclude, this set of experiments suggests that the concept we propose is valid and provides good results even when it is instantiated with classical tools. Moreover, we have shown that more challenging scenarios can be handled using more advanced techniques. A deeper investigation of these scenarios is the natural next step now that this preliminary work has shown promising results.

6   Conclusion and Future Works

This paper introduced, defined and proposed a first instantiation of SPH infrastructure, as a flexible and efficient way to protect the IP of integrated systems.

Experimental results in the context of software implementations confirm the relevance of the approach. Namely, we are able to discriminate proprietary IP using our instance of SPH, in the challenging scenario where the source code and inputs of the IP to protect remain unknown to the detection infrastructure, with minimum data complexity. Quite naturally, the strong contribution of the control logic in a software implementation makes it a target of choice for our IP detection infrastructure. Hence, the investigation of other contexts such as FPGA, hardware or more complex implementations is an interesting scope for further research. In view of the strong results obtained with simple tools in software, we expect the method to remain applicable in those cases, in particular in known input scenario (taking advantage of the strong literature in side-channel attacks) and/or if the source code is available to the detector (in order to take advantage of Hidden Markov Model cryptanalysis techniques such as in [33,10]). Eventually, another potentially interesting research direction would be the definition of design strategies (or code modifications) that could be applied to the IP before its release in order to facilitate the future detection of this IP with SPH.

Acknowledgements. This work has been funded in part by the ERC project 280141 (acronym CRASH) and the Walloon Region MIPSs project. Stéphanie Kerckhof is a PhD student funded by a FRIA grant, Belgium. F.-X. Standaert is a Research Associate of the Belgian Fund for Scientic Research (FNRS-F.R.S).

References

1. Abdel-Hamid, A.T., Tahar, S., Aboulhamid, E.M.: A survey on IP watermarking techniques. Design Autom. for Emb. Sys. 9(3), 211–227 (2004)
2. Armknecht, F., Maes, R., Sadeghi, A.-R., Standaert, F.-X., Wachsmann, C.: A formalization of the security features of physical functions. In: IEEE Symposium on Security and Privacy, pp. 397–412. IEEE Computer Society (2011)
3. Baetoniu, C.: FPGA IFF copy protection using Dallas semiconductor/Maxim DS2432 secure EEPROMs. XAPP780 (May 28, 2010)
4. Becker, G.T., Kasper, M., Moradi, A., Paar, C.: Side-channel based watermarks for integrated circuits. In: Plusquellic, J., Mai, K. (eds.) HOST, pp. 30–35. IEEE Computer Society (2010)
5. Brier, E., Clavier, C., Olivier, F.: Correlation Power Analysis with a Leakage Model. In: Joye, M., Quisquater, J.-J. (eds.) CHES 2004. LNCS, vol. 3156, pp. 16–29. Springer, Heidelberg (2004)
6. Chari, S., Rao, J.R., Rohatgi, P.: Template Attacks. In: Kaliski Jr., B.S., Koç, Ç.K., Paar, C. (eds.) CHES 2002. LNCS, vol. 2523, pp. 13–28. Springer, Heidelberg (2003)
7. Collberg, C.S., Thomborson, C.D.: Watermarking, tamper-proofing, and obfuscation-tools for software protection. IEEE Trans. Software Eng. 28(8), 735–746 (2002)
8. Daudigny, R., Ledig, H., Muller, F., Valette, F.: SCARE of the DES. In: Ioannidis, J., Keromytis, A.D., Yung, M. (eds.) ACNS 2005. LNCS, vol. 3531, pp. 393–406. Springer, Heidelberg (2005)

9. Drimer, S.: Authentication of FPGA Bitstreams: Why and How. In: Diniz, P.C., Marques, E., Bertels, K., Fernandes, M.M., Cardoso, J.M.P. (eds.) ARCS 2007. LNCS, vol. 4419, pp. 73–84. Springer, Heidelberg (2007)
10. Durvaux, F., Renauld, M., Standaert, F.-X., van Oldeneel tot Oldenzeel, L., Veyrat-Charvillon, N.: Cryptanalysis of the ches 2009/2010 random delay countermeasure. Cryptology ePrint Archive, Report 2012/038 (2012), http://eprint.iacr.org/
11. Eisenbarth, T., Gong, Z., Güneysu, T., Heyse, S., Kerckhof Sebastiaan Indesteege, S., Koeune, F., Nad, T., Plos, T., Regazzoni, F., Standaert, F.-X., van Oldeneel tot Oldenzeel, L.: Compact implementation and performance evaluation of block ciphers in ATtiny devices (2011)
12. Eisenbarth, T., Paar, C., Weghenkel, B.: Building a side channel based disassembler. Transactions on Computational Science 10, 78–99 (2010)
13. Fridrich, J., Goljan, M.: Robust hash functions for digital watermarking. In: ITCC, pp. 178–183. IEEE Computer Society (2000)
14. Gandolfi, K., Mourtel, C., Olivier, F.: Electromagnetic Analysis: Concrete Results. In: Koç, Ç.K., Naccache, D., Paar, C. (eds.) CHES 2001. LNCS, vol. 2162, pp. 251–261. Springer, Heidelberg (2001)
15. Goubin, L., Matsui, M. (eds.): CHES 2006. LNCS, vol. 4249. Springer, Heidelberg (2006)
16. Guajardo, J., Kumar, S.S., Schrijen, G.-J., Tuyls, P.: FPGA Intrinsic PUFs and Their Use for IP Protection. In: Paillier, P., Verbauwhede, I. (eds.) CHES 2007. LNCS, vol. 4727, pp. 63–80. Springer, Heidelberg (2007)
17. Guilley, S., Sauvage, L., Micolod, J., Réal, D., Valette, F.: Defeating Any Secret Cryptography with SCARE Attacks. In: Abdalla, M., Barreto, P.S.L.M. (eds.) LATINCRYPT 2010. LNCS, vol. 6212, pp. 273–293. Springer, Heidelberg (2010)
18. Kahng, A.B., Lach, J., Mangione-Smith, W.H., Mantik, S., Markov, I.L., Potkonjak, M., Tucker, P., Wang, H., Wolfe, G.: Watermarking techniques for intellectual property protection. In: DAC, pp. 776–781 (1998)
19. Kahng, A.B., Mantik, S., Markov, I.L., Potkonjak, M., Tucker, P., Wang, H., Wolfe, G.: Robust IP watermarking methodologies for physical design. In: DAC, pp. 782–787 (1998)
20. Kocher, P.C., Jaffe, J., Jun, B.: Differential Power Analysis. In: Wiener, M. (ed.) CRYPTO 1999. LNCS, vol. 1666, pp. 388–397. Springer, Heidelberg (1999)
21. Lefèbvre, F., Czyz, J., Macq, B.M.: A robust soft hash algorithm for digital image signature. In: ICIP (2), pp. 495–498 (2003)
22. Linke, B.: Xilinx FPGA IFF copy protection with 1-wire SHA-1 secure memories. XAPP3826 (July 21, 2006)
23. Monga, V., Evans, B.L.: Perceptual image hashing via feature points: Performance evaluation and tradeoffs. IEEE Transactions on Image Processing 15(11), 3452–3465 (2006)
24. Moradi, A., Barenghi, A., Kasper, T., Paar, C.: On the vulnerability of FPGA bitstream encryption against power analysis attacks: extracting keys from Xilinx Virtex-ii FPGAs. In: Chen, Y., Danezis, G., Shmatikov, V. (eds.) ACM Conference on Computer and Communications Security, pp. 111–124. ACM (2011)
25. Myles, G.: Using software watermarking to discourage piracy. ACM Crossroads 12(1), 4 (2005)
26. B. Poettering. Fast AES implementation for Atmel's AVR microcontrollers, http://point-at-infinity.org/avraes/
27. Réal, D., Dubois, V., Guilloux, A.-M., Valette, F., Drissi, M.: SCARE of an Unknown Hardware Feistel Implementation. In: Grimaud, G., Standaert, F.-X. (eds.) CARDIS 2008. LNCS, vol. 5189, pp. 218–227. Springer, Heidelberg (2008)

28. Semico Research. Semiconductor intellectual property: The market hits its stride, http://www.design-reuse.com/news/11069/semico-research-report-semiconductor-%intellectual-property-market-hits-stride.html

29. Simpson, E., Schaumont, P.: Offline hardware/software authentication for reconfigurable platforms. In: Goubin, Matsui (eds.) [15], pp. 311–323

30. Torrance, R., James, D.: The State-of-the-Art in IC Reverse Engineering. In: Clavier, C., Gaj, K. (eds.) CHES 2009. LNCS, vol. 5747, pp. 363–381. Springer, Heidelberg (2009)

31. Tuyls, P., Schrijen, G.J., Skoric, B., van Geloven, J., Verhaegh, N., Wolters, R.: Read-proof hardware from protective coatings. In: Goubin, Matsui (eds.) [15], pp. 369–383

32. Venkatesan, R., Koon, S.-M., Jakubowski, M.H., Moulin, P.: Robust image hashing. In: ICIP (2000)

33. Walter, C.D., Koç, Ç.K., Paar, C. (eds.): CHES 2003. LNCS, vol. 2779. Springer, Heidelberg (2003)

34. Wollinger, T.J., Guajardo, J., Paar, C.: Security on FPGAs: State-of-the-art implementations and attacks. ACM Trans. Embedded Comput. Syst. 3(3), 534–574 (2004)

35. Ziener, D., Teich, J.: Power signature watermarking of IP cores for FPGAs. Signal Processing Systems 51(1), 123–136 (2008)

N-Victims: An Approach to Determine N-Victims for APT Investigations

Shun-Te Liu[1,2], Yi-Ming Chen[1], and Hui-Ching Hung[2]

[1] Department of Information Management, National Central University
Taoyuan, Taiwan(R.O.C.)
{964403004,cym}@cc.ncu.edu.tw
[2] Information & Communication Security Lab, TL, Chunghwa Telecom co., Ltd.,
Taoyuan, Taiwan(R.O.C.)
{rogerliu,hushpuppy}@cht.com.tw

Abstract. The advanced Persistent Threat (APT) is a sophisticated and target-oriented cyber attack for accessing valuable information. The attacker leverages the customized malware as the stepping stone to intrude into the enterprise network. For enterprises and forensic analysts, finding the victims and investigating them to evaluate the damages are critical, but the investigation is often limited by resources and time. In this paper, we propose an N-Victims approach that starts from a known malware-infected computer to determine the top N most likely victims. We test our approach in a real APT case that happened in a large enterprise network consisting of several thousand computers, which run a commercial antivirus system. N-Victims can find more malware-infected computers than N-Gram based approaches. In the top 20 detected computers, N-Victims also had a higher detection rate and a lower false positive rate than N-Gram based approaches.

Keywords: advanced persistent threat, incident investigation, malware detection, botnet detection.

1 Introduction

Many studies have considered APT as a sophisticated and target-oriented cyber attack for accessing valuable information [1–5]. The attacks often go undetected for significant periods of time by using a slow and stealthy approach [6]. In the cases of APT attacks, the attacker leverages advanced social engineering techniques or software vulnerabilities to install a customized malware on the victim's computers [1, 3, 4, 7, 8]. The computers will become the stepping stones for the attackers to remotely control them to attack the other internal computers of a company [9]. The attack model inferred from the above APT cases is shown in Fig 1.

To reduce the damages caused by the APTs, the company needs to know the APT malware-infected computers as quickly as possible. The forensic analysts also need to take advantage of this information for planning the investigations.

D.H. Lee and M. Yung (Eds.): WISA 2012, LNCS 7690, pp. 226–240, 2012.

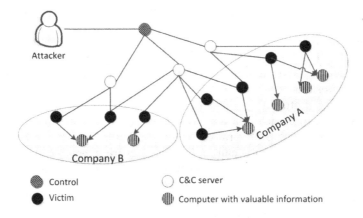

Fig. 1. The attack model inferred from the known APT cases

Therefore, determining possible victims is very important for both the company being attacked and the forensic analysts. However, this is a challenge because of the three problems. First, the APT malware samples are few and specific for a target so that it has a little chance to define a general signature for other similar malware programs. Second, the attackers may clean their footprints and damage the protective mechanism (e.g., antivirus software) on the victim's computers so that the information gathered from the computers may be incomplete or poisoned, making it difficult to determine the attacks. Third, finding a victim often means that the attack happened several weeks or months before. To solve these problems, we attempt to inspect the APTs in depth to find out the other useful information.

As shown in Fig 1, the APT attack model looks likely a botnet. Some research also considers that APT is running on a sophisticated but smaller botnet [9]. Instinctively, it is possible to modify previous botnet detection approaches to detect the APT malware-infected computers. These botnet detection approaches can be roughly divided into two categories: detecting bot behavior [10–13] and bot-infected computers [14, 15]. The research proves that they can detect bot-infected computers but these approaches require more bot samples to train a feasible model. However, there is only a slight chance to implement them in practice as APT malware is often few in number and specific to a target. Retrospective detection approach may be a solution for finding the APT malware-infected computers.

Retrospective detection is a mechanism which allows one to identify exactly which computer has similar symptom from historical information once a threat is identified [16, 17]. As web-related protocols are allowed almost everywhere, the APT malware is often equipped with remote access ability under the HTTP-based command and control (C&C) infrastructure to facilitate the attacks on the Intranet[7, 8]. Therefore, the logs of HTTP requests provide us an opportunity to uncover them retrospectively.

In this paper, we define a matching scheme for HTTP requests and propose an HTTP tree structure to construct the relationship among the clients and the servers on the Internet based on HTTP request logs. Our approach finds the possible victims based on the similar C&C servers and similar HTTP request's behavior. Once an APT malware-infected found, by giving a seed N, this approach can determine the N most possible malware-infected computers. This approach is very useful in an incident investigation limited by resources and time. We test our approach in a real APT case that happened in a large enterprise network consisting of several thousand computers that run a commercial anti-virus program. N-Victims can find more malware-infected computers than N-Gram approaches [10, 11]. In the top 20 detected computers, N-Victims also has a higher detection rate and a lower false positive rate than N-Gram based approaches.

This paper contributes to network security in the following areas:

1. Propose an approach to detect the victims starting from a found malware-infected computer.
2. Propose a method to determine the scope of the APT investigations.
3. Prove the usefulness of our approach on a real APT investigation case.

The organization of this paper is as follows. Section 2 describes the previous research in APT attacks and botnet detection. In Section 3, we propose an N-Victim approach to determine the N most likely victims. Section 4 shows our experimental results and the comparison with N-Gram approaches [10, 11]. Section 5 concludes and describes the future work.

2   Previous Research

2.1   APT Definition

The term "advance persistent threat" can be traced back to the research by Daly in 2009 [1]. In the case study of the research, the attacker combined the social engineering attack and PDF vulnerability to install a customized malware with remote-control ability on the victim. Then, the attacker can control the victim to steal valuable information. The similar case had ever happened while it was called The New E-spionage Threat in 2008 [18]. A cyber attack against Google occurred in 2009 recently was also considered an APT [5, 19].

As the name implies, the advanced persistent threat (APT) uses a highly targeted method persistently for compromising data security, but the definition of APT in academic research is still unclear. We extract the attributes of APT incidents from reports [2, 3, 18, 19] and research [1, 6–9, 20]. The findings are listed as follows: target-oriented, cyber crime, customized malware, remote access, slow and stealthy, advanced attack technologies and valuable information. Based on these findings, we give a definition of APT in this paper as "a sophisticated and target-oriented cyber attack for accessing valuable information."

To understand the APT attacks, we infer a general attack model, as shown in Fig 1, from the known APT attack cases [1, 3, 4, 7, 8]. The attackers compromise the systems using various approaches and then install a customized malware on them. The malware is controlled by the attacker through the command and control (C&C) servers which are responding for sending commands and receiving results. Therefore, the attackers can intrude into the enterprise's network for obtaining valuable information behind the C&C servers [9]. As the attack model looks likely a botnet and some research has also considered that APTs are running on a sophisticated but smaller botnet [9], botnet detection approaches may provide us a chance to deal with APT investigations.

2.2   Botnet Detection

Based on the communication methods, botnets can be divided into four types: 1)IRC (Internet Relay Chat) botnet, 2)HTTP botnet, 3)P2P (Peer-to-Peer) botnet, and 4)Fast-flux Networks [21]. As web-related protocols are allowed almost everywhere, the APT malware is often equipped with remote access ability under the HTTP-based command and control (C&C) infrastructure to facilitate the attacks on the Intranet [7, 8]. Therefore, the HTTP botnet detection approaches may be useful for detecting the APT malware.

In [11], the authors focus on detecting C&C channels masquerading as web traffic. They use 2v-gram based anomaly detection approach to distinguish the C&C traffic from web traffic. In [14], the authors leverage the IRC nickname to detect bot contaminated hosts. They can also detect an HTTP bot by the common strings in the URL of the bot servers. Botzilla [10] captures malware traffic to detect the phoning home behavior. The phoning home traffic will be tokenized to generate the signature for detecting a malware-infected computer. In [12], the authors present a malware clustering system. They analyze the structural similarities among malicious HTTP traffic and automatically generate HTTP-based malware signatures for further detection. All of these mentioned approaches require a lot of malware samples to train a feasible model for detection. However, it was difficult for us because the APT malware is often few in number and specific to a target. Therefore, a new approach is required to deal with this problem.

3   The Proposed Approach

3.1   Overview

Firewall is an important defense mechanism to prevent the enterprise network from the threats coming from the Internet nowadays. It can filter out the incoming or outgoing network traffic by the predefined rules. Mostly, the Web related protocols are allowed to go out rather than to enter by the firewalls. Therefore, the HTTP bots inside the enterprise network will invoke the HTTP requests continuously to contact with the C&C servers and then get new commands for further actions. This behavior is called "phoning home" [10].

To avoid to being detected, the APT malware may slow the HTTP requests [6], change the HTTP requests algorithmically and flux the C&C server fast [22].

Even so, their footprints are still left in the outgoing traffic. As most enterprises leverage proxy servers to intermediate the HTTP requests between internal computers and the Internet, proxy logs provide us an opportunity to uncover them. However, we can't expect that the behavior of APT malware can be modeled. If we could identify APT malware by a model, we wouldn't call them "advanced persistent threats." Therefore, we need additional information to complement the APT malware-infected computers determination.

A found malware can be extracted the C&C servers and corresponding malicious HTTP requests. The C&C servers can be used as the signatures (black list) for detecting the other malware-infected computers. They provide a higher precision rate but low coverage rate of the detection. Oppositely, the malicious HTTP requests can be leveraged to build a general model for further malware detection. They have a higher coverage rate of the detection but they prone to lack the precision of the detection when few malware samples. Unluckily, this dilemma will occur when facing APTs. In this situation, we attempt to combine the advantages of C&C servers with that of HTTP requests.

Let W be websites, V be computers and R be the HTTP requests. As the malware-infected computers may connect to the websites with similar domain names, such as fast flux techniques, we define a function h which is equal to 1 if v and v' connect to the websites with similar domain names w, where v and $v' \subseteq V$ and $w \subseteq W$, otherwise it is equal to 0. Meanwhile, the malware-infected computers may invoke similar malicious HTTP requests for phoning home. We define another function $d(r, r')$ which is the similarity between r and r', where r and $r' \subseteq R$. The relationships among computers and websites are defined as follows:

- **Definition 1:** Neighborhood of a computer v in respect of the websites w, denoted by $N(v,w)$, is defined by $N(v,w) = \{v' \subseteq V \mid ser(v,v',w) =1\}$.
- **Definition 2:** Neighborhood of a set websites w, denoted by $G(w, r_w)$, is defined by $G(w,r_w)=\{w' \subseteq W \mid d(r_w,r_{w'}) > \lambda\}$ where r_w is the major behavior of w and λ is a threshold.

To make the bots available, the bots may be designed to connect to more than one C&C servers for failover [23]. This feature makes it more efficiently to find unknown C&C servers from the HTTP requests invoked by victims than that invoked by all the computes. Therefore, we design an algorithm, called N-Victims, to realize the determination of top N possible victims. The N-Victims starts from a found malware-infected computer v and corresponding C&C servers w and continue to add the neighborhood of v and w to enlarge the scope of possible victims. The working concept is shown in Fig 2 and simply described as follows:

1. finds $N(v,w)=\{a,b,c\}$ and a set C&C servers w_m.
2. determines the major malicious behavior r_m of the $N(v,w)$.
3. finds $G(w_m, r_m)$ on the HTTP requests invoked by $N(v,w)$.
4. appends $G(w_m,r_m)$ to w and goes back step 1 until the number of $N(v,w)$ is to be N.

The details of the N-Victims are described in the following sections.

3.2   The Similarity of HTTP Requests

Some research had leveraged the similarity of HTTP requests to detect the bots. In [24], the authors divided an Uniform Resource Locator (URL) into two part: the hostname and the path. For example, with the URL *www.example.com/usr/index.html*, the hostname portion is *www.example.com* and the path portion is *usr/index.html*. In [12], the authors chose the features of HTTP requests including request method, path, page name, parameters names and values to determine the structural similarity among sequences of HTTP requests.

Two factors were ignored by both of these studies: 1) hostname or called domain name is a tree structure. The similarity of two hostnames is determined by the relationship of domain name structure rather than the strings in the hostname and 2) the relationship between protocol and port number often constrained by a firewall or a proxy, such as *<HTTP, 80>* and *<HTTPS, 443>*. In this paper, we take advantage of some attributes from the HTTP request as illustrated in Fig 3, where s represents the IP address and invokes the HTTP requests and h denotes the domain name. The other attributes form a behavior $b = <p, n, m, d, f, t>$ and is described as follows:

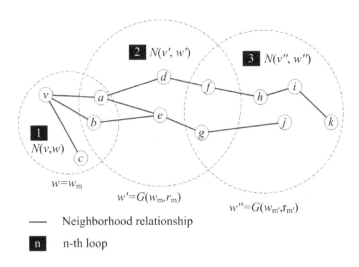

Fig. 2. The concept of top N victims determination

- p represents the request protocol such HTTP or HTTPS; n represents port number such as 80 or 443; m represents the request method such as GET or POST and t represents the file type of page file such as ASP and PHP. The similarity functions of the four attributes, d_p, d_n, d_m and d_t, are Boolean functions. For example, let two HTTP requests be r_i and r_j, the similarity function $d_p(r_i, r_j) = 1$ if r_i and r_j use the same request protocol, otherwise it is equal to 0.

- d represents the path of URL. As the path is referred to the tree structure file system of the websites, the longer the common postfix string to the paths is, the higher possibility the HTTP requests belong to the same service. Therefore, the similarity function $d_d(r_i, r_j)$ is calculated by Longest Common Pretfix (Pre) between the strings to the path of r_i and r_j.

$$d_d(r_i, r_j) = \frac{Pre(d_i, d_j)}{Max\{Length(d_i), Length(d_j)\}} \qquad (1)$$

- f represents the page file name. As the page files are opened by different interpreters of the browsers based on the file type. The similarity of the page file names should be determined by the postfix common string to the names. Therefore, the similarity function $d_f(r_i, r_j)$ is defined to be Longest Common Postfix (Pos) between the strings to the page file name of r_i and r_j.

$$d_f(r_i, r_j) = \frac{Pos(f_i, f_j)}{Max\{Length(f_i), Length(f_j)\}} \qquad (2)$$

The similarity d of two HTTP request r_i and r_j is defined as

$$d(r_i, r_j) = w_p d_p(r_i, r_j) + w_m d_m(r_i, r_j) + w_n d_n(r_i, r_j) + \\ w_d d_d(r_i, r_j) + w_f d_f(r_i, r_j) + w_t d_t(r_i, r_j) \qquad (3)$$

3.3   Building HTTP Tree

To determine the similar domain names, we introduce the domain name tree structure to design an HTTP tree structure. The design will also help for speeding up the traversal from step 1 to step 4 of the determining process. A HTTP tree $T=(R, W, V, L, C)$ consists of a root node $R=<0>$, a set $W=<h>$ of internal nodes, a set $V=<s>$ of external nodes, a set $L=<W_x, W_y>$ of links among internal nodes and a set $C=<V_x, W_y, B>$ of links between internal nodes and external nodes. W_x is the sub domain of W_y and B is a set of behavior b defined in above description.

The process of building the HTTP tree is similar to the general tree-building process. At first, the HTTP requests in the proxy logs are decomposed into the defined elements as shown in Fig 3. Generally, a HTTP request will generate one internal node w, one external node v and one link c, where $w \subseteq W$, $v \subseteq V$ and $c \subseteq C$. Then, the building process will decompose w by the domain name tree

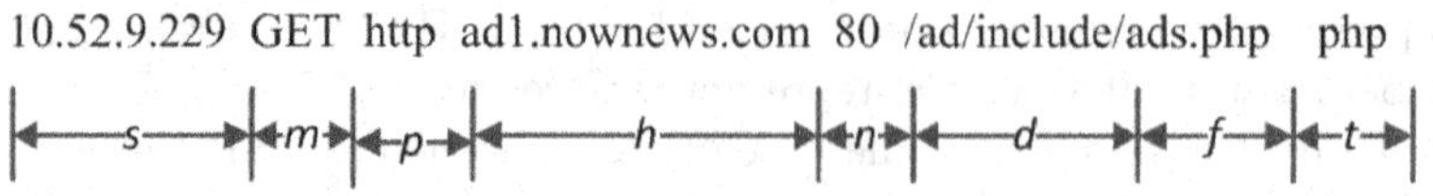

10.52.9.229 GET http ad1.nownews.com 80 /ad/include/ads.php   php

Fig. 3. HTTP request structure in proxy log. s=source ip; m=method; h=hostname; p=protocol; n=port; d=path; f=page file; t=file type.

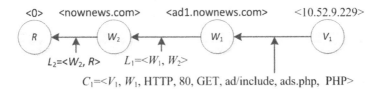

Fig. 4. The HTTP tree generated from the HTTP request of Fig 3

structure to generate the other internal nodes and corresponding link l, where l $\subseteq L$, until reach the root node R. Fig 4 is an example path of the HTTP tree which is generated according to the example HTTP requests in Fig 3. The HTTP requests are processed continuously. Finally, the proxy logs will be transferred to be an HTTP tree.

This HTTP tree will be used for finding the similar malware-infected computers and extracting the malicious HTTP requests when a victim is found.

3.4 Determine the Malware-Infected Computers

Once a victim is found, the N-Victim approach can be started. The victim provides us with the C&C servers and a sort of malicious behavior between the victim and the C&C servers. Let the C&C server be W_1, the victim be V_1, and the number of other possible victims we attempt to find be N. The algorithm of N-Victims is shown in Fig 5. We explain the N-Victims by walking through its execution in Fig 6:

1. Finding $N(v_1, w_1)$: As the top-level internal node of W_1 is W_2, the external nodes belonging to W_2 are the possible victims as they connect to the tree with root W_2. Therefore, V_2, V_3 and V_4 are the possible victims and are added to the list.
2. Determine the major behavior b between V_1 and W_1 and extracting the links C' of the possible victims (V_2, V_3 and V_4). b will be used for finding the other C&C servers among the detected possible victims. (We believe a victim has a higher chance to connect more than one C&C server.)
3. Finding $G(b)$: once the similarity between b and the behavior of the extracted links is larger than the threshold , the internal node of the link is the new C&C server, such as W_4.
4. The new C&C server and victims will be the inputs to find the other possible victims. In the case of Fig 6, V_5 is found because of W_4.
5. If the number of detected victims is smaller than N, the threshold is reduced by 0.1 until is smaller than λ, where λ is the minimum acceptable similarity.
6. Once the number of detected victims is still smaller than N, we find the similar behavior on the residual HTTP requests, such as $<V_6, W_6>$. The threshold is reduced by 0.1 until the N possible victims are determined.

In this paper, the major behavior of a set behavior is extracted by an association rules mining approach, Apriori [25], with Eq(3).

function N-victim
input
    T HTTP tree; w The found C&C servers; v The found victims; N The number of victims
output
    γ The possible victims
begin
(1) $\gamma = N(w, v)$; //Get the external nodes which belongs to the top level domain of of v
(2) b = Aprior (w, v); // Determine the major behavior between w and v
    C' = Extract(γ); // Extract the links of γ
    $\delta := 1$;
(3) For $\delta := 1$; $\delta > \lambda$; $\delta := \delta - 0.1$
        For $i := 1$; $i := M$; $i := i+1$; //M=size of C'
            if the elements on $\gamma \geq N$ then return γ;
(4)   if $d(C'_i(b), b) \geq \delta$ and $C'_i(W) \notin V$ then
                append $N(C'_i(W), C'_i(V))$ to γ;
        End For
    End For
    $\delta := 1$; //reset δ
(6) For $\delta := 1$; $\delta > \lambda$; $\delta := \delta - 0.1$
        For i:=1; $i := M'$; i:=i+1 // M' = size of $\overline{C}$, where $\overline{C}'$ is C exclusive of C'
            if $d(\overline{C}'_i(b), b) \geq \delta$ and $\overline{C}'_i(W) \notin V$ then
                append $N(\overline{C}'_i(W), \overline{C}'_i(V))$ to γ;
            if the elements on $\gamma \geq N$ then return γ;
        End For
    End For
    return γ;
end

Fig. 5. The algorithm of N-Victims

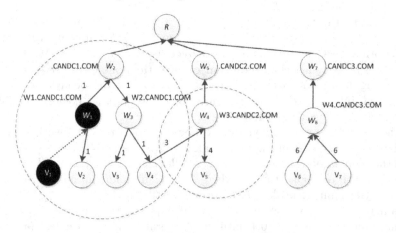

Fig. 6. The example of detecting malware-infected computers on the HTTP tree

4   Experiments and Evaluation

4.1   The Experimental Setup

To evaluate the effectiveness of our approach, we try to prepare the experimental data as close to the real environments as possible. At first, we collect the raw disk images of 20 APT victims which were compromised from May 1 to July 31, 2011. There are 27 malware samples, which can be classified into three malware families by their behavior, on the victims. These malware can evade the commercial antivirus detection at that time. We scanned the malware samples by Trendmicro and Symantec antivirus software and only one family was detected and classified as "Lurid" and "Meciv" respectively on February 20, 2012. The 20 raw disk images were transferred into VMware images by a tool "Liveview" [26], and only 10 raw disk images were transferred successfully. The transferred image was booted up on the experimental environments as shown in Fig 7 to gather the malicious HTTP requests invoked by the malware for three days. Meanwhile, we collect the HTTP requests generated by 30 legitimate computers for two weeks from the proxy servers. The source IPs of the malicious HTTP requests were replaced with 10 random legitimate computer's IP. The modified malicious HTTP requests were inserted into the legitimate HTTP requests to be the first experimental data.

In addition, we tested our approach in a large enterprise network consisting of several thousand computers that run a commercial anti-virus system. As the network traffic is filtered by a firewall and more than five proxy servers are deployed to intermediate the requests from clients to other servers on the Internet, we collected the proxy log from all the proxy servers for a period of two weeks, from October 11 to October 24, 2011, as the second experimental data. The attributes of the experimental data are shown in Table 1.

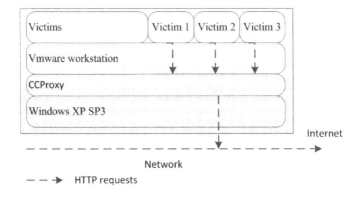

Fig. 7. The experimental environment. The version of CCProxy is 7.2 and that of VMware workstation is 7.0.

Table 1. The attributes of the second experimental data

Size	Clients	Hostnames	HTTP requests
440GB	10,486	102,253	167,219,262

The experimental data consists of the HTTP requests of a malware-infected computer that was discovered in December 14, 2011. Two reasons make us believe this is an APT attack: 1) the computer was compromised and installed a malware. The attack footprints can be traced back to the eight months ago and 2) the malware has the similar abilities, such as remote access, key logger, packet forward, DLL injection and so on, as described in [1, 8, 9].

Finally, as we don't know how many computers were actually infected in the data, our best effort was to investigate manually the top 20 possible victims detected by our approach and N-Gram approach [10, 11]. The investigations are used for evaluating the detection rate and false positive rate.

4.2   Determining Parameters

It is difficult to determine the parameters w_p, w_m, w_n, w_d, and w_f because of low number of APT malware samples. Instead of aggregating each HTTP attribute's similarities, we used a prune process that removes the lower-priority attributes one by one. The priority of the attributes is determined by the network environment:

As the protocols and ports are controlled by a firewall, the malware has to utilize the legitimate protocols and ports to pass the firewall. Therefore, the protocols and ports are seldom changed if compared with other HTTP request attributes. Similarly, the HTTP request methods are often limited by proxy, so it won't be changed frequently. From the above analysis, we define the priority of the attributes as $p > n > m > d, f, t$.

4.3   Results

The First Experiment. The distribution of the malware families and the major malicious HTTP requests generated by Apriori are shown in Table 2. Notably, the values of method (m), protocol (p), port (n), and file type (t) are consistent in each malicious behavior on the priority. These results are the same as the finding in [9, 27]. Therefore, the attributes p, n, m, and t are used by Apriori for determining the major behavior and Eq(3) is replaced with Eq(4) as the following equation.

$$d(r_i, r_j) = w_d d_d(r_i, r_j) + w_f d_f(r_i, r_j) \qquad (4)$$

To observe the impact of the attributes, path (d) and file name (f), we refer to the distribution in the experimental data. The results in Table 3 show that the

Table 2. The distribution of the victims and corresponding malware families

The victims infected by the same malware family	Major malicious behavior $<m, p, n, d, f, t>$
V_1, V_2, V_6, V_6	$<GET, HTTP, 443, /FC001/, ms.php, PHP>$
V_3, V_5, V_7	$<GET, HTTP, 443, /, sb.php, PHP>$
V_8, V_9, V_{10}	$<POST, HTTP, 80, /cgi-bin/, owpq4.cgi, CGI>$

Table 3. The distribution of path, file name and file type in the first experimental data

Data	Number of path	Number of file name
Legitimate HTTP requests	3,487	13,543
Malicious HTTP requests	3	17

file name is the key factor to diver the HTTP requests. To verify the observations, three sets of weight vector $<w_d, w_f,>$ are given and star from three victims, each of which is infected by individual malware family. The results in Table 4 show that f has a greater impact than that of d to the detection. Therefore, weight vector $<w_d, w_f,>$ is given to be $<0.3, 0.7>$ for the next experiment.

In addition, the starting victim is an important factor to influence the detection results. In the case of starting from V1, as the criteria "$p=HTTP$ and $n=443$" filter out all legitimate HTTP requests, the detection rate is 100%. However, if the detection is starting from V_8, we will get a higher false-positive rate because most legitimate HTTP requests match the criteria "$p=HTTP$ and $n=80$" and the path "$cgi-bin$" is a common path of websites.

The Second Experiment. Similarly, the major behavior b of the victim's malicious behavior is determined by Apriori with Eq(4), where $b= <GET, http, 443, /, 90ad.asp, asp>$. The values of m, p, n, and t are consistent in each malicious behavior. Again, to observe the impact of the attributes, d and f, three sets of weight vector $<w_d, w_f>$ are given and starts the detection. The results in Table 5 show that f is the key factor to influence the number of possible victims and C&C servers. The higher threshold of similarity, the fewer possible victims are found.

To evaluate the detection rate and false positive rate, the λ is given to be 0.5 and 0.7, and the weight vector $<w_d, w_f>$ is given to be $<0.7, 0.3>$. The results in Table 6 show that N-Victims can detect more possible victims and C&C servers than the N-Gram approach. In the case of $\lambda= 0.5$, only two legitimate web server, ic.flashcom.shtyle.userplane.com and www.trendsecure.com, are mistaken as C&C servers. More importantly, all possible C&C servers are actual C&C servers when λ is given as 0.7. This proves that the coverage of N-Victims is larger than N-Gram approach. In the case of the top 20 possible victims, no

Table 4. The number of possible victims detected by different weight vectors. The total number of victims is 10. The value p/q means that p is the real victim and q is the detected possible victims.

| $<w_d, w_f>$ | $\lambda=0.5$ | | | $\lambda=0.7$ | | | $\lambda=0.9$ | | |
Starting victim	V_1	V_3	V_8	V_1	V_3	V_8	V_1	V_3	V_8
$<0.7, 0.3>$	4/4	3/3	3/17	4/4	3/3	3/17	4/4	3/3	3/3
$<0.5, 0.5>$	4/4	3/3	3/17	4/4	3/3	3/3	4/4	3/3	3/3
$<0.3, 0.7>$	8/8	8/8	3/17	4/4	3/3	3/3	4/4	3/3	3/3

Table 5. The number of possible victims (NV) and possible C&C servers (NC)

| $<w_d, w_f>$ | $\lambda=0.5$ | | $\lambda=0.7$ | | $\lambda=0.9$ | |
	NV	NC	NV	NC	NV	NC
$<0.7, 0.3>$	2212	273	221	273	2212	273
$<0.5, 0.5>$	46	3	0	0	0	0
$<0.3, 0.7>$	46	3	0	0	0	0

Table 6. Detection rate and false positve rate of N-Victims and N-gram approach.

| | N-Victims | | N-Gram | | |
	$\lambda=0.5$	$\lambda=0.7$	$N=4$	$N=3$	$N=2$
Number of possible victims	67	31	0	8	2280
Number of possible C&C server	19	11	0	4	147
Top 20 possible victims					
Detection rate	100%	100%	0%	100%	5%
False positive rate	0%	0%	0%	0%	95%

matter if λ is given as 0.7 or 0.5, the detection rate and false-positive rate of our approach are the same as N-Gram with N given as 3 and 4. When N is equal to 2, thousands of possible victims are found so that we randomly selected 20 and only one was a real victim.

5   Conclusion and Future Work

This paper proposes an approach called N-Victims. In a real APT investigation, we prove the N-Victims approach has a higher detection rate and a lower false-positive rate than the approaches based on N-Gram. The number of the discovered C&C servers and victims is also larger than that of N-Gram approaches.

There is some future work. First, the major behavior extraction can be improved by using a better classification or clustering approach. Second, the worst case of N-Victims' complexity is $O(C^2)$, where C is the number of the HTTP requests. The process should be parallelized to improve the performance. Third, we only compare our approach with N-gram approaches. It would be necessary to compare with other existing approaches for proving the improvements strongly.

Acknowledgement. The authors would like to thank reviewers' helpful comments. This research is partially supported by the Information & Communication Security Lab, Telecommunication Laboratories, Chunghwa Telecom co., Ltd, the National Science Council of Taiwan, ROC under Grant No. NSC100-2218-E-008-006 and the Software Research Center of National Central University.

References

1. Daly, M. K.: The Advanced Persistent Threat (2009),
   http://static.useeix.org/event/lisa09/tech/slides/daly.pdf
2. Damballa. Advanced Persistent Threats (APT) (2010),
   http://www.damballa.com/knowledge/advanced-persistent-threats.php
3. Hoglund, G.: Advanced Persistent Threat (2010), http://www.issa-sac.org/
   info_resources/ISSA_20100219_HBGary_Advanced_Persistent_Threat.pdf
4. Juels, A., Yen, T.F.: Sherlock Holmes and The Case of the Advanced Persistent Threat. In: 5th USENIX Workshop on Large-Scale Exxploits and Emergent Threats (2012)
5. Winder, D.: Persistent and Evasive Attacks Uncovered. Infosecurity 8(5), 40–43 (2011)
6. Tankard, C.: Advanced Persistent threats and how to monitor and deter them. Network Security 2011(8), 16–19 (2011)
7. Li, F., Lai, A., Ddl, D.: Evidence of Advanced Persistent Threat: A case study of malware for political espionage. In: 6th International Conference on Malicious and Unwanted Software, MALWARE (2011)
8. Frankie Li, A.A.: A Detailed Analysis of an Advanced Persistent Threat Malware. SANS Institute InfoSec Reading Room (2011)
9. Alperovitch, D., McAfee: Revealed: operation shady RAT (2011),
   http://www.mcafee.com/us/resources/white-papers/
   wp-operation-shady-rat.pdf
10. Rieck, K., et al.: Botzilla: detecting the "phoning home" of malicious software. In: Proceedings of the 2010 ACM Symposium on Applied Computing, pp. 1978–1984. ACM, Sierre (2010)
11. Warmer, M.: Detection of web based command & control channels (2011),
    http://essay.utwente.nl/61232/
12. Perdisci, R., Lee, W., Feamster, N.: Behavioral clustering of HTTP-based malware and signature generation using malicious network traces. In: Proceedings of the 7th USENIX Conference on Networked Systems Design and Implementation, p. 26. USENIX Association, San Jose (2010)
13. Gu, G., Zhang, J., Lee, W.: BotSniffer: Detecting botnet command and control channels in network traffic. In: Proceedings of the 15th Annual Network and Distributed System Security Symposium (2008)
14. Goebel, J., Holz, T.: Rishi: identify bot contaminated hosts by IRC nickname evaluation. In: roceedings of the first conference on First Workshop on Hot Topics in Understanding Botnets, p. 8. USENIX Association, Cambridge (2007)

15. Brustoloni, J., et al.: Efficient Detection of Bots in Subscribers' Computers. In: IEEE International Conference on Communications, ICC 2009 (2009)
16. Liu, S.T., Chen, Y.M.: Retrospective Detection of Malware Attacks by Cloud Computing. In: 2010 IEEE International Conference on Cyber-Enabled Distributed Computing and Knowledge Discovery (2010)
17. Oberheide, J., Cooke, E., Jahanian, F.: Cloudav: N-version antivirus in the network cloud. In: The Proceedings of 17th USENIX Security Symposium (2008)
18. Brian Grow, K.E., Tschang, C.-C.: The New E-spionage Threat (2008), http://www.businessweek.com/magazine/content/08_16/b4080032218430.html
19. Websense. Advanced attack or APT (2011), http://www.websense.com/content/advanced-attacks-in-the-news.aspx
20. Gordon, T.: APTs: a poorly understood challenge. Network Security 11, 9–11 (2011)
21. Zhaosheng, Z., et al.: Botnet Research Survey. In: Proceedings of the 32th Annual IEEE International Computer Software and Applications Conference (2008)
22. Yadav, S., et al.: Detecting Algorithmically Generated Domain-Flux Attacks With DNS Traffic Analysis. IEEE/ACM Transactions on Networking 99, 1 (2012)
23. Neugschwandtner, M., Comparetti, P.M., Platzer, C.: Detecting malware's failover C&C strategies with squeeze. In: Proceedings of the 27th Annual Computer Security Applications Conference, Orlando, Florida, pp. 21–30 (2011)
24. Ma, J., et al.: Beyond blacklists: learning to detect malicious web sites from suspicious URLs. In: Proceedings of the 15th ACM SIGKDD International Conference on Knowledge Discovery and Data Mining, pp. 1245–1254. ACM, Paris (2009)
25. Kantardzic, M.: Data mining: concepts, models, methods, and algorithms. Wiley-IEEE Press (2011)
26. Live View (2009), http://liveview.sourceforge.net/
27. Binde, B., McRee, R., O'Connor, T.J.: Assessing Outbound Traffic to Uncover Advanced Persistent Threat. Sans Institute (2011), http://www.sans.edu/student-files/projects/JWP-Binde-McRee-OConnor.pdf

An Efficient Filtering Method
for Detecting Malicous Web Pages

Jaeun Choi[1,*], Gisung Kim[2], Tae Ghyoon Kim[1], and Sehun Kim[3]

[1] Department of Industrial and Systems Engineering, KAIST, Daehak-ro 291,
Yuseong-gu, Daejeon, 305-701, Republic of Korea
{juchoi,tgkimahn}@kaist.ac.kr
[2] KAIST Institute for Information Technology Convergence, Daehak-ro 291,
Yuseong-gu, Daejeon, 305-701, Republic of Korea
kks00@kaist.ac.kr
[3] Department of Industrial and Systems Engineering and Graduate School of
Information Security, KAIST, Daehak-ro 291, Yuseong-gu, Daejeon, 305-701,
Republic of Korea
shkim@kaist.ac.kr

Abstract. There are ways to detect malicious web pages, two of which
are dynamic detection and static detection. Dynamic detection has a
high detection rate but uses a high amount of resources and takes a long
time, whereas static analysis only uses a small amount of resources but
its detection rate is low. To minimize the weaknesses of these two methods, a filtering method was suggested. This method uses static analysis
first to filter normal web pages and then uses dynamic analysis to test
only the remaining suspicious web pages. In this filtering method, if a
page is classified as normal at the filtering stage, it is not being tested any
more. However, the existing filtering method does not consider this problem. In this paper, to solve this problem, our proposed filtering method
utilizes a cost-sensitive method. Also, to increase the efficiency of the
filter, features are grouped as three subsets depending on the difficulty
of the extraction. The efficiency of the proposed filter can be increased,
as our method only uses the necessary feature subset according to the
characteristics of the web pages. An experiment showed that the proposed method shows fewer false negatives and greater efficiency than an
existing filtering method.

Keywords: Internet security, Malicious web page, Filtering method,
Cost-sensitive analysis, Machine learning.

1 Introduction

As the Internet is accessible anytime and anywhere due to the development of
network technology, many people use various Internet services which are provided
via web applications. Web applications are coded by computer languages such
as HTML code, JavaScript and VBScript [6]. These languages can easily be
modified and used as tool for attacks. If a user accesses a web page coded by

D.H. Lee and M. Yung (Eds.): WISA 2012, LNCS 7690, pp. 241–253, 2012.

malicious scripts, a computer of the user could be infected by a virus or worm. The infected computer can cause problems not only within the infected computer itself, but also on other computers connected to the network, which increases the seriousness of the problem. Therefore, detecting malicious web pages efficiently and blocking them in advance are very important strategies.

Attacks by malicious web pages are increasing; therefore, creating prevention techniques is important. One existing malicious web page detection technique involves the use of what are known as dynamic detection using a honeyclient [10], [15], [16]. These methods run the scripts associated with web pages on a virtual machine to detect if the page is malicious. By fully running the contents of the web pages, the detection rate of dynamic approaches is high, but the analysis of web pages takes a long time. Owing to this characteristic, many web pages which have a complex structure cannot be tested in a short time [2]. Therefore, dynamic detection is not very applicable to large-scale, real time classification [1]. Another detection technique is known as a static detection technique, which uses data mining and machine learning [1], [6], [8], [13], [14]. In these methods, a machine learns the patterns of normal and malicious data and uses the learnt data during the actual test. The detection time of static detection methods is faster than that of dynamic detection methods but the detection rate is lower than that of dynamic detection methods [5]. Also, new types of malware are difficult to detect by the static detection as this method only has information about existing malware and is only able to detect similar types.

Given that both static and dynamic detection methods have disadvantages, Canali et al. suggested a filtering method known as Prophiler, which combines static and dynamic detection [2]. In Prophiler, first, static detection is used to classify all web pages quickly. Only suspicious pages classified by static detection are then tested by dynamic detection. By filtering most normal pages by fast static detection and testing only the rest with dynamic detection, the detection time is reduced. The overall process is shown in Fig. 1.

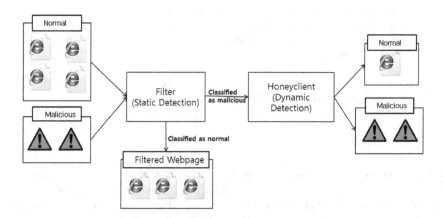

Fig. 1. The framework of filtering method

In this method, web pages which are classified as normal via static detection will no longer be tested; thus, it is important that no malicious web pages are among those web pages. However, the Prophiler method does not consider these false negative errors, which means that a malicious web page may be misclassified as normal. In the Prophiler method, web pages that classified as malicious will be tested by a dynamic detection such as a honeyclient. Therefore, if a page is suspicious, it is better to mark it as malicious and run a dynamic detection rather than marking it as normal and leaving it untested. Therefore, lowering the false negative error rate is important in the filtering method.

In this paper, we suggest a filtering method based on machine learning that filters normal web pages while reducing the false negative error rate. To achieve this goal, if a web page is a somewhat suspicious, the page will be classified as malicious to avoid the possibility of any malicious web pages being classified as normal. To reflect this characteristic in the filtering process, we apply a MetaCost scheme [4], which is a variation of a cost-sensitive method used part of our proposed method. The MetaCost scheme considers cost of classification errors and attempts to minimize this cost. During the learning process, we set the cost of malicious web pages misclassified as normal so that it is much higher than the cost of other types of error. As the cost of false negative errors is higher than other costs, our filtering method can prevent false negative errors.

Also, in this paper, a filtering method with higher efficiency than Prophiler is introduced. There are numerous web pages existing on a network, which necessitates an efficient filtering method. Our filtering method is based on machine learning. To improve the efficiency and performance of machine learning, the proper selection of features is important. Various features can be extracted from web pages, from simple one to complex. One existing filtering method extracts all features and uses them for detection at once, which increases the complexity of the detection model. In this paper, features are grouped into three subsets according to their complexity and are used successively. First, all of the web pages are classified using the simplest feature subset. Web pages confirmed as normal will not be classified in the next step. The remaining web pages are classified using the simplest feature subset among the remaining subset. The same process continues until all of the feature subsets are used. Accordingly, not all feature subsets are used to classify all of the web pages, thus reducing the detection time and amount of resources that are used.

The proposed filtering method makes the following contributions. First, by applying a cost-sensitive method, we can reduce the false negative rate because only normal pages are filtered. Also, the filtering efficiency is increased through the application of a sequential filtering phase. The existing filtering method uses all of the features but the proposed method selectively uses a feature subset, which increases the level of efficiency. The experimental result shows that most normal web pages were filtered and that the dynamic detection load was decreased. The false negative rate and the detection time were also decreased compared to the existing filtering method.

This paper is organized as follows: Section 2 reviews related work. Section 3 describes the proposed algorithm in detail. In Section 4, the algorithm is evaluated. Finally, we summarize our study and conclude the paper in Section 5.

2   Related Work

The latest types of malware frequently use a drive-by download scheme, which means that malicious code is downloaded and executed without the permission of the user [2]. Malware downloaded without the user noticing can steal personal information and send spam emails. If an infected web page is popular, many users PCs can be infected in a very short time. Therefore, to detect malicious web pages causing drive-by downloads, dynamic detection and static detection technologies are under study.

The dynamic approach visits web pages or extracts the source code of a web page and tests if the page is malicious. This line of research analyzes the malware activity patterns in a virtual environment in which malware can operate. Dynamic detection methods use honeyclient systems. Some of these systems are low-interaction systems which provide a very limited environment to attackers, while others are high-interaction systems which contain the actual system and services [2]. Typical client honeypots are MITRE HoneyClient [15], Microsofts Honeymonkey [16] and Capture-HPC [10], all of which are high-interaction honeyclients [2]. Low-interaction honeyclients, such as Wepawet [3], PhoneyC [9] and JSUnpack [7], provides a limited environment for the malware and therefore has difficulties when undertaking what is known as malware crawling. Also, because the malicious scripts used by drive-by download attempts are generated dynamically within the users browser, collection from low-interaction honeyclients which use a web crawler is difficult.

Numerous honeyclient technologies have been introduced to collect malicious codes spreading through web sites. However, high-interaction client honeypot systems are expensive to establish and require a large amount of time to collect malicious codes, whereas low-interaction client honeypot systems cannot easily collect malicious codes which cause infection through a dynamically generated script.

A static approach based on machine learning generates the signatures of malicious activities at existing web pages and detects attacks through these. During a given amount of time, more web pages can be tested by a static approach than by a dynamic approach, but the level of accuracy is lower. Nonetheless, due to its efficiency, research on malicious web pages using machine learning is very active [1], [6], [8], [13], [14]. In this study, our filtering method utilizes the strengths of dynamic detection and static detection.

3   Proposed Method

In this paper, we suggest a filtering method which filters normal web pages using machine learning before using a honeyclient to test whether the web pages are malicious. Because the honeyclient tests web pages in detail, if every web page is tested using the honeyclient, it requires too much time and uses too high a level of system resources. There are numerous web pages on the internet, and most of them are not harmful. Therefore, only using a honeyclient takes a long time and requires a considerable amount of resources to test the normal web sites, which are the majority of pages on the internet. More time and resources are used to test normal web pages than to test malicious pages, which lowers the efficiency of the honeyclient. Therefore, if we can decrease the number of web pages to be tested by the honeyclient using a filtering method, the detection performance will increase.

In this section, the features that the filter uses are explained, and the framework of the detection technique that uses these features will also be explained.

3.1   Features

The filters suggested in this paper use machine learning, and the data is classified based on the relevant features. The features used in this study were based on the features used in a previous study [6] based on detecting malicious web pages using machine learning. Features that can be extracted from web pages vary from simple features of a source code analysis to complex features that show the characteristics of the functions. In this paper, the features of entire web pages are categorized according to the complexity of the extraction after referring to earlier research [6]. The entire set of features can be grouped into three subsets according to their levels of complexity of extraction.

Document Features. Document features are the simplest features that can be extracted from HTML documents [6]. The length of the source code, the average number of words, the number of lines, the average number of words on a line and the number of NULL characters are the characteristics of the document features. Hackers use obfuscation methods to make code analysis difficult. Through these obfuscation methods, executable malicious code unreadable by humans is included in a web page. In this case, the number of characters in HTML functions is abnormally large [6]. These types of web pages have more characters than normal pages, and malicious web pages can therefore be detected considering this characteristic. Also, to hide elements performing the malicious activity, a hacker often uses an iframe tag to make the elements size close to 0. Therefore, malicious web pages can be detected if invisible elements that have an iframe size of 0 or close to 0 are set to feature. In this paper, the document features used are listed in Table 1.

Some malicious web pages can be detected by simple document features. However if a page consists of complex functions, it cannot be detected merely with document features. Therefore, JavaScript, which hackers often use to conceal malicious activity, often needs to be analyzed.

JavaScript Features. JavaScript features are count of the use of each JavaScript function. There are hundreds of JavaScript functions, and among them, *eval()*, *unescape()*, *escape()*, *exec()* and *uboud()* are commonly used by malicious codes [6]. Therefore, we can detect malicious web pages which use malicious JavaScript functions by checking how often these functions are used. In this paper, we consider the 154 JavaScript functions used in the aforementioned study [6].

ActiveX Features. ActiveX features are the hardest features that can be extracted from web pages. ActiveX is a strong function which enables the distribution of applications through a web browser. Normally, it is designed to be downloaded and run by a web browser. Therefore, hackers often attempt to insert malicious codes inside ActiveX to infect users PCs. For example, attackers can use WScript.Shell so that users computers will perform the malicious activity instructed by the shell code, or they will use Adob.Stream to download malicious files onto users computers. Therefore, by learning the patterns of ActiveX functions that are often used for malicious activity, malicious web pages using these functions can be detected. In this paper, we consider the eight ActiveX features used in the earlier study [6].

Table 1. Selected features

Feature name	Feature used
Document features	1. Number of lines 2. Number of null spaces 3. Number of words 4. Number of distinct words 5. Number of words per line 6. Average word length 7. Number of script tags 8. Wherther a script tag is symmetric 9. The size of an iframe 10. Number of delimiters
JavaScript features	Count of each JavaScript function
ActiveX features	Count of each ActiveX object

3.2 Framework

To uncover suspicious web pages out of numerous web pages efficiently, filter is necessary. The filtering method suggested in this study is based on machine learning. To apply machine learning, features are selected and extracted from web pages. As explained earlier, various features extracted from web pages exist, including simple features that can be easily extracted via a HTML analysis to the complex to extract features to test if ActiveX is used. The existing filtering method, Prophiler, used all of the features without considering their characteristics and levels of complexity. However, some malicious web pages can be detected using only simple features. Using complex features to test these web pages is a waste of time and system resources. Therefore, in this paper, features are grouped into three subsets depending on how difficult it is to obtain the characteristics and use them. After extracting the features, these are used as input to the classifiers. In this paper, the classification algorithm is a decision tree [11]. The detailed structures of our filter are shown in Fig. 2.

As shown in Fig. 2, every web page is initially classified according to the document feature subset, which is the easiest to extract. Pages considered to be clearly normal by this classification will not be tested any longer and are diagnosed as normal. Web pages, which were not filtered using document features, are classified using JavaScript features. Also, any pages considered to be clearly normal by this classification system are no longer tested. Pages that are still suspicious up to this stage are classified finally according to their ActiveX features. After being classified by three feature subsets, pages classified as normal are no longer tested, and the remaining suspicious web pages are tested by a honeyclient. With sequential filters, the number of features utilized by our method is fewer than that of Prophiler, which uses all of the features. Therefore, the amount of time and the system resources taken to detect malicious web pages are decreased, allowing the detection process to be more efficient than the existing detection method.

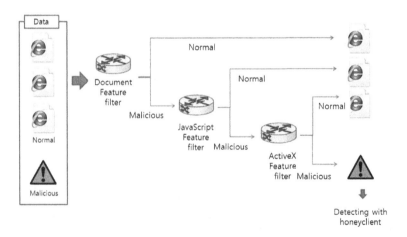

Fig. 2. The proposed filter framework

3.3   Cost Sensitive Classifier

The filtering method suggested in this paper does not test anymore if any web page is classified once as normal at any filtering stage. Therefore, if malicious web pages are often classified as normal, it becomes a serious problem. Therefore, in this paper, filtering of only the pages which are undoubtedly normal during the filtering stage is done, and remaining pages are tested by the honeyclient test. To do this, we apply MetaCost, which minimizes the cost of classification errors [4].

In MetaCost scheme, class of each instance is decided by following equation.

$$x\text{'s class} = \arg\min_i \sum_j P(j|x)C(i,j) \tag{1}$$

where, $p(j|x)$ is the probability of each class j and $C(i,j)$ is the cost of errors predicting that an instance x belongs to class i when in fact it belongs to class j. By considering cost of classification errors, MetaCost can minimize the expected cost of predicting the class of each instance. The detailed cost minimizing procedure is shown in Table 2 [4].

Table 2. The MetaCost algorithm

Inputs:
    S is the training set,
    L is a classification learning algorithm,
    C is a cost matrix,
    m is the number of resamples to generate,
    n is the number of examples in each resample,
    p is $True$ iff L produces class probabilities,
    q is $True$ iff all resamples are to be used for each example.

Producre MetaCost (S, L, C, m, n, p, q)

For $i=1$ to m
    Let S_i be a resample of S with n examples.
    Let M_i = Model produced by applying L to S_i.

For each example x in S
    For each class j
        Let $P(j|x) = \frac{1}{\sum_i 1} \sum_i P(j|x, M_i)$
        Where
            If p then $P(j|x, M_i)$ is produced by M_i
            Else $P(j|x, M_i) = 1$ for the class predicted
                by M_i for x, and 0 for all others.
            If q then i ranges over all M_i
            Else i ranges over all M_i such that $x \notin S_i$.
        Let x's class = $\arg\min_i \sum_j P(j|x)C(i,j)$.

Let M = Model produced by applying L to S.

Return M

In general, machine learning methods assume that every error has the same cost. However, in a filtering method, errors of malicious pages that are misclassified as normal are more serious than the opposite case. Therefore, the cost in both cases should be set differently. Thus, in this paper, with MetaCost, the cost of a malicious page being misclassified as normal is much higher than in the other case. By applying MetaCost to all filtering stages, if a page has any suspicious components, it will be classified as malicious and the number of malicious pages within the normal web page group will be reduced.

4 Experiments

4.1 Experimental Environment

To verify the proposed method, we collected 3,068 of normal web pages and 363 malicious web pages from the Internet. Normal web pages were collected by a RafaBot web crawler directly. Among collected web pages, 363 web pages were classified as malicious according to JSUnpack [7]. The experiment was done by WEKA, which is a machine learning tool [17], and the J48 decision tree [12] was used as a classifier. Training and testing of data were done by a 10-fold cross-validation scheme. When applying MetaCost, the cost of false negative errors was set to 50 and the cost of the other error type is set to 1.

4.2 Filtering Results

The purpose of the filter used in this study is to filter out clearly normal web pages so that the load at the honeyclient test will be reduced. To increase the filtering efficiency, a sequential filtering method is suggested. Table 3 shows the result after the entire filtering process is complete.

Table 3. Detection and error rate of the proposed filter

	Predicted Normal	Predicted Malicous
Real Normal	0.875	0.125
Real Malicious	0.058	0.942

The detection rate for malicious pages is 94.2% and the false negative rate for malicious pages is 5.8%, which is considerably low. With MetaCost, the proposed method worked to reduce the false negative rate. In the proposed method, the false negative rate is low but the false positive rate is relatively high. However, lowering the false negative rate is more important than lowering the false positive rate due to the characteristics of the filtering method.

Here, the efficiency of the filtering method is analyzed. Table 4 shows how many web pages are being processed at each filtering stage. At the first filter, all of 3,068 normal web pages and 363 malicious web pages were classified. Pages marked as malicious were classified at the second filter, and the same process was run at each filter. Finally, the number of normal web pages being tested at the honeyclient was 384, about 12.5% of all normal web pages. The filtering

Table 4. Numbers of web pages processed at each stage

	Document feature filter	JavaScript feature filter	ActiveX feature filter	Honeyclient
Normal	3,068	913	403	384
Malicious	363	352	347	342
Total	3,431	1,265	750	726

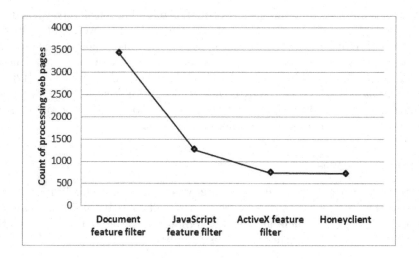

Fig. 3. Total number of web pages at each stage

method proposed in this study effectively filtered out most normal web pages and thus increased the efficiency of the honeyclient. For the malicious web pages, the theoretically best result is that a malicious web page should not be filtered by any filter. However, some malicious pages have similar characteristics compared to the normal pages; therefore, 21 malicious web pages were classified as normal. Fig. 3 shows that the number of web pages being tested at the final honeyclient was greatly reduced. Without applying the filter, the honeyclient tested 3,431 web pages, but when the filter was applied, only 726 pages were tested. Because the honeyclient is a detection method which opens every web page in sequence to determine if there is any harmful activity, reducing the number of web pages to be tested will increase the efficiency. As shown in the result, by applying the filtering method, only about 21.2% of the pages needed to be tested. Hence, a more thorough and detailed analysis is possible.

4.3   Comparing Error Rate

The filter proposed in this paper uses the MetaCost method to prevent malicious web pages from being misclassified as normal. To check this, the false negative rates of the proposed filter and an existing filter were compared. For comparison, an existing filtering method, Prophiler, used the J48 decision tree. The features used in this paper were also applied in Prophiler.

Table 5 shows that the proposed filter shows a lower false negative rate than the existing scheme. This occurs because the proposed method used MetaCost to prevent malicious pages from being misclassified as normal. Therefore, when using the proposed filter, there are fewer malicious web pages among the pages classified as normal.

4.4   Comparing the Detection Time

The filter used in this study is designed more efficiently. To test this, the detection time was compared. The detection time of the existing filter is measured as time taken by one classifier when using all of the features for detection. The detection time of the proposed filter is measured as the sum of the time taken at each of three filters. The specifications of PC used for time measuring are as follows: AMD 2.6GHz for the CPU and 4GB of RAM.

Table 5 shows that the detection time taken by the filter proposed in this paper is less than that by the existing filter. The proposed filter completed the testing in three steps but used only the necessary features. Thus, fewer web pages were tested at each step, which reduced the detection time. Comparing detection times proved that the proposed method is more efficient than the existing methods.

When testing 3,431 web pages, the detection time of the proposed method was faster than that of the existing method by 1.20 seconds. If the proposed filtering method is applied to a real situation where billions of web pages exist, the difference between the detection time of the proposed filter and that of existing filter will be larger.

Table 5. Comparison to existing filtering method

	False negative rate(%)	Detection time(s)
Proposed filter	**5.8**	**1.67**
Existing filter	16.3	2.87

5   Conclusion

In this paper, we proposed a filtering method that combines the strengths of static detection and dynamic detection. When using filtering methods, the false negative errors may be fatal. To decrease false negative errors where malicious pages are misclassified as normal, a cost-sensitive method is applied to our filtering method. Also, to increase the efficiency of the existing filtering method, we proposed a sequential filtering method. It was confirmed that when we applied the proposed method, less of a load is applied to the honeyclient, which is a dynamic detection methods. Also, it was proven from the experiment that the proposed method shows a lower false negative rate and greater efficiency than the existing filtering method.

In the future, to increase the detection accuracy, we will consider using other classifiers aside from a decision tree. Also, we will consider other features in an attempt to increase the detection performance.

Acknowledgments. This research was supported by the MKE(The Ministry of Knowledge Economy), Korea, under the CYBER SECURITY RESEARCH CENTER supervised by the NIPA(National IT Industry Promotion Agency), NIPA-C1000-1101-0001.

References

1. Bannur, S.N., Saul, L.K., Savage, S.: Judging a site by its content: learning the textual, structural, and visual features of malicious web pages. In: Proceedings of the 4th ACM Workshop on Security and Artificial Intelligence, pp. 1–10. ACM (2011)
2. Canali, D., Cova, M., Vigna, G., Kruegel, C.: Prophiler: A fast filter for the large-scale detection of malicious web pages. In: Proceedings of the 20th International Conference on World Wide Web, pp. 197–206. ACM (2011)
3. Cova, M., Kruegel, C., Vigna, G.: Detection and analysis of drive-by-download attacks and malicious javascript code. In: Proceedings of the 19th International Conference on World Wide Web, pp. 281–290. ACM (2010)
4. Domingos, P.: Metacost: A general method for making classifiers cost-sensitive. In: Proceedings of the Fifth ACM SIGKDD International Conference on Knowledge Discovery and Data Mining, pp. 155–164. ACM (1999)
5. Eshete, B., Villafiorita, A., Weldemariam, K.: Malicious website detection: Effectiveness and efficiency issues. In: First SysSec Workshop (SysSec 2011), pp. 123–126. IEEE (2011)
6. Hou, Y.T., Chang, Y., Chen, T., Laih, C.S., Chen, C.M.: Malicious web content detection by machine learning. Expert Systems with Applications 37(1), 55–60 (2010)
7. JSUnpack, http://jsunpack.jeek.org
8. Likarish, P., Jung, E., Jo, I.: Obfuscated malicious javascript detection using classification techniques. In: 4th International Conference on Malicious and Unwanted Software (MALWARE 2009), pp. 47–54. IEEE (2009)
9. Nazario, J.: Phoneyc: a virtual client honeypot. In: Proceedings of the 2nd USENIX Conference on Large-Scale Exploits and Emergent Threats: Botnets, Spyware, Worms, and More, p. 6. USENIX Association (2009)
10. The Honeynet Project. Capture-hpc, https://projects.honeynet.org/capture-hpc/
11. Quinlan, J.R.: Induction of decision trees. Machine Learning 1(1), 81–106 (1986)
12. Quinlan, J.R.: C4. 5: programs for machine learning. Morgan Kaufmann (1993)
13. Seifert, C., Welch, I., Komisarczuk, P.: Identification of malicious web pages with static heuristics. In: Australasian Telecommunication Networks and Applications Conference, ATNAC 2008, pp. 91–96. IEEE (2008)

14. Tao, W., Shunzheng, Y., Bailin, X.: A novel framework for learning to detect malicious web pages. In: 2010 International Forum onInformation Technology and Applications (IFITA), vol. 2, pp. 353–357. IEEE (2010)
15. Wang, K.: Mitre honeyclient development project. Internet, `http://honeyclient.org` (accessed: March 2009)
16. Wang, Y.M., Beck, D., Jiang, X., Roussev, R., Verbowski, C., Chen, S., King, S.: Automated web patrol with strider honeymonkeys. In: Proceedings of the 2006 Network and Distributed System Security Symposium, pp. 35–49 (2006)
17. Weka, `http://www.cs.waikato.ac.nz/ml/weka/`

Lightweight Client-Side Methods
for Detecting Email Forgery

Eric Lin[1], John Aycock[1,*], and Mohammad Mannan[2]

[1] Department of Computer Science, University of Calgary,
2500 University Drive NW, Calgary, Alberta, Canada T2N 1N4
{linyc,aycock}@ucalgary.ca
[2] Concordia Institute for Information Systems Engineering,
Faculty of Engineering and Computer Science, Concordia University,
1515 Ste-Catherine Street West, EV7 640, Montreal, Quebec, Canada H3G 2W1
mmannan@ciise.concordia.ca

Abstract. We examine a related, but distinct, problem to spam detection. Instead of trying to decide if email is spam or ham, we try to determine if email purporting to be from a known correspondent actually comes from that person – this may be seen as a way to address a class of targeted email attacks. We propose two methods, geolocation and stylometry analysis. The efficacy of geolocation was evaluated using over 73,000 emails collected from real users; stylometry, for comparison with related work from the area of computer forensics, was evaluated using selections from the Enron corpus. Both methods show promise for addressing the problem, and are complementary to existing anti-spam techniques. Neither requires global changes to email infrastructure, and both are done on the email client side, a practical means to empower end users with respect to security. Furthermore, both methods are lightweight in the sense that they leverage existing information and software in new ways, instead of needing massive deployments of untried applications.

1 Introduction

It is safe to say that very few people have friends and family who legitimately contact them about penis enlargement, Canadian pharmaceuticals, and lonely Russian women. However, email `From:` lines are trivial to forge, and passwords to user email accounts and social networking sites are easy to phish; usernames and accounts belonging to legitimate users may be co-opted to send spam.

More insidious is the threat of targeted attacks via email, which have gone up many-fold in the last few years; one report [23] noted these attacks have increased from 1–2 attacks/week in 2005 to 77 attacks/day in 2010. The same report stated that 6.3% of all phishing emails blocked in 2010 were targeted (spear) phishing attacks. In these attacks, an attacker may customize the email content for the target user, and/or masquerade as someone the target knows [8,14]. Targeted phishing emails are more effective than bulk spam; e.g., one experiment

---

* Corresponding author.

D.H. Lee and M. Yung (Eds.): WISA 2012, LNCS 7690, pp. 254–269, 2012.
© Springer-Verlag Berlin Heidelberg 2012

reported [18] significant differences in success rates of socially targeted phishing attacks (72%) vs. regular phishing attacks (16%).

Victims of these attacks come from all walks of life, including everyday users (e.g., friends/contacts of a target are asked to send money to help the target in need, stuck in a foreign country [8,14]); government and defense executives (e.g., malicious attachments were received by a U.S. defense contractor purporting to be from a legitimate Pentagon sender [6]); and IT security professionals (e.g., targeted employees of RSA opened a malicious Excel attachment, entitled "2011 Recruitment Plan", allowing attackers to compromise sensitive information on widely used SecurID tokens [30]). Although very simple, these attacks have already caused significant financial damages, as well as increased risks to national security. From an attacker's point of view, these attacks are much less detectable, and estimated to yield much higher return than traditional spam (e.g., see [9]).

How can such targeted emails from seemingly legitimate sources be detected? We propose the use of IP geolocation (of known email-sending users and their email servers) and text stylometry analysis (of email content from known senders) to empower email recipients in detecting email forgery. The basic idea follows from familiar real-world experiences. For example, if a resident in the USA receives postal mail with a stamp from Nigeria, they are likely to be suspicious about the content of the mail, if it claims to be coming from the the IRS (Internal Revenue Service). In the same manner, when users receive a telephone call (assume a spoofed phone number) from someone purporting to be a friend/relative, users may detect the spoof from the differences in voice and language styles. We explore whether such "common sense" approaches can be used for email forgery detection.

The goal here is to provide more information to an end user for helping them decide whether the sender appears authentic or not. This information may be presented to the user by their MUA[1] based on classification done by the MUA itself or in the user's MTA or MDA; no global changes need be enacted to support our techniques. In fact, we have developed a client-side plug-in for the Thunderbird MUA that currently implements our IP geolocation method. However, we must determine the viability of anti-forgery techniques in real-world settings – the problem we address in this paper.

Looking at anti-spam techniques, it is easy to pick apart any new proposed method by attacking the assumptions that underlie it.[2] *All anti-spam technologies operate based on assumptions about spammer behavior. None of them are perfect and we do not claim that our forgery detection methods are either.* We are more concerned with having a wide range of anti-forgery methods so that defense in depth can be employed.

In terms of the threat model, we try to detect email forgery from two sources. First, compromised email accounts, where an attacker has access to a legitimate email account belonging to someone known to the target user. We observe that methods like SPF [32] and DKIM [1] do not help in this case. Second, arbitrary

---

[1] MUA = mail user agent; MTA = mail transfer agent; MDA = mail delivery agent.

[2] For a categorization of anti-spam techniques by assumption, see [16].

mail transmissions, where an attacker has forged the From: header to appear as if it comes from a sender known to the target user. We assume that attackers do not control the target's or the sender's email client or software platform. Common spam is not our focus. We also do not address phishing/scam emails from *unknown* senders (e.g., typical advance-fee frauds).

Our contributions may be summarized as follows. First, we have proposed and evaluated two methods for email forgery detection. Second, these methods purposely leverage existing information – in email headers, on the Internet – and existing, tested software, making our methods lightweight in terms of their requirements and implementation. Third, we tested our methods with real email. Getting access to spam samples is trivial, of course, but experiments like ours that require nonspam (i.e., ham) samples are much trickier, and demands that research be conducted observing ethical constraints (and sometimes the inability to capture certain data) to ensure privacy. Fourth, our methods are readily-deployable on the client side with no changes to email infrastructure needed.

The remainder of this paper looks at the classification techniques we have studied, with geolocation in Section 2 and stylometry in Section 3. Section 4 discusses related work, and Section 5 concludes.

2 Geolocation

The intuition behind geolocation for forgery detection is that most correspondents will send email from only a small number of physical locations. For example, an email arriving from China, claiming to be from a person who has only ever mailed from Canada previously, should be treated with a great degree of suspicion. This intuition will not always hold true, of course, and we revisit that and other limitations in the discussion below.

2.1 Experimental Design

To test our intuition, we performed a study on IP address information we found in saved email headers;[3] IP addresses can be mapped into a geographic location, and their stability may also provide a similar means to detect forgery, even if the IP addresses are not converted into a geolocation. It is important to note that we are not interested in the accuracy of geolocation or IP addresses. The purpose of our study is to find the *consistency* of senders' IP addresses and geolocation.

A script we wrote for data collection, run in study participants' accounts, looked for mailbox files in both mbox and dbx format. The script automatically extracted each sender's email address, domain, recipients, and IP address from a participant's saved email. Due to privacy issues, we only collected the (MD5) hash of a sender's mail address, the hash of a sender's domain, and the hash of a recipient's email address. None of the email body was read.

---

[3] Ethics approval for data collection (and restrictions on data collection) granted by University of Calgary Conjoint Faculties Research Ethics Board, file #6515.

Specifically, we were looking at the last `Received: from` header in each message (i.e., the first one added). We refer to these as *RF headers*. There are some problems with the IP addresses in the RF headers such as

1. The last RF header does not always contain an external (public) IP address. In this case, if the last RF header's IP address is internal, then we find the second to the last and so on, until the first external IP is found. That IP is taken as the sender's IP address.
2. Some mails are sent internally, so there are no external IP addresses at all. We discard all emails that only have internal IP addresses because internal IP addresses cannot be used to geolocate senders.

In both cases, we use the list of private IP address blocks from RFC 1918 [27].

We assume that most people don't save spam (anti-spam researchers not being "most people"), so we assume data collected is mostly from legitimate senders. We do, however, filter out common spam folders in the study, like "Spam" and "Junk."

A total of ten subjects participated in our study, selected via convenience sampling. After filtering out the emails without an external IP address, a total number of 73,652 emails were collected. Out of 73,652 emails, 6909 unique senders were extracted and 2838 unique domains were found.

2.2 Analysis

Looking at the number of unique IP addresses a sender has shows a large range (Figure 1). 72% of senders have only one IP address, 85% of senders have one or two IP addresses, and 15% of senders have three or more IP addresses. However, these results are tempered by the number of emails that are sent from different numbers of IP addresses. Only 16% of emails were sent by senders with one

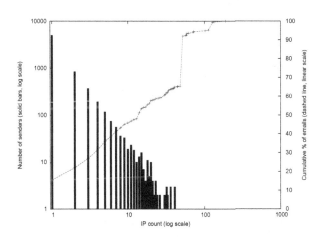

Fig. 1. IP address counts vs. number of senders and amount of email sent

IP address, 22% of emails were sent by senders with one or two IP addresses, and the majority, 78%, of emails were sent by senders with more than three IP addresses.

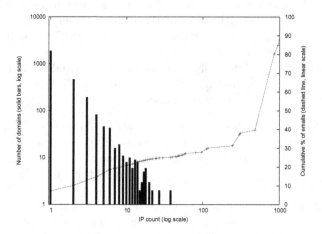

Fig. 2. IP address counts vs. number of domains and amount of email sent

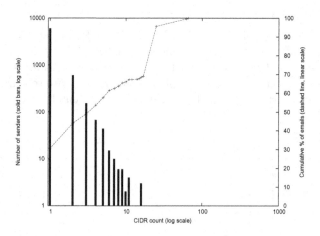

Fig. 3. CIDR address counts vs. number of senders and amount of email sent

A sender's email address also relates to a domain, which is the email provider's name that the email address is hosted at. Figure 2 shows an even larger variance of IP addresses amongst the domains. 66% of domains have only one IP address, 82% have one or two IP addresses, and the remaining 18% domains have three or more IP addresses. Furthermore, there is one domain (not shown) that has 1128 different IP addresses. We observed most emails were sent from domains with

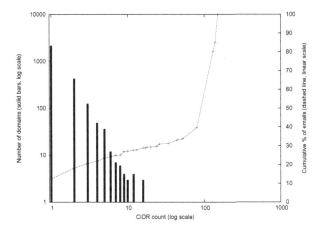

Fig. 4. CIDR address counts vs. number of domains and amount of email sent

more than three IP addresses. That is, 90% of emails were sent from domains which have more than three IP addresses, and the remaining 10% of emails were sent from domains which have one or two IP addresses.

One factor that might cause large sets of IP addresses for some senders is dynamic IP addresses. In an attempt to mitigate this effect, we used `whois` to map senders' IP addresses into their corresponding CIDR address. With CIDR lookups, the IPs for a single sender reduced significantly (Figure 3). That is, 87% of senders have one CIDR address and 95% of senders have one or two CIDR addresses, and only 5% of senders have three or more CIDR addresses. In terms of number of emails, we observed an increase in the emails sent from senders with one or two CIDR addresses to 44%, and a decrease in emails sent from senders with three or more CIDR addresses to 56%.

We performed the same analysis on the domains' CIDR addresses. Figure 4 shows that the number of CIDR addresses of domains also reduced significantly. 76% of domains have only one CIDR address, 91% have one or two CIDR addresses, and the remaining 9% of domains have three or more CIDR addresses. After mapping IP addresses to CIDR addresses, there is a significant difference in the total number of emails sent from different groups of CIDR addresses: the 91% of domains with one or two CIDR addresses contribute 18% of total emails.

Turning now to geolocation, we mapped senders' IP addresses into city and country granularity using `IPInfoDB`.[4] Again, we are interested in consistency rather than mapping accuracy.

A total number of 1310 unique cities and 113 unique countries were found in our data. From Figure 5a we observed 92% of senders were only located in one city, over 97% senders were located in one or two cities, and just 3% of senders were located in three or more cities.

Figure 5b shows an even stronger correlation between senders and their countries. 96% of senders only send email from one country, 99% of senders were

---

[4] `http://ipinfodb.com`

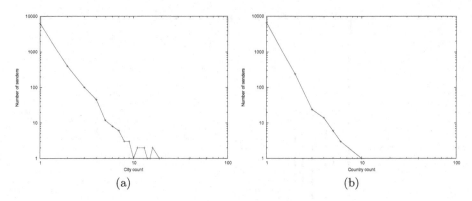

Fig. 5. Number of senders vs. city (a) and country (b) counts, log-log scale

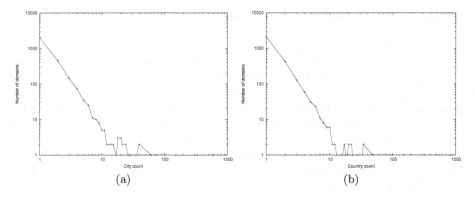

Fig. 6. Number of domains vs. city (a) and country (b) counts, log-log scale

located in one or two countries, and only 1% of senders were located in three or more countries.

We find there is a strong correlation between senders and their city/country location, but this is less so for the domains. In Figure 6a we observed 72% of domains located in one city, 88% domains located in one or two cities, and 12% of domains located in three or more cities. Figure 6b shows 74% of domains send email from one country, 89% of domains are located in one or two countries, and the remaining 11% of domains are located in three or more countries.

2.3 Discussion

Our results indicate that the majority of senders have four properties. They have a small set of IP addresses; they have a small set of CIDR addresses; they have highly consistent city geolocation; they have highly consistent country geolocation. From any or all of these, we may construct an email forgery classifier that will flag emails from known senders whose email comes from an unexpected location. The fact that many emails, in terms of volume, do not fit this profile is not a major concern, as we are not trying to construct a general anti-spam solution, but detect forgery for known senders – the important criterion is that the vast majority of senders *do* have these properties.

Domain information was less stable and, for example, we observed a large number of emails were sent from domains with more than three IP and CIDR addresses. This might indicate large web-based mail providers (e.g., Yahoo!, Gmail, Hotmail), or may be attributable to some participants retaining some spam in their saved mail.

There are several limitations with our data analysis. First, while we collected a large number of real emails, the sample may be biased, and it would be helpful to repeat this experiment with a larger sample size. Demographic information about the study participants would be interesting to collect in a larger study, although the demographic of email senders may be equally interesting (but much harder to collect). Second, emails which are sent from some web-based email clients (e.g., Gmail) do not reveal their true IP addresses. Often, the only traceable IP is the the email provider's mail server IPs, and the sender's true IP address is not shown in the RF header. If a forged email is sent from the same web-based mail provider as a legitimate email, then it is not possible to distinguish them by IP addresses. In order to solve this problem, we recommend that web-based email providers log the sender's IP from their TCP connection into the email header; this can be used to detect forged emails sent from web-based providers. Third, geolocation databases will inevitably have some minor inaccuracies that may affect city and country mapping. If more accuracy is needed, it is possible to query multiple geolocation databases. Finally, some senders might never have a consistent geolocation. That is, it is possible that a person travels consistently and sends email from different geolocations, or a person always uses anonymous proxies (e.g., Tor [12]). For this type of user, no geolocation-based technique will apply. While we know our method is not a perfect solution that is suitable for all senders, it can be used for a majority of senders, and it can be combined with other forgery detection mechanisms, like stylometry.

3   Stylometry

The stylometry problem may be stated informally as follows. Say that Alice receives a piece of email that purports to be from Bob. Alice and Bob have exchanged emails in the past, and consequently Alice has a collection of past email messages from Bob. Can the characteristics of Bob's past email be used to determine if the latest email is really from Bob? Any solution, as part of an email system, must be fully automated and not require preselection of features, have low overhead, make a decision using short inputs, and be scalable from one past email correspondent to arbitrarily many. Ideally, a solution should not be limited to English text; obviously, a solution should have high accuracy.

It seemed to be a straightforward application of existing computer forensic techniques, at first. However, upon closer examination, most previous work on authorship analysis addresses a different problem: let $\{S_1, S_2...., S_n\}$, $n \geq 2$, be the set of senders in the training database. There is a collection of email E_i for each $S_i \in \{S_1, S_2...., S_n\}$, and $|E_i| \geq 1$. Upon receiving a suspect email, M, with unknown authorship, identify the author S_a from $\{S_1, S_2...., S_n\}$ whose writing style most closely matches the writing style of M.

In other words, the "usual suspects" have already been rounded up; it is simply a question of "whodunnit?" This unfortunately does not work in our case. Our solution has to work even if there is only one sender present in the training database, and there is no guarantee that the sender comes from a known set. Much seemingly related work is thus not applicable.

Instead, our problem falls into a subarea of authorship analysis called "author identification" in Zheng et al.'s taxonomy, which computes 'the likelihood of a particular author having written a piece of work by examining other works produced by that author' [34, page 60]. Formally, let $\{S_1, S_2...., S_n\}$, $n \geq 1$, be the set of senders in the training database. There is a collection of email E_i for each $S_i \in \{S_1, S_2...., S_n\}$, and $|E_i| \geq 1$. Upon receiving a suspect email, M, which claims it is from author S_a, where $S_a \in \{S_1, S_2...., S_n\}$, identify how likely it is that M is written by S_a.

3.1 Our Method

We based our stylometry system on the SpamBayes statistical spam filter[5] [24] inheriting, among other things, various canonicalizations of emails and a χ^2 method of combining the probability scores for individual tokens in a new email. We switched the tokenizer to an N-gram tokenizer (N = 5), because we found it gave us better accuracy in our experiments (similar to Kanaris et al. [20]) and also allows our system to be language-independent.

The usual approach would be to train SpamBayes with ham and spam, and create a single database. Instead, we had a separate database for each known email sender, training on legitimate email from each respective sender and telling SpamBayes that the email was all ham.

As a consequence of training on ham from a given sender only, the assumption that the training corpora are half ham and half spam no longer applies. Therefore, when classifying a new email, we have moved away from Robinson's calculation [28] and instead compute a token's probability score using the simplified formula

$$prob = \frac{P \times S + n}{S + n} \qquad (1)$$

Here, n = number of times the token occurs in the dictionary; P is the probability of an unknown token. From testing on the Enron corpus, $P = 0.3$ yields the best result. S is the strength of an unknown token. It adjusts the weight of probability of this token by counting n. $S = 0$ means the token is always believed 100%; from testing of the Enron corpus, $S = 0.6$ yields the best result.

---

[5] http://spambayes.sourceforge.net, version 1.0.4.

3.2   Experiments

The Enron corpus [19] is the data source used in our experiment; it contains 200,399 real emails from 158 users.

Forwarded emails written by other people can affect author identification results, so they must be removed. The Enron corpus contains many different formats for forwarding information in emails, so we manually filtered out forwarded content.[6] Manual selection might bias the result, but we tried to minimize the impact: we only filtered out forwarded contents of each email, and other than stripping out forwarded content, the original text remained unchanged.

Each experiment was run 30 times and the arithmetic mean is reported here. Each experiment included a training and testing phase. Training and testing emails were selected randomly for each test to reduce bias.

We first trained the engine with a set of legitimate emails from a sender, S. Emails from other senders were taken as the testing emails. The From: header from all testing emails was forged to the email address of the sender S, then each testing email was sent to the engine to query for the probability of the email being written by the sender S.

Table 1. Confusion matrix

		Predicted Class	
		Positive	Negative
Actual	Positive	True Positive (TP)	False Negative (FN)
Class	Negative	False Positive (FP)	True Negative (TN)

We use the matrix in Table 1 to calculate statistical measurement in this experiment. True negative (TN) measurement, which means the engine classifying a forged email as not legitimate, is the most important measurement because it represents whether or not our method successfully classifies a forged email, so our precision and recall are focused on it rather than true positives; F_1 is the normalized mean of precision and recall.

$$Recall\ (R)\ =\ \frac{TN}{TN + FP} \tag{2}$$

$$Precision\ (P)\ =\ \frac{TN}{TN + FN} \tag{3}$$

$$F_1\ =\ \frac{2PR}{P + R} \tag{4}$$

The probability of classifying a forged email with our method is further broken into five intervals for detailed analysis: $[0, 0.25)$, $[0.25, 0.5)$, 0.5, $(0.5, 0.75)$, and

---

[6] We note that Iqbal et al. [17] also manually filtered Enron emails in their study. A production system would, of course, do this automatically, but we wanted to ensure a clean data set for experiments.

[0.75, 1]. A probability of 0 means the email is most likely not composed by the author, 1 means it most likely is, and 0.5 means not sure. Any value below 0.5 implies TN, 0.5 implies neutral, and greater than 0.5 implies FP.

We ran this experiment with four different sets of training emails: 10, 20, 30, and 40. Testing against different numbers of training emails is important because of two things that occur in real world conditions. First, it is not necessarily the case that users always train a large fraction of total emails across all senders – some senders might have more training emails than the others, and they will not be perfectly balanced. Second, users might only train the engine with a fixed number of training emails from a sender and use the fixed set of training emails for all further classification.

We randomly selected six authors for this experiment. For each author, we first trained the engine with a fixed number of emails (randomly selected), then we took all emails from all other authors (5 authors, 50 emails each, for a total of 250 emails). These 250 testing emails' From: header email address was forged to the email address of the author trained in the engine. Then each testing email was sent to the engine for querying the probability score.

Table 2. Forging emails: classification scores divided into intervals of forging email senders, training 10 emails

	Authors					
	Allen	Beck	Blair	Cash	Haedicke	Heard
[0, 0.25)	0	0	0	0	0	0
[0.25,0.5)	6942	7292	7112	7100	7124	7037
0.5	528	152	315	352	345	405
(0.5, 0.75)	0	56	43	18	1	28
[0.75, 1]	0	0	0	0	0	0

Table 3. Forging emails: precision, recall, and F_1 of forging email senders, training 10 emails

	Authors					
	Allen	Beck	Blair	Cash	Haedicke	Heard
R	100%	99.0%	99.4%	99.7%	100%	99.6%
P	100%	100%	100%	100%	100%	100%
F_1	100%	99.6%	99.7%	99.9%	99.9%	99.8%

We show the detailed classification scores of 10 training emails divided into intervals in Table 2; Table 3 shows the corresponding precision, recall, and F_1 values. Our method was almost perfect on recall, precision, and F_1 against forged emails with only 10 training emails from each author. Table 4 gives the F_1 values computed from the tests of all different numbers of training emails (e.g. 10, 20, 30, and 40). In general, our method is still able to produce close to 100% F_1 values against forged emails.

Table 4. Forging emails: F_1 values of different number of training emails

	Authors					
	Allen	Beck	Blair	Cash	Haedicke	Heard
F_1 (T=10)	100.00%	99.60%	99.70%	99.90%	99.90%	99.80%
F_1 (T=20)	99.80%	98.00%	98.60%	99.10%	99.40%	98.80%
F_1 (T=30)	99.30%	95.60%	97.60%	97.50%	98.90%	97.40%
F_1 (T=40)	99.00%	92.70%	96.40%	94.90%	97.70%	96.00%

Of course, forged emails will (hopefully) be the exception rather than the norm, and we also looked at the classification accuracy for the sender's own emails. For each sender, we took 14 emails of the sender and trained the engine, and then the remaining emails from the sender were used for testing emails. Table 5 shows the results of testing a sender's own emails. Our method is able to perform adequately in terms of precision, recall, and F_1.

Table 5. Precision, recall, and F_1 of each sender's own emails: 14 training emails

	Authors					
	Allen	Beck	Blair	Cash	Haedicke	Heard
R	100%	100%	100%	100%	100%	100%
P	62%	82%	91%	84%	65%	98%
F_1	77%	90%	95%	91%	79%	99%

3.3 Discussion

Our method is able to classify both legitimate and forged emails with good classification accuracy. As with geolocation, the classification need not be perfect, as it can be used in conjunction with other methods.

We assume that an attacker does not know about the writing style of a sender; thus, one limitation of our method is that it might not work as well when the attacker gains knowledge about the sender. A possible scenario: what if a sender's computer is compromised and becomes a zombie machine, giving the attacker access to emails saved on the machine? The attacker can make use of the saved emails and forge emails with a very similar writing style to the legitimate sender; this type of attack was discussed in [3]. Manual attempts to imitate writing style are examined with respect to authorship analysis in [5]. In the case of automated or manual style imitation, our method might not be able to distinguish between legitimate and forged emails because the writing styles would be very similar.

4 Related Work

Related geolocation work. There is much existing work that examines the characteristics of spam, spammers, and IP addresses.

Ramachandran et al. [26] studied spammers' traffic at the network level. Among other things, they found that both spam and legitimate emails can come from similar IP address spaces, so it is impossible to distinguish spam and non-spam email by IP addresses alone, in general. However, they did not examine legitimate emails in depth, and did not examine the role played by persistence in legitimate senders' IP addresses.

Cook et al. [10] looked to see if there were any indicators that spam was about to be sent from an IP address, but did not find any strong signs that conclusively flagged forthcoming spam. Again, this work is not looking at the same problem that we are.

Gomes et al. [15] collected 360,000 emails sent to a university and used SpamAssassin to classify the emails into spam and ham, gathering data about both. Most relevant is their observation that 'on average, a single sender domain is associated with 15 different IP addresses, whereas the average number of different domains per sender IP address is only 6' (page 359). However, this is only an aside and they do not discuss or analyze this further.

Sanchez et al. [29] want to find out whether or not spammers lie about their IP addresses in `Received:` headers. Their results showed this was a rarity, which is good news for forgery detection based on this information.

Xie et al. [33] studied dynamic IP addresses, discovering 'IP-to-host bindings changing from several hours to several days' (page 302). This suggests that the CIDR or city/country geolocation may be preferable for anti-forgery than the IP address itself.

The situation does not improve for emails sent from mobile phones. Balakrishnan et al. [4] studied geolocation for mobile phones' IP addresses, finding it wildly inaccurate at times. While they concluded that geolocation was 'impossible,' we observe that this does not mean that the accuracy will not improve over time, and in any case we only require consistency.

Email IP address geolocation falls into the subproblem of IP geolocation in Muir et al.'s [25] classification because, in our case, we will have an IP address but not necessarily an active TCP connection. Although IP address geolocation has many limitations as Muir et al. discussed, again we are interested in consistency rather than mapping accuracy.

Related stylometry work. A wide variety of techniques have been brought to bear on stylometry. Calix et al. [7] used a K-nearest neighbor (KNN) algorithm along with 55 stylistic features to classify the author of unknown emails. Corney [11] used a support vector machine (SVM) technique with extensive experiments to determine good features. Iqbal et al. [17] used features combined to create what they called 'write-prints,' meant to be analogous to fingerprints. Argamon et al. [2] used an exponentiated gradient learning algorithm. Frantzeskou et al. [13] used an N-gram tokenizer for analyzing source code authorship, along with a similarity measure of their own devising. A χ^2 approach was used by Vogel and Lynch [31] for classical works, and also by Luyckx and Daelemans [22]. The work we have found in this area typically suffers from one or more difficulties with respect to our problem criteria. For example, manually selecting features rather than automatically discovering them; expecting a small set of "suspects" to choose from; needing large amounts of text; not being language-independent. In comparison, our solution based on SpamBayes is both simple and effective.

5   Conclusion and Future Work

This paper examined the detection of email forgeries, mails that claim to be from a known sender, which includes a class of targeted email attacks. We addressed the problem by using two characteristics of the legitimate sender's email – geolocation and stylometry. While neither proffers perfect detection, they can be used in combination with each other or existing anti-spam techniques. All analysis can be done on the targeted user's side, without requiring a global overhaul of email, and leverages information and software that exists today.

Besides adding stylometry into our client-side plug-in, future work will examine other sources of sender location data. For example, using a sender's location from Facebook or Foursquare, or a special mobile application that posts encrypted location data to Twitter, may yield useful data for validating senders.

Acknowledgments. The authors' research is supported by the Natural Sciences and Engineering Research Council of Canada via ISSNet, the Internetworked Systems Security Network. This paper is based on the first author's thesis [21].

References

1. Allman, E., Callas, J., Delany, M., Libbey, M., Fenton, J., Thomas, M.: DomainKeys Identified Mail (DKIM) Signatures. RFC 4871 (Proposed Standard), Updated by RFC 5672 (May 2007)
2. Argamon, S., Šarić, M., Stein, S.S.: Style mining of electronic messages for multiple authorship discrimination: first results. In: 9th ACM SIGKDD International Conference on Knowledge Discovery and Data Mining, pp. 475–480 (2003)
3. Aycock, J., Friess, N.: Spam zombies from outer space. In: 15th Annual EICAR Conference, pp. 164–179 (2006)
4. Balakrishnan, M., Mohomed, I., Ramasubramanian, V.: Where's that phone?: geolocating IP addresses on 3G networks. In: 9th ACM SIGCOMM Conference on Internet Measurement, pp. 294–300 (2009)
5. Brennan, M., Greenstadt, R.: Practical attacks against authorship recognition techniques. In: 21st Innovative Applications of Artificial Intelligence Conference, pp. 60–65 (2009)
6. BusinessWeek. The new e-spionage threat. Cover story (April 10, 2008), http://www.businessweek.com/magazine/content/08_16/b4080032218430.htm
7. Calix, K., Connors, M., Levy, D., Manzar, H., McCabe, G., Westcott, S.: Stylometry for e-mail author identification and authentication. In: Proceedings of CSIS Research Day. Pace University (2008)
8. CBC News. Ottawa man victim of Facebook, email scam. News article (March 2, 2011), http://www.cbc.ca/news/canada/ottawa/story/2011/03/02/ottawa-facebook-scam.html

9. Cisco.com. Email attacks: This time its personal. Online resource (June 2011), http://www.cisco.com/en/US/prod/collateral/vpndevc/ps10128/ps10339/ps10354/targeted_attacks.pdf

10. Cook, D., Hartnett, J., Manderson, K., Scanlan, J.: Catching spam before it arrives: domain specific dynamic blacklists. In: 2006 Australasian Workshops on Grid Computing and e-Research, pp. 193–202 (2006)

11. Corney, M.: Analysing e-mail text authorship for forensic purposes. Master of Information Technology thesis, Queensland University of Technology (2003)

12. Dingledine, R., Mathewson, N., Syverson, P.: Tor: The second-generation onion router. In: 13th USENIX Security Symposium, pp. 303–320 (2004)

13. Frantzeskou, G., Stamatatos, E., Gritzalis, S., Katsikas, S.: Source code author identification based on n-gram author profiles. In: IFIP International Federation for Information Processing, pp. 508–515 (2006)

14. Gallagher, D.F.: E-mail scammers ask your friends for money. New York Times. Blog article (November 9, 2007). http://bits.blogs.nytimes.com/2007/11/09/e-mail-scammers-ask-your-friends-for-money/

15. Gomes, L.H., Cazita, C., Almeida, J.M., Almeida, V., Meira Jr., W.: Characterizing a spam traffic. In: 4th ACM SIGCOMM Conference on Internet Measurement, pp. 356–369 (2004)

16. Hemmingsen, R., Aycock, J., Jacobson Jr., M.: Spam, phishing, and the looming challenge of big botnets. In: EU Spam Symposium (2007)

17. Iqbal, F., Hadjidj, R., Fung, B.C., Debbabi, M.: A novel approach of mining write-prints for authorship attribution in e-mail forensics. Digital Investigation 5(suppl. 1), S42–S51 (2008)

18. Jagatic, T., Johnson, N., Jakobsson, M., Menczer, F.: Social phishing. Commun. ACM 50(10), 94–100 (2007)

19. Kaelbling, L.: Enron email dataset. CALO Project (August 21, 2009), http://www.cs.cmu.edu/~enron/

20. Kanaris, I., Kanaris, K., Houvardas, J., Stamatatos, E.: Words vs. character n-grams for anti-spam filtering. Int. Journal on Artificial Intelligence Tools (2007)

21. Lin, E.: Detecting email forgery. Master's thesis, University of Calgary (2011)

22. Luyckx, K., Daelemans, W.: Authorship attribution and verification with many authors and limited data. In: 22nd International Conference on Computational Linguistics, pp. 513–520 (2008)

23. MessageLabs. MessageLabs intelligence: 2010 annual security report, http://www.messagelabs.com/mlireport/MessageLabsIntelligence_2010_Annual_Report_FINAL.pdf

24. Meyer, T.A., Whateley, B.: SpamBayes: Effective open-source, Bayesian based, email classification system. In: 1st Conference on Email and Anti-Spam (2004)

25. Muir, J.A., Van Oorschot, P.C.: Internet geolocation: Evasion and counterevasion. ACM Comput. Surv. 42(1), 1–23 (2009)

26. Ramachandran, A., Feamster, N.: Understanding the network-level behavior of spammers. SIGCOMM Comput. Commun. Rev. 36(4), 291–302 (2006)

27. Rekhter, Y., Moskowitz, B., Karrenberg, D., de Groot, G.J., Lear, E.: Address Allocation for Private Internets. RFC 1918 (Best Current Practice) (February 1996)

28. Robinson, G.: A statistical approach to the spam problem. Linux Journal 107 (March 2003)

29. Sanchez, F., Duan, Z., Dong, Y.: Understanding forgery properties of spam delivery paths. In: Proc. 7th Annual Collaboration, Electronic Messaging, Anti-Abuse and Spam Conference (CEAS), pp. 13–14 (July 2010)

30. ThreatPost.com. RSA: SecurID attack was phishing via an Excel spreadsheet. Blog article (April 1, 2011), `http://threatpost.com/en_us/blogs/rsa-securid-attack-was-phishing-excel-spreadsheet-040111`
31. Vogel, C., Lynch, G.: Computational stylometry: Who's in a play? In: Verbal and Nonverbal Features of Human-Human and Human-Machine Interaction: COST Action 2102 International Conference, Revised Papers, pp. 169–186 (2008)
32. Wong, M., Schlitt, W.: Sender Policy Framework (SPF) for Authorizing Use of Domains in E-Mail, Version 1. RFC 4408 (Experimental) (April 2006)
33. Xie, Y., Yu, F., Achan, K., Gillum, E., Goldszmidt, M., Wobber, T.: How dynamic are IP addresses? In: 2007 Conference on Applications, Technologies, Architectures, and Protocols for Computer Communications, pp. 301–312 (2007)
34. Zheng, R., Qin, Y., Huang, Z., Chen, H.: Authorship Analysis in Cybercrime Investigation. In: Chen, H., Miranda, R., Zeng, D.D., Demchak, C.C., Schroeder, J., Madhusudan, T. (eds.) ISI 2003. LNCS, vol. 2665, pp. 59–73. Springer, Heidelberg (2003)

AIGG Threshold Based HTTP GET Flooding Attack Detection

Yang-seo Choi, Ik-Kyun Kim, Jin-Tae Oh, and Jong-Soo Jang

Cyber Security-Convergence Research Department, ETRI
218, Gajeong-no, Yuseong-gu, Daejeon, 305-700, South Korea
{yschoi92,ikkim21,showme,jsjang}@etri.re.kr
http://www.etri.re.kr

Abstract. Distributed denial-of-service (DDoS) attacks still pose un-predictable threats to the Internet infrastructure and Internet-based businesses. As the attackers focus on economic gain, the HTTP GET Flooding attacks against the business web servers become one of the most frequently attempted attacks. Furthermore, the attack is becoming more sophisticated. In order to detect those attacks, several algorithms are developed. However, even though the developed technologies can de-tect the sophisticated attacks some of them need lots of system resources [12,13]. Sometimes due to the time consuming processes the whole per-formance of DDoS defense systems is degraded and it becomes another problem. For that, we propose a simple threshold based HTTP GET flooding attack detection algorithm. The threshold is generated from the characteristics of HTTP GET Request behaviors. In this algorithm, based on the defined monitoring period (MP) and Time Slot (TS), we cal-culate the Average **Inter-GET_Request_Packet_Exist_TS-Gap** ($AIGG$). The $AIGG$ is used for threshold extraction. For effective detection, the optimized MP, TS and the threshold value, are extracted. In addition, the proposed algorithm doesn't need to analyze every HTTP GET re-quest packet so it needs less CPU resources than the algorithms which have to analyze all the request packets.

Keywords: DDoS Attack, HTTP GET Flooding Attack Detection, Network Security.

1 Introduction

While more than ten years have passed since the first DDoS attack was dis-covered, it still remains one of the most dangerous attacks against current IT environments such as 7.7 DDoS attack [1] and 3.4 DDoS attack [2]. There are various DDoS attack types such as simple flooding attacks, which utilize Internet protocols (TCP, ICMP, etc.), and sophisticated application layer DDoS attacks, which are dedicated to specific applications [4]. Among these, one of the most popular attacks is the HTTP GET flooding attack [3].

In the past, the purpose of a DDoS attack was to render a network inaccessible by generating a high amount of network traffic that would crash servers, over-whelm routers, or otherwise prevent network devices from functioning properly

D.H. Lee and M. Yung (Eds.): WISA 2012, LNCS 7690, pp. 270–284, 2012.
© Springer-Verlag Berlin Heidelberg 2012

[4]. Recently, however, DDoS attack trends have been altered and now focus on economic gain. For example, a hacker may demand payment from a company in exchange for not being attacked. For this type of attack, the perpetrators do not want to paralyze an entire network and its systems. They only need the target application layer service to be unavailable to legitimate users.

In order to bring down only specified target services, the attackers do not have to generate a massive amount of attack traffic. In fact, if we examine each sophisticatedly generated attack traffic, they appear to be the same as a normal legitimate traffic and their volumes are also equally small. In other words, it is very difficult to detect an HTTP GET Flooding attack using only an attack traffic bandwidth analysis that is widely applied to current anti-DDoS attack detection systems.

In order to overcome this situations, many researchers have developed the HTTP GET Flooding detection methods with complicated statistical algorithms. However, due to the high complexity of the proposed techniques, some of them have to spend a lot of time for detecting the attacks. This is because these techniques have to analyze various pieces of information gathered from a lot of network packets or Web server log files. In some cases, if massive HTTP GET Flooding attack is occurred the detection methods couldn't handle the situations. Therefore, even though the various kind of information is utilized, the detection mechanism should be very simple.

In order to overcome this situation, we propose a new threshold-based detection method that can detect the attack based on the abstracted information of the HTTP GET request packet transmission behavior. In fact, we utilize the HTTP GET Request behavior. Basically, the HTTP GET flooding attack transmits more HTTP GET request packets to the target server than the server can handle. So, the characteristics of HTTP GET request packets are different between normal and attack traffics. Beside, the threshold-based detection method is very simple so it doesn't need that much CPU time. And, the proposed method does not need to investigate every network packet so it is relatively simpler and faster than other methods and utilizes the HTTP GET request behaviors as well.

The remainder of this paper is organized as follows. In section 2, we present related works and current problems. In section 3, we describe the details of the HTTP GET request traffic characteristics. In section 4, the detection mechanism will be depicted and in Section 5 we evaluate the proposed method and provide comparison results with previously developed defense methods. Finally, we conclude this paper in section 6.

2 Related Works

Currently, a number of researches on defending network layer DDoS attacks have been conducted using various methods such as anomaly detection [5], ingress/egress filtering [6], IP trace back [7,8], ISP collaborative defense [9], etc. However, the main attack types have been changed to sophisticated application layer DDoS attacks. And the HTTP GET Flooding attack became the most critical and frequently attempted attacks.

S. Ranjan et al. proposed a counter-mechanism that consists of a suspicion assignment mechanism and DDoS-resilient scheduler, DDoS Shield, by building a legitimate user model for each service and detecting suspicious requests based on their content [13]. Jie Yu et al. proposed the trust management helmet (TMH). Its key insight is that a server should give priority to protecting the connectivity of good users during application layer DDoS attacks, instead of identifying all attack requests. The trust in clients is evaluated based on their visit history, and is used to schedule service to their requests [17]. T. Yatagai et al. proposed a HTTP-GET flooding attack detection method that utilizes page browsing orders. If the browsing orders of pages are the same between different sessions, then all systems that request the same web pages are decided as attackers [10]. W. Lu et al. proposed a DDoS attack detection method that detects abnormalities of distribution in a requests arrival time. An attack decision is made using a hidden semi-Markov model (HSMM) [11]. Y. Xie et al. proposed an anomaly detector based on an HSMM to describe the dynamics of an access matrix and to detect attacks. The entropy of document popularity fitting to the model was used to detect potential application-layer DDoS attacks [12]. Jaydip Sen proposed a statistic information based web server protection method. The load of the attacked system is calculated and used for attack detection [14]. Debasish Das et al. proposed an multi scenarios detection methods. In this paper, they utilized the HTTP request arrival rates. In an index reflection attack [16], the clients in a P2P network are utilized as attackers and do not need to control any botnets. Thus, it is very easy to perform this type of attack. Since application layer DDoS attacks are non-intrusive and protocol-compliant, attackers are indistinguishable based on packets or protocols, and thus these attacks cannot be defended against using network layer solutions. Clearly, new defense mechanisms are required for application layer DDoS attacks.

These detection methods are mainly focused on HTTP GET Flooding attacks, and some of them require a high amount of computation. However, we propose an effective HTTP GET flooding attack detection method that utilizes the continuity and repetition of service request behavior.

3   HTTP GET Request Traffic Characteristics

3.1   Normal HTTP GET Request Traffic

Under a normal situation, when a user requests a web page in a web server via a web browser, the server provides the content as a web page. During the web browsing process, when the requested web page is arrived at client side, the web browser parsing the arrived page and requests in-line objects automatically in a very short period of time. When all the contents are arrived, the user reads the contents of the web page. After a while, the user requests another web page based on the links gathered from the first page.

In this normal web page exploring sequence, however, HTTP GET request packets are generated in a very short period of time and there are no requests for a while. It is because, a user needs to identify the contents of the web page and decide the next action, for that it usually takes more than several seconds. This time period is called as a think time. It means in a normal situation, the service request and reply process is a kind of spot transaction in a certain time period. It's not continuous and repeated during a specified monitoring period. This web page requesting process is depicted in Fig. 1.

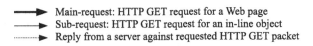

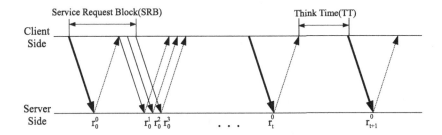

Fig. 1. HTTP GET request and reply process. This shows there are several in-line objects in a Web page, and many HTTP GET request packets are generated automatically for them in a very short period of time.

In this paper, we call the series of HTTP GET request packets from the main-request to the last sub-request for the last in-line object in a Web page a Service Request Block (SRB), and the time period of SRB is called the Service Request Block Time (SRBT). In addition, we call the Think Time as TT.

All the normal traffics which are used for the experiments in this paper are gathered from a real network during the real sites access. However, the attack traffics are collected from a testbed. The network in our testbed is configured with 23 1U size servers, two layer-2 gigabit switches, one 10 gigabit switch with 24 gigabit interfaces and two 10 gigabit interfaces and two routers. We installed the real botnet and 7.7 DDoS attack tools in the testbed and generated the attack traffics.

3.2   Comparison between Normal and Attack Traffic

The most different characteristics between attack and normal HTTP GET request traffic are the `Inter-GET_Request_Packet-Gap` and the HTTP GET Request count. So, those are utilized for threshold based HTTP GET Flooding detection. However, these days, the characteristics of attack traffic are very much similar to normal one. So, it is very difficult to detect the attack with those thresholds.

First, as we can see in Fig. 2, the `Inter-GET_Request_Packet-Gaps` between sub-requests are very short. Usually, they are less than the gaps of requests from the sophisticatedly generated attack traffic. This is why the `Inter-GET_Request_Packet-Gap` threshold cannot be used for HTTP GET flooding attack detection.

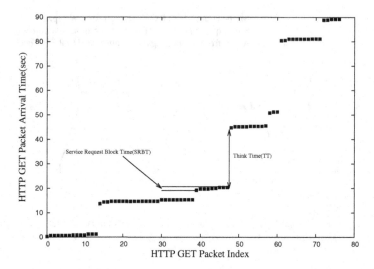

Fig. 2. HTTP GET Request packet arrival time (https://www.auction.co.kr). In this figure, each mark identifies each session and the traffic is captured from the beginning of the web site access.

Second, as we can see in Fig. 3, in some time period, the number of HTTP GET request count from a normal traffic is bigger than that of attack traffic, so it is not possible to use this character to detect it.

3.3   HTTP GET Flooding Attack Scenarios

The HTTP GET flooding attack can be classified into four categories based on its traffic characteristics. The first type is a simple flooding attack that generates as many HTTP GET request packets as possible with the full performance of zombie PCs. The second type is a sophisticatedly generated attack whose bandwidth and `Inter-GET_Request_Packet-Gap` lies between normal ranges, but generates attacks continuously and repeatedly. The third type is a one-shot type attack in which the traffic characteristics are very similar to a flash cloud. Lastly, the fourth type is attacks that utilize the vulnerabilities of application protocols or specific Web servers such as Slowloris [22] and R.U.D.Y [23].

Among these types of attacks, the second type is the most frequently attempted because it is quite difficult to detect. In fact, the first type of attack could be detected easily with the count of GET request or Inter_GET_Packet_Gap

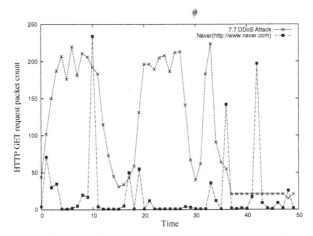

Fig. 3. The number of HTTP GET request packets per two seconds from 7.7 DDoS attack traffic and a normal portal site accessing traffic

based threshold. The black and white list based attacker filtering method can handle the third type of attack. And the fourth type of attack is not a flooding attack. It is a kind of exploit which utilizes a vulnerability in a system. Therefore, if the vulnerability is removed then the attack doesn't work anymore.

So, in this paper, we are focusing on the second type of attack. The traffic characteristics of this type of attacks are very similar to normal traffic, and thus it is difficult to detect this type of attack with a simple threshold-based detection method. In fact, the 7.7 DDoS and 3.4 DDoS attacks are also included in this type of attack. We call this type of attack as the sophisticated HTTP GET Flooding attack.

4   Detection Algorithm

4.1   Main Idea

In fact, the `Inter-GET_Request_Packet-Gap` and the number of HTTP GET request count shows quite good characteristics for HTTP GET Flooding attack detection. However, in some normal traffics, the `Inter-GET_Request_Packet-Gap` is shorter and the number of HTTP GET request count is bigger than attack traffic. It is because of the sub-requests.

The `Inter-GET_Request_Packet-Gap` of normal traffic is shorter because the sub-requests are generated in a very short period of time. Also, the number of HTTP GET request count is bigger than and attack traffic because in some cases, there are too many in-line objects that have to be automatically requested right after the main-request.

Therefore,   if   the   sub-request   can   be   removed   then   the `Inter-GET_Request_Packet-Gap` and the number of HTTP GET request count could be quite suitable characteristics for sophisticated HTTP GET

Flooding attack. In other words, if it is possible not to add the sub-requests to the total count of HTTP GET request count then the count could be used for the attack detection. Also, if it is possible to get rid of the sub-requests while measuring the `Inter-GET_Request_Packet-Gap` then it also could be used for the attack detection. In a normal situation, as we can see in Fig. 2, the sub-request are occurred in a very short period time right after the main-request is generated. Therefore, if we count only one request among SRB, then the sub-requests could be abstracted and removed. For that the best way is to know SRBT and TT. In a normal case there would be only one main-request during SRBT and TT. So, if we can monitor the traffic during SRBT and TT, the traffic characteristics would be different between normal traffic and attack traffic.

However, to measure the TT in a session, the URI in every HTTP GET request packet has to be investigated in order to determine whether the request is a main-request or sub-request. Also, we have to have all information about every object in the Web server. This is almost impossible because many Web pages and in-line objects in a Web server are dynamically created and removed. Even though we can handle the information, the requested object identification, HTTP packet detection, URI extraction, and URI comparison processes are time consuming processes, and thus it is very difficult to measure the TT quickly enough for real-time DDoS attack detection.

So, we define two monitoring periods which can be used instead of SRBT and TT. They are Monitoring Period(MP) and Time Slot(TS). MP and TS is calculated before the detection phase and will be utilized for attack detection.

Definition 1. Monitoring Period (MP). The monitoring period (MP) is defined as the biggest time period that is bigger than the SRBT and less than SRBT + RTT + TT in a session. The MP consists of N Time Slots. The entire fixed time period and number of Time Slots are decided by the HTTP GET Request traffic characteristics.

Definition 2. Time Slot (TS). The Time Slot is defined as the smallest time period that is bigger than the SRBT in a session. The TS is the unit time and N TSs make up one monitoring period.

In a normal situation, the TT is much bigger than the SRBT, and thus the length of the MP is also much bigger than that of the TS. Therefore, there could be many TS in one MP. Also, in a normal session, the HTTP GET request packets can exist only at the first TS. However, in an attack situation, the TT is relatively short, and therefore there could be many more HTTP GET request exist TS than normal traffic. Thus, if we calculate the average `Inter-GET_Packet_Exist_TS-Gap` (AIGG) during an MP then the AIGG in normal traffic is bigger than the AIGG in attack traffic. We use this characteristic to detect the HTTP GET flooding attacks.

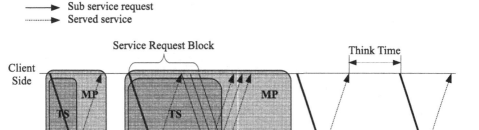

Fig. 4. Monitoring period (MP) and Time Slot (TS)

4.2   Optimal Duration Selection for an MP and TS

The time periods of MP and TS are different for each session. Thus, to use exact MP and TS for the dedicated sessions, the periods have to be identified during the detection process. However, if it is calculated during the detection process, it also a burden for detection system. So, we calculate it before the detection process and use it. For that, we analyzed normal traffic which captured from a university in Daejeon, South Korea, and attack traffic captured from our lab with 7.7 DDoS attack tools. The analysis process is as follows:

☐ Average SRBT and TT calculations from normal traffic

☐ Based on the calculated average SRBT and TT, select some candidate time periods of MP and TS

☐ AIGG calculation with selected candidates from attack and normal traffic

☐ Euclidean distance (ED) calculation between AIGG of attack traffic and normal traffic with same MP and TS periods.

☐ Normalization of calculated ED

☐ Select the MP and TS period for the biggest ED as the optimized period

The average SRBT and TT from normal traffic were 214 msec and 5.884 sec. Thus, we have selected 1/2/4 sec as the time period candidates of MP and 100/200/400 msec for the TS. With these candidates, we calculated the AIGG with normal and attack traffic. During the AIGG calculation against the various MP candidates, the TS period was fixed at 100 msec, while the MP was fixed at 2 sec during the AIGG calculation against the various TS candidates.

Afterward, the EDs with the AIGGs were calculated and normalized by dividing them with the number of TS. The calculated AIGG, ED, and normalized ED for the candidates are shown in Table 1 and 2. Based on the results, we

Table 1. Optimized MP selection with fixed TS (100 msec)

MP (sec)	1	2	4
AIGG (Normal)	7.0428	13.8155	26.0355
AIGG (Attack)	1.4149	1.5052	1.6999
ED	5.6279	12.3103	24.3356
Normalized ED	0.56279	**0.61552**	0.60839

Table 2. Optimized TS selection with fixed MP (2 sec)

Timeslot (msec)	100	200	400
AIGG (Normal)	14.2155	7.3478	4.0716
AIGG (Attack)	1.5052	1.0779	1.0702
ED	12.7103	6.2699	3.0014
Normalized ED	**0.63552**	0.62699	0.60028

selected the time period of the MP and TS as 2 sec and 100 msec for HTTP GET flooding attack detection.

4.3 Threshold Selection

To select the optimal threshold we investigated the detection rates and false positive rates with every possible threshold against attack and normal traffic based on the selected time periods of the MP and TS. The results are shown in Fig. 5, 6 and Table 3. Based on the results, we selected 1.9 as the optimal threshold.

Table 3. Detection and false positive rates for threshold selection

Threshold	1.7	1.8	1.9	2.0	2.1
Detection Rates	0.5143	0.5143	0.9714	0.9714	0.9714
False Positive Rates	0.0170	0.0170	0.0222	0.0286	0.0286

4.4 Detection Process

When a new HTTP GET request packet is detected, the session is monitored during an MP. During this monitoring period, only one HTTP GET packet is counted and used for IGG calculation per TS. When an MP is passed, then the AIGG of the session is calculated and compared with the selected threshold. After that, if the calculated AIGG is smaller than the threshold it is then classified as an attack session. A detailed explanation of the detection process is shown in Fig. 7.

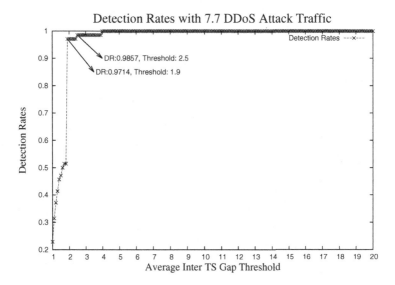

Fig. 5. Detection rates with 7.7 DDoS attack traffic

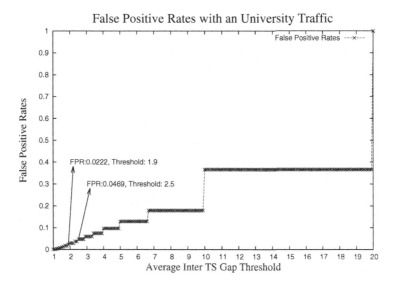

Fig. 6. False positive rates with normal traffic at a university

5   Experimental Results

5.1   Detection Performance

For a detection performance evaluation, we tested the following 10 traffics shown in Table 4 with the selected parameters: TS, 100 msec, MP, 2 sec; and threshold, 1.9.

Table 4. Traffic list for detection performance evaluation

Traffic Type	Name	Period	Traffic volume
Normal	Shopping mall (http://www.auction.co.kr/)	2m 1s	57MB
	Bank (http://www.wooribank.co.kr/)	1m 34s	4MB
	Portal site1 (http://www.daum.net/)	2m 48s	9MB
	Portal site2 (http://www.naver.com/)	2m 26s	20MB
	Research institute (http://www.etri.re.kr/)	1m 54s	4MB
	Government (http://www.metro.daejeon.kr/)	3m 54s	4MB
	An university in Daejeon	49m 8s	375GB
Attack	7.7 DDoS Attack	2m 51sec	231MB
	Black Energy [19]	5m 50s	23MB
	Netbot [20]	3m 9s	53MB

The detection rates (DR) against attack traffic and false positive rates (FPR) against normal traffic are shown in Table 5. The average DR and FPR are 98.84% and 4.97%. The DR and FPR of the proposed method are compared with other detection techniques and they are shown in Table 6.

Table 5. Detection and false positive rates for each traffic

Traffic Type		Total num. of new sessions	Attack session	Normal session	Detection rates	False positive rates
Normal	Shopping mall	66	1	65	-	1.52%
	Bank	28	0	28	-	0.00%
	Portal site1	112	0	112	-	0.00%
	Portal site2	110	0	110	-	0.00%
	Research institute	38	0	38	-	0.00%
	Government	59	1	58	-	1.69%
	University	4511	243	4268	-	5.39%
Attack	7.7 DDoS Attack	69	67	2	97.10%	-
	Black Energy	23	23	0	100.00%	-
	Netbot	80	80	0	100.00%	-

5.2 Execution Performance

Unfortunately, we can't compare the execution performances with other algorithms because we can't get their original source codes. So, in this section we add our own execution time for new session management, TS information update and attack decision.

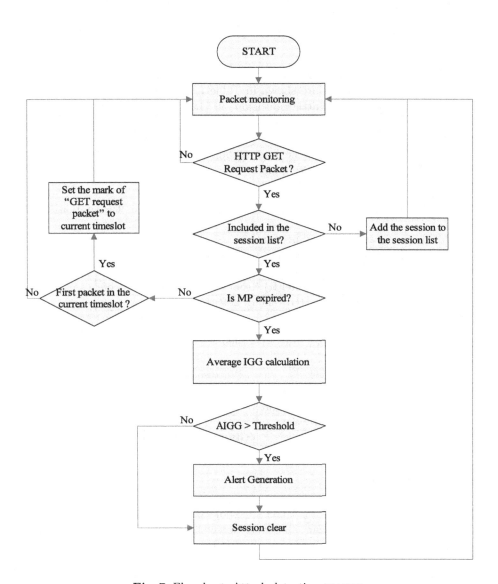

Fig. 7. Flowchart: Attack detection process

Table 6. Detection performance comparison

Algorithms	Proposed method	[10]	[11]	[12]
Detection Rates	98.84%	100.0%	98.43%	98.0%
False positive rates	4.97%	9.0%	6.6%	1.5%

We have implemented this proposed algorithm on the Linux system. The exact system specifications are shown in Table 7. For the new session creation, TS information update and attack decision, 36.5185 sec, 25.8786 sec, 11.6316 sec are needed respectively. The total average processing time for each HTTP GET request packet was 25.8432 sec. It means the proposed method can handle about 40,000 HTTP GET request packets per second. It would be more if the omitted HTTP GET request packets are added.

Table 7. A system specifications for proposed algorithm implementation

Classification	Specifications
Operating System	CentOS 5.4(Linux)
Kernel version	2.6.9-67.0.15.ELsmp
CPU	Intel(R) Xeon(TM) 3.60GHz Quad core
Memory	4GB(main), 2MB(Cache)

Table 8. Average processing time of simple method (sec)

Task	Processing time(sec)
New session creation	36.5185
TS information update	25.8786
Attack decision	11.6316
Memory	4GB(main), 2MB(Cache)

6 Conclusions

In this paper, we proposed an AIGG threshold based HTTP GET flooding attack detection method. It can effectively detect the most popular HTTP GET Flooding attack type, and is also applicable to the 7.7 DDoS attack, Netbot, Black Energy, and etc.

The proposed method is a threshold based detection method and needs only one HTTP GET packet in the same session during the same TS for attack detection. Therefore, it doesn't have to analyze every packet so it can reduce the workload of the attack detection process more effectively than other detection methods, as other methods have to analyze all the HTTP GET request packets or large log files. The detection rates and false positive rates are 98.84% and 4.97%.

In this paper, while we evaluate the detection performance of this method, the attacks are detected when a session is detected as an attack during an MP. However, the detection count could be managed. In other words, if we decide a session as an attack if three MPs consecutive MPs are detected an attacks, then the whole false positives rates could be dropped. In the future, this parameters will be analyzed for more accurate detection.

Acknowledgments. This work was supported by the IT R&D program of MKE/KIAT. [Development of Analysis Technologies against Unknown Virtualization-based Malicious Activity for Trusted Cloud Computing Service].

References

1. Arbor Networks ASERT Team: South Korea and US DDoS Attacks. ARBOR Networks (July 10, 2009)
2. Youm, H.Y.: Korea's experience of massive DDoS attacks from Botnet, ITU-T SG 17, Geneva (April 12, 2011), http://www.itu.int/en/ITU-T/studygroups/com17/Documents/tutorials/2011/ITU-T-ddos-tutorial-20110412-hyyoum.pdf
3. Monthly Internet Incidents Trends and Analysis, 2011. vol.12, Korea Internet & Security Agency (January 2012)
4. Mirkovic, J., Reiher, P.: A taxonomy of DDoS attack and DDoS defense mechanisms. ACM SIGCOMM Computer Communication 34(2), 39–53 (2004)
5. Mirkovic, J., Prier, G., Reiher, P.: Attacking DDoS at the Source. In: Proceedings of ICNP 2002, Paris, France, pp. 312–321 (November 2002)
6. Tupakula, U., Varadharajan, V.: A Practical Method to Counteract Denial of Service Attacks. In: Proceedings of ACSC 2003, Adelaide, Australia, pp. 275–284 (2003)
7. Lu, L., Chan, M., Chang, E.: Analysis of a General Probabilistic Packet Marking Model for IP Traceback. In: Proceedings of ASIACCS 2008 (2008)
8. Stone, R.: CenterTrack: An IP Overlay Network for Tracking DoS Floods. In: Proceeding of 9th Usenix Security Symposium (2002)
9. Chen, Y., Hwang, K., Ku, W.: Collaborative Detection of DDoS Attacks over Multiple Network Domains. IEEE Transations on Parallel and Distributed Systems (2007)
10. Yatagai, T., Isohara, T., Sasase, I.: Detection of HTTP-GET flood Attack Based on Analysis of Page Access Behavior. In: Proceeding of PACRIM 2007, pp. 232–235 (2007)
11. Lu, W.Z., Yu, S.Z.: An HTTP Flooding Detection Method Based on Browser Behavior. In: International Conference on IEEE Computational Intelligence and Security 2006, vol. 2, pp. 1151–1154 (November 2006)
12. Xie, Y., Yu, S.: A Large-Scale Hidden Semi-Markov Model for Anomaly Detection on User Browsing Behaviors. IEEE/ACM Transactions on Networking (2009)
13. Ranjan, S., Swaminathan, R., Uysal, M., et al.: DDoS-Shield: DDoS-Resilient Scheduling to Counter Application Layer Attacks. IEEE/ACM Transactions on Networking 7(1), 26–39 (2009)
14. Sen, J.: A Robust Mechanism for Defending Distributed Denial of Service Attacks On Web Servers. International Journal of Network Security & Its Applications (IJNSA) 3(2) (March 2011)

15. Das, D., Sharma, U., Bhattacharyya, D.K.: Detection of HTTP Flooding Attacks in Multiple Scenarios. In: Proceedings of the 2011 International Conference on Communication, Computing & Security (ICCCS 2011), pp. 517–522 (2011)
16. Liang, J., Naoumov, N., Ross, K.W.: The Index Poisoning Attack in P2P File Sharing Systems. In: Proceedings of INFOCOM 2006 (2006)
17. Yu, J., Fang, C., Lu, L., Li, Z.: A Lightweight Mechanism to Mitigate Application Layer DDoS Attacks. In: The 4th International ICST Conference on Scalable Information Systems (INFOSCALE 2009), Hong Kong, China, June 10-11 (2009)
18. Xie, Y., Yu, S.: Monitoring the Application-Layer DDoS Attacks for Popular Websites. IEEE/ACM Transactions on Networking (2009)
19. Nazario, J.: BlackEnergy DDoS Bot Anaysis. ARBOR Networks (October 2007)
20. Han, K., Im, E.: A Study on the Analysis of Netbot and Design of Detection Framework. In: Proceedings of JWIS 2009 (2009)
21. Electronics and Communications Research Institute (ETRI), http://www.etri.re.kr
22. Slowloris, http://ha.ckers.org/slowloris/
23. R.U.D.Y, http://code.google.com/p/r-u-dead-yet/
24. Universal HTTP Denial-of-Service,Hybrid Security, http://www.hybridsec.com/papers/OWASP-Universal-HTTP-DoS.ppt

Implementation of GESNIC for Web Server Protection against HTTP GET Flooding Attacks

Hyunjoo Kim[1], Byoungkoo Kim[2], Daewon Kim[2], Ik-Kyun Kim[2],
and Tai-Myoung Chung[1]

[1] Internet Management Technology Laboratory,
Department of Electronic and Computer Engineering, Sungkyunkwan University,
300 Chenchen-dong, Jangan-gu, Suwon, Gyeonggi-do, 440-746, Republic of Korea
H.JooKim76@gmail.com, tmchung@imtl.skku.ac.kr
[2] Network System Security Research Team,
Electronics and Telecommunications Research Institute,
218 Gajeongno, Yuseong-gu, Daejeon, 305-700, Republic of Korea
{bkkim05,dwkim77,ikkim21}@etri.re.kr

Abstract. Distributed Denial-of-Service (DDoS) attacks are made in such a way that a plurality of zombie computers infected with malicious code simultaneously makes Denial-of-Service (DoS) attacks. These DDoS attacks still dominate the ranking of cyber threats. It is a great challenge to accurately detect and intercept the DDoS attacks on high speed network. Most of all, HTTP GET flooding attacks increase day by day. Therefore, we propose the web server protection scheme against HTTP GET flooding attacks. The proposed technique easily can detect HTTP GET flooding attacks. Most of all, it was implemented in our Gigabit Ethernet Secure Network Interface Controller (GESNIC) for the high performance DDoS prevention. Our GESNIC let IT administrators protect their Internet servers against various DDoS attacks. GESNIC provides the high performance secure logics, which is a kind of security offload engine against TCP and HTTP related DDoS attacks on network interface card. Besides, the secure offload engine has robustness against various DDoS attacks itself and it is independent on server's OS and external network configuration. Its performance is almost a carrier-class level as latency time of 7×10^{-6} seconds. In summary, installing our GESNIC can make the more secure, highly available, and easier to manage - which is exactly the kind of innovation.

Keywords: DDoS attack, GESNIC, Server Protection, HTTP GET flooding.

1 Introduction

Generally, DoS attacks are made against websites, domain name servers or the like, and deteriorate the availability of networks or servers. In particular, DDoS attacks are performed such that an unspecified number of attackers transmit a large amount of data for the purpose of disturbing the normal service of a system,

D.H. Lee and M. Yung (Eds.): WISA 2012, LNCS 7690, pp. 285–295, 2012.

so that the perfor-mance of a target network or system is rapidly deteriorated, thereby disabling the service provided from the corresponding system from being used[3]. A DDoS attack is divided into two attack types. One is a network-level attack and the other is an application-level attack. The network-level attack designates a network layer attack such as TCP flooding, UDP flooding, and ICMP flooding. The application-level attack designates an application layer at-tack such as HTTP related flooding, SIP flooding, and DNS flooding[1][4][6]. Since the attack properties of the two types of attacks are different from each other, the detection and response methods thereof are different from each other. Most of existing DDoS prevention techniques use a simple method of measur-ing the amount of traffic, such as Bit per Second (BPS) or Packet per Second (PPS), and blocking packets for a predetermined time if the amount of traffic is greater than a predetermined threshold. Further, Intrusion Detection Sys-tem/Intrusion Prevention System (IDS/IPS) products use a method of applying string patterns, which mainly appear in a DDoS attack tool, to detection rules, performing a pattern matching function, and instantly blocking a corresponding packet when the packet is detected[7]. However, since there are limits on simple pattern matching, attempts at effective response have been recently made by providing priority queues combined with Quality of Service (QoS) or applying a rate limiting technique. However, such existing DDoS prevention techniques perform detection and response based on the basically simple amount of traf-fic and string patterns, so that there are limits on realizing rapid and accurate prevention in an actual DDoS attack situation.

The remainder of the paper is structured as follows. The next section summa-rizes our GESNIC. Then, section 3 presents our approach for server protection against HTTP GET flooding attacks. Section 4 shows the implementation and experimental results in our test-bed environment. Finally, we conclude and sug-gest directions for further research in section 5.

2   Architecture of GESNIC

In this section, we briefly introduce the architecture of our GESNIC. It let IT administrators protect their Internet servers against DDoS attacks. GESNIC provides the high performance secure logics, which is a kind of security offload engine against TCP and HTTP related DDoS attacks on network interface card. The secure offload engine has robustness against DDoS attacks itself and it is independent on servers OS and external network configuration. It supports not only IP address-based filtering method but also packet-level filtering, therefore it can ma-nipulate attacks from NAT-based user group. Fig. 1 denotes a basic concept of GESNIC. As shown the figure, GESNIC has a CPU independent ar-chitecture that secure logics for a server protection are located in a reconfiguring hardware (Server Protection H/W). Therefore, all arriving packets to the server are inspected and fil-tered by our secure logics. As shown in the Fig. 2, the server protection hardware named GESNIC is composed of four secure blocks and one coordination block.

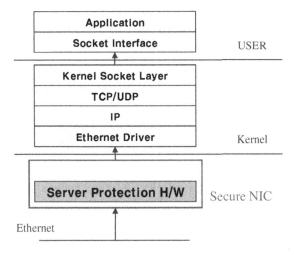

Fig. 1. Basic Concept of GESNIC

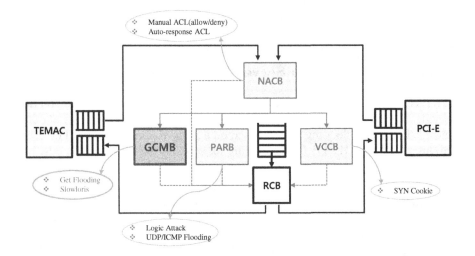

Fig. 2. Secure Logic Components of GESNIC

The summary of the internal logic blocks is following;

☐ NACB (Network Access Control Block): NACB processes IP-Address level packet filtering. Most of all, it can deal with the filtering requests from other blocks on the front line of GESNIC. Therefore, it can reduce the unnecessary packet processing load of other blocks.

☐ VCCB (Valid Client Check-out Block): VCCB processes a defense against TCP SYN flooding attack through the TCP SYN cookie operation. Besides, TCP related flooding attacks are handled.

☐ PARB (Protocol Anomaly Response Block): PARB processes a defense against UDP/ICMP related flooding attacks. It is simply performed by a threshold based rate-limiting technique.

☐ GCMB (Guaranteed Connection Management Block): GCMB employs the pro-posed web server protection scheme against HTTP GET flooding attacks.

☐ RCB (Response Coordination Block): RCB receive analysis results from all other blocks, and handles an actual packet forwarding and blocking operation about ar-riving packets.

Besides, there are a TEMAC interfacing logic for gigabit networking with external system and a PCI-E interfacing for networking with internal CPU. Through the interoperability of these components, Our GESNIC performs the server protection mechanisms against various DDoS flooding attacks. Namely, the major functionality of our GESNIC is to perform the high performance DDoS prevention on secure logics. Therefore, we focus on effective prevention strategies applied FPGA logics.

3   The Proposed Web Server Protection Scheme

In this section, we introduce the proposed HTTP GET flooding attack detection methods. The proposed methods focus on two types of attacks. One is about a typical HTTP GET flooding attack based on a large volume of traffic. The other is about a row-rate HTTP GET flooding attack. Through these methods, our GESNIC performs a web server protection against HTTP related DDoS attacks.

3.1   Detection Mechanism against a Typical HTTP GET Flooding Attack

In this type of attacks, malicious clients send a large number of HTTP GET request messages to the target web server automatically[9][10]. The main feature of HTTP GET request messages from each malicious client is a continuous repetition of HTTP GET messages with same URI (Uniform Resource Identifier). Besides, these messages are consistently transmitted to target server for no more than a few milliseconds. It is impossible that this traffic pattern is generated by a normal user behavior.

Fig. 3 shows a comparison normal GET request messages with GET request messages causing HTTP GET flooding based on a large volume of traffic. Generally, most web pages are completed by information involved in various URIs. Therefore, normal GET request messages from one client are composed of messages with various URI requests for accessing an intended web page. On the

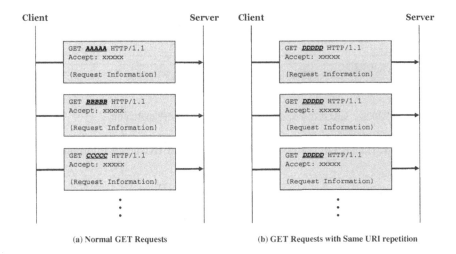

(a) Normal GET Requests   (b) GET Requests with Same URI repetition

Fig. 3. Main feature of a Typical HTTP GET flooding attack

other hand, HTTP GET flooding attack is performed by GET request messages with same URI repetition.

Our web server protection mechanism against this attack type is performed by the packet analysis based on this feature. Put simply, it is processed by tracing technique about source IP and URI content extracted from arriving packets. Fig. 4 shows an arriving packet analysis method for HTTP GET request message identification and analysis source extraction. Regardless of which version of HTTP, HTTP GET request message starts from *"GET (0x47 45 45 20)"* pattern and includes *" HTTP/1.(0x20 48 54 54 50 2f 31 2e)"* pattern at the end position of URI content. That is, HTTP GET message can be identified through the pattern matching about *"GET "* and *" HTTP/1."*. Therefore, if an arriving packet to Web service port has a payload and contains the string, it can be determined to HTTP GET request message. After such an identification process, URI content and URI size are extracted. Finally, source IP information is extracted from a header of the arriving packet.

Fig. 5 shows a table configuration for source IP and URI content tracing of the proposed mechanism. For each source IP of arriving packets, the hash function generates an index h, and the corresponding slot in the hash table is accessed. As shown in the figure, the corresponding slot is composed of multiple entries for hash collision avoidance, and each entry has several fields as following;

☐ Source IP : a source IP address value

☐ URI hash(uh) : a hash value generated from the URI content

☐ URI size : a length of the URI content

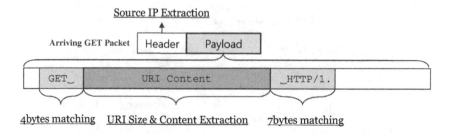

Fig. 4. HTTP GET Message Identification and Extracted Information

☐ Time stamp : an entry allocation or modification time

☐ Alloc. : if the entry exists, then 1, otherwise 0

Here, we use the URI hash and the URI size for the URI content tracing. The reason is that the URI content extracted from each arriving packet has a variable length. That is, an URI content comparison of arriving packets with an identical source IP is performed through a matching about the URI hash and the URI size.

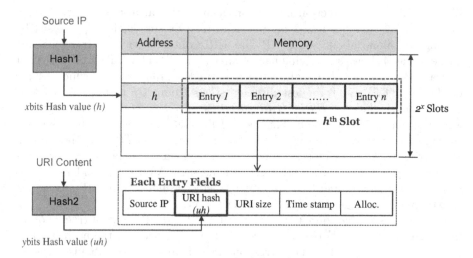

Fig. 5. Table Configuration for the Proposed Mechanism

Fig. 6 briefly shows an example of web server protection scenario against HTTP GET flooding attack based on a large volume of traffic.

First, the hash value A' is generated about an arriving GET packet with source IP A and URI content a, and the corresponding slot in the hash table is accessed. The first entry of the accessed slot is filled with source IP A and the hash value a' of URI content (URI size, Timestamp and allocation bit is

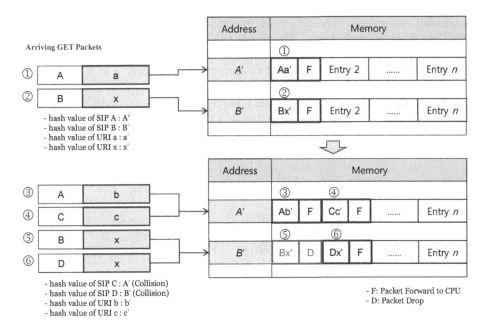

Fig. 6. An Example of HTTP GET flooding Prevention

skipped for an abridged description). Next, the same operation is performed for an arriving GET packet with source IP B and URI content x. The third packet has an identical source IP to the first packet, but the URI content is different. In this case, the previous entry is modified to source IP A and the hash value b' of URI content. Continuously, the hash value A' generated from source IP C is identical to that of the third packet. That is, a hash collision happens. Therefore, the second entry of the same slot is filled to source IP C and the hash value c' of URI content. Until now, all arriving packets are forwarded to CPU. However, the fifth packet is identical to the second packet. That is, the existing source IP B and the hash value x' are generated. In this case, HTTP GET flooding attack is detected, and the fifth packet is dropped. Furthermore, the source IP causing HTTP GET flooding can be registered to IP-based packet filtering block, and all packets from the malicious source IP can be filtered within a fixed period. Finally, the sixth packet is processed as the same way to the forth packet.

3.2   Detection Mechanism against a Low-Rate HTTP GET Flooding Attack

In this type of attacks, malicious clients try to keep many connections to the target web server as long as possible. It accomplishes this by opening connections to the target web server and sending a partial HTTP GET request message. Periodically, it will send subsequent HTTP GET request messages, but the message is never completed. Affected servers will keep these connections open, filling their maximum concurrent connection pool, eventually denying additional connection attempts from normal clients. Therefore, this attack type is possible to cause the DDoS attack by a small quantity of packets[2][8]. Most of all, these messages are not necessary to be transmitted to target server quickly. Fig. 7 shows the main feature of a GET request message causing the low-rate HTTP GET flooding attack. Generally, most normal GET request messages are completed to one message with an appointed string at the end position. On the other hand, this low-rate HTTP GET flooding attack is performed by incomplete GET request messages with a short message length.

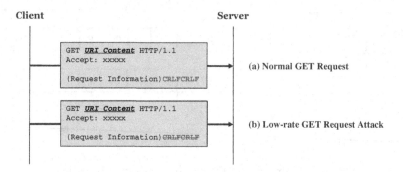

Fig. 7. Main feature of a low-rate HTTP GET flooding attack

As shown in the previous mechanism, the web server protection mechanism against this attack type is also performed by the simple packet analysis based on the above feature. Fig. 8 shows the requested information for an incomplete HTTP GET request message identification. Here, a method for the HTTP GET request message identification is the same as those described in the previous 3.1 section. In addition, total packet length of an arriving packet is required. If an arriving HTTP GET request packet is less than general MTU (Maximum Transmission Unit) and doesnt contain the string *"CRLFCRLF(0x0d 0a 0d 0a)"* at the end position of the payload, it can be regarded to low-rate HTTP GET flooding attack. In this case, the arriving packet is dropped. Furthermore, the source IP can be controlled by IP-based packet filtering block as described in the previous section.

Basically, the above operations are performed about all arriving packets on the high performance secure logic. That is, our web server protection scheme can perform a defense against these HTTP GET flooding attacks without lowing of performance and packet loss.

4   Implementation and Experimental Results

4.1   Implementation

We have developed our prototype based on our GESNIC architecture. The secure logics of our GESNIC are implemented in Verilog HDL (Hardware Description

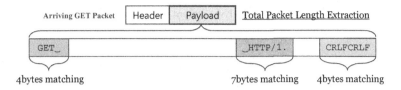

Fig. 8. Incomplete HTTP GET Message Identification

Language) that is best suited for high performance packet processing. Fig. 9 shows our GESNIC prototype and installing image. As shown in the figure, our prototype uses the security offload engine on Xilinx virtex5 platform. Besides, it employs 10/100/1000 RJ-45, GE SFP and PCI-E connectors for an external interfacing. Here, a SRAM is used for IP address based filtering, and holds up to 2 million IP address. Therefore, our GESNIC can handle enough malicious clients. Overall, our GESNIC helps the server protection against TCP and HTTP related DDoS attack. It supports wire-speed TCP Proxy and HTTP flooding protector, which are compatible with TCPv4. Intelligent GESNIC processing offloads and powerful traffic-control features reduce the burden imposed on the server CPU and accelerate system performance. Furthermore, Optimized for Windows 2008 Server, Linux operating systems, the security processor significantly accelerates system and application through the watchdog control of process. Besides, GESNIC management assistant gives end users and support staff one easy-to-use tool for management, troubleshooting, and repair. Its automated interface provides options for either self or assisted service, helping users get and stay connected.

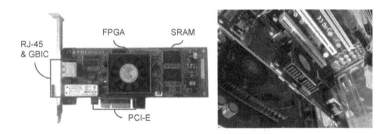

Fig. 9. GESNIC Prototype and Installation

4.2 Experimental Results

In this experiment, we use two web servers. One is our GESNIC installing server, and the other is a general server. Here, the specification of two servers is identical. Next, we prepared two attack tools in our test-bed. One is for a typical HTTP GET flooding attack, and the other is for a low-rate HTTP GET flooding attack. The attack tools are NetBot attacker[5] and slowloris, respectively. Here, our test-bed has several computers as the attack sources. However, we show the

Table 1. Experimental Results

Time	NetBot attacker				Slowloris			
	GESNIC Server		General Server		GESNIC Server		General Server	
(second)	Packets	CPU	Packets	CPU	Packets	Session	Packets	Session
5	56(12)	1%	15813	4%	398(8)	1	1023	180
10	26(4)	2%	17752	4%	418(2)	1	995	340
15	4(1)	1%	17392	4%	441(3)	1	616	385
20	4(0)	1%	17576	3%	441(6)	1	498	385
25	128(14)	1%	17689	4%	440(4)	1	465	385

experimental results for one attack source to present them exactly and easily. Table 1 shows the experimental results.

In this above table, *Packets* indicates the number of all arriving packets and the value given in brackets indicates the number of packets sent to CPU. In case of a general server, the number of all arriving packets is identical to the number of packets sent to CPU. *CPU* indicates a CPU usage rate, and *Session* is the number of concurrent established sessions. As a result, our GESNIC installing server was not directly affected by HTTP GET flooding attacks. On the other hands, the general server fell into out of service state in a few seconds. In summary, our web server protection scheme can perform a suitable defense against HTTP GET flooding attacks.

5   Conclusions

In this paper, we present the architecture of our GESNIC. Then we introduce the web server protection scheme against HTTP GET flooding attacks. The proposed technique is implemented in our GESNIC for the high performance DDoS Prevention. It is independent on server's OS and external network configuration. Therefore, it enables the web server protection against the DDoS attacks without an additional CPU power. Most of all, our approach easily and accurately can detect the HTTP related DDoS attacks. Finally, we reported the experimental results of our approach. As shown in the experimental result, our approach can guarantee a service continuity of the target web server under HTTP GET flooding attacks. However, the current approach is very preliminary and a thorough evaluation will require experimentation in a real world environment. In future, we need to focus on reducing its false rate as the further study through more experimental results. Besides, we will keep up our efforts for improvement in performance of detection mechanism on real world environment.

Acknowledgments. This work was supported by the IT R&D program of MKE/KIAT [Development of Analysis Technologies against Unknown Virtualization-based Malicious Activity for Trusted Cloud Computing Service].

References

1. Zade, A.R., Patil, S.H.: A Survey On Various Defense Mechanisms Against Application Layer DDoS Attack. International Journal on Computer Science and Engineering (IJCSE) 3(11), 3558–3563 (2011)
2. Wu, Z., Wang, C., Zeng, H.: Research on the comparison of Flood DDoS and Low-rate DDoS. In: 2011 International Conference on Mul-timedia Technology (ICMT), pp. 5503–5506 (July 2011)
3. Choi, Y.-S., Oh, J.-T., Jang, J.-S., Ryou, J.-C.: Integrated DDoS Attack Defense Infrastructure for Effective Attack Prevention. In: 2nd International Conference on Information Technology Convergence and Services, pp. 1–6 (August 2010)
4. Xie, Y., Yu, S.: Monitoring the Application-Layer DDoS Attacks for Popular Websites. IEEE/ACM Transactions on Networking (2009)
5. Han, K., Im, E.: A Study on the Analysis of Netbot and Design of Detection Framework. In: JWIS 2009 (2009)
6. Ranjan, S., Swaminathan, R., Uysal, M., et al.: DDoS-Shield: DDoSResilient Scheduling to Counter Application Layer Atttacks. IEEE/ACM Transactions on Networking 7(1), 26–39 (2009)
7. Yu, J., Fang, C., Lu, L., Li, Z.: A Lightweight Mechanism to Mitigate Application Layer DDoS Attacks. In: Mueller, P., Cao, J.-N., Wang, C.-L. (eds.) INFOSCALE 2009. LNICST, vol. 18, pp. 175–191. Springer, Heidelberg (2009)
8. Yatagai, T., Isohara, T., Sasase, I.: Detection of HTTP-GET flood Attack Based on Analysis of Page Access Behavior. In: 2007 IEEE Pacific Rim Conference on Communications, Computers and Signal Processing, pp. 232–235 (August 2007)
9. Yu, J., Li, Z., Chen, H., Chen, X.: A Detection and Offense Mechanism to Defend Against Application Layer DDoS Attacks. In: Third International Conference on Networking and Services(ICNS 2007), pp. 54–59 (2007)
10. Lu, W.Z., Yu, S.Z.: A HTTP Flooding Detection Method Based on Browser Behavior. In: 2006 International Conference on IEEE Computational Intelligence and Security, vol. 2, pp. 1151–1154 (November 2006)

Privacy-Aware VANET Security: Putting Data-Centric Misbehavior and Sybil Attack Detection Schemes into Practice *,**

Rasheed Hussain[1], Sangjin Kim[2], and Heekuck Oh[1]

[1] Hanyang University, Department of Computer Science and Engineering,
Republic of Korea
{rasheed,hkoh}@hanyang.ac.kr
[2] Korea University of Technology and Education
School of Computer Science and Engineering, Republic of Korea
sangjin@koreatech.ac.kr

Abstract. The past decade has witnessed a growing interest in VANET (Vehicular Ad Hoc NETwork) and its myriad potential applications. Nevertheless, despite the surge in VANET research, security and privacy issues have been the root cause of impeded momentum in VANET deployment. In this paper we focus on misbehavior and Sybil attacks from VANET standpoint. With intrusion capabilities in hand, malicious users in VANET can inject false information and launch Sybil attack. Sybil attack refers to pretending one physical node to be many and in worst case almost all kinds of attacks can be launched in the presence of Sybil attack. Misbehavior in VANET can be categorized as a sub-effect of Sybil attack where a malicious vehicular node(s) spoof legitimate identities. There are two main strategies for avoiding misbehavior in VANET; Entity-centric strategies that focus on the revocation of misbehaving nodes by revocation authorities. On the other hand, Data-centric approach mainly focuses on the soundness of information rather than the source of information. We cover both strategies where decision on which strategy to be used, is taken on the basis of traffic situation. In a dense traffic regime, we propose SADS (Sybil Attack Detection Scheme) whereas in sparse traffic regime, we propose LMDS (Location-Based Misbehavior Detection Scheme). Our proposed schemes leverage position verification of the immediate source of warning message. Furthermore, we guarantee security and privacy (conditional anonymity) for both beacons and warning messages.

Keywords: VANET Security, Data-centric Misbehavior, Privacy, Sybil Attacks.

* This research was supported by the MKE (The Ministry of Knowledge Economy), Korea, under the ITRC (Information Technology Research Center) support program (NIPA-2012-H0301-12-4004) supervised by the NIPA (National IT Industry Promotion Agency).
** This research was supported by Basic Science Research Program through the NRF (National Research Foundation of Korea) funded by the Ministry of Education, Science and Technology (2012009152).

D.H. Lee and M. Yung (Eds.): WISA 2012, LNCS 7690, pp. 296–311, 2012.
© Springer-Verlag Berlin Heidelberg 2012

1   Introduction

The complete deployment of VANET (Vehicular Ad Hoc NETwork) is still rapidly ahead and its success and adaptation in end-users (drivers), consumers, and governments will depend on viable security solutions. Since VANET is a form of ephemeral networks, mobility issues have to be dealt with. Additionally VANET is prone to traditional security issues like authentication, non-repudiation, integrity, and privacy. Moreover VANET inherits all its parental characteristics from MANET (Mobile Ad Hoc Networks) with more stringent security requirements [1, 2, 3 , 4, 5]. Since VANET deals with the lives of human beings, the proper and authorized functioning of VANET demands prime concern from security standpoint. Besides, VANET requires that sensitive user information such as identity and location must not be abused as a result of non-legal tracing and profiling. On the contrary, due to liability issues, traceability is inevitable where identity information needs to be revealed by revocation authorities in extreme cases such as deadly accidents. A number of security schemes have already been proposed [2,6,7] which cover different security primitives in VANET [8,9]. According to Dedicated Short-range Communication (DSRC) [10] in traffic safety applications, vehicular nodes broadcast scheduled beacon messages with certain frequency. Among variety of different messages in VANET, aforementioned beacons and critical warning messages are most prominent [11]. Most of the previously proposed schemes used public-key cryptography to provide security for such messages [6, 12, 13]. Group signatures, multiple pseudonyms, identity-based cryptosystems, and certificates-based schemes can be found in literature [8, 14, 15, 16, 17]. For ephemeral and resource constrained networks such as VANET itself, group signatures and certificates are not an ideal choice for security and privacy especially in case of high frequency beacons. The signing and verification cost may become bottleneck for the network [9]. As a remedy, symmetric cryptography was adopted in some proposed schemes, which is a viable solution for VANET. In [18], the authors outlined such schemes. In addition, Identityless beaconing scheme was proposed for secure and privacy-aware beaconing [19].

In this paper we focus on privacy, misbehavior and Sybil attacks detection schemes. There are two categories of MDS (Misbehavior Detection Schemes) in wireless networks, and in VANET in particular; Data-centric MDS and Entity-centric MDS. In Data-centric MDS approach, the underlying system is only concerned about the soundness of information rather than the source of information. The system singles out only wrong information instead of revoking the source of information. In other words data-centric MDS schemes deal with message revocation. In contrast, Entity-centric approaches leverage the revocation function in VANET where misbehaving vehicular nodes are revoked. To date, the focus has been put on entity-centric approaches only [20, 21, 22, 23, 24]. To the best of our knowledge, [25] is the only proposed scheme where authors envisioned data-centric approach for VANET security.

A strong authentication and confidential scheme would keep outsiders [2] from causing severe consequences. However, keeping insiders from misbehaving is a

challenging task because the impact of their misbehavior is far larger than outsiders. Traditional authentication schemes are not sufficient to keep insiders from
misbehaving. It is worth noting that privacy and Sybil attacks [21] are two opposite poles. Working out at one end, creates devastating problems at the other
end. For instance strong privacy preservation where messages are not linkable
to each other and to the sender, Sybil attackers get an edge.

1.1 Problem Statement

In a privacy-aware VANET environment with privacy-aware beaconing (for instance *identityless* beaconing) where two messages provide *unlinkability*, how
to prevent and/or detect misbehavior on the part of vehicular nodes and how
to avoid and/or detect Sybil attacks? As outlined before, privacy and misbe-
havior/Sybil attacks are the two conflicting requirements in VANET. They are
indirectly proportional to each other. More precisely if A_S denotes Sybil attack
in VANET and P denotes privacy, then the relation between these two primitives
is given by partial equality; $A_S \propto 1/P$. The remainder of the paper is organized
as follows:

In the following section we outline detailed state of the art regarding previously carried out research on misbehavior and Sybil attacks in VANET. In
section 3, we provide the readers with a bird's view of the underlying VANET
architecture. We discuss our proposed scheme in detail in section 4. In section 5,
we evaluate our proposed scheme followed by concluding remarks in section 6.

2   State of the Art

Despite the fact that strong user and location privacy must be preserved in
VANET but due to liability issues, revocation must be possible [26]. The common approaches towards privacy preserving in VANET are anonymous certificates, group signatures [5,12,13], batch verification schemes [27], pseudonyms
[21], mix zones and silent-periods [28], and identityless schemes [19]. The concept of group signatures was first introduced by Chaum and Heyst [29] and the
main advantage of group-signature-based schemes is that, any public entity cannot reveal the identity of the message originator thereby preserving privacy [13],
but the limitation of group signatures is that the cost of signing and verification is very high. Moreover, group signature-based schemes are prone to identity
escrow problem, because a group manager who possesses the group master key
can arbitrarily reveal the identity of any group member.

The pseudonym-based schemes leverage both public-key cryptography [2, 6,
16, and 17] and symmetric-key cryptography [18]. Raya et al. [2] proposed a
pseudonym-based authentication scheme where each vehicle stores a large number of pseudonymous certificates with pseudo-identities and it randomly chooses
one of the available pseudonymous certificates to sign the outgoing messages.
However if a vehicle is revoked, all identities stored in the vehicle must be added
to Certificate Revocation List (CRL) thereby drastically increasing the size of

CRL. Wasef et al. [30] proposed an RSU-assisted distributed certificate services in VANET by employing batch verification scheme.

2.1 Sybil Attack Detection in VANET

Sybil attacks in VANET are inherited from Wireless Sensor Networks (WSNs). It was first introduced by Douceur et al. [31] in p2p networks. In Sybil attack, a malicious node pretends to be many physical nodes and the fake nodes created by malicious node are called Sybil nodes. There are number of proposed schemes to avoid such attacks beforehand or, detect the attack and take countermeasures afterwards [21]. Nevertheless there must be some tradeoff between the privacy requirements in VANET and Sybil attack detection.

Public-key cryptography based algorithms are widely used in the literature to defend against Sybil attacks [2]. Raya et al. [2] proposed a scheme to detect and revoke malicious nodes. In their scheme, each node has several pseudonyms. Corresponding to each pseudonym, there is one public/private key pair and a certificate issued by CA (Certification Authority). To revoke a node, its corresponding certificates are revoked. Self-certified pseudonyms are leveraged by Martucci et al. [32] in their proposed scheme to prevent Sybil attacks.

In [21], authors propose a scheme called P^2DAP (Privacy-preserving Detection of Abuses of Pseudonyms). In their scheme, vehicles are issued with a large pool of pseudonyms and the pseudonyms are grouped base on two functions H_c and H_f called coarse-grained and fine-grained hash functions respectively. Each pseudonym has a fine grained hash value $H_f(p_i|k_f)$ and a coarse-grained hash value $H_c(p_i|k_c)$ where p_i is ith pseudonym and k_f, k_c are freshness keys. The fine-grained hash value of all the pseudonyms of a node must be same. Any two fine-grained hash values of pseudonyms belonging to different nodes must be different. RSU checks if there are two pseudonyms that hash to the same coarse-grained value, then either they are from the same vehicle or from different vehicles which hash to the same coarse-grained value. RSU accuses such messages to CA which investigates it further for the possibility of potential Sybil attack.

2.2 Misbehavior Detection Schemes in Anonymous VANETs

Misbehavior is a severe threat to safety-related applications in VANET because important decisions have to be made depending upon the information in hand. Malicious nodes can violate the normal flow of the VANET functionalities and inject wrong and/or bogus information which may cause devastating consequences such as deadly accidents. There must be a way to find out the authenticity of the information in hand before safety-related application takes any decision on that information.

In VANET, MDS can be divided into two strategies: Entity-Centric MDS [20] and Data-Centric MDS [25]. Entity-Centric MDS means eviction of misbehaving nodes regardless of the fact that the eviction will have adverse effect on the normal VANET functionality. For instance Sun et al. [24] proposed a scheme to evict misbehaving nodes from VANET. Golle et al. [33] incorporated sensors information to detect misbehavior in VANET. In their scheme, vehicular nodes exchange sensor information and then crosscheck it with their own information to find any sign of misbehavior. Moore et al. [34] proposed a *suicide*-based mechanism called *sting*, in which revocation is done locally. A node accusing a misbehaving node is also blacklisted by the neighboring nodes along with the accused node. This sacrificing behavior demonstrates that the accusing node is honest. Nevertheless this scheme can be attacked in a scenario where a benign vehicle is surrounded by malicious nodes. Furthermore, two game theoretic based revocation schemes are outlined in [22]. The main theme of the proposed schemes in [22] is that a node has 3 choices; it can vote, abstain from voting or commit suicide. Each of the aforementioned actions has associated cost and payoffs.

3   Underlying VANET Architecture

In this section we outline the underline baseline VANET architecture and the threat model for our proposed scheme. Our proposed VANET framework, at least in part, has resemblance with Hussain et al.'s [19] and Sun et al.'s scheme [7]. We consider a typical hierarchical VANET framework where DMV (Department of Motor Vehicles[1]) is at the top of the hierarchy and can be split up into two functional bodies named RA (Revocation Authority) and CA (Certification Authority). It is worth mentioning that due to seriousness of liability issues, the revocation functionality maybe distributed among several physical entities which then collaboratively revoke a node and/or a message in case of a dispute. If a single entity (e.g. police department) is given the capability to revoke a message or a vehicle, the privilege that a node can be revoked maybe abused [7]. By splitting the revocation functionality into several entities has twofold advantages; it will keep corrupt authorities from abusing users' privacy and stop malicious authorities from framing benign users.

Fig. 1 illustrates the hierarchy of functional entities in VANET. It must be noted that each RCA is an autonomous certification authority and controls a specific domain under its jurisdiction. RSI (Road-Side Infrastructure) is divided into two physical entities namely RSUs (Road-Side Units), hereafter termed as RSSE (Road-Side Static Entity) and RSME[2] (Road-Side Mobile Entity). DMV is trusted body and as a root of the management hierarchy, the function of DMV includes entity registration, initialization, and overall management. Without loss of generality, DMV decides the deployment of RSI at roadsides according to the law, rules, and regulations which are specific to countries. Certification task is physically distributed across the network by dividing VANET into physical domains and each domain is administered by a particular RCA. Note that the

---

[1] The notion of DMV can be different depending upon the government structure hierarchy of a particular country.

[2] We believe that patrolling of police vans on highways round the clock, is a common practice and with current technologies, we argue that these vans can be used as mobile RSUs.

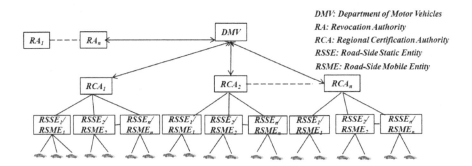

Fig. 1. Funcational Entities in VANET

size of domain might be different depending upon the volume of traffic (for instance a district) in a region. RSI provides the source of *intermediacy* between VANET users and managerial authorities. Moreover, it also plays partial role in key updates but does not supervise the update process. More precisely, RSI does not have the fresh keys for vehicles; but it can produce its share for the keys. Vehicles and RSI are equipped with OBU (On-Board Unit), TRM (Tamper-Resistant Module), and omni-directional radar (which we call *virtual eyes*).

3.1   Attacker Model

In order to misbehave or launch a Sybil attack in VANET, we assume the attacker to be insider [2] and have more resources and capabilities than a common legitimate node. We term any node as an *attacker* if it deviates from normal VANET behavior or infringes with users' privacy. The attacker is assumed to have capability to eavesdrop, forge identities, spoof them, and/or impersonate other vehicles. Moreover the attacker can track other nodes (*profile generation*) and diffuse wrong information into the network. Since there are many voting-based schemes for decision-making processes in VANET, if the attacker succeeds in presenting multiple identities, the decision can easily be biased and affect the normal VANET behavior. We also assume that the attacker can manipulate with input data for message construction. For our proposed scheme, the security requirements include *authentication,nonrepudiation, pivacy, misbehavior countermeasures*, and *Sybil attack detection*. Our proposed scheme must meet the aforementioned security requirements.

3.2   Our Contributions

Our contributions are enlisted below.

1. We define privacy preserving beaconing and warning mechanisms, which is an extension of our previous work [19].
2. Algorithms are devised for privacy-preserved LMDS and SAD mechanisms.

3. We leverage scheduled beacons to calculate privacy-aware, and realistic threshold-based traffic density.
4. Virtual eyes (*radar*) and virtual ears (*beacons*) are exploited to crosscheck the location information for soundness.
5. We combine data-centric MDS with SAD to provide security in conditional privacy-preserved VANET. Fig. 2 illustrates our proposed VANET architecture.

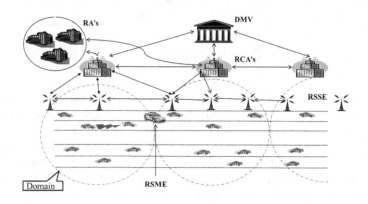

Fig. 2. An illustration of proposed VANET architecture

4   Proposed Scheme

4.1   Beaconing and Critical Warning Messages

We divide VANET messages into two basic forms; beacons (M_b) and critical warning messages (M_W). The format of beacon message is given below.

$$M_b = (m\|G_{id}\|\sigma\|\delta) \tag{1}$$

Where m is beacon data, $\sigma = HMAC.K_{d_i}(T\|G_{id}\|Data)$ and $\delta = HMAC.$ $K_{V_i}(T\|G_{id}\|Data\|\sigma)$. Due to high frequency of beacon messages, we do not need any sophisticated authentication mechanism. Instead, we use loose authentication in beacon messages employing HMACs (Hashed Message Authentication Code). Vehicles carry two types of keys for beacon messages, K_{d_i} and K_{V_i}. K_{d_i} is the domain-level common secret key and used by vehicles [3] in the same domain to check the integrity of entire message including σ while K_{V_i} is the individual secret key, used by nodes for liability issues. In case of a dispute, this key is used to revoke a message or a node. RCAs divide the vehicles into virtual groups to reduce the effect of partial brute-force revocatio. For that purpose, group ID

---

[3] Terms '*vehicles*', '*vehicular nodes*', and '*nodes*'are used in this paper interchangeably.

(G_{id}) is included in beacons. For more detail about grouping techniques and revocation process, we refer the readers to [19]. The second type of messages is critical warning messages. In case of critical scenarios in VANET, for instance accident on the road, fog, traffic jam, and ambulance approaching, the observer reports the event to nearby vehicles to avoid any further hazard situation for the vehicles following the observer. The format of warning message is given in Fig. 3.

Type	E_{ID}	L_{ID}	G_{id}	T	loc_{iT}	Sig. $K_{TRH_i}(E_{ID}, L_{ID}, G_{id}, T, loc_{iT})$
1	1	16	2	8	16	42

Fig. 3. Warning message (M_W) format

Where $Type$ is the type of warning (also indicating whether the message is relayed message or sensed), E_{ID} is event ID, L_{ID} is location where the event occurred, G_{id} is group ID from beacon message, T is timestamp for freshness, loc_{iT} is the current location of the immediate source of the warning message at time T, and the message is signed by the sender with its K_{TRH_i} (TRHs individual secret key and it is different from K_{V_i}). The second row in Fig. 3 shows the size of each field in the message in bytes [30, 35]. Additionally, the warning message travels relatively farther than the normally scheduled beacons. Depending upon relaying mechanism (efficient flooding) in place, warning messages must be relayed to reach a maximum distance to cover REI (Region of Expected Infection). The format of relayed message is shown in Fig. 4.

Type	T	loc_{iT}	G_{id}	λ	Sig. $K_{TRH_i}(T, loc_{iT}, G_{id}, \lambda)$
1	8	16	2	22	42

Fig. 4. Relayed warning message (M_{RW}) format

Where $\lambda = (E_{ID}, L_{ID}, G_{ids}, \Delta L, \Delta T)$. Instead of using explicit location information and timestamp we use relative difference in location difference (ΔL) and time difference (ΔT). G_{ids} is the group ID of the immediate source of the warning message. The advantage of such approach is twofold: it will reduce the number of bytes, hence reducing communication overhead and the time difference will make sure that the message is not stale. We assume that different types of warning messages and their expected actions after warning are already stored in the OBUs beforehand.

4.2   Hybrid Mechanism

Our goal is to combine data-centric and entity-centric approaches to secure VANET from both misbehavior and Sybil attacks. Basically our proposed hybrid scheme depends upon current traffic regime. Due to ephemeral nature of VANET, the traffic regime can vary from one extreme to the other at any instant of time. There are three well known traffic regimes namely Dense Traffic Regime (DTR), Sparse Traffic Regime (STR), and Disconnected Traffic Regime (DcTR) [36]. However the authors in [36] have their own notion of different traffic regimes. Without loss of generality, we only consider DTR and STR.

4.3   Traffic Density Calculation

We leverage scheduled beacon messages to calculate privacy-aware vehicular density. There are many previously proposed schemes to calculate traffic density using neighbor lists [36]. Since we use *identityless* beaconing scheme at base level, it becomes very challenging to calculate vehicular density on the top of aforementioned beaconing mechanism where messages are unlinkable to each other and to their sources. Therefore we define a threshold density calculation mechanism. The core idea is to collect the beacon messages in a particular time interval and then use the following formula to calculate the traffic density.

$$X_b = \begin{cases} 1 & \textit{if the source of the beacon is ahead} \\ 0 & \textit{if the source of the beacon is behind or in opposite direction} \end{cases}$$

$$D(v)_t = \frac{\sum_{i=t_k}^{t_{k+1}} X_b b_i}{f_b} + \varepsilon \qquad (2)$$

Where $D(v)_t$ is the traffic density at time t. Since we are concerned only about the vehicles ahead of the density calculating node, we need to eliminate the vehicles behind and the vehicles moving in opposite direction of the density calculating node. We define an indicator variable X_b which eliminates the aforementioned vehicles from the equation. b_i represents the beacon at time t_i and f_b is the frequency of beacons defined by DSRC. To compensate the packet loss due to noise or other reasons in the wireless communication, we define an error margin denoted by ε. To this end, we define vehicular density calculation mechanism in an *identityless* beaconing mechanism.

4.4   Sybil Attack Detection

The underlying idea for Sybil attack detection is same as that of density calculation. Only one additional concern is that we have to take care of redundancy in W_M. Warning messages are collected in an interval Δt for a particular Event E_{ID}, and then crosschecked with $D(v)_{\Delta t}$. For the sake of understanding, we assume that there is at least one relay on the part of each receiver of the warning message. Nevertheless there must be some efficient flooding and/or forwarding mechanism in place. When an event[4] is reported, the receiver collects all the event reporting messages and crosscheck them with the number of vehicles in the vicinity at that particular time $(D(v)_{\Delta t})$. However the redundant event messages must be taken care of because the receiver might already have received it from other vehicles (relayers).

The receiver removes the redundant messages and collects only distinct sensed and relayed messages. Then it crosschecks the number of messages with vehicular density. If $[number\ of\ warning\ messages]_{\Delta t} > D(v)_{\Delta t}$, then the situation is reported to RSI which then reports it to RCA for further investigation. Nevertheless such scenario maybe detected with the location verification in first place.

4.5   Location Verification

The vehicles overhear messages through their virtual ears (messages received containing location information) and then verify them with virtual eyes (omnidirectional radar). Verifying location gives an edge to MDS in our scheme. There are many proposed schemes in the literature to verify position information in privacy preserving environment. We use cosine-similarity based approach by Yan et al [37]. Due to space constraints, for more details we refer the readers to [37].

4.6   Combining Sub-funcations

In the previous subsections we outlined the sub-functions of our proposed scheme. Here we combine those sub-functions to form a hybrid mechanism for misbehavior and Sybil attack detection in VANET. Fig. 5 illustrates the functional flow of our proposed scheme.

Generally at the receivers end, we put certain checks on the intermediate source of the warning messages. These checks include *spatial checks*, *temporal checks*, *behavioral checks*, and *integrity checks*.

When a vehicular node receives any M_W, it first checks for freshness by making sure that $t_{cur} - t_i \geq \tau$. Where t_{cur} is the current time, t_i is the time when this message was sent from the source and τ is the validity threshold. It is not desirable for outdated warning message to linger around in the network. Then, the vehicle checks if it already received this warning from any other node beforehand. The vehicle checks movement trajectory after non-duplicity confirms. The physical locality of the sender and receiver of warning message must be either $(E - V_y - V_x)$ or $(V_x - V_y - E)$, where E is the event, V_x is the receiver of the message and V_y is the source of the warning message. $(V_x - V_y - E)$ scenario will be most likely in many cases, for instance if there is an accident on a freeway,

---

[4] When some event occurs, then a warning message (M_W) is broadcasted in the network. Moreover 'events'and 'warnings'are used interchangeably in this paper.

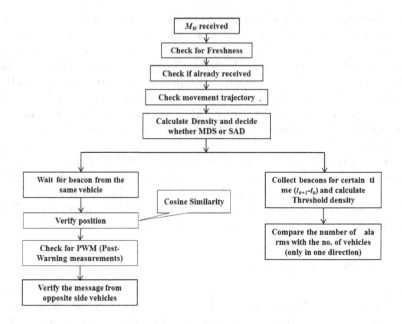

Fig. 5. Proposed Scheme: Functional Flow

then V_y sends warning message to V_x in order to avoid further hazards. The logical PWM of the event reporting vehicle would be either to change the road or reduce the speed.

The vehicle calculates the vehicular density of the vehicles ahead of it using equation 2. On the basis of vehicular density, the system decides whether to activate MDS function or SADs. Practically these two functions could run in parallel because misbehavior and Sybil attacks might overlap and/or Sybil attack might have caused misbehavior. To this end, we argue that in dense traffic regime, the system checks for SADs and in sparse traffic regime, the system checks for MDS. In case of sparse traffic regime, the traffic situation might be visible through naked eye as well, so we only check for misbehavior and in case of dense traffic regime, we single out the possibility of Sybil attack as well. After going through a series of checks, the receiver of the warning message waits for a beacon from the immediate source of the M_W. It is most likely that the receiver will receive beacons from the intermediate source of M_W, provided that it is within the transmission range of the source. Nevertheless, a vehicle cannot link a beacon message to a particular vehicle, but we argue that location information could be leveraged to estimate the sender of the message. If the location of source is sound, then the receiver checks for PWM and crosschecks the behavior of the vehicle against the concerned entry in table which is already stored in the OBU. Note that beacons are closely scrutinized for this purpose. We exploit the two-way traffic scenario and the vehicles moving in opposite direction are used to verify the soundness of the message in parallel with the checks we just performed on the source. However there is a possibility that colluding malicious nodes might cooperate to launch misbehavior attack and in worst case, the colluding vehicles might be in the opposite direction. In such case our argument does not hold. But in the meantime we assume that keeping in mind the ephemeral nature of VANET, colluding malicious nodes might have a very less room to cooperate in such scenarios and their target would be very limited. The procedure for detecting Sybil attack is already outlined in the previous subsection.

5   Evaluation

We evaluate our proposed scheme from the following perspectives.

1. Security (M_b and M_W)
2. Conditional privacy and revocation
3. Comparison with other schemes

5.1   Security (M_b and M_W)

Security of both beacon messages and critical warning messages is essential in our proposed scheme. Due to the high frequency of scheduled beacons, we use loose authentication using hashed MAC with domain-level common secret key K_{d_i}. In case of warning message, we use ECMV [30] scheme for authentication. The reason for assuming ECMV as authentication scheme is because it fits to our proposed hierarchical framework structure. The security requirements in aforementioned two message scenarios are *message authentication, message integrity, privacy protection, anonymity revocability*, and *non-frameability*. It is worth noting that the notion *revocation* differs from message and user standpoint. Message revocation refers to linking a message to a particular node whereas user revocation means to abandon the revoked user from using VANET functionalities. In our proposed scheme we emphasize on message revocation and leave the latter case for extreme scenarios where revocation is inevitable. In extreme cases user revocation takes place by collaboration of the authorized RAs.

Our beacon messages do not carry any identity information which could be traced back to a user; hence the privacy of the user is naturally preserved. Additionally, since beacon messages are not able to be linked to each other or to a particular vehicle; message privacy is preserved as well. Due to the nature of beacon messages, confidentiality is not a concern in beacons. In other words, the information contained in beacon message is only used in safety application by the vehicles in vicinity, hence there is no reason to encrypt the information. Nevertheless, content security is still an issue. We argue that other means for content security would be beneficial (for instance modular security in case of beacon assembling beforehand). To this end, the security requirements are fulfilled by our proposed scheme.

5.2   Conditional Privacy and Revocation

The privacy has already been discussed in the previous subsection. We consider both message revocation and user revocation in beacon messages and warning messages. In case of beacons we used G_{id}, and individual secret key K_{V_i} for revocation. To revoke a beacon message, domain information is extracted from the beacon followed by group information and then a partial brute-force is applied on that group to revoke the message. Note that the security credentials are stored against each vehicle at the time of issuing keys by the competent authorities. The order of revocation in case of beacon message is $O(d+g)$ where d is the size of domain and g is the size of the group. Since $(d \ll g)$, we can ignore d; so the order of revocation in case of beacon message is $O(g)$.

In case of warning messages, G_{id} is leveraged to revoke the anonymity of the message. Nevertheless, the scope of the brute-force will be larger than in case of beacon messages. The order of revocation in case of warning message is $O(d.g)$ because RAs must traverse through domains to find the group ID that was extracted from the warning message. Computational overhead will be included in the extended version of this paper.

5.3   Comparison with Other Schemes

We compare our scheme with previously proposed Sybil attack detection schemes and data-centric misbehavior schemes as illustrated in Table 1. The comparison matrices are *signatures and certificates, privacy preservation, RSUs being bottleneck, profile generation* and *computational overhead*. Note that in Table 1, T_p represents the time required to perform pairing operation, T_m is the time required to perform point multiplication, T_H represents the time required to perform hash operation, and H represents hash operations. It can be argued from Table 1 that our proposed scheme outperforms previous schemes in terms of aforementioned comparison matrices. However our proposed scheme differs from the aforementioned scheme in certain aspects like underlying network model yet

Table 1. Comparison with other systems

Scheme	Certificates with Beacons	Profile Generation	RSU as Bottleneck	Privacy	Computations M_b	M_W
Zhou et al.	x	✓	✓	Dependent on Pseudonyms Change	N/A	N/A
Ruj et al.	✓	✓	✓	Dependent on Pseudonyms Change	T_p+ $3T_m+$ $2T_H$	$2T_p+$ $6T_m+$ $4T_H$
Our Scheme	x	x	x	✓	$2H$	T_p+ $3T_m+$ $2T_H$

the goal is almost same. We do not include any signatures or certificates in normal beacons whereas the other schemes do. Our scheme is repellant to profile generation; however conditional privacy is preserved whereas Ruj et al. [25] used signatures and certificates in normal beacons which are still highly questionable in VANET. Zhou et al. [21] did not discuss the format of normally sent beacons. The privacy of Zhou et al.'s [21] scheme and Ruj et al.'s [25] scheme depends upon the rate of change of pseudonyms whereas our beaconing mechanism does not use any pseudonyms in beacons. So clearly, our proposed scheme has advantages over the previously proposed schemes.

6 Conclusions

We propose a hybrid mechanism to handle both misbehavior and Sybil attacks in VANET. Our strategy towards misbehavior is data-centric. The proposed scheme leverages identityless beaconing for privacy and a signature-based scheme for warning messages. The immediate source of warning message is observed for PWM (Post-Warning Measurements) and the measurements taken are crosschecked against the normal expected behavior where the expected action to be taken after warning is already stored in OBUs beforehand. Moreover, oppositeside traffic is exploited to prove the soundness of the information in hand. Our proposed scheme guarantees security and conditional privacy. After comparing with other schemes, we argue that our proposed scheme outperforms the previously proposed schemes.

References

1. Jung, C.D., Sur, C., Park, Y., Rhee, K.-H.: A Robust Conditional Privacy-Preserving Authentication Protocol in VANET. In: Schmidt, A.U., Lian, S. (eds.) MobiSec 2009. LNICST, vol. 17, pp. 35–45. Springer, Heidelberg (2009)
2. Raya, M.H., Hubaux, J.-P.: Securing Vehicular Ad Hoc Networks. J. Computer Security 15, 30 (2007)
3. Leinmuller, T., Schoch, E., Maihofer, C.: Security requirements and solution concepts in vehicular ad hoc networks. In: Fourth Annual Conference on Wireless on Demand Network Systems and Services, WONS 2007, pp. 84–91 (2007)
4. Dötzer, F.: Privacy Issues in Vehicular Ad Hoc Networks. In: Danezis, G., Martin, D. (eds.) PET 2005. LNCS, vol. 3856, pp. 197–209. Springer, Heidelberg (2006)
5. Antolino Rivas, D., Barcel-Ordinas, J.M., Guerrero Zapata, M., Morillo-Pozo, J.D.: Security on VANETs: Privacy, misbehaving nodes, false information and secure data aggregation. Journal of Network and Computer Applications 34, 1942–1955 (2011)
6. Rongxing, L., Xiaodong, L., Haojin, Z., Pin-Han, H., Xuemin, S.: ECPP: Efficient Conditional Privacy Preservation Protocol for Secure Vehicular Communications. In: INFOCOM 2008. The 27th Conference on Computer Communications, pp. 1229–1237. IEEE (2008)

7. Jinyuan, S., Chi, Z., Yanchao, Z., Yuguang, F.: An Identity-Based Security System for User Privacy in Vehicular Ad Hoc Networks. IEEE Transactions on Parallel and Distributed Systems 21, 1227–1239 (2010)
8. Lei, Z., Qianhong, W., Solanas, A., Domingo-Ferrer, J.: A Scalable Robust Authentication Protocol for Secure Vehicular Communications. IEEE Transactions on Vehicular Technology 59, 1606–1617 (2010)
9. Plößl, K., Federrath, H.: A privacy aware and efficient security infrastructure for vehicular ad hoc networks. Computer Standards and Interfaces 30, 390–397 (2008)
10. DSRC (Dedicated Short-Range Communication) Home, http://www.leearmstrong.com/Dsrc/DSRCHomeset.html
11. Schmidt, R.K., Leinmuller, T., Schoch, E., Held, A., Schafer, G.: Vehicle Behavior Analysis to Enhance Security in VANETs. In: Fourth Workshop on Vehicle to Vehicle Communications, V2VCOM 2008 (2008)
12. Yipin, S., Ronxing, L., Xiaodong, L., Xuemin, S., Jinshu, S.: A Secure and Efficient Revocation Scheme for Anonymous Vehicular Communications. In: 2010 IEEE International Conference onCommunications (ICC), pp. 1–6 (2010)
13. Studer, A., Shi, E., Fan, B., Perrig, A.: TACKing Together Efficient Authentication, Revocation, and Privacy in VANETs. In: 6th Annual IEEE Communications Society Conference on Sensor, Mesh and Ad Hoc Communications and Networks, SECON 2009, pp. 1–9 (2009)
14. Daza, V., Domingo-Ferrer, J., Sebe, F., Viejo, A.: Trustworthy Privacy-Preserving Car-Generated Announcements in Vehicular Ad Hoc Networks. IEEE Transactions on Vehicular Technology 58, 1876–1886 (2009)
15. Calandriello, G., Papadimitratos, P., Hubaux, J.-P., Lioy, A.: Efficient and robust pseudonymous authentication in VANET. In: Proceedings of the Fourth ACM International Workshop on Vehicular Ad Hoc Networks, pp. 19–28. ACM, Montreal (2007)
16. Yixin, J., Minghui, S., Xuemin, S., Chuang, L.: A robust signature scheme for vehicular networks using Binary Authentication Tree. IEEE Transactions on Wireless Communications 8, 1974–1983 (2009)
17. Wasef, A., Yixin, J., Xuemin, S.: DCS: An Efficient Distributed-Certificate- Service Scheme for Vehicular Networks. IEEE Transactions on Vehicular Technology 59, 533–549 (2010)
18. Scheuer, F., Posse, K., Federrath, H.: Preventing Profile Generation in Vehicular Networks. In: IEEE International Conference on Wireless and Mobile Computing Networking and Communications, WIMOB 2008, pp. 520–525 (2008)
19. Hussain, R., Kim, S., Oh, H.: Towards Privacy Aware Pseudonymless Strategy for Avoiding Profile Generation in VANET. In: Youm, H.Y., Yung, M. (eds.) WISA 2009. LNCS, vol. 5932, pp. 268–280. Springer, Heidelberg (2009)
20. Raya, M., Papadimitratos, P., Aad, I., Jungels, D., Hubaux, J.P.: Eviction of Misbehaving and Faulty Nodes in Vehicular Networks. IEEE Journal on Selected Areas in Communications 25, 1557–1568 (2007)
21. Tong, Z., Choudhury, R.R., Peng, N., Chakrabarty, K.: P^2DAP: Sybil Attacks Detection in Vehicular Ad Hoc Networks. IEEE Journal on Selected Areas in Communications 29, 582–594 (2011)
22. Raya, M., Manshaei, M.H., Felegyhazi, M., Hubaux, J.-P.: Revocation games in ephemeral networks. In: Proceedings of the 15th ACM Conference on Computer and Communications Security, pp. 199–210. ACM, Alexandria (2008)
23. Ghosh, M., Varghese, A., Gupta, A., Kherani, A.A., Muthaiah, S.N.: Detecting misbehaviors in VANET with integrated root-cause analysis. Ad Hoc Networks 8, 778–790 (2010)

24. Sun, J., Fang, Y.: Defense against misbehavior in anonymous vehicular ad hoc networks. Ad Hoc Networks 7, 1515–1525 (2009)
25. Ruj, S., Cavenaghi, M.A., Zhen, H., Nayak, A., Stojmenovic, I.: On Data- Centric Misbehavior Detection in VANETs. In: 2011 Vehicular Technology Conference (VTC Fall), pp. 1–5. IEEE (2011)
26. Kamat, P., Baliga, A., Trappe, W.: Secure, pseudonymous, and auditable communication in vehicular ad hoc networks. Security and Communication Networks 1, 233–244 (2008)
27. Chenxi, Z., Rongxing, L., Xiaodong, L., Pin-Han, H., Xuemin, S.: An Efficient Identity-Based Batch Verification Scheme for Vehicular Sensor Networks. In: The 27th Conference on Computer Communications, INFOCOM 2008, pp. 246–250. IEEE (2008)
28. Beresford, A.R., Stajano, F.: Mix zones: user privacy in location-aware services. In: Proceedings of the Second IEEE Annual Conference on Pervasive Computing and Communications Workshops, pp. 127–131 (2004)
29. Chaum, D., van Heyst, E.: Group Signatures. In: Davies, D.W. (ed.) EUROCRYPT 1991. LNCS, vol. 547, pp. 257–265. Springer, Heidelberg (1991)
30. Wasef, A., Yixin, J., Xuemin, S.: ECMV: Efficient Certificate Management Scheme for Vehicular Networks. In: Global Telecommunications Conference, IEEE GLOBECOM 2008, pp. 1–5. IEEE (2008)
31. Douceur, J.R.: The Sybil Attack. In: International Workship on Peer to Peer Systems, pp. 251–260 (2002)
32. Martucci, L.A., Kohlweiss, M., Andersson, C., Panchenko, A.: Self-certified Sybil-free pseudonyms. In: Proceedings of the First ACM Conference on Wireless Network Security, pp. 154–159. ACM, Alexandria (2008)
33. Golle, P., Greene, D., Staddon, J.: Detecting and correcting malicious data in VANETs. In: Proceedings of the 1st ACM International Workshop on Vehicular Ad Hoc Networks, pp. 29–37. ACM, Philadelphia (2004)
34. Moore, T., Raya, M., Clulow, J., Papadimitratos, P., Anderson, R., Hubaux, J.P.: Fast Exclusion of Errant Devices from Vehicular Networks. In: 5th Annual IEEE Communications Society Conference on Sensor, Mesh and Ad Hoc Communications and Networks, SECON 2008, pp. 135–143 (2008)
35. Ibrahim, K., Weigle, M.C.: CASCADE: Cluster-Based Accurate Syntactic Compression of Aggregated Data in VANETs. In: GLOBECOM Workshops, pp. 1–10. IEEE (2008)
36. Yan, G., Olariu, S., Weigle, M.C.: Providing VANET security through active position detection. Computer Communications 31, 2883–2897 (2008)

On Trigger Detection against Reactive Jamming Attacks: A Localized Solution

Incheol Shin, Sinkyu Kim, and Jungtaek Seo

The Attached Institute of ETRI
{icshin,skkim,seojt}@ensec.re.kr

Abstract. Reactive jamming attacks have been considered as the most critical and fatally adversarial threats to subvert or disrupt the networks since they attack the broadcast nature of transmission mediums by injecting interfering signals. Existing countermeasures against reactive jamming attacks, i.e. frequency hopping or channel surfing, requires excessive computational capabilities, which are infeasible for low cost resource constraint Wireless Sensor Networks (WSNs). To overcome the problems for normal lower power sensors, we propose an efficient localized jamming-resistant approach against reactive jamming attacks by identifying *trigger nodes* whose transmissions invoke the jammer. By constraining the trigger nodes to be receivers only, we can avoid invoking the jammers and completely nullify the reactive jamming attack. The triggers identification approach utilizes a hexagon tiling coloring and sequential Group Testing (GT), which does not demand any sophisticated hardware. Theoretical analyses and simulation results endorse the suitability of our localized algorithm in terms of time and message complexity.

1 Introduction

Wireless Sensor Networks (WSNs) have enormous critical applications in different realms such as military surveillance and reconnaissance to keep track of the enemy, health monitoring, smart homes, and disaster area monitoring. Nodes in WSNs communicate over radio transmissions and due to the broadcast advantage, a transmitter can send a message to all its receivers in a single radio transmission. However, this increases the vulnerability in communication to various security challenges such as Denial of Service attacks [1].

There are several types of DoS attacks, among which, jamming attacks have been known as the most significant threats because of their effectiveness and lethal damage against WSNs. In jamming attack, malice disseminates out adversarial signals into busy channels which are filled with legitimate sensor transmissions without following any legitimate protocols. This will result in the slump of the Signal to Noise Ratio (SNR) and network throughput. The jammers do not need to explore lots of internal information of the network components, so this light weight attack is easy to launch and favored by attackers.

In the scope of jamming attacks, *reactive jamming* poses the maximum threats while requires the lowest attacker energy against WSNs. In essence, the reactive

D.H. Lee and M. Yung (Eds.): WISA 2012, LNCS 7690, pp. 312–327, 2012.

jamming attack is the most efficient attack strategy and extremely difficult to be discovered, in which a malicious node (jammer) quietly scans all the available channels to sense any activity and blatantly starts injecting adversarial signal on that channel.

Existing countermeasures against reactive jamming attacks can be broadly classified into: 1) Physical layer approaches, 2) MAC layer approaches, 3) Network layer approaches. Firstly, the physical layer approaches [5, 2, 4, 3, 7] generally use Frequency Hopping (FH) and Code Division Multiple Access (CDMA) which requires a high computational cost. MAC layer approaches [8, 9] are either inherently based on FH or repositioning the sensor nodes, which may result in network partitioning and bring in high computation overhead. Finally, in the network layer approach, [6] introduces a new scheme to quarantine possible jammed areas and re-route all the messages that originally pass this area. However, this approach can create unnecessarily big jammed region and result in isolated networks. Additionally, the message overhead is relatively high during its mapping processing.

In our previous work [10, 11], we proposed a novel concept of *trigger nodes*, which refers to the sensor nodes whose broadcasting activate the reactive jammers The detection of trigger nodes have several benefits for the defense of reactive jammings: (1) Routing algorithm could be constructed in which the triggers are only the receivers, thus avoiding activating the jammers and minimizing the damage of jamming attacks. This can overcome the limitations of channel surfing and frequency hopping methods. In case of a trigger node needs to send a message, we may still utilize the use of channel surfing, however, only a few nodes may require this operation, thus greatly reducing the computational costs required by existing methods. In addition, the identification of trigger nodes will not create an unnecessary large size of jammed regions as in [6]. (2) After identifying trigger nodes, victim nodes would be scheduled to transmit messages based on the identification results such that no jammer would be activated, and whenever the trigger nodes start to broadcast, all other victim nodes stop their transmission. thus preventing from being jammed. (3) The location information of trigger nodes can be used to locate the jammers as well. Therefore, with accurate and efficient identification of trigger nodes, a number of effective defense strategies can be developed.

However, this trigger detection procedure is non-trivial, due to the unknown and dynamic locations of jammers and their various behaviors. To this end, we propose a localized trigger detection algorithm which employs two techniques: a hexagon tiling coloring scheme and a sequential group testing (GT), which efficiently identifies all the *trigger nodes* without requiring any extra hardware on sensors. Different from our previous work, this method can be distributedly implemented with a low time and message complexity. Furthermore, we investigate a more sophisticated behavior of jammers where they do not start injecting noise as soon as they sense some signals. Instead, jammers randomly start jamming with some probability p under this new model.

The rest of the paper is organized as follows: In section 2, we introduce the network and the jamming model along with the problem definition. Section 3 discusses the fundamental results of our approach along with our proposed hexagon tiling coloring technique. The localized algorithm for identification of the trigger nodes is presented in section 4 with the theoretical analyses. Section 5 shows how to avoid the activation of reactive jammers by a routing protocol, and section 6 concludes the paper.

2   Network and Jamming Models

2.1   Network Model

We consider a Wireless Sensor Network (WSN) consisting of n sensor nodes. Each sensor node has a uniform transmission radius r. Thus the WSN can be modeled as a *Unit Disk Graph* (UDG) $G = (V, E)$, where V represents the set of sensor nodes and E represents the set of wireless communication links. Between any two sensor nodes $u, v \in V$ there exists an edge $(u, v) \in E$ iff $d(u, v) \leq r$ where $d(u, v)$ denotes the Euclidean distance between u and v.

We further consider a set of jammers J existing at unknown locations in the network having a transmission range at most $R = \alpha r$ where $\alpha > 1$. Note that if two jammers have distance less or equal to R, they may consider the signals from each other as some activity in the network and keep injecting *Noise* until they get depleted of their energy. Thus we may consider the distance between any two jammers is greater than R.

Any sensor node $u \in V$ is said to be a **trigger node** if there is a jammer $j \in J$, such that $d(u, j) \leq r$. That is, when u transmits, it inevitably invokes the jammer j. A sensor node v is said to be a **victim node**, iff $d(v, j) \leq R$. (Note that by definition, a trigger node is always a victim node). If a jammer is invoked then all the victim nodes within its transmission range are jammed from receiving any messages.

2.2   Jamming Model

The **Reactive Jamming Attack** (RJA) model was first defined in [12]. In this model, a jammer continuously scans all the available channels in the network to sense some activity. *As soon as* it senses a signal on some channels, it injects adversarial signal (we call this signal *Noise* in this paper) to drastically decrease the signal to noise ratio and communication throughput of that channel.

In this paper, we consider the above RJA model. Generally, the duration for the transmission of *Noise* by the jammer is larger than or equal to the duration for transmission of a trigger node. For instance, let the duration for transmission of a trigger node is Δt_t and the duration for the transmission of *Noise* from the jammer is Δt_j. Then if $\Delta t_t > \Delta t_j$, after Δt_j time the jammer will be done with its transmission, but still it will sense some signal on the channel. So, the jammer will again start sending the *Noise* signal and it repeats this till it detects no signal on the channel. Therefore, Δt_t should be less than or equal to Δt_j.

Besides the above simplistic attacking model, we further consider a more sophisticated one. In practice, jammers usual adopt more sophisticated scheme to prevent themselves from being caught such as varying their power level or choose not to respond to the *Noise* for some cases. These makes detecting of jammers and triggers in the network become more challenging. We formally define this sophisticated model as follows:

Random Reactive Jamming Model: We relax the jamming model and consider that after sensing some signal, a jammer randomly starts jamming with probability $p < 1$. Note that if the jamming probability p is too small i.e. $p \leq 1/2$, the jammers may fail to jam the communication in the network as in that case, the communication in the network is still possible (with at least half of the normal efficiency). Hence, it is a reasonable assumption that jamming probability $p > 1/2$.

2.3 Problem Statement

Given a WSN $G = (V, E)$ and a set of jammers J. Considering the above network and jamming models, our objective is to efficiently identify all the trigger nodes in the network with low time and message complexities.

We can use the triggers information to construct an overlying routing protocol where trigger nodes are receivers only, so that the invoking of any jammer is avoided and the reactive jamming attack is completely nullified.

3 Identification of Trigger Nodes

In this section, we introduce an efficient localized algorithm which can be used as a network maintenance service and can be periodically invoked to identifying all the *trigger* nodes. The basic idea of jamming-resistant routing approach underlies the observation that transmission of *trigger* nodes activate the jammers and invoke adversarial signals. In addition, the overlaying network protocol would be able to avoid forwarding alarm messages over *trigger* nodes by converting them into receivers only. Hence, an effective identification of trigger nodes is a promising approach to nullify the reactive jamming attack and locate jammers.

3.1 Overview of Identification Procedure

The overview of trigger identification procedure is depicted as follows: The sets of nodes are geographically divided into hexagonal groups, and each hexagonal group is colored into interference-free disjoint groups, where the transmission of nodes within a group will not activate the same jammer whose adversarial signals will disrupt the communications with other groups. These groups are called *testing groups* in remainder of this paper. The set of nodes within *testing groups* with the same color are then scheduled to fulfill a sequential group testing procedure simultaneously in order to identify all trigger nodes over each *testing group*. Notice that all nodes in a network do not need to exchange additional messages in order to partition themselves into disjoint groups (to be explained in detail) and run a sequential group testing procedure since the basic premise of our network systems are loosely synchronized in the order of seconds.

The trigger identification algorithm within each pool has two phases: (1) The first phase of the trigger detection procedure is to identify six *trigger nodes* in order to estimate the possible location of a jammer. Each *testing group* corresponding to a hexagon of diagonal size at most r has possible Δ number of nodes where Δ is the maximum degree of WSN, and sensors have an uniform transmission radius r. That is, identification of a single *trigger node* by sequential testing will be done within $O(\log \Delta)$ rounds, and the location of a jammer would be estimated by these identified six *trigger nodes*. (2) The rest of *trigger nodes* within each hexagon would be discovered by the estimated location of a jammer and another *trigger node* as described in Section 3.

In principle, the flow of the identification procedure is: (1) Partition the set of nodes into hexagonal *testing groups*; (2) Assign colors to hexagons in order to maximize the number of disjoint interference-free *testing groups* and schedule them according to the colors; (3) Perform sequential group testing within each hexagonal *testing group* during the assigned time slot for the each group, and discover six *trigger nodes* to estimate the location of a jammer. (4) Discover the additional *trigger node* which has the maximum distance to the estimated location of a jammer so as to identify rest of *trigger nodes* within each hexagon.

How to divide the set of nodes into interference-free testing groups and *how to discover all trigger nodes within minimum latency* play fatal role in our localized approach against reactive jamming attack. These will be illustrated along with theoretical analysis in the following sections.

3.2 Hexagon Tiling Coloring

In this section, we propose a hexagon tiling coloring, which we later use in section 4 to locally partition the set of sensor nodes in WSN into groups in order to exploit the available spacial parallelism.

In order to study the hexagon tiling coloring, we formulate the following new problem:

Definition 1. Hexagon tiling coloring problem: *Given a distance $d \in \Re^+$ and a hexagon tiling H dividing the 2D plane into regular hexagons of sides $\frac{1}{2}$. Find the minimum number of colors needed to color H, such that any two hexagons h_1 and h_2 in H with same color are at distance greater than d.*

The distance between two hexagons h_1, h_2, denoted as $d(h_1, h_2)$ is defined as the Euclidean distance between any two closest points p_1 and p_2, such that p_1 is located in h_1 and p_2 is located in h_2. This makes the hexagon tiling coloring problem different from the channel assignment problem [13] in cellular network, where the distance between two hexagon cells is measured from their centers.

It can be observed in Figure 1 that in a hexagonal tilling, centers of all the hexagons are placed on a triangular lattice. So, we consider a new coordinate

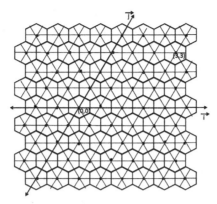

Fig. 1. A Hexagonal Tilling

system in the 2D plane, with axes inclined at 60°. This new coordinates system has two units vectors $\overrightarrow{i}$ $(\frac{\sqrt{3}}{2}, 0)$ and $\overrightarrow{j}$ $(\frac{\sqrt{3}}{4}, \frac{3}{4})$ as shown in Figure 1. The centers of each hexagon h coincide with the integral coordinates in this coordinate system. Now, each hexagon h can be identified by the coordinates (i, j) of its center as $h(i, j)$. The Euclidean distance between two hexagon centers $h(i_1, j_1)$ and $h(i_2, j_2)$ is given as $d_c(h_1, h_2) = \frac{\sqrt{3}}{2}\sqrt{(i_1 - i_2)^2 + (i_1 - i_2)(j_1 - j_2) + (j_1 - j_2)^2}$

3.3   The k^2-coloring Algorithm

We now present our k^2-coloring algorithm for the hexagon tiling coloring problem. For a given distance $d \in \Re^+$, the k^2-coloring algorithm uses k^2 colors, where $k = \left\lceil \frac{2d}{\sqrt{3}} + 1 \right\rceil$, to color the entire hexagon tiling and guarantees that any two hexagons $h_1, h_2 \in H$ with $d(h_1, h_2) \leq d$ have different colors. Figure 3 shows the coloring pattern generated by the k^2-coloring algorithm for $d = \frac{3\sqrt{3}}{2}$ and $k = 4$. The k^2-coloring algorithm is used by the sensor nodes in our proposed localized algorithm to locally identify the group they belong to.

Algorithm 1. k^2-coloring algorithm

Input: Given a hexagon tiling H and a distance $d \in \Re^+$
Output: Colored H
Compute $k = \left\lceil \frac{2d}{\sqrt{3}} + 1 \right\rceil$
for all hexagon $h(i, j) \in H$ **do**
    $Color_{h(i,j)} \leftarrow (j \bmod k)k + (i \bmod k) + 1$
end for

Lemma 1. *For a given $d \in \Re^+$, the k^2-coloring algorithm colors the hexagon tiling H, such that two hexagons $h_1, h_2 \in H$ have different colors if $d(h_1, h_2) \leq d$.*

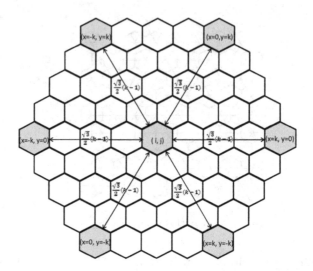

Fig. 2. The Minimum Distance Between Two Nodes with Same Color

Proof. The lemma can be proved by showing that in the color assignment generated by the k^2-coloring algorithm, for any two hexagons $h_1(i_1, j_1), h_2(i_2, j_2) \in H$, the distance $d(h_1, h_2)$ will be greater than $\frac{\sqrt{3}}{2}(k-1)$ (where $k = \left\lceil \frac{2d}{\sqrt{3}} + 1 \right\rceil$).

If $h_1(i_1, j_1)$ and $h_2(i_2, j_2)$ are assigned the same color by the k^2-coloring algorithm, then $j_1 \pmod{k} \times k + i_1 \pmod{k} + 1 = j_2 \pmod{k} \times k + i_2 \pmod{k} + 1$. This happens iff

$$i_1 \equiv i_2 \pmod{k}$$
$$j_1 \equiv j_2 \pmod{k}$$

Let $x = i_1 - i_2$ and $y = j_1 - j_2$. It follows that x and y will be multiple of k. The distance between the centers of $h_1(i_1, j_1)$ and $h_2(i_2, j_2)$ is given by

$$d_c(h_1, h_2) = \frac{\sqrt{3}}{2}\sqrt{x^2 + xy + y^2}$$

Consider the following cases:

- If $|x| \geq 2k$: We have $d_c(h_1, h_2) = \frac{\sqrt{3}}{2}\sqrt{(\frac{x}{2} + y)^2 + \frac{3}{4}x^2} \geq \frac{\sqrt{3}}{2}\sqrt{\frac{3}{4}(2k)^2} > \frac{\sqrt{3}}{2}(k-1) + 1$. Note that for every hexagon the distance from a point inside it to its center is at most $\frac{1}{2}$. Hence, the distance between two hexagons $d(h_1, h_2)$ will be at least $d_c(h_1, h_2) - 2(\frac{1}{2}) > \frac{\sqrt{3}}{2}(k-1)$.
- If $|y| \geq 2k$: We also obtain the same result as in the case $|x| \geq 2k$.
- If $|x|$ and $|y| < 2k$: If $x = y = \pm k$, then the distance between two hexagons $d(h_1, h_2)$ will be at least $d_c(h_1, h_2) - 2(\frac{1}{2}) > \frac{\sqrt{3}}{2}\sqrt{3k^2} - 1 > \frac{\sqrt{3}}{2}(k-1)$. Otherwise there are only six left cases of x, y as shown in the figure 2. The distance between two hexagons in all of these cases is exactly $\frac{\sqrt{3}}{2}(k-1)$.

Hence, the lemma is completely proved.

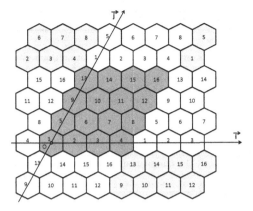

Fig. 3. The Coloring Pattern for $k = 4$

4 Localized Trigger Identification Algorithm

In this section, we introduce a localized algorithm which can be used as a network maintenance service and can be periodically invoked to identifying all trigger nodes and the location of jammers in the WSN. On the basis of this information, the overlying network protocol could avoid relaying the messages over the trigger nodes, considering them as receivers only. With this no trigger node will invoke the jammers and jamming attack can be completely nullified. If possible we can also destroy the jammers after knowing their location.

An overview of our localized trigger identification algorithm is given in Algorithm 2. The basic idea is to first geographically partition the nodes in the WSN into disjoint groups. Each group is then scheduled to run an algorithm that identifies the trigger nodes within itself along with the location of the jammer they are triggering. Based on this, our localized Trigger Identification algorithm has two phases. The first phase results in partitioning of set of nodes in the WSN into disjoint groups, such that the nodes located in the same hexagon forms a group. Each group has a color based on Algorithm 1. In the second phase, based on the color assignment different groups are scheduled to individually executes a localized trigger nodes identification algorithm to identify the trigger nodes within them along with the location of the jammer they trigger. All the groups with same color are scheduled in the same time slot.

4.1 Partition of Nodes Based on Hexagon Tiling and Coloring

In this subsection we discuss the localized partitioning of the WSN nodes into groups. We consider 2D plane on which the WSN is deployed is partitioned into regular hexagons forming a hexagon tiling, all the nodes located in the same hexagon form a group. Let D_h be the diameter of a hexagon as follows:

- If $1 < \alpha \le 2$, then the diameter of the hexagons D_h will be r
- If $2 < \alpha \le 3$, then the diameter of the hexagons D_h will be $R - 2r$
- If $\alpha > 3$, then the diameter of the hexagons D_h will be r

---

Algorithm 2. Localized Trigger Identification Algorithm

PHASE 1:

- Using hexagon tiling coloring partition the WSN into disjoint groups, such that all nodes located in a hexagon forms a group.
- On the basis of color assignment on the set of hexagons in the hexagon tiling of the WSN, generate a schedule $\{t_1, t_2, \ldots, t_c\}$ for all the groups. Groups located on different hexagons with same color i (where $1 \leq i \leq c$) are assigned the same time slot in the schedule.

PHASE 2:

- In accordance to the schedule generated in PHASE 1, different groups run the trigger node identification algorithm to identify the trigger nodes along with the location of the jammer.
- After the time slot t_c, all the trigger nodes are identified along with the location of the jammer.

In all the above cases, the nodes located within same hexagon will have distance less than or equal to r. Hence, they can communicate with each other in one hop.

We now discuss a method which can be using which a sensor node can locally identify the hexagon it belongs to and so it can find the group it belongs to. Further, using Algorithm 1 the node can identify the color of its hexagon and also the time slot assigned to its group in the schedule. We consider that a node $v \in V$ knows its neighbors $N(v)$ since the time of deployment of the WSN and using some ad hoc positioning method [14, 15] it can identify its location as (x_v, y_v) with respect to some reference node. We consider the sink node $s \in V$ in the WSN as the reference node such that $(x_s, y_s) = (0, 0)$. Now, we show that if a node v knows its coordinates (x_v, y_v) in the Cartesian system then without having the global view of the hexagon tiling, it can locally compute its coordinates (x_v^h, y_v^h) in new coordinate system on the hexagon tiling and further, it can identify the hexagon it belongs to. For instance a node v at coordinates (x_v, y_v) in the Cartesian coordinates can compute its coordinates (x_v^h, y_v^h) in the new coordinate system as: The coordinates of the hexagon $h(i, j)$ in which node v is located is given as:

In order to show the correctness of our method we prove the following lemmas:

Lemma 2. *When $\alpha > 2$, all trigger nodes located in a hexagon h trigger a single common jammer.*

Proof. Assume that there exists a hexagon h which has two trigger nodes v_{t1} and v_{t2} triggering two different jammers j_1 and j_2, respectively. Now, when $2 < \alpha \leq 3$, $D_h = R - 2r$, then $\max\{d(v_{t1}, v_{t2})\} = R - 2r$ and $\max\{d(v_{t1}, j_1)\} = \max\{d(v_{t2}, j_2)\} = r$, hence, in this case $\max\{d(j_1, j_2)\} = R$, which is a contradiction as $d(j_1, j_2) > R$. Similarly, when $\alpha > 3$, $D_h = r$, $\max\{d(v_{t1}, v_{t2})\} = \max\{d(v_{t1}, j_1)\} = \max\{d(v_{t2}, j_2)\} = r$, hence, $\max\{d(j_1, j_2)\} = 3r$ which is again a contradiction.

Lemma 3. *A node v located in a hexagon h_1 cannot be affected by the Noise injected by a jammer j invoked by a trigger nodes v_t located in another hexagon h_2, where $d(h_1, h_2) > R + r$.*

Proof. Assume that the *Noise* injected by the jammer j affects node v, then $d(j, v) \leq R$ and as $\max\{d(v_t, j)\} = r$, so $\max\{d(v_t, v)\} = R + r$, but as $d(h_1, h_2) > R + r$, so $d(v_t, v) > R + r$, which is a contradiction.

Lemma 4. *Given $d = (R + r)$, the number of colors c use by Algorithm 1 to color the entire hexagon tiling is:*

- $\left\lceil (\frac{2}{\sqrt{3}}(\alpha + 1) + 1) \right\rceil^2$, *when $D_h = r$.*
- $\left\lceil (\frac{2}{\sqrt{3}} \frac{(\alpha+1)}{(\alpha-2)} + 1) \right\rceil^2$, *when $D_h = R - 2r$.*

Proof. In general, if a hexagon tiling H has hexagons of diameter D_h, then considering a distance $d \in \Re^+$ the k^2-coloring algorithm needs $\left\lceil \frac{2d}{D_h \sqrt{3}} + 1 \right\rceil^2$ colors, hence, it is straightforward to show that when :

- $D_h = r$ and $d = R + r = (\alpha + 1)r$,
  k^2-coloring algorithm needs $c = \left\lceil \frac{2}{\sqrt{3}}(\alpha + 1) + 1 \right\rceil^2$ colors
- $D_h = R - 2r = (\alpha - 2)r$ and $d = R + r = (\alpha + 1)r$,
  k^2-coloring algorithm needs $c = \left\lceil (\frac{2}{\sqrt{3}} \frac{(\alpha+1)}{(\alpha-2)} + 1) \right\rceil^2$ colors

Remark 1. Using the above method mentioned in this section, a sensor node in the WSN, without having a global view of the hexagon tiling can locally identify the hexagon in which it is located along with its color.

4.2   Trigger Nodes Identification Procedure

We resort to sequential group testing to identify all trigger nodes out of testing groups. This subsection illustrates detail idea of the trigger nodes detection algorithm based on sequential group testing within each hexagon.

For each *testing group* in hexagons of color i, we devised the

we only necessitate to discover only six trigger nodes so as to determine all trigger nodes within a hexagon of diagonal size r at most. Therefore, each hexagonal *testing group* would obviously require a deterministic upperbound of testing rounds $6 \times \log \Delta$. Based on this observation, the duration to run the identification algorithm of trigger nodes would be practically set by reasonable amount of time since we consider that our network systems are loosely synchronized in the order of seconds. We call this discrete time slots **epochs**. **Epochs** are amortized running time due to the fact that the testing groups with the same color can run the identification algorithm in parallel. Furthermore, each epoch is further divided into sub-time slots called **trice**. We consider the time duration of a trice is $\Delta t \geq 2t_{prop} + t_{trans}^{jam}$, where t_{prop} is the propagation delay of a transmitted signal for a distance equal to r and t_{trans}^{jam} is the time duration for which a jammer injects interference signal *noise* after listening to a signal from some trigger node. *Notice that the deterministic upper bound of testing rounds enables our approach applicable against reactive jamming attack in practical WSNs.*

**Sequential Group Testing Based Trigger Node Identification Algo-
rithm (SGTNI)** As stated Lemma 2, based on the constraint on distance
between any two jammers j_1 and j_2, $d(j_1, j_2) > R$ in order to avoid mutual invocation between them, we proved that in two cases when $2 < \alpha \leq 3$, $D_h = R - 2r$
and $\alpha > 3$, $D_h = r$ only one jammer can be activated by nodes within a hexagon.
The SGTNI algorithm has following five steps:

- Step1: Identify two trigger nodes v and u with maximum distance between
  them within a hexagon using sequential group testing.
- Step2: Construct a disk D centered at each of the two trigger nodes from
  step1 with radius $d(v, u)$ in order to determine suspicious trigger nodes. The
  intersection of those two D disks is *triggering area* where all trigger nodes
  should be located.
- Step3: Discover two nodes w and z with the minimum distances to each
  intersection point of two disks D respectively from step2 If both w and z are
  trigger nodes, all nodes withing triggering area are trigger nodes.
- Step4: Determine two trigger nodes u' and v' with the minimum distances
  from the intersection point which is closer to the non-trigger node if either
  of w or z is a non-trigger node.

**Detect a set of *suspicious trigger nodes* by discovering two trigger
nodes which have the maximum distance between them using sequential group testing:**

For the sake of covering all the *suspicious trigger nodes* within a testing group,
we initially detect two trigger nodes v and u with the maximum distance between
them and construct two disks D centered by v and u. Obviously, the radius of
D will be less than equal to r. The intersection of those disks is called *triggering
area* since all trigger nodes should be placed in here. In addition, all nodes within
this area called *suspicious trigger nodes* the nodes which might be *trigger nodes*.
Likewise, as illustrated in Fig. 4, the *triggered area* with blue thick line is the
area where the jammer is supposed to be located at.

Lemma 5. *All trigger nodes locate in the intersection of two D disks centered
at each of two trigger nodes, where they have the maximum distance among any
trigger nodes in testing group.*

Proof. As shown in Fig. 4, suppose that two identified trigger nodes v and u
have the maximum distance among any other trigger nodes in a hexagon. It is
straightforward that if there is a trigger node outside of the intersection, then
the maximum distance between any two trigger nodes should not be the distance
between v and u. Notice that as introduced in 4.1 the diagonal of hexagon is
adjusted adequately, so that all trigger nodes within a hexagon activate the same
jammer.

Discovering two trigger nodes away each other with maximum distance are conducted using sequential group testing within two phases: (1) identification of the
trigger node located farthest away from the center of hexagon. In this sense,

we create a non-increasing sorted list of nodes based on the distances to the center of hexagon and perform a sequential group testing with the list. Detail procedure of sequential group testing is to be discussed. (2) Creation of another non-increasing sorted list of nodes according to the distances from all nodes to the trigger node with maximum distance to the center. We conduct one more sequential group testing to identify the trigger with this sorted list. Then we would be able to discover two trigger nodes with maximum distance to each other.

The localized algorithm for identifying a trigger node is illustrated in Algorithm 3. We assume that sensors have own unique identifications , and a sensor node v knows the IDs and locations of its neighbors in $N(v)$ along with hexagons they belong to. Hence, if v is located in the hexagon h and belongs to the respective group N_h of nodes located in h, then it can find out all the other nodes in N_h. Based on this information, we could run sequential group testing with parametrized data structure called $NodeList$ which contains list of nodes sorted in a certain criteria. Further, all the nodes $v \in N_h$ synchronously runs Algorithm 3. The algorithm takes at most $\log_2(|N_h|)$ trice to identify a trigger node. And as the data structure $NodeList$ could be individually computed by all the nodes in N_h, hence, all nodes have the uniform information about the identified trigger node.

Identification of All Trigger Nodes within a Hexagon

By discovering a set of *suspicious trigger nodes*, we will introduce how to identify an exact set of trigger nodes out of the set. As illustrated in Fig. 4, there will be two intersection points $p1$ and $p2$ from two D disks centered by u and v. Each node in a hexagonal testing group checks two sensors w and z with the minimum distances to $p1$ and $p2$ respectively.

A hexagonal testing have two cases that either all nodes could be trigger nodes or part of nodes could be trigger nodes. As illustrated in 4(a), if both w and z are trigger nodes, then no further action is required since all the nodes in the testing group are trigger nodes. However, either w or z could be a non-trigger node and w is a non-trigger node in Fig. 4(b) , which requires additional two more identified trigger nodes u' and v' with minimum distances to a intersection point $p2$ which is closer to the non-trigger node w. We consider that each u' and v' is located away exactly r from the location of the jammer and construct a disk with radius r passing through both u' and v' including u and v in order to get the center of the disk because other nodes closer to $p2$ are non-trigger nodes and out of triggering range r. Any nodes in the testing group with distances less than r to the center are the trigger nodes.

5   The *TNLT-CDS* Routing Algorithm

One of the benefits for identifying the trigger nodes is to help construct a routing protocol which does not activate any reactive jammer. In this section, we propose a simple routing algorithm called **Trigger Nodes Leaves Tree based on Connected Dominating Set** (*TNLT-CDS*) which uses trigger nodes as

---

Algorithm 3. Trigger Nodes Identification Algorithm

All nodes in a group N_h synchronously performs the following to identify three trigger nodes in N_h.
INPUT: $TestingGroup$
OUTPUT: $Triggers$
$Triggers \leftarrow \emptyset$

/* In order to discover a node v with maximum distance to the center of the hexagon, each node sorts all neighbors based on the distance to the center of the hexagon in non-increasing order */
$SortedNodes \leftarrow DecSort(d(N_h, d_c))$
In a new **trice** Δt do the following:
$v \leftarrow ISTN(SortedNodes)$

/* In order to discover a node u with maximum distance to v , each node sorts all neighbors based on the distance to v in non-increasing order */
$SortedNodes \leftarrow DecSort(d(N_h, v))$
In a new **trice** Δt do the following:
$u \leftarrow ISTN(SortedNodes)$

if $v == u$ **then**
    $Triggers \leftarrow v$
else
    Construct two disks D_v and D_u centered by v and u with radius $d(u, v)$
    Pick two nodes w and z which have the closest intersection points from D_v and D_u. w is the node with smaller ID.
    In a new **trice** Δt do the following:
    if $ID == w$ **then**
        Perform individual testing on w
    else
        Listen to the $Noise$
    end if
    In a new **trice** Δt do the following:
    if $ID == z$ **then**
        Perform individual testing on z
    else
        Listen to the $Noise$
    end if
    if $w == TriggerNode$ and $z == TriggerNode$ **then**
        $Triggers \leftarrow N_h$
    else
        if $w == TriggerNode$ **then**
            $w \leftarrow z$
        end if
        Coordinate $p \leftarrow$ the closest intersection of D_v and D_u from w
        $SortedNodes \leftarrow IncSort(d(N_h, p))$
        In a new **trice** Δt do the following:
        $u' \leftarrow ISTN(SortedNodes)$
        $SortedNodes \leftarrow SortedNodes \setminus u'$
        In a new **trice** Δt do the following:
        $v' \leftarrow ISTN(SortedNodes)$
        $C_j \leftarrow$ center of the disk with radius r which includes both v and u, passing through v' and u'.
        for $i = 0; i \leq |N_h|; i + +$ **do**
            if $d(C_j, N_h^i) \leq r$ **then**
                $Triggers \cup N_h^i$
            end if
        end for
    end if
end if

Algorithm 4. Identification of A Single Trigger Node Algorithm *ISTN* based on Sequential Group Testing

```
INPUT: NodeList
OUTPUT: Trigger
Trigger ← ∅
Beg = 0; End = NodeList.length() − 1; Mid = ⌊(Beg+End)/2⌋
while Beg ≤ End do
    In a new trice Δt do the following:
    if v ∈ NodeList(Beg, End) then
        Transmit TEST₁ packet in t_test time and Listen to the Noise
    else
        Just Listen to the Noise
    end if
    if Noise exists after t_test + r/s time then
        if Beg==End then
            Trigger = Trigger ∪ NodeList[Beg];
            NodeList = NodeList \ Trigger;
            break;
        end if
        End = Mid; Mid = ⌊(Beg+End)/2⌋;
    else
        Beg = Mid; Mid = ⌊(Beg+End)/2⌋
    end if
end while
return Trigger
```

only end receivers. Together with the *ITN* algorithm, *TNLT-CDS* will complete an efficient countermeasure for reactive jamming attacks.

We will utilize the Connected Dominating Set (CDS) to construct our *TNLT-CDS* as CDS has been shown as one of the most efficient methods for constructing a broadcast protocol. Again, consider network $G = (V, E)$ with $U \subset V$ as a set of trigger nodes identified by *ITN*. We will construct a directed graph $G' = (V, E')$ by changing all the undirected edges $(u, v) \in E$ where $u \in V \setminus U$ and $v \in U$ to the directed edge (u, v). We then deploy any CDS algorithm in directed graph [16] on G'. It is easy to see that the obtained CDS S will not consist of any node

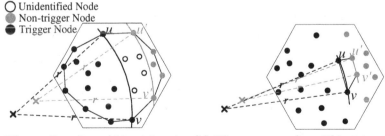

(a) When *all* nodes within *triggering area* are trigger nodes

(b) When *some* nodes within *triggering area* are trigger nodes

Fig. 4. Various edge detection algorithms

in U. Finally, we construct a broadcast tree T by connecting nodes in S to the rest using newly added directed edges.

6   Conclusion and Further Discussion

In this paper, we devise a novel localized algorithm to efficiently tackle reactive jamming attack problem in WSN by identifying *trigger nodes*. Our local identification of all trigger nodes achieves high feasibility with low overhead in terms of time and message complexity by leveraging sequential GT and hexagon tiling scheme. We propose the hexagon tiling coloring to exploit the available spacial parallelism to test the WSN for identifying trigger nodes. Based on the color assignment, all testing groups are scheduled to conduct the localized trigger node detection algorithm using the sequential GT. Besides the analytical complexity analysis, an intensive series of experiments has shown an outstanding performance of our solution on various WSN settings in terms of scalability and stability. Furthermore, investigation on more stealthy and energy efficient jamming model with simulations indicates robustness and potential of our scheme as well.

By embedding identifying the location of jammers based on identified trigger nodes, improved countermeasure for more robust WSNs could be realized since elimination of attackers is inevitably the best way to maintain the soundness of WSNs.

Acknowledgement. This work was supported by the International Cooperative R&D Project of the Korea Institute of Energy Technology Evaluation and Planning(KETEP) grant funded by the Korea government Ministry of Knowledge Economy (20111030100020).

References

[1]   Bellardo, J., Savage, S.: 802.11 Denail-of-Service Sttacks: Real Vulnerabilities and Practical Solutions. In: Proceedings of the 12th Conference on USENIX Security Symposium (2003)

[2]   Sidek, O., Yahya, A.: Reed Solomon Coding for Frequency Hopping Spread Spectrum in Jamming Environment. American Journal of Applied Sciences (2008)

[3]   Chiang, T., Hu, Y.: Dynamic Jamming Mitigation for Wireless Broadcast Networks. In: INFOCOM (2008)

[4]   Desmedt, Y., Safavi-Naini, R., Wang, H., Charnes, C., Pieprzyk, J.: Broadcast Anti-Jamming Systems. Computer Networks, 349–355 (1999)

[5]   Ling, Q., Ren, J., Li, T.: Message-Driven Frequency Hopping — Design and Analysis. In: Li, Y., Huynh, D.T., Das, S.K., Du, D.-Z. (eds.) WASA 2008. LNCS, vol. 5258, pp. 373–384. Springer, Heidelberg (2008)

[6]   Wood, A., Stankovic, J., Son, S.: A Jammed-Area Mapping Service for Sensor Networks. In: Proceedings of the 24th IEEE International Real-Time System Symposium, vol. 78, pp. 286–297 (2003)

[7] Strasser, M., Popper, C., Capkun, S., Cagalj, M.: Jamming-resistant Key Estab-
     lishment using Uncoordinated Frequency Hopping. In: Proceedings of the 2008
     IEEE Symposium on Security and Privacy, pp. 80–89 (2008)
[8] Xu, W., Wood, T., Trappe, W., Zhang, Y.: Channel Surfing and Spatial Retreats:
     Defenses against Wireless Denial of Service. In: Proceedings of the 3rd ACM Work-
     shop on Wireless Security, pp. 80–89 (2004)
[9] Xu, W., Trappe, W., Zhang, Y.: Channel Surfing: Defending Wireless Sensor Net-
     works from Interference. In: Proceedings of the 6th International Conference on
     Information Processing in Sensor Networks, pp. 499–508 (2007)
[10] Shin, I., Shen, Y., Xuan, Y., Thai, M., Znati, T.: Reactive Jamming Attacks
     in Multi-Radio Wireless Sensor Networks: an Efficient Mitigating Measure by
     Identifying Trigger Nodes. In: Proceedings of the 2nd ACM International Work-
     shop on Foundations of Wireless Ad Hoc and Sensor Networking and Computing,
     FOWANC 2009, pp. 87–96 (2009)
[11] Xuan, Y., Shin, I., Thai, M.: On Trigger Detection against Reactive Jamming
     Attacks: A Clique-Independent Set Based Approach. In: Performance Computing
     and Communications Conference (IPCCC), pp. 223–230 (2009)
[12] Xu, W., Trappe, W., Zhang, Y., Wood, T.: The Feasibility of Launching and
     Detecting Jamming Attacks in Wireless Networks. In: Proceedings of the 6th
     ACM International Symposium on Mobile Ad Hoc Networking and Computing,
     pp. 46–57 (2005)
[13] Sen, A., Roxborough, T., Sinha, B.: On an Optimal Algorithm for Channel Assign-
     ment in Cellular Networks. In: IEEE International Conference on Communications
     (1999)
[14] Niculescu, D., Nath, B.: Ad Hoc Positioning System (APS) using AOA. In:
     Twenty-Second Annual Joint Conference of the IEEE Computer and Commu-
     nications Societies, INFOCOM 2003 (2003)
[15] Niculescu, D., Nath, B.: Ad Hoc Positioning System (APS) using AOA. In:
     GLOBECOM 2001 (2001)
[16] Thai, M., Tiwari, R., Du, D.: On Construction of Virtual Backbone in Wireless
     Ad Hoc Networks with Unidirectional Links. IEEE Transactions on Mobile Com-
     puting, TMC (2008)

Efficient Self-organized Trust Management in Location Privacy Enhanced VANETs

Yu-Chih Wei[1,2] and Yi-Ming Chen[2]

[1] Information & Communication Security Lab, TL, Chunghwa Telecom co., Ltd.,
Taoyuan, Taiwan(R.O.C.)
[2] Department of Information Management,National Central University
Taoyuan, Taiwan(R.O.C.)
vickrey@cht.com.tw,cym@cc.ncu.edu.tw

Abstract. Improving the safety of transportation system is the main
purpose of vehicle ad-hoc networks (VANETs). In order to improve traffic safety and ensure the event messages reliability, more and more researches have been focused on trust management to resolve the problems.
However, in these researches, little attention has been paid to the location
privacy due to the natural conflict between trust and anonymity, which is
the basic protection of privacy. Although traffic safety remains the most
crucial requirement in VANETs, location privacy can be just as important for drivers, and neither can be ignored. In this paper, we propose
a self-organized trust management system that aims to thwart internal
attackers from sending false messages in privacy-enhanced VANETS. To
evaluate the reliability and performance of the proposed system, we conducted a set of simulations under collusion and non-collusion attacks.
The simulation results show that the proposed system is highly resilient
to adversarial attacks, no matter whether it is under a fixed silent period
(FSP) or random silent period (RSP) location privacy-enhanced scheme.

Keywords: VANET, Trust Management, Safety, Self-Organized.

1 Introduction

In order to improve traffic safety, vehicles are equipped with communication devices, which can share useful information to other vehicles in the vicinity. In addition to traffic safety, vehicular ad-hoc networks (VANETs) can also be used for
traffic efficiency improvement and entertainment. However, traffic safety is still
the most important issue in VANETs. In order to enhance traffic safety, many
VANETs safety applications require vehicles to periodically broadcast single-hop
messages to other vehicles. These periodic broadcast messages are called beacon
messages. In addition to beacon message, vehicles also broadcast event-driven
warning messages, such as Electronic Emergency Break Lights (EEBL), and
Post-Crash Notifications (PCN) etc. [1], to neighboring vehicles. These event-
driven warning messages are called event messages. If these event messages were
abused, it may raise new safety risks for the whole transportation system [2].

D.H. Lee and M. Yung (Eds.): WISA 2012, LNCS 7690, pp. 328–344, 2012.
© Springer-Verlag Berlin Heidelberg 2012

Message authentication is one common method to resolve the safety risks of VANETs, which can ensure the integrity of transmitted messages. In message authentication, cryptographic mechanisms have been widely employed to protect VANETs against unauthorized message alterations. However, the message authentication method can only ensure that messages are sent from legitimate senders. It cannot prevent a legitimate sender from broadcasting bogus or altered messages malevolently to neighbor vehicles. These bogus or altered messages may not only decrease the transportation efficiency, but also in the worst cases, they will cause accidental events that can threaten human life. In order to treat the internal threat, establishing trust relationships can enable vehicles to distinguish trustworthy vehicles or messages from untrustworthy ones. This can reduce the risk of vehicles being misled by other malicious vehicles. However, if vehicles collude to cheat message receiving vehicle by altering the opinion message, a vehicle will be misled due to too many malicious vehicles forward the event message with their opinions to support the bogus messages or opposite the normal messages. Besides, if adversaries cooperate together, it is much easier to mislead vehicle to make the wrong decision. More than one adversary might collude to launch an attack by cooperatively injecting false messages in order to en-large the effectiveness of the attacks [3]. Due to strategic cooperation for lying, collusion attacks are still an open problem in existing works [4,5].

In order to overcome the problems mentioned above, in this paper, we propose an efficient self-organized trust management model, which can not only treat event messages but also collect beacon messages for establishing trust relationship with entity and event message. Given this capability, we can reduce both the false positive rate and false negative rate for making decision about the received event messages. We evaluate the proposed system under fixed silent period (FSP) and random silent period (RSP) location privacy enhanced schemes through extensive simulations. All of the simulations consider different adversary models, including opinion alteration at-tacks and bogus message attacks under collusion or non-collusion scheme. The simulation results show that the proposed system performs outstanding than the comparison baseline in location privacy-enhanced schemes.

The rest of this paper is organized as following: Section 2 describes the related work. Section 3 depicts the trust management framework and module functions. Section 4 describes the evaluation methods and simulation results of the proposed system, and Section 5 presents our conclusions and future work.

2 Related Work

2.1 Misbehavior Detection in VANETs

In misbehavior detection, position verification is the most widely adopted mechanism [6,7]. In [7], Leinmller et al. proposed a position verification approach, which considered with autonomous sensors such as acceptance range threshold (ART), mobility grade threshold (MGT) etc. With this mechanism, the nodes cheating about their positions in beacons can be recognized. In [8], Schmidt et al. enhanced a position verification approach with Sudden Appearance Warning (SAW) and Maximum Beaconing Frequency (MBF) to improve their misbehavior detection mechanisms and proposed a reputation system to maintain the trust relation with historical data. Raya et al. [9] proposed a misbehavior detection scheme (MDS) to discover misbehaving or faulty nodes by detecting their deviation from normal behavior. The MDS they proposed can distinguish between two types of misbehaviors: known misbehaviors and data anomalies. In known misbehavior detection, they adopted the position-verification approach mentioned in [6]; In data anomalies, their method leveraged the entropy and outlier detection algorithm to detect the malicious event messages. Ghosh et al. also proposed an MDS integrated with root-cause analysis [10], in which they first constructed a cause-tree, then they used the logical reduction to indicate the root cause of the misbehavior.

2.2   Trust Management in VANETs

In VANETs, entity trust is the traditional notion of trust. A network of nodes with trust relationship can easily distinguish normal behavior nodes from misbehavior nodes. In VANETs, such capability can help to ensure the safety of vehicles. Dotzer et al. [11] proposed a distributed entity-centric reputation system named VARS, which can share trust opinions among neighboring vehicles in VANETs. In their proposed system, every message forwarder appends their opinion about the vehicles trustworthiness to the message. However, VARS is not suitable in an ephemeral environment for the message size will become larger and larger due to the piggybacking of opinions. Based on the assumption that most vehicles are honest and will not endorse any message containing false data [12]. Ostermaier et al. [13] proposed a simple and straightforward voting scheme to evaluate the plausibility of received hazard messages. Lo and Tsai [14] also proposed an event-based reputation system to prevent the spread of false traffic warning messages in VANETs. They introduced a dynamic reputation-evaluation mechanism to determine the trustworthiness of the event messages. In order to overcome the dependence of slow-to-change entity trust, Raya et al. [15] proposed a data-centric trust management model for VANETs. In their proposed system, data trustworthiness would focus on data per se, such as position and timestamp of event message, rather than merely on the trustworthiness of the data-reporting vehicles. Besides, they also evaluated some decision logic, such as voting, Bayesian inference (BI) and the Dempster-Shafer Theory (DST). Their model, however, focuses only on the data and they do not leverage the trustworthiness of sender or forwarder of event messages.

Existing researches on reputation systems [11,12,13,14,15] for VANETs mainly collect event-based messages for decision-making, while neglecting beacon messages, which are also useful in determining the trustworthiness of event messages in reputation systems. Regarding to collusion resistance reputation system, as far as we know, little research tries to examine trust establishment with collusion attacks in VANETs. Most collusion attacks prevention researches still focus on routing mechanism but merely focus on traffic safety. Take [16] as an example, the authors proposed a new collusion attack prevention model against OLSR routing protocol in MANETs, but the proposed model is suitable for VANETs. Golle et al. [17] also proposed a special kind of collusion attack prevention model, however, the scheme only works in the simplest scenario regarding the collusion attack [5]. Other researches such as [18] and [11] have mentioned collusion attacks, however, their works did not provide any solution.

In the next section, we will introduce our research assumptions and the description of the proposed methods in detail.

3   Methodology

3.1   Assumptions

In order to make the proposed model work properly, throughout this paper, we made the following assumptions:

- All on-board units (OBUs) are equipped with GPS and wireless interfaces. The system time of the OBUs are synchronized via GPS in real-time.
- OBUs periodically broadcast single-hop beaconing messages, which contain at least position, velocity, and headway direction.
- OBUs adopt pseudonyms to prevent identity tracking while beaconing and sending message, and all pseudonyms are changed after a short period and do not repeat.
- OBUs have the ability to collect beacon and event messages, and they enable the linkability of these messages.
- There exists a public key infrastructure (PKI) in VANETs and a fully trustworthy third party that conforms to standardize key management, verification, and revocation.

3.2   Adversary Model

In this paper, we consider an adversary to be a vehicle equipped with an OBU in a certain area of the VANET. The attacker can actively participate in the network and violate the integrity of messages, such as by broadcasting or forwarding malicious messages. The basic trust attack models focus on bogus message attack and alteration attack [19]. These basic attacks may cause legitimate drivers to change their driving behavior, such as decelerating or choosing alternative routes, which may succeed in confusing honest drivers behavior. In addition to the basic trust attack methods, combination attacks such as collusion attacks are also introduced in the following.

Non-collusion Attack. A non-collusion attack is assumed that malicious vehicles are all selfish one, besides they all make their selfish decisions independently. Each malicious vehicle can send a forged bogus message, while another multi-hop message forwarder can decide to support this event message or not. It is assumed that on non-collusion attack model, all of their decisions are always for their own selfish purpose. For example, to make a good traffic quality of the alternative route, a selfish vehicle may decide to forward a PCN message to other vehicles with its opposite opinion to prevent other vehicle reroute to another road.

Collusion Attack. In [20], Yu and Liu mentioned that collusion attacks are attackers working together in order to improve the attack capability. In other words, collusion attacks are hard to resistant or prevent. In this paper, it is assumed that vehicles can collude with other colluders and make use of above basic attack methods to let vehicles make wrong decisions. For example, as shown in Fig. 1, it is assumed that vehicle S, A, B are colluders. In Fig. 1(a), when colluder S send a bogus message to others in the vicinity, colluder A and B will send support opinion messages while only honest vehicle C sends opposite opinion message to deny this bogus event message. This may make receiver R believe this bogus event message and then make a wrong decision to react to this forged event. Besides, as shown in Fig. 1(b), if honest vehicle H sends an event message, colluder A, B may forward the event message with their opposite opinions in order to confuse the message receiver R. The collusion scenarios depend on the number of basic attack models. In this paper, to simplify the simulation, we choose bogus message attack, and alternation attacks for this evaluation.

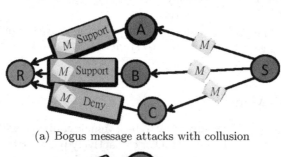

(a) Bogus message attacks with collusion

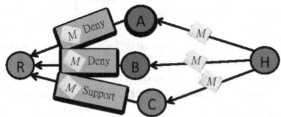

(b) Alteration attacks with collusion

Fig. 1. Illustration of Collusion attacks

3.3   System Architecture

As show in Fig. 2, the proposed system can be divided into three parts: trust gathering, trust compositing, and trust combining and decision.

Trust gathering contains two modules: beacon trustworthiness gathering module and event message trustworthiness gathering module. The beacon trustworthiness gathering module is responsible for establishing vehicles entity trustworthiness from historical beacon messages. Due to the basic requirement of periodically beaconing in VANETs safety applications, beacon trustworthiness gathering module can determine the entity trustworthiness in real-time by cross-checking the reasonability of vehicle movement from beacon messages. Event message trustworthiness gathering module is different from beacon trustworthiness module as it determines the event message trustworthiness by the reasonability of the received event messages and beacon messages. According to the count of forwarding hops in the event message, these are two types of trust relations among entities: direct and indirect, which will be discussed in the next section.

The trust compositing part composites the trust values from different sensors and maintain the historical reputation. In historical reputation maintaining module, the reinforcement and discourage of the historical reputation is its major job. Finally, the trust combining and decision part is comprise of trust combining module and decision making module. Trust combining module is responsible for fusion the trustworthiness of event message sent from different vehicles. The decision making module makes decisions based on the final trust value to decide whether forwarding with support opinion or warning vehicle in the vicinity with denial opinion.

3.4   Trust Gathering

In general, trust information gathering methods in VANETs can be classified into three major categories: direct, indirect, and hybrid [21]. Direct trust means that trust information is observed or obtained by a vehicle itself. Information that is received from neighboring vehicles is the first-hand information. Beacon messages and direct received event messages from other vehicles are both first-hand information. Indirect trust relation is also known as second-hand information trust relation, which is obtained via the recommendation or opinion given from other vehicles. Of course, hybrid trust relation construct the trust relations not only from direct information but also from second-hand information, which can composite the advantages of them and complement their disadvantages. In this paper, the hybrid trust relation model is adopted by which we obtain direct trust information from beacon messages and direct received event messages and indirect trust from the traditional event message trust opinion method. In the following context, we give a detailed description of how to compute the direct and indirect trustworthiness of beacon and event message.

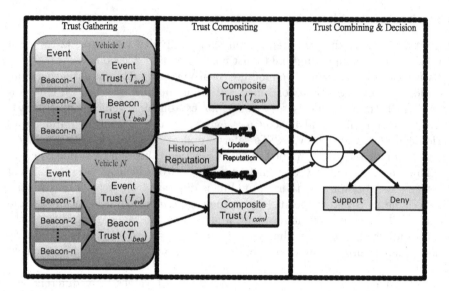

Fig. 2. The framework of the proposed self-organized trust management system

Beacon Trust. In order to enhance drive safety, many VANETs applications require vehicles to periodically broadcast single-hop messages to other vehicles, called beaconing. The content of the beacon messages contain the current position, velocity, headway direction and so, so that other vehicles in the vicinity can be aware of this vehicles movement. In addition to ensuring drive safety, beaconing is also the basic supporting mechanism for geographic routing and message transmission [22]. In general, beacon messages are broadcast in low latency, such as a few hundred milliseconds, and in plain text with digital signatures for non-repudiation. In order to provide privacy in VANETs, pseudonyms will be used while vehicles are beaconing. The pseudonyms will make it difficult to link vehicle-movement pattern together.

The main idea of beacon-based trust is to estimate and to verify constantly a vehicle's position, velocity, and drive direction. By computing the similarity between the claimed position, velocity, and direction with the estimated values, we can determine the trustworthiness of the vehicle that sending the beacons. In this paper, cosine similarity [23], Sim_{Cos}, is used to compute the angle between the estimated vector and the claimed vector, where vector is the set of vehicles position, velocity and direction values. This angle belongs to the inner product family and is also called the angular metric .[24]. In order to maintain the historical beacon-trust information of neighboring vehicles, in the following, we propose a time-based weighting method to calculate the trustworthiness of beacon messages. In (1), the beacon trustworthiness of a neighboring vehicle is denoted as T_{bea}. where $\overrightarrow{E}$ is the estimated vector based on the latest observations and $\overrightarrow{O}$ represents the claimed vector obtained in the latest beacon message.I is the number of beacons that should be taken into consideration, when the larger the value of I, the longer the time that the beacon messages can influence the trustworthiness. w_i is the weight of the last i beacons and n is the exponent value. Where n is the importance of the similarity, which decays over time.

$$T_{bea} = \frac{\sum\limits_{i=1}^{I} Sim_{Cos}(\overrightarrow{E}_i, \overrightarrow{O}_i)(w_i)^n}{\sum\limits_{i=1}^{I} (w_i)^n} \tag{1}$$

Event Trust. For public safety, vehicles broadcast event-driven warning messages, such as Approaching Emergency Vehicle Warnings, SOS Services, EE-BLs, and PCNs [1], to vehicles in the vicinity. In this paper, we call such an event-driven warning messages as "event-based message". It is assume that each message forwarder can give their opinion about the forwarding event message in order to assist message receiver to identify whether the message is trustworthy or not. In the forwarding event message, their opinion can be {*support, denial* }. Besides, each opinion attached with their trustworthiness of the their opinion. Let T_{evt} represents the trustworthiness of an event message. A greater value of T_{evt} indicates that the event message forwarder believes their opinion is trustworthier. Like beacon messages, each event-based message also contains authentication information to validate the authenticity of itself.

As mentioned earlier, there is two types of trust relation among vehicles: direct and indirect trust relations. Fig. 3 shows that trust relations among a set of vehicles, where it is assumed that vehicles A and B, C and D, D and E, E and F are radio-reachable. As shown in Fig. 3(a), vehicle A can transmit event message M_1 to vehicle B directly, the trust relation between A and B is a direct trust one, thus, the trustworthiness of the M_1 to vehicle B is a direct trust event message. While, in Fig. 3(b), an event message M_2 is transmitted multi-hop in order to notify vehicle F, an indirect trust relation occurs. In this example, M_2 needs to be forwarded by vehicles D and Ebefore reaching vehicle F. Hence, the trust relation between receiver F and original sender C is an indirect trust relation. It is noted that in this example, the trust relation between sender C and forwarder D is a direct trust relation because they are directly radio-reachable, and the relations of vehicles D and E and vehicles E and F are direct trust relations, too.

In order to compute the trustworthiness of a direct event-based message, we propose a position- and movement-verification mechanism. By this mechanism, a receiving vehicle is able to evaluate the trustworthiness of the sender vehicle by analyzing both the received event messages and the beacon messages from a vehicle. In the following, our proposed vehicle behavior-analysis method is presented. For determining direct event trust value, Tanimoto coefficient [25] is adopted, which is most widely used for binary fingerprints, to obtain the similarity between historical beacon messages and received event messages. Unlike cosine similarity, the Tanimoto coefficient belongs to the intersection family,

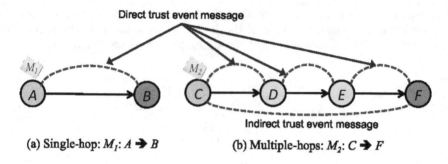

(a) Single-hop: M_1: $A \rightarrow B$ (b) Multiple-hops: M_2: $C \rightarrow F$

Fig. 3. The relationship between direct and indirect event message

which is different from cosine similarity [24]. The Tanimoto coefficient is defined as:

$$Sim_{Tan}(\vec{E}, \vec{R}) = \frac{\vec{E} \cdot \vec{R}}{\left|\vec{E}\right|^2 + \left|\vec{R}\right|^2 - \vec{E} \cdot \vec{R}} \tag{2}$$

where $\vec{R}$ is the vector of the location information from the received event message, and $\vec{E}$ is the vector of the location information estimated from the beacon message. In order to verify event-message plausibility and maintain trustworthiness, Equation (3) is used to compute the direct event trust T_{devt}, where Δd denotes the distance between the message receiver and the message sender, and Δt denotes the time delay between the original event message timestamp and the current timestamp of the message receiver. In equation (3), in addition to the trustworthiness value, we consider two more plausibility measurements: maximum transmission distance verification and maximum transmission delay verification. If Δd is larger than maximum transmission distance D_{max} or Δt is greater than maximum event message delay T_{max}, then the trustworthiness of direct event message T_{devt} will be set to zero. After passing the plausibility verification, T_{devt} will be assigned by the value of Tanimoto similarity.

$$T_{devt}(\vec{E}, \vec{R}) = \begin{cases} 0, \text{if}(\Delta d > D_{max} \ or \ \Delta t > T_{max}) \\ Sim_{Tan}(\vec{E}, \vec{R}), \text{else} \end{cases} \tag{3}$$

If a receiving vehicle recognizes that the sender of an event message is not the original transmitter, then the message will be classified as a type of indirect event message. To deal with the trust of indirect information, some researchers, such as Sun et al. [26], Dotzer et al. [11], and Luo et al. [27], have proposed indirect trust relation or recommendation methods. Luo et al. [27] divided indirect trust into transitivity and consensus recommendation trust models, and they proposed fuzzy trust recommendation models. However, in their research, they did not discuss in detail the axiom of indirect trust propagation. In this paper, we adopt the method proposed by Sun et al. [26]. When a receiving vehicle establishes a trust relationship through the recommendation of other vehicle, the trustworthiness between the sender and receiver should not be more than the trust value between the receiver and the forwarder, as well as the trust value between the sender and the forwarder. The indirect trustworthiness of the event message T_{evt} is calculated according to (4):

$$T_{evt}(e) = \begin{cases} T_{devt}, if(e \text{ is direct event}) \\ \min(T_{opn}, T_{devt}), otherwise \end{cases} \qquad (4)$$

Let e represent the event message identifier. If e is a direct event message, T_{evt} is assigned by T_{devt}, otherwise, T_{evt} is assigned by the minimum between the trustworthiness of the forwarder opinion T_{opn} and T_{devt}.

3.5   Trust Compositing

The event reputation value T_{rep} of a vehicle can be computed as in the following equation:

$$T_{rep}(t) = \begin{cases} \alpha T_{rep}(t-1), if(T_{evt}(t) = 0) \\ \beta T_{evt}(t) + (1 - \beta)T_{rep}(t-1), else \end{cases} \qquad (5)$$

In order to prevent huge degrading of reputation value, if T_{evt} is zero, T_{rep} will be punished by α, which is a constant for smoothly degrade the reputation value. β is the weighted value of current reputation value, while $(1-\beta)$ is the weighted value for the previous reputation value. After a vehicle computes the event trust value T_{evt}, it updates the previous reputation value in order to take the historical event trust value into consideration.

In this paper, we composite the vehicle's beacon trust T_{bea}, event trust T_{evt}, and the reputation trust T_{rep} to illustrate the trustworthiness of the event message. T_{com} is used for compositing the trustworthiness of the sensors. T_{com} is calculated as:

$$T_{com} = T_{bea} \times w_{bea} + T_{evt} \times w_{evt} + T_{rep} \times w_{rep} \qquad (6)$$

$w_{bea}, w_{evt}, w_{rep}$ are the weights of beacon trust, event trust, and reputation respectively, and $w_{bea} + w_{evt} + w_{rep} = 1$.

3.6   Trust Combining and Decision Making

When a vehicle receives a direct event message or an indirect event message opinion transmitted from multiple vehicles, it needs to find an effective solution to combine the received opinions and then to determine the overall trustworthiness of this event message. In [15], Raya et al. proposed a data-centric trust-establishment scheme. In addition to the trust-establishment scheme, they also evaluated several methods for comparing performance, such as Majority Voting (MV), Weighted Voting (WV), BI, and DST. They concluded that DST performed more consistently than other methods under the conditions of fast changes and high uncertainty. However, VANETs are ephemeral and fast-movement networks, in which there is not always a fixed infrastructure available to support security mechanisms. Besides, event messages may be lost due to the high uncertainty of the VANET. Thus, vehicles have to organize the trustworthiness of each vehicle and implement security protection schemes themselves.

The Dempster-Shafer evidence combination method provides a convenient numerical computing method for aggregating multiple pieces of data [28]. In addition, DST is not like BI, which requires prior probability to compute the posterior probability of an event message, something that is difficult to determine in practice [29]. Hence, DST is more suitable for dealing with the problems of uncertainty, and it minimizes the performance downgrade introduced by node mobility. In this paper, in order to accommodate the nature of uncertainty of VANETs, we adopt DST for opinion combination. The combined trust value Tds corresponding to an event is represented as in (7):

$$T_{ds}(i) = \overset{|N|}{\underset{n=1}{\oplus}} m_n(H_i) \tag{7}$$

N is the set of vehicles that transmitted or forwarded the event messages while the T_{bea} of the forwarding vehicle less than T_{thld}, it will be excluded from N. $|N|$ is the number of vehicles in N. If the opinion of the event message is trustworthy, and the trustworthiness of this vehicle n is T_{com}, then its probability assignment will be: $m_n(T) = T_{com}$, $m_n(\tilde{\ }T)=0$, $m_n(\Omega) =1-T_{com}$. If the opinion of the event message is not trustworthy, the probability assignment will be: $m_n(T) =0$, $m_n(\tilde{\ }T)= T_{com}$, $m_n(\Omega) =1-T_{com}$.

If an observation vehicle can receive event opinions from other vehicles in the vicinity, the result of trust combination can be used to compare with the threshold of trust degree. If T_{ds} greater than T_{thld}, observation vehicle will trust the event message and forward this event message with support opinion. Otherwise, observation vehicle will forward the event message with denial opinion in order to warn neighboring vehicles.

4   Evaluation

In this paper, we consider an adversary to be a vehicle equipped with an OBU in a certain area of the VANET. The internal attacker can actively participate in the network and violate the integrity of messages, such as by broadcasting or forwarding malicious messages. Focused basic attack models are alteration attacks and bogus message attacks [19]. In order to simulate the different adversary models in our proposed scheme, the attack behavior of an attack vehicle can be simulated through the assignment of attack functions. Three function parameters $\delta, \varepsilon, \omega$ have been used in the adversary models: δ is the rate of misbehavior vehicle, and ε is the alteration attack rate, and ω represents the bogus message rate. In addition to basic attacks, we also evaluate the proposed trust management model under collusion attacks in order to compare the proposed trust management system with comparison baseline.

4.1   Evaluation Model

In order to investigate the difference of the simulation results, we conduct both collusion and non-collusion attack scenarios to evaluate the trust models. In the simulations, all of the honest vehicle decisions will be logged and evaluated. If a vehicle forwards normal event messages under attack, the decisions are true negative (TN) opinion when receiving vehicle decides these event messages are trustworthy. In contrast, if receiving vehicle decides to send out opinion, which recognizes the original normal event message as untrustworthy, these decisions are false positive (FP) opinion. A vehicle makes a false negative (FN) decision if it is attacked and forwarded a malicious event as a trustworthy one. On the other hand, a vehicle makes a true positive (TP) opinion if it receives a malicious event and sent out an opinion to indicate that message is untrustworthy. After determining TN, TP, FN, and TP, we use these parameters to obtain both precision rate and recall rate. In this paper, we adopt F-measure (denoted as F) [30], as shown in (8), to measure the overall efficiently of the evaluated system. It is important to evaluate precision and recall in conjunction, owing to the easiness of optimizing either one separately. The F-measure is a weighted combination of precision, and its value ranges from 0 to 1. However, the F-measure does not take the true negative rate into account.

$$F = \frac{2 \times Precision \times Recall}{Precision + Recall} \tag{8}$$

4.2   Evaluation Environment

We simulate the proposed system using ns-2 with the MAC layer parameters of IEEE 802.11. An omnidirectional antenna with a TwoRayGround propagation model within a 250-meter transmission radius is used. The simulation scenario is set on a Manhattan street map, which is constructed from 5 x 5 street blocks, and the size of each block is 300 square meters. For each simulation, 300 vehicles are randomly generated with random trips on paths routed across the street map, and the average velocity in this simulation is 11.26 m/s.

After the simulation ends, the decision results of the misbehaving vehicles are excluded. When a vehicle receives an event message, the system computes the trustworthiness of the received event message and decides whether the message is trustworthy or not. During the simulation, both normal and attack messages are transmitted in the VANETs. We evaluate the performance of the proposed scheme under non-collusion and collusion attack models. In addition to the adversarial models, we also compare location privacy enhancement scheme FSP with RSP. In the comparison experiments, we take the method proposed by Leinmller et al. [7] with weighted vote as a comparison baseline, named WV. It is assumed that information collection, misbehavior detection, and reputation systems are computed locally in the OBU of vehicle. All of the above evaluation results will be shown in the following sections.

4.3   Simulation Results

We evaluate the performance of the proposed scheme for different rates of mis-behaving vehicles δ with $\varepsilon = 0.5$ and $\omega = 1$ under FSP with a beaconing interval of 1 second and RSP with a beacon interval from 300 millisecond to 3 second. As shown in Fig. 4, with a higher rate of the adversary vehicles, the detection results worsened. We can also see that our proposed system can perform better than WV under both collusion and non-collusion attacks. In FSP, the overall results for F are still close to 0.7, 0.8 with an adversary ratio of up to 90% under collusion and non-collusion attack respectively. The average F value of the proposed system is greater than 14.15%, 9.35% in comparison with the WV method. In addition to the misbehaving vehicle rate, we also simulate with different densities. In Fig. 5, we simulate with different number of vehicles on the same topology, ranging from 30 to 300 vehicles. The greater the number of ve-hicles on the road is, the higher the density of the topology is. In Fig. 5, we can see that the proposed system can still perform better than the WV schemes. The average detection rate in the proposed system is higher than that of WV by about 7.86%, 10.36% respectively. This could indicate that our proposed system can still suit a high-density environment no matter under collusion and non-collusion attacks. The outstanding results of the proposed system on collusion attacks due to the contribution of trust gathering module by crosschecking the plausibility of the beacon message and the event message. If colluders attempt to collude together, their beacon message and event message are likely conflicted each other, and lead to the low trustworthiness.

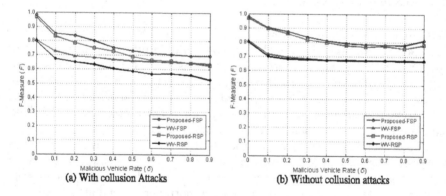

Fig. 4. Performance of the simulation results with respect to the rate of malicious vehicles ($\varepsilon = 0.5$, $\omega = 1$)

If a vehicle enhances its location privacy by adopting RSP, it will continu-ously send beaconing at random intervals. The RSP scheme may influence the detection result of the proposed trust-management system. In order to evaluate the effect of a location privacy-enhancement scheme in the proposed system, we also compare an RSP with an FSP location privacy-enhancement scheme in Fig. 4 and Fig. 5. Similar to previous evaluations, we also evaluate these two schemes under collusion and non-collusion attacks. In the simulation, we choose the random beaconing interval to be from 0.3 seconds to 3 seconds under the RSP scheme. In Fig.4 and Fig. 5, we can see that the proposed system still perform better than WV method under above mentioned attacks. As shown in Fig. 4(b), the F-measure is not degraded enormously (less than 2 percent) in comparison with detection rate under FSP. However, we can see that under RSP scheme, as shown in Fig. 4, the detection results degrade larger than that under FSP scheme. We can also see that the proposed self-organized trust management system can still perform well under the location privacy-enhancement scheme. Besides on the degrading of detection result, the proposed system degrades less than WV under collusion attacks. The detection rate of the proposed system can still perform greater than 11.78% and 13.85% in comparison with WV method on different misbehaving vehicle rate and vehicle amount.

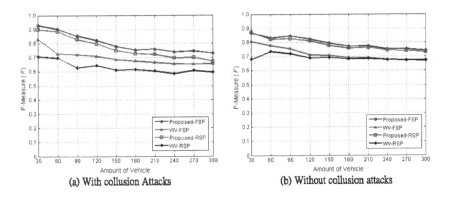

(a) With collusion Attacks   (b) Without collusion attacks

Fig. 5. Performance of the simulation results with number of vehicles ($\delta = 0.5$, $\varepsilon = 0.5$, $\omega = 1$)

5   Conclusion and Future Work

In this paper, we propose a self-organized trust management system aiming to thwart internal malicious attackers in location privacy-enhanced VANETs. In the proposed system, a vehicle can utilize not only direct or indirect event messages, but also beacon messages to construct trustworthiness values in order to distinguish trustworthy event messages from the VANET. The simulation results suggest that the proposed scheme is highly resilient to collusion and non-collusion attacks. Another important contribution of the proposed system is that it is suitable for both FSP and RSP location privacy-enhancement schemes.

In the evaluation, the average F-Measure value of the proposed system is 14.15% greater than comparison baseline in FSP scheme and 13.15% in RSP scheme under non-collusion attacks, and 9.35%, 11.78% under collusion attacks respectively. Thus, we can conclude that the proposed self-organized trust management system cannot only withstand collusion and non-collusion attacks, but also is viable for location privacy-enhancement schemes.

In the future, we intend to improve the detection rate of the proposed system and to evaluate the performance of the proposed scheme with different average velocities. Moreover, making comparisons with other trust-management systems and evaluate the efficiency of the proposed system will also be an important investigation topic in our future work.

References

1. The CAMP Vehicle Safety Communications Consortium: Vehicle Safety Communications Project Task 3 Final Report: Identify intelligent vehicle safety applications enabled by DSRC. National Highway Traffic Safety Administration (2005)
2. Lin, X., Lu, R., Zhang, C., Zhu, H., Ho, P., Shen, X.: Security in vehicular ad hoc networks. IEEE Communications Magazine 46, 88–95 (2008)
3. Haojin, Z., Xiaodong, L., Rongxing, L., Pin-Han, H., Xuemin, S.: AEMA: An Aggregated Emergency Message Authentication Scheme for Enhancing the Security of Vehicular Ad Hoc Networks. In: IEEE International Conference on Communications, ICC 2008, pp. 1436–1440 (2008)
4. Jie, Z.: A Survey on Trust Management for VANETs. In: 2011 IEEE International Conference on Advanced Information Networking and Applications (AINA), pp. 105–112 (2011)
5. Ma, S., Wolfson, O., Lin, J.: A survey on trust management for intelligent transportation system. In: Proceedings of the 4th ACM SIGSPATIAL International Workshop on Computational Transportation Science, pp. 18–23. ACM, Chicago (2011)
6. Leinmüller, T., Maihöfer, C., Schoch, E., Kargl, F.: Improved security in geographic ad hoc routing through autonomous position verification. In: Proceedings of the 3rd International Workshop on Vehicular Ad Hoc Networks, pp. 57–66. ACM, Los Angeles (2006)
7. Leinmüller, T., Schoch, E., Kargl, F.: Position verification approaches for vehicular ad hoc networks. IEEE Wireless Communications 13, 16–21 (2006)
8. Schmidt, R.K., Leinmüller, T., Schoch, E., Held, A., Schäfer, G.: Vehicle Behavior Analysis to Enhance Security in VANETs. In: 4th Workshop on Vehicle to Vehicle Communications (V2VCOM 2008), Eindhoven, The Netherlands (2008)
9. Raya, M., Papadimitratos, P., Aad, I., Jungels, D., Hubaux, J.-P.: Eviction of Misbehaving and Faulty Nodes in Vehicular Networks. IEEE Journal on Selected Areas in Communications 25, 1557–1568 (2007)
10. Ghosh, M., Varghese, A., Gupta, A., Kherani, A.A., Muthaiah, S.N.: Detecting misbehaviors in VANET with integrated root-cause analysis. Ad Hoc Networks 8, 778–790 (2010)

11. Dotzer, F., Fischer, L., Magiera, P.: VARS: A Vehicle Ad-Hoc Network Reputation System. In: Proceedings of the Sixth IEEE International Symposium on World of Wireless Mobile and Multimedia Networks, pp. 454–456. IEEE Computer Society (2005)

12. Wu, Q., Domingo-Ferrer, J., Gonzalez-Nicolas, U.: Balanced Trustworthiness, Safety, and Privacy in Vehicle-to-Vehicle Communications. IEEE Transactions on Vehicular Technology 59, 559–573 (2010)

13. Ostermaier, B., Dotzer, F., Strassberger, M.: Enhancing the Security of Local DangerWarnings in VANETs - A Simulative Analysis of Voting Schemes. In: Proceedings of the Second International Conference on Availability, Reliability and Security, pp. 422–431. IEEE Computer Society, Vienna (2007)

14. Lo, N.-W., Tsai, H.-C.: A Reputation System for Traffic Safety Event on Vehicular Ad Hoc Networks. EURASIP Journal on Wireless Communications and Networking 2009 (2009)

15. Raya, M., Papadimitratos, P., Gligor, V.D., Hubaux, J.-P.: On Data-Centric Trust Establishment in Ephemeral Ad Hoc Networks. In: The 27th Conference on Computer Communications, INFOCOM 2008, Phoenix, AZ, pp. 1238–1246. IEEE (2008)

16. Kannhavong, B., Nakayama, H., Jamalipour, A.: NIS01-2: A Collusion Attack Against OLSR-based Mobile Ad Hoc Networks. In: Global Telecommunications Conference, GLOBECOM 2006, pp. 1–5. IEEE (2006)

17. Philippe, G., Dan, G., Jessica, S.: Detecting and correcting malicious data in VANETs. In: Proceedings of the 1st ACM International Workshop on Vehicular Ad Hoc Networks. ACM, Philadelphia (2004)

18. Chen, C., Jie, Z., Cohen, R., Pin-Han, H.: A Trust Modeling Framework for Message Propagation and Evaluation in VANETs. In: 2010 2nd International Conference on Information Technology Convergence and Services (ITCS), pp. 1–8 (2010)

19. Aslam, B., Park, S., Zou, C., Turgut, D.: Secure Traffic Data Propagation in Vehicular Ad hoc Networks. Int. J. Ad Hoc and Ubiquitous Computing 6, 24–39 (2010)

20. Wei, Y., Liu, K.J.R.: Attack-resistant cooperation stimulation in autonomous ad hoc networks. IEEE Journal on Selected Areas in Communications 23, 2260–2271 (2005)

21. Wex, P., Breuer, J., Held, A., Leinmüller, T., Delgrossi, L.: Trust Issues for Vehicular Ad Hoc Networks. In: Vehicular Technology Conference, VTC Spring 2008, pp. 2800–2804. IEEE (2008)

22. Schmidt, R., Leinmüller, T., Schoch, E., Kargl, F., Schafer, G.: Exploration of adaptive beaconing for efficient intervehicle safety communication. IEEE Network 24, 14–19 (2010)

23. Yan, G., Olariu, S., Weigle, M.C.: Providing VANET security through active position detection. Computer Communications 31, 2883–2897 (2008)

24. Cha, S.-H.: Comprehensive survey on distance/similarity measures between probability density functions. International Journal of Mathematical Models and Methods in Applied Sciences 1, 300–307 (2008)

25. Zahera, H., El Hady, G., El-Wahed, W.: Query Recommendation for Improving Search Engine Results. In: World Congress on Engineering and Computer Science (WCECS), San Francisco, USA, vol. 1 (2010)

26. Sun, Y.L., Yu, W., Han, Z., Liu, K.J.R.: Information theoretic framework of trust modeling and evaluation for ad hoc networks. IEEE Journal on Selected Areas in Communications 24, 305–317 (2006)

27. Luo, J., Liu, X., Fan, M.: A trust model based on fuzzy recommendation for mobile ad-hoc networks. Computer Networks 53, 2396–2407 (2009)
28. Chen, T.M., Venkataramanan, V.: Dempster-Shafer theory for intrusion detection in ad hoc networks. IEEE Internet Computing 9, 35–41 (2005)
29. Li, W., Joshi, A.: Outlier Detection in Ad Hoc Networks Using Dempster-Shafer Theory. In: Proceedings of the 2009 Tenth International Conference on Mobile Data Management: Systems, Services and Middleware. IEEE Computer Society (2009)
30. Yang, Y., Liu, X.: A re-examination of text categorization methods. In: Proceedings of the 22nd Annual International ACM SIGIR Conference on Research and Development in Information Retrieval, pp. 42–49. ACM, Berkeley (1999)

A Trust Management Model for QoS-Based Service Selection

Yukyong Kim and Kyung-Goo Doh*

Department of Computer Science and Engineering, Hanyang University ERICA,
Ansan, Korea
{yukyong,doh}@hanyang.ac.kr

Abstract. As the number of available services increases on the Web, it becomes greatly vital in service-oriented computing to discover a trustworthy service that best fits users' requirements. Once a set of services fulfilling user's functional requirements are founded, one of these services invoked by the users depends mostly on the Quality of Services (QoS), particularly security, trust, and reputation. This paper proposes a trust management model to support service discovery and selection based on trust and QoS. We propose a novel trustworthy service discovery and selection mechanism to make service consumers get trustworthy services possible. The mechanism uses consumers' feedback to describe service's and service provider's trustworthy level. The service selection using the quantitative measurement rather than consumers' intuitive selection allows selecting a high reliable service accomplishing their quality requirements well. Finally, we give experimental results by implementing the prototype for verifying the trust evaluation method.

Keywords: Service Oriented Architecture, trust management, service selection, Quality of Service (QoS).

1 Introduction

Service Oriented Architecture (SOA) is an architectural style that builds enterprise solutions by combining loosely-coupled and interoperable services. SOA provides a way to integrate widely disparate applications on multiple implementation platforms. Because SOA can help businesses respond more quickly and more cost-effectively to changing market conditions, it is increasingly used in enterprise information systems, especially in the form of Web services.

In adopting SOA, one obvious challenge faced relates to provide appropriate levels of security. As security is one aspect of confidence, in particular, security focuses on those aspects of assurance that involve the accidental or malign intent of other people to damage or compromise trust in the system and on the availability of SOA-based systems to perform desired capability. Trust is an assertion as to the behavior of participants in relation to each other. In terms of security

---

* Corresponding author.

D.H. Lee and M. Yung (Eds.): WISA 2012, LNCS 7690, pp. 345–357, 2012.

assurance, trust often refers to the confidence that target systems may have as to the identity and validity of a participant as they interact with the system [1].

In the context of an SOA, services are used by many people and there may not be a single repository for information that can justify trust. Often different aspects of trust are managed by different entities. Trust between participants that are established by participants who introduce other participants into the chain of trust. Because application-managed security is not the right model for securing services, therefore, the impact of changing a service that touches multiple business domains will require a higher level of change management governance [2].

Trust is a meaningful factor for achieving successful online interaction as it is in real life communities. With an increasing number of services providing similar functionalities, recently, trust is becoming more and more imperative for service consumers. In distributed and heterogeneous SOA computing environments, the critical quality attributes such as availability and reliability of services are uncertain because the potential number of services can be extremely large and there is no guarantee that the service will be available at a particular time. Since the service providers also may have varying levels of trust, to select the trustworthy service provider is a challenging problem for users. Service consumers have to decide which services satisfy closely to their needs and worry about the reliability of the service provider. Consequently, trust is a highly influential factor for selecting services. We need a way to efficiently find and select trustworthy services.

However, it is difficult to solve this problem by the current service discovery technique based on Universal Description, Discovery and Integration (UDDI). The current UDDI registries provide service discovery mechanisms using only the functional aspect of services without considering non-functional aspects. In this paper, we present a trust management model for supporting QoS-based service discovery and selection. This paper focuses on the definition of trust and information required to build trust. We first derive a trust definition to cover different aspects of trust. Then we define a trust mediator to discharge the establishment of trust. The trust mediator manages trust-related information for service providers as well as services, and evaluates trust degrees using the applicable metrics on the trust information.

The QoS requirements can provide a finer constraint to find services. By facilitating QoS-driven discovery and selection, users can easily and efficiently select a trustworthy service that is more suitable to their needs. We propose a trust management model for finding and selecting services on the trust mediator. From the user's functional and QoS requirements including trust, the mediator contacts the service registry to find services that match the given requirements. The mediator is also responsible for processing ratings of services from users, then assigning and updating the trust rate of the related service.

The mediator receives and aggregates ratings for a service from users over a specific period of time. Using the ratings, the trust levels of the services and service providers are computed. This provides a general and overall estimate of the reliability of the service provider as well as the service. We assume that the ratings of the mediator are trustworthy. Our model contains service matching and selection algorithms to find services that fulfill user's requirements and to select services based on the trust level and QoS information.

The motivation of this work originates from the need that trust enables service consumers to support efficiently the trustworthy selection as a social control mechanism in SOA environments. This paper contributes to the field of trust evaluation by providing formal trust model expressed in qualitative perspective using a complementary methodology for trust. The model is consolidated in an SOA infrastructure as a trust management solution.

The rest of the paper is organized as follows: Section 2 reviews related works on trust management for SOA and QoS issues. Section 3 introduces a trust model and trust assessment metrics, and then formalizes a trustworthy service selection approach. The trust mediator and a QoS-based service matching algorithm are defined in Section 4. In Section 5, we present the result of experiments. Finally, Section 6 summarizes and discusses future works.

2   State of the Art

Existing OASIS WS-* standards such as WS-Security [3] and WS-Trust [4] ensure hard security mechanisms of SOA applications. They define how to pass data securely between autonomous Web services. At its core, however, trust is not covered as an essential service that reflects the nature of trust. WS-Trust represents an extension built on to the WS-Security standard, which provides secure messaging and adding extensions for security token exchange within different trust domains. WS-Trust provides a framework for requesting, issuing, renewing, and validating security tokens as well as brokering trust relationships. Although WS-Trust is the standard trust mechanism at the messaging level, WS-Trust is limited in addressing important trust aspects and requirements as well as various trust challenges. Security tokens in the SOAP messages of WS-Trust cannot provide evidence for some trust aspects or address certain challenges because they are irrelevant to these security tokens. WS-Trust cannot identify entities with hidden motives, consider reputation, or determine levels of trustworthiness of entities. Moreover, WS-Trust have an overhead over requestors that have only basic knowledge and cannot understand complex trust processes or participate in a complex trust negotiation process, such as obtaining or validating a security token. A requestor needs, simply, to obtain the trust ratings of different entities and to select among these entities [5].

Many researches have been devised to extend the UDDI standard and described service's quality capabilities. However, the literatures about SOA trust are still immature. Zhengping et al. present a trust framework for designing trustworthy service oriented applications [6]. The trust framework includes service selection and service behavior surveillance. They describe the formalized model to verify the integrity of the design, as well as the correctness and consistency of the implementation. In [7], a trust-based service-selection method is proposed to establish trust for services and support service selection based on trust. The method considers building trust for service providers as well as rating services. In [8], a conceptual model of web-service reputation is defined. The model using the web service agent proxy is to pick the correct service implementation by looking at the reputation of the various services based on the conceptual model. It is just a preliminary model, and the evaluation about service is not comprehensive. The factors which affect the trustworthiness of service from service entity are explicated in [9]. However, it lacks three roles of SOA which are all needed to be considered. In [10], the trustworthiness of service provider in SOA is discussed. The service selection using the existing methods is practically complicated. In addition, they define the reputation value which is too abstract and difficult to use, and the fitness of service is not explained. Chang et al. propose a trust and reputation ontology, introduce trust modeling techniques, explain different trust factors of agents, and discuss the assignment of trustworthiness values. The authors take into account that trust has a dynamic nature and is a social phenomenon [11]. In multi-agent systems, the trust management is implemented with a reputation mechanism [12]. The propagation and transferability of trust is discussed in [13] [14]. These works about trust management remain just at the abstract level. A system has many services with lots of inputs and outputs and then a feasible management method is needed to manage them.

Moreover, there are traditional trust and reputation (T&R) systems that have been developed to establish mutual trust between service providers and service consumers for electronic marketplace and online collaboration systems. T&R model by Yu and Singh, flexible and adaptive Bayesian Reputation System by Jsang et al., and the TRAOVS (Trust and Reputation model for Agent-based Virtual Organizations) system are introduced in [15]. Traditional T&R systems, however, focus on evaluating the reliability and credibility of the participants such that recommendation can be made when needed. Existing trust management systems such as KeyNote rely on a strict boundary between the trusted and untrusted zones. As a traditional mechanism such as authentication and access control, the KeyNote model works well for small scale applications in which there are well defined administrative and topological boundaries between internal and external services [16].

For the concept of trust, the social component is vital because it uses interactive methods for identifying and sanctioning community members. Although SOA continues to be broadly adopted, there have been surprisingly little interests in the trust management of service in runtime. The comprehensive trustworthy analysis and management in services and application levels should be presented in detail.

3   A Model for Managing Trust

According to the WS-trust specification, trust is defined as "the characteristic that one entity is willing to rely upon a second entity to execute a set of actions and/or to make assertions about a set of subjects and/or scopes" [4]. As described in [17], however, trust is a complex mental state of agent A towards B

as for a given action and goal. The concept of trust incorporates trust management to establish, monitor and adjust trust relationships among participants. The core concept of trust management is represented by the trust model that defines primary factors of trust relationships and describes how to calculate the resulting trust values.

To establish trust model for SOA, we consider the trust as the belief that one agent has in the other agent's capability to deliver a quality of service in a given context and in a given time slot. We assume that an agent can be an abstract entity in a distributed network and can represent an ordinary service user, a service, or a service provider.

Definition 1. *Trust is realized by the concept of a trust relationship between agent a_i and a_j from the set of agents A and is expressed as a binary relation $R \subseteq A \times A$. The trust relation $a_i R a_j$ represents a directed link between agent a_i and a_j in a directed graph which is called a trust graph denoted by an ordered pair $TG = (A, R)$.*

The knowledge such as past experiences can be formulated as trustworthiness in time and context. The time dimension T is a set of time values t_i when the interaction between agents took place. The context dimension C contains a set of propositions that can be formulated as a sequence of possible events. Actual trust relationships between agents are reflexive because an agent trusts himself/herself implicitly. That is, for all $a_i \in A$, $a_i R a_i$.

Definition 2. *An element $r \in R$ has a degree of trust from a domain set of possible trust values D. When $r = (a_i, a_j)$ for a_i and $a_j \in A$, the **trust level** is defined that the trust degree of an agent a_i towards agent a_j in time t and context c, and represented by $\tau_{ij}(t, c) \in D$ where $t \in T$ and $c \in C$.*

Figure 1 presents an example of trust graph in a specific time t_0 and context c_0. The directed links have weight values τ from the domain set D. Because a graph can be represented by a matrix, we define a trust matrix of Figure 1.

$$TM(t_0, c_0) = \begin{bmatrix} - & \tau_{1,2} & \tau_{1,3} \\ \tau_{2,1} & - & \tau_{2,3} \\ \tau_{3,1} & \infty & - \end{bmatrix}$$

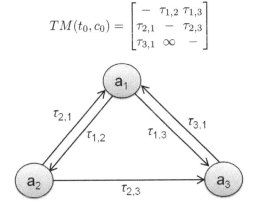

Fig. 1. A trust graph

We assume that the service consumer can assess trustworthiness of service providers for every transaction. That is, before agent a_i makes interaction with agent a_j, a_i has to be assessed its trustworthiness towards a_j according to the feedback on the history from the trust system. To select QoS guaranteed services or credible service providers, we define the trust model to evaluate and assign the trust level to each service and service provider. The trust level is determined by the trust mediator using equation (1) based on the history data of past invocations. We assume that service consumers provide a feedback indicating the level of satisfaction after use and the ratings are available and valid.

$$\tau_{i,j}(t, c) = E_{i,j} \times Credits(i, j) + (1 - E_{i,j}) \times RepScore(j) \qquad (1)$$

In equation (1), $E_{i,j}$ is an *experience factor* which means the knowledge of agent a_i towards agent a_j acquiring through direct interaction between a_i and a_j. We assume that with the augmenting quantity of interaction, the knowledge of agent a_i towards agent a_j is increased. However, with the lapse of time, the knowledge does not increase any more to the reasonable level. This paper defines the experience factor as a logarithmic growth curve:

$$E_{i,j} = 1 - e^{(-0.5 \times N_{i,j})} \qquad (2)$$

In equation (2), $N_{i,j}$ is the total number of interactions between agents a_i and a_j, and e is a constant approximately equal to 2.7183 as a base of the natural logarithm. Exponential decay models of this form can model learning curves. Exponential decay models of this form will increase very rapidly at first, and then level off to become asymptotic to the upper limit as shown in Figure 2.

In equation (1), $Credits(i, j)$ represents a satisfaction degree of an agent a_i towards an agent a_j according to QoS attributes such as price, response time, availability, and throughput. To evaluate these QoS attributes, we use existing QoS metrics and quality evaluation framework [21][22] [23]. Then, the measured values of QoS attributes are normalized into the range [0,1]. Let $Q1, Q2, Q3$, and $Q4$ stand for price, response time, availability, and throughput, respectively. For each QoS attribute Q_i (i=1, 2, 3, 4), we give a weight w_i as an importance degree under the condition $0 \leq w_i \leq 1$ and $\sum w_i = 1$. Through the interaction between agent a_i and a_j, each QoS attribute is measured on the history data of

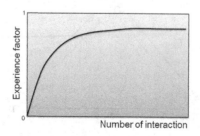

Fig. 2. A learning curve representing experience factor

past invocations such as logging data, actual execution time, and the number of response times to user's requests.

$$Credits(i,j) = \sum_{1 \le k \le 4} Q_k(i,j) \times w_k \qquad (3)$$

In equation (1), $RepScore(j)$ is defined by reputation for the agent a_j. When the set of all agents who have been interacted with an agent a_j is $A_j = \{a_1, a_2, ..., a_m\}$, the reference factor $\upsilon(k,j)$ is a certainty of which an agent $a_k \in A_j$ towards agent a_j. The satisfaction factor $S(k,j)$ is determined on five scales (distrusted, partially distrusted, undecided, partially trusted, and trusted) by $a_k \in A_j$, and the domain set of values is $\{0.2, 0.4, 0.6, 0.8, 1.0\}$. These values are based on feedback directly provided by $a_k \in A_j$ towards a_j.

$$RepScore(j) = \frac{\sum_{k=1}^{m} \upsilon(k,j) \times S(k,j)}{m}, \qquad (4)$$

$$where\ \upsilon(k,j) = \prod_{k=1}^{m} \left(s_{k,j} - \frac{f_{k,j}}{1 - min\{s_{k,j}, f_{k,j}\}} \right)$$

In equation (4), $s_{k,j}$ is the number of times that an agent $a_k \in A_j$ provides a feedback of successful execution against the total number of requests. On the contrary, $f_{k,j}$ is the number of failures against the total number of requests. That is, the total number of requests equals to $s_{k,j} + f_{k,j}$.

Each interaction between agents has to carry information about the sequence of events that occurred. In addition, every agent should have its own trust policy to check compliance with trust related requirements. Declarative policy languages such as WS-Policy [24] are used to express the capabilities and requirements of the entities in a Web-service-based system.

4   Trustworthy Service Discovery and Selection

In this section, we present a conceptual framework which enables trust and QoS-based service discovery and selection. Then service matching and selection algorithm is described.

4.1   Trust Mediator

The traditional SOA model has three roles: service provider, service consumer and service registry. In our framework, a new role, trust mediator as a QoS broker, is added as shown in Figure 3.

The trust mediator is added into the QoS broker as a trusted third party, and is responsible for governing the trust process. The trust mediator·extracts the information from service descriptions which are submitted by service providers, and verifies its compatibility when service providers want to publish their services along with the trust information. The mediator gets the service request from

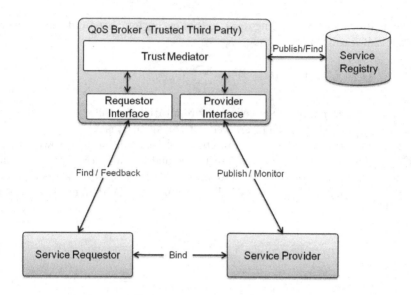

Fig. 3. Trust based SOA framework

consumer, and validates its compatibility before invoking service discovering API to get a list of services. It also filters services based on QoS properties and selects the service with maximum trust level. As the core component of the framework, the mediator maintains and manages service descriptions, service providers' information and service trust rates. The trust mediator has a rating registry to maintain the trust information. Trust establishment is performed by evaluating and storing trust level for services on advertised service information and history data using equation (1).

4.2   Service Discovery and Selection Algorithm

Discovering services should support the selection of services based on their functional properties and trustworthiness on a set of requestors' preferences. In this operation, the service consumer requests to find out the service fulfilling his/her QoS requirements as well as functional requirements through the service requestor interface. The mediator searches the service registry for discovering services that match the functional properties. Then, the trust mediator selects services that match well the non-functional properties, QoS and trustworthiness, of services from the rating registry. Consequently, the best services satisfying the requestor's functional, non-functional and trust preferences are returned to the service requestor.

In this framework, the trust mediator is responsible for selecting the optimal service with the highest value of trust level. If the match does not succeed, the mediator. will provide a highly QoS service that meets the user's functional requirements with an acknowledgement containing the trusted match is failed. Table 1 shows the detailed steps of how the trust mediator finds services that meet the user's QoS needs including trust as well as functional requirements.

When using this discovery scheme, a consumer can choose the service with the maximum value of trust level, or choose the set of services such that the trust level is less than or equal to the threshold.

Table 1. Service discovery steps

```
// Functional matching
1: Find services that meet the user's functional requirements
2: Add the service entity to the service candidate list if the services
      meet the user's requirements

// Trust matching
For each service that meets the user's functional requirements,
3: Compute the trust level for each service in the candidate list
4: Find a subset of services the meet the user's trust requirement in
      the service candidate list

// Selection
5: Rank the services in the candidate list based on trust levels
6: Select and return the specified number of services based on the
      user's requirements
```

The UDDI registry stores advertisements provided by service providers. The advertised information includes the basic ability description and the QoS specification of the service. After receiving a user's request, the mediator chooses the advertisements that are relevant to the current request from the UDDI registry. An advertisement matches a request, when the advertisement and the request describe exactly the same service. We thus define the matching as subsume matching where the inputs and outputs of the advertisement are a subclass of the inputs and outputs of the request.

5   Analysis and Evaluation

In this paper, we consider services providing similar functionalities as a logical group, and data structures for service descriptions including trust information are maintained in the service registry to compute trust level. When the service provider enrolls service descriptions in the service registry, the mediator constructs trust level information of the service and the service providers. If there is no trust information about the service or service provider, the mediator assigns the lowest value approximately to zero to the service as a default value. After assessing service's trust information, the mediator modifies the past service profile about the trust level.

Table 2. Data structures for transactions

ID	N	Q	υ	s	f
$ID_{i,1}$	$N_{i,1}$	Q_{k1}	$\upsilon(k1,1)$	$s_{k1,1}$	$f_{k1,1}$
$ID_{i,2}$	$N_{i,2}$	Q_{k1}	$\upsilon(k1,2)$	$s_{k1,2}$	$f_{k1,2}$
...	...	...	...	...	...
$ID_{i,j}$	$N_{i,j}$	Q_{k1}	$\upsilon(k1,j)$	$s_{k1,j}$	$f_{k1,j}$
...	...	...	...	...	...

Table 3. QoS attributes

Attributes	Data type	Description
Price	Float	Service price per transaction
Response Time	Float	Average response time (x.xx seconds)
Availability	Float	Available time rate (xx.xxx%)
Throughput	Integer	Transaction numbers per second

The service registry should have an event structure as shown in Table 2. This is a condensed data about transactions during the specific time intervals. When there is a change on the trust level of services in a group is changed, it has no effect on other service groups. This is to manage efficiently the trust information.

To implement the trust management model, we need a way to describe the QoS information of a service. The QoS information of the service can be attached to the *Service Profile* in OWL-S. We derive a new class as a subclass of the *ServiceParameter* class already defined in OWL-S. Table 3 shows an example of the definition of QoS attributes. We can extend QoS attributes using subclass derivation, and represent QoS requirements as well as functional requirements. Table 4 is an example of QoS requirements described in OWL-S.

As part of the empirical analysis, a number of experiments are conducted to provide evidence for assessing the robustness of the proposed trust bootstrapping solution.

To validate the proposed model, we simulate the proposed evaluation method on the service registry using jUDDI(ver3.1) and MySQL. We enter 27 services with different quality levels for Online DVD rental systems. They are divided into three logical groups with similar functionality. The service requests are performed by executing the service request program written in Java programming language.

The goal of this experiment is to verify the fact that the proposed trust evaluation method provides the optimal trusted service fulfilling user's requirements. We compare the service having the highest value of trust level using the equation (1) with the selected service based on QoS information. Assume that services having appropriate quality level for QoS attributes are first selected. Then some of them are chosen for evaluating the reputation because the reputation is the only factor to select services without trustworthiness. For 50 requests per group, 34 times (68%), 39 times (78%), and 37 times (74%) are agree on the service selection.

Table 4. OWL-S description of service requirements

```
<Service Quality rdf:ID="ServiceQuality_1">
<profile:sParameter>
    <ServiceQualityInfo rdf:ID="ServiceQualityInfo_11">
        <ServicePrice rdf:datatype="http://.../XMLSchema#float"> 0.1
        </ServicePrice>
        <ResponseTime rdf:datatype="http://.../XMLSchema#float"> 0.03
        </ResponseTime >
        <Availability rdf:datatype="http://.../XMLSchema#float"> 99.95
        </Availability >
        <Throughput rdf:datatype="http://.../XMLSchema#integer"> 700
        </Throughput >
        <TrustLevel rdf:datatype="http://.../XMLSchema#float"> 0.8
        </TrustLevel >
    </ServiceQualityInfo>
</profile:sParameter>
<profile:serviceParameterName
        rdf:datatype="http://.../XMLSchema#string"> ServiceQuality
</profile:serviceParameterName>
</ServiceQuality>
<profile:Profile rdf:ID="serviceUser1_Profile">
<profile:serviceParameter rdf:resource"#ServiceQuality_1">
  ...
</profile:Profile>
```

6   Conclusion

In SOA computing environments, the potential number of services providing similar functionalities can be extremely large. In this context, to discover the really useful services for consumers, the environment in which services exist is steady and all the services are trustworthy. Otherwise consumers may find that, although the descriptions of services match their requirements perfectly, they cannot invoke these services. Thus a way to efficiently find and select trusted services is needed.

By facilitating QoS driven discovery and selection, users can easily and efficiently select a trustworthy service that is more suitable to their needs. In this paper, we present a trust management model for discovering and selecting trustworthy service using trust evaluation based on QoS properties and past history data. The QoS requirement can be used as a finer constraint to find optimal services. We define a trust mediator which is responsible for governing trust process. From the user's functional and QoS requirements including trust, the mediator contacts the service registry to find services that match the given requirements. The trust mediator is responsible for processing ratings of services from users, then assigning and updating the trust rate of the related service. The aim of this work is to propose a trust evaluation method as a trust management model. Our model contains a service matching algorithm that finds services that match a user's requirements and selects services based on the trust level and QoS information. As the mediator manages the trustworthy degree of the service providers as well as services, it provides a method to improve the possibility to find services that match a user's QoS and trust requirements. Because we use the reputation by considering feedback from service users over a specific period of time, advertised QoS information may be verified. Using the feedback and QoS metrics, we compute the trust level of the service and service providers. It provides a general and overall estimate of the reliability of the service provider as well as services.

We assume the service ratings are all trustworthy but it could be invalid. Thus the trust evaluation should be refined. In addition, service discovery and selection process require a further refinement to classify and measure on the user's preference and more QoS attributes.

Acknowledgement. This work was supported by the Engineering Research Center of Excellence Program of Korea Ministry of Education, Science and Technology(MEST)/National Research Foundation of Korea(NRF) (Grant 2012-0000469).

References

1. OASIS: Reference Architecture for Service Oriented Architecture Version 1.0. (2008)
2. Wik, P.: Confronting SOA's Four Horsemen of the Apocalypse. Service Technology Magazine (LI) (2011)
3. OASIS WSS TC: Web Services Security - SOAP Message Security 1.1. (2006)
4. Kelvin, L., Chris, K., Anthony, N., Marc, G., Martin, G., Abbie, B., Hans, G.: Ws-Trust 1.4. Technical report, OASIS Standard (2009)
5. Zhao, W., Varadharajan, V.: Trust management for web services. In: Proceedings of the 2008 IEEE International Conference on Web Services, pp. 818–821 (2008)
6. Zhengping, L., Xiaoli, L., Guoqing, W., Min, Y., Fan, Z.: A formal Framework for Trust management of Service-oriented Systems. In: Proceedings of the IEEE International Conference on Service-Oriented Computing and Applications, pp. 241–248 (2007)
7. Aljazzaf, Z. M.: Trust based Service Selection. Ph.D. Thesis, The University of Western Ontario, London, Ontario, Canada (2011)
8. Maximilien, E.M., Singh, M.P.: Conceptual Model of Web Service Reputation. SIGMOD Record 31(4), 36–41 (2002)
9. Hussain, F.K., Chang, E., Dillon, T.S.: Aspects Influencing Trustworthiness in Service Oriented Environments. In: Proceedings of Data Engineering Workshop, p. 99 (2006)
10. Jin-dian, S., He-qing, G., Ying, G.: An adaptive trust model of Web services. Wuhan University Journal of Natural Sciences 10(1), 21–25 (2005)

11. Zacharia, G.: Trust Management Through Reputation Mechanisms. Applied Artificial Intelligence, 881–907 (2000)
12. Wolfe, S., Ahamed, S., Zulkernine, M.: A Trust Framework for Pervasive Computing Environments. In: Proceeding of theACS/IEEE International Conference on Computer Systems and Applications (AICCSA), pp. 312–319 (2006)
13. Dimitrakos, T.: A Service-Oriented Trust Management Framework. In: Falcone, R., Barber, S.K., Korba, L., Singh, M.P. (eds.) AAMAS 2002. LNCS (LNAI), vol. 2631, pp. 53–72. Springer, Heidelberg (2003)
14. Yanchuk, A., Ivanyukovich, A., Marchese, M.: A Lightweight Formal Framework for Service-Oriented Applications Design. In: Benatallah, B., Casati, F., Traverso, P. (eds.) ICSOC 2005. LNCS, vol. 3826, pp. 545–551. Springer, Heidelberg (2005)
15. Noorian, Z., Ulieru, M.: The State of the Art in Trust and Reputation Systems: A Framework for Comparison. Journal of Theoretical and Applied Electronic Commerce Research 5(2), 97–117 (2010)
16. Blaze, M., Kannan, S., Lee, I., Sokolsky, O., Smith, J.M., Keromytis, A.D., Lee, W.: Dynamic Trust Management. IEEE Computer 42(2), 44–52 (2009)
17. Kova, D., Trek, D.: Qualitative trust modeling in SOA. Journal of Systems Architecture 55, 255–263 (2009)
18. Dragoni, N.: Toward trustworthy web services - approaches, weaknesses and trust-by- contract framework. In: IEEE/WIC/ACM International Conference on Web Intelligence and Intelligent Agent Technology, pp. 599–606 (2009)
19. Matai, J., Han, D.-S.: Learning-Based Trust Model for Optimization of Selecting Web Services. In: Dong, G., Lin, X., Wang, W., Yang, Y., Yu, J.X. (eds.) APWeb/WAIM 2007. LNCS, vol. 4505, pp. 642–649. Springer, Heidelberg (2007)
20. Kim, Y., Ko, B.S.: A Service Selection Method using Trust Evaluation in QoS Based Web Services Composition. Journal of KIISE: Software and Applications 36(1), 1–9 (2009) (in Korean)
21. Bianco, P., Kotermanski, R., Merson, P.: Evaluating a Service-Oriented Architecture. Carnegie Mellon University (2007)
22. Choi, S.W., Her, J.S., Kim, S.D.: Modeling QoS Attributes and Metrics for Evaluating Services in SOA Considering Consumers' Perspective as the First Class Requirement. In: Proceedings of the IEEE Asia-Pacific Service Computing Conference, pp. 398–405 (2007)
23. Jeong, B., Hyunbo, C., Choonghyun, L.: On the Functional Quality of Service(FQoS) to Discover and Compose Interoperable Web Services. Expert Systems with Applications 36, 5411–5418 (2009)
24. W3C: Web Services Policy 1.2. W3C Member Submission (2006)

Multilevel Secure Database on Security Enhanced Linux for System High Distributed Systems

Haklin Kimm and Norkee Sherpa

Computer Science Department
East Stroudsburg University of Pennsylvania
East Stroudsburg, PA 18301
haklkimm@esu.edu

Abstract. There has been increasing interest for numerous organizations to access, integrate and process data securely while protecting individual privacy. The confidentiality as well as privacy of the organizations will be ensured if the concepts of multilevel secure system are applied. A multilevel secure (MLS) system is defined as a system with a mode of operation that allows two or more sensitivity levels of information to be processed simultaneously within the same system when not all users have a clearance or formal access approval for all data. In MLS there is no super-user since administrators also should be under the control of fine-grained MAC policy. Security Enhanced Linux (SELinux) operating system, promises to change the way Linux users practice computer security from a reactive posture based upon applying independent patches to close published vulnerabilities, to a proactive posture that seeks to prevent even unpublished vulnerabilities from compromising systems. In this paper, SELinux policy that enforces an active MLS on file system and DBMS- SELinux PostgreSQL is tested and demonstrated to develop a practical prototype of distributed heterogeneous multilevel secure database systems.

Keywords: Multilevel Security, Security Enhanced Linux, SELinux PostreSQL.

1 Introduction

The rapid expansion of the Internet and development of information systems, digitizing unlimited data of human society, have been tremendously fast and non-stopping processes. On the basis of benchmark study of U.S companies by Ponemon Institute [15], it is clear that the rate of cyber crime attacks on information systems and leakage of information have increased dramatically. It is easily seen that security of information systems is the biggest and most costly issue in the world today. Hence building a secure information system, enhancing security features on existing systems, and integrating and sharing secured information among the organizations have been a great deal of interest among the information system specialists and computer scientists.

The integration of data among the trusted organizations can be more efficient if the autonomous databases are linked by a secured information tool that integrates

D.H. Lee and M. Yung (Eds.): WISA 2012, LNCS 7690, pp. 358–370, 2012.

distributed multilevel database systems. It would be beneficial to see a prototype that can retrieve data stored in different secure level databases on various orgranizations, especially in multilevel secure way. However, it is a difficult task to connect autonomous databases in multilevel secure systems and implement them as one heterogeneous distributed database system. It is more difficult building a distributed database system in multilevel secure environment than integrating conventional standard database systems into a distributed database system.

Security Enhanced Linux (SELinux) operating system, which implements Mandatory Access Control (MAC), promises to change the way Linux users practice computer security from a reactive posture base on applying independent patches to close published vulnerabilities, to a proactive posture that seeks to prevent even unpublished vulnerabilities from compromising systems. As mentioned in [1] SELinux is the most important technology for Linux users that has been introduced in the last several years, even though it is not easy enough for dependable use by Linux system administrators. SELinux significantly enhances the Linux security against attackers and intruders by providing Linux system administrators with access to the sophisticated security technology previously available only to administrators of high security systems running expensive, military-grade operating systems.

SEPostgreSQL (Security Enhanced PostgreSQL) is a reference monitor built in the popular database PostgreSQL, and works in conjunction with SELinux security policy to provide a centralized system-wide access control between the database and the operating system. Unlike traditional database systems, which maintain a separate database access control or user authentication from the OS, the SEPostgreSQL database system works with SELinux security policy to provide a layer of system-wide kernel level security over the existing access control [9]. For example, if a user with a low security clearance in the file system tries to connect to the database system using a high level user authentication, the connection will be rejected. It is because the SEPostgreSQL consults with SELinux policy definition before the decision. Security policy defines a clear explanation of 'who' (subject) 'does' (action) 'to what' (object). Any actions that violate the policy definition are denied and reported immediately.

Multi Level Security (MLS) is a specific MAC security scheme in the SELinux, which solely focuses on confidentiality or controlling the information flow. The default SELinux policy does not support MLS, but it provides a Multi Category Security (MCS). MCS is analogous to MLS in the sense that MCS enhances SELinux security providing a layer of security over previously existing access control constraints. MCS security has been successfully implemented over file system and the database system, i.e., SELinux and SEPostgreSQL [4, 5, 7, 8].

Enforcing MLS in Database Management System (DBMS) is a complex and not-so-easy task to users. First of all each data can have associated with security label (category or sensitivity), secondly database users are also controlled by similar security labels, and lastly such security labels are mandatory or cannot be altered. In the present, there are very few numbers of database systems, such as SEPG, Trusted-Rubix [17], and Oracle OLS [18] that support MLS at some extend [16]. Those databases are highly professional and out of reach to most regular users. The successful application of SELinux MCS/MLS in the file system and the DBMS has given researchers, open source institutions, or developers a great hope that the SELinux MLS policy can be applied to file system and the DBMS.

As of now, the SELinux MLS policy has been resealed, but it is under the testing phase. Therefore, the SELinux with an active MLS policy does not support the GUI mode yet, and command mode is the default option. In this work comparative study/research between the MCS of SELinux default policy and MLS SELinux policies is conducted, and trying to apply to a prototype example of integrating distributed MLS database systems.

The remainder of this paper is organized as follows: section 2 introduces history of SELinux as well as its overview. Section 3 describes the Security Enhanced PostgreSQL that has been illustrated and installed onto SELinux. Section 4 describes the SEPostgreSQL with MLS. Section 5 presents the implementation SEPostgreSQL with MLS. Section 6 concludes and provides the feature direction of the paper.

2   SELinux Overview

Security Extended Linux (SELinux) was originally a development project from the National Security Agency (NSA). It was released under the GPL in late 2000 by NSA's office of information assurance. Since then it has been developed by the open source community in collaboration with NSA. SELinux currently ships as a part of Fedora Core, and it is supported by Red Hat as a part of Red Hat Enterprise Linux [3, 6].

SELinux implements the Flask operating system architecture [2]. Flask architecture is based on MAC, which focuses on providing a strictly and administratively-defined security policy that can control all the subjects and objects basing decisions on all security-relevant information. The main focus of Flux Advanced Security Kernel (Flask) is "least privilege", which means that a process is given exactly the privileges that are necessary for performing a given task; nothing more and nothing less. The Flask architecture provides flexible support for mandatory access control policies and flexibility in labeling transition and access decision. Instead of being tied to a rigidly defined lattice of relationships, Flask can define other labels based on user identity (UID), role attributes, domain or type attributes, MLS levels, and so forth. Flask implementation in SELinux supports multiple major points such as encapsulation of security labels, flexibility in labeling decision, and flexibility in access decision, and support for policy change.

Linux Security Module is a framework that allows the Linux Kernel to provide everything needed to successfully implement a Mandatory Access Control module, while imposing the fewest changes to the Linux Kernel. NSA integrated the SELinux module in the traditional Linux kernel using the LSM framework. The basic idea behind the LSM is to insert security function calls and security data structures in the various kernel services to allow access control to be applied over and above that already implemented via DAC, allow registration and initialization services for the third-party security modules, allow process security attributes to be available to user-space services, support file-systems that use extended attributes, and consolidate the Linux security and access control capabilities into an optional module [4, 5].

SELinux subjects (users, processes, applications) and objects (files, application, and devices) have a security context associated with them. A set of attributes on the basis of a MAC model forms the security context, which is also loosely referred as

Security Identity (SID), an identity of individual subjects and objects. The identity attribute is taken from the User Identity (UI) model, the domain or type attributes is taken from the Type Enforcement (TE) model. The role attribute is taken from the RBAC model and the level attribute is taken from the MLS model [16]. At one point, it makes you believe that SELinux makes security decisions based on the security contexts or the SID. Each subject or object is labeled with a security context or SID, which contains the security permission available to it. More precisely, SELinux makes security decisions based on SIDs, thereby gaining some efficiency since SIDs are represented as integers and are therefore efficiently manipulated by the CPU [1]. Actually, the security context is a string consisting of a user, role, type, and level (*optional*) separated by colon (:) as following: *<user>:<role>:<type>:<level>* [4, 5].

3   Security Enhanced PostgreSQL

PostgreSQL is a powerful, open source object-relational database management system (ORDBMS) based on Postgres (version 2.4) developed by the Computer Science Department at the University of California Berkeley [11]. It runs on all major Operating Systems (Linux, Windows) and includes most SQL: 2008 standards and supports storage of binary large objects, including picture, sound and videos [10]. PostgreSQL is one of the best known open-source database systems in the world today. PostgreSQL provides the specific features such as the client/server database for a multi-user environment, networking with TCP/IP, the three authentication methods (Kerberos, host/user based and username/password authentication), SQL as query language (Most of all), multiple index types, unique indexes and multi-column indices, user-defined functions (SQL, C), operators, data types, sequences and trigger functions, and the language interfaces for C, C++, Objective-C, Java, Perl, Tcl/Tk and Python, others.

SEPostgreSQL (Security Enhanced PostgreSQL) is a built-in enhancement of PostgreSQL, providing additional access controls based on Security-Enhanced Linux (SELinux) security policy [9]. SEPostgreSQL was meant to provide the same kinds of fine-grained access controls to the PostgreSQL database engine, integrating those policies with SELinux [10]. SEPostgreSQL works as a reference monitor within relational database management system, and provides fine-grained mandatory access control features collaboration with SELinux and its security policy [13]. SEPostgresSQL is summazied mostly based upon the SEPostgresSQL documents shown in [12, 13, 14].

Traditional database systems use a permissions model that is similar to, but separate from, the underlying operating system permissions. Database admin creates users within the database and grants access permission to various database capabilities, some of which they can pass to others. Database Management System (DBMS) have a super-privileged user that bypasses all of the permission checks. This sort of privilege model lacks a centralized access permission control and it has risk of information leakage. Fortunately, SEPostgreSQL works with SELinux to apply its policies on top of the DBMS permissions, allowing the administrator the fine-grained access control, enforced by SELinux, within PostgreSQL [10].

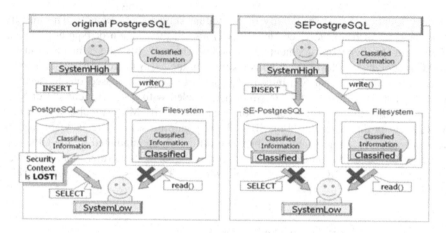

Fig. 1. Comparing PostgreSQL with SEPostgreSQL [13]

The comparison shown in Figure 1 makes a clear point that SELinux OS has secured the file system. Therefore, when the user with "SystemHigh" clearance writes on a file (in file system), the file is labeled by security context called "classified". The user with "SystemLow" clearance cannot read the classified file, because SELinux security prevents any user with low clearance accessing any classified files or objects that belongs to high clearance users. However, in the database system, the original PostgreSQL does not have the Extended Security feature like in the SEPostgreSQL, in other words original PostgreSQL does not cooperate with SELinux to apply its security policy on top of the dabatabse management system permission. As shown in the Figure 2 (original PostgreSQL), the user with "SystemHigh" clearance inserts classified information into the database. Since there is no cooperation between OS and database system, the data inserted by high clearance user lacks the security context "classified" and hence the data can be accessed by users with "SystemLow" clearance. The SEPostgreSQL database system works together with SELinux creating a system wide (certralized) security authentication. Therefore, the data (classified information) inserted into database by the user with "SystemHigh" clearance (Figure 1: SEPostgreSQL) has labeled as "classified" by SELinux policy. When the user with "SystemLow" clearance tried to access the data, his request was denied by the SELinux policy, which prevents users with low security clearance to access data of users with high security clearance [4].

SEPostgreSQL database system assigns a security context to each database object (table, row, column, tuples, procedures, etc.), and makes access control decisions based on the security context as if SELinux applies them in the kernel. The SELinux policy in the kernel is consulted for each database operation and they are either allowed or denied based on the combination of the user security context and database object security context.

If the security sensitive data of the file system is migrating to database table and the data have to remain with same security label as in file system, then the security context of the data (from file system) can be inserted into the table as a part of data. The row of the data will inherit the inserted security context. Once the data is inserted into table with specific security label, the data will be protected and only allowed users can access the information. If a user with less security clearance queries the table which contains rows and columns of classified data, the user will not be able to see those classified data. The user only will see the query result of unclassified data or the data that he/she is allowed to access [9,10].

SEPostgreSQL performs as a client of the security server [12]. Any query coming from clients is checked as if SELinux checks any system call invocation, and asks in-kernel SELinux for decision. Then, SEPostgreSQL prevents the client from accessing the requested database object if no security criteria are met. Since access control decisions are made by the SELinux security server based on its common criteria, this design is also known as system-wide consistency in access controls. For example, a user without clearance to read the information labeled as "credential' shall be prevented even if it is stored as either a file or a database record.

Communication between SEPostgreSQL and SELinux requires a context-switch due to the system call invocation, which is a heavy operation, so it is necessary to reduce the number of system call invocations to minimize the performance loss due to additional security check. Especially, a query can fetch massive number of tuples in a single query, so it might be insufferable if it has invoked a system call for each check. The userspace AVC (Access Vector Cache) works to minimize this overhead. In the SELinux security model, massive numbers of objects tend to share a limited number of security context, and the same result shall be returned for the identical combination of the security context and actions, so we can cache recently asked pattern in the userspace.

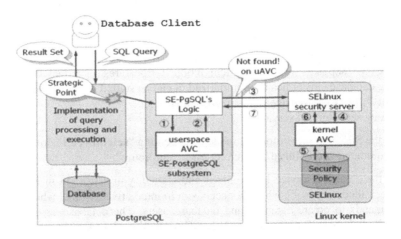

Fig. 2. SEPostgreSQL Architecture [12]

4   SEPostgreSQL with MLS

MLS is a specific MAC security scheme, which solely focuses on information confidentiality or controlling the flow of information. Although, it is believed that MCS and MLS are analogous security features, the MLS security constraint is much more advance and sophisticated. Category is optional part in the MLS security label. The SELinux with active MLS policy type supports all sixteen sensitivity levels and 1024 categories. Combining the sensitivities and categories, one can design vast number of strong security labels.

In the MLS policy, the Security Labels (SLs), the sensitivity level and categories are defined in the "/etc/selinux/mls/setrans.conf" file. In the files, "s0=SystemLow" defines a translation of "s0" the lowest sensitivity level with no category; "s15:c0.c1023=SystemHigh" defines a translation of "s15:c0.c1023" to SystemHigh, where c0.c1023 is shorthand for all the categories and the colon (:) separates the sensitivity level and category. The "s0-s15:c0.c1023=SystemLow-SystemHigh" defines a translation of "s0-s15:c0.c1023 to SystemLow-SystemHigh." Two sensitivity ranges are separated by a dash (-). And two category ranges are separated.

During the installation processes of sepostgresql, an init script (/etc/init.d/sepostgresql) was added, which manages the database service initialization. To initialize the database "service sepostgresql initdb" is executed as root user:

[root@npc11 ~]# service sepostgresql initdb
- env: /etc/init.d/sepostgresql: **Permission denied**

Unfortunately database could not initialize and start in active MLS mode. Therefore, the SELinux or MLS are changed to permissive mode manually editing the "/etc/selinux/config" file to set SELINUX=permissive. The system is rebooted and started in run-level 3 again, and logged in as root to execute the command "*service sepostgresql initdb*" to initialize the database. The process of initialization of database service builds the database cluster in /var/lib/sepgsql/data.

[root@npc11 ~]#ls –Z /var/lib/sepgsql/
drwx------. sepgsql   sepgsql system_u:object_r:postgresql_db_t:s0 backups
drwx------. sepgsql   sepgsql system_u:object_r:postgresql_db_t:s0 data
Once database cluster has been initialized, it can be started as following:
[root@npc11 ~]# service sepostgresql start
Starting sepostgresql service:

Then set the SELinux into enforcing mode by executing "**setenforce 1**" command and run the command "**getenforce**", which returned "enforcing".

Once the database service is initialized and started, you can login in as database super user called "sepgsql", which connects you to interactive terminal where you can run commands to create database and database users. The database super-user and group called "sepgsql" are added as part of installation. Logging in as super user "**sepgsql**" with su command:
[root@npc11 ~]#su – sepgsql
su: warning: cannot change directory to /home/sepgsql: No such file or directory

This warning says that there is no **/home/sepgsql** directory (directory for superuser sepgsql); hence the directory "sepgsql" is created under home dir by command "mkdir." Creating a database called "myDatabase" with owner "Admin by **createdb**" command:
-bash-4.1$ createdb –U sepgsql –O Admin myDatabase

In order to connect to database and be able to run PostgregreSQL commands, the PostgreSQL interactive terminal "psql" need to be loaded. The following command loads "psql" and connects to "myDatabase" database with user Admin.

-bash-4.1$psql –d myDatabase –U Admin –W
psql: FATAL: Ident authentication failed for user "Admin"

To allow user_name and password authentication, the "pg_hba.conf" file at /var/lib/sepgsql/data/ is to be upadated. After the updating, you must restart/ reload the service:

[root@npc11 ~]#service sepostgresql restart
env: /etc/init.d/sepostgresql: **Permission denied**

As mentioned earlier, it was not allowed to set up and/or initialize/start services while MLS is active (enforcing mode). Tried to execute "setenforce 0" to set MLS into permissive mode, but this command failed, so set the SELinux Permissive manually in "config" file and rebooted the system. Finally restarted the 'sepostgresql" service and set SELinux to enforcing mode.

[root@npc11 ~]#service sepostgresql restart
Stopping sepostgresql service   [OK]
Starting sepostgresql service   [OK]

[root@npc11 ~]#setenforce 1

Repeat more steps to connect to the database with user_name and password authentication as earlier.

-bash-4.1$psql –d myDatabase –U Admin –W
Psql (8.4.8, server 9.0.1)
WARNING: psql version 8.4, server version 9.0. Some psql feature might not work.
myDatabase=#

5   SEPostgreSQL Implementation

When active MLS did not allow running any commands related to policy file configuration or policy management with "semanage" command, as suggested on Fedora user manual, SELinux MLS is changed to permissive mode and performed policy management task, made all the policy configuration files with settings as desired. Once changes were made and system files were relabeled, even active SELinux MLS supported the changes. Upon testing the SEPostgreSQL, we were curious about how active SELinux MLS may response to those database and database-objects that are created in MLS permissive mode. Therefore we set the SELinux MLS into permissive mode and created database, tables and performed comparative database operations as following.

Creating a Database

myDatabase=#CREATE DATABASE testdb WITH OWNER mydbuser
SECURITY LABEL='system_u:object_r:sepgsql_db_t:s0-s5:c0.c99';
ERROR: Syntax error at or near security_label ......

Note: There is no syntax error in above statement, however the statement could not execute for unknown reason. Hence, we first created a database with default security label and then altered the database with desired security label as following.

myDatabase=#CREATE DATABASE testdb WITH OWNER mydbuser;
CREATE DATABASE
myDatabase=#SELECT datname, security_label from pg_database where datname='testdb';
datnema | *security_label*

----------------------+--

testdb | *root:object_r:sepgsql:db_t:s0*

Altering the database with desired security label:

myDatabase=#ALTER   DATABASE   testdb   SECURITY   LABEL   TO
'system_u:object_r:sepgsql_db_t:s0-s5:c0.c99';
ALTER DATABASE

myDatabase=#SELECT   datname,   security_label   from   pg_database   where
datname='testdb';
datnema | *security_label*

----------------------+--------------------------------------

testdb | *system_u:object_r:sepgsql:db_t:s0-s5:c0.c99*

Creating a Table

Column_label is the security label to be set on newly created column and **table_label** is the security label to be set on newly create table. Creating a table with default security_label is shown below'

testdb=#SELECT relname, security_label from pg_class where relname='staff';
relname | security_lbel

----------------------+--

staff | root:object_r:sepgsql_table_t:**s0**
(1 row)

While one terminal is still connected to "testdb" as user "mydbuser" who has higher sensitivity, new terminal is opened, logged in as root and set SELinux into enforcing mode. Then a low sensitivity level database with user authentication performs the following operations.

a.   Altering Database in active MLS mode:
**myDatabase=#ALTER   DATABASE   testdb   SECURITY   LABEL   TO
'system_u:object_r:sepgsql_db_t:s0:c0.c99';**
ERROR: SELinux: security policy violation

b.   Selecting database with security label from myDatabase:
myDatabase=#SELECT datname, security_label from pg_database where datname='testdb';
<pre>
datnema | security_label
---------------- +---------------------------------------
</pre>
(0 rows)

c.   Shifted to "**testdb**" terminal and run SELECT statement against table "**staff**":
testdb=#SELECT relname, security_label from pg_class where relname='staff';
ERROR: SELinux: security policy violation

d.   Inserting data into the table "staff" in active MLS mode:
testdb=#INSERT INTO staff (stfId, stfname, stfgender, stfssn)
     VALUES(1, 'Dana', 'F', '306453892');
ERROR: SELinux: security policy violation

e.   Deleting the table in active MLS mode:
testdb=#DROP TABLE staff;
ERROR: SELinux: security policy violation

f.   Quit from the "testdb" executing "\q" command.

g.   Connecting back to database with user authentication:
     $ psql –d testdb –U mydbuser –W

psql: FATAL: permission denied for database "testdb"
h.   Shift to the terminal of "**myDatabase**", and ran the SELECT statement against pg_authid system catalog.
myDatabase=#SELECT rolname, security_label from pg_authid where rolname='mydbuser';
<pre>
rolname | security_lbel
---------------- +--------------------+--------------------
</pre>
     (0 row)
Note that *the user (mydbuser) is still in the database system, but not showing.*

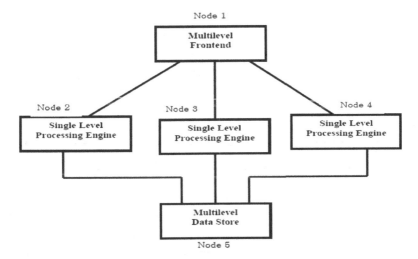

Fig. 3. Distributed Multiple MLS database system

6   Feature Directions and Conclusions

Government Security Agencies have been investing great amount of budget for securing information from outliers and information leakages happening from internal authorized persons by mistake or by intention. Therefore, SELinux (Security Enhanced Linux) O/S, which enforces Mandatory Access Control (MAC); thus enforces MLS or MCS security policy, was born at NSA (National Security Agency). Releasing the SELinux as open source OS in late 2000 by NSA has given great opportunity to open source developers and institutes to enhance and use SELinux security for free of cost. Today, only handful of expensive professional DBMS, such as ORACLE, Rubix are able to provide certain level of MLS in DBMS. SELinux MLS policy, which is under testing phase, is not supported in DBMS. Implementation of MCS in DBMS has given a hope for policy developers that SELinux MLS could enforce on DBMS in the future. Successful enforcement of MLS in SELinux and DBMS can bring a revolution in field of information/data security and economy of DBMS.

The SELinux MLS policy, which focuses on confidentiality and controls information flow, supports both sensitivity and categories. It is learned that the security labels designed by combining sensitivities and categories provide a very strong and narrow set of MLS security in the file system. However, this research has found that the active MLS mode is not well function in the present. For example, the active MLS does not support GUI mode. Active MLS is problematic especially when executing any policy management commands or tools, making any configuration changes in policy files. Any urgent administrative configuration and Boolean value changes in policy files were need to be done in MLS troubleshooting mode (permissive mode). Every Boolean setting or TE rule application needed system rebooted to bring changes into effect and that was really inconvenient and extremely time consuming process. However, these problematic parts of the SELinux could no longer exist during final release of MLS policy in the future.

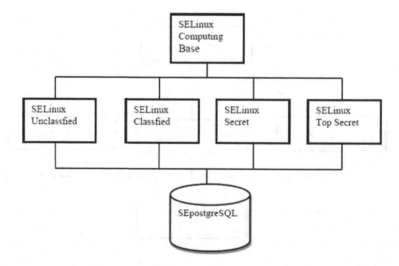

Fig. 4. Distributed MLS database system with SELinux systems and SEPostgresSQL

This research would be a stepping stone for integrating and developing a distributed multilevel database systems as an example shown in Figure 3 and 4, where multiple different MLS database could be integrated into an extended MLS database system. When integrating the systems based MLS, especially heterogeneous MLS components, integration risks exist as follows [19,20]: the integrated components might not work correctly, not provide complete or correct enforcement of security policies, invalidate the security of individual component products, and introduce new security problems outside the scope of any single component. In our prototype design, the host is being used as a gateway to retrieve information from other local databases. If an unlabeled machine is in a physically secure location, and can be trusted to well-behaved in a security sense, this unlabeled machine is also allowed to be on the same Ethernet. Information label and sensitivity label are assigned to all the machines on the network by changing trusted networking databases in the proposed system. In our proposed system, the information and sensitivity labels are allocated to corresponding MLS systems. Anytime, users in the host are allowed to read data at the local sites with their corresponding sensitivity levels, which are lower than or equal to the sensitivity level of users. This satisfies the operational restrictions specified in [20]. In our architecture for the information retrieval tool in heterogeneous MLS systems, users at the local sites are not paid much attention. Users at local sites are not allowed to retrieve information from the host system. And users at each local MLS system work on their system based on the security of their own MLS systems.

Our prototype is a distributed system which consists of different SElinux MLS systems and single-level systems which are connected by a computer network, shown in Figure 4. It is recommended in the proposed system that users are easy to work on different security levels. Furthermore, the abilities to label ports or external addresses are required data to manually import via air gap and sneaker net. When integrating the systems based MLS, especially heterogeneous MLS components, integration risks exist as follows [20]: the integrated components might not work correctly, not provide complete or correct enforcement of security policies, invalidate the security of individual component products, and introduce new security problems outside the scope of any single component. In our prototype design, the host is being used as a gateway to retrieve information from other local databases. If an unlabeled machine is in a physically secure location, and can be trusted to well-behaved in a security sense, this unlabeled machine is also allowed to be on the same Ethernet. Information label and sensitivity label are assigned to all the SELinux machines on the network by changing trusted networking databases in the proposed system. In our proposed system, the information and sensitivity labels are allocated to corresponding SELinux MLS systems and SEpostgreSQL database system.

Anytime, users in each SELinux machine are allowed to read data at the local sites with their corresponding sensitivity levels, which are lower than or equal to the sensitivity level of users. This satisfies the operational restrictions specified in MLS systems. In our architecture for heterogeneous MLS systems, users at the local sites are not paid much attention. Users at each local MLS system work on their system based on the security of their own MLS systems. In order to provide name and location transparencies in our proposed architecture, a global data dictionary what we call metadatabase is applied. In our prototype since users at local sites are not required to retrieve information from a host, metadatabase is kept at the host machine. Users at the host do not need to provide information about location, file name or file types to retrieve information from local sites, since name and location transparencies are provided by using metadatabase at a host. Security labels are also given to a metadatabase table. The security level of a global query is labeled by the security level of the current user. Then data will be retrieved from the distributed secure database systems up to this security level. For example, the global query with Classified which are the sensitivity level of the current window opened may not retrieve the data with Secret even if the user has the classification with Top Secret.

References

1. McCarty, B., Schultz, U.P., Consel, C., Muller, G.: ELinux: NSA's Open Source Security Enhanced Linux. O'Reilly Media, Inc. (2004)
2. Stephen, S.: History of Flask, National Security Agency, NSA (2000)
3. Hicks, B., Rueda, S.: A Logical Specification and Analysis for SELinux MLS Policy, Pennsylvania State University, USA
4. Kimm, H.: Introduction to SELinux. In: International ACM Symposium on Applied Computing, Seoul, Korea (March 11, 2007)
5. Hanson, C.: SELinux and MLS: Putting the Pieces Together Trusted Computer Solutions, Inc.
6. Hallyn, S.E.: Role-based Access Control in SELinux, IBM: Software Engineer (2008)
7. Lugo, P.C., Garcia, J.M.G., Flores, J.J.: A System for Distributed SELinux Policy Management. In: Third International Conference on Network and System Security (2009)
8. Lugo, P.C., Garcia, J.M.G., Flores, J.J.: Architecture for Systematic Administration of SELinux Policies in Distributed Environments. International Journal of Computers and Communications 1(4) (2007)
9. SEPostgreSQL Introduction, http://wiki.postgresql.org/wiki/SEPostgreSQL_Introduction
10. Edge, J.: SEPostgreSQL uses SELinux for Database Security (2007)
11. PostgreSQL:About, http://www.postgresql.org/about/
12. SEPostgreSQL Architecture (2009), http://wiki.postgresql.org/wiki/SEPostgreSQL_Architecture
13. Kohei, K.: sepgsql: Security Enhanced PostgreSQL - What is SEPostgreSQL? (2010), http://code.google.com/p/sepgsql/wiki/WhatIsSEPostgreSQL
14. Kohei, K.: sepgsql: Why we need SEPostgreSQL? (2010), http://code.google.com/p/sepgsql/wiki/WhatIsSEPostgreSQL
15. (2010-2011), http://engardelinux.net/modules/index/list_archives.cgi?list=selinux&page=0068.html&month=2011-01
16. Caplan, D., MacMillan, K., Mayer, F.: Type Enforcement Access Control (2006), http://www.informit.com/articles/article.aspx?p=606586&seqNum=2
17. Trused Rubix, http://rubix.com/cms/features
18. Oracle MLS, http://www.oracle.com/webapps/dialogue/ns/dlgwelcome.jsp
19. Kimm, H., Rhi, J.: Architecture for Confidential Information Retrieval in Health Care Organizations. Journal of Personal Data Protection, Korea Information Security Agency, 1–12 (December 2002)
20. Neugent, B.: General Issues To Be Resolved in Achieving Multilevel Security (MLS). In: Proceedings of the 15th National Computer Security Conference, Baltimore, MD, pp. 213–220 (October 1992)

Author Index